Church, Faith and Culture in the Medieval West

General Editors
Brenda Bolton, Anne J. Duggan, and
Damian J. Smith

About the volume

Who can concentrate on thoughts of Scripture or philosophy and be able to endure babies crying...? Will he put up with the constant muddle and squalor which small children bring into the home? The wealthy can do so ... but philosophers lead a very different life ...

So, according to Peter Abelard, did his wife Heloise state in characteristically stark terms the antithetical demands of family and scholarship. Heloise was not alone in making this assumption. Sources from Jerome onward never cease to remind us that the life of the mind stands at odds with life in the family. For all that we have moved in the past two generations beyond kings and battles, fiefs and barons, motherhood has remained a blind spot for medieval historians. Whatever the reasons, the result is that the historiography of the medieval period is largely motherless. The aim of this book is to insist that this picture is intolerably one-dimensional, and to begin to change it.

The volume is focused on the paradox of motherhood in the European Middle Ages: to be a mother is at once to hold great power, and by the same token to be acutely vulnerable. The essays look to analyse the powers and the dangers of motherhood within the warp and weft of social history, beginning with the premise that religious discourse or practice served as a medium in which mothers (and others) could assess their situation, defend claims, and make accusations. Within this frame, three main themes emerge: survival, agency, and institutionalization. The volume spans the length and breadth of the Middle Ages, from late Roman North Africa through ninth-century Byzantium to late medieval Somerset, drawing in a range of types of historian, including textual scholars, literary critics, students of religion and economic historians. The unity of the volume arises from the very diversity of approaches within it, all addressed to the central topic.

Church, Faith and Culture in the Medieval West

General Editors
Brenda Bolton, Anne J. Duggan
and Damian J. Smith

Other titles in the series:

Hugh of Amiens and the Twelfth-Century Renaissance
Ryan P. Freeburn

Commemorating the Dead in Late Medieval Strasbourg
The Cathedral's Book of Donors and Its Use (1320–1521)
Charlotte A. Stanford

Ansgar, Rimbert and the Forged Foundations of Hamburg-Bremen
Eric Knibbs

Saving the Souls of Medieval London
Perpetual Chantries at St Paul's Cathedral, c.1200–1548
Marie-Hélène Rousseau

Readers, Texts and Compilers in the Earlier Middle Ages
Studies in Medieval Canon Law in Honour of Linda Fowler-Magerl
Edited by Martin Brett and Kathleen G. Cushing

Shaping Church Law Around the Year 1000
The *Decretum* of Burchard of Worms
Greta Austin

Pope Celestine III (1191–1198)
Diplomat and Pastor
Edited by John Doran and Damian J. Smith

Bishops, Texts and the Use of Canon Law around 1100
Essays in Honour of Martin Brett
Edited by Bruce C. Brasington and Kathleen G. Cushing

Roma Felix – Formation and Reflections of Medieval Rome
Edited by Éamonn Ó Carragáin and Carol Neuman de Vegvar

MOTHERHOOD, RELIGION, AND SOCIETY
IN MEDIEVAL EUROPE, 400–1400

Henrietta Leyser with grandchild

Motherhood, Religion, and Society in Medieval Europe, 400–1400

Essays Presented to Henrietta Leyser

Edited by

CONRAD LEYSER and LESLEY SMITH
University of Oxford, UK

Routledge
Taylor & Francis Group

LONDON AND NEW YORK

First published 2011 by Ashgate Publishing

Published 2016 by Routledge
2 Park Square, Milton Park, Abingdon, Oxon OX14 4RN
711 Third Avenue, New York, NY 10017, USA

Routledge is an imprint of the Taylor & Francis Group, an informa business

British Library Cataloguing in Publication Data
Motherhood, religion, and society in medieval Europe,
  400-1400. -- (Church, faith and culture in the medieval West)
  1. Motherhood--Europe--History--To 1500. 2. Motherhood--Religious aspects.
  I. Series II. Smith, Lesley (Lesley Janette) III. Leyser, Conrad.
  306.8'743-dc22

Library of Congress Cataloging-in-Publication Data
Motherhood, religion, and society in medieval Europe, 400-1400 : essays
presented to Henrietta Leyser / [edited by] Conrad Leyser and Lesley Smith.
  p. cm. -- (Church, faith, and culture in the medieval west)
  Includes bibliographical references and index.
  ISBN 978-1-4094-3145-9 (hardcover)
  1. Motherhood--Europe--History. 2. Motherhood--Religious aspects--Christianity.
  3. Middle Ages. 4. Church history. I. Leyser, Conrad. II. Smith, Lesley (Lesley Janette)

HQ759.M873423 2011
306.874'30940902--dc22

2011015462

ISBN 9781409431459 (hbk)

Contents

List of Figures and Tables

Figures

Tables

Notes on Contributors

Caroline M. Barron is a Professorial Research Fellow at Royal Holloway, University of London. Her latest book, *London in the Later Middle Ages: Government and People* was published by the Oxford University Press in 2004.

James Campbell was formerly Professor of Modern History, University of Oxford, with particular interests in the Anglo-Saxons. He is an Emeritus Fellow of Worcester College, Oxford.

Michael Clanchy is Emeritus Professor of Medieval History at the Institute of Historical Research, University of London. He specializes in the history of literacy and scholasticism in the central Middle Ages and also in law and politics in medieval England.

Kate Cooper is Professor of Ancient History at the University of Manchester, specializing in late-Roman Christianity and the family.

Samuel Fanous is Head of Publishing at the Bodleian Library. His research interests focus on medieval religious texts, autobiography and saints' lives.

Monica H. Green is Professor of History at Arizona State University, with affiliations in the Program of Women and Gender Studies and the Global Health Program in the School of Human Evolution and Social Change. She specializes in the history of medieval medicine, and is currently working on studies of the so-called 'school' of Salerno in the twelfth century. She is also exploring how history and the historicist sciences (palaeopathology, palaeomicrobiology and genomics) can better reconstruct the history of disease.

Tony Hunt is a Senior Research Fellow at St Peter's College, Oxford, where he specializes in editing texts, including medical texts, in Continental Old French and Anglo-Norman.

Conrad Leyser is Fellow and Tutor in History at Worcester College, Oxford, specializing in the early medieval Church.

Claire A. Martin read history at St Peter's College, Oxford and then completed her PhD at Royal Holloway, University of London in 2008 on the subject of 'Transport for London 1250–1550'.

Henry Mayr-Harting is Emeritus Regius Professor of Ecclesiastical History, University of Oxford, and Emeritus Fellow of St Peter's College, Oxford. His most recent book is *Religion, Politics and Society in Britain, 1066–1272* (Pearson, 2011).

Brian Patrick McGuire is Professor of Medieval History at Roskilde University, Denmark. He publishes on monastic topics and has recently reissued, with a new review of research, his 1988 *Friendship and Community: The Monastic Experience 350–1250*.

Janet L. Nelson is Professor Emerita of History at King's College London, specializing in Carolingian social and political history.

Lesley Smith is Fellow and Tutor in Politics and Senior Tutor of Harris Manchester College, Oxford. She specializes in intellectual history, working particularly in biblical exegesis and the history of the manuscript book.

Sethina Watson is Lecturer in Medieval History at the University of York. She works on the religious and social history of the High Middle Ages in England, focusing on the medieval hospital.

Mark Whittow is University Lecturer and Fellow in Byzantine Studies at Corpus Christi College Oxford, specializing in the comparative history of medieval Europe and the Near East, with a focus on Byzantium.

Jocelyn Wogan-Browne is Thomas F.X. Mullarkey Chair in Literature, English Department, Fordham University and formerly Professor of Medieval Literature, University of York, UK. She works on medieval women's writing, the French of England, medieval vernacularity and saints' lives.

Preface

Who can concentrate on thoughts of Scripture or philosophy and be able to endure babies crying ...? Will he put up with the constant muddle and squalor which small children bring into the home? The wealthy can do so ... but philosophers lead a very different life.[1]

So, according to Peter Abelard, did his wife Heloise state in characteristically stark terms the antithetical demands of family and scholarship. It was Heloise, the less conventional of the pair, who argued against their marriage, fearing that her husband's brilliance would be dimmed by a life of genteel poverty lived with her and their infant son. She speaks of the scholar as 'he' – assuming, for all her own remarkable education and academic gifts, that it was Abelard who would be disturbed. The death of her own scholarly life must be taken for granted.

Heloise was not alone in making this assumption. Sources from Jerome onward never cease to remind us that the life of the mind stands at odds with life in the family. (Only in the 1880s, for example, were fellows at Oxford Colleges finally free to marry.) Marriage and fatherhood were bad enough, even given a supply of nannies, but motherhood was the last straw. Even today, statistics repeatedly insist, women continue to shoulder the majority of housework and childcare, even in families where both parents work full time. Being a mother subsumes any other roles a woman might play, and motherhood is so consuming that anything else of interest in a woman's life must disappear. For all that we have moved in the past two generations beyond kings and battles, fiefs and barons, motherhood has remained a blind spot for medieval historians. While the study of women, gender and the family has expanded almost beyond measure, it is still the case that one can count on one hand the number of studies devoted specifically to medieval mothers and motherhood. The reasons for this may lie deep within the collective psyche – or they may be bathetically easy to discern. However delightful, children are generally speaking an obstacle to historical research: when they finally get to their desks, many scholars with obligations to their kin, both young and old, may wish to escape. Whatever the reasons, the result is that the historiography of the

---

[1] *The Letters of Abelard and Heloise*, trans. and intro. Betty Radice (Harmondsworth, 1974), pp. 71–2.

medieval period is largely motherless. The aim of this book is to insist that this picture is intolerably one-dimensional, and to begin to change it.

Our central focus is on the paradox of motherhood in the European Middle Ages. To be a mother is at once to hold great power, and by the same token to be acutely vulnerable. This is by no means a new observation, nor is it specific to motherhood: the same could be said of other roles for women within the family – wife, widow, sister, daughter. However, where previous studies of medieval motherhood have tended to explore this paradox in terms of cultural poetics, our volume looks to analyse the powers and the dangers of motherhood within the warp and weft of social history.

The best evidence for this kind of context-specific investigation often comes from religious sources. Here we run into another familiar debate in the study of women and gender. Some scholars regard medieval Christianity as a source of power for women, mitigating the disadvantages built into their social position; in the view of others, however, religious norms systematically curtailed female agency. Hence the well-known crux, was the Virgin Mary 'good' or 'bad' for women? If however we take the paradox of motherhood seriously – that maternal powers *entailed* maternal vulnerability – then we must abandon the 'either–or' format of the question. Christianity is neither the problem nor the solution for medieval mothers: at the very least it is both. Our volume starts from the premise that religious discourse or practice served as a medium in which mothers (and others) could assess their situation, defend claims and make accusations. This is what we have in mind in promising a study of 'Motherhood, Religion, and Society'.

Within this frame, three main themes emerge: survival, agency and institutionalization. The first of these, 'survival', has two aspects. Some of the contributors (Green, Hunt) start with basic questions of evidence, recovering texts for and about mothers hitherto lost or ignored. For others (Cooper, Watson, Wogan-Browne), the starting point is the basic social fact in the pre-modern world: mortality. A mother's fertility was never enough: her primary experience as it has come down to us was one of loss.

In this context, several contributors ask what the social agency of mothers was actually like. To what extent could mothers prepare their children for the social future (Cooper, Nelson, Clanchy), or fight for the property rights of the dynasty if that future was cut short by death (Mayr-Harting, Watson, Barron)? Conversely, how dependent were they on their children to protect them (Smith)? Under what circumstances might mothers turn away from their own offspring (Whittow)?

Thirdly, in what senses did 'motherhood' become an institution, detachable from the persons of mothers themselves? From the ninth century on, and gathering pace in the eleventh, we can observe the articulation of Motherhood as an 'office'. Initially at least, this discourse seems to have arisen in the context of the development of the male clerical hierarchy. Devotion to Mary, and indeed to Jesus as Mother, had remarkably little to do with women (Leyser, McGuire); a mother could be a social choice, not a biological given (Fanous, Smith). Once mothers joined the ranks of women to think with, what effect did this have on mothers themselves (Fanous, Mayr-Harting, Wogan-Browne)?

Our volume spans the length and breadth of the Middle Ages, from late Roman North Africa through ninth-century Byzantium to late medieval Somerset. We do not, however, aspire either to coverage or to an overall synthesis. The subject is still too little developed for that, and a series of specific interventions represent a more useful contribution at this stage. This allows us to draw in a range of different types of historian, including textual scholars, literary critics, students of religion, and economic historians. The rationale is that the unity of the volume arises from the very diversity of approaches within it, all addressed to the central topic. Rather like the segmented societies of decolonizing Africa, of such allure to British anthropologists in the 1950s, the cohesion of the whole is here not a product of a 'top-down' structure or message – it inheres in the very plurality of points of view, often in tension, to which the book gives voice.

The collected essay format also allows contributors to honour the work of Henrietta Leyser – mother of one editor, friend to the other; mother-in-law to one contributor, student of another: colleague, remarkably, to all. Her book on medieval women not only had much to say about medieval motherhood – it is also the case that her life and work together offer an example of how scholarship and motherhood might not, after all, be at odds.

List of Abbreviations

A&P	*Acta et processus canonizacionis beate Birgitte*, ed. Isak Collijn, SSFS 2, 1 (Uppsala, 1924–1931)
AND²	*Anglo-Norman Dictionary*, edited by Stewart Gregory, William Rothwell and David Trotter, 2nd edn (London, 2005)
AND⁰	*Anglo-Norman Dictionary online:* see www.anglo-norman.net
CCCM	*Corpus Christianorum, Continuatio Mediaevalis*
CCSA	*Corpus Christianorum, Series Apocryphorum*
CCSL	*Corpus Christianorum, Series Latina*
CP	*The Complete Peerage of England, Scotland Ireland, Great Britain and the United Kingdom*, ed. G.E. Cockayne (13 vols in 6, Gloucester: Alan Sutton, 1987; repr. of London, 1910–1959 edn)
CSEL	*Corpus Scriptorum Ecclesiasticorum Latinorum*
HW	*Calendar of Wills proved and Enrolled in the Court of Husting*
KVHAA	*Kungl. Vitterhets Historie och Antikvitets Handlingar*
LB	*Calendar of the Letter Books of the City of London*
MGH SS	*Monumenta Germaniae Historica Scriptores*
MGH	*Monumenta Germaniae Historica*
PG	*Patrologia Graeca*, ed. J.-P. Migne, 162 vols
PL	*Patrologia Latina*, ed. J.-P. Migne, 221 vols + suppl.
SC	*Sources chrétiennes*
SSFS	*Samlingar utgivna av Svenska Fornskriftsäilskapet*

Introduction

Henrietta Leyser

James Campbell

I first met Henrietta more than forty years ago, when I taught her for a Further Subject, Stubbs's *Select Charters*. (Her future husband, Karl Leyser, had taught me the same subject ten years before.) She was an intelligent, cool, notably individual pupil.

These qualities showed in her *Hermits and the New Monasticism. A Study of Religious Communities in Western Europe 1000–1150* (London, 1984). Some of her originality and, not least, her economy in words appear, in a minor key, on the dust-jacket. The front flap states: 'For a note on the author please see the back flap'. Turn to the back flap. 'Henrietta Leyser lives near Oxford. This is her first book.' That is all. The first words of the book strike an original note. 'Talking about hermits provokes mirth; if you do not believe this, try working on hermits and keeping a goat'. The point is that Henrietta not only worked on hermits, but she and Karl *did* keep a goat. (It is questionable whether Karl, left to himself, would have done anything of the kind. I expect Henrietta thought it was good and interesting for their four children, and surely it was.)

The book ultimately derived from her B.Litt. thesis, and it is an original account of an important subject. Its central difficulty is indicated by the book's full title. This implies some such question as: 'When is a hermit not a hermit?', requiring an answer of the kind which has to fall over itself, for example 'When he is a member of the Cistercian order or of one of the other twelfth-century monastic associations which had eremitical influences on their origins and aspirations'. These movements have many diversities, if also underlying coherences. The story is shot through with paradoxes. One is the conflict or contrast between people seeking their individual way to God and the need they felt for ordered rule, indeed an Order. This was one of the many dilemmas that faced the participants in the eremitical movement, and necessarily face its historians. Another is this. Essential initiatives for the movement often came from laymen. Why then, in the twelfth century, is it that 'the influence of the laity vanishes, as it were overnight,[1] leaving *conversi* as distinctly and greatly subordinated? The old monastic dilemma raises its head: how to abjure the world yet try to change the world. Henrietta Leyser has a gift for informed sympathy, for entering into the anguish of such dilemmas and the feelings of protagonists. This is expressed in her deployment of sources. She is widely read in, and beyond, the secondary literature, can deploy modern anthropological learning and is unusual among medievalists in being able to quote four lines from Louis MacNeice on her first page. However, most striking is the sensitive use she makes of numerous and sometimes vivid contemporary sources. They can be touching, as in the story of Stephen of Obazine and his companions borrowing shoes to go to church and always remembering the woman who gave them half a loaf and some milk when they were famished. Henrietta uses her wide knowledge of the sources to introduce a note of humour, no less welcome than discreet[2] as when she indicates that, among the 'temptations and trials' of hermits, could be visitations from 'vultures and Ethiopians'.[3]

Prominent among the virtues of *Hermits and the New Monasticism* is its brevity, a complex theme lucidly and thoughtfully surveyed in 135 pages. Wordiness is the curse of modern historiography. Who can write history when there is far too much to read? A remedy, already adopted by at least one very eminent ancient historian, is to skip secondary literature.[4] Henrietta Leyser's first book is not one to skip.

Women play an interesting but ambiguous role in the tale told by this book. Only one of the monasteries concerned seems to have been founded by a woman, Springiersbach, in Trier. Yet women played a large part in the movement and the movement did something for women, even though 'the Cistercians and the Premonstratensians did their best (however unsuccessfully) to disown or ignore their women followers'.[5]

Henrietta Leyser's second book, *Medieval Women. A Social History of Women in England 450–1500* (London, 1995) is all about women and is a remarkable achievement. She modestly lays no claim to originality, misleadingly, for this is no mere textbook but, on the contrary, an informed, carefully reflective, and quite

---

[1]   Henrietta Leyser, *Hermits and the New Monasticism: A Study of Religious Communities in Western Europe 1000–1150* (London, 1984), p. 47.

[2]   Ibid., p. 41.

[3]   Ibid., p. 21.

[4]   A.H.M. Jones, *The Later Roman Empire 284–602* (2 vols, Oxford, 1964), I, p. vi: 'I early realised that if in a field so vast I tried to read the modern literature exhaustively and keep abreast of modern scholarship I should not have time to read the sources. I therefore abandoned the former attempt'.

[5]   Leyser, *Hermits*, p. 51.

often original survey. It deals with a once-neglected subject that has become the theme of a torrent of historiography. What was there to read in 1960 on the history of secular women in medieval England? There were some fine essays by Eileen Power and a recently (1957) published work by D.M. Stenton, which were solid, but not such as to set the mind alight.[6] Women's history was a not-very-important theme which one might pursue if one were interested in that kind of thing. It could be seen as more significant than, say, the history of bee-keeping, but nothing compared with, say, the history of the art of war. *Medieval Women* is not only an account of the fairly distant past but also evidence for a great change in our own day.

Not the least ingenious thing about the book is its arrangement. Henrietta Leyser has had to face the historian's normal problem of combining narrative and themes, but also has had to reckon with the difficulty that most women's history makes sense only in the context of general social and economic movements.

Four chapters go to the Anglo-Saxons. In one she makes heroic efforts to dig out something about Anglo-Saxon women from cemeteries. Something emerges, but there is no escaping the fact that most attempts to illuminate Anglo-Saxon society from Anglo-Saxon graves have something of the attraction and lightness of hot air balloons. The chapter on Anglo-Saxon law is again thoughtful and cogent. The difficulty here is that the legislation deals chiefly with the affairs of the propertied. Indeed for many centuries historians can say little more about the poor than that they know that they are always with them. Throughout her book Henrietta makes sterling efforts to illuminate the lives of poor women and does so, particularly in regard to late medieval towns. However, even she has to leave stark questions unanswered. Where and what could a poor housewife cook? How did she store water?

Perhaps the most significant part of the analysis of laws is that devoted to the Penitential of Theodore, where Henrietta thoughtfully brings out the possibly revolutionary effects of Christian marriage law. This theme recurs in her book, not least in her stressing the importance of the Fourth Lateran Council's emphasis on the sacramental as compared with the contractual view of marriage. The history of women, or at least what can be known of the history of women in Anglo-Saxon times, is largely a matter of religion: the wonderful greatness of the seventh- and eighth-century abbesses; the uniqueness of Anglo-Saxon missionary women. Henrietta has a chapter on women in vernacular literature. It is a subject that is easily distorted. I once heard (admittedly in California) how Grendel's mother (poor thing) had been demonized by a patriarchal society. Such extravagant fancies are not for Henrietta Leyser. Her reaction to

---

[6]   D.M. Stenton, *The English Woman in History* (London, 1957).

the poems is often that intended by their authors, being carried along by the stories while showing how little the role of the women in them can sustain simple interpretation. Occasionally she adds a welcome touch of humour to this lugubrious literature, humour, for example, in her attractive account of *Judith*: the heroine, having decapitated Holofernes, 'pops the head into her lunch-bag'.[7]

The centuries immediately after the Conquest are treated with selective skill, illuminating key issues. An example is the extent to which the fate of the English language must have been affected by the English wives and servants of the conquerors. Henrietta emphasizes the major consequences of the relatively new insecurity of bastards and the apparently growing legal security given to widows and heiresses, particularly by Magna Carta, clauses seven and eight.[8] Her treatment of Magna Carta is part of an element in her work that does something to ease the sense of guilt that the present reviewer feels on reading the first sentences of the preface to her book. She relates how, on attending Sir Richard Southern's inaugural lecture in 1961, she was filled with 'fascinated horror'. (Not an emotion than even the most distinguished lecturer can often hope to inspire.) He maintained that the devisers of the Oxford history syllabus had left out 'that which is most interesting in the past in order to concentrate on what was practically and academically most serviceable'. There was a fair amount of truth in what Southern said. Constitutional History (and in particular the study of Stubbs) had been made a key part of the syllabus because it provided a firm framework of difficult, demanding learning. It was required by the Modern History syllabus for about a century.[9] Perhaps I should blush for having been an instrument for imposing on Henrietta an element in a horrifying system. However, the care with which she deals with law, in particular urban and manorial laws, leads one to suppose that there may have been at least a little to be said for Stubbs after all.

Indeed, one of the demands of writing a comprehensive book on women's history is that it demands something more than a casual acquaintance with a number of historical fields. Thus Henrietta Leyser shows good knowledge and a sensitive appreciation not only of legal but also of medical and economic history; she does not just retail what others have written but gives it analytical

---

[7]   Henrietta Leyser, *Medieval Women: a Social History of Women in England, 450–1500* (London, 1995), p. 58.

[8]   Ibid., pp. 171–2.

[9]   Maitland commented as early as 1901 that 'Literature and art, religion and law, rents and prices, creeds and superstitions have burst the political barrier and are no longer to be expelled'. F.W. Maitland et al., *Essays on the Teaching of History* (Cambridge, 1901), p. xx; cf. p. 54: J.R. Tanner on the fading of the 'beneficient superstition' of the key importance of Stubbs.

consideration, for example in her examination of the importance and complications for women's medicine of Greek humoral theory.

Perhaps the most impressive section in the book is that which deals with the religious lives of medieval women. The most distinguished of Henrietta's predecessors in this was Eileen Power. The 724 learned and fascinating pages of her *Medieval English Nunneries c. 1275–1535* (Cambridge, 1922) represent a magnificent, an almost incredible, achievement for someone aged 33. It deals with many aspects of nunnery life in learned and brilliantly presented detail. Only one aspect receives inadequate attention: religion. Religion was not Power's scene. Henrietta, by contrast, deals with beliefs and cults with knowledge and sympathy. There are many examples in that work, for example, on the power of the extraordinary Christina of Markyate,[10] or again in her account of the sculptures of the Virgin Mary on the Eleanor crosses:

> The statues of Eleanor ... underlined her relationship to the Virgin in ways undreamed of in the iconography of the tenth-century *Benedictional of Æthelwold*. In this period the regality of the Virgin had been a necessary buttress to the still fragile position of the queen; by the fourteenth century it was the compassion of the queen that was called upon in order to soften, though not to challenge, the arbitrary power of royal rule.[11]

Or yet again her treatment of female mysticism shown, for example, in Richard Rolle's connection with the former Cistercian nun Margaret Kirkby.[12]

A special feature of the book is the well-chosen and largely unfamiliar illustrations. Most remarkable is a thirteenth-century illumination showing a cow. Henrietta (who is very good at slipping in useful information) tells us what the possession of a single cow could mean to a peasant family: 80 pounds of cheese in a year. (One almost wonders whether she had been thinking of acquiring a cow herself.)

Medieval Women has become a standard work. Few books deserve this status, but this one does. It is full of reflective, very fair-minded learning, happily unaccompanied by the note of strident indignation which hovers round some feminist history.

Its qualities can inspire an incidental thought. For over a century a high proportion of the best books on medieval history have been written by women. A list of just some of those who made a mark before 1914 is impressive enough:

---

[10]   Leyser, *Medieval Women*, p. 87.

[11]   Ibid., p. 85.

[12]   Ibid., p. 217.

for example, Mary Green (formerly Wood), Alice Green, Kate Norgate, Agnes Strickland, Mary Bateson, Bertha Phillpotts, Helen Cam and Bertha Putnam. The list would be far, far longer if extended towards today. Medieval history is one of the branches of learning to which women have made major contributions for a long, long time. When someone writes a book about women medievalists, Henrietta Leyser should have a deserved place in it.

Chapter 1
Augustine and Monnica

Kate Cooper

The relationship between mothers and children in antiquity is often elusive for modern historians, because it was for the most part not the kind of thing that our ancient predecessors cared to write about. What we know of it has been pieced together as a mosaic from disparate sources: from laws and inscriptions, and from occasional references in poetry and the ancient romances. For one family of the provincial gentry in late Roman North Africa, however, a window has been left open to shed a dazzling light. Monnica, the mother of Augustine, bishop of Hippo, is the subject of an extended memoir that forms part of Augustine's *Confessions*, the meditation on human frailty and the love of God that her son wrote upon becoming a bishop.[1]

Born in 354, Augustine was the son of Patricius, a clubbable member of the town council of Thagaste, a market town in the fertile valley of the Mejerda river (modern Souk Arras in eastern Algeria). In light of the father's good relations with one of the more powerful local landowners, the son's early brilliance meant that through him the family had the chance to raise its status. By the time

---

[1] I am grateful to Conrad Leyser, Mark Vessey, and Emily Spencer for saving me from various (but perhaps not all!) errors. Tom Heffernan and the members of his National Endowment for the Humanities seminar on Perpetua and Augustine, July–August 2010, offered stimulating debate on virtually every passage discussed. Margaret Miles and Clarissa Atkinson first introduced me to the subject, and I am as grateful as ever for their generosity and inspiration.

Monnica is a figure who has finally begun to attract the attention she deserves. Although I have not systematically cited studies that did not directly influence my thinking in writing this piece, I would like to call the reader's attention to a number of valuable recent studies. Clarissa W. Atkinson, '"Your Servant, My Mother"': the Figure of Saint Monica in the Ideology of Christian Motherhood', in Clarissa W. Atkinson, Constance H. Buchanan, Margaret R. Miles (eds), *Immaculate and Powerful: the Female in Sacred Image and Social Reality* (Boston, 1985), pp. 139–72, has influenced virtually everyone who came after her. The essays in Judith Chelius Stark (ed.), *Feminist Interpretations of Augustine* (State College, PA, 2007) offer a wonderful variety of approaches to Monnica, and Catherine Conybeare, *The Irrational Augustine* (Oxford, 2006), offers a sustained and fascinating comparison of Monnica with Plato's Diotima. The present study neglects, but does not ignore, James J. O'Donnell's discussion of Monnica's Donatist background, *Augustine: a New Biography* (New York, 2005), pp. 55–7.

Augustine's career was properly launched, it was within reason to aspire to an office that could confer promotion to the senatorial class. Augustine's education stretched the modest resources of his parents to breaking point, but it was a sound investment. Yet when Augustine reached sixteen the money ran out, and he was forced to suspend his studies, kicking his heels at home, until resources were found to send him back to school and then university.

We know very little about the family standing of Monnica's people, beyond the fact that they were of citizen status. According to the practice of the time, Patricius would have tried to marry the daughter of a local landowner slightly more powerful than his own father, and there is no reason to believe that he did not succeed. The story Augustine tells of his mother is that of a woman whose vivid imagination and human warmth had allowed her to expand her own horizons from the minor provincial town of Thagaste to the heights of Milan, then the empire's Western capital. It is possible that she had her own wealth and connections. Augustine's choice to bring his by then widowed mother with him to Milan when he went to the imperial city to make his career may have been a matter less of charity towards a widowed mother than of a sense – correct, as it turned out – that the social skills and contacts of an experienced provincial *matrona* could serve him well in establishing his standing at court.

Augustine's story of Monnica is coloured by his ambivalence about her worldly ambitions, and he tends to downplay her considerable nous. If he writes about her with great fondness, there is also a certain narcissism in his point of view. His memoir shows interest not in the mother's dreams, but in the son's conscience with respect to the disappointments he knows himself to have caused. Still, he reports with relief that, in the end, he had somehow managed to reconcile his mother's contradictory hopes for him.

There were other more painful memories to contend with, however. The *Confessions* also give us a glimpse of a second mother–son relationship, that of Augustine's son by the love of his life, the woman with whom he lived and whom he was forced to leave in the brutal game of arranged marriage and social climbing at court. When Augustine wrote the *Confessions* he had concluded his precipitous climb, retiring from public office, accepting baptism, and allowing himself to be ordained first as a Christian priest and then as a consecrated bishop. While he was unwilling to share with his readers even the name of his lost love, whom he had betrayed for the sake of ambition, he was able to muse freely on his years with Monnica. He was now far older than his mother had been at the time of his own childhood, and looked back at their years together with affection only mildly coloured by regret.

Monnica married at around fourteen, to Patricius, a man substantially older than herself. To a modern sensibility, it is difficult to imagine the challenge faced by the young Monnica when she first went as a bride to her husband's house. Augustine says that she was brought up 'in modesty and sobriety', and that she married early. 'When she reached marriageable age, she was given to a man and served him as her lord. She tried to win him for you, speaking to him of her virtues through which you made her beautiful, so that her husband loved, respected and admired her' (*Confessions*, 9.8.17).[2] It is somewhat shocking to remember that in Roman law the 'marriageable age' to which Augustine refers here was only twelve – although there is some evidence that Roman women normally married slightly later, in their mid-teens, and Monnica may have done so as well.

Augustine remembered his father as hot-tempered, and the marriage was not an easy one. Monnica and Patricius seem to have had three children. The first, probably the older son Navigius, must have been born when Monnica was in her mid teens, and there was also a girl. Augustine was born when his mother was twenty-three, and he may have been the last. Augustine rarely mentions his sister, but there is a hint of sibling rivalry when he writes about Navigius. The older brother appears repeatedly in Augustine's writings as a foil for the younger brother's brilliance and sensitivity. Navigius fails to follow his younger brother's train of thought, or his obtuseness leads him to miss a moment of complicity when Augustine and Monnica understand each other perfectly. The younger son was clearly possessive about his closeness to his mother.

The father, by contrast, does not seem to have been an important rival for her affections. As an older man, Augustine remembered Patricius as having been repeatedly unfaithful to Monnica, and he remembered Monnica as having turned a blind eye. It is possible that she was in fact grateful for his infidelities, since they may have allowed her to escape the cycle of almost continuous pregnancy and childbirth experienced by many other women. However, it is also possible, given the public health conditions of late Roman North Africa, that there were many pregnancies but only three that produced a surviving child.

Augustine offers us a window into the austere upbringing that prepared his mother for the task of holding her own when faced with a difficult older man and an equally difficult mother-in-law. Although she had been brought up by Christian parents, it seems to have been the relationship with the household's female slaves that left the most lasting impression on the child. Most important of these, in Monnica's memory, was an old woman who had been with the family since Augustine's grandfather's childhood. 'She used to speak highly not so much of her mother's diligence in training her as of a decrepit maidservant who

2   The most useful modern version of Augustine's text is Augustine, *Confessions*, ed. James J. O'Donnell (Oxford, 1992). I have cited, with minor amendments, Henry Chadwick's translation (Oxford, 1991).

had carried her father when he was an infant, in the way that infants are often carried on the back of older girls' (9.8.17). The old woman was an important figure in the household, both loved and feared.

> Because of this long service and for her seniority and high moral standards in a Christian house, she was held in great honour by her masters. So she was entrusted with responsibility for her master's daughters and discharged it with diligence and, when necessary, was vehement with a holy severity in administering correction. (9.8.17)

At points, her strategies for developing the girls' sense of self-control seem somewhat alarming. For example, the children were denied drinking water despite the North African heat. 'Outside those times when were fed a most modest meal at their parents' table, she allowed them to drink not even water, even if they were burning with thirst, wishing to avert the formation of a bad habit' (9.8.17). The Spartan training would serve Monnica well in her future life.

Another story, this time told of one of Monnica's childish companions, a slave-girl with whom she often did errands for her parents, makes vivid the awkward balance of power in the household. In even minor instances, the master's daughter had to show herself worthy of her privilege, or she would be made to feel it by the other children in the house. When Monnica was asked to fetch wine from the storage cask to fill the jug with which it was served at table, she would sometimes take a sip of the wine she was carrying, and eventually she acquired a taste for it. This left an opening for one of her playmates to wound her pride: 'The slave-girl who used to accompany her to the cask had a dispute with her young mistress which happened when they were alone together. Bitterly she insulted her by bringing up the accusation that she was a drunkard. The taunt hurt' (9.8.18). Augustine commends the child's reaction to the accusation: instead of trying to defend herself, 'she reflected ... and stopped the habit.'

The moral of the story (which Augustine may have heard from his mother) seems to be that the wise child Monnica was humble enough – or self-possessed enough – to find opportunity in even the most humiliating of childhood dramas. Even the malicious attention of other children who envied her virtue – or her position – and wanted to 'catch her out' could be taken as a valuable chance for moral betterment. '... The maidservant in her anger sought to wound her little mistress, not to cure her. But You, Lord, ruler of heaven and earth, turn to your own purposes the deep torrents. Even from the fury of one soul you brought healing to another' (9.8.18). This ability of Monnica's to find valuable correction where others would have seen only pointless humiliation was to be one of her great gifts.

When Monnica married, she was again the target of spiteful tactics from her inferiors, this time from the female slaves of her husband's household. 'Monnica's mother-in-law was at first stirred up to hostility towards her by the whisperings of malicious maidservants', Augustine tells us. However, she won her husband's mother over, 'by her respectful manner, and by persistence in patience and gentleness. The result was that her mother-in-law denounced the interfering tongues of the slave-girls to her son' (9.9.20). We must imagine here a household in which the mother-in-law is a widow living with her adult son; otherwise it would have been to the father-in-law that disputes among the household's women were reported.

The power of punishment wielded by the *paterfamilias* is seen here as an instrument of good order. The mother-in-law applies to her son to cut short a situation that has spun out of control. 'The domestic harmony between herself and her daughter-in-law was being disturbed, and she asked for them to be punished. He met his mother's wish by subjecting the girls of whom she complained to a whipping'. We are led to believe that order was thus successfully restored. 'From then on, no one dared to utter a word, and they lived with a memorably gentle benevolence towards each other' (9.9.20).

Yet the bishop betrays ambivalence about his father's power, which was not always applied with justice. As a beloved younger son, Augustine's natural instinct was to take his mother's side as he watched her efforts to cope with a difficult husband, and this sympathy colours his account of the relationship between his parents, written long after both of them were dead. He paints his father as warm-hearted if somewhat volatile – 'He was exceptional both for his kindness and for his quick temper' (9.9.19) – and as someone who could not be trusted to manage his temper. In this, Patricius was probably not unlike many Roman husbands of his day.

Augustine was grateful for his mother's pragmatic attitude to her situation. Again, her patient willingness to look for opportunities where others saw only difficulty would stand her in good stead. 'She knew that an angry husband should not be opposed, not only by anything she did, but even by a word.' He did not see her as allowing herself to be walked upon, but rather as having the self-control to choose her moment. She could be trusted to make her own case when she was met with unjust criticism, but she was cautious about the timing. 'Once she saw that he had become calm and quiet, and that the occasion was opportune, she would explain the reason for her action, in case perhaps he had reacted without sufficient consideration' (9.9.19).

In his desire to celebrate his mother's adept handling of a potentially threatening imbalance of power, Augustine steers perhaps rather too close to blaming those women who were not so fortunate for the difficulties they experienced with their own husbands. When other women complained about the behaviour of their husbands, Monnica was more practical than sympathetic. 'Speaking as if in jest but offering serious advice, Monnica used to blame their tongues. she thought that they should remember their condition and not proudly withstand their masters' (9.9.19).

All concerned seem to have taken it for granted that wives who did not manage their husbands' tempers successfully could expect physical abuse. When Monnica gave advice to her friends, she was met with admiration. 'The wives were astounded, knowing what a violent husband she had to put up with. Yet it was unheard of, nor was there ever a mark to show, that Patrick had beaten his wife or that a domestic quarrel had caused dissension between them.' In any event, Augustine's impression was that Monnica's advice was useful to those women who took it to heart. 'Those who followed her advice found by experience that they were grateful for it, while those who did not were treated as subordinate and mistreated' (9.9.19).

Years later as a bishop, when he wrote letters of advice to married women, Augustine would suggest a similar tactic of charm and patience for dealing with difficult husbands. He has sometimes been criticized for this: since it was certainly a bishop's duty to admonish a man who was misbehaving toward his wife, some scholars have thought that it was wrong to encourage the wives to make light of any difficulty with their husbands. However, if Augustine reveals any weakness of judgement in this arena, he came by it honestly. It is characteristic of children who grow up in abusive households to internalize the distress caused by a parent's outbursts, and to believe, however wrongly, that if only one could find the right formula to soothe the nerves of the abuser, the abusive behaviour would cease. Augustine clearly believed that his mother had somehow found the magic formula, and he wished to dwell on her victory.

One imagines that, as he tells the story, the now-grown son is looking for a way to put an uncomfortable memory to rest. Even if the young Monnica's attempts to steer her husband away from intimidating behaviour and even violence were largely successful, having to witness them must have been distressing to her children. For the mother, the presence of a sympathetic son must have been a source of strength, especially a son who paid as close attention to her struggles as Augustine's memoir reveals that he did. One can understand why the boy was the object of such intense affection.

One wonders, too, whether Monnica's ambition for her son – the ambition that drove him first to Carthage and then to Rome and Milan – was not a way of imagining a different future, not only for him but also for herself. The life he chose in early adulthood, which took him far from Thagaste to the imperial capital at Milan, must have seemed a provocative answer to the years of enduring the temper of a swaggering provincial *paterfamilias*.

One of the petty humiliations to be endured in Thagaste seems to have been the routine expressions of the father's masculine self-importance:

> when one day at the baths my father saw that I was showing signs of virility and the stirrings of adolescence, he was overjoyed to suppose that he would now be having grandchildren, and told my mother so. His delight was that of the intoxication which makes the world oblivious to You, its Creator, and to love your creation instead of you. (2.3.6)[3]

Behind the charge that Patricius had forgotten to honour God one senses an understandable feeling of discomfort with the father's jubilation at the son's sexual development.

Years later, when Augustine came to tell the story, he was safely past his own years as a Roman husband and father. If he had felt pride in his own boy's emerging sexuality, he had nonetheless rejected the culture of the baths – his own father's culture – with its easy male sexual display. By the time Augustine's son Adeodatus was a teenager, both he and his father were living together in a monastic community – an atmosphere of male sociability, to be sure, but one where talk about sex was firmly discouraged. By the time Augustine wrote his *Confessions*, Adeodatus had been dead for a decade.

This is something we must remember when we return to the story of Monnica. Among many losses, the loss of his mother was one that Augustine was drawn to talking about. However, if he was willing to speak expansively about her, this is by no means because this loss was the most painful. Rather, it was somehow the most manageable. There were regrets, but they were regrets that could be laid to rest. He was able to tell himself – and to believe it – that whatever the petty deceptions and betrayals of their long relationship, he had in the end been true to her.

The relationship with Monnica had been, as Augustine now saw it, a perfect instrument for drawing him towards God. Sometimes unwittingly, Monnica's desires had been aligned with God's deeper purpose for her son, and the most bitter of her disappointments had turned out to be indispensable steps towards realizing the dearest hopes of her heart.

This point is nowhere more visible than in Augustine's account of his departure for Rome. At twenty-eight, after he had been teaching rhetoric at

---

[3]   Garry Wills, *Saint Augustine* (London, 2000), pp. xvii–xix, sheds valuable light on this passage. On this scene, and on Augustine's family life more generally, see Brent D. Shaw, 'The Family in Late Antiquity: the Experience of Augustine', *Past and Present*, 115 (1987): 3–51.

Carthage for a number of years, he had been met with a blow that had darkened his outlook. Augustine had long waited for the opportunity to consult with the Manichaean bishop Faustus, whose arrival in Carthage, it had been promised, would offer a resolution to some inconsistencies in the Manichaen teaching that were a source of intellectual agitation to the younger man. Yet Faustus brought only disappointment. Augustine could see why others loved him – he was a generous and humane teacher – but he was by no means a great light intellectually, and could do little to reconcile the contradictions that his brilliant pupil had discovered. At this juncture, Augustine was offered the chance of a lifetime. Through Manichaean friends, Augustine was offered the chance to continue his teaching career in Rome, where he would find not only better compensation and greater glory but also, word had it, students who were far more serious about their studies than the rabble-rousers of Carthage.

Augustine's friends encouraged him warmly, but against his going he had to count the formidable will of Monnica.

> You knew, God, why I left Carthage and went to Rome, yet of that you gave no hint either to me or to my mother, who was fearfully upset at my going and followed me down to the sea. But as she vehemently held onto me, calling me back or saying she would come with me, I deceived her ... I lied to my mother – to such a mother – and I gave her the slip ... By her floods of tears what was she begging of you, my God, but that you would not allow me to sail? Yet in your deep counsel you heard the central point of her longing, namely that you would make me what she continually prayed for, though not granting what she then asked. The wind blew, and filled our sails, and the shore was lost to sight. (5.8.15)

It has long been remarked that Monnica's weeping on the shore intentionally echoes that of Dido weeping for Aeneas, about which Augustine has much to say in the *Confessions*. Some of the most interesting approaches have emphasized Augustine's self-irony in telling the story in the way he does.

> Augustine was making a point, and part of the point is to demonstrate the falseness of his self-conception as a Vergilian hero ... Aeneas had fled his mistress, the enraged queen of Carthage, on a divine mission to build an empire; Augustine sneaked away by night from his mother, in search of more docile students.[4]

The episode also evokes an earlier reading of Dido, in Book One, where Augustine describes his education and his love for tales of suffering. 'What is

---

[4]   Camille Bennett, 'The Conversion of Vergil: the *Aeneid* in Augustine's *Confessions*', *Revue des Études Augustiniennes*, 34 (1988): 47–69, at 61.

more pitiable than a wretch without pity from himself who weeps over the death of Dido dying for love of Aeneas, but not weeping over himself dying for his lack of love for you, my God, light of my heart?' (1.13.21).

William Werpehowski has explored how Augustine invokes a parallel in Book One between Dido's love for Aeneas and Augustine's own misguided love, as a youth, for worldly pleasure. As he looks back, he sees his pleasure in Dido's suffering as misguided. It is only his mother, he tells us, who sees the real reason to weep, which is that her son has been trapped, by his earthly passions, in the world of death. 'When the boy weeps, he does not weep well. His mother weeps well, and for him, instead. Monnica, insistently faithful, the very voice of God speaking in her cries and warnings (II, 3), stands as contrast and challenge to her son's weeping over Dido.'⁵ Werpehowski makes the important point here that, just as Augustine the schoolboy is encouraged to weep over Dido, who has committed suicide for the sake of love, so 'the tears of Monnica concern a suicide whose loves have led him to death' (61). It is *Augustine*, not Monnica, who most resembles Dido in the *Confessions*.

When Monnica takes her turn as Dido in Book Five, however, a different point is being made. Augustine's own desires are being put to the service of God's purpose, however obliquely. 'You applied the pricks which made me tear myself away from Carthage, and you put before me the attractions of Rome to draw me there, using people who love a life of death committing insane action in this world, promising vain rewards in the next' (5.8.14).

So Monnica's temporary disappointment in her son is not a matter for regret on Augustine's part, but rather for musing on the opacity of God's purpose in both their lives.

> As mothers do, she loved to have me with her, but much more than most mothers, and she did not understand that you were to use my absence as a means of bringing her joy. She did not know that. So she wept and lamented ... and yet after accusing me of deception and cruelty, she turned again to pray for me. (5.8.15)

There is a point here to be made about how Augustine sees human attachments. Kim Power has noted that he repeatedly sounds a note of caution about human affections, and in particular encourages his male friends to try to wean their mothers of a human affection for their sons that is focused too sharply on the creature rather than the Creator.⁶

---

5   William Werpehowski, 'Weeping at the Death of Dido: Sorrow, Virtue, and Augustine's Confessions', *The Journal of Religious Ethics*, 19 (1991): 175–91, at 180.

6   Kim Power, *Veiled Desire: Augustine's Writing on Women* (London, 1995), p. 85, citing *Letter* 243: 'Years later his advice to the youth Laetus about the appropriate way to deal

By contrast, when Augustine tells of his parting with the mother of his son, none of the same reassurances are in place. When Augustine reached Milan, before his conversion to Christianity, it became clear that if he could find 'a wife with some money' (6.11.19) his gift for rhetoric would allow him to pursue a political career, perhaps as the governor of a Roman province. His friend Alypius tried to convince him to remain a bachelor and pursue the life of philosophy, but Monnica was able to find a powerful family who would betroth their charming ten-year-old daughter to Augustine, now in his thirties, if he would give up the concubine with whom he had lived for over a decade. Augustine makes it clear, in this passage, that he had essentially allowed himself to be sold, in exchange for the wealth and hope of preferment his prospective parents-in-law could offer.

His first task, now that he had sold himself, was to send the mother of his son back to Africa. 'Meanwhile, my sins multiplied. My concubine was torn from my side because she was a hindrance to my marriage. My heart, which clung to her, was torn and wounded till it bled. And she went back to Africa, vowing that she would never know any other man' (6.15.25).

It is probably for this reason that Augustine's spiritual crisis in the summer of 386 turned on the question of whether or not he would marry after all. Most scholars have assumed that, having fallen under the influence of Alypius and the circle of Ambrose, Augustine believed that the only true form of Christianity was ascetic Christianity, but this is not what the text says. In fact, Augustine says he had won the debate with Alypius over the respective virtues of marriage and continence, largely through the example of the loving harmony of his relationship with his concubine. 'If the honourable name of marriage had been added to my life, he would have had no reason to be surprised that I could not despise married life. So he himself began to desire marriage' (6.12.22).

Indeed, Augustine's later writings as a bishop persistently accord a spiritual value and a moral obligation to the relationship between a man and his concubine.[7] While others saw the liaison as entirely exploitative – with the man acquiring no long-term obligation toward his partner or her children – Augustine would argue that in moral terms it should be seen as equivalent to the legal bond of marriage. Looking back, Augustine commented on the naïve male self-centredness of his debate with Alypius: 'Neither of us considered it more than a marginal issue how the beauty of having a wife lies in the obligation to respect the discipline of marriage, and to bring up children' (6.12.22).

---

with a possessive mother perhaps rings with the authenticity of experience … "the very private and personal love for you [must] be killed in her, in case she thinks it a more important bond than your unity as Christians".

[7]   On marriage and concubinage in Augustine's thought, see Kate Cooper, *The Fall of the Roman Household* (Cambridge, 2007), chapter 4, 'Such Trustful Partnership'.

So in Augustine's own case, the problem was not sex and marriage *per se*, but rather the immoral aspect of his own willingness to betray the mother of his child for the sake of money and worldly honour. It is therefore no surprise that, at the climax of Book Eight of the *Confessions*, when during the famous moment in the garden Augustine decides to dedicate his life to God, the momentous change in his life is interpreted in light of his relationship with women. Certainly, he was guilty of a terrible sexual sin, but the sin was not sleeping with his concubine, it was casting her away.

Where Monnica figured in all this is difficult to plot. If Augustine blamed her for insisting on the career match and the dismissal of his partner, he is careful not to say so, although he famously criticized his parents for holding him back from marriage in his youth (5.2.3). Instead, he tries to exonerate her by suggesting that her reasoning was based on the notion that, if he were to marry a good Catholic girl, it would be easier to steer him towards baptism. However, there is reason to suspect that his concubine was herself a Catholic, so the same aim – minus the social ambitions – could have been realized through her.[8]

All this leads to a reading of Augustine's conversion to asceticism as a way out of a morally untenable position. He finds his chance in a flash of illumination while reading Romans 13: 14 ('put on the Lord Jesus Christ and make no provision for the flesh in its lusts'). 'At once, with the last words of this sentence, it was as if a light of relief from anxiety flooded into my heart' (8.11.29). Augustine felt that he had been given a sign that God's watchful eye had been present in his struggle.

In turning from his moment of insight towards thinking about how it will shape his future, Augustine again stresses Monnica's role as an unwitting agent of the divine will. He tells us that, once he had recovered himself, he told his friend Alypius, who was with him in the garden, what had happened, and the two went together to tell Monnica, who was indoors. 'She was filled with joy ... she blessed You, who "have the power to do more than we ask or think" (Eph. 3: 20) She saw that You had granted her far more than she had long been praying for in her painful and tearful murmurings' (8.12.30). The watchful eye of God and the passionate prayers of his mother, Augustine and Monnica discover together, had been working in unison all along. His story ends not in marriage, but in baptism: he is united neither with his concubine, nor with the Milanese heiress, but with the Lord.

It is the same theme of conformity between Monnica's blind love for her son and God's all-knowing plan for him that characterizes Augustine's moving account of Monnica's death, which took place some months after the scene in

---

8   Power, *Veiled Desire*, pp. 95–6, offers an illuminating discussion of Augustine's failure to marry his concubine.

the garden. The episode begins with Augustine and Monnica pausing at Ostia, the port of Rome, where the two were preparing to embark for Africa and there to make a new life once Augustine had decided, as a result of his change of heart, to renounce his professorship in the imperial capital.

> The day now approached when she was to depart this life, a day which You knew and we did not. I believe it came about through Your hidden ways that she and I were standing and leaning out of a window, overlooking a garden. It was the house where we were staying at Ostia on the Tiber, where, far removed from the crowds, after the exhaustion of a long journey, we were recovering our strength for the voyage. (9.9.23)

Here Augustine not only alerts the reader to how far they had come in their homeward journey; he is also invoking, with the window and the garden, the *locus amoenus*, the stereotypical setting where the Roman reader would expect a philosophical dialogue to take place. 'Alone with each other, we talked very intimately ... we asked what quality the eternal life of the saints will have, a life which "neither eye has seen nor ear heard, nor has it entered into the heart of man"' (I Cor. 2: 9; *Conf* 9.9.23). United in their musing they found themselves able to reach beyond the limits of reason and into a deeper kind of contemplation.

> Our minds were lifted up by an ardent affection towards eternal being itself ... in this wisdom there is no past and future, but only Being, since it is eternal ... And while we talked and sighed after it, we touched it in some small degree, by a moment of total concentration of the heart. (9.9.24)

Augustine is conscious that, in that moment, he and Monnica had understood something of the nature of eternity, the fuller life beyond this earthly life.

> We would hear His word, not through the tongue of the flesh, or through the voice of an angel, not through the sound of thunder, nor through the obscurity of a symbolic utterance. Him, whom in these things we love, we would hear in person. at that moment we extended our reach and in a flash of mental energy made contact with the eternal wisdom which abides beyond all things. (9.9.25)

Now the reader is ready, emotionally if not mentally, for what comes next. It is not Augustine, but Monnica, who sees where the vision is leading.

> Lord, you know that on that day. my mother said "My son, as for myself, I now find no pleasure in this life. What I have still to do here, and why I am here, I do

not know. My hope in this world is already fulfilled. The one reason I wanted to stay longer in this world was my desire to see you a Catholic Christian before I die. My God has granted this. what have I to do here?" (9.9.26)

Augustine does not say so, but we may suspect that, if he is remembering the conversation as it really happened, it could well be that Monnica herself had steered the conversation toward thoughts of eternity and the life beyond the body. She may well have anticipated that in her fragile condition the long sea-journey from Ostia back to Africa would prove too much for her, and wanted to prepare her son for the likelihood that he would have to make the journey without her.

In any event, before the week was out Monnica had fallen into a fever; she slipped into unconsciousness and then rallied long enough to tell Augustine and Navigius, who were at her bedside, that they should not worry if they had to bury her in Italy instead of bringing her back with them to Africa. 'Bury my body anywhere you like; let no anxiety about that disturb you. I have only one request to make of you, that you remember me at the altar of the Lord, wherever you may be' (9.9.27). Augustine tells us that she died on the ninth day of her illness.

The next few paragraphs record the efforts of Augustine and the men around him to channel their grief into a confident expectation of the afterlife. Here, the boy Adeodatus emerges as the one who gives outward expression to the grief that all of them must have felt, a wailing which the older men were quick to silence. Yet Augustine tells us he himself felt it desperately, 'a very affectionate and precious bond suddenly torn apart' (9.9.30). Augustine begins to muse on his last days with his mother, grateful for her kindness in telling him, as he tended to her, how much she valued his devotion to her as a son. He recognized, too, what she had done for him: 'Now that I had lost the immense support she gave, my soul was wounded, and, as it were, my life torn to pieces, since my life and hers had become a single thing' (9.9.30). As the chanting of Psalms and the preparations for the burial of the body began, Augustine went to a place apart, to struggle with his feelings. When his friends followed him, he found himself able – barely – to maintain his composure. 'They listened to me intently, and supposed me to have no feeling of grief' (9.9.31). This performance – of command over what he felt – was of paramount importance in the culture of the Roman male, a culture which Augustine did not question, although he often strayed beyond its boundaries.

Later, however, alone with his thoughts and with God, he was able to find an opportunity to weep freely, and he did not hesitate to admit it. 'Now I let flow the tears which I had held back, so that they ran as freely as they wished. My heart rested upon them, and it reclined upon them because it was Your ears that were present, not those of some human critic who would put a proud interpretation on my weeping' (9.9.33). Although Augustine shared the view of his contemporaries, that for a man to give in to his emotions was somehow to lose honour, he understood, at the same time, that in the sight of God it had not been wrong to confess how deeply his life had been connected to that of another one of his creatures, and how painful he had found the prospect of going forward without her.

With this episode, Augustine concluded the story of Monnica's life, but also of his own. After the account of Monnica's death, he turns to face his audience in the present, eliding the nine years between his departure from Ostia and his assumption of office as Bishop of Hippo. It was to be all but thirty years before he began to write retrospectively again. Thus the *Confessions* is the story of how Augustine lost, one by one, the people whom he most loved.

Among Augustine's many losses, that of Monnica was the one on which he could most comfortably permit himself to dwell. There were a number of reasons for this. First, perhaps, it could never be wrong for a Roman son – or for a Christian – to reflect on what he owed his parents: the value of filial piety ran as a deep current in both traditions. Second, Augustine's intervening years as a priest and then as a bishop had taught him that there might be others who could learn from his mother's story: from her fortitude in working for her son's salvation even when the prospect was at its most bleak, or from her pluck in finding a way to way to mediate the peculiar difficulties of her lot as a wife and mother.

At the same time, the loss of Monnica was the most tractable of his losses, and the safest to explore in detail. It was right and natural that a grown man should lose his parents, and it could be said, in many ways, that Monnica's life on earth had ended well. Augustine's own role in her story was certainly imperfect, but in the end he had been true to her, and could now in all honesty remain true to her memory. If it was a story of loss, it was also a story with a happy ending.

Chapter 2

From Maternal Kin to Jesus as Mother: Royal Genealogy and Marian Devotion in the Ninth-century West

Conrad Leyser

When, in the Middle Ages, did men discuss motherhood? One answer is, in the twelfth century, with the ascent of the cult of the Virgin Mary.[1] In a series of prayers and treatises – above all, Eadmer of Canterbury's treatise on the Immaculate Conception – a remarkable generation of men articulated rich patterns of complex devotion to Mary as Virgin and Mother that were to endure for centuries.[2] Yet what of the period beforehand? This essay explores an earlier, less familiar, epoch of Marian piety.[3] In the ninth century, what we find is a devotional culture held in thrall by the power of the ruling family, the Carolingians. Mary herself was imagined as a royal Queen of Heaven, adored by dynasts male and female, and by well-born churchmen. In this era, then, 'motherhood' was yet to be fully abstracted from the family matrix.

Twelfth-century contemplation of Mary as a mother changed the way men thought about motherhood. 'But you, Jesus, good lord, are you not also a mother?': so said Anselm of Canterbury, Eadmer's mentor.[4] His prayers featured Jesus as a mother hen, raising her chicks. In the following generation, Bernard

---

[1] See R.W. Southern, *The Making of the Middle Ages* (London, 1953), pp. 246–54. My thanks to Helmut Reimitz for his help and advice. My debt to the work of Kate Cooper will be obvious: in need of acknowledgement is her galvanizing orientation of my thinking in relation to this piece. The dedicatee, meanwhile, will recall the author's early Marian efforts.

[2] Eadmer of Canterbury, *Tractatus de conceptione sanctae Mariae*, ed. H. Thurston and P.T. Slater (Breisgau, 1904).

[3] See further Rachel Fulton, *From Judgement to Passion: Devotion to Christ and the Virgin Mary, 800–1200* (New York, 2002); Henry Mayr-Harting, 'The Idea of the Assumption of Mary in the West, 800–1200', in R.N. Swanson (ed.), *The Church and Mary*, Studies in Church History 39 (Woodbridge, 2004), pp. 86–111.

[4] Anselm, Prayer 10 to St Paul, as cited and discussed by Caroline Bynum, *Jesus as Mother: Studies in the Spirituality of the High Middle Ages* (Berkeley, 1982), pp. 110–69 at p. 114.

of Clairvaux and other Cistercian monks began to imagine the crucifixion, startlingly, in terms of a mother nursing her children: the piercing of Jesus' side became, in this perspective, a scene of lactation.

This devotion to Jesus as Mother found its modern interpreter in Caroline Bynum.[5] Offered over a generation ago, Bynum's analysis began by insisting that the imagination of Jesus as Mother did not reflect in any direct way a culture of maternity. In the later Middle Ages, female mystics might seek to refashion Jesus in their own image – but in the first instance, those who imagined Jesus as Mother were not themselves mothers, nor were they female. They were male ascetics.

Bynum's explanation of this apparent paradox was that men interested in motherhood were making a statement about themselves and their authority. In the twelfth century, male lords, whether secular or ecclesiastical, were expected to rule through fear, or even savagery. However there emerged a group of men who sought to defy this culture of brutality, even if they continued to enjoy the privileges of lordship. To profess devotion to Jesus as Mother was to broadcast the possibility that power over others could be exerted without terror or exploitation. In their embrace of the language of motherhood, men such as Anselm and Bernard witnessed the hope that authority could even be nurturing.

The context for Bynum's analysis was the new society of Latin Europe that took shape after the first millennium. An intensification of the regime of agricultural production was the basis for the first indigenous urban society in the West, as opposed to one imported from the Mediterranean.[6] The most obvious social cost was borne by those who laboured in the fields – but there was also a price paid by the landholding elite. The new dispensation called for a drastic reorganization of inheritance customs. If land was to function effectively as a profitable economic unit, it could no longer be shared equally among the next generation. Partible inheritance gave way to primogeniture, resulting in the disinheritance of younger sons and daughters.[7]

For the disinherited, and especially for disinherited men, there was, however, the possibility of reinvention. If they entered the Church, they could enjoy the fruits of institutional property in the great monasteries or cathedral churches of the West. The price for this was permanent foreswearing of participation in the biological family, and the adoption of a life of celibacy. Such a division of sexual

---

[5]   Bynum, *Jesus as Mother*, an early version of which appeared first in *Harvard Theological Review*, 70 (1977): 257–84. Bynum's theme is taken up by Brian McGuire elsewhere in this volume.

[6]   See, for example, R.I. Moore, *The First European Revolution, c. 970–1215* (Oxford, 2000) for an analysis in these terms.

[7]   See, for example, Georges Duby, *The Chivalrous Society*, trans. Cynthia Postan (London, 1977).

labour between the clergy and laymen had been mooted since the fourth century, but it was not regularized across the Latin West until the eleventh and twelfth centuries. This was the achievement of the movement for Church Reform; and it has been the achievement of the past generation of scholarship to begin to understand Reform in terms of the wider transformation of the social order.[8] While some of the premises of this analysis have been the subject of intensive debate – such as the extent to which enserfment or primogeniture was the rule across the Latin West – it is much harder to doubt that the campaign for clerical celibacy and its corollary, the campaign against simoniac acquisition of office, were European-wide phenomena.[9]

This newly established clerical elite were at the cutting edge of devotional fashion. New developments in the cult of the Virgin and devotion to Jesus as Mother were the product of the imagination of men displaced from the family and challenged with producing an institutional identity. Changes in high medieval Marian piety, then, can be directly correlated with changes in family structure and kinship strategies.

Is this correlation a fleeting coincidence or a more lasting phenomenon? In the course of the long arc from the seventh to the twelfth centuries, most would agree that the structure of the European family altered profoundly. The early medieval kin group was expansive, even polymorphous. Descent was traced in both the male and the female lines, with the result that one's kin could stretch far and wide. 'Kinship' was a not a delimited biological given, but a superabundance of claims and social obligations, likely to produce both enmity and solidarity in equal measure. Five hundred years later, the family was a tightly defined lineage, in which descent was traced in the single male line. This basic contrast between the early and the high medieval family was conceived by Karl Schmid, on whose work Georges Duby drew substantially in his account of the rise of primogeniture at the turn of the first millennium.[10]

---

[8]   An initiative taken by R.I. Moore, 'Family, Community, and Cult on the Eve of the Gregorian Reform', *Transactions of the Royal Historical Society*, 30 (1980): 49–69.

[9]   On the family, see Pauline Stafford, 'La Mutation Familiale: a Suitable Case for Caution', in J. Hill and M. Swan (eds), *The Community, the Family and the Saint: Patterns of Power in Early Medieval Europe* (Turnhout, 1998), pp. 103–25. From a huge bibliography, the essays collected in Lester K. Little and Barbara H. Rosenwein, *Debating the Middle Ages: Issues and Readings* (Oxford, 1998) provide perhaps the best introduction to the debate over the 'Transformation of the Year 1000'.

[10]   For Anglophone introductions, see Karl Schmid, 'The Structure of the Nobility in the Earlier Middle Ages', in Timothy Reuter (ed. and trans.), *The Medieval Nobility* (Amsterdam, 1979), pp. 37–59; and R.I. Moore, 'Duby's Eleventh Century', *History*, 69 (1984): 36–54. See now Régine Le Jan, *Famille et pouvoir dans le monde franc (viie–xe siècle). Essai d'anthropologie sociale* (Paris, 2003).

In the late 1960s, however, Karl Leyser offered a critique of the Schmid thesis.[11] Firstly, he issued a note of caution. Schmid's study of *Libri memoriales*, the compendious records of names kept by the great Geman monasteries, did not necessarily reflect social reality so much as family self-consciousness. Secondly, in studying the German aristocracy from the ninth to the twelfth centuries, what struck Leyser most forcibly was the element of continuity. Kin groups east of the Rhine did not contract to a patrilineage: maternal kin remained important across the tenth eleventh, and twelfth centuries. Deep into the age of Church Reform, churchmen in Germany found that they could not rise above family networks. A clear division of biological dynasties and institutional identities did not obtain. Other scholars have subsequently suggested that the German case is not, in fact, exceptional: much the same may actually be true in the lands west of the Rhine.[12]

If the high medieval cult of Mary among male celibates relates to the narrowing of kinship in the eleventh and twelfth centuries, in the earlier era of sprawling kinship networks, we would expect to find a more inclusive devotional culture. In a world where mothers and maternal kin were still central to the representation of families, and in which churchmen and lay dynasts were not so clearly separated out, Mary did indeed assume a central place as a mother with a royal lineage.

Mary as a Dynast

Mary, her son and her husband appear well suited as a devotional model for elites with complex, ramifying kin relations. Mary and Jesus were, after all, Joseph's second family: in one well-established tradition, he was understood to be a much older man, a widower with children from a first marriage. One of these, James, was believed to have written an apocryphal account of his stepmother Mary's family history, to which we turn in a moment.

---

[11]   Karl Leyser, 'The German Aristocracy from the Ninth to the Twelfth Centuries. A Historical and Cultural Sketch', *Past and Present*, 41 (1968): 25–53. A debate ensued on terminology, which deflected attention from Leyser's original critique of Schmid: see Donald Bullough, 'Early Medieval Social Groupings: the Terminology of Kinship', *Past and Present*, 45 (1969): 3–18, and Karl Leyser, 'Maternal Kin in Early Medieval Germany: a Reply', *Past and Present*, 49 (1970): 126–34.

[12]   See in particular Anita Guerreau-Jalabert, 'Sur les structures de parenté dans l'Europe mediévale', *Annales: économies, sociétés, civilizations*, 36 (1981): 1028–49; eadem, 'La désignation des relations et des groupes de parenté en latin mediéval', *Archivium latinitatis medii aevi (Bulletin du Cange)*, 46–47 (1988): 65–108.

Mary herself, 'prompts genealogical thinking', as one scholar has put it.[13] The canonical Gospels set up something of a conundrum with regard to her lineage. Readers of Matthew, in particular, are left puzzled. The evangelist asserts that Jesus is of royal descent, announcing his work as 'the book of the generation of Jesus Christ, the son of David' (Matt. 1: 1). Then, in a baffling *non-sequitur*, great attention is devoted to establishing the genealogy of Joseph, a bystander in the begetting of Jesus. Jesus' claim to royalty must depend on Mary, and so on maternal kin – but Matthew and the other Gospels say nothing about Mary's family.

One way to solve the problem was simply to insist that Mary also was descended from David. From the second century onward, apologists developed the interpretation that Matthew's 'book of generations' was in fact, a genealogy of Mary. Exegetes offered the reassurance that biblical genealogies never referred to women, and so nothing sinister should be read into the exclusive focus on Joseph. 'For Joseph, read Mary', exegetes from Origen onwards proposed.[14]

Another strategy was to 'backfill' Mary's history. Supplementary narrative relating to her birth took its point of departure from the second-century Protoevangelium of James, the stepbrother of Jesus.[15] Here the story of Mary's birth is unfolded on the pattern of the miraculous fertility of Sarah, the wife of Abraham. Anna, the wife of the patriarch Joachim, barren for many years, yearns for a child. Her prayers are answered, and Mary is born. Aged twelve, she is betrothed to Joseph, but before the marriage she is summoned to the Temple to assist in the making of a veil. The task requires 'pure virgins of the tribe of David', and Mary is one such, the narrator asserts, before leading into the scene of the annunciation.[16] The Protoevangelium of James proved extremely successful with readers in the ancient Mediterranean and beyond. For early medieval societies, Mary's royal lineage was a given of sacred history.

In modern times, this dynastic Mary has been understudied, and indeed Mary in the early Middle Ages as a whole has received comparatively little attention.

---

[13]   Dominique Iogna-Prat, 'Le culte de la Vierge sous le règne de Charles le Chauve', *Les Cahiers de Saint-Michel de Cuxa*, 22 (1992): 97–116 at p. 99 (repr. in Iogna-Prat (ed.), *Marie: Le culte de la vierge dans la société médiévale* (Paris, 1996), pp. 65–98. In the same volume, see further Anita Guerreau-Jalabert, 'L'Arbre de Jessé et l'ordre chrétien de la parenté', pp. 137–70.

[14]   See Geoffrey Dunn, 'The Ancestry of Jesus According to Tertullian: *ex David per Mariam*', *Studia Patristica*, 36 (2001): 349–55 for a discussion and further references.

[15]   See Edgar Hennecke and William Schneemelcher (eds), *New Testament Apocrypha*, trans. R.McL. Wilson (2 vols, Philadelphia, 1963), vol. 1, pp. 370–88. Citations below are from this edition.

[16]   Protoevangelium of James 10, p. 379.

Mariologists have tended to devote their attentions to the periods on either side – to Mary in the later Roman Empire, or in high medieval Europe. These are indeed the formative periods with regard to Marian doctrine. If the twelfth century proposed the Immaculate Conception, the corresponding landmark for the Church in late antiquity is the Council of Ephesus in 431. At this gathering, Mary was officially proclaimed Theotokos, or in Latin *Dei genetrix*, Mother of God. This declaration formed part of the intensive discussion in this period of the nature, or natures, of Christ. To affirm Mary as Theotokos was to insist that Christ was both fully human and fully divine, against those who wished to diminish or adjust either side of his nature.[17] After Ephesus, and before Eadmer and his generation, from a strictly theological point of view, there is little to report by way of change or progress on Mariology.

This theologically driven approach carries the risks of superficiality and anachronism. If all we look for is doctrinal innovation, we will miss the creative energies poured into Marian devotion by early medieval societies. We are also in danger of assuming that 'theology' as such was socially important. No doubt it became so in the world of Anselm and Bernard. The schools of Paris and Oxford, founded in the twelfth century, were designed precisely to formulate and to teach the discipline of theology – but to assume that 'doctrine' was at the centre of Christian society or even intellectual culture in previous eras is to read backwards. Specifically, it is to presume that churchmen had attained a sufficient degree of institutional autonomy to be able to launch and sustain an abstract discourse of Christian teaching. This process of institutionalization may already have been underway before the first millennium – but the task is to trace its development, not to assume its prior existence.[18]

Recent work on Mary as Theotokos in the later Roman Empire demonstrates what may be accomplished if we abandon theology as a starting point. Kenneth Holum, Vassiliki Limberis and Kate Cooper have shown that to regard late Roman Marian doctrine as a handmaiden of Christology is to miss the point.[19] The status of Mary was at the very centre of the discussion, for concrete political

---

[17]   On the term Theotokos, see D.F. Wright, 'From "God-Bearer" to "Mother of God" in the Later Fathers', in Swanson (ed.), *Church and Mary*, pp. 22–30.

[18]   See now Steffen Patzold, *Episcopus. Wissen über Bischöfe im Frankenreich des späten 8. bis frühen 10. Jahrhunderts* (Ostfildern, 2008).

[19]   Kenneth Holum, *Theodosian Empresses: Women and Imperial Dominion in Late antiquity* (Berkeley, 1982); Vassiliki Limberis, *Divine Heiress: the Virgin Mary and the Creation of Christian Constantinople* (London, 1994); Kate Cooper, 'Contesting the Nativity: Wives, Virgins, and Pulcheria's Imitatio Mariae', *Scottish Journal of Religious Studies*, 19 (1998): 31–43; Cooper, 'Empress and *Theotokos*: Gender and Patronage in the Christological Controversy', in Swanson (ed.), *Church and Mary*, pp. 39–51.

reasons. If Mary was not the Mother of God, this threatened to cast a slur on the imperial family, the chief impresarios of the religious cult in the Empire. Thus the initiative at the Council of Ephesus lay not, or not only, with the bishops charged with reaching a decision, but with the Empress Pulcheria. Her goal, crudely put, was to achieve the condemnation of the Patriarch Nestorius, whose reluctance to accord Mary the title of Theotokos was a slight on the honour of her family.

The Marian legacy of the later Roman Empire was less a body of doctrine than a model of Mary as a dynast whose rule in Heaven mirrored the earthly rule of the imperial family. Pulcheria's victory at Ephesus ensured that the cult of the Virgin was lodged at the very centre of Byzantine devotional and political culture. By the end of the sixth century, as Averil Cameron has shown, Mary was venerated as the special patron of the imperial capital Constantinople.[20] Her care for the city involved fierce military defence as much as any maternal tenderness. To what extent was this also true in the Latin West – and in particular at the court of the Carolingians, the family who claimed, in the face of Byzantium, to be rightful emperors of the Romans?

Carolingian Genealogy, Sacred and Secular

Carolingian Marian piety, sure enough, was squarely centred on Mary as Queen of Heaven.[21] Charlemagne dedicated his court chapel at Aachen to Mary. He surrounded himself with intellectuals, one of whose first self-appointed tasks was to refight the Council of Ephesus. In the teachings of the Spanish divines Elipandus of Toledo and Felix of Urgel, Alcuin saw the spectre of the Patriarch Nestorius, and took it upon himself to recondemn his position. Alcuin wrote to insist that Jesus was not the son of God by any kind of adoption: the Godhead was born directly of the Virgin. In short, the so-called Adoptionist controversy can be seen, like the Council of Ephesus, as driven by a concern with Mary and the family, as much as by abstract theological concerns to do with Christ.[22]

---

[20]   Averil Cameron, 'The Theotokos in Sixth-century Constantinople: a City Finds its Symbol', *Journal of Theological Studies*, 29 (1978): 79–108.

[21]   Leo Scheffzyck, *Das Mariengeheimnis in Frömmigkeit und Lehre der Karolingerzeit* (Leipzig, 1959) remains the principal survey. For a recent stock-taking, see Irene Scaravelli, 'Per una mariologia carolingia: autori, opere e linee di ricerca', in Celia Piastra (ed.), *Gli studi de mariologia medievale: Bilancio storiografico* (Florence, 2001), pp. 65–85.

[22]   John Cavadini, *The Last Christology of the West: Adoptionism in Spain and Gaul, 785–820* (Philadelphia, 1993), the standard modern survey of the controversy, does not include Mary. By contrast, Celia Chazelle, *The Crucified God in the Carolingian Era: Theology*

That said, in Carolingian devotion, Mary Queen of Heaven is never a ruler in her own right. She is always a consort – or a daughter, or a mother.[23] As Katrien Heene has shown, Carolingian moralists valued motherhood positively – witness the moral treatise composed by the *matrona* Dhuoda for her son William – but the main function of mothers was dynastic.[24] Mothers sustained lineage, and notions of lineage provided a matrix of collaboration, albeit often tense and competitive, between male and female dynasts, churchmen and churchwomen.

Genealogy, in fact, was one of the secrets of Carolingian success, and one of the family's enduring legacies.[25] For 137 years, the Carolingians ruled as kings of the Franks, insisting that they were the only legitimate ruling family.[26] The mechanics of this remarkable political fiction remain, to a degree, elusive. What we can say is that no other continental dynasty was so systematic in its use of genealogy as an ideological tool.[27] The dynasty was of course to falter in the late ninth century, running out of legitimate candidates for the imperial title, and a century later it died out completely. The genre of geneaology persisted, however. Familes in the eleventh and twelfth centuries assumed that a noble family had a clear genealogy, and they sought to trace their descent specifically into the Carolingian line.[28]

---

and the Art of Christ's Passion (Cambridge, 2001) is consistently alert to the interdependence of Christ and Mary, see for example, pp. 82–6.

[23]   Janet Nelson, 'Women at the Court of Charlemagne: a Case of Monstrous Regiment?', in her *The Frankish World, 750–900* (London, 1996), pp. 223–42, at 230–31. See further Pauline Stafford, *Queens, Concubines, and Dowagers: the King's Wife in the Early Middle Ages* (London, 1983); Simon Maclean, 'Queenship, Nunneries and Royal Widowhood in Carolingian Europe', *Past and Present*, 178 (2003): 3–38.

[24]   Katrien Heene, *The Legacy of Paradise: Marriage, Motherhood and Woman in Carolingian Edifying Literature* (Frankfurt, 1997), and the contribution of Jinty Nelson elsewhere in this volume.

[25]   See Léopold Genicot, *Les Généalogies*, Typologie des sources du moyen âge occidental, Fasc. 15 (Turnhout, 1998); and in particular Helmut Reimitz, 'Anleitung zur Interpretation. Schrift und Genealogie in der Karolingerzeit', in Walter Pohl and Paul Herold (eds), *Vom Nutzen des Schreibens. Soziales Gedächtnis, Herrschaft und Besitz im Mittelalter* (Vienna, 2002), pp. 167–81, with further references.

[26]   On this theme, see Stuart Airlie, '*Semper fideles*? Loyauté envers les Carolingiens comme constituant de l'identité aristocratique', in Regine Le Jan (ed.), *La royauté et les élites dans l'Europe carolingienne* (Lille, 1998), pp. 129–43.

[27]   On the profusion of insular genealogies, see David Dumville, 'Kingship, Genealogies, and Regnal Lists', in Peter Sawyer and Ian Wood (eds), *Early Medieval Kingship* (Leeds, 1977), pp. 72–104.

[28]   See further Gabrielle M. Spiegel, 'Genealogy. Form and Function in Medieval Historiography', in her *The Past as Text. The Theory and Practice of Medieval Historiography* (Baltimore, 1997).

These later genealogies were simplified stories of fathers and sons. In the Carolingian family tree, women and bishops play a prominent role, as their most recent commentators have observed.[29] The earliest surviving example is the *Commemoratio genealogiae domni Karoli gloriosissimi imperatoris*, which was transmitted in a mid ninth-century manuscript, and rapidly diffused and adapted.[30] In all its variants, this text begins with a (mythical) senator Ansbert who married into the Merovingians through the (no less mythical) Blithildis. Ansbert's grandson is given as the (historically attested) blessed Bishop Arnulf of Metz (d. 643). He is not the only bishop of Metz mentioned. The *Commemoratio* has been dated to the early ninth century (800–814), when the bishopric of Metz was vacant. It has been argued that, in compiling the genealogy, clerics at the cathedral sought to keep the see prominent in the eyes of the Emperor.[31]

The Carolingians knew that their family survived only through maternal kin.[32] The line would have died out had it not been for the daughters of Pippin I, Gertrude and Begga, who maintained family honour and biological continuity after the disgrace and death without issue of their brother Grimoald. Gertrude became an abbess of Nivelles, and Begga the wife of Bishop Ansbert's son Ansegisl, and mother of Pippin II. The *Annals of Metz* do not stint in the praise of these women, Begga in particular. She is identified as the great woman behind the throne of Pippin II:

> As support in the administration of such a large estate, he had his glorious mother, Begga by name, worthy of all praise. Filled with every good sense, she daily instructed her son Pippin with the salutary exhortation that, with the Lord helping, he should keep himself in his coming rule among the teachings of his youth without the contagion of iniquity.[33]

---

[29] See Ian Wood, 'Genealogy Defined by Women: the Case of the Pippinids', in Leslie Brubaker and Julia M.H. Smith (eds), *Gender in the Early Medieval World: East and West, 300–900* (Cambridge, 2004), pp. 234–56; Helmut Reimitz, 'Geschlechterrollen und Genealogie in der fränkischen Historiographie, in Christoph Ulf and Robert Rollinger (eds), *Frauenbild und Geschlechterrollen bei antiken Autoren an der Wende von der Spätantike zum Mittelalter* (Cologne, 2007), pp. 335–54.

[30] For this text and its successors, see *Genealogiae Karolorum*, ed. Georg Waitz, MGH SS 13 (Hannover. 1881), pp. 242–8.

[31] Gerhard Oexle, 'Die Karolinger und die Stadt des heiligen Arnulf', *Frühmittelalterliche Studien*, 1 (1967): 250–364.

[32] Wood, 'Genealogy Defined by Women'.

[33] *Annales Mettenses Priores* s.v. 688, ed. B. von Simson, MGH SS rerum Germanicarum in usum scholarum [10] (Hannover, 1905), trans. Paul Fouracre and Richard A. Gerberding, *Late Merovingian France: History and Hagiography 640–720* (Manchester, 1996), p. 351.

Pippin 'surpassed the salutary teachings of his mother', but Begga, *gloriosa genetrix*, here underwrote the moral integrity of the dynasty.

After Begga, the dynasty was seen to descend in the male line, but wives were not forgotten. The wives of Pippin II (Alpaida and Plectrude), and Charlemagne's wife Hildegard (d. 783) were all commemorated in Carolingian genealogies or family histories. In the 830s, several decades after her death, Hildegard's descent was given full biblical treatment by Thegan in his biography of Louis the Pious.

> The aforesaid emperor [Charlemagne], when he was a young man, pledged himself in marriage to a girl of a most noble Swabian family, by the name of Hildegard, who was related to Godfrey, duke of the Alemanni. Duke Godfrey begat Loching, who begat Nebi; Nebi begat Emma, who begat the most blessed Queen Hildegard.[34]

Karl Leyser suggested that this passage has a specific peace-weaving function, in seeking to flatter a line with whom the imperial family had clashed. In broader terms, as the text's editor remarks, what Thegan shows is that when Carolingian churchmen thought of family, their template was 'the book of generations', the Gospel of Matthew.[35]

We can correlate the production of Carolingian genealogical texts with contemporary commentary on Matthew. Ninth-century exegetes necessarily began their works with a discussion of the royalty of Mary. On this point, they inherited a solid body of patristic teaching. As we have seen, early Christian apologists had developed the reassuring reading that Matthew's genealogy of Joseph was in fact describing Mary's descent. In the same vein, they had reasoned, there were good social and cosmic reasons for the evangelist to describe Joseph and Mary as man and wife (and therefore Jesus as their son). The 'cover story' of their marriage ensured that Mary was not stoned for adultery; it meant that she had a companion when they were forced to fly to Egypt to seek refuge from Herod's persecution; and finally, it was a ruse to fool the Devil. Jesus appeared as a human child, tricked the Devil into subjecting him to death – and then confounded Satan by escaping the grave. So far from being accidental, the confusion sown at the beginning of Matthew about Jesus' lineage was part of the Lord's brilliantly waged campaign to secure human salvation.

---

[34]   Thegan, *Vita Hludowici imperatoris* 2, ed. E. Tremp, MGH SS rerum Germanicarum in usum scholarum 64 (Hannover, 1995), trans. Paul Dutton, *Carolingian Civilization: a Reader* (New York, 1996), p. 141.

[35]   See Leyser, 'The German Aristocracy', p. 35; Ernst Tremp, *Studien zu den Gesta Hludowici imperatoris des Trierer Chorbischofs Thegan* (Hannover, 1988), pp. 131–45.

Carolingian scribes did not tire of copying the works of Jerome and Augustine in which these points were made, nor did exegetes tire of repeating them in their own commentaries on Matthew.[36] Especially from the reign of Louis the Pious onwards, Matthew commentary was one of modes in which aspirant court intellectuals sought to establish their credentials. Claudius of Turin, Hrabanus Maurus, Paschasius Radbertus, Sedulius Scottus, Walahfrid Strabo, Christian of Stavelot and Remi of Auxerre have all left compendious Matthew commentaries (as have at least two others whom we cannot identify, transmitted as Ps.-Alcuin, and Ps.-Bede, both dependent on Hrabanus). Discussion of these commentaries began over a century ago, and has been helped recently by the production of new editions – but some important commentaries, in particular that by Claudius of Turin, have not been edited, and a sustained comparison remains to be undertaken.[37]

Early medieval reception of the narrative tradition celebrating Mary's Davidic descent was no less enthusiastic: we return to the Protoevangelium of James.[38] A witness to its success is the condemnation of apocrypha regarding 'the birth of Mary' by the (probably sixth-century) Pseudo-Gelasian decree.[39] By 800, there was in circulation in the Latin West an adaptation of the Protoevangelium, named 'the Pseudo-Matthew' by its nineteenth-century editor, for reasons we explain below.[40] The Pseudo-Matthew is a systematic rewriting of the Protoevangelium of James. Accenting the royalty of Mary, and exploring its connection with her virginity, seems to be a particular goal of the text. Both Joachim and Anna, Pseudo-Matthew specifies, are from the tribe of David; and he lends emphasis to Mary's descent as a pure virgin of David. The date of the text is uncertain; its most recent editor has suggested the early seventh century.[41]

However obscure in origin, the Carolingian career of the Pseudo-Matthew is something we can follow. In the earliest witness to this text, a lectionary copied

---

[36] See for example, Paschasius Radbertus, *Expositio in Matthaeum Libri XII*, I. 16, ed. Beda Paulus, CCSL 56, 56A, 56B (3 vols, Turnhout, 1984), vol. 1, pp. 73–4.

[37] See Anton E. Schönbach, 'Über Evangelionkommentare des Mittelalters', *Sitzungeberichte Wien*, 146 (1903): 1–176; Brigitta Stoll, 'Drei karolingische Matthäus-Kommentare (Claudius von Turin, Hrabanus Maurus, Ps. Beda) und ihre Quellen zur Bergpredgt', *Mittellateinisches Jahrbuch*, 26 (1991): 36–55.

[38] See in particular Mary Clayton, *The Apocryphal Gospels of Mary in Anglo-Saxon England* (Cambridge, 1998).

[39] *Decretum Gelasianum de libris recipiendis et non recipiendis*, ed. Ernst von Dobschütz. *Texte und Untersuchungen* 38.4 (Leipzig, 1912), pp. 50–51.

[40] See now *Pseudo-Matthaei Evangelium*, ed. Jan Gijsel, CCSA, 9 (Turnhout, 1997), building on his earlier study *Die unmittelbare Textüberlieferung des sog. Pseudo-Matthäus* (Brussels, 1981).

[41] *Pseudo-Matthaei*, ed. Gijsel, pp. 59–67.

c. 800, the Pseudo-Matthew is combined with the original Protoevangelium to produce a hybrid account of Mary's birth and early life; and this is in turn juxtaposed with another apocryphal text on Mary's Assumption. It is tantalizing to note that this manuscript, with its dossier of Marian texts, was copied in Metz, the epicentre of genealogical discourse on the Carolingians.[42]

By 830, Marian enthusiasts had gone further, creating a new preface for the Pseudo-Matthew in order to increase its appeal.[43] The original preface casts the text in the mould of the Protoevangelium, as the work of Jesus' step-brother James. The new preface names Matthew as the author, by means of a forged correspondence between Jerome and two bishops, Chromatius and Heliodorus. The bishops beg Jerome to give them a copy of a translation of a text about Mary composed by Matthew, but kept hidden by him. Jerome agrees to comply only because he wishes to wrest control of the text from the Manichee Leucius, who has put out a misleading version.[44] There follows the text of Pseudo-Matthew, now understood as a complement to Matthew's Book of the Generation of Jesus. The likely goal of this new preface is to efface the condemnation in the Pseudo-Gelasian decree of apocryphal narrative regarding Mary's birth by looking to lend full canonical authority to the revision of the Protoevangelium. A further effect of the new preface was to eliminate James: in the Pseudo-Matthew, all attention is focused on Mary, her lineage and her son Jesus.

The cult of Mary as a royal queen and the genealogical self-promotion of the Carolingians converged under the rule of Charles the Bald (840–77). From the outset of his reign, and with the active collaboration of Archbishop Hincmar of Rheims, Charles seems to have encouraged the exploration of the theocratic possibilities of female rulership. In 841, for example, the relics of the Empress Helena were transferred to Rheims, at Hincmar's behest.[45] It is not inconceivable that the new King Charles here sought to rehabilitate his mother, the Empress Judith, who had been the subject of intense vilification in the struggles of the previous decade, as Charles's half-brothers rose up against their father Louis.[46]

---

[42]   Montpellier, Bibliothèque de la Faculté de médecine, MS 55 described with further references in *Pseudo-Matthaei*, ed. Gijsel, p. 213.

[43]   *Pseudo-Matthaei*, ed. Gijsel, p. 71–88. The new preface appears first in two MSS, datable to the 820s: London, British Library, Add. MS 11880 (written in Regensburg) and Budapest, Széchényi Bibl. nat., clma 316 (written in Salzburg 825).

[44]   On Leucius, see Eric Junod and J.-D. Kaestli, *L'histoire des Actes Apocryphes des Apôtres du III au IX siècle. Le cas des Actes de Jean* (Geneva, 1982), pp. 137–44, which shows that the Pseudo-Matthew preface develops out of the preface to the Pseudo-Melitan text on the Assumption.

[45]   See Iogna-Prat, 'Culte de la Vierge', p. 114.

[46]   For an introduction, see Elizabeth Ward, 'Caesar's Wife: the Career of the Empress

A brilliant group of Mariologues gathered at Charles's court. Pre-eminent among these were Paschasius Radbertus and Ratramnus, both monks of Corbie, who engaged each other in a lively debate on Mary's perpetual virginity.[47] Radbertus had previously composed a text on the Assumption of the Virgin, dedicated to Charlemagne's cousin Theodrada and her daughter Emma, of the convent of St Mary at Soissons, where Radbertus had grown up as an oblate.[48] Paschasius's text plays down Mary's bodily assumption, but as Henry Mayr-Harting has emphasized, it focuses instead on Mary's status as Queen in Heaven, at the head of the serried ranks of the angelic hosts, a heavenly hierarchy designed to mirror those on earth.[49]

Paschasius's goal was also to transport himself and his dedicatees back to the Roman Empire.[50] Following the cue of the author of the new pseudo-hieronymian preface to the Pseudo-Matthew, Radbertus cast himself as Jerome addressing his patrons Paula and Eustochium.[51]

> You compel me, Paula and Eustochium, or rather the love of Christ compels me, as one who has long been accustomed to speak to you through treatises, to adopt a new way of speaking, in a way that will be worthy of you as holy virgins, using Latin, for the sake of your edification – to compose a sermon about the Assumption of the blessed and eternally glorious Virgin Mary, in the manner of those who are used to declaiming in church to the people. Never before have I practised such a manner of teaching.[52]

Judith', in Peter Godman (ed.), *Charlemagne's Heir: New Perspectives on the Reign of Louis the Pious* (Oxford, 1990), pp. 205–27.

[47]   Paschasius Radbertus, *De partu virginis*, ed. E.A. Matter, CCCM, 56C (Turnhout, 1985); Ratramnus of Corbie, *De partu sanctae Mariae*, ed. J.M. Canal, *Marianum*, 30 (1968): 53–160.

[48]   Pascasius Radbertus, *Cogitis me/Epistula beati Hieronymi ad Paulum et Eustochium de assumptione sanctae Mariae virginis*, ed. A. Ripberger (Fribourg, 1962), text repr. CCCM, 56C.

[49]   Mayr-Harting, 'Idea of the Assumption of Mary', pp. 87–90.

[50]   On Paschasius as an ideologue, see Mayke de Jong, 'Becoming Jeremiah: Paschasius Radbertus on Wala, Himself, and Others', in Richard Corradini et al. (eds), *Ego-Trouble: Authors and Their Identities in the Early Middle Ages* (Vienna, 2010), pp. 185–96.

[51]   Rita Beyers, '*De nativitate Mariae*: problèmes d'origine', *Revue de théologie et de philosophie*, 122 (1990): 171–88 discusses the possibility that Radbertus was the author of the pseudo-Jerome preface.

[52]   Paschasius Radbertus, *Cogitis me*, I.1, CCCM, 56A, p. 109 (my translation).

Passing as Jerome's, Paschasius's text was to provide the liturgy for the Feast of the Assumption for the Latin Church down to the twelfth century.[53] His literary pretence fooled few of his contemporaries – and certainly not his adversary Ratramnus – but Hincmar was keen to promote the text and to defend its authenticity.[54] He himself penned verses on the Virgin to attach to it, which he had copied in a luxury volume for donation to the cathedral of Rheims, itself dedicated to the Virgin.[55]

Charles's final decade appears as an apotheosis of the Marian project. In 869, he was crowned king of Lotharingia. Hincmar staged the coronation and recounted it in the *Annals of St Bertin* as a celebration of Carolingian genealogy under the sign of Mary. Hincmar recalled Charles's ancestry.

> His father of holy memory the Lord Louis, pious and august emperor, was descended from Louis famous king of the Franks, who was converted through the catholic preaching of St Remigius, the apostle of the Franks, and baptised along with 3,000 of the Franks, not counting children and women, on the vigil of holy Easter at the metropolis of Rheims, and anointed and consecrated king with chrism got from heaven, of which we still have some. And from him St Arnulf was descended; and from his flesh the pious and august Emperor Louis drew his carnal origin. This Emperor Louis was crowned emperor by the Roman Pope Stephen at Rheims before the altar of the holy Mother of God and ever Virgin Mary.[56]

To buttress the genealogical claims made at the coronation, Hincmar commissioned a major historical compilation from the scriptorium of St Amand. As Helmut Reimitz has powerfully shown, a concern to establish a fitting lineage and historical narrative to legitimate Charles's West Frankish takeover of Lotharingia undergirds the whole codex. The compendium

---

[53]   See Rachel Fulton, '"Quae est ista quae ascendit sicut aurora consurgens?": the Song of Songs as the Historia for the Office of the Assumption', *Mediaeval Studies*, 60 (1998): 55–122.

[54]   See the landmark article of Cyril Lambot, 'L'Homélie du Pseudo-Jérôme sur l'Assomption et l'Évangile de la Nativité de Marie d'après une lettre inédit d'Hincmar', *Revue Bénédictine*, 46 (1934): 265–82; Iogna-Prat, 'Culte de la Vierge', p. 112.

[55]   For Hincmar's verses, see MGH Poetae III, pp. 410–12; and Flodoard, *Hist Rem Eccl* I. III. 5, MGH SS 13, 478–9. While the codex to which Flodoard refers there has been lost, we have in Rheims 1395 a mid ninth-century Rheims manuscript which preserves a Marian dossier including the Pseudo-Matthew and comparable to the dossier in Montpellier, Bibl. Fac. Méd., MS 55.

[56]   *Annales Bertiniani*, s.v. 869, ed. F. Grat, J. Vielliard and S. Clémencet (Paris, 1964), trans. Janet L. Nelson (Manchester, 1991), p. 161.

concludes with a version of the Metz *Commemoratio*, and with an additional genealogy of the Frankish kings.[57]

There was, then, a synergy between Mary, Carolingian kings, their womenfolk, and their bishops. These elements, however, did not always pull in the same direction. Mary as she develops in the ninth century is a figure for the celebration of maternal kin – but we may start to see the outlines of Mary as she later becomes, a 'theological' figure, whose principal acolytes are celibate men.

Mary against Maternal Kin

Theocratic power comes at a price. The more kings sought to avail themselves of the ideological resources wielded by religious specialists, the more they played a game whose rules they did not in the end determine – and which they might lose.[58] In this context, we may turn to the Carolingian 'King's Great Matter', the divorce of Lothar II and Teutberga, and the decisive role played in it by Hincmar and the Virgin Mary. Here we see the Virgin turned against a reigning Carolingian and his maternal kin.

In the mid 850s, Lothar II, who succeeded his father Lothar in 855, began to look to repudiate his wife Teutberga, in favour of another woman, Waldrada, by whom he had already had a child. To secure his divorce, Lothar accused Teutberga of sodomitical incest with her own brother.[59] In his great treatise, *De Divortio Lothari et Teutberga*, Hincmar gravely considers the possibility, concluding that the only woman known to have conceived other than through vaginal intercourse was the Virgin.[60] Here Hincmar drew on the discussion of the Virgin birth at Corbie between Radertus and Ratramnus. The text is often read as a misogynist investigation of Teutberga, but the net effect of Hincmar's

[57] Helmut Reimitz, 'Ein karolingisches Geschichtsbuch aus Saint-Amand. Der Cvp 473', in C. Egger and H. Weigl (eds), *Text – Schrift – Codex. Quellenkundliche Arbeiten aus dem Institut für Österreichische Geschichtsforschung, Mitteilungen des Instituts für Österreichische Geschichtsforschung*, Erg. bd. 35 (Vienna, 2000), pp. 34–90.

[58] A general theme of Walter Ullmann's work (see, for example, his *A Short History of the Papacy* [London, 1972]), and of Stuart Airlie, 'Private Bodies and the Body Politic in the Divorce Case of Lothar II', *Past and Present*, 161 (1998): 3–38.

[59] A clear account is Karl Heidecker, *The Divorce of Lothar II: Christian Marriage and Political Power in the Carolingian World*, trans. Tanis Guest (Ithaca, NY, 2010).

[60] Hincmar of Rheims, *De divortio Lotharii regis et Theutbergae reginae*, ed. L. Böhringer, MGH Concilia IV.I (Hannover, 1992), as discussed in Airlie, 'Private Bodies', pp. 22–3.

intervention, however prurient, was to cast doubt on her accusers, and indeed to save her life.[61]

In terms of power politics, Hincmar's narrative in the *Annals of St Bertin* makes it clear that this was a battle between uncles. The case was watched with extreme interest by Lothar's paternal uncles, Louis the German and Charles the Bald, both of whom, Lothar (rightly) suspected were casting greedy eyes on his kingdom. To defend himself, Lothar turned to his maternal uncle, Liutfrid, ensuring his support for his union with Waldrada, and sending him to Rome to secure papal letters against Charles and Louis. Lothar also seems to have enjoyed the good will of Charles's own maternal uncle, Conrad, much to Hincmar's chagrin.[62]

For Hincmar, Mary was a weapon to deploy against the lustful Lothar and the malign influence of these maternal kin. In the *Annals of St Bertin*, he punctuates the narrative with Marian liturgy. Thus we read that, on the morning 15 August 862, a slave woman in Thérouanne began to iron her master's linen shirt, so that he could wear it when he went to mass. The shirt turned bloody, again and again, impelling the bishop to institute the Feast of the Assumption in the diocese. Later that month, Hincmar records, Lothar married Waldrada, with the backing of Liutfrid and the 'arrogant yet superficial' Conrad. Hincmar, meanwhile, summoned Charles and his bishops to Rheims, and dedicated the cathedral there to the Virgin.[63]

In August of 865, Hincmar records with satisfaction, Lothar was forcibly reconciled with Teutberga. On 15 August, the Feast of the Assumption, the pair celebrated mass together. When he continued to seek out Waldrada, Lothar found himself hounded by the Pope and by Adventius of Metz. Adventius excommunicated him on the Feast of the Purification of the Virgin in 866, charging him to reconcile within a year, so that he could celebrate mass at the cathedral of his ancester Arnulf.[64]

The denouement came in 869. Lothar, supported only by adulterers (Hincmar again), relentlessly pursued his suit at the papal court in Rome. Some of his supporters thought he was successful – but on the return journey, an unmistakeable and definitive judgement came from God. A fever struck his party at Lucca: 'He watched them dying in heaps before his eyes.' Within the gravitational pull of the Feast of the Assumption (8 August), Lothar died.[65] His

---

[61]   I owe this observation to Kate Cooper.

[62]   *Annales Bertiniani*, s.v. 862 on Liutfrid and Conrad; see also Heidecker, *Divorce of Lothar II*, pp. 69–71, 143–8.

[63]   *Annales Bertiniani*, s.v. 862.

[64]   Ibid., 865, 866.

[65]   Ibid.. 869.

paternal uncle Charles made haste to Metz, and a month later, as we have seen, staged the coronation.

Three years later, Charles and his queen Ermengarde were to dedicate a chapel at Compiègne to the Virgin. The royal couple, it is admitted in the charter, may not have been able to secure tenure of Aachen, but they had the more important element, it is argued, a shrine to the Virgin.[66] Charlemagne had dedicated the chapel at Aachen to Mary: in the reign of his grandson, she herself is hailed as the token of rulership.

Before the decade was out, however, Charles was dead, and a non-Carolingian had challenged for the throne;[67] a decade later again, there were no legitimate Carolingians left to succeed to the imperial title.[68] The genealogical tradition was to continue, as was the apocryphal tradition of Mary's childhood. For the dynasty, however, the story was over. Marian devotion was not enough. 'In the end, neither piety nor propaganda could compensate where fertility failed.'[69]

Conclusion: From Maternal Kin to Jesus as Mother

What made the Carolingians special was their ability to monumentalize themselves as a family. No small part of this effort, we have suggested, involved devotion to Mary as a royal queen of heaven. Conceived of in these terms, Mary was integral to the discourse of Carolingian genealogy. Her presence was a necessary, if not a sufficient, condition for a dynasty which knew itself to have relied upon maternal kin for its existence.

Mary, we should stress, was more than 'a woman to think with' in discussions about the family: she *was* the family. As one scholar has pointed out, the Middle Ages owed its language of kinship directly to late Roman Marian piety. Isidore of Seville's famous definition of 'agnatic' and 'cognatic' relations draws substantially on Jerome's discussion of the different meanings of 'brother' in his *Contra Helvidium*, composed in Rome in 383 to defend the perpetual

---

[66] See Iogna-Prat, 'Culte de la Vierge', pp. 98–9.

[67] See Stuart Airlie, 'The Nearly Men: Boso of Vienne and Arnulf of Bavaria', in Anne J. Duggan (ed.), *Nobles and Nobility in Medieval Europe: Concepts, Origins, Transformations* (Woodbridge, 2000), pp. 25–41.

[68] Simon MacLean, *Kingship and Politics in the Late Ninth Century: Charles the Fat and the End of the Carolingian Empire* (Cambridge, 2003) warns against an overly fatalist account of the 880s.

[69] Cooper, 'Empress and *Theotokos*', p. 51.

virginity of Mary against what Jerome perceived to be the slurs of Helvidius.[70]
Isidore's discussion in turn undergirds the terminology of kinship in subsequent
centuries. A renewed discussion of medieval kinship, then, would start with the
texts of late Roman Marian polemic and its reception in the early Middle Ages.[71]

Jerome's Marian treatise supplies a language of spiritual as well as biological
kindred, to describe those bound not by nature but by 'affect'.[72] This, too, was
a legacy greedily received and exploited in the Carolingian era. Consider this
passage from the *Life of Adalard of Corbie*, by the self-appointed voice of Jerome
in the ninth century, Paschasius Radbertus.

> He [Adalard] was, O good Jesus, one whom I found the complete and only abbot,
> whom of all I found seeking the welfare of another more than of his own. As a
> mother loves her only son, so he loved most tenderly, inviting all to take the solider
> matters. Behold, O men, and see, all people: Mother Corbie, beehive of monks,
> weeping, weeping, and saying "My illustrious one has been taken from me."

Motherhood abounds in this lament for the death of Adalard, composed by
Radbertus in 826. Adalard is a mother to his monks, the monastery is a mother
mourning her son, the monks themselves return Adalard's love the more strongly:
'maternal love would perish before we could cease loving you.'[73] To find such an
abundance of metaphorical mothering in the ninth century may be surprising:
conventional wisdom would have us wait until after the millennium to find such
an overwrought display of feeling from a male community.

Have we, then, misdated the rise of affective piety by some two or three
centuries? In general, Carolingian churchmen were less exuberant than was
Paschasius and more restricted in their metaphorical play with motherhood.[74]

---

[70]   See David Hunter, *Marriage, Celibacy, and Heresy in Ancient Christianity: the
Jovinianist Controversy* (Oxford, 2007); Iogna-Prat, 'Culte de la Vierge', p. 108. A full
examination of Isidore's use of Jerome remains a key desideratum. See, for example, the
following chapter, on *affines*, where Mary herself makes an entrance. Isidore explains that
coniuges are so called from the point at which they are *desponsata*: 'Sicut Maria Ioseph coniux
vocatur, inter quos nec fuerat nec futura erat carnis ulla commixtio' (*Etym.* IX.vii).

[71]   See for example, Leyser, 'Maternal Kin', p. 130.

[72]   'Quattuor modis in Scripturis divinis fratres dici: natura, gente, cognatione, affectu'.
Jerome, *Liber de perpetua virginitate* PL 23, 107–108; Isidore, *Etymologiae*, IX, vi, ed. W.M.
Lindsay (Oxford, 1911).

[73]   Radbertus, *Vita Adalardi* 82, PL 120: 1549, trans. Allen Cabaniss, *Charlemagne's
Cousins: Contemporary Lives of Adalard and Wala* (Syracuse, NY, 1967), pp. 73–4: 'ipse
enim erat, bone Iesu, quem in toto ex omnibus solum abbatem reperi ... qui sicut mater amat
unicum ita quosque tenerrime diligebat, atque ut solidiora caperent invitabat'.

[74]   But see Chazelle, *Crucified God*, pp. 222–3 for another exception, from Hincmar.

However, this may not be the best way to put the question. It is unlikely that Paschasius would have seen a contradiction between ties of nature and ties of affect, or between Mary as a dynast, and a 'theological' Mary. Adalard and Theodrada, his spiritual father and mother respectively, were both themselves from the royal lineage, and Radbertus could assume the person of Jerome to speak to both of them. Like the medium of Marian genealogy which his texts helped to resource, 'Jerome' as a figure was himself a symbolic matrix, and a capacious one. What is perhaps most distinctive here is the triumphant conviction that Jerome's world, the later Roman Empire, could be reinhabited. Within this magical realist frame, tensions between family identity and institutional obligation melted away. If the voice of Jerome was one portal to this world, then devotion to Mary was a yet more powerful mode of access: it was on these terms that men in the ninth century discussed her motherhood.

Chapter 3

Dhuoda on Dreams

Janet L. Nelson

In recent years, Dhuoda's *Handbook for her son William* has become familiar to historians of earlier medieval Europe, in a surprising but wholly welcome way: surprising because it languished for so long in a limbo of obscure yet difficult texts, despised for its allegedly poor latinity and very limited contemporary impact in or after the ninth century, and consigned to a shelf marked 'spirituality'; welcome because it is recognized nowadays as the original work of an able writer with a distinctive take, and hence valuable evidence, on contemporary politics, social life and cultural values. It is a sad comment on an increasingly anglolexic international scholarly world that it took more than the interest of Joachim Wollasch and Pierre Riché to get Dhuoda's work better known.[1] A happier comment would focus on the growing interest in the history of women and of gender in the USA and the UK, which inspired, and was in turn greatly promoted by, two excellent English translations.[2] When in 1971 I chose the *Handbook* to make my contribution to an in-house lecture series at King's College London on medieval Latin texts, few if any of my audience had even heard of Dhuoda.[3] Now Dhuoda is being not just cited in scholarship on the Carolingian state, but credited with aspiring to address a contemporary audience and inspiring, if not herself assembling, a collection of texts that

---

[1] J. Wollasch, 'Eine adlige Familie des frühen Mittelalters. Ihr Selbstverständnis und ihre Wirklichkeit', *Archiv für Kulturgeschichte*, 39 (1957): 150–88; P. Riché, 'Les bibliothèques de trois aristocrates laïcs carolingiens', *Le Moyen Âge*, 69 (1963): 87–104, at 88–96, repr. in Riché, *Instruction et vie religieuse dans le Haut Moyen Âge* (London, 1981), Chapter 8; *Dhuoda. Manuel pour mon fils*, ed. P. Riché with trans. by B. de Vregille and C. Montdésert, Sources chrétiennes, 225 (Paris, 1975).

[2] *Handbook for William: a Carolingian Woman's Counsel for her Son*, trans. with introduction C. Neel (Lincoln, NE, 1991, repr. with Addendum on historiography, 1999); Dhuoda. *Handbook for her Warrior Son: Liber Manualis*, trans. M. Thiébaux (Cambridge, 1998): Latin text with English trans.

[3] The edition by E. Bondurand, *L'éducation carolingienne, Le Manuel de Dhuoda (843)* (Paris, 1887) was then the only one available.

together formed a Carolingian programme in moral education.[4] The fact that, of all the Carolingian moralists, Dhuoda alone was a parent, and a woman, means that her take might also be considered in certain respects more representative than those of other contemporary mirrors for laity, and certainly has a bearing on my decision to write this paper, rather than another, for Henrietta Leyser, in a Festschrift devoted to the theme of motherhood. This theme, on which Henrietta herself wrote luminously in the later-medieval section of *Medieval Women*, no longer needs any apology as a subject for an early medievalist, and it has, as a close look at the historiography shows, the signal merit of enthusing scholars of different generations.[5] I offer this *munusculum* or giftie, then, as an expression of far more than conventional thanks for long-term friendship which has turned out to be long-haul as well.

Dhuoda demands to be taken seriously as an author. Her prefatory materials provide explanations of her choice of genre and her motives for writing, an eighty-seven-line acrostic poem and short prose prologue dedicating her *opus* to her son, and an account of the context in which she wrote, while the concluding section gives the exact dates on which she began and ended her work (30 November 841; 2 February [843]).[6] This means, amongst other things, that the reader is asked to recognize the thinking behind the *Handbook*'s structure and balance. There is clearly no direct correlation between book or chapter length and significance. In the first part of the *Handbook*, Books 1–6, the setting out of religious fundamentals occupies Books 1 and 2, Books 3 and 4 offer guidance on social and moral conduct in light of those fundamentals, while in the very much shorter Books 5 and 6, Dhuoda returns to spiritual matters, to consider how

---

[4]   J.L. Nelson, *Charles the Bald* (London, 1992), pp. 41, 48–9; S. Airlie, 'Semper fideles? Loyauté envers les Carolingiens comme constituant de l'identité aristocratique', in R. Le Jan (ed.), *La royauté et les élites dans l'Europe carolingienne* (Lille, 1998), pp. 129–43, at pp. 133–4; J.L. Nelson, 'Dhuoda', in P. Wormald and J.L. Nelson (eds), *Lay Intellectuals in the Carolingian World* (Cambridge, 2007), pp. 106–120; C.J. Chandler, 'Barcelona BC 569 and a Carolingian Programme on the Virtues', *Early Medieval Europe*, 18 (2010): 265–91.

[5]   M. Claussen, 'Fathers of Power and Women of Authority: Dhuoda and the *Liber Manualis*', *French Historical Studies*, 19 (1996): 785–809; Chandler, 'Barcelona'; S. Stofferahn, 'The Many Faces in Dhuoda's Mirror: the *Liber Manualis* and a Century of Scholarship', *Magistra: a Journal of Women's Spirituality in History*, 4 (1998): 89–134; V.J. Garver, 'The Influence of Monastic Ideals upon Carolingian Conceptions of Childhood', in A. Classen (ed.) *Childhood in the Middle Ages and Renaissance* (Berlin, 2005), pp. 67–85.

[6]   See Riché, *Manuel*, pp. 11–21 for invaluable discussion of all these points. P. Dronke, *Women Writers of the Middle Ages* (Cambridge, 1984), pp. 36–54 (with notes at pp. 290–93) proved just how seriously Dhuoda's work deserves to be taken by historians of literature and of thought.

trials and tribulations can be met.[7] The answer to the question of why Dhuoda chose to say anything about dreams (and, so far as I know, no-one has yet claimed that she has anything special to say on this subject) will not lie in quantity, then, but in quality. Dhuoda has in fact rather little to say about dreams, but she does select them for special attention in so far as she places them strategically, in chapters dealing with fundamentals.

The first moment in her book when Dhuoda came to dreaming was when, in Book 2, she instructed her son about prayer, and especially prayer at bedtime. She wrote:

> When you lie, quiet, in your bed, say three times, "O God make haste to deliver me! O Lord make haste to help me!" Say the "*Gloria*", and then the Lord's Prayer. When you have done, say, "Guard me, Lord, through the day, and guard me this night if it is your command. May I deserve to be shielded 'under the shadow of your wings' ... and encircled by a guard of angels, so that, though resting only a little, I may capture the dream of peace. And if I should awaken at any time, may I feel that through my sleeping I am beneath you, my guardian, you who, as saviour, appeared on the ladder to the blessed Jacob." When you have done all this, make the sign of the cross on your forehead and over your bed ... like this +, and say: "I worship your cross, Lord, and I believe in your holy resurrection ... The cross is my salvation, the cross my defence, the cross my protection, my refuge forever. The cross is life to me, but death to you, Devil, enemy of truth, bringer-forth of what is vain; the cross is life to me, but death to you, always!" ... May this cross and blessing always be with those whom I in my frailty have so often been talking about earlier ... and may the anointing of Jesus Christ, God's son, flow down on you and remain with you wherever you go, and upon your brother, who was second after you to come forth from my womb. And if, by God's help, there should be more children, may they have together with you what I have just prayed for here ... Amen.[8]

---

[7]   Rough indications of relative length are the following, derived from Thiébaux's Latin text: Book 1, 7 pp.; Book 2, just over 5 pp.; Book 3, just over 19 pp.; Book 4, 19 pp.; Book 5, 8½ pp.; Book 6, 3½ pp.; Book 7, 2½ pp.; Book 8, just over 6 pp.; Book 9, just over 3 pp.; Book 10, just over 6 pp. (mostly Dhuoda's verses); Book 11, just over 3 pp. (by way of an appendix, on psalm-readings). The division into Books is Riché's, following the thematic sections indicated by the chapters (*capitula*), which are Dhuoda's own, although the numbering in her table of contents varies slightly between the three extant manuscripts: Riché, *Manuel*, pp. 15–17, 53–9. For the divide between the work's two parts (Books 1–6, 7–10), see Nelson, 'Dhuoda', p. 112. In what follows, Dhuoda's *Manual* is cited from Thiébaux, with book, chapter and page number(s), with a few minor changes in the translation.

[8]   *Dhuoda*, ed. Thiébaux, 2, 3, pp. 78–81 (Chapter IX in Dhuoda's numbering). There is a brief but telling comment on this passage by P.E. Dutton, *The Politics of Dreaming in the*

In this extraordinarily intimate passage, the instruction in prayer, and the presenting of an exemplary prayer in William's voice, turns into a prayer itself, in Dhuoda's own voice, and not just for William, but for his little brother and any future siblings. The thought of the night evokes the sense of vulnerability and need for protection, and at the same time the sense of God's closeness in sleep and in dreams; invocations to the saving Cross become exorcism of the Devil who is death and whom the Cross kills. She recalls her own family, 'those I have often spoken about earlier': William himself, and his little brother, and possible future children. In the prayer practice Dhuoda advocates, penitential psalms and invocations of the cross are connected, and specifically at night. Her recommendations are inspired and informed directly by the liturgy and by private prayer, and indirectly by monastic spirituality. Perhaps they derive, too, from religious practice using the family psalter and family prayerbook? If *feminae potentes* were held by churchmen to be 'especially' responsible for the moral education of their households, for instance in ensuring that 'everyone' learned the *Pater Noster* and the *Credo* by heart, is it fanciful to credit *this* elite woman with teaching her own son to read, and then reading and studying the psalter with him?[9] In the instructions of the *Handbook*, was not Dhuoda literally transcribing William's experience in his early years of being taught to pray in spoken words, and using the gesture of the cross, 'like this'? This is not to leave chaplain and nanny out of the picture: it is to highlight a maternal contribution.

In the title of Book 5, Chapter 1, *tribulationes*, trials and tribulations, and *temperamenta*, ways of disciplining the self, are side by side.[10] Dhuoda looks for inspiration and information to St Paul, and to Alcuin's *Virtues and Vices* (without directly referencing this work, however).[11] She also looks to Augustine, who wrote of the perils of the night when the Devil stalked, and it is worth pausing here to consider how and why Augustine's discussion of ideal and reality intersects with his – and Dhuoda's – thinking on dreams. In the *Enarrationes in Psalmos*, Augustine addressed a collective 'beloved' in a sermon on Psalm 48, v. 15:

Carolingian Empire (Lincoln, NE, 1994), pp. 16–17.

[9]   For *feminae potentes*, see Council of Meaux–Paris (845), c. 70, ed. A. Boretius, MGH *Capitularia regum Francorum* (Hannover, 1893), II, no. 293, p. 419.

[10]   '*De diversarum tribulationum temperamentis*', as in MS 'P'. *Dhuoda*, ed. Thiébaux, p. 165, translates: 'On observing self-control under various hardships', which well represents a possible (and attractive) meaning of *temperamenta*; cf. the variant form of the title in MS 'B': '*tribulationibus temperamenta*', Riché, *Manuel*, p. [260], note at l. 1. Vregille and Montdésert translate: '*Les diverses formes d'épreuves*'; Neel, *Dhuoda. Handbook*, p. 65 translates: 'On being tested in various troubles'.

[11]   Alcuin, *De virtutibus et vitiis* 33, PL 107: 633C. See now Chandler, 'Barcelona', pp. 285–6.

Sicut oves in inferno positi sunt;

Mors depascet eos.

Et dominabuntur eorum justi in matutino.[12]

Augustine, interpreting 'Death' here as the Devil, the 'shepherd' leading the sheep astray, said: 'Bear the night. Desire the morning'. In a passage a little further on, Augustine cited St Paul, II Corinthians 6: 10, on how Christian should comport themselves: 'quasi tristes, semper autem gaudentes', 'always as if sad, yet always joyful'. Augustine commented: 'our joy has no "as if", because it is in certain hope. Why does our sorrow have "as if"? Because it passes like a dream.'[13] Augustine went on: 'Whoever is telling about a dream adds an "as if": [it was] "as if" I was sitting, "as if" I was talking, "as if" I was having a meal, "as if" I was riding, "as if" I was arguing. The whole of this is "as if", because when the person wakes up, they can't find what they saw.' Augustine returning to Paul, and wanting, as ever, to contrast the transient with the eternal, pitted the "as if" against the true, or real. 'The dreamers' "as if" is the happiness of the *saeculum*, the true is their suffering. But our [that is, Christians'] "as if" is sadness, and our joy is not the "as if"'. A few lines on, pondering Paul's 'quasi nihil habentes', Augustine declared: 'that "having nothing" was the Apostle's "as if"' – in other words, we Christians are those who really have it all.

Near the beginning of Book 5, Chapter 1, Dhuoda herself considers the *quasi* and the *verum*.[14] First she quotes the Apostle, II Corinthians 7: 10, on the wrong kind of *tristitia*: 'seculi ... tristitia mortem operatur'. To this Dhuoda responds, 'Tristitia autem spiritualis vitam atque laetitiam adtrahit sempiternam', which could be read as a paraphrase of Paul's immediately preceding statement in the same verse, 'Quae enim secundum Deum tristitia est, poenitentiam in salute stabilem operatur'.[15] Dhuoda notes, in a passing allusion (without reference) to Alcuin's *Virtues and Vices*, 'the two branches' of human sadness, the carnal and spiritual. Then she says that *peritissimi*, wise people, people with experience, say that it is better to think hard about sorrow than to forget or suppress it. Corinthians 6: 10 is now à propos, and Dhuoda quotes it: 'Quasi tristes, semper autem gaudentes. Quasi nichil habentes, et omnia possidentes'. Then, not mentioning Augustine by name, but in fact summarizing his thought on this

---

[12]   *Enarrationes in Psalmos*, ed. E. Dekkers and I. Fraipont, CCSL 38, Pss I–L (Turnholt, 1956), in Ps. 48, serm. ii, 5, p. 565; compare *King James Version*, Ps. 49: 14.

[13]   Ibid., pp. 569–70, for this and what follows.

[14]   *Dhuoda*, ed. Thiébaux, 5, 1, pp. 164–7.

[15]   II Cor. 7: 10, 'For godly sorrow worketh repentance to salvation not to be repented of: but the sorrow of the world worketh death'. Cf. *Dhuoda*, ed. Thiebaux, p. 165: 'but spiritual sorrow leads to life and eternal joy'; cf. Neel, *Dhuoda. Handbook*, p. 65.

subject, Dhuoda writes: "'Quasi' dicimus quod non est verum: verum quod non est 'quasi'" ('we call the "as if" that which is not true, and the true, that which is not the "as if"'). She immediately illustrates this:

Dicit quidam captor somnii: "Quasi equitabam, quasi currebam; quasi epulans pocula, ni prius atque cibus, cuncta manibus tenebam; ferculis in pomis, sapor gusti quo triplectabant; huc illucque me volvens, equestrium sessor aderam. Expergefactus a somno, nichil cernens valui amplecti; inanis et fragilis, demensque et palpans, totus cum 'quasi' remansi. O si fuisset verum quod annuens oculis, manu palpans, pedem terens!" "O", dicit doctor, "si talis vel quisque futurus 'quasi' cerneret 'verum', lapsus per umbras, surgeret ad dapes! Transit moriens, et ecce 'quasi' felicitas rerum temporalium, cum ab insipientibus et negligentibus relinquitur; nichil aliud per funebra carminum restat dampnatio morti perpetualis illorum. Cernentium temporaliter cuncta quid aliud a sapientibus computatur, nisi 'quasi'?" Audi auctorem qui dicit: "Vidi omnia sub sole et ecce vanitas, vanitas vanitatum et omnia vanitas". En habes "quasi" cum somno vanitatis, vinculorum inretitu conexibus. Quare? Quia, ut ait Psalmista: "Turbati sunt omnes insipientes corde, dormitaverunt qui ascenderunt equos"; expergefacti a somno "nihil in manibus invenerunt suis", transierunt irrevocabili gressu. O somnum durum et inexcitabile his qui nequiter vivunt et absque poenitentiae fructum ad imam recurrunt! Quid in talibus, nisi "quasi"?[16]

---

[16] *Dhuoda*, ed. Thiébaux, pp. 164–7, with her translation (which I could hardly seek to better): 'A man struck by a dream recounts this: "It was 'as if' I rode a horse, 'as if' I were running, and 'as if' at a banquet. I held all the goblets in my hands, not to mention the dainties and the platters of fruit whose savour made me three times hungrier than usual. Ranging here and there, I thought I sat on horseback. Wakened from sleep, I neither saw nor held anything. I was worn out and weak, distracted and stumbling. I remained alone with my 'as if'. Oh, if only that had been true, the things I caressed with my eyes, and touched with my hand, and trod with my feet!" "Oh", says the Teacher, "if that man or some other in a future time were to take this delusory 'as if' for the truth, he would, deceived by phantoms, run to a banquet. A man passes and he dies. And see how the 'as if' of worldly felicity is left behind by the foolish and the careless! Nothing is left during the funeral chants except the 'as if'! Why is this? Because these people's goods fade away and all that is left is their eternal condemnation to death. As for people who view everything from the temporal viewpoint, don't wise men consider what they only regard the world "as if"? Heed the writer who said, "I have seen everything under the sun, and it was vanity, the vanity of vanities, all is vanity". Here you have "as if" bound up in the net of its fetters by the sleep of vanity. Why? Because, as the Psalmist says, "all fools are troubled in their hearts; those who have mounted horses have grown drowsy with sleep". Once roused from their sleep, "they found nothing in their hands". They have passed over on a journey from which they cannot be called back. Oh, the deep, heavy sleep from which there is no awakening for those who live badly and who race toward the abyss without the fruit of penance!'

Pierre Riché and his colleagues were perplexed by this passage. 'Here begins a long and very interesting borrowed passage, but it is difficult to identify. Is this an unknown Carolingian sermon? If so, [its author] was inspired by Augustine [in the passage quoted from *Enarr. in Psalm* 48, cf. n. 6 above]. Here the initial dream story recalls classical vocabulary and style but it is badly transmitted and very hard to translate. In the end, it is not easy to distinguish between what is quotation and what Dhuoda herself adds.'[17] I am not sure it is possible to go much further, pending the discovery of the hypothetical lost sermon. Riché and colleagues list 'triplecto' amongst 'mots rares'. I do wonder if Dhuoda herself, perhaps with a little help, could not have pieced together the biblical quotations, and Augustine on Psalm 38, with a dash of imagination, to produce something like the passage in *Handbook* 5, 1. Dhuoda's use of Augustine is remarkable and has been duly remarked on by commentators, although it would be only fair to say that the *quasi/verum* passage is the prime witness.[18] Dhuoda's use of the psalms is much more extensive, evenly distributed throughout the *Handbook*, and suggestive of deep and independent reflection. Her use of Psalm 75 is notably free (as is her use of St Paul too, for that matter): scriptural texts were there to be manipulated. A remarkable fact is that, although she quoted psalms nearly 400 times – she is a one-woman exemplar of psalm-centred lay piety in the Carolingian age – in only ten cases does she cite a single psalm-verse as many as four times, and not only is Psalm 75 one of the ten but all four of her citations of Psalm 75: 6 are concentrated in Book 5, Chapter 1.[19]

The question I want to re-focus on, finally, is what drew Dhuoda to Psalm 75. I should like to move in on this from two rather different directions. The first resumes my earlier point about the psalms as an education for the Frankish elite,

---

[17]   Riché, *Manuel*, pp. 262–3, n. 2 (my translation); cf. Neel, *Dhuoda, Handbook*, p. 136, n. 4: 'Dhuoda seems to expand on the explanation of an unknown source, apparently a commentary on Psalm 75'. But that unidentified commentator certainly was not Augustine, whose comments on Psalm 75 do not pursue the *'quasi'/verum* distinction, but instead pursue the horses and riders: 'Who are those who mount horses? They are those who reject humility. It is no sin to ride a horse, but it is [a sin] to raise the neck of power against God and to think yourself in some position of honour.' Augustine moves on to consider Pharoah and his host of riders: models of hardness of heart who refuse to repent. 'But it is better not to mount a horse so that then you don't fall asleep when you ought to be vigilant and listen to the voice of Christ': *Enarrationes in Psalmos*, 75: 9–10, ed. Dekkers and Fraipont, CCSL 39, Pss. L–C (Turnholt, 1956), p. 1045.

[18]   P.-A. Becker, 'Dhuodas Handbuch', *Zeitschrift für romanische Philologie*, 21 (1897): 73–101, at 85–6; Riché, *Manuel*, pp. 262–3, n. 2; Nelson, 'Dhuoda', p. 116.

[19]   Psalm 83: 8 is unique in being cited six times. Dhuoda's use of the Book of Job is equally assured. Ten out of Dhuoda's 58 citations of Job are in Book 5, Chapter 1 (where she also uses Gregory's *Moralia*).

personified by William. Of all the aspects of the noble life of prime social and symbolic importance for a young man in William's position, recently sent to the royal court and with a career to make, membership of the retinue, centred on martial service, and the companionship of *comilitones*, was the most absorbing and required most explicit demonstration. It was epitomized and displayed by the receiving and use of horses, often in ritual settings like war-games and gift-givings, when kings typically distributed horses to their young followers. Prowess at hunting, one of the group's badges of distinction, identified the noble youth, and cemented the group's identity.[20] Riding and managing horses were necessary skills. Dhuoda understood the importance of the retinue, but her *Handbook* was not concerned with the military aspects of youth-training. Another collective activity was feasting and commensality, likewise important in group-bonding of the participants, and the giving and receiving of dinner invitations were aspects of courtly life on which Dhuoda did have something, although not much, to say.[21] These activities, important as they were to the aspiring youth, were likely also to have been sources of competitiveness and anxiety. With these considerations in mind, recall Augustine's list of activities that characterized the world of the 'as if': sitting [at table], talking, feasting, riding, arguing. Recall the dream recounted by Dhuoda, and the abrupt awakening of the dreamer to the realization of being 'alone with my "as if"'.[22] Then, re-read Psalm 75, vv. 6–7:

Turbati sunt omnes insipientes corde.

Dormierunt somnum suum,

Et nihil invenerunt omnes viri divitiarum in manibus suis.

Ab increpatione tua, Deus Jacob,

Dormitaverunt qui ascenderunt equos.

---

[20]   J.L. Nelson, *The Frankish World, 750–900* (London, 1996), pp. 75–87, 120–24; J.L. Nelson, 'Was Charlemagne's Court a Courtly Society?', and M. Innes, 'A Place of Discipline: Carolingian Court and Aristocratic Youth', both in C. Cubitt (ed.) *Court Culture in the Early Middle Ages* (Turnhout, 2003), pp. 39–57, 59–76.

[21]   *Dhuoda*, ed. Thiébaux, 3, 11, p. 122 (*convivia* with priests); cf. *De ordine palatii*, ed. T. Gross and R. Schieffer, MGH, *Fontes iuris germanici antique* (Hannover, 1980), cap. V (c. 27), ll. 446–51, p. 80 (*milites* dining with *capitanei ministeriales*). Note in *Dhuoda*, ed. Thiébaux , 4, 8, pp. 148–9, the association of reining in of mind and tongue with a kind of peaceful enjoyment of feasts: 'Tu si patiens fueris et mentem et linguam refraenaveris tuam, beatus eris et quasi inter epulas iugis convivantium turmis, mens tua absque terrore undique secura quiescet. Scripta namque est: Secura mens ut iuge convivium' (Proverbs 15: 15).

[22]   Cf. Hincmar of Rheims's terrifying vision of the king after death: alone, without followers or family: Quierzy letter (858), MGH, *Concilia aevi Karolini* III, ed. W. Hartmann (Hannover, 1984), no. 41, c. 4, p. 410.

My suggestion is that these word pictures caused exceptional anxiety for young *aulici*: 'turbati sunt', and in particular by the thought of the rider who had fallen asleep. This *quidam captor sompnii* had been struck by divine reproof (*increpatio*), his God no longer the God of Jacob, who sent a dream of peace, of comfort, but a God who sent a vision of dysfunction and punishment, the body without any self-discipline, the beast in control. The dream had turned to a nightmare: 'O somnum durum et inexcitabile'. It was in such dreams that demons found entry to the mind.[23] In the same mind, the word picture, embedded since youth, was fitfully remembered with dread.

There is another, lateral, line of approach that takes us into the chamber of the household where youthful psalter-reading was practised, and the memory tracks were laid. I have talked of word pictures. What of actual images? Only members of the highest elite could have owned illustrated psalters, but Dhuoda and William belonged to that elite, and the books they owned included psalters. The two earliest surviving illustrated western psalters were both produced in western Francia during Dhuoda's lifetime, probably in the years around 830: the Stuttgart Psalter, made at St-Germain-des-Prés, and the Utrecht Psalter, made at Rheims.[24] Between them they give an idea of what kind of book Dhuoda and her husband Bernard, at the height of his power and influence, might have been able to commission or acquire. Both these psalters include vivid depictions of Psalm 75, vv. 6–7.[25] The suggestion being proposed here is that Dhuoda and William might together have studied the psalms from such a book, or a rather less grand one, and that the images of the rider 'cast into a dead sleep by demons',[26] and of

---

[23] On demons in dreams, see Dutton, *The Politics of Dreaming*, pp. 95–6, 213–19, and Index s.v. 'dream symbols of punishment: demons'. Dutton's book is of fundamental importance on the understanding of dreams in this period.

[24] For dating of both these psalters to 'before 830', see Dutton, *The Politics of Dreaming*, pp. 11, 17, with illustrations of Psalm 75: 6–7 at Figures 7 and 8, following p. 160. See further for a similar dating of the Utrecht Psalter with a suggested *terminus ante quem* of 833, K. van der Horst, 'The Utrecht Psalter: Picturing the Psalms of David', in van der Horst et al. (eds), *The Utrecht Psalter in Medieval Art* (Utrecht, 1996), pp. 23–84, at 24, 81–3. The size of the Stuttgart Psalter, at 265 x 175 mm, considerably smaller than the Utrecht Psalter, allows the possibility of something approaching domestic use.

[25] The relevant images are in The Stuttgart Psalter, Württembergerische Landesbibliothek, Cod. Bibl. 2° 23, fol. 88v, facsimile, ed. E. DeWald, *The Stuttgart Psalter* (Princeton, NJ, 1930), and The Utrecht Psalter, Bibliotheek der Rijksuniversiteit, Utrecht, cod. 32, fol. 43v., facsimile ed. by K. van der Horst and J.H.A. Engelbregt, *Utrecht Psalter. Vollständige Faksimile-Ausgabe* (Graz, 1984), 2 vols, I. As Thiébaux notes (*Dhuoda*, p. 263, n. 4), Dutton, *The Politics of Dreaming* offers no comment on Dhuoda's remarks on dreaming in Book 5, Chapter 1.

[26] Dutton, *The Politics of Dreaming*, Figure 8, caption.

other demons whispering to sleepers of feasting and riches, had been fixed in William's mind, unsettling, disturbing, but provoking. When Dhuoda came to write her *Handbook*, to provide both reassurance, and stimulus to virtue, as part of the most important *rite de passage* her son would undergo, she confronted – believed she *must* confront – the demons and the nightmare sleeper, lay bare the fears and confusions revealed by the dream she recounted – and what could be more fearful and confusing than the absurdity of sleeping while riding and feasting at the same time? Dhuoda could expose the dream as illusion, part of the 'as if' of the night, oppose nightmare experience to the truth of reality as seen by the awakened in the light of day, and so, for William and his *comilitones* whom she hoped would constitute her extended audience, convert fears and confusions into clear perception and self-discipline. For Dhuoda, dealing with the dream was not an option but a necessity. In accomplishing this, by opposing dreamt 'as ifs' to real moral exemplars in historic time, she showed more than intellectual resourcefulness: she left an indelible impression of a mother's special sense of responsibility to awaken both conscience and consciousness.

Figure 3.1 Stuttgart Psalter, Psalm 75

(King James Version Ps. 76): 6–7 [6] 'Turbati sunt omnes insipientes corde./Dormierunt somnium suum,/et nihil invenerunt omnes viri divitiarum in manibus suis. [7] Ab increpatione tua, Deus Jacob,/dormitaverunt qui ascenderunt equos.' [6] All those who are fools in their hearts have been thrown into confusion./They have slept their dream,/And all those men have found in their hands not a thing of the riches [they dreamt of]. [7] From your curse, O God of Jacob,/Those who mounted [their] horses have fallen asleep.' In the Stuttgart Psalter, Württembergerische Landesbibliothek Stuttgart, Cod. Bibl. 2°23, fol. 88v, reproduced by kind permission of the Württembergerische Landesbibliothek Stuttgart, a rider has been cast into sleep (left), while a demon whispers of riches to a fool who sleeps (right).

Figure 3.2 Utrecht Psalter, Psalm 75: 6–7

In the Utrecht Psalter, Utrecht, University Library, MS 32, fol. 43v., reproduced by kind permission of the Utrecht University Library, a group of horsemen are cast into sleep by demons (centre), while other demons whisper of riches to fools who sleep (right).

Figure 3.3 Utrecht Psalter, Psalm 72

(King James Version Ps. 73): 14–20, esp. 18–20: '[18] Verumtamen propter dolos posuisti eis; dejecisti eos dum allevarentur. [19] Quomodo facti sunt in desolationem?/Subito defecerunt; perierunt propter iniquitatem suam. [20] Velut somnium surgentium, Domine,/ in civitate tua imaginem ipsorum ad nihilum rediges.' '[18] But indeed for [their] deceits you have ordained [something] for them: while they were arising, you have cast them down. [19] How have been they brought to desolation? Suddenly they have failed: they have perished because of their iniquity. [20] As the dream of those that wake up, O Lord,/even so in your city you shall bring their imagining to nought.' In the Utrecht Psalter, University Library MS 32, fol. 41v., reproduced by kind permission of the Utrecht University Library, dreamers are depicted on their beds (?camp-beds), (left, middle), 'set in slippery places' (so, the King James Version; cf. 'set on slippery ground', NEB), and liable to be cast down with the damned (left, below) rather than united with the saved (left, above).

Chapter 4

Motherhood and Power in Early Medieval Europe, West and East: The Strange Case of the Empress Eirene

Mark Whittow

Over the last quarter-century, one of the key advances in our understanding of European society during the middle ages – an advance in which the work of Henrietta Leyser has been seminal – has been a much sharper appreciation of the political role of women, and its potentially central importance. A previous generation of historians not unreasonably saw their position as marginal. Medieval Europe was by any standards a highly gendered society where all frontline roles appeared to be played by men. In a society addicted to war, played out in campaigns that could take participants away for months at a time, women were not warriors; in a world where politics was far more personal than institutional, where warbands and hunting parties were so often the places where relationships were forged and fostered, women were not there; in a culture where charismatic sacral authority was exercised by male priests, women were unavoidably excluded. The default sex of a ruler was male. God was male. Yet, real though these factors were, they have come to be seen as only a part of the picture.

Thanks to Henrietta's work, along with that of other scholars, the problem is now no longer to put the case for female power as such, but to explain the varying forms it took in different societies at different times. In other words what is needed is a comparative history, and one not just of female power in isolation, but understood in the context of each society as a whole. The attraction of such an approach is obviously in part the classic justification of comparative history that, by looking at an aspect of one society in the context of another, one defamiliarizes it and highlights peculiarities that one would otherwise accept as unremarkably normal. However, there is also a purpose that goes beyond the study of female power as such. Following the theme of women in power across cultures offers a trace element that can illuminate the differences between societies. The study of women in power is not just an important topic in itself, but a means to the larger end of writing analytical comparative history on the grand scale. One recent and successful attempt has been Chris Wickham's *Framing the Early Middle Ages*, which uses a variety of trace elements, particularly the structures of revenue raising and land exploitation, to compare the component parts of the early medieval world in Europe and the Near East. Women are not absent from Wickham's work, but the theme of women in power does not take centre stage.[1] As Julia Smith noted ten years ago, there is clearly something to be learnt by trying to put it there.[2]

Motherhood and Power

Power in any society comes in a variety of forms, and ranges from the highly circumscribed, limited to the workings of very small worlds, to the acknowledged leadership of peoples and states. Not all female power in the middle ages depended upon motherhood.[3] An empress or queen was de facto an aristocrat with patronage to dispense and access to resources that made them dangerous for lesser mortals of either sex to cross. The woman who shared a king's bed had a peculiarly close form of königsnähe that could be exploited whether or not she bore children.[4] The sixth-century Empress Theodora, whatever Procopius's exaggerations, was a powerful woman, but she bore Justinian no children. Her power rested, one must presume, on the acknowledged role of an intercessor played by all empresses and queens, on her access to wealth and service, and possibly on an ability to deputize for the emperor in his absence.[5] Such observations, however, are essentially no more than preliminary caveats.

---

[1]   Chris Wickham, *Framing the Early Middle Ages* (Oxford, 2005), pp. 554–7 is the closest he comes to this theme.

[2]   Julia M.H. Smith, 'Did Women have a Transformation of the Roman World?', *Gender and History*, 12 (2000): 552–71.

[3]   A point well made in Liz James, *Empresses and Power in Early Byzantium* (Leicester, 2001), see esp. pp. 59–65.

[4]   Cf. Anthony Trollope, *The Warden* (London, 1855), p. 121: 'Whatever of submissive humility may have appeared in the gait and visage of the archdeacon during his colloquy with his wife in the sanctum of their dressing-rooms was dispelled as he entered his breakfast-parlour with erect head and powerful step. In the presence of a third person he assumed the lord and master; and that wise and talented lady too well knew the man to whom her lot for life was bound, to stretch her authority beyond the point at which it would be borne'.

[5]   Clive Foss, 'Theodora and Evita: Two Women in Power', in Claudia Sode and Sarolta Takács (eds), *Novum Millennium: Studies in Byzantine History and Culture Presented to Paul Speck* (Aldershot, 2001), pp. 113–22.

Legitimate autonomous power that did not rest simply on a husband was in practice almost always a factor of motherhood.

> Ortu magna, viro major, sed maxima partu
> Hic jacet Henrici filia, sponsa, parens.
> [Great by birth, greater by marriage, greatest in her offspring
> Here lies the daughter, wife, and mother of Henry.][6]

The epitaph of the Empress Matilda (1102–1167) from her now destroyed tomb at Bec in Normandy neatly sums up her career as the daughter of Henry I (1068/9–1135, son of William the Conqueror, King of England and Duke of Normandy), wife of Henry V (1086–1125, Emperor of the Romans and King of Germany), and mother of Henry II (1133–1189, King of England, Duke of Normandy and Aquitaine, Count of Anjou). On one level the epitaph is an elegantly phrased statement of fact about her relationship to the three Henries and about the three Henries themselves. Matilda was significant as the daughter of a powerful king of England, more important as the wife of the greatest European ruler of the early twelfth century, and most important of all as the mother of the political phenomenon of his age, the dynast who already by 1167 ruled an empire that stretched from the Cheviot Hills to the Pyrenées and included the whole of western France. However, it is also the expression of a truism, that women were most powerful through their sons. Matilda was only noteworthy as a daughter of Henry I because, after the wreck of the *White Ship* in 1120, he had no legitimate male heir, and even then, despite having sworn oaths to accept her as queen, the Anglo-Norman nobility promptly rejected her in 1135 in favour of her male cousin, Stephen of Blois. As Henry V's queen and then empress, Matilda was a much more significant power broker as long as her husband lived, but in 1125 this power was shown to have been hollow. Had she been the mother of a male heir, Matilda would have been a key player in imperial politics for the rest of her life; as it was she was a powerless irrelevance and less than a year after her husband's death she was back at her father's court in England. What then gave her importance and a degree of lasting political power was not so much her second marriage in 1128 to Geoffrey, ten years her junior and at the time of the betrothal not even Count of Anjou (and significantly not mentioned on her epitaph), but the fact that in 1133 she gave birth to a son, which made her the mother of the potential heir to Anjou, England and Normandy. Matilda was not a great politician. Her mistakes in 1141 allowed what appeared to be

---

[6]   Marjorie Chibnall, *The Empress Matilda: Queen Consort, Queen Mother and Lady of the English* (Oxford, 1991), p. 191.

total victory in the civil war against Stephen to slip from her grasp. Yet, unlike her situation in Germany in 1125, she never became powerless. The fact of her being the mother of a potential and then actual king gave her power that lasted to her death.[7] Another face of female power in the age of Matilda was that of the virgin charismatic, a description that would not apply to the empress, but can be illustrated by two of her contemporaries, the German visionary abbess, Hildegard of Bingen, and on a less spectacular scale the Hertfordshire anchoress, Christina of Markyate, who has been the subject of a series of Henrietta's penetrating studies.[8] The important point to note, however, is that these virgin charismatics paradoxically confirm the normal centrality of motherhood in the makeup of female power. A crucial aspect of saintly power, as Peter Brown has long emphasized in his work on holy men, is its social liminality.[9] The saint can effect reconciliation because she or he is not one of the contesting parties. Either they are an outsider or by their behaviour they act as such. Witness the hermit living in the desert, the stylite on a column, or in this case the saintly woman, 'forgetful of her sex', which in this context covers, above all, eschewing motherhood.[10] There were saints who were mothers, mostly concentrated in the seventh and eighth centuries, and in the west. Some, such as the tenth-century Ottonian matriarchs Mathilda and Adelheid, were queens whose status as saints reflected the pre-Gregorian sanctification of aristocratic power, but in most cases women were recognized as saints despite their motherhood and not because of it.[11] As Jane Schulenburg notes, female saints who were mothers 'did not often

---

[7]   Marjorie Chibnall, 'Matilda (1102–1167)', *Oxford Dictionary of National Biography* (Oxford, 2004), http://www.oxforddnb.com/view/article/18338.

[8]   Sabina Flanagan, *Hildegard of Bingen: a Visionary Life* (London, 1989); Samuel Fanous and Henrietta Leyser (eds), *Christina of Markyate: a Twelfth-century Holy Woman* (London, 2005); *The Life of Christina of Markyate*, trans. C.H. Talbot, Rev. with Intro. and Notes by Samuel Fanous and Henrietta Leyser (Oxford, 2008).

[9]   Although the concept of liminality is clear enough in Peter Brown, 'The Rise and Function of the Holyman in Late Antiquity', *Journal of Roman Studies*, 61 (1971): 83–4, 86, 91–2, Brown had not come across Turner's usage until he came to Berkeley in 1978. See Peter Brown, *A Life of Learning*, Charles Homer Haskins Lecture for 2003, American Council of Learned Societies Occasional Paper, 55 (2003), p. 11 and cf. Brown, *The Cult of the Saints: Its Rise and Function in Latin Christianity* (Chicago, 1981), pp. 42–3.

[10]   *Oblita sexus*: Jerome, *Letters*, 77.9.2, 108.14.3, ed. Isidor Hilberg, editio altera supplementis aucta, CSEL 55.2 (Vienna, 1996), pp. 46, 325; Jane Tibbets Schulenburg, *Forgetful of Their Sex: Female Sanctity and Society, ca. 500–1100* (Chicago, 1998), pp. 127–75.

[11]   Schulenburg, *Forgetful of Their Sex*, pp. 211–69; Anneke B. Mulder-Bakker, 'Introduction', in Anneke B. Mulder-Bakker (ed.), *Sanctity and Motherhood: Essays on Holy Mothers in the Middle Ages* (New York, 1995), pp. 16–23; Ineke van't Spijker, 'Family Ties: Mothers and Virgins in the Ninth Century', in ibid., pp. 165–90; Sean Gilsdorf, *Queenship*

warrant consideration for full membership in the celestial gynaeceum'.[12] The natural denizens of that place were saintly virgins who had deliberately cut themselves off from the normal root of female power, and by doing so made it potentially possible to access the liminal status of the charismatic. Nothing could illustrate more clearly the extent to which the association of motherhood and power were the social norm.

Very few women in power during the middle ages or even the early modern period are even potential exceptions to this rule. One might be Queen Elizabeth I (1533–1603), virgin queen regnant of England from 1558 to 1603. However, her spinsterhood was the product of highly peculiar circumstances. A royal princess would normally have been married while still young to a foreign royal groom, but as Elizabeth's mother had been executed by her father and she had formally been declared a bastard (a status her half-sister, Queen Mary, was keen to maintain), this was unlikely to happen. Furthermore, as someone brought up to be a convinced Protestant in a divided Europe, the realistic options were limited. When, rather against the odds, she finally became queen, Elizabeth seems to have thought seriously of marrying one of her already married subjects, Robert Dudley, until the objections of her councillors and the scandal of the death of Dudley's existing wife in highly suspicious circumstances made it effectively impossible. Elizabeth appears to have been close to marrying the Duke of Anjou in 1579, but in this case serious objections to a Catholic marriage from some of her leading councillors made her step back. After that it was too late. She was stuck with the image of the virgin queen, whether she liked it or not. As such Elizabeth's role, like that of the medieval virgin saint, acted not so much to overturn the normal association of motherhood and power as to confirm it. Elizabeth could be a charismatic peacemaker because she stood outside the normal bounds of political behaviour, and this underlined her exceptionality and the normal centrality of motherhood to female power.[13] Another possible exception is the Chinese empress, Wu Zhao (or Wu Zetian as she is also termed), who having entered the imperial court as a fifth-rank concubine in about 640, rose by 655 to become principal consort of the emperor Gaozong and an increasingly dominant figure in the regime. After his death, their son Li Xian succeeded, but his reign lasted a mere six weeks before his mother deposed him

---

and Sanctity: the Lives *of Mathilda and the* Epitaph *of Adelheid* (Washington DC, 2004), pp. 35–60.

[12]   Schulenburg, *Forgetful of Their Sex*, p. 269.

[13]   Susan Doran, *Monarchy and Matrimony: the Courtships of Elizabeth I* (London, 1996); Kevin Sharpe, *Selling the Tudor Monarchy: Authority and Image in Sixteenth-century England* (New Haven, 2009), pp. 324–416. I am grateful to John Watts for pointing me to Doran's important book.

and put his younger and more pliant brother, Li Dan, in his place. In 690 Li Dan was made to stand down and Wu Zhao ruled in her own right from 690 to 705, at which point the elderly empress, now in her eighties, was removed from power and Li Xian restored.[14] The Empress Wu has a lurid reputation thanks to the Chinese Confucian tradition of historical writing, which regarded female rulership as an unnatural aberration. She is accused, amongst other things, of murdering her daughter in 652 to frame Gaozong's previous consort, the Empress Wang; of murdering the empress Wang herself in 655 (cutting off her limbs and throwing them into a vat of wine); of killing two half brothers and an uncle in 666, a nephew in 670, her eldest son, the heir apparent, Li Hong, in 675, and framing her second son, Li Hsien, in 679, so that he was banished and eventually committed suicide. Later sources suggest she killed Gaozong too. In 684, having crushed a rebellion against her, she presided over a bloody reign of terror that lasted until 691. Another rebellion in 688 provided an excuse to attack the imperial Li family. She was also described as sexually voracious into her eighties, when the number of aphrodisiacs she took made her grow new teeth and eyebrows.[15] As a historian of the west of medieval Eurasia rather than the far east, it is hard to know what to make of this, but it sounds wildly unlikely. None of the sources are strictly contemporary, and in any case, given that they are for the most part extremely hostile, it is difficult to see why they should be believed.[16] However, even taking them at something like face value, it is clear that there is nothing to show Wu Zhao breaking the link between motherhood and power. She initially came to attention because she gave birth to one or possibly two sons, while the Empress Wang was childless, and later she produced more. As Richard Guisso points out, there is actually no reason to think that Li Hong

---

[14]   N. Harry Rothschild, *Wu Zhao: China's Only Woman Emperor* (New York, 2008); Denis Twitchett and Howard J. Wechsler, 'Kao-tsung (reign 649–83) and the Empress Wu: the Inheritor and the Usurper', in *Cambridge History of China*, iii: *Sui and T'ang China, 589–906*, part 1, ed. Denis Twitchett (Cambridge, 1979), pp. 242–89; Richard W.L. Guisso, 'The Reigns of the Empress Wu, Chung-tsung and Jui-tsung (684–712)', in ibid., pp. 290–332. (Twitchett, Wechsler and Guisso use the Wade–Giles romanization of Chinese rather than currently standard Pinyin. Hence Kao-tsung = Gaozung; Chung-tsung = Zhongzong, also known by his personal name of Li Xian, and Jui-tsung = Ruizong, personal name Li Dan.)

[15]   Twitchett and Wechsler, 'Kao-tsung (reign 649–83) and the Empress Wu', pp. 248, 251, 265, 267, 270–71, 273; Guisso, 'The Reigns of the Empress Wu, Chung-tsung and Jui-tsung', pp. 294, 297, 302. For Wu Zhao's later reputation as sexually voracious see the sixteenth-century erotic novel, the *Ruyijun zhuan*, ed. and trans. C.R. Stone, *The Fountainhead of Chinese Erotica: the Lord of Perfect Satisfaction* (Ruyijun zhuan) (Honolulu, 2003).

[16]   Rothschild, *Wu Zhao*, pp. ix–xii, 206–10; Twitchett and Wechsler, 'Kao-tsung (reign 649–83) and the Empress Wu', pp. 244–5; Richard W.L. Guisso, *Wu Tse-T'ien and the Politics of Legitimisation in T'ang China* (Bellingham, WA, 1978), p. 8.

died of other than natural causes, or that Li Hsien (who may not have been her son) was framed.[17] In 684 she had already been acting as effective ruler for more than two decades, and in any case she replaced one son (whom she exiled but later recalled) with another. Only from 690 did she rule unabashedly in her own right, and even then she did so with one son, Ruizong, as the emperor expectant. At this point she took the title of 'sage mother, sovereign divine' following the convenient finding the year before of a white stone in the river Lo which bore the prophetic inscription, 'A sage mother shall come to rule mankind; and her rule shall bring eternal prosperity'.[18] Sage mothers need sons. Even less than England's virgin queen did the Empress Wu, in this respect at least, break the expected mould.

The third candidate as an exception to the rule that female rule rests directly or indirectly on motherhood is the late eighth-century Byzantine empress Eirene. Her career has left traces in a variety of sources, but for a detailed narrative we are dependent on the account given in the early ninth-century *Chronographia* of Theophanes.[19] Originally from the province of Hellas, in other words central Greece, and quite likely from Athens itself, Eirene had been brought to Constantinople in 769 to marry Constantine V's eldest son and teenage co-emperor Leo IV.[20] She may have been related to the Serantapechys family, and as such from the provincial elite of Hellas, but otherwise one can only speculate as to why Constantine thought her a suitable bride for his son.[21] Leo himself was the son of Constantine's first marriage to a Khazar princess called Çiçek,

---

[17]   Guisso, *Wu Tse-T'ien*, p. 23.

[18]   Guisso, 'The Reigns of the Empress Wu, Chung-tsung and Jui-tsung', p. 302.

[19]   There is a substantial and important bibliography on Eirene, and I have drawn on the following: 'Eirene # 1439', *Prosopographie der mittelbyzantinischen Zeit*, ed. Ralph-Johannes Lilie, et al. (6 vols, Berlin, 1998–2002), i, p. 454; 'Eirene 1', *Prosopography of the Byzantine Empire*, I, 641–867, CD ROM, ed. John Robert Martindale (Aldershot, 2001); Judith Herrin, *Women in Purple: Rulers of Medieval Byzantium* (London, 2001); Ralph-Johannes Lilie, with Ilse Roschow, *Byzanz unter Eirene und Konstantin VI. (780–802)* (Frankfurt am Main, 1996); Paul Speck, *Kaiser Konstantin VI: Die Legitimation einer fremden und der Versuch einer eigenen Herrschaft: Quellenkritzsche Darstellung von 25 Jahren byzantinischer Geschichte nach dem ersten Ikonoklasmus* (2 vols, Munich, 1978). Referring to episodes in Eirene's career, however, I shall only cite Theophanes, who is usually the sole source.

[20]   Theophanes, *Chronographia*, ed. Karl de Boor (2 vols, Leipzig, 1883–1885), i, pp. 444; trans. Cyril Mango and Roger Scott, *The Chronicle of Theophanes Confessor: Byzantine and Near Eastern History, AD 284–813* (Oxford, 1997), p. 613.

[21]   The case that Eirene was part of the Serantapechys or Tessarandapechys family rests solely on a less than clear passage in Theophanes: *Chronographia*, i, p. 474; trans. Mango and Scott, pp. 651–2, and n. 6; cf. Herrin, *Women in Purple*, pp. 55–6; Lilie and Roschow, *Byzanz unter Eirene und Konstantin VI.*, pp. 36–41.

'Flower', who had died in 750. The emperor's second wife, Maria, lasted less than two years. His third wife, Eudokia, was still alive in 769, and had given birth to five sons and a daughter.[22] Eirene's marriage to Leo was accompanied by a new imperial coronation for both bride and groom, which served as an unequivocal statement that Leo was the heir apparent.

In January 771, Eirene gave birth to a son, Constantine. Four years later in 775, Constantine V died, Leo IV became emperor and Eirene replaced the widowed Eudokia as senior empress. The next year, on 14 April 776, which was Easter Sunday, the infant Constantine was crowned as co-emperor. The nature of the new order was made clear in May when Leo's half-brother, the Caesar Nikephoros, was accused of plotting, deprived of his title (and hence of his income) and sent into exile in the Crimea.[23] On 7 September 780, Leo IV, then aged 30, died without warning. Eirene, as a crowned empress and mother of the nine-year-old surviving emperor Constantine VI, became regent. Hardly more than a month later, the former Caesar Nikephoros was again accused of plotting to seize power. The supposed conspirators, who included a number of high-ranking military and civil officials, were arrested, flogged, tonsured, and sent into exile. At this point the remainder of Constantine V's sons, Eirene's half-brothers-in-law, were forcibly ordained, and to ensure as much as possible that this status was irrevocable, they were made to participate in the Christmas Day liturgy at Hagia Sophia and very publicly to administer communion to the people.[24] Some coins dating from the 780s present Eirene as the junior partner to her son Constantine, but in the majority of designs it is she who appears as the senior ruler.[25] At the council of Nicaea in 787 most references are to 'Constantine and Eirene', in that order, but on what were probably the two most important ceremonial occasions in which the emperors were involved at the Council, namely the end of the first and the end of the final sessions, Eirene took precedence, being acclaimed before her son on the first occasion, and subscribing the canons before Constantine in the second. The implication that she was the senior ruler was plain enough.[26] By this date, however, this was an aberration.

---

[22]   'Leo IV # 4243', *Prosopographie der mittelbyzantinischen Zeit*, ii, p. 668 'Leo 4', *Prosopography of the Byzantine Empire*.

[23]   Theophanes, *Chronographia*, i, pp. 450–51, 454; trans. Mango and Scott, pp. 621, 627.

[24]   Theophanes, *Chronographia*, i, p. 454; trans. Mango and Scott, p. 627.

[25]   Philip Grierson, *Catalogue of the Byzantine Coins in the Dumbarton Oaks Collection and the Whittemore Collection, III: Leo III to Nikephoros III 717–1081. Part 1: Leo III to Michael III (717–867)* (Washington DC, 1973), pp. 108–9, 139, 337, 347.

[26]   *Concilium Universale Nicaenum Secundum. Concilii Actiones I–III*, ed. Erich Lamberz, Acta Conciliorum Oecumenicorum, series ii, vol. 3.1 (Berlin, 2008), pp. 42, 110

In 787 Constantine, now sixteen, was easily of age to rule in his own right. If the normal patterns of Byzantine politics had been followed, Eirene should already have stepped aside. However, they were not, in ways that, according to Theophanes's account, became increasingly extraordinary.

Constantine made a first attempt to seize power in February 790, but failed. Eirene arrested and punished his supporters, and Constantine himself was flogged and imprisoned. The army was then asked to take an oath never to accept Constantine as emperor. However, Eirene's authority did not prove secure, and over the course of the year began to unravel. By October the army had moved to support Constantine and he was now able to arrest his mother's supporters, punish them, and place her under house arrest in the palace of Eleutherios. Yet even this did not prove the end of her role. At the beginning of 792 she was restored to her status as empress, and once again acclaimed at court alongside her son. This situation lasted until 797, when Eirene's backers among the army managed to arrest the emperor.[27] What happened next is described by Theophanes as follows.

> About the 9th hour they blinded him in a cruel and grievous manner with a view to making him die at the behest of his mother and her advisers. The sun was darkened for seventeen days and did not emit its rays so that ships lost course and drifted about. Everyone acknowledged that the sun withheld its rays because the emperor had been blinded. In this manner Eirene acceded to power.[28]

There is some debate as whether Constantine did actually die at this point. Much later chronicles tell what sound like fanciful stories involving hidden treasure that require him to have survived into the reign of Nikephoros I (802–811); however, since the only piece of direct testimony, two letters written by the iconophile abbot, Theodore the Stoudite, would support any date for his death between 797 and 805, there seems no compelling reason to question the implication of Theophanes's account that he died either at the time or very soon afterwards as a result of his injuries.[29] Had he survived, someone would

---

(Eirene acclaimed before Constantine), 112, 280; *Sacrorum conciliorum nova et amplissima collectio*, ed. Giovanni Domenico Mansi (31 vols, Florence and Venice: Antonius Zatta, 1758–1798), cols 1, 129 (Eirene preceding Constantine), 157, 201, 203, 364, 376, 397, 398, 413 (synod called by God-protected empress Eirene), 415 (Eirene subscribes canons before Constantine).

[27] Theophanes, *Chronographia*, i, pp .465–72; trans. Mango and Scott, pp. 640–48.

[28] Theophanes, *Chronographia*, i, p. 472; trans. Mango and Scott, pp. 648–9.

[29] E.W. Brooks, 'On the Date of the Death of Constantine the Son of Irene', *Byzantinische Zeitschift*, 9 (1900): 654–7; Lilie and Roschow, *Byzanz unter Eirene und*

have tried to make political capital out the fact, and hence the silence seems significant. After what I therefore take to be the effective murder of her son, for the next five years Eirene was sole ruler of the empire. She survived until 802, when she was toppled in a coup that brought one of her former allies, the logothete of the genikon, Nikephoros to power. The new emperor exiled her to Lesbos and she died there in 803.[30] Much of what Theophanes has to say should obviously be discounted. No more than the stories told by Procopius of the Empress Theodora, or those recorded about the Empress Wu by the authors of the Old and New Tang Histories, should Theophanes's stories of Eirene be taken at face value. The *Chronographia* is a near-contemporary source for the Empress's career, but it is certainly not a disinterested record. The reader needs always to be alert for the hum of grinding axes.[31] That said, the essential narrative is not fiction. There is enough independent evidence that survives from coins and seals, documents and inscriptions, and entirely independent sources such as the letters of Theodore the Stoudite or the Frankish annals, to corroborate that Eirene did rule as regent after Leo IV's death, that her son, Constantine, did remain under his mother's authority through the 780s, and that after a short period of independent rule in the 790s, he was blinded and his mother resumed rule in her own name. It is quite possible that much of the agency that Theophanes attributes to the Empress should actually be credited to others, but the fact remains that Eirene was the only female ruler of the middle ages who at the least acquiesced in the murder of her son, and then carried on ruling in her own right. It is a remarkable story. What are we to make of it? What light does it shed on Byzantium, and on Byzantium in comparison with other societies, notably the other half of the formerly united Roman empire, the Christian west?

Byzantium and the West

Before heading west, though, there is another Byzantine story that is relevant, namely that of Metrios, as principally told in the *synexarion* of Constantinople. A synexarion is a collection of abbreviated saints' lives arranged so that each life appears under the day on which the saint's feast is celebrated. The synexarion of Constantinople is a record of the feasts celebrated in the imperial city, and one

---

Konstantin VI., pp. 273–7.

[30]   Theophanes, *Chronographia*, i, pp. 473–80; trans. Mango and Scott, pp. 650–58.

[31]   Cf. Leslie Brubaker, 'Sex, Lies and Textuality: the *Secret History* of Prokopios and the Rhetoric of Gender in Sixth-Century Byzantium', in Leslie Brubaker and Julia M.H. Smith (eds), *Gender in the Early Medieval World: East and West, 300–900* (Cambridge, 2004), pp. 83–101.

manuscript that dates to 1301 but is a compilation of older material includes the life of Metrios, an independent farmer from Paphlagonia in the north of Asia Minor, who lived in the ninth century and was rewarded for virtuous behaviour. The story tells how the pious Metrios wanted a son. He had seen how his neighbours had sons, whom they castrated and sent to Constantinople to make their fortunes, and he wanted to do the same. However, despite his prayers nothing happened. One day, however, on his way back from market, he found a bag of gold that had been dropped by an itinerant merchant. Rather than pocketing the find, Metrios waited until the next market day, found the merchant who had lost it, and gave it back, even refusing a reward for his action. The Virgin Mary was naturally impressed by this good deed, and Metrios was rewarded by the birth of a son, whom the good man promptly had castrated, and sent to be a eunuch in Constantinople, where he made his father rich, and they all lived happily ever after.[32] From the point of view of a western reader in the middle ages, let alone now, the story is bizarre. It is a simple tale of virtue rewarded, but in the west the whole point of being rewarded with a son would have been for the son to marry the princess and for them to produce a quiver of children. To have castrated the boy would have been pointless and unthinkable.

Byzantium and the west were both heirs of the Roman empire, and if one looks at the early medieval west in the age of the Merovingians and Carolingians, it is possible to see certain basic aspects of western society that broadly speaking can be parallelled in Byzantium. One is that the west was, like Byzantium, a society characterized by the fairly wide political participation of a substantial class of landed freemen. The Franks during the early middle ages did not imagine themselves to include slaves, but equally not all Franks were noble aristocrats either. There were many others whom we might want to label peasants and whom contemporaries were likely to think of as the poor. They were not destitute, but not rich and powerful either, and it was one characteristics of this society that these people had a full stake in its political life, at least at the local level, bearing arms, serving on campaigns, attending court, whether the king's or the local count's, and there ensuring that justice was done.[33] In other words, they were men rather like Metrios.

---

[32] *Synaxarium Ecclesiae Constantinopolitanae: Propylaeum ad Acta Sanctorum Novembris*, ed. H. Delehaye (Brussels, 1902), p. xli, cols 721–4 (1 June, Synexaria Selecta). A variant of the story appears in the tenth- or eleventh-century chronicle conventionally known as the Pseudo-Symeon Magister published as Symeon, Magister, *Annales*, ed. Immanuel Bekker, Corpus scriptorum historiae Byzantinae, 33 (Bonn, 1838), pp. 713–4. See too Kathryn M. Ringrose, *The Perfect Servant: Eunuchs and the Social Construction of Gender in Byzantium* (Chicago, IL, 2003), pp. 188–91.

[33] Régine Le Jan, *La société du haut Moyen Âge, vi^e–ixe siècle* (Paris, 2003), pp. 142–3.

Like Byzantium, the Frankish world was also one of powerful rulers, until 800 termed kings rather than emperors, but whatever they were called, playing a recognizably similar role to their eastern counterparts. Like the imperial court in Constantinople, the royal court under both the Merovingians and the Carolingians was a vital focus of attraction, and the kingdom, like the Byzantine empire, was a real unit of political action and identity.[34] However, this is where the differences begin to emerge. The usual explanation for the wealth of the Byzantine court and its ability to act as the political focus for an area that was still very large indeed, even after the Arab conquests of the seventh century, is the survival of a tax system and a bureaucracy to run it.[35] Despite the arguments of some historians to the contrary, there is no convincing case that anything like this existed in the west.[36] Yet the riches and power of so many Merovingian and Carolingian monarchs are strikingly impressive.

This disjuncture between the wealth and power of Frankish kings and their lack of a bureaucracy has for a long time been a puzzle to historians, since it seems to contradict one of the master narratives of European history, namely the rise of the modern state. What defines the modern state, as in the conventional periodization that sees an early modern period begin around 1500, is a new ability to exercise power, to act as a centralizing authority and as a focus of identity on a new scale. Conventional wisdom would look above all to the rising costs of war from the fifteenth century onwards and the concomitant need to tax and control a subject population that might hopefully be encouraged to identify itself in terms of the state: Normans and Picards into Frenchmen, Valencians and Galicians into Spaniards, Pomeranians and Magdeburgers into Prussians, or whatever.[37] From this viewpoint, the authority of the early Frankish kings seems an aberration because neither the Merovingians nor the Carolingians deployed an administrative machine on a sixteenth-century scale, let alone anything later. It may be a mistake to portray the Carolingian or even the Merovingian state in excessively primitive terms. The lack of documentary evidence is far more a reflection of the vagaries of its survival than the basis for a true picture of Frankish capabilities in the early middle ages. Charlemagne, the ruler of most

---

[34]   Wickham, *Framing the Early Middle Ages*, pp. 102–15.

[35]   Ibid., pp. 124–9; Mark Whittow, *The Making of Orthodox Byzantium, 600–1025* (Basingstoke, 1996), pp. 104–13.

[36]   Chris Wickham, 'La chute de Rome n'aura pas lieu', *Le moyen âge*, 99 (1993): 107–26; cf. Elisabeth Magnou-Nortier, 'La chute de Rome a-t-elle eu lieu?', *Bibliothèque de l'Ecole de Chartes*, 152 (1994): 521–41.

[37]   Charles Tilly, *Coercion, Capital and European States, AD 990–1990* (Oxford, 1990), pp. 1–37; Richard Bonney, 'The Rise of the Fiscal State in Europe, c. 1200–1815', in Richard Bonney (ed.), *The Rise of the Fiscal State in Europe, c. 1200–1815* (Oxford, 1999), pp. 1–14.

of western Europe, a builder of palaces and canals, a relentless issuer of laws and decrees, and an implacable campaigner against his enemies, did not run his empire with the help of a couple of clerics on the basis of a box under the bed.[38] Even so it would be a bigger mistake to think in terms of a Frankish bureaucracy. The power of Frankish kings evidently must have rested on other bases.

Timothy Reuter, an old friend of Henrietta's, once elegantly argued that the key to this mystery lay once again in war, but unlike the early modern state, not in the developments necessary to bear the costs of war, but rather in its profits. A golden age for the Franks was a dark age for their neighbours. Most famously, according to Einhard, cartloads of treasure were brought to Aachen from the defeat of the Avars and the sack of the Avar Ring, making this the most profitable victory the Franks had ever achieved. Other than the scale, Reuter's view was that this was not out of the ordinary. The Franks had been waging generally successful war against Aquitainians, Lombards, Alamanni and Bavarians for generations. The profits these wars brought had flowed into royal coffers and out to their loyal supporters with the effects of a virtuous circle for generations by the time of Charlemagne. Frankish kings were the most powerful rulers in western Europe because their military machine operated on a larger and more relentless scale than that of any of their contemporaries. In turn, the larger scale and the greater profits attracted and bound followers to them in a way no smaller kingdom could match, making the Frank's military capabilities yet more formidable, and the consequences of disloyalty yet more serious. Even supposing the king could not punish you for your failure to attend court or to go on campaign, could you afford to see the rewards of loyal service on this scale go into the hands of your rivals?[39] A clear and neat narrative of the rise and decline of the Frankish state thus emerges according to which early military success beginning as early as the sixth century snowballed into the great Frankish state that culminated with that of Charlemagne at the end of the eighth and the beginning of the ninth century. However, after that the pickings became much thinner. The Arabs in Spain proved tough opponents, and what else was there? After the Avars potential victims tended to be too poor to justify the effort, or in the case of the Vikings, they were themselves eying the treasure houses of Francia as suitable targets to rob. The Frankish kingdoms did not collapse overnight, but with the waning opportunities for profitable war at reasonable cost, the

---

[38]   Rosamund McKitterick, *The Carolingians and the Written Word* (Cambridge, 1989).

[39]   Timothy Reuter, 'Plunder and Tribute in the Carolingian Empire', *Transactions of the Royal Historical Society*, 35 (1985): 75–94; Reuter, 'The End of Carolingian Military Expansion', in Peter Godman and Roger Collins (eds), *Charlemagne's Heir* (Oxford, 1990), pp. 391–405.

momentum behind these previously so impressive early medieval states wound down in an era of internal war and intradynastic competition.

Reuter's model is elegant, but not wholly persuasive. What is just as striking about the political history of the Frankish kingdoms is not so much the coincidence between profitable military success and the power of kings as the disjuncture. One might explain Charlemagne's ability to wage an unprofitable war against stubborn Saxon opponents for over thirty years from 772 in terms of the political capital already amassed or being amassed elsewhere at the same time, but that is a harder argument to sustain for the reign of Charlemagne's grandson, Charles the Bald (840–877), a lengthy period of remarkable political effectiveness and almost consistent military failure.[40] The same point can be made for many Merovingian rulers in the sixth and seventh centuries. Kings appear as the powerful focus of political life whether or not their armies win on the battlefield, conquer new lands or plunder wealthy enemies.

Over recent years the answer to this conundrum has come more and more to be seen to lie in another aspect of Frankish society. In addition to the numerous class of free peasants, actively involved in political life, and to the powerful kings able to exercise their influence over very large portions of western Europe, the Merovingian and Carolingian world has also increasingly come to be appreciated as an age of aristocracy.[41] Thanks to the survival of the remarkable documents that record in detail their huge land-holdings, two individuals have come to be emblematic of the Frankish aristocracy in their pomp, Bertram of Le Mans and Abbo of Provence. Bertram was born no later than 540. His father was a landowning aristocrat with numerous estates in the lower Seine valley city territories of Paris, Rouen, possibly Sens and certainly and extensively Le Mans. His mother's family came from Aquitaine, and were landowners on a similar if slightly smaller scale around Bordeaux and the Saintonge.[42] One of his mother's family estates was at Plassac on the right bank of the Gironde, 30 km north of Bordeaux. What was presumably Bertram's villa was excavated in the 1960s and 1970s, and it is a rare example of an originally first-century AD foundation

---

[40]   Einhard, *Vita Karoli*, c. 7, ed. L. Halphen (Paris, 1938), pp. 22–6; Janet L. Nelson, *Charles the Bald* (London, 1992), pp. 67–8.

[41]   Among an extensive and interesting literature to this effect, see Matthew Innes, *State and Society in the Early Middle Ages: the Middle Rhine Valley, 400–1000* (Cambridge, 2000), pp. 259–63, and Wickham, *Framing the Early Middle Ages*, pp. 123–4, 197–203.

[42]   Margarete Weidemann, *Das Testament des Bischofs Berthramn von Le Mans vom 27. März 616*, Römisch-Germanisches Zentralmuseum Monographien, 9 (Mainz, 1986), pp. 173–6.

with a continuous history through to a named seventh-century owner.[43] It has been speculatively suggested that Bertram was related to the Merovingian royal family through queens Ingundis and Aregundis, sisters and successive queens of Chlothar I; however what is certain is that Bertram's kinsmen on both sides were powerful players in Frankish politics and that together they made up a family grouping whose resources and influence any effective king would have had to either harness or break. Bertram began his career at a date before 561 in royal service to Chlothar I. Possibly in the late 560s, he left secular service to become a priest and by 580 he was a deacon at the basilica of St Vincent in Paris and by 585 archdeacon of Paris.[44] These were years of high tension and violent competition within the Merovingian family. Since Chlothar I's death in 561 more than six Merovingians at various times had been recognized as kings and in various permutations had divided the kingdom between them. Suspicious and competitive, urged on by aristocratic clans like Bertram's, whose interests were tied to the fortunes of one or other Merovingian, the tensions and rivalries exploded into intermittent civil war. In 586 Bertram was elected Bishop of Le Mans by King Guntram acting as guardian for his infant nephew, Chlothar II, whose father had been murdered two years earlier. In 592 Guntram died, leaving Chlothar II to the mercy of his cousin, Childebert II, who promptly expelled Bertram from Le Mans and installed a new bishop, who was given not just the lands of the church but also those belong personally to Bertram. In 595 Childebert II died, the now teenaged Chlothar II recovered his inheritance and Bertram was restored to his see. In 600 the process was repeated. Childebert II's sons, Theuderic II and Theudebert II, recaptured Le Mans and ejected Bertram for a second time. However, Chlothar II's fortunes were in the ascendant. In 604 he recovered Le Mans, this time permanently, and restored Bertram once again to his estates. By 613 Theuderic II and Theudebert II were both dead and Bertram's loyalty to Chlothar II, who was now the sole Merovingian king, was triumphantly and profitably vindicated.[45] Bertram drew up his will, in accordance with proper Roman legal norms, in March 616. The original, a roll more than seven metres long and half a metre wide, was destroyed in the French Revolution, but not before a number of copies and a printed edition

---

[43]   Weidemann, *Das Testament des Bischofs Berthramn*, pp. 27–8. For Plassac, as well as Catherine Balmelle, *Les demeures aristocratiques d'Aquitaine: Société et culture de l'Antiquité tardive dans le Sud-Ouest de la Gaule*, Aquitainia Supplément, 10 (Bordeaux, 2001), pp. 394–6, see the website of the current Plassac villa project at http://plassac.gironde.fr/pagesEditos.asp?IDPAGE=82.

[44]   Weidemann, *Das Testament des Bischofs Berthramn*, pp. 132–4, 173.

[45]   Weidemann, *Das Testament des Bischofs Berthramn*, pp. 148–67, 173–5; Ian Wood, *The Merovingian Kingdoms, 450–751* (London, 1994), pp. 140–41.

had been produced. What the will lists, in a rather confusing order, which may suggest that the bishop was working from earlier wills he had made, are 135 units of land, most referred to as *villae* or groups of *villae*, in other words estates. This colossal body of land, estimated by one commentator as adding up to more than 300,000 hectares, was distributed over much that is now France, from Normandy and the Ile de France to the Pyrenées, and from Lorraine to the Atlantic, with concentrations in the lower Seine valley, in Aquitaine, in Burgundy, and in Provence.[46] Recent commentators have stressed how much of this property empire came to Bertram from Chlothar II's generosity, and that is an important and a valid point, but it is worth emphasizing the extent to which Bertram is less specific about the property he inherited from his parents than he is about that which came from the king.[47] In view of the political upheavals of the previous quarter century, it was perhaps more important to be specific about such property where his claim had no other basis than political fortune. In any case, given the uncertainty of the full extent of Bertram's inherited properties, it may well be misleading to underplay the extent to which landed wealth that undoubtedly came from royal patronage was matched or at least balanced by estates that had been passed down within the family.

The point matters because it affects what inferences are to be drawn from Bertram's will. If the bulk of Bertram's fortune came from Chlothar II, then it suggests a strikingly unfettered royal power capable of making and breaking an aristocracy of essentially royal placemen. If on the other hand a significant proportion of Bertram's wealth came from his ancestors, then even if that was matched by royal generosity, the point would be that aristocratic wealth was a separate phenomenon to powerful kingship. Or rather, that the relationship was at the least one of symbiosis.

The case for a Frankish aristocracy with its own inherited resources separate from or at least not entirely reliant on royal generosity gains support from the other aristocratic will to which I have referred, that of Abbo, conventionally known as Abbo of Provence or Abbo of Maurienne.[48] The will dates to 739, and like that of Bertram, survives (in a later but seemingly reliable medieval copy)

---

[46] Weidemann, *Das Testament des Bischofs Berthramn*, pp. 1–5, 7–49 (text), 50–62 (summary), 79–112 (analysis); 300,000 hectares: Henri Leclercq, 'L'épiscopat de saint Bertrand', in Fernand Cabrol and Henri Leclercq (eds), *Dictionaire d'Archéologie Chrétienne et de Liturgie* (15 vols, Paris, 1924–1953), x, col. 1495.

[47] Wood, *The Merovingian Kingdoms*, p. 209; Wickham, *Framing the Early Middle Ages*, p. 187.

[48] Patrick J. Geary, *Aristocracy in Provence: the Rhône Basin at the Dawn of the Carolingian Age*, Monographien zur Geschichte des Mittelalters, 31 (Stuttgart, 1985), pp. 38–78 (text).

thanks to the fact that the childless donor was giving the bulk of his property to an ecclesiastical institution, in Abbo's case the monastery of Novalesa in Piedmont that he had founded just over a decade earlier, in 726.[49] Abbo's career parallels Bertram's too in the sense that he benefited from conspicuous loyalty to what turned out to be the winning side, in Abbo's case loyalty to Charles Martel and the Carolingian cause in the 730s. Assuming, as seems likely, that the Abbo of the will can be identified with the *patricius* Abbo who appears in documents from St Victor at Marseilles as the ruler of Provence in the 740s, then he can be identified as the Carolingians' leading supporter in south-east Gaul from the 730s up to this death in about 750. To judge by the will, however, loyalty to the Carolingians did not bring Abbo the same scale of reward in land that support for Chlothar II had brought Bertram. Only a very small proportion of the extensive network of properties Abbo owned throughout the Alps, the Rhône valley and Provence had come to him from Charles Martel, and it seems to be confined to a mere three or four instances of properties confiscated from defeated rebels. That is not say that Abbo was not rewarded in other ways. No doubt booty came his way, possibly other gifts of treasure too, and his rule over Provence was no doubt a highly profitable form of reward too, but the fact remains that his landed fortune came not from a king, or in Charles Martel's case a mayor of the palace, but from his parents and ancestors. There are other clues too to Abbo's established status before the Carolingians arrived. It has been plausibly suggested that Abbo was related to the family of Waldelenus, one of the early supporters of the Irish monk Columbanus in seventh-century Burgundy, and it is possibly significant that one of Abbo's cousins was called Eustathius, the name of Columbanus's successor at Luxeuil. Furthermore, Jonas, Columbanus's biographer, came from Susa, an important centre in the western Alps, of which Abbo could describe himself as rector in 726. In other words, the will and the few other tantalizing scraps of evidence, make it quite clear that Abbo was not made by the Carolingians, rather his support, as a powerful landowner with very extensive properties in the region, from a long-standing family based in south-east Gaul, as far as this region is concerned, made them.[50] One could go on. There are fourteen more wills of more or less interest and detail that could be brought into the discussion, and more narrative material, particularly hagiography, that can be used to shed light on Frankish aristocratic society.[51] However, it is not necessary to labour the point. None of these ideas about Merovingian and Carolingian society is

---

[49]   Geary, *Aristocracy in Provence*, pp. 12–35.

[50]   Geary, *Aristocracy in Provence*, pp. 34, 101–48; Ian Wood, 'Review of P. Geary, *Aristocracy in Provence*', *French History*, 1 (1987): 118–9; Wood, *The Merovingian Kingdoms*, pp. 210–11.

[51]   Wood, *The Merovingian Kingdoms*, pp. 206–7.

particularly new as such, in the sense that historians have been talking about free peasants, powerful kings and wealthy landowning aristocrats in this context on and off since the nineteenth century. What is new is the growing appreciation that each of these characterizations of Merovingian and Carolingian society can be equally valid, and were to a large degree mutually reinforcing.

A substantial free peasantry gave kings a force to offset a powerful aristocracy. Aristocrats with extensive landed fortunes needed the sort of coordination and security that only effective kings could give. A powerful aristocracy with its sights focused on levels above the local was quite willing to allow peasants considerable freedom and had no need to pressure them for heavier labour services or larger revenues – and so on. Yet more recently still (I am thinking especially of the work of Paul Fouracre and Chris Wickham) has come the appreciation that in this case the question of which came first in this system, the chicken or the egg, may have a definitive answer in an aristocratic chicken.[52] What is so striking about the wills of Bertram and Abbo, and especially the former, is not just the fact of aristocratic landed wealth on such an impressive scale, but that it was not new with the individuals whose wills have come down to us. In fact, by definition, since their property subsequently ended up in ecclesiastical hands, they were the end of the line. Abbo's inheritance can be traced back into the seventh century and Bertram's into the sixth. What is also clear in Bertram's will is the healthy survival of what were clearly centuries-old patterns of land division and management. The villa at Plassac that belonged to Bertram's mother is only a particularly vivid example. The will as a whole is strong evidence that the Merovingian and Carolingian aristocracy was not a creation of the Frankish period, but an inheritance from Rome. It has of course been argued that this was not the case, and that we should recognize a fifth- and sixth-century break when the free peasants and the powerful kings emerge (both Frankish in their own imagination), and only see wealthy landowning aristocrats as a phenomenon of a new age that began in the late sixth or seventh century. However, reading Bertram's will, where a picture is set out in front of us very much of the agrarian world that had underpinned Roman aristocratic power in the age of Ausonius and Sidonius Apollinaris, still essentially intact a century and more after the fall of the western empire, it is hard to understand how this can possibly be the case. If all three ways of characterizing Merovingian and Carolingian society are valid, it looks increasingly convincing that it was the existence of a substantial aristocratic class, landowners on a large scale and ultimately the descendants of a Gallo-Roman aristocratic class famous for its wealth, that conditioned so much

---

[52]   Paul Fouracre, *The Age of Charles Martel* (Harlow, 2000), pp. 18–23; Wickham, *Framing the Early Middle Ages*, pp. 168–203.

of its social and political culture; moreover, it explains the power of the Frankish kings, despite their lack of a bureaucracy or a system of general taxation.[53] Going back to the story of Metrios castrating his son to make his fortune, the fact that at the heart of Frankish society was an aristocracy where wealth was built up within the family over generations, and who shared it was determined by the roulette wheel of marriage and inheritance, makes it quite obvious why acting as Metrios did would have been so unthinkable in the west. For castration to be the route to success requires a political system where institutions can trump the family. Early medieval Byzantium was not a society without aristocrats who owned large estates and passed those resources on to their children, but it was not a society founded on aristocracy in the same way as Francia.[54] Aristocrats and their family strategies were not at the very fulcrum of political life. Hence it was possible for a man like Metrios to send off a castrated boy to Constantinople in the hope that he might strike it rich. The castrato who rose, as Metrios's son did, to become *parakoimomenos*, keeper of the imperial bedchamber, had achieved an institutional position that did not require the buttressing of aristocratic family connections.

Eirene: The Female Eunuch?

Should Eirene's murder of her son be viewed in a similar light, as another case illuminating what made Byzantium different from the west? Certainly it is impossible to imagine Eirene's career as we know it largely from Theophanes taking place in the west. To go back to the metaphor of the roulette wheel, if early medieval Francia was a world where the control of wealth was fundamentally determined by the roulette wheel of marriage and inheritance, with bets placed on the procreation and survival of heirs, then as work since the 1970s has so usefully emphasized, it was bound to be one where women were almost unavoidably at the centre of the game, and at the heart of their power would be their status as mothers.[55] The importance of women as political actors

---

[53] Wickham, *Framing the Early Middle Ages*, pp. 178–86; cf. Guy Halsall, *Settlement and Social Organization: the Merovingian Region of Metz* (Cambridge, 1995), pp. 33–45.

[54] Mark Whittow, 'Early Medieval Byzantium and the End of the Ancient World', *Journal of Agrarian Change*, 9 (2009): 134–53; Leslie Brubaker and John Haldon, *Byzantium in the Iconoclast Era, c. 680–850* (Cambridge, 2011), pp. 575–91.

[55] See, seminally, Janet L. Nelson, 'Queens as Jezebels: the Careers of Brunhild and Balthild in Merovingian History', in Derek Baker (ed.), *Medieval Women: Dedicated and Presented to Professor Rosalind M.T. Hill on the Occasion of her Seventieth Birthday*, Studies in Church History, Subsidia 1 (Oxford, 1978), pp. 32–4, 35, 74; and for a synthesis which

in the early medieval west emerges in a variety of ways, some obvious, some less so. Starting with the wills of Bertram and Abbo that we have already discussed, women feature most obviously as the means of transferring property from the legal entity of one family to another. Bertram's mother, who like Bertram's father is not named, brought the properties in Aquitaine that created a new landed empire linking the maternal Aquitaine of the Garonne with the paternal Neustria of the lower Seine. Another close kinswoman of Bertram's created a similar north–south alliance by marrying a certain Avitus, possibly the later bishop of Clermont, who owned substantial properties in the city territories of Bourges, Albi, Cahors and Agen.[56] A little more can be said about Abbo's mother largely because, on top of the fact that she had brought him substantial properties in the region of Arles and Marseilles, which suggests a family well established in the region, he tells us her name, Rusticia, and those of several members of her family, Dodina, Goda and Doda. Rusticia points to various Rusticii who had long been important in the Lyons and Vaison region; Dodina, Goda and Doda point to links with the Austrasian Franks and the Rhineland. As Geary suggests, was it the links created by his maternal kin that lay at the origin of Abbo's alliance with Charles Martel?[57] His father's family came from the Alps, and Abbo's female relations on this side included Widegunda, Rigaberga and Siagria, who all left or sold him substantial properties. Siagria's name suggests a link with the Syagrii who had been leading aristocratic landowners over a swathe of southern Gaul for generations. The first known member of the family appears in the fourth century.[58] As relations and property owners, and in the case of Queen Berchetrude (second wife of Chlothar II, to whom Bertram left a property in Paris) as a legatee, high-status women appear quite frequently in both wills.[59] That said, the wills inevitably reveal little or nothing about the agency of any of the women mentioned. They reveal the web of property and kinship that a women might be able to draw on; they do not prove that she did so. For women in political action one needs to turn to narrative sources, and most obviously those of Gregory of Tours and Fredegar, which describe the careers of the Merovingian queens, Fredegund and Brunhild.

Fredegund was the second wife of Chilperic II (561–584), and mother of Bertram of Le Mans's patron, Clothar II. In the 560s Chilperic dismissed Fredegund in favour of a new wife, the Visigothic princess, Galswinth, but

places female power in the context of land and inheritance, Fouracre, *The Age of Charles Martel*, pp. 18–21.

[56] Weidemann, *Das Testament des Bischofs Berthramn*, pp. 83–4, 122–3, 136–7.
[57] Geary, *Aristocracy in Provence*, p. 116.
[58] Ibid., pp. 82, 103, 117–8.
[59] Weidemann, *Das Testament des Bischofs Berthramn*, p. 15.

after the princess's death, which followed only shortly afterwards, the king took her back. Fredegund bore Chilperic at least six children, of whom Chlothar II, born after his father's death, was ultimately the only one to live to succeed him. Gregory of Tours, the main source for her career, hated her, and in his *History* she is portrayed as a ruthless murderer, motivated by the desire to see her sons on their father's throne. Gregory's Fredegund is responsible for a list of victims, including Chilperic's sons by other wives, and a number of unfortunates whom she unjustly blamed for the early deaths of her own children.[60] Brunhild was Galswinth's younger sister. In 566 or 567 she married Sigibert I, who was Chilperic II's elder brother, making Fredegund her sister-in-law. Gregory admired her, and in the History she appears as a wise woman, who made the best of difficult circumstances after Sigibert's murder in 575 left her with the child heir, Childebert II. Her story, however, is carried on after 591 in the *Chronicle* of Fredegar, who in effect did for Brunhild what Gregory had done for Fredegund. She is described as a manipulative murderer, a second Jezebel, who fully deserved her final dreadful fate, dragged to death behind an unbroken horse in 613 on the orders of her victorious nephew, Chlothar II.[61] Modern historians have obviously been alert to Gregory and Fredegar's biases, but at the same time they have sometimes been curiously trusting of the specific information they give us. In fact we know nothing about the veracity of any of the charges made against either Fredegund or Brunhild. The lurid list of their crimes may rest on no more than hearsay, innuendo, a biblically influenced assumption that these were the sorts of things that bad queens did, or a natural wish to believe the worst of an enemy. The episodes they report usually date to several decades before they were written down, and by their nature assassinations and murders are intended to be kept secret. It is quite likely that neither Gregory nor Fredegar had any privileged information about either of the two queens, and in any case, if they did, we would not be able to distinguish the genuine from the fictitious. These stories sound convincing, but they do so against a picture of Merovingian society almost entirely based on what Gregory and Fredegar tell us in the first place.

However, that is only partly the point. Gregory and Fredegar tell us stories that made sense to them, and that they assumed would be believed by their readers. Even if everything they have to say about the queens is fiction, their stories reliably report how female power was perceived in Merovingian Francia, and since power is to a large extent perceived and imagined power (in other words the power of the powerful depends at least as much on widespread social

---

[60]   Wood, *The Merovingian Kingdoms*, pp. 124–6; Ian Wood, 'The Secret Histories of Gregory of Tours', *Revue belge de philologie et d'histoire*, 71 (1993): 257–9.

[61]   Nelson, 'Queens as Jezebels', pp. 39–46; Wood, *The Merovingian Kingdoms*, pp. 126–36.

assumptions as to what the powerful can do as it does on any real coercive force), such stories can still convey important truths about how female power operated. In the first place, and quite clearly, Gregory and Fredegar believed that queens were powerful figures who could make or break their allies and opponents. At one level Gregory had personal experience of this when he was forced to appear before the royal court on charges of having slandered Fredegund, but it is worth nothing that he came back safely from this experience, and in his account of the whole episode the queen was only a device to justify charges and counter-charges rather than a leading actor in her own right.[62] Paradoxically Fredegund appears more powerful when Gregory has no personal experience to describe.

Behind both authors' stories lies two related facts. One was that queens were not warleaders. If they were powerful and they could not destroy their enemies by simple force, then it followed that their weapons were bound to be the assassin's dagger, the poisoner's vial and the denunciation. The other fact was that the significance of queens lay in their position as the king's odalisque and consequently the mother of his children, and in particular mother of his sons and potential heirs. To go back once again to the metaphor of the roulette wheel, each spin brought new winners and losers, as older wives were replaced by younger, prettier versions with new friends and enemies, and sons became step-sons, and former heirs candidates for the priesthood.[63] The fortunes won and lost on each spin might be treated philosophically as the random workings of chance or the arcane judgement of God, but in practice there would always be the temptation, especially for a historian attempting to discern pattern and meaning in events, to explain the result by pointing at who had gained and to suggest that the wheel had been fixed, and that the convenient deaths of husbands or wives, step-sons or nephews had not been fortuitous. None of the stories of murder and assassination may be true in a literal sense, but they can still express an underlying truth that these facts and therefore these events were at the heart of queenly politics. This was a world where motherhood (potential and actual) and power were inextricably linked.

Paradoxically, the same point is implied by the other category of powerful women in the Frankish west, the sainted abbesses, who come to particular prominence in the seventh century. Saints are of course a cultural construct, and fashions change. Men and women are only saints because they have been recognized as such, attracted a cult following, and more importantly if posterity is to have any awareness of their existence, a Life has been written. By such

---

62   Gregory of Tours, *Decem Libri Historiarum* V. 49, ed. Bruno Krusch and Wilhelm Levison, MGH SS Rerum Merovingicarum, I.1 (Hannover, 1951), pp. 258–63.

63   Pauline Stafford, 'Sons and Mothers: Family Politics in the Early Middle Ages', in Baker (ed.), *Medieval Women*, pp. 81–91.

standards sixth-century saints in Francia had tended to be wonder-working hermits, while the fashion in the seventh century was for holy bishops and saintly aristocratic abbesses. Neither the sixth-century hermits nor the seventh-century bishops need cause any surprise. The hermits fitted a pattern fixed by hundreds of saints' Lives from the fourth century onwards. Gregory of Tours wrote many such Lives consciously following what was clearly to him a very familiar model. The bishops are equally what you would expect from a male church led by bishops who, as Bertram of Le Mans so notably exemplifies, controlled often huge resources. It would be strange if bishops had not been treated as saints. The saintly aristocratic abbesses are no more remarkable, provided one accepts the pivotal role of female power in this society. By deliberately and ostentatiously stepping back from motherhood, and thereby, potentially at least, accessing the power inherent in charismatic liminality, the aristocratic virgin sets herself outside the power game but at the same time confirms its normative force.[64] From such a point of view, Eirene is the female eunuch: a regendered figure, female but acting as emperor in an unfemale way. Her story can be told as that of an ambitious person who enjoyed power, and was sure that her ability was much greater than that of her son. Unwillingly forced out by her son in 790, she was soon back, and working to marginalize Constantine's authority. According to Theophanes, he was tricked by his mother into blinding the general of the Armeniakon, Alexios Mouselem, which destroyed the loyalty this provincial army had once felt for Constantine, and left him without committed military support.[65] Constantine's rejection of his second wife Maria is also blamed by Theophanes on the machinations of his mother. 'She was yearning for power and wanted him to be universally condemned.'[66] The divorce followed by Constantine's third marriage to a court lady-in-waiting, Theodote, provoked bitter opposition from the church. In 796 Theodote gave birth to a son, christened Leo after his grandfather. Eirene now moved to have Constantine overthrown. Acting directly as well as through members of her household, Eirene persuaded and bribed the commanders of the tagmata to agree to depose her son and accept

---

[64]   František Graus, *Volk, Herrscher und Heiliger im Reich der Merowinger: Studien zur Hagiographie der Merowingerzeit* (Prague, 1965), pp. 106–20; Friedrich Prinz, *Frühes Mönchtum im Frankenreich: Kultur und Gesellschaft in Gallien, den Rheinlanden und Bayern am Beispiel der monastischen Entwicklung (4. bis 8. Jahrhundert)*, 2nd edn (Munich, 1988), pp. 481–501. See also the careful comments in Paul Fouracre, 'The Origins of the Carolingian Attempts to Regulate the Cult of Saints', in James Howard-Johnston and Paul Antony Hayward (eds), *The Cult of Saints in Late Antiquity and the Early Middle Ages: Essays on the Contribution of Peter Brown* (Oxford, 1999), pp. 146–61.

[65]   Theophanes, *Chronographia*, i, pp. 467–8; trans. Mango and Scott, pp. 642–3.

[66]   Ibid., i, p. 469; trans. p. 645.

her as sole ruler in his place.[67] The coup took place in July 797. Constantine had been in Constantinople to mourn the death of his baby son. Discovering that he was in danger, he set out in a warship for the army of the Anatolikon that was camped on the Asian shore, but he was actually already in the hands of her supporters. They dithered, but it was clear to Eirene that if he reached an army the coup would be over and vengeance would follow. If that happened, she made it clear that her fall would bring them disaster too. She would denounce them all as traitors who had been ready to betray the emperor. Such a threat concentrated minds. The boat turned round, Constantine was brought back to Constantinople, taken to the purple chamber in the imperial palace where he had been born, and on his mother's orders blinded in such a way that he died from his injuries.[68] Now sole emperor with no co-ruler, Eirene issued coins that show her image as empress on both sides. Earlier coins had shown her as part of a dynastic college. Now she appeared alone.[69] The coins are inscribed *basilissa* (empress), but at least on documents that stated new laws, such as two dealing with oaths and remarriage, she appeared quite bluntly as emperor, *basileus*, the ordinary masculine term, and as such she continued to reign until 802.[70] Like the story of Metrios and his son, this could not have happened in the west. It was only conceivable under a system where power was centralized and more to the point, institutionalized. Eirene's career was possible because in Byzantium the survival of the Roman system of general taxation allowed salaried offices with recognized responsibilities. Eirene's supplanter, Nikephoros, had been logothete of the genikon, in other words the official in charge of taxation.[71] The post was not hereditary, and its duties were broadly fixed. Similarly, the empire's armed forces were raised and paid by the state, commanded by generals appointed by the emperor and replaced when their term had come to an end.[72] This was an institutionalized system in a way that in the west not even the church could fully match. Bishops, for example, were office holders, but even they were not

---

[67]   Ibid., i, pp. 469–71; trans. pp. 645–8.

[68]   Ibid., i, pp. 471–2; trans. pp. 648–9.

[69]   Grierson, *Catalogue of the Byzantine Coins ...Leo III to Michael III*, p. 347.

[70]   Ludwig Burgmann, 'Die Novellen der Kaiserin Eirene', *Fontes Minores*, 4 (1981): 16, 26. For various shades of interpretation see Lilie and Roschow, *Byzanz unter Eirene und Konstantin VI.*, pp. 277–9; James, *Empresses and Power*, pp. 126–7; Herrin, *Women in Purple*, pp. 100–101.

[71]   Theophanes, *Chronographia*, i, p. 476; trans. Mango and Scott, p. 655.

[72]   Wolfram Brandes, *Finanzverwaltung in Krisenzeiten: Untersuchungen zur byzantinischen Administration im 6.–9. Jahrhundert*, Forschungen zur byzantinischen Rechtsgeschichte, 25 (Frankfurt am Main, 2002), pp. 180–98; Brubaker and Haldon, *Byzantium in the Iconoclast Era*, pp. 608–16.

appointed by a central authority and moved to a new post after a set number of years. As such, Byzantine rulers could give orders and expect designated officials to carry them out. If they were unwilling or incompetent, new ones could be appointed who would do the job. Behind them was a system that transcended the patrimonial and affective power of an individual or a family. In Byzantium there were levers of power that an emperor could pull, even if he were a woman, and that she could pull even if she were not a mother.

Politics, Ideology and Gender: Byzantium in the Age of Eirene

This is an attractive model for the differences between Byzantium and the west, and it may not be wrong, but as an argument based on the story of Metrios, and on Eirene's ability to reign alone and with fair success for five years after murdering her only son, it is a house of cards. Like the equivalently emblematic career of the Empress Wu, on closer inspection things are not quite what they seem.

To begin with Metrios, a story concerning eunuchs certainly highlights aspects of Byzantine society that have no parallel in the west, or at least not until the castrati stars of the seventeenth- and eighteenth-century Italian musical world. However, what is equally striking is the fact that, beyond the immediate topos of virtue rewarded, this is also a story of an individual's successful efforts to make his family rich. The particular means are peculiar to Byzantium, Islam and China, but the idea of someone coming to court, attracting the ruler's attention through good service and subsequently making the family's fortune is not. The stories told in the west about a number of aristocratic dynasties, that their founder was a poor man who saved the king's life in battle or came to his attention in some other way, prove that at least the idea was present in the west, even if the reality was about as common as winning the lottery or learning that your eunuch son had become an imperial parakoimomenos.[73] The story of Metrios does not so much show that Byzantium was not a patrimonial society, as highlight the alternative ways patrimonial strategies might work. The process in Byzantium looks rather similar to the way celibate priests in papal Rome advanced their nephews as part of an overall strategy to advance the family, an outcome that took concrete form in the city's great baroque palazzi, shared by a clerical breadwinner and the lay begetters of the next generation.[74] The story of the empress Eirene also looks a little less extraordinary when considered more

---

[73] Karl Ferdinand Werner, 'Untersuchungen zur Frühzeit des Französischen Fürstentums (9–10 Jahrhundert)', *Die Welt als Geschichte*, 20 (1960): 116–8.

[74] Tracy L. Ehrlich, *Landscape and Identity in Early Modern Rome: Villa Culture at Frascati in the Borghese Era* (Cambridge, 2002), pp. 20–21.

closely and critically. The picture of her as an ambitious politician, given by the structure of Byzantine political system a freedom and an agency denied to her female contemporaries in the early medieval west, rests to a large extent entirely on the *Chronographia* attributed to Theophanes. As Cyril Mango has explained, the chronicle is effectively a cut and pasted collection of roughly edited excerpts taken from other sources. Mango has also argued that the work should be attributed to George the Synkellos rather than Theophanes, but in this context that does not make much difference.[75] Up to 780, whoever he was, the compiler's sources are for the most part obvious enough. From 780 to the end of the chronicle the source or sources are unknown. It might even be the compiler's own creation, but that is less significant than the fact that it dates to before the end of 814.[76] (The date is fixed by the favourable judgement of the emperor Leo V. Given the compiler's consistent hostility to iconoclasm it must have been written before Leo's public avowal of the heresy at the end of that year.[77]) A text that throughout shows a concern, however flawed in practice, to get dates right, can be relied upon to be broadly accurate, in so far as compiler knew the facts, when it talks of events such as accessions, deaths, battles, marriages or the like.[78] On the other hand, a text that equally betrays a consistent wish to identify a pattern in the empire's affairs, whereby orthodoxy is rewarded and heresy leads to perdition, cannot be trusted for its interpretation for anything beyond the bare facts, and least of all can it be trusted for agency or motive.[79] So when, for example, the chronicle tells us that in April 795 Constantine made an expedition against the Arabs and later in the same year married Theodote, we should believe him; but when we are told that Constantine 'had conceived an aversion towards his wife Maria through the machinations of his mother (for she was yearning for power and wanted him to be universally condemned)', there is no reason to do so.[80] Just as the judgements of the Confucian historians of Tan'g China distort our view of the Empress Wu, so the chronicle attributed to Theophanes is no certain guide to the Empress Eirene. It is quite possible that Eirene was the ambitious power-hungry manipulator of the chronicle's account, but we have no means of knowing, and it cannot be the basis for any coherent analysis.

---

[75]   Mango and Scott, *The Chronicle of Theophanes*, pp. xliii–lxiii.

[76]   Ibid., pp. lv–lxii.

[77]   Ibid., pp. lvi–lvii.

[78]   Ibid., pp. lxiii–lxxiv.

[79]   Jenny Ferber, 'Theophanes' Account of the Reign of Heraclius', in Elizabeth Jeffreys, Michael Jeffreys and Anne Moffat (eds), *Byzantine Papers: Proceedings of the First Australian Byzantine Studies Conference, Canberra, 17–19 May 1978* (Canberra, 1981), pp. 32–42.

[80]   Theophanes, *Chronographia*, i, pp. 470–71; trans. Mango and Scott, p. 645.

Reading Theophanes's account with these points in mind suggests a picture of Eirene's career that makes her look, not exactly typical of female rulers, but less of an aberration, and at the same time less exotically Byzantine. It also serves to restore motherhood as an element of her power. To begin in 780, the role she played after her husband's death was an unremarkable instance of the link between motherhood and power. She was the mother of the nine-year-old emperor, and according to custom and law, in charge of the boy, responsible for his interests, and therefore responsible for ruling the empire too.[81] What gradually gave Eirene's power a different dimension was a combination of the uncomfortable weakness of her position as the mother of a small boy with five elder half-brothers who might easily supplant him and her, together with the important political opportunities offered by taking sides in the empire's current religious controversy, namely that over icons. The latter was the crucial context for everything that followed. Whether or not the canons of the Second Council of Nicaea give a fair or a misleading impression of iconoclasm under Leo III, Constantine V, and Eirene's husband, Leo IV, is in this context.[82] The Council quite clearly set a mark in Byzantine politics. It interpreted the past in a way that defined politics in the present. You were either a supporter of the Council, deserving to be rewarded with the fruits of office, or you were not. From Eirene's point of view, such a polarization of politics had considerable advantages. Her survival in power and ability to fend off her half-brothers-in-law depended on creating a party that needed her to legitimize their hold on office. By characterizing her late husband's policy as heresy, she won over a group of iconophiles who from that point on had no option but to stick with her.

Through most of the 780s, to judge from the ability to mount military expeditions against the Arabs and Slavs, and the absence of revolts, the deal between Eirene and the iconophiles delivered a fairly stable regime, but as the decade wore on and Constantine reached and passed the age at which a young emperor would normally exercise power in his own right, tensions among the various parties in the imperial court flared up. The announcement of a prophecy that 'It is ordained by God that your son should not obtain the Empire, for it is yours, given to you by God', was, as Theophanes says, quite obviously the device of a party that wanted to keep a hold on office.[83] However, more generally, it is a strong indication that the political world was split into factions, and that some were very alarmed at the prospect of Constantine as sole ruler.

---

[81]   Aikaterina Christophilopoulou, 'He antibasileia eis ton Byzantion', *Symmeikta*, 2 (1970): 20–29, 132–6.

[82]   For a reinterpretation of what 'iconoclasm' might mean in the eighth century, see now Brubaker and Haldon, *Byzantium in the Iconoclast Era*, pp. 69–356.

[83]   Theophanes, *Chronographia*, i, pp. 464; trans. Mango and Scott, pp. 638–9.

Initially the events of Constantine's sole reign must have suggested that
these concerns were unjustified, or at the least there was room in the regime for
Eirene's supporters too. At first sight this might look surprising. In February 790
it must have appeared that Eirene and her supporters had destroyed any room
for compromise when they had Constantine flogged and imprisoned.[84] When
the emperor did manage to seize power for himself in October of the same
year, one of the first things he did was to have the eunuch Staurakios flogged,
tonsured and exiled, and Aëtios, another of Eirene's eunuchs and closest allies,
exiled too. Yet early in 792 they were all back in favour.[85] The fact that we rely
on iconophile sources, and that the iconophiles won in the end, has the effect
of making us imagine that, outside certain sections of the army, they had the
majority of opinion on their side. However, there is no good reason to think this
was the case, and certainly one way of interpreting the return of Eirene and her
supporters is that the iconophile cause needed to be united if it were to survive.

What then happened between 792 and 797 that caused Constantine to be
murdered? The explanation seems to lie in a split between the various factions
among Eirene's supporters, triggered it appears by the emperor's divorce in 795
and remarriage. Constantine had originally been betrothed to Charlemagne's
daughter, Rotrud, an arrangement that allowed Eirene to choose a bride for her
son outside the factions of Byzantine domestic politics.[86] In 788 that promise
was broken, according to Theophanes, on Eirene's instructions, and Constantine
was married instead to Maria of Amnia.[87] In 795 he divorced her and married
Theodote who, as well as being a lady-in-waiting in the imperial bedchamber,
came from a leading Constantinopolitan family related to such ecclesiastical
aristocrats as Theodore the Stoudite and Platon of Sakkoudion.[88] Amnia was
in Paphlagonia, in northern Asia Minor, a region famous for eunuchs. Metrios's
son, who lived in the late ninth century, is only one of the many known to have
come from there, and it is a telling detail in the story, confirming the reputation
of Paphlagonia, that Metrios was envious of his neighbours who had all had
sons whom they had castrated and sent off to Constantinople with a view to
making their families' fortunes.[89] This was clearly what a Constantinopolitan

[84]   Ibid., i, pp. 464–5; trans. p. 639.

[85]   Ibid., i, pp. 466–8; trans. pp. 641, 643.

[86]   Ibid., i, pp. 455; trans. p. 628; 'Erythro #1606', *Prosopographie der mittelbyzantinischen Zeit*, i. p. 510.

[87]   Theophanes, *Chronographia*, i, pp. 463; trans. Mango and Scott, p. 637; 'Maria #1606', *Prosopographie der mittelbyzantinischen Zeit*, iii. pp. 147–9.

[88]   Theophanes, *Chronographia*, i, pp. 469–70; trans. Mango and Scott, pp. 645–6; 'Theodote #7899', *Prosopographie der mittelbyzantinischen Zeit*, iv. pp. 530–32.

[89]   *Synaxarium Ecclesiae Constantinopolitanae*, cols 721–2.

readership expected, rightly or wrongly, Paphlagonians to do with small boys.[90] An important faction among Eirene's closest supporters, preeminently Staurakios and Aëtios, were eunuchs.[91] On those grounds alone one might have guessed that Constantine's marriage to a Paphlagonian bride was a mark of their ascendancy, but there is more. Maria of Amnia's father, Philaretos, was later written up as a saint. The Life describes her marriage to Constantine as the result of a bride show, which, as the story goes, involved searching the empire for the best and most beautiful girls, bringing them to Constantinople, and allowing the emperor to choose the one he preferred. According to the Life all this was the work of Staurakios.[92] Putting this all together, it is hard not to interpret the marriage to Maria as a Paphlagonian putsch, intended very likely to put Staurakios's kinsmen in power for the future.[93] If that is so, then the crisis of 797 that led to Constantine's murder seems to be quite explicable. The divorce of Maria amounted to the overthrow of a Paphlagonian nexus in favour of a rival Constantinopolitan faction. When Theodote gave birth to a son in October 796, Staurakios and Aëtios, and the associated network of their kinsmen, could see that the future would no longer lie with them.[94] Others in Constantinople and in the provinces would have known that too. Theodote's relatives would henceforth be the people to look to for patronage and influence at court. When the infant Leo died less than a year later, all these hopes ended. The only obstacle to the Paphlagonians was now Constantine himself, and with no male heir, the interest of any uncommited figures in the court, church and army, no longer so obviously lay in supporting him. Constantine seems to have realized what was happening and tried to escape to potential allies in the Anatolikon theme, but it was too late, and he was brought back to the imperial palace, to the purple

---

[90]   Paul Magdalino, 'Paphlagonians in Byzantine High Society', in Stelios Lampakis (ed.), *Byzantine Asia Minor (6th–12th c.)*, Institute for Byzantine Research, International Symposium 6 (Athens, 1998), pp. 141–50.

[91]   'Staurakios #6880', *Prosopographie der mittelbyzantinischen Zeit*, iv, pp. 187–9; 'Aëtios #106', *Prosopographie der mittelbyzantinischen Zeit*, i, pp. 32–3.

[92]   *Life of St Philaretos the Merciful Written by His Grandson Niketas: a Critical Edition*, ed. Lennart Rydén, Studia Byzantina Upsaliensia, 8 (Uppsala: 2002), pp. 82–104.

[93]   It is claimed in the eleventh-century Menologium of Basil II that the Paphlagonian eunuch Niketas was a kinsman of Eirene, but there is no reason to think this detail is anything more than the later hagiographer's wish to link an iconophile saint with an iconophile empress. The abbreviated lives in the Menologium are not a reliable independent source for events two centuries earlier: *Menologium Graecorum Basilii Porphyrogeniti imperatoris jussu editum*, PG 117: 93; cf. Lilie and Roschow, *Byzanz unter Eirene und Konstantin VI.*, p. 37; 'Niketas # 5424'.

[94]   Theophanes, *Chronographia*, i, p. 471; trans. Mango and Scott, p. 648.

chamber, and murdered.[95] Only the Paphlagonians may have positively wished for Constantine's death, but for a spectrum of factions, Eirene ruling alone may have seemed preferable to the triumph of any of their rivals. If that was the case then her continued rule required the court to remain divided. The fewer the factions, or the less balanced their power, the less room for manoeuvre Eirene was bound to have, and the more likely it was that one of them could put together enough support to seize the throne. In this context the reliability of the particular stories told about the quarrels between Staurakios and Aëtios is less important than the fact that after 800 Staurakios was dead, and only two years later Eirene had lost her throne.[96] A single childless empress was only in sole power as long as there was no agreement on a male replacement.

From this point of view Eirene, that rare example of a regnant maternal filicide, looks rather less peculiar. Neither a phenomenon peculiar to the Byzantine world, nor a personality uniquely driven by ambition, so much as a product of the unusual but not unparalleled combination of factional divisions and an age of deep ideological difference. Protestant divines of the early modern era were among the first English scholars to be interested in the rulers of Byzantium, although their sympathies were with the iconoclasts whom they cast as proto-Protestants, rather than Eirene, the restorer of idolatrous graven images, whom they associated with Bloody Mary.[97] An Eirene who used her alliance with one side of an ideological war to establish and keep herself in power, who refused offers of marriage that would upset her supporters, and was maintained in power by a male court strongly opposed to women rulers, but even more strongly opposed to any of their rivals replacing her, sounds more like Elizabeth than Mary. Neither ruler was what their male subjects wanted. They simply wanted the alternatives less.

---

[95]   Ibid., i, pp. 471–2; trans. pp. 648–9.

[96]   Ibid., i, pp. 474–5; trans. pp. 651–3.

[97]   Margaret Aston, *England's Iconoclasts, I: Laws Against Images* (Oxford, 1988), pp. 47–61; Lancelot Andrewes, *A Pattern of Catechistical Doctrine* (London, 1641) in *A Pattern of Catechistical Doctrine and Other Minor Works*, Minor Works of Bishop Andrewes (Oxford, 1846), p. 130: 'the second council of Nicea, at which there were more unlearned and evil disposed men than ever at any. Constantia [sic] was their president, an heathen and unnatural woman, who plucked out her son's eye because he loved not images'. (Cited by Aston, p. 55.)

Chapter 5

In Search of the Good Mother: Twelfth-century Celibacy and Affectivity

Brian Patrick McGuire

The Gregorian reform of the eleventh century and its aftermath in the twelfth made it impossible for priests to live together with women, have legitimate offspring with them, and be in the good graces of the Church. However much one might argue that the reform rarely was implemented on the parish level, it now became unacceptable for priests to form bonds with women that combined sexuality with legitimacy of offspring.[1] In the few cases where we can see the impact of the reform on an individual priest, such as Eilaf, the father of Aelred of Rievaulx, it looks as though he was allowed to live out his married life, but his successor would not be allowed to form a bond with a woman.[2]

In what follows here I will attempt to consider some of the emotional, spiritual and social consequences of the imposition of celibacy on the clergy.[3] Because we have such limited information about parish priests, however, I will also consider the situation of some of the monks who are known to us through hagiographical materials. My question is how clerical and monastic men of the twelfth century coped with celibacy and how they formed bonds of affectivity that replaced or substituted for the bonds they no longer could have with their wives or mistresses. Years ago I looked at celibacy in terms of the friendships that developed in the monastic life,[4] while now I will especially be considering the bonds of affection that existed between clerical and monastic men and their

---

[1] For background, see Henrietta Leyser's superb 'Clerical Purity and the Re-ordered World', in Miri Rubin and Walter Simons (eds), *Christianity in Western Europe c. 1100–c. 1500*, Cambridge History of Christianity 4 (Cambridge, 2009), pp. 11–21.

[2] For Eilaf, see Brian Patrick McGuire, *Brother and Lover: Aelred of Rievaulx* (New York, 1994), pp. 23–5.

[3] The classic study is still Henry C. Lea, *History of Sacerdotal Celibacy in the Christian Church*, 4th edn (London, 1932), even though Lea was almost universally negative about the effects of the reform.

[4] B.P. McGuire, *Friendship and Community: the Monastic Experience 350–1250* (Kalamazoo, MI, 1988), which is in the process of being reprinted by Cornell University Press.

mothers. I will be searching for good mothers, even though I will also be dealing with one or two bad ones.

Before beginning this enquiry I think it is important to emphasize our relative ignorance about the question of married priests and how they lived before the twelfth century. We assume that most priests did have wives, but we do not know these wives at all. We take it for granted that the Gregorian reform made a difference and made it necessary for some priests to put away their wives or mistresses. In the words of Henrietta Leyser, 'The way out chosen by the West brought in its wake hardship, both for clergy and for their discarded women'.[5] We know from the Roskilde Chronicle in its description of the events of the 1130s that clerical celibacy was not accepted in the north, even though a faction of peasants is said to have demanded it.[6] It seems obvious that the imposition of clerical celibacy brought with it great suffering for the forgotten women who now had no rights and were looked upon as concubines or simply ignored, but we have virtually no sources about such women, and we cannot consider their affective lives.

In the midst of these gaps in our knowledge, there is no doubt that clerical and monastic men were dependent on their mothers. We also can take into account the greatest mother of them all, the Virgin Mother Mary.[7] We know some of the paradoxes and pitfalls of medieval culture, and we think we know its mothers, but do we? I will try to consider some of the mothers who appear in sources dealing with celibacy and affectivity in Western Europe in the twelfth and early thirteenth centuries.

The Decisions of the Councils: Mothers are Acceptable

The seventh statute of the First Lateran Council (1123) makes it clear that any clerical person, from subdeacon on upwards in the hierarchy, was not allowed to live together with any woman, unless she was his 'mother, sister, maternal or paternal aunt or someone else of this kind, of whom no suspicion can rightly arise'.[8] The statute refers to the decision of the Council of Nicaea (325). We are

---

    [5]   Leyser, 'Clerical Purity', p. 20.

    [6]   *Chronicon Roskildense* in *Scriptores Rerum Danicarum* 2, ed. M.Cl. Gertz (Copenhagen, 1970), p. 26: 'incepit questionem contra clericos, quatinus habentes uxores dimitterent, et non habentes nequaquam ducerent'.

    [7]   There are many studies, but now we have an ambitious overview in Miri Rubin, *Mother of God. A History of the Virgin Mary* (London, 2009).

    [8]   *Conciliorum Oecumenicorum Decreta*, ed. Joseph Alberigo (Basil, 1962), p. 167, §7: 'Presbyteris, diaconibus vel subdiaconibus concubinarum et uxorum contubernia penitus

thus reminded that the Church in Late Antiquity did try to impose celibacy on the clergy, but it did not succeed. Now, centuries later, the Council of Nicaea was used as an authority to make sure that members of the clergy were not seen to be living with women with whom they might have a sexual bond. By implication, cousins were on the forbidden list: a priest could not live together with a female cousin. Mothers and female members of her generation, however, were acceptable to share in the priest's household.

The Second Lateran Council (1139) goes further and deprives priests who have wives or concubines of office (§6). It is made clear that such bonds are not marriages at all: *matrimonium non esse censemur.*[9] The same strictures are to be found in the decisions of the Third Lateran Council (1179): clerics who are known to have *mulierculas* (a very disparaging term) in their homes and to be living in incontinence are to be deprived of office and benefice.[10] Canon 14 of the Fourth Lateran Council (1215) says the same, but the language was reformulated in order to emphasize the gravity of the fault and it was now decided that a priest who, because of incontinence, was suspended from office should also pay a temporal penalty.[11]

The last sentence of Canon 14 mentions the fact that in some geographical areas priests can still be married. If such men fall into impurity, they are to be more severely punished 'since they can use matrimony lawfully'. In most of the western Church, however, the twelfth century witnessed a massive effort to make clerical celibacy the norm and not the exception. The decision of Lateran I to forbid wives but allow mothers, sisters and aunts in the priest's home shows a desire to make it possible for the priest to have a household where women were present, but where there was no wife. The fact that this decision, taken from the Council of Nicaea, was not repeated in the later Lateran Councils could indicate that it was generally accepted and not a problem. Mothers and aunts were not under suspicion, and so the permission did not need to be repeated. The problem was the clerical wife, whom the Third Lateran Council said legally did not exist.

It is always difficult, if not impossible, to use legal sources in order to provide social history, but the decisions of the four Lateran Councils from 1123–1215 indicate a concern about the married clergy and a demand to separate priests from their wives. In removing the wives from the rectory, the twelfth-century

---

interdicimus et aliarum mulierum cohabitationem, praeter quas synodus Nicaena propter solas necessitudinum causas habitare permisit, videlicet matrem sororem amitam vel materam aut alias huiusmodi, de quibus nulla iuste valeat suspicio oriri'.

[9] Ibid., §7, p. 174.
[10] Ibid., §11, p. 193.
[11] Ibid., §14, p. 218.

Church made the position of the priest's mother, aunt or sister more central than it previously may have been. Without wives and lovers, priests were handed over to their mothers. In the monasteries mothers theoretically had no such access, but in some of our sources I will show how mothers continued to be a spiritual and emotional presence.

Powerful Mothers and Good Sons

For any medieval monk or priest who read his Saint Augustine, his long-suffering and devout mother Monnica could be a source of great inspiration and perhaps also provoke a sense of insufficiency or even guilt. Monnica was the mother whose tears and prayers brought her son to the baptismal font. As a bishop whom Monnica pestered about her son answered her in his frustration: 'Leave me and go in peace. It cannot be that the son of these tears should be lost'.[12] Such a remark sums up the situation of any mother worried about her son and how he is to do in life.

Monnica from the beginning thought she knew what was best for her son, even though Augustine reveals that his father Patricius was concerned about his education.[13] However, Augustine criticizes Patricius for his lack of concern about his son's religious belief and his chastity. The father's death is mentioned in a phrase, while Monnica is everywhere in the first books of the Confessions: 'I was now in my nineteenth year and she supported me, because my father had died two years before'.[14] Monnica was, naturally, the first person to whom Augustine broke the news of his conversion to the Christian faith, and she remained with him for the rest of her life. Once he tried to escape her by sailing away to Italy, but he came to regret his action.[15] He was bound to his mother and could never dismiss her as he came to send away the unnamed woman who had given him a son and with whom he had lived for years.

In the life of Augustine as he told it, his mother was central, while his lover was expendable. Around Monnica, of course, were other mothers and probably also sisters of Augustine's friends.[16] Here was a thriving male world of educated men excited about philosophy and biblical studies, but provided for by women

---

[12]   Augustine, *Confessiones*, Book 3, chapter 12: 'Vade a me, ita vivas, fieri non potest, ut filius istarum lacrimarum pereat', trans. R.S. Pine-Coffin (Harmondsworth, 1961), p. 70.

[13]   Ibid., Book 2, chapter 3.

[14]   Ibid., Book 3, chapter 4; trans. p. 59.

[15]   Ibid., Book 5, chapter 8.

[16]   For background, see Peter Brown's outstanding *Augustine of Hippo. A Biography* (Berkeley, CA, 2000), chapter 6, p. 50: 'Friends': 'Augustine will never be alone'.

who were there when they were needed. In Augustine's idealization of male intellectual and emotional friendships, there are always the women serving in word and deed. The first woman, of course, is the mother, who remains with the son until the end of her days.

Whatever limitations we can see in Monnica and whatever tensions we detect in Augustine's relationship with her, she became for the medieval cleric or monk who read Latin a paragon of virtue and service. Her death a few months after the baptism of Augustine in 387 provides a fitting end to a life of service and devotion. Augustine as the model of the medieval priest and bishop, serving his diocese and looking after its people, became the true son of the mother who had dedicated her life so that her son would live the truth that makes one free.

Thanks to the Gregorian reform, Augustine's experience could have become a model for any medieval cleric who distanced himself from all women except those to whom he was closely related. The best twelfth-century example of such a pattern is Guibert of Nogent and his mother. Guibert describes how she went to live in a small house next to the monastery of Fly. This took place when he was still a boy, so his mother was actually abandoning him to the care of others: 'She knew then that I would be exposed to this neglect, but the fear and the love she bore for you, my God, gave her the resolve she needed'.[17] Guibert describes how painful it was for his mother to travel through the town where her son lived, and how she kept from looking at his house.

There is no breath of criticism in this description of a mother abandoning her son, for Guibert interprets his mother's action as being in harmony with the precept of the Gospel to leave all those whom we love in order to follow Jesus. He even quotes the Song of Songs to show that his mother's love for God was 'strong as death' (Song 8: 6).

In the meantime Guibert applied for entrance to the monastery of Saint Germer, while remaining emotionally close to his mother. Here he began to write biblical commentaries, but it was his mother's words and visions that dominated his consciousness: 'She consciously urged me to imitate her way of life'.[18] Guibert competed with his mother in determining the best way of life. He was also emotionally dependent on his tutor and the man's requirements for his pupil, but it is the mother who is the dominant figure. In the twentieth century outstanding medieval historians such as John Benton tried to understand

---

[17]   *Guibert de Nogent, Autobiographie,* ed. Edmond-René Labande (Paris, 1981), lib. 1, c. 14, trans. Paul J. Archambault, *A Monk's Confession. The Memoirs of Guibert of Nogent* (University Park, PA, 1995), p. 45.

[18]   *Autobiographie,* lib. 1, c. 18, trans. Archambault, p. 64.

Guibert in psychological terms.[19] Today he can be seen as a man who thought he could find in the *Confessions* of Augustine a model for his life and who saw in his mother a new Monnica.

However little this parallel works in our minds, it is a reminder that for a twelfth-century cleric there was an unmistakable pattern: the son clings to the mother, even when he is an adult, for the mother shows the way in matters of faith: 'She was always lamenting the immorality of youth, and she would keep my fantasies in check as they did tend to wander. To hear her talk about these matters you would have thought her a mellifluous bishop rather than the illiterate woman she was.'[20]

From this point onwards in the narrative, Guibert concentrates on Nogent, the monastery which elected him as abbot. His mother was against the choice, 'because she feared that I was dangerously inexperienced at this stage of my life'.[21] Guibert claims to agree with her, but he accepted the position, and his mother disappears from view. What has been an intensely personal account of his life becomes a chronicle of the monastery and the region, as in his well-known description of the commune at Laon (Book 3). The biological mother is replaced by Mary the Mother of God, as when Guibert saw her image beneath the crucifix. It had changed from 'her usual serenity' to that of someone troubled. Guibert relates this transformation to the fact that lightning had struck the monastery. God was angry with the monks, but as soon as they accepted their just punishment, Mary's face again became calm.[22]

Just as he had tried to please his mother, Guibert did his best to please Mary the Mother of God. So did Saint Anselm. As a young man in Aosta, his devotion to his mother is said to have restrained him from dissipating himself.[23] When she died, however, he lost his bearings and began to drift. The young man had difficulties with his father, who in the Canterbury monk Eadmer's portrait is said to have persecuted his son. The result was Anselm's decision to leave home and cross the Alps for a better life. Here he found an alternative father figure in

---

[19]   John F. Benton, *Self and Society in Medieval France* (New York, 1970), p. 26: 'Compelled as a boy to be rational, self-controlled, and sexually pure, Guibert had trouble dealing with the hostile, aggressive, lustful side of his nature'. Benton, who was a dear friend, once confided in me that, after himself going through psychoanalysis, he decided to try to understand Guibert in the same terms. Whatever one thinks of his approach, Benton provoked his colleagues into thinking about medieval people in new ways.

[20]   *Autobiographie*, lib. I, c. 18, trans. Archambault, p. 73.

[21]   Ibid., lib. I, c. 18, trans. Archambault, p. 73.

[22]   Ibid., lib. I, c. 23, trans. Archambault, p. 80.

[23]   *The Life of St. Anselm*, ed. R.W. Southern (Oxford, 1972), c. iv, p. 6: 'Veruntamen pia dilectio et diligens pietas quas in matrem suam habebat, nonnichil eum ab istis restringebant'.

Lanfranc, and the rest of the story is well known, thanks to Eadmer and, in the twentieth century, to the two very different biographies of Anselm written by Sir Richard Southern.[24]

It is still possible, however, to supplement the story of Anselm in considering his prayers. He was dissatisfied with how he expressed himself to Mary and so composed three prayers to her. These are not pale imitations of each other; they are different declarations of love and affection. The first is meant to be said 'when the mind is weighed down with heaviness'.[25] As in Anselm's first meditation, he describes the filth and stench of sin that he experienced in himself and fears that Mary will turn away from him. The second prayer 'when the mind is anxious with fear' concentrates less on Anselm's sense of sin and more on what can await him because of God's anger with him. He throws himself into the care of Mary: 'there in your mercy you will not be found wanting'.[26] The third and final prayer dwells on the love that Mary and her son provide. Here Anselm sees Mary as renewing the world and all its life forces. There are confidence, praise and joy in this prayer in a manner not found in the others: 'Desiring to be always with you, my heart is sick of love'.[27] Anselm does his best to balance devotion to Mary with worship of her son, but it is the loving mother who emerges more convincingly from this prayer, which summarizes his quest for love and comfort.

It can be argued that Anselm's devotion to Mary replaced the love that he once had for his biological mother. The same process may have taken place with Saint Bernard, who also lost his mother when he was young and held her in reverence. In Bernard's *Vita prima* we are told by his friend William of Saint Thierry how his mother, Aleth of Montbard, made sure to nourish her children with her own milk instead of handing them over to a nurse.[28] The remarks about Aleth are conventional in the genre of hagiography, as with her dream while she was pregnant with Bernard that she had a barking dog inside of her. It is noticeable, however, that it is Aleth who is said to have concerned herself with Bernard's education, in handing him over to the priests at Châtillon.[29]

---

[24] *Saint Anselm and his Biographer. A Study of Monastic Life and Thought 1059–c. 1130* (Cambridge, 1966) and *Saint Anselm. A Portrait in a Landscape* (Cambridge, 1990).

[25] 'Oratio ad sanctam Mariam cum mens gravatur torpore', *Anselmi Opera Omnia*, ed. F.S. Schmitt (Stuttgart, 1984), vol. 2, p. 13, trans. Benedicta Ward, *The Prayers and Meditations of Saint Anselm* (Harmondsworth, 1973), p. 107.

[26] 'in eo misericordiae vestrae non dignentur deficere', *Anselmi Opera*, vol. 2, p. 17, trans. Ward, p. 114.

[27] 'Vestro continuo amore langueat cor meum', *Anselmi Opera*, vol. 2 p. 24, trans. Ward, p. 124.

[28] *Sancti Bernardi Vita Prima*, lib. 1.1, in PL 185: 227C.

[29] Ibid., I.3, PL 185: 228B.

Aleth is described as a model wife but also as one who would have preferred to have become a nun or even a hermit. Instead she lived as such in her own home, where she ate sparingly and held vigils and compensated 'for what was lacking in her newfound profession by almsdeeds and various works of mercy'.[30] It is possible that it was not Bernard himself who described Aleth to William of Saint Thierry but one of Bernard's brothers. However, in view of the fact that Bernard and William spent so much time together, I think it likely that the portrait of Aleth in substance comes from Bernard. She was in his mind a woman who had developed on the path of holiness. Her death meant that the teenage Bernard had to find his way virtually alone. The father was still present, but his role in Bernard's life seems to have been secondary.

Bernard is described at this point in his life as turning to his friends, but their example could be dangerous. It is now that he is said to have experienced the sexual temptations which he managed to overcome. When his brothers discovered that he was considering becoming a monk, they did their best to stop him and make him return to secular learning, in which he had already excelled. However, the recollection of his mother made him resist their arguments: 'Time and again he seemed to see her coming to meet him, reproach him, rebuke him – not for such trifles had she educated him with such tender care, nor for such hopes had she trained him!'[31]

Bernard's experience of conversion is thus intimately associated with his devotion to and memory of his mother. Her rebuke could be narrowly construed as the response of a mother who did not want to waste resources on a wanton son, but we can also interpret the desire to avoid 'trifles' as Aleth's hope that he would offer his life to God.

In Bernard's hagiographical portrait the mother triumphs, first the mother Aleth and later the mother of God.[32] In Bernard's *Homilies in Praise of the Blessed Virgin Mary* he formulated a biblical and theological language for the cult of the Virgin. He saw her as the 'valiant woman' described in Proverbs (31: 10): 'The price of this valiant woman is not known to man (Job 28: 13) on earth but is

---

[30]   Ibid., I.5, PL 185: 229D–230A, trans. Martinus Cawley, *Bernard of Clairvaux. Early Biographies* (Lafayette, OR, 2000), p. 7.

[31]   Ibid., I.9, PL 185: 231D–232A, trans. Cawley, p. 10.

[32]   I realize that I am dependent on sources which were meant to contribute to the view of the person described as a saint. This literary purpose does not necessarily make it impossible for us to make use of the source's contents to tell us about the person portrayed. One must exercise caution, but it is precisely now in the twelfth century that hagiography becomes more vivid and attentive to the inner life and the sayings of the saint.

found in the heights of heaven' (Ecclus 1: 3).[33] Bernard did nothing more than bring together the Jewish Bible with the New Testament in finding a language to describe the role of Mary in being a virgin mother to God's son.

What is perhaps new in Bernard's narrative is his consideration of Joseph, who is said to have known what was best for Mary: 'To avoid telling lies and exposing an innocent woman to public shame, he very rightly resolved to send her away quietly'.[34] However, Joseph in spite of being a good man does not come close to Mary's status: 'he was neither the husband of the mother nor the father of the Son'.[35] Bernard conceded, however, that Joseph had a special privilege, for he imagined how it was for him to be with the Christ child, 'even to carry him, to take him by the hand, to hug and kiss him, to feed him and to keep him safe'.[36] This is a rare moment in twelfth-century theology when the affectivity of father for son becomes evident. Later Joseph will take on added significance,[37] but for now it is Mary who is the central object of attention. Even though Bernard's father is described in a more positive manner than Anselm's, the father for the clerical or monastic figure is often much less prominent than the mother.

Bernard's awareness of the centrality of the mother, whether it was his own or the Blessed Mother, can also be seen in his *Life of Malachy*, the only saint's life that he himself wrote. Malachy as Archbishop of Armagh had come in the last months of his life to Clairvaux, where he died on 2 November 1148. Bernard wrote about him as a friend who in his dying moments gave the abbot of Clairvaux his blessing.[38] In describing Malachy's background Bernard used a typical hagiographical cliché and said his mother was more noble in mind than in lineage.[39] She cultivated in him both worldly learning and sacred learning: the first he got at school from his teacher; the second at home from his mother: 'From his mother's breast he was imbibing the waters of saving wisdom (Ecclus 15: 3) instead of milk, and day by day he waxed more prudent'.[40]

---

[33]   *Sermones in laudibus Virginis Matris*, II.5, in *Opera Bernardi*, ed. Jean Leclercq and Henri Rochais, vol. 4, p. 24, trans. Marie-Bernard Saïd, *Homilies in Praise of the Blessed Virgin Mary* (Kalamazoo, MI, 1993), p. 18.

[34]   Ibid., II.14, *Opera Bernardi* 4, p. 32, trans. p. 26.

[35]   Ibid., II.15, *Opera Bernardi* 4, p. 33, trans. p. 28.

[36]   Ibid., II.16, *Opera Bernardi* 4, p. 34, trans. p. 29: 'sed etiam portare, deducere, amplecti, deosculari, nutrire et custodire'.

[37]   See Paul Payan, *Joseph. Une image de la paternité dans l'Occident médiévale* (Paris, 2006).

[38]   *Vita Sancti Malachiae, præfatio, Opera Bernardi* 3, p. 309: 'Accucurri ego, ut benedictio morituri super me veniret'.

[39]   Ibid., p. 310, I.1, 'mente quam sanguine generosior'.

[40]   Ibid., p. 310, trans. Robert T. Meyer, *The Life and Death of Saint Malachy the Irishman* (Kalamazoo, MI, 1978), p. 15.

One thinks of Bernard as a baby drinking the milk of his mother's breast, and then of the later story (first appearing in the thirteenth century) of Bernard drinking the milk of the Virgin's breasts, as a source of his wisdom.[41] Bernard in describing Malachy certainly saw the importance of what mothers give their sons, and so he saw Malachy as having a good and generous mother. She does not appear again in the narrative, but we do hear of Malachy's sister, who criticized her brother for participating in works of mercy, such as burying the dead, which she considered to be beneath their social position: 'What are you doing, you idiot? Let the dead bury the dead.' Malachy replied, 'Wretched woman, you keep to the pure word, but you are unaware of its meaning'.[42] Bernard frames this incident in the story of Eve. Malachy's sister is a temptress, but she is saved, for he has a dream after her death that reveals her need for his prayers and offering of the Eucharist on her behalf.[43]

Powerful mothers and good clerical or monastic sons populate the twelfth century. In the aftermath of the Gregorian reform the Church favoured strong women who would see to it that their sons got good educations and formed habits of piety. We rarely see the pattern of a Monnica staying with her son Augustine, but there is the story of how Herluin, the first abbot of Bec, lived there with his mother, who took care of practical tasks.[44] Such an arrangement was possible in a house following the Rule of Saint Benedict but not reformed in the way that Cîteaux would be. Mothers were not considered to be dangerous, and there was rarely the ambivalence about them as nurturers that there could be about fathers. Mother Church and the Mother of God favoured the devout mother who would care for the youth devoting his life to God.

Missing Mothers and a Bad Mother

In emphasizing the importance of continuing bonds between mothers and clerical or monastic sons, I do not want to leave the impression that the mothers

---

[41]   See 'Bernard and Mary's Milk: a Northern Contribution', in B.P. McGuire, *The Difficult Saint. Bernard of Clairvaux and his Tradition* (Kalamazoo, MI, 1991), pp. 189–225, esp. 196–202.

[42]   *Vita ... Malachiae*, III.6, p. 314, trans. Meyer, p. 21.

[43]   Ibid., V.11, p. 320, trans. Meyer p. 28.

[44]   *Vita Herluini* 42, in *The Works of Gilbert Crispin*, ed. Anna Sapir Abulafia and G.R. Evans, Auctores Britannici Medii Aevi 8 (London, 1986), p. 193: 'nobilis mater eius addixit, et concessit Deo prediis que habebat, ancille fungebatur officio, seruientium Deo pannos abluens et quicquid iniungebatur extremi operis accuratissime agens'.

always were present in the minds and hearts of their sons. There are central ecclesiastical figures of the twelfth century who apparently made do without their mothers. This is the case, for example, with Hugh, the Carthusian monk who became bishop of Lincoln. We have but a single line about his relation to his mother: 'Being deprived of a mother's care when still a young child, he was shortly afterwards admitted with his father into a community of canons regular'.[45] The Latin indicates that Hugh became an orphan, so the mother must have died, but no time is spent on her, and the hagiographer's main concern is to show that Hugh did not waste his time on the distractions of childhood: 'I never knew or learnt how to play'.[46]

Hugh is perhaps one of the most affable saints of the twelfth century, but his gentleness is not seen as a maternal gift. He is the good boy who does everything correctly, and there is no room in him for the doubts and excesses that Augustine experienced. However, the hagiography does convey Hugh's love for his father, especially in telling how he looked after the man in his old age and decrepitude: 'He used often to relate with great pleasure how for the rest of his father's life, he used to lead him and carry him about, dress him and undress him, wash him, dry him and make his bed and when he grew feebler and weaker, prepare his food and even feed him.'[47] Hugh thus became the mother of his father, a role that should be understandable today at a time when many children grow up to become the parents of their aged mothers and fathers. However, here the point is that the age of powerful mothers does not exclude the presence of fathers as objects of love and devotion.

Sometimes, however, mothers are not mentioned at all. In the case of Aelred of Rievaulx, he tells of his priest father, who is described as a good man, even if he did not live up to the requirement of celibacy. Aelred's mother, however, is almost totally absent from his works.[48] Aelred's biographer, Walter Daniel, dealt with his abbot's embarrassing lineage by saying absolutely nothing about it. He says that Aelred was *mirabilis* in his youth 'and even when of tender years had

---

45   *Magna Vita Sancti Hugonis. The Life of Saint Hugh of Lincoln*, ed. Decima L. Douie and Hugh Farmer (London, 1961), chapter 1, p. 5: 'Et genitricis quidem solatio, cum prime necdum etatis metas excessisset, orbatus est'.

46   Ibid., chapter 1, p. 6: 'iocos numquam didici, numquam scivi'. It is, of course, a hagiographical cliché that children who become saints do not play.

47   Ibid., chapter 3, p. 15.

48   Walter Daniel, *The Life of Ailred of Rievaulx*, ed. F.M. Powicke, Introduction pp. xxxiv–xxxv. Also McGuire, *Brother and Lover*, chapter 3, 'An Absent Mother'. Walter's 'Letter to Maurice' does mention the mother in connection with a wonder ascribed to the infant Aelred, but her name is never given (p. 71).

the makings of a fine man'.[49] Jocelin of Furness in his *Life of Saint Waldef* suffices with asserting that Aelred came from 'fine old English stock'.[50]

Through such omissions we get the sense of how difficult it was for Aelred's contemporaries to cope with his family background. Historians are not to argue on the basis of silence in the sources, but sometimes a silence can be pregnant with meaning. If it were not for Aelred's own ability later in life to come to terms with his origins, we would be very much in the dark about his connection to the married priests of Hexham.

Even when the mother presumably was not an embarrassment to the clerical or monastic son, she could be left out of the information given about childhood and family. This is the case with the monk and historian Orderic Vitalis, who at age sixty-seven looked back over the course of his life and gave thanks for what he had received. He wrote of his baptism and of the priest Siward, who taught him Latin for five years. Orderic's father built a monastery, but there was concern 'that I might be distracted among kinsfolk' and kept from obeying God's law *per parentum carnalem affectum*, which could be translated as physical attachment to members of his family.[51] So Orderic was sent to Normandy: 'I abandoned my country and my kinsfolk, my friends and all with whom I was acquainted.'[52] He was ten years old and was sent to a place where he did not understand the language, the abbey of Saint Evroul, where he was to live as a monk for fifty-six years before he wrote this description of himself and his times. Orderic may at this point in his life have had no strong recollection of his mother.

This is a moving tale but also a disturbing one. The major decision was made on the child's behalf by his father, the old style of child oblation that the Cistercians were to eliminate. Orderic claims his experience was a good one, for he found 'nothing but kindness and friendship among strangers'.[53] His narrative indicates that, for some men who had been given as children to monastic communities, the love of their mother became a dim memory that could completely disappear.

Another hagiographical narrative with a missing mother is that of Wulfric of Haselbury, parish priest and anchorite near Bristol. The Cistercian John of Ford described how Wulfric functioned as priest in Compton Martin. At first he lived in what is called a frivolous manner, engaging in hunting and hawking.[54] Wulfric

---

49   Daniel, *Life of Ailred*, p. 2

50   Powicke in Daniel, *Life of Ailred*, p. xxxiii.

51   *The Ecclesiastical History of Orderic Vitalis*, ed. Marjorie Chibnall, vol. 6, Books 11–13 (Oxford, 1978), Book 13, chapter 45, p. 553.

52   Ibid., pp. 553–5.

53   Ibid., p. 554–5: 'inter exteros omnem mansuetudinem et familiaritatem repperi'.

54   *Wulfric of Haselbury, by John, Abbott of Ford*, ed. Maurice Bell, Somerset Record Society 47 (London, 1933); trans. Pauline Matarasso in *The Cistercian World. Monastic*

changed his ways, and his modern translator Pauline Matarasso points out the importance of such a narrative that 'takes us outside the cloister' and gives us a sense of how it was to be a parish priest.

I have been unable to find narratives describing bad mothers who kept their sons from entering into clerical or monastic life. I could have overlooked such sources, but even in this age of googling, obscure Latin sources can be bypassed. Perhaps mothers did not have the power to hold back their sons. However, we do have a bad mother in the life of Christina of Markyate. In recognition of the manner in which Henrietta Leyser has helped make Christina visible, it is worth returning to the text and seeing what it tells of a mother–daughter relationship. Our source tells of a relationship between two women, instead of the woman–man bond in the relationship of mother to son.

In the first place we are given the name of the mother, Beatrix, and we are told that she did what she could to satisfy the sexual desires of the Norman prelate Ralph Flambard by offering him her daughter. When Christina refused to marry the man chosen by Flambard and approved by her parents, the mother unleashed her anger on the daughter: 'from then onwards she persecuted her with unheard-of cruelty, sometimes openly, at other times secretly'.[55] She spent money on charms and potions to enhance Christina's sexual appetite. Once Beatrix removed Christina from a banquet and pulled her hair and beat her, then brought her back to the guests and made fun of her.[56]

The narrative approaches the style of a martyr's tale, and we must remember, of course, that it is told from Christina's point of view, while her mother may have perceived events in a completely different manner. She may even have thought that she was doing her best for her child's welfare. However, Christina is said to have found comfort in the Virgin Mary. She had a vision of being brought into a beautiful church, where she found a man dressed as a priest and about to say mass. He gave her a branch with leaves and flowers and told her to offer it to 'the lady'. Nearby sat a lady looking like an empress (*similem imperatrici*).[57] The grand lady received the branch and gave Christina back a twig. She asked her how she was and assured her that she would deliver her from her persecutors.

Writings of the Twelfth Century (London, 1993), p. 235. A full translation of this delightful and useful source is in the making for Cistercian Publications.

[55] *The Life of Christina of Markyate, a twelfth-century recluse*, ed. C.H. Talbot (Oxford, 1959), 23, p. 73. See C. Stephen Jaeger, 'The Loves of Christina of Markyate', in Samuel Fanous and Henrietta Leyser (eds), *Christina of Markyate: a Twelfth-century Holy Woman* (London, 2005), pp. 99–115.

[56] *The Life of Christina*, 23, p. 75.

[57] Ibid., 24, p. 75.

She saw Christina's husband Burthred on the ground with his face turned down. He groaned and watched her, but he could not touch her.[58]

The Mary who appeared to Christina was no gentle friend. She was a powerful queen who challenged her and said: 'Why are you gazing upon me so intently? I am the greatest of women. Do you wish to know how great? As I stand here it is quite easy for me to touch the highest point of heaven.'[59] The Mary that we find in this period can be haughty and distant, but as far as Christina was concerned, this mother was a welcome substitute for the one who abused her. Christ's mother could make up for and overcome a cruel and unloving biological mother.

Seeking Holy Mother Church and the Mother of God

When biological mothers became enemies or simply disappeared from view, then Mary was not the only mother who could compensate. Holy Mother Church could become a substitute for clerical or monastic men in search of affectivity. Already in the third century, Cyprian, bishop of Carthage, had written of the Church as mother: 'He can no longer have God for his Father who has not the Church for his mother'.[60] In the centuries to come the Church took on the role of nurturer and caretaker: it was here that male youth came in order to learn Latin and become part of the clerical culture that especially flourished after the reforms of the eleventh century.

In this process we find what Colin Morris called the discovery of the individual, and even if his analysis has been challenged, there seems to be a general consensus that the twelfth century in western Europe brought a greater awareness of the person as a unique product of God's creation.[61] Here the historian John Benton saw the emergence of mother figures. As he wrote in the early 1980s, 'as we seek to know more about the growth of self-awareness in the

[58]   Ibid., 24, p. 77.

[59]   Ibid., 26, p. 79.

[60]   Cyprian, *On the Unity of the Catholic Church*, chapter 6; Christian Classics Ethereal Library, http://www.ccel.org/ccel/schaff/anf05.iv.v.i.html.

[61]   *The Discovery of the Individual 1050–1200*, first published in 1972 and reprinted as a Medieval Academy text for teaching (Toronto, 1987), a distinction shared with *The Life of Christina*. See Caroline Walker Bynum's important 'Did the Twelfth Century Discover the Individual?', in *Jesus as Mother. Studies in the Spirituality of the High Middle Ages* (Berkeley, CA, 1982), pp. 82–109. Bynum's main article in this important book emphasizes the motherhood of Jesus and provides a further dimension to the place of spiritual motherhood in this period.

renaissance of the twelfth century we should look most closely at the influence of Mother Church and biological mothers'.[62]

Benton was in the 1970s one of the leading historians to insist upon the place of childhood in medieval history, and so he concluded that our understanding of the individual has to take its point of departure in affective bonds within the family, and especially between sons and mothers. This may seem so obvious that it hardly needs to be stated, but the prominence of good mothers in the twelfth century is very much in contrast with the sixteenth century, 'when fathers ruled'.[63] Even when biological mothers are largely absent from historical narrative, we find the presence of Holy Mother Church.

This is the case, for example, in Thomas of Celano's First Life of Francis of Assisi, a story we think we know so well that we can forget what it tells us. We see Francis unclothing himself of his father's property and stripping naked in front of the bishop of Assisi as the representative of the Church. Francis had been kept at home like a prisoner, but once his father was away, then his mother spoke to him and became convinced of his intention to live a devout life. She released him, and in so doing 'she was moved by maternal instinct'.[64] Here we find a good mother, the opposite of Christina's, who makes it possible for her son to do what he has to do.

The father returned and was only interested in getting back the money that Francis had taken. Francis then came before the bishop and 'threw down all his clothes and returned them to his father'.[65] The bishop immediately covered him with his own mantle. Francis no longer belonged to his father. He could enjoy the protection and blessing of the Church. From this time onwards he needed no other mother. However idealized this description may be, the movement from loving biological mother to loving Mother Church is clear. The one makes the other possible, for Francis's mother released him from captivity and opened his way to Holy Mother Church. The father understood nothing except how to reduce everything to his possessions, and so he had to give up his son.[66]

---

[62] John F. Benton, 'Consciousness of Self and Perceptions of Individuality', in Benton, *Culture, Power and Personality in Medieval France*, ed. Thomas N. Bisson (London, 1991), p. 355.

[63] Steven Ozment, *When Fathers Ruled. Family Life in Reformation Europe* (Cambridge, MA, 1983).

[64] *The Life of Saint Francis by Thomas of Celano*, I.6, p. 192 in *Francis of Assisi. The Saint. Early Documents*, ed. Regis Armstrong, J.A. Wayne Hellmann, William J. Short.

[65] Ibid., I.6, p. 193.

[66] Lesley Smith has kindly suggested to me an alternative reading of Francis's gesture: the father was 'very aware of Francis moving away from him and the family business, but

With Mother Church is the Mother Mary who takes the clerical or monastic man under her protection. The twelfth century brought an explosive spread of stories about the miracles of the Virgin, as shown decades ago in the work of Sir Richard Southern.[67] In the early thirteenth century the Cistercian writer Caesarius of Heisterbach collected dozens of these stories, especially those connected with monastic houses of his order. One of the most remarkable of these tales concerns a monk in a Spanish Cistercian monastery who was especially devout to Mary: 'He was attentive and devout in singing her hours'.[68] After seventeen years as a monk he became gravely ill, and the prior allowed a friend who had entered the monastery with him to look after the sick man. He told his friend that Mary had visited him and that he would die soon. He added that Mary had grasped his neck with her arms and kissed him.

Caesarius guaranteed the veracity of the story by attributing it to Arnold, who had been abbot of the monastery, and who had narrated the story at Trier, not far from Heisterbach. We hear in the next story about a lay brother who was worn out with fatigue, so Mary told him to go back to bed and she took care of singing in church for him. Mary looks after those who show devotion to her, as in the story which once convinced the eighteen-year-old Caesarius to convert to the Cistercians: the abbot of Heisterbach told him how Mary had been seen descending from the hills behind Clairvaux at harvest time and together with her ladies had wiped the brows of the sweating monks in the fields.[69]

Jo Ann McNamara, whose work on monastic women has inspired many of us and whose recent death is a loss for our field, once wrote a seminal article about the emotional difficulties men experienced in the Church once they were deprived of their wives: 'If celibacy redefined masculinity, it also redefined femininity. Clerical celibacy and indissoluble secular marriage drove many men and women into syneisactic refuges. This precipitated the *Herrenfrage*, a crisis of masculine identity'.[70] I agree that for men deprived of women, there can have been such a crisis, but in the rich cultural and religious life of the twelfth century men could look to women for advice and counsel, as in the spectacular case of the powerful abbot of Saint Albans, Geoffrey, going to the seemingly powerless

---

not knowing how to make contact with his son, he asks for the money back in a desperate attempt to get Francis to react to him, to speak to him; but it backfires terribly'.

[67]   R.W. Southern, *The Making of the Middle Ages* (London, 1953), pp. 246–55.

[68]   *Dialogus miraculorum*, ed. J. Strange (Cologne, 1851, repr. 1966), vol. 2, dist. 7, c. 50, p. 70.

[69]   Ibid., vol. 1, dist. 1, c. 17, pp. 24–5.

[70]   'The *Herrenfrage*: the Restructuring of the Gender System, 1050–1150', in Clare A. Lees (ed.) *Medieval Masculinities. Regarding Men in the Middle Ages* (Minneapolis, MN, 1994), pp. 3–29, esp. p. 22.

Christina for advice and counsel. Geoffrey could continue to be the Norman lord while he looked forward to his next conversation with Christina, who here can be thought of as a mother figure for him, even though their relationship is primarily described as a friendship:

> Christina's thoughts were with her dear friend abbot Geoffrey ... night and day, and she busied herself with his interests by fasting, watching, calling upon God, the angels, and other holy folk in heaven and on earth, asking for the mercy of God with humble prayers, sensibly reproving him when his actions were not quite right.[71]

So ends the Life of Christina, with her spiritual care for Geoffrey. As Stephen Jaeger has put it, Christina is abbot Geoffrey's spiritual mentor.[72]

Conclusion: Mothers as Vehicles of Grace

Any monk or cleric in twelfth-century Europe knew the story of the Annunciation, with Mary humbly accepting the will of God and letting it be done to her. This demonstration of humility can also be seen as an assertion of power: God can only be incarnated if a woman lets herself be used as a vehicle of divine grace. It is my contention that many clerical sons in this period could have seen their mothers as other Marys, who let God's will be done in entrusting their sons to the Church. Certainly Francis's mother accepted that this choice was right for her son, while Bernard's mother, Aleth, did everything possible to see that her boy was prepared for a life in the Church.

The mother is thus the vehicle of grace for her son. She protects him from a punishing father or encourages him to accept the life that God has prepared for him. Only rarely is it the father who takes on this role, as in the life of Orderic Vitalis. Yet what about the aunts or sisters who according to the First Lateran Council could be accepted as living with the priest? We hear very little about them, while sisters do not do well. Bernard tried to reject his sister when she came to visit him at Clairvaux, and it was only the urging of his biological brothers that made it possible for a meeting between the two.[73] As for Aelred, he wrote a superb set of directions for his sister about how she was to live as a recluse, but she remains a shadowy figure and has even been called a literary

---

[71] *The Life of Christina*, 86, p. 193.
[72] Jaeger, 'The Loves of Christina', p. 109.
[73] *Vita prima* I, c. 30, PL 185: 244D–245AB.

fiction.[74] I am not convinced by this approach, but if this interpretation is right, then Aelred's sister, as his mother, becomes inaccessible. Only the father remains in his life.

In the end mothers were what mattered. I do not want to idealize this arrangement. The memory of the good mother could be an incentive to sons, but the mother could also be an unattainable object who reminded the son of his limitations, as in the case of Guibert of Nogent. Ultimately the only mother who never let down her son was Mary herself, and there is no doubt that her importance grew in Church and society during this period. Meanwhile the father became less significant, even if he sometimes plays a positive role, as in the narrative of Orderic Vitalis.

It may seem a truism to emphasize the position of mothers in the twelfth century, but truisms can be worth repeating. As wives and mistresses were edged out in the clerical world and monks reformed their lives, mothers came to take on a more prominent role. Women were deprived of the position they had previously had in the Church, but as spiritual friends and mothers they made their presence felt. However much the reformed Church feared women, it had to admit that its very Latin name was feminine and that theologians since Cyprian had seen the institution as a mother. At the same time Mary became ever more present and powerful in the lives of clerics and perhaps also of lay people. Thanks to holy mothers, the world of twelfth century Western Europe may have become just a little gentler and more loving than its eleventh-century predecessor.

---

[74]   As was suggested in a paper given at the Cistercian Studies Conference, the Medieval Congress, Western Michigan University, by Marsha Dutton of Ohio State University.

Chapter 6
Twelfth-century English Mothers

Henry Mayr-Harting

Mothers are not often encountered in the indexes of social histories of the high middle ages or of collections of medieval documents. For every mother in indexes relating to the twelfth century, there must be at least ten widows; and even widows are not thick on the ground. The scourer of such indexes is quickly made aware of how much more interested authors and editors seem to be in windows or wine! It may be observed, of course, that we often get two things for the price of one, namely that when we get widows we are often (more often than not) getting mothers as well. But more of that shortly. An honourable exception to our generalization, about content at least, is one of the finest possible mothers as well as one of the finest of scholars, namely Henrietta Leyser. Within sixteen years of publication, her book *Medieval Women* (in England) has established itself as a classic, and it has a lengthy section of one chapter on Motherhood and the Upbringing of Children, and another whole chapter on Widows.[1] Besides what is in the section on Motherhood, there is much about mothers scattered throughout other parts of the book. Something of the quality of Henrietta's writing, as well as her scrupulous acknowledgement of the work of other scholars, can be gathered from quoting part of one passage – about high aristocratic mothers of the late Anglo-Saxon period:[2]

> It was in just such circumstances [that is, there being too many or too few heirs in a royal succession], as Pauline Stafford has shown, that the mothers in question were able to acquire considerable power both for themselves and for their sons. That they were able to do so is testimony both to their own attributes and to the personal and familial character of royal government in tenth- and eleventh-century England. If this power seems fragile so too was men's. If women's power was particularly precarious, their lives at least were more secure. Royal women who got in the way had a better chance of being sent off to convents than of being murdered.

---

[1] Henrietta Leyser, *Medieval Women: a Social History of Women in England 450–1500* (London, 1995), pp. 122–41, and chapter 8.

[2] Leyser, *Medieval Women*, p. 76.

Not for nothing is Henrietta herself both mother and widow, widow of Karl Leyser. In his fundamental study of women in the whole structure of Ottonian, or tenth-century Saxon, society, Karl was characteristically discerning of what was poignant within outwardly formal documentary evidence. For example, he writes at one point about how, for demographic reasons, fathers, and more particularly mothers, became the heirs of their own offspring. He also lights upon a charter of the Emperor Otto I, recording that the widow Aeddila had in 960 transferred four *curtes* (farms or manors) to Otto for the endowment of the nunnery of Hilwartshausen, which she had received from the inheritances of her dying sons.[3] Important or interesting issues of women's history naturally often change from one period to another, and I know of no similar case that comes to the fore in twelfth-century England, even though it cannot be that such a thing never happened. However, given that much of women's history has to be extracted from male-produced sources, it requires a certain quality of intuition to bring out its human side, a quality which both Leysers have shared.

My initial and principal focus in this paper is on the *Rotuli de Dominabus*, sometimes translated as *The Ladies' Rolls*, of 1185, a source produced about women from the male angle if ever there was one. These rolls, the records of a survey by English royal itinerant justices with the help of groups of local jurors, were part of the records of Henry II's Exchequer. The survey was of all women who needed the licence of the king, as their feudal lord, to marry, or more likely to re-marry as the overwhelming majority of them were widows. Part of the idea in this was to prevent marriages which for one reason or another could be regarded as harmful to royal power, but a large part of it was money. Marriage was one of the 'incidents' of feudal lordship, the others being reliefs, wardships and escheats. They were not called incidents because they were incidental, but because they were the windfalls of lordship, extremely lucrative windfalls, and none more so than marriage and wardships, to which we shall come.

Henry II saw that there was a market in marriage, above all for the king himself, charging for licences to marry, or, in the cynical management of the Angevin government's 'marriage rights', using women to marry them off to sometimes low-born if clever administrators in their own government, and forcing them to marry to their own social disparagement. Yet how could he possibly know how much to charge, or how valuable a woman he was 'giving' in marriage was, unless he had a fact-finding exercise to discover the relevant factors about them – their wealth, the number of children who might be a drain on their wealth or have inheritance expectations, their age, and so

---

[3]   Karl Leyser, *Rule and Conflict in an Early Medieval Society: Ottonian Saxony* (London, 1979), chapters 5, 6, and esp. pp. 59–60.

on?[4] The fact-finding element of Henry II's government is written all over its records. Before you sack half your sheriffs, you hold an inquest into their illicit activities and extortions (1170).[5] Before you rectify an alleged unjust disseisin, the sheriff is ordered to get a jury together to give factual answers about the seisin in question.[6] And so with the *Rotuli de Dominabus.*

It is clear that in the latter case there had been a previous survey (1176–1177) of which the justices of our survey had the records (although they are now lost to us), for they make several references to the situation eight years previously. These earlier records must have been a response to the order given by the Assize of Northampton (1176), clause 9, that the justices about to go out on eyre inquire about escheats, churches, lands and *women who are in the gift of the lord king.*[7]

This fact-finding trait in Henry II's government was new at least in degree, not perhaps in comparison with Carolingian government of more than three centuries previously, but in comparison with the recent English past.[8] Henry I, for instance, was said to have used the legislation of papal legates against clerical marriage to sell licences for clergy to get married.[9] Whether this is true or not, we have no indication that he could have had any means of knowing up to what limit he could price them. Similarly with disseisins, Henry I was very keen to remedy disseisins by the exercise of royal power and justice, but he often had no means of knowing the facts of the case, and was said to act on the representations of one party in the absence of the other.[10] To many historians, Henry II's more

---

[4]   *Rotuli de Dominabus et Pueris et Puellis de XII Comitatibus* (1185), ed. J.H. Round, Pipe Roll Society 35 (London, 1913), Round's Introduction; Susan M. Johns, *Noblewomen, Aristocracy and Power in the Twelfth-Century Anglo-Norman Realm* (Manchester, 2003), chapter 9; A.L. Poole, *Obligations of Society in the XII and XIII Centuries* (Oxford, 1946), chapter 6. For 'feudal incidents' in general, and their financial importance above all for the king, see Susan Reynolds, *Fiefs and Vassals* (Oxford, 1994), pp. 369–70.

[5]   *English Historical Documents 1042–1189*, ed. D.C. Douglas and G.W. Greenaway (London, 1953), pp. 437–8.

[6]   *Royal Writs from the Conquest to Glanvill*, ed. R.C. Van Caenegem, Selden Society 77 (London, 1959), pp. 51–103.

[7]   *Select Charters and Other Illustrations of English Constitutional History from the Earliest Times to the Reign of Edward the First*, arranged and edited by William Stubbs, 9th edn, ed. H.W.C. Davis (Oxford, 1921), p. 180.

[8]   See, for example, Rosamond McKitterick, *The Carolingians and the Written Word* (Cambridge, 1989), pp. 27–40; F.L. Ganshof, *Frankish Institutions under Charlemagne*, trans. B. Lyon and M. Lyon (New York, 1970), esp. pp. 3–55.

[9]   Henry of Huntingdon, *Historia Anglorum*, ed. Diana Greenway (Oxford, 1996), pp. 484–5.

[10]   *Royal Writs*, ed. Van Caenegem, p. 273. Literally, a litigant easily persuaded Henry I, 'quia defuit qui resisteret': *History of the Church of Abingdon*, ii, ed. John Hudson (Oxford,

empirical and disciplined way of government action has seemed, and probably with some justification, the consequence of absorption into administration of graduates and *magistri* from the rising cathedral schools and universities of twelfth-century western Europe.[11]

Often the daughters of aristocratic widows, as well as their widowed mothers, could not marry without the king's licence, or could be given in marriage to a favourite. Often the children of widows, boys more than girls, were wards of a feudal lord (in this case the king). That meant that, while they were minors, the incomes of the boys' inheritances from their deceased fathers (their mothers living on their dower or *maritagium*, or sometimes an independent inheritance) would be at the disposal of the king or whomever he bestowed the wardship on or sold it to. Thus the survey of 1185 was very much about children as well as about women.

Susan Johns has called the *Rotuli* 'a complex and under-utilized source', and they were indeed under-utilized before her own book on twelfth-century noblewomen appeared, with its excellent and original chapter on the *Rotuli*.[12] Her chapter makes a number of important points, first of all about how the women are identified, whether by their husbands, or by whose mother they were, or by their pre-marriage family, or even by their mother's name, or by one of these in one context and another in another context. She concludes that patrilineal association was important but not predominant. She goes on to consider widows in the source who had custody of their children. Although only sixteen out of the eighty widows listed as having children had custody of their children, and these had had to fine with the royal government for it, there are various reasons why the situation was not so bleak in the all-important issue of their motherhood as may appear. Other widows could well have had custody where this does not appear, and the children of yet others could have been grown up in 1185 and the question would not arise. She argues that the *Rotuli* show a higher proportion of widows re-marrying than had hitherto been generally thought; and also that in many cases the wealth of widows was likely to have been much greater than transpires from the rolls, not least because they could have held property in others of the numerous shires whose records have not survived from 1185. The governing idea of the whole chapter, indeed of the

---

2002), pp. 234–5.

[11]   For example, R.N. Swanson, *The Twelfth-century Renaissance* (Manchester, 1999), chapter 4; R.W. Southern, 'The Place of England in the Twelfth-Century Renaissance', in his *Medieval Humanism and Other Studies* (Oxford, 1970), esp. pp. 175–9. The best discussion of Glanvill's 'scholastic methods' that I have ever heard was in an unpublished lecture of the late John Prestwich in 1957.

[12]   Johns, *Noblewomen*, p. 7; cf. n. 4 above.

book, is that women should not be perceived as victims, but rather as people who had considerable power and room for action, and that the Rolls (as I now call the *Rotuli*) were far from necessarily only a sign of the weakness of widows in the face of royal justice. Indeed, she maintains, the survey could have helped to *clarify* the claims of widows and wards on dower and inheritance, and thus benefited them by short-circuiting the tortuous legal process to seek redress for land or dower withheld.

It must be made clear at the outset that I have not at all raised this book in order to criticize it, rather than in some ways to build on it. The *Rotuli* have interested me since I studied *Stubbs' Charters* as a student, and I have long thought of looking a little more closely into them as a source. In this, Johns's book has been a help and a stimulus. She and I have somewhat different purposes. Hers is to survey and analyse the role of female power within the interaction of gender and lordship in twelfth-century society.[13] Mine, dictated by the theme of this volume, is to try and see the widows of the Rolls as mothers.

My first point about widow–mothers in the Rolls is a seldom noticed one, that several of them held at least some of their land, presumably and sometimes explicitly their dower, from their sons. Only in nos 1, 2, 4 and 7 below is dower explicitly mentioned, but one may probably assume it in the other cases.

1. In Lincolnshire, a mother holds her dower of her son, for which she does service.[14]

There are four more cases in Norfolk:[15]

2. Alicia de Hainford holds Hainford in dower by the gift of Gilbert Blund. It is worth £8 but could if better stocked be worth £10. She is forty and holds Hainford of Hubert, her son, who is twenty and is a ward of the Bishop of Ely (the notorious curialist and former opponent of Becket, Geoffrey Ridel).
3. Agnes de Montchensy, daughter of Payn FitzJohn, is sixty. One of her daughters is married to Stephen de Glanvill. Her land in Holkham is held (in dower) of her eldest son, Ralph, who himself holds of the Earl of Sussex.
4. Ada de Tony is thirty; she has one son, Baldwin, who is fifteen, and five daughters. In Holkham she has 100s worth of land held of the fief of

---

13 Johns, *Noblewomen*, p. 6.
14 *Rotuli de Dominabus*, p. 10.
15 Ibid., pp. 47, 50, 51 (bis).

Roger de Tony. This she holds in dower of Baldwin, her son (that is, like Agnes above, she has been inserted into the tenurial links as a sub-tenant).

5. Amicia de Limesia is sixty. She has two sons, both knights, the elder called John de Limesia. She also has many daughters. She has 60s of land of the fief of John de Limesia, and holds it of him (*et de eo tenet*).

Then there are two more cases from Essex.[16]

6. One is of the Countess Juliana, sister of Earl Alberic. Part of her land, Lexedene, is worth £10 and is of the fief of Earl Alberic. So this is a brother, not a son, but the principle is in important ways the same.
7. The other is Alicia of Essex, who is eighty (a few other women in the Rolls have reached this age, but not many) and holds Clavering as her dower of the fief of Henry of Essex, who was in fact her son. (Thirty years earlier, at the beginning of Henry II's reign, Henry was royal constable and had acted as an itinerant justice for the king.)

One may note that in the Rolls the jurors of different shires varied in how much detail and what kind of detail they gave. Therefore, it is much more likely that holding dower of a son was a widespread custom, only noted in Norfolk and occasionally elsewhere, than that it was confined predominantly to Norfolk. Indeed it is quite clear from Glanvill's *De Legibus et Consuetudinibus Anglie* that it was normal for a woman to hold her dower from the heir of her dead husband, who would most often though by no means always be her eldest son.[17] Probably this fact was so taken for granted in Glanvill, composed in the same half-decade as the Rolls were compiled, that that is the very reason why it is not more often stated in the latter.

The word 'dower' should be distinguished from the word 'dowry'. By dower was meant the portion of a husband's property which he bestowed on his wife, notionally a third, to be hers for her life after his death, a kind of life insurance policy for her. It reverted to the patrilineal inheritance after her death. Dowry is what is given to a woman by her own family when she marries. Glanvill says that the word *dos* (dower) has two meanings. In common English law usage it means what a free man gives to his wife on marriage; in Roman Law it has a different

---

16   Ibid., pp. 71, 77, and 77 n. 1.

17   Glanvill, *De Legibus et Consuetudinibus Anglie = The Treatise on the Laws and Customs of the Realm of England, Commonly Called Glanvill*, ed. G.D.G. Hall (London, 1965), pp. 60–61, 63.

meaning, that is, what is given *with* a woman to her husband, commonly called (in English law) *maritagium*, or marriage-portion.[18]

My question is: what did this tenurial relationship between mother and son mean for their human relations generally? Very often it clearly had bad implications. Sons might recognize too little dower or drag their feet altogether, when as heirs they would be responsible for ensuring that their widowed mothers had seisin of their dower. Widowed mothers on their side were not above claiming too much or engaging in skulduggery.[19] Glanvill and the forms of writs concerning dower anticipate a great deal of litigation on the subject; when we start to get the evidence of the Curia Regis Rolls, that is, the records of the royal courts, beginning around 1200, we see (a) that Glanvill had left much room for argument about how a 'reasonable dower' should be calculated,[20] and (b) how much feeling and litigation was generated by the subject of dower in general.

S.F.C. Milsom, who has shown how rich a source of litigation the inheritance of sisters by parage was when there were no sons to inherit, has also brought out a fundamental problem about dower. A widow had been given dower on her marriage in a ceremonial sense, but even if the land had then been specified, it remained within her husband's control. This explains why her action to recover dower after her husband's death from his heir is one of the most frequent of all actions on the early plea rolls.[21]

Janet S. Loengard has stressed the huge quantity of litigation about dower seen in the Curia Regis Rolls, or plea rolls, of the first half of the thirteenth century. Although Magna Carta, Clause 7, saying that widows should not pay for their dower, improved their legal position at that time, disgruntled sons, stepsons, brothers-in-law and lords continued to find ways to redress the balance – by simple inaction, by negotiation, by collusive suit, and even by violence. 'When they did', she continues, 'another recruit would be added to the army of doweresses whose complaints march across the plea rolls'.[22] In what I have just quoted, it will be obvious that, besides sons, there were stepsons and others with whom widows might have their suit. Moreover there might be many reasons

---

[18]   Ibid., pp. 58–9, 69.

[19]   For such widows, see Leyser, *Medieval Women*, p. 170; Janet S. Leongard, 'Rationabilis dos', in S. Sheridan Walker (ed.), *Wife and Widow in Medieval England* (Ann Arbor, MI, 1993), p. 61. This is implicit at several points in Glanvill's chapter on dower, chapter 6, pp. 58–69.

[20]   Leongard, 'Rationabilis dos', esp. pp. 63–8.

[21]   S.F.C. Milsom, 'Inheritance by Women in the Twelfth and Thirteenth Centuries', in Morris S. Arnold, et al. (eds), *On the Laws and Customs of England: Essays to Samuel E. Thorne* (Chapel Hill, NC, 1981), esp. p. 83.

[22]   Leongard, 'Rationabilis dos', p. 72.

why writs of dower were taken out other than that an heir was actually claimed to be withholding a widow's dower at that moment. One, for instance, might be a challenge to the legitimacy or freedom of one claiming to be the heir. Another might be the wish to have a record made of an indisputable claim to land.[23] Therefore one need not think that the Curia Regis Rolls represent a general picture of mainly embittered relations between mothers and sons. Such cases, where either things had broken down or clarification was needed, must surely represent a small minority. Glanvill opines, in upholding the rights of an eldest son, that fathers tend to have a greater affection for younger sons,[24] but he says nothing here about mothers.

Loengard gives no idea of how many of the dower cases in the Curia Regis Rolls are straightforward battles between a mother and son. That is no doubt partly because such an analysis, a high desideratum, would go well beyond the scope of her article, as it would beyond the scope of mine. It may also be partly because she is not particularly interested in her widows as mothers, as the theme of the present volume forces myself to be. Indeed one may wonder whether the one downside of her generally excellent article is that it concentrates on women as victims, the very approach that Susan Johns tries to get away from, rather than seeing their opportunities, in this case not only their opportunities as independent holders of dower, but also their opportunities to develop a creative mother–son relationship.

We are here in the territory of a very fine article by Paul Hyams on warranty in twelfth-century England. The writ given in Glanvill for summoning 'the son and heir' of the deceased husband to 'warrant', or guarantee, the dower, if he has refused to do so or has dragged his feet (which shows that mother/son problems cannot have been infrequent, whatever one thinks about their not being the norm), requires him either to give warranty or to show why he was not bound to do so.[25] Warranty involved the idea that a lord protect his vassals and their rights against all counter-claimants. Such warranty, Hyams shows, increasingly became the hallmark of good lordship in the twelfth century. On this showing, sons and heirs were required to be good lords to their widowed mothers, and if they were also heirs to their dower, they normally had every inducement to be so. Hyams also observes that a proffer of service made publicly in the lord's court was sufficient to establish warranty in the king's court.[26] The form of the writ of right for land belonging to dower, as given in Glanvill, refers to 'the free

---

[23]   Ibid., pp. 60–61.

[24]   Glanvill, *De Legibus*, p. 70.

[25]   Ibid., p. 63.

[26]   Paul R. Hyams, 'Warranty and Good Lordship in Twelfth-century England', *Law and History Review*, 5 (1987): 437–503, esp. pp. 448–51, 463.

service of ten shillings a year for all service', which the widow pays to the heir.[27] That probably explains the reference (no. 1, p. 107 above) to the dower of the Lincolnshire mother, for which 'she does service' to her son.

What if widows remarried? Would they not take their dower with them, and thus might not the dower be lost in favour of another line of patrilineal descent? The answer to this is no, not normally. In the Rolls under Northants, Sibilla, wife of Geoffrey Ridel/Basset, has two sons and one daughter, but none is heir of her dower. Richard Basset is, who was born of her husband's first wife.[28] Sibilla herself hung onto her dower in her second marriage, but her heir to it was acknowledged to be the son of her first and deceased husband.

In fact, the whole law relating to dower was structured to reduce impediments to, and facilitate, good relations between mothers and eldest sons. It would be strange were it otherwise. In many historical societies widows have been thought to have their dangers because of their vulnerability in terms of sexuality and property, but such societies have therefore organized themselves to provide very necessary protection for them. This is written all over both testaments of the Bible. In some societies protection has been the widow's re-marriage to one of her deceased husband's male kin (a brother perhaps).[29] This had the added advantage of keeping property within the patrilineal family. However, it was regarded as tantamount to incest in Christian law. In early Christian communities widows would often become dignified, chaste and matronly adherents of a church. This had the disadvantage to the deceased husband's family that large amounts of its property might be permanently alienated to the church.[30] In twelfth- and early-thirteenth-century England, society's way of protecting the aristocratic widow was predominantly through her dower. Certainly Magna Carta and its early re-issues threw their weight behind the widow. This had the advantage, as we have remarked, that it helped to keep the patrimonial inheritance together, and it put a premium on the eldest son's role in his widowed mother's protection.

The *Rotuli de Dominabus* deal with aristocratic women, although some of them were of very modest means. However, by a coincidence we have another great survey from exactly the same year, 1185. It is the very professional Inquest by the military order of the Templars into all their widely scattered English

---

[27] Glanvill, *De Legibus*, p. 61.

[28] *Rotuli de Dominabus*, pp. 24–5.

[29] That is, the levirate, for example, John Beattie, *Other Cultures: Aims, Methods and Achievements in Social Anthropology* (London, 1964), pp. 119–20.

[30] Jack Goody, *The Development of the Family and Marriage in Europe* (Cambridge, 1983), chapter 4, esp. pp. 62–4; Peter Brown, *The Body and Society: Men, Women and Sexual Renunciation in Early Christianity* (New York, 1988), esp. pp. 147–51, and cf. pp. 261–4; and for c10, Leyser, *Rule and Conflict*, esp. pp. 60–62.

rents and revenues. It is packed with all kinds of interest, and a fine edition of it was published by Beatrice Lees in 1935, with an introduction of book length. From this we can carry study of the property relations of widowed mothers and their sons a little further, and at a much lower level of society. For example, at Cardington and Enchmarsh (Shropshire) the widow Hingrid holds 3 acres for which she owes a rent of 8d p.a., while her son Ovietus (probably the only known Ovietus in twelfth-century England and a name itself worthy of investigation!) held 1 acre for a rent of 2d.[31] This is small beer indeed, although whether Ingrid and Ovietus held other land by other lords one cannot tell. Again, at Weston (Hertfordshire), Matilda the widow of Ailmar the tailor has 6 acres for 12d p.a. and one day's labour service every second week. Hugh her son (presumably, that is, Hugo filius Ailmari) holds 18 acres and does two days of labour services each week. Her son, Walter, holds 12 acres, and Matilda has 1 acre in addition which the Templars received from Walter FitzHubert.[32] In the latter of these two cases, at least, the references to labour services make it clear that the people concerned must be unfree peasants, that is, villeins, and any division of land must be of a customary nature within the manor. However, that does not mean that they could not prosper, and in both cases we seem to see some kind of joint agrarian enterprise of mother and son or sons.

One wonders also about Alice the widow and Geoffrey Hasard, who hold 2 bovates (between 40 and 50 acres)[33] of the fief of Heppo Arblaster (the crossbowman) in Blankney (Lincolnshire) for 3s 6d rent, labour services (*opus*) and commuted food-rents (*present*).[34] The labour services show that these too are villeins, albeit seemingly prosperous ones, so there can of course be no question of Alice being Heppo's mother and holding by dower. However, could she be Geoffrey Hasard's mother, again in a joint enterprise with her son? The Templars were only interested in their rents and services, not in the relationships of those who paid them, so we cannot know. Several other widows appear in the Inquest, and for all we know their sons might also lie unidentified in the record. Maybe we are just lucky to have as many as two fairly clear instances of a more common arrangement. An intriguing urban instance of a possibly similar case is so relevant to Henrietta herself that I bring it in. At Oxford the Templars had a measure of land (*unam terram*) within the castle bailey, not many yards from where Henrietta has sat for many years as a Fellow of the College of St Peter-le-Bailey, which yielded 18d rent, which William the goldsmith and Leveva the

---

[31]   *Records of the Templars in England in the Twelfth Century: the Inquest of 1185*, ed. Beatrice A. Lees (London, 1935), p. 38.

[32]   Ibid., p. 65, and cf. pp. cxxxviii–ix.

[33]   Ibid., pp. clxxi–ii.

[34]   Ibid., p. 85, and 85 n. 11.

widow paid.[35] Oxford being an important town, it is quite possible that this was nothing more than a business relationship. William, however, may have been quite young in 1185, because he was not one of the two goldsmiths listed among the sixty-three leading citizens of Oxford in its municipal charter of 1191.[36] Again, this may be a mother–son business.

The 1185 survey of women in the *Rotuli de Dominabus* was never more a survey also of children than when it concerned the wardship of minors, and most especially the sons of widows (girls could be heirs only if there were no boys) whose deceased husbands had held their land in one way or another directly of the king. The king might hold the wardship himself, or much more likely grant it to someone else for money or to a courtier whom he wanted to favour (or both). While a boy was a minor, whoever held the wardship drew the revenues of his inheritance until he came of age, and could arrange a marriage for him. The trade in wardships was a highly lucrative one to the king and his favourites, as we can see from the accounts of a guardian's takings in some cases in the Rolls of 1185.[37] However, it was also one of the most hated aspects of Angevin government. Magna Carta deals with the subject very early on, in its clauses 3–6, immediately before it comes to widows, not in order to abolish wardship of course, but to say that guardians must not be irresponsible or exploitative in the way they managed the estates of a minor and that heirs should be married 'without disparagement' and with due notice to those nearest in blood to the heir. In the last respect, of marriage, the citizens of Bristol had wrung the ultimate concession out of Count John (later king) in 1189–1191: that they could marry themselves and their sons and daughters and widows without the licence of their lords.[38] This grant was made at a time when John was more desperate for support even than at the time of Magna Carta, hence the extreme nature of the concession, but it shows what large numbers of people wanted, if they could have got it. Earlier the Earls of Gloucester had granted the same liberties to their burgesses of Cardiff and Tewkesbury.[39]

What compounded the evil of wardship as seen by the tenants of lords, including the king, was that, while the majority for the sons or heirs of freemen was reached at the age of fifteen, it was twenty-one for the sons and heirs of knights or tenants of military fiefs.[40] Thus there are several mentions in the Rolls

---

[35] Ibid., p. 42.

[36] R.H.C. Davis, 'An Oxford Charter of 1191' in his *From Alfred the Great to Stephen* (London, 1991), pp. 265–79, esp. p. 266.

[37] For example, *Rotuli de Dominabus*, pp. 63–4, 68–9.

[38] *Earldom of Gloucester Charters*, ed. R.B. Patterson (Oxford, 1973), p. 37, no. 10.

[39] Ibid., p. 61, no. 46.

[40] Glanvill, *De Legibus*, p. 82.

of minors aged eighteen or even twenty.[41] An exploitative guardian could have many years in which to waste the resources of an inheritance, even though the inheritance itself had in theory to be given back intact to an heir on his or her coming of age, and to exploit those resources for his own profit rather than for the good of the estate; and he could have plenty of time to force a ward into a disparaging marriage.

It is obvious where mothers come into this picture. The widowed mothers of sons in the Rolls are often seen fighting like tigers to secure the wardship of their own sons. Sixteen out of eighty widows in the Rolls who had under-age minors, according to the comprehensive analysis of Susan Johns, fined with the king to have custody of their own sons, that is, they paid sums of money well beyond what they should have paid, and in many cases what on the face of it they could afford.[42] Alina d'Arci had recovered custody of her son and her barony for £200, double the maximum 'reasonable' relief for any barony, in 1182, only to die herself at the end of that year. The Rolls contain quite a detailed account of William Basset's own rake-off after her death while he had custody.[43] Matilda, widow of Angot de Wicombe, fined with the king for forty marks to have custody of Robert, her thirteen-year-old son.[44] That looks well beyond her means to pay, although we have always to remember that, because of the differences of juries in the various shires about what they recorded and the many shires not represented in the Rolls at all, some part of a woman's total wealth may often be hidden from us. The widow of William Granvel, whose eldest son was eighteen, held one-third of a knight's fee. She fined with the king for the custody of her land and her sons, and for her relief, to the tune of 8 marks, that is, £5 6s 8d.[45] Her relief, according to Glanvill's stated principle of a 'reasonable' relief, should have been at most one-third of 100 shillings, that is, £1 13s 4d, and it may be assumed that, like the citizens of Bristol, she thought she ought to pay nothing for the custody, rather than another £3 13s 4d. When we read that someone has fined with the king for anything, it usually ends by being bad financial news for that person.

We learn that the son of William FitzChetell, falconer or goshawk keeper of the king, was twelve years old and in the custody of his mother through Ranulf de Glanvill, Chief Justiciar, and that his mother had fined with Glanvill for 10 marks to get this custody; and here we see a motive for mothers wanting to pay such money, which was probably more powerful than a purely economic one. She paid it so that he might marry at his own will (*ut liceret ei nubere ad*

41   *Rotuli de Dominabus*, for example, pp. 2–3, 12, 47, 60–61, 81.
42   Johns, *Noblewomen*, p. 176.
43   *Rotuli de Dominabus*, pp. 2–3.
44   Ibid., p. 36.
45   Ibid., p. 81.

voluntatem suam).[46] We have already touched upon this subject. There are two backdrops to it that appear rather in conflict with each other; and within the scope of this paper I cannot resolve the question. Perhaps it has already been resolved in work of which I am ignorant, in which case I sincerely apologize to the author/s. On the one hand, with marriage being taken ever more seriously as a sacrament during the twelfth century, canonists and moralists were increasingly stressing the importance of entering into it voluntarily and without coercion. That in itself raised the emotional expectations of teenagers. On the other hand there are signs that, at least at peasant level, parental authority over marriage was on the up, with lords only interested in taking their licence fee (*merchet*) and otherwise unconcerned about who the partner actually was.[47] However, parents were not unconcerned, for this was at all levels a matter of family honour. The story of Christina of Markyate, for example, is that of her parents wanting to keep face in Huntingdon, her mother if anything more than her father (cf. *Pride and Prejudice*), by marrying her to an eligible citizen of that town.[48] The wording of the Rolls in the case of William FitzChetell's son might suggest that his mother wanted him to be able to marry when and whom he would. However, might she not have wanted her own say?

The system of wardship, however, was not all doom and gloom for relations between a mother and her children. It had occasional humane mitigations. For a start, it usually applied only to eldest sons, or to daughters when they were heirs. The son of Peter de Pelleville, for instance, is a ward of the king; his brother, not yet one year old, and two sisters are with their mother.[49] Beatrice, widow of Robert Mantel, is thirty and has three sons and one daughter. The heir is ten and is in the custody of Robert de Saucei through the king. The other boys, or children (*pueri*), are with their mother.[50] Often, indeed, elder sons and heirs were clearly separated from their mothers and placed in the households of their guardians to be brought up. Whether this was more like being sent to a boarding school at a young age, or like adoption where the links with the natural family were completely severed, is difficult to say. The case of the ten-year-old who was in the custody of Robert de Saucei is one of several in point. Since Robert had fined with the king to have custody of the boy, with the land that he

---

[46]   Ibid., p. 9.

[47]   Henry Mayr-Harting, 'The Miracles of St Frideswide', in Henry Mayr-Harting and R.I. Moore (eds), *Studies in Medieval History, presented to R.H.C. Davis* (London, 1985), pp. 199–201.

[48]   *The Life of Christina of Markyate, a Twelfth-century Recluse*, ed. C.H. Talbot (Oxford, 1959), esp. pp. 46, 72–4, for her mother.

[49]   *Rotuli de Dominabus*, p. 52.

[50]   Ibid., p. 26.

would inherit, it looks as if the boy must have been separated from his mother in person and gone into de Saucei's custody. However, it was not necessarily so. The Rolls of 1185 sometimes make a distinction between custody of the land and custody of the person. The wife of Everard de Ros has two sons, the elder thirteen, but only the land is said to be in the custody of Ranulf de Glanvill (the Chief Justiciar).[51] The heir of Gilbert Hansard is in the custody of his mother, by the gift of the Bishop of Durham, but his land at Suchelsea is in the hands of Hugh de Morewich.[52] In another case, the land with the heir (implying that that needed to be said) is in the custody of Alexander Medarius.[53] The wife of Simon de Crevecuer is twenty-four and has two sons aged five and four. Her land in Hackthorn (Lincolnshire) is in the hands of the king, and by the king's order to the sheriff, the wife and sons were to have what was necessary, although he could hardly find the wherewithal and got nothing for himself, he complains.[54] Here the sheriff administered the land, but the mother looked after the young boys. Henry II does not show himself uniformly a monster in these Rolls, unlovable as he often appears in the narrative sources of his reign. In the case of older boys they are sometimes said to be with the king, that is, receiving a training in the royal household, and that can have been no bad start to their adult life. Nor did it necessarily mean that they were cut off from their widowed mothers, who might have had every reason to be proud of them. In one case the elder son was twenty-four, a leper and a ward of the king; he had his upkeep paid for in a hospice or leper hospital. The second son was not yet one![55] He was presumably with his mother. (What a 'story' in journalists' terms, there might have been there!)

When the custody of the person of a boy was concerned, much obviously depended on his age. It is not easy to find in these Rolls boys under the age of ten who were personally not in the custody of their mothers, and when they were not so, as in the case of the son of Thomas de Bello Fago (two-and-a-half years old), where no mention is made of a mother, the likely reason is that they were orphaned.[56] Most strikingly must this have been the case when the king gave to the son of Thomas FitzBernard, called John, the daughter of Walter de Caune, together with Fambridge, worth the goodly sum of £20 p.a. The five-year-old heiress, not named in the Rolls, was apparently given to John with her land, in the sense that she would be married to him when she came of age to be

51   Ibid., p. 1.
52   Ibid., p. 5.
53   Ibid., p. 36.
54   Ibid., p. 18, cf. p. 7.
55   Ibid., p. 53.
56   Ibid., pp. 57–8.

so. Meanwhile, John's mother was custodian of the little girl's person.[57] She was being brought up by her future mother-in-law, having clearly been orphaned.

There is a peculiar tweak to the story of another child, the heir of Ralph de Haudebovill', not yet one, who was by the king put in the custody of Ranulf de Glanvill. The Rolls show that Ranulf, besides writing his treatise and acting as Chief Justiciar, found time to manage on the side quite a little trading empire in wardships. In this case two-thirds of the heir's land in Acton (Suffolk) was worth, again, £20 p.a., a tidy sum for the Justiciar to have the prospect of drawing over twenty more years. The other third of the land was held, presumably as dower, by Ralph's widow. That widow turns out to have been Glanvill's niece, herself in his custody (regarding any future marriage she might make)![58] So the one-year-old was obviously cared for by his mother after all.

To anyone who thinks that late-twelfth-century people would not have been so concerned about a mother's care as we are in the early twenty-first century, I refer for a contrary example to Adam of Eynsham's *Magna vita* of St Hugh, Bishop of Lincoln (1186–1200). Adam explains Hugh's entry together with his solicitous father into a community of regular canons when he was barely eight by saying that he was deprived of a mother's care when still a young child.[59]

One of the points involved in aristocratic mothers' upbringing of their young children is their likely role in the initial education of both girls and boys. This has been brought out by both Henrietta Leyser and Michael Clanchy, amongst others.[60] There is quite a lot of evidence from the twelfth century for boys being taught in schools or by individual schoolmasters, while we know that Robert of Bethune, the future bishop of Hereford (1130–1148), had acted as the teacher of his nieces and nephews.[61] There is not, however, much concrete evidence for mothers doing the job, although it must have happened widely. Clanchy points out that, when in the mid-thirteenth century Walter of Bibblesworth wrote his treatise on French for the widow, Denise de Montchensy, he assumed that it would be she who would be teaching her children, and that both she and her children would be familiar with the Latin primer.[62] Walter composed his treatise

---

[57] Ibid., p. 77.

[58] Ibid., pp. 60–61.

[59] *Magna Vita S. Hugonis*, I, ed. Decima Douie and Hugh Farmer (London, 1961), p. 5.

[60] Leyser, *Medieval Women*, pp. 138–9; Michael Clanchy, *From Memory to Written Record* (London, 1979), pp. 152, 194, 196.

[61] *The Life of Robert of Bethune by William of Wycombe*, trans. with intro. and notes by B.J. Parkinson, unpub. B.Litt. thesis (Oxford, 1952), chapters 2 and 3. Robert had himself been taught his letters by his eldest brother, Gunfrid. For this *Life*, see also Henry Wharton, *Anglia Sacra ii* (London, 1691), pp. 293–321.

[62] Clanchy, *From Memory*, esp. p. 196.

in particular so that the mother could teach her children the kind of French they would need for 'husbandry and management', and by the mid-thirteenth century many more aristocrats were engaged in the direct management of their own estates than had been the case in the twelfth century, when leasing out was more the order of the day. All the same, if it was the *assumption* of Walter's time that mothers would generally be the teachers of their young children, that assumption could hardly be invalid for the late twelfth century. From Walter, we would deduce that many boys who would become clergymen, who of course scarcely figure in our Rolls, took their first steps in Latin (to mix the metaphor) on their mother's knee.[63]

Since the Rolls of 1185 are so much concerned with heirs, usually males, they tell us in the nature of the case more about mothers and sons, but there are insights to be had about mothers and daughters too. At Burton (? Buckinghamshire), for instance, low in the social scale of females covered by the Rolls was the daughter of Walter de Burton. She was ten, and was heir to half a hide of land, which she should hold of the king by the serjeanty (or service) of store-keeping (*dispensarie*) land worth 12s a year without stock, 19s if stocked. In demesne this girl only holds one virgate, the other being held by her mother in dower.[64] It looks as if the girl was worth too little, particularly if payment for the service had to be made, to be of much interest to anyone as a ward, and as if her unnamed mother (who presumably needed the royal licence to re-marry) ran the daughter's affairs along with her own dower.

As we mentioned, the justices who made the survey of 1185 were interested in the number of a widow's children, particularly their daughters, who might act as a present and future drain on her resources and thus lower her value in the marriage market. This is where mothers and daughters most come into play. If a daughter were in future to be married, that could mean a considerable *maritagium*, but widowed mothers felt a strong compulsion, certainly sometimes and one imagines usually, to provide as best they could for unmarried daughters. A touching example of this is the charter that a great heiress, Aelina de Rullos, drew up for Margaret her younger (*recte* youngest) daughter in the early 1160s. Aelina, who was apparently dying at the time, left to Margaret all the lands that her husband Baldwin FitzGilbert left her when he was dying, and that look as if they had originally come out of her own inheritance from her father, Richard de Rullos, 'so that', Aelina adds, 'this daughter should not remain unprovided for (*inconsulta*) while her other daughters were provided for'.[65]

---

[63]   Cf. Leyser, *Rule and Conflict*, p. 55.

[64]   *Rotuli de Dominabus*, p. 43.

[65]   *Facsimiles of Early Charters from Northamptonshire Collections*, ed. F.M. Stenton, Northants Record Society 4 (Lincoln, 1930), pp. 82–3.

Two widows in the Rolls, at least, had veritable quiverfuls of daughters to provide for. Emma, widow of Hugh FitzRobert and previously wife of Robert of St Paul, and daughter of Henry Tiart, was in the gift of the king and was forty. From her first husband she had dower worth 50s a year and she also had a *maritagium*, presumably from her father, worth 63s; so on this showing, she was comfortable without being rich. Her eldest son was twenty, in the king's custody, but nearly of an age to inherit. She had an engaged daughter of eighteen, a girl of sixteen, two nuns and two other younger daughters.[66] Hawis of Windsor had a male heir who was eighteen, and she had seven daughters. Two were abroad (as she herself was, so her age was not known), two again were nuns, and three were in the gift of the king.[67]

Of particular interest in these two cases are the daughters who were nuns. There are two other cases where one of the daughters was a nun.[68] Given that all these cases are in the relatively restricted area of Northamptonshire, Buckinghamshire and Bedfordshire, it could well be that there were many other cases in the Rolls, in other shires, where daughters were nuns but where this was not stated by the jurors because they would be of only marginal relevance to the enquiry. To provide for a daughter by placing her in a nunnery did not cost nearly as much as a dowry, but it was by no means without cost.[69] It was normal either for a family to give an endowment (this applies also to monks) sufficient for it always to be able to place one of its members in the religious house concerned, or for a donation of land, money or valuables to be made on the entry of a member.[70] Margaret de Rullos could have used her mother's endowment as a *maritagium* if she were about to get married or would do so subsequently, like the interestingly named Pavia of Westminster, widow of a butler of Hurley (Berkshire), who in the early thirteenth century gave some land at Longditch via an intermediary to her daughter, Joanna, for her marriage portion.[71] However, equally, and for all we know, Margaret could have used her mother's endowment to enter a nunnery. She was unmarried and probably in her late twenties. Had she taken this course of action she would have had honour and protection, to put it no higher.

---

[66]   *Rotuli de Dominabus*, pp. 22–3.

[67]   Ibid., p. 35.

[68]   Ibid., pp. 31, 38.

[69]   Robert Bartlett, *England under the Norman and Angevin Kings, 1075–1225* (Oxford, 2000), p. 436.

[70]   Sharon Elkins, *Holy Women of Twelfth-Century England* (Chapel Hill, NC, 1988), p. 68.

[71]   *The Beauchamp Cartulary Charters, 1100–1268*, ed. Emma Mason, Pipe Roll Society, n.s. 43 (London, 1980), pp. 112–13, no. 191.

We have many possible examples of perpetual endowments to Gilbertine houses in Lincolnshire, although I can nowhere find it to be stated in the charters that placing girls in nunneries was the motive for the grants (there was no reason why it should be stated). For example, when in the first decade of the thirteenth century Walter de Neville made a substantial grant of land to the nunnery of Bullington, with the consent of Cecily, his wife, and Alexander his heir,[72] this could well have been intended to endow a place for a family member, or in the case of so significant a baron, for a dependent family, even though that is not stated. However, it is clear that this had happened, either as a perpetual endowment of a place or as a one-off placement of a young woman in the Gilbertine nunnery of Catley, for a charter of the time of Henry III contains confirmation of a grant of land made to Catley by Beatrice Cressy when her daughter Juliana became a nun there.[73] Paul Hyams has mentioned that if there was a state of feud between two families in medieval England, the killer might even fund one of the deceased's relatives into the religious life 'as the best guarantee of full-hearted intercession'.[74] That is not a specifically 'mother' point, but it must include mothers and daughters.

Twelfth-century England saw the new foundation of many nunneries, most of them rather small, middle-class institutions.[75] The Rolls of 1185 hint at one reason for this and suggest a demographic imperative behind the phenomenon, but we need not assume that that was all there was to it. When we know that women became nuns, we do not generally know where they came in the order, by age, of their siblings, and it may be that they were not the younger or for various reasons the hardest to marry off so much as the ones most disposed to take on the religious life. The large number of Irish catholic priests and nuns in England during the twentieth century equally had a demographic imperative behind it, but that did not mean that most of them were unsuited to their way of life. There could have been, if it does not sound self-contradictory to say so, an almost Darwinian principle of natural selection at work for families in the way vocations were implanted into the hearts of boys and girls. To have (especially) a priest in a working-class family raised the family's social standing, trimmed its numbers advantageously of those seeking to make respectable marriages, and

---

[72]   *Transcripts of Charters relating to Gilbertine Houses*, ed. F.M. Stenton, Lincoln Record Society 18 (Horncastle, 1922). For Walter, Cecily and Alexander de Neville, see I.J. Sanders, *English Baronies* (Oxford, 1960), p. 74.

[73]   *Transcripts of Charters*, ed. Stenton, p. 88.

[74]   Paul R. Hyams, *Rancor and Reconciliation in Medieval England* (Ithaca, NY, 2003), p. 200.

[75]   Sally Thompson, *Women Religious: the Founding of English Nunneries after the Norman Conquest* (Oxford, 1991), pp. 1–4; Leyser, *Medieval Women*, chapter 9.

often seemed to be a fruit of parental religious devotion. Although there was occasional parental psychological pressure in such 'vocations', mostly this was not a discernible factor. There seems no reason why things should have been much different in twelfth-century England.

In fact to follow again Susan Johns's point that we should not only see the victimization of women but also their opportunities for creative action, there is plenty of creative possibility in the kind of mother/nun-daughter relationships seen in the Rolls of 1185. The nunneries of the period in the country may look to us now as if they were placed in remote locations, and indeed the vocations of many of the women tended to the eremitical, but they were very much part of the society to which they belonged, as Roberta Gilchrist has said of these 'small gentry foundations'. They often 'remained linked to gentry of their locality, people concerned with local parish and village affairs and local family ties'.[76] The same was true of urban nunneries, like Clerkenwell in London or Clementhorpe on the outskirts of York. Clementhorpe's main revenues were from York rents and from nearby land next to the River Ouse. Over time, it developed multiple bonds of kinship and friendship between the prioress or nuns and the wealthier members of urban or surrounding rural society, and daughters of York merchants became nuns.[77] A justly famous article by Elisabeth van Houts shows how in the earlier Middle Ages the women in royal and high aristocratic nunneries played a pivotal role in keeping alive their family traditions and knowledge about the male and female members of their dynasty.[78] At a lower level of society in England around 1185, the same could probably be said about the women in many of the nunneries, who thereby helped to preserve the cohesion and identity of their families. It is a pity that we do not know to which institutions the six nuns mentioned in the Rolls of 1185 belonged, although with a concerted effort it could be possible to find out. However, it is unlikely that their being nuns cut them off from their widowed mothers. Rather the contrary.

The relations of mothers with their sons and daughters is one that is always heavy and sometimes fraught with emotion, and yet all the evidence that I have so far presented is either devoid of emotion or is in its emotional aspects highly speculative. At first sight it seems impossible to bring into play the kind of history of emotions that medieval historians like Barbara Rosenwein and

---

[76]   Roberta Gilchrist, *Gender and Material Culture: the Archaeology of Religious Women* (London, 1994), p. 50.

[77]   Leyser, *Medieval Women*, pp. 202–203; R.B. Dobson and S. Donaghey, *The History of Clementhorpe Nunnery* (London, 1994), esp. p. 14.

[78]   Elisabeth van Houts, 'Women and the Writing of History in the Early Middle Ages: the Case of Abbess Matilda of Essen and Aethelweard', *Early Medieval History*, 1 (1992): 53–68.

Paul Hyams have recently and imaginatively been calling for and practising.[79] Sometimes there is evidence of emotions, not least from snatches of recorded talk, while sometimes, as in our present case, there is little or none. However, historians have always to bear in mind what must be present and important, albeit not directly in evidence. In particular, this prevents him or her from making dubious assumptions. I can never forget Keith Thomas's masterly review of Lawrence Stone's *History of Childhood*, in which he cast serious doubt on Stone's idea that, because of the large size of families and the number of child deaths that parents had to get used to in seventeenth-century England, they could not have had the same degree of love for their children as we have in our time. This review put me in mind of the touching monument to a twenty-nine-year-old mother and her dead child (1634) in Croome d'Abitot church (Worcestershire).[80]

It is hard to think of ways to study the emotional investment in English motherhood during the twelfth century. We do not have the resources of evidence in such writers as Gregory the Great, Fortunatus and Gregory of Tours (so far as I am aware) that have enabled Barbara Rosenwein to say so much that is important and interesting about mothers in the sixth century – about motherly love, about bereavement of mothers, about mothers perceived as possessive or over-emotional, and about more besides.[81]

One possible way, however, is to consider developing attitudes to the motherhood of Mary in our period. That is what I propose to do in the last paragraphs of this paper. This may look to some like sheer naiveté, as if I were applying to English mothers evidence of emotions attaching to the motherhood of Mary when I lack any other evidence to go on, but I in no way seek to apply the evidence for attitudes to Mary's motherhood to any of the evidence of mothers that I have already adduced, only to give a general context in which many people's thoughts or feelings about motherhood could have run. The

---

[79]   Hyams, *Rancor and Reconciliation*, for example, pp. 37–8; Barbara Rosenwein, *Emotional Communities in the Early Middle Ages* (Ithaca, NY, 2006), and the important collection of papers about anger edited by her in *Anger's Past* (Ithaca, NY, 1998).

[80]   Keith Thomas's review: *Times Literary Supplement* 21 October 1977, pp. 1226–7; Croome d'Abitot: Graham Hutton and Edwin Smith, *English Parish Churches* (London, 1952, 1957), ill. 201.

[81]   Rosenwein, *Emotional Communities*, esp. pp. 66–7, 93, 115–18, 149–55, 192. Two mothers in the twelfth century who had a considerable influence on their son's religious life were those of Godric of Finchale, who insisted on accompanying him on his pilgrimages in his younger days (*De Vita et miraculis S. Godrici*, ed. J. Stevenson, Surtees Society 20 (1847), c. 7, pp. 37–8), and of St Edmund of Abingdon, who when he and his brother were studying at Paris, sent them parcels of linen with hair shirts also enclosed (Matthew Paris, in C.H. Lawrence, *The Life of St Edmund of Abingdon by Matthew Paris* [Oxford, 1996], pp. 118–19).

devil's advocate might say that, if that is all, I am not saying much. My answer is that I can only leave it to the reader to judge how much or how little I am saying.

The twelfth-century view of Mary's motherhood is far from uniform and it was multi-layered. Although there was an undoubted tenderization of the idea of Mary's motherhood in the twelfth century, we should not overlook that, as a mother, she also remained a figure of authority. The Gregorian Reform may have helped to unleash a new surge of Marian devotion, but it had the effect in this of reaffirming her image as queen of heaven and a paradigmatic ruler.[82]

A twelfth-century English example of Mary's motherhood viewed as a position of authority, requiring obedience, comes in the *Ormulum*. The *Ormulum* is a manuscript of gospel readings for the year, translated from Latin into Middle English, and each reading followed by a 'twenty-minute sermon' in English.[83] It was composed with very idiosyncratic orthography by an Augustinian canon called Orm. Although as a collection of vernacular sermons this is close to being unique in twelfth-century England, given the importance of the Augustinian canons in the pastoral care of parishes at that time,[84] the points made in the sermons are likely to have been influential, if not commonplace. Our example comes in the sermon on the gospel reading (Luke 2: 41–51) about Jesus aged twelve. Jesus had been lost in Jerusalem and was eventually found by Mary and Joseph amidst the teachers in the Temple. Mary said to him, 'Why have you treated us so? Your father (that is, Joseph) and I have been looking for you anxiously', and Jesus replied that he must be about his Father's (that is, God's) business. Nonetheless he went back with them to Nazareth, 'and was obedient to them'. This is what the sermon says about it:[85]

> Mary said to her dear son, 'I and your father have both sought you anxiously';
> for she wanted to think well of him and to show how he came to mankind [that

---

[82]   Henry Mayr-Harting, 'The Idea of the Assumption of Mary in the West, 800–1200', in R.N. Swanson (ed.), *The Church and Mary*, Studies in Church History 39 (Woodbridge, 2004), pp. 99–103. Similarly, an image of Mary as ruler may be seen in some twelfth-century English seals, see T.A. Heslop, 'The Virgin Mary's Regalia and Twelfth-century English Seals', in A. Borg and A. Martindale (eds), *The Vanishing Past: Studies Presented to Christopher Hohler* (Oxford, 1981), pp. 53–62.

[83]   Bartlett, *England under the Norman*, p. 496. His phrase, 'twenty-minute sermons', came in his Oxford Ford Lectures of 2004.

[84]   J.C. Dickinson, *The Origins of the Austin Canons and their Introduction into England* (London, 1950), chapter 6; and further, Henry Mayr-Harting, *Religion, Politics and Society in Britain, 1066–1272* (Harlow, 2011), chapter 6. See also *Twelfth-century Homilies* in Ms. Bodley 343, ed. A.O. Belfour, Early English Text Society 137 (1909; repr. 1962).

[85]   *The Ormulum, with the Notes and Glossary of Dr R.M. White*, ed. Robert Holt (Oxford, 1878), I, pp. 312–17, esp. p. 315.

is, through her womb], and to show that the Lord Jesus Christ was obedient to
them both, and was ever humble and joyful and eager to follow their will. Indeed,
he gave us all an example to please well both our father and our mother, to obey
them, to honour them, and to serve them eagerly.

This subject, of Mary and Joseph finding the boy Jesus in the Temple, figures in
one of the wall paintings of Hardham church, Sussex (c. 1160). Hardham is a
rare twelfth-century English parish church to have preserved virtually its whole
scheme of twelfth-century wall-paintings. Our painting is high up on the left of
the chancel arch, one of the most visible to a congregation in the nave, and the
figures of Mary and Joseph have particular prominence in it.[86]

One of the best known apparent examples of disobedience to one's mother
in twelfth-century England is that of Christina of Markyate, refusing to enter
a marriage ordered by her parents. However, the *Life of Christina*, written in
the mid-twelfth century by a monk of St Albans, struggles to show that she was
not being disobedient. 'If I do all in my power to fulfil the vow (of virginity)
which I made to Christ', the *Life* has her say, 'I shall not be disobedient to my
parents'.[87] Special pleading, no doubt, but special pleading by a writer who knew
his readers' or listeners' imperative about obedience to parents.

The view of Mary as a mother of tenderness was far from new in the twelfth
century. In twelfth-century England it seems to have been given new momentum
by the prayers of St Anselm. Ailred of Rievaulx, for instance, writing his *De
Institutione inclusarum* (c. 1160) for his sister, much of which suggests that she
pray and meditate particularly by imagining herself to be one of the women
around Jesus, picks up touchingly a theme from Anselm's prayers – Christ on the
Cross giving Mary to John to be his mother and John to Mary to be her son:[88]

And you, virgin (that is, Ailred's sister), you who can be more confident with
the Virgin's (that is, Mary's) son than the women who stand afar, approach the
Cross with his mother and the virgin disciple (that is, John), and look at close

[86]   *Twelfth-century Paintings at Hardham and Clayton*, introductory essay by Clive Bell
(Lewes, 1947). See one page of text on Hardham (unpaginated). Otto Demus, *Romanesque
Mural Painting*, trans. M. Whittal (London, 1970), p. 507. This particular painting is not in
a good state of preservation, but good enough for its main features to be decipherable.

[87]   *Life of Christina*, pp. 62–3.

[88]   *Aelredi Rievallensis Opera Omnia*, I, ed. A. Hoste and C.H. Talbot, CCCM 1
(Turnhout, 1971), p. 671. See also André Wilmart, *Auteurs Spirituels* (Paris, 1932, 1971),
505–7. For similar affectus in art, see for instance the way Mary kisses the hand of the dead
Jesus in the Descent from the Cross in the St Albans Psalter, p. 47, in *The St Albans Psalter*,
ed. O. Pächt, et al. (London, 1960), frontispiece.

quarters upon that face, moist and pale. What then? Can you view the tears of the loving mother without tears of your own? Can you remain dry-eyed while the sword of sorrow pierces her soul? Can you hear without sobs his saying to his mother, "woman behold your son", and to John, "behold your mother", when he committed his mother to the disciple and promised paradise to the thief?

Walter Daniel, Ailred's hagiographer, gives Ailred himself the image of a tender mother. He writes that, when Ailred lay on his sick-bed, the brethren walked or lay about his bed, 'and talked with him as a little child prattles with its mother'.[89] At the same time, the mention of the promise of paradise to the thief, in the *De Institutione inclusarum* immediately after Mary's motherhood of John, draws us to another developing aspect of her compassionate motherhood, seen in the collections of *Miracles of the Virgin*. The authors of many twelfth-century English miracle narratives make rather a point of beneficiaries of a miracle having to confess their sins before being cured or whatever. Yet not in the *Miracles of the Virgin*, where the most unworthy or outrageous sinners were beneficiaries. The one qualification was that they love Mary. So the sacristan of a monastery, who said an *Ave Maria* every time he passed her altar, was drowned on his way to visit his mistress, but survived. So a certain thief, who was in the habit of saluting the Virgin even on his criminal expeditions, was caught and hanged, but Mary's hands prevented the rope from gripping his throat.[90]

In her famous essay, 'Jesus as Mother', Caroline Walker Bynum associates a transference of the tenderness of Mary to Jesus himself particularly with the twelfth-century Cistercians. She quotes, for instance, a letter of St Bernard to the parents of a novice, saying, 'I will be for him both a mother and a father'.[91] St Bernard also spoke of the motherliness required by abbots and preachers, saying that they must offer their breasts to be suckled as the Bridegroom (Christ) offers his. In this thought world, sexual stereotypes consistently lie behind maternal imagery – gentleness, compassion, tenderness, emotionality and love. Judgement, discipline and command are seen as more male. The stereotypes, according to Bynum, are invariable, but they can be evaluated in such a way that women may be associated with strength. Bynum here develops an important argument, which she does tentatively but which is a striking one. It is that Cistercians felt the need to develop a certain concept of authority whereby authority was

---

[89] *The Life of Ailred by Walter Daniel*, ed. F. M. Powicke (London, 1950), p. 40.

[90] R.W. Southern, *The Making of the Middle Ages* (London, 1953), pp. 246–54.

[91] Caroline Walker Bynum, *Jesus as Mother: Studies in the Spirituality of the High Middle Ages* (Berkeley, CA, 1982). The title essay of this book is pp. 110–69, here p. 116. See also good remarks about Mary and twelfth-century Cistercians in Miri Rubin, *Mother of God: a History of the Virgin Mary* (London, 2009), pp. 149–57.

supplemented with love. Cistercian abbots were experiencing something akin to a crisis of authority, causing many of them to resign. Cistercians rejected child oblates, putting a greater emphasis on adult choice and conversion, which was a pressure on abbots to rule with greater sensitivity to souls, greater intuition in their spiritual guidance, and, one might add, greater acceptability of abbatial authority to those whose experience of religion was increasingly interior and decreasingly one of primarily following external rules,[92] for this crisis of religious authority in the twelfth century was far from confined to the Cistercians. One would hardly expect that it would be so in a period rife with papal schism (from which St Bernard and the Cistercians by no means stepped aside). Hildegard of Bingen, for instance, once she had become a famous visionary, received letters from abbots, abbesses and others wanting to resign their ecclesiastical positions. Each time she said 'don't', and tried to stiffen their sinews.[93]

Is it not possible that there was a similar crisis of authority amongst twelfth-century parents, mothers very much included, most particularly when it came to the marriage of their children? That like abbots they had to preserve their authority and to be loving and understanding at the same time? There they were, confronted on the one hand with the need to preserve the honour and economic status of their family, sometimes in face of the harsh exigencies of lordship, and on the other hand with the growing idea of the canonists (and the Cistercians) that love and friendship and consent ought to be paramount in marriage.[94] Or if girls (and boys) wanted to take up a religious vocation at all, parents and other relatives had to sympathize or be cut off. It was said of St Bernard, such was his eloquence and magnetism, that mothers hid their sons when he was around.[95]

---

[92]   Bynum, *Jesus*, esp. pp. 146–69. It may be of interest to note in this connection that, when Thomas Gailor, the great Episcopalian Bishop of Tennessee (1893–1935), spoke at a service in Stanford University, California, on 5 February 1915, as he noted in his diary, 'a girl said prayer and began: "Dear father and mother God"'. He made no comment. Thomas Frank Gailor, *Some Memories* (Kingsport, TN, 1937), p. 208.

[93]   For example, Sabina Flanagan, *Hildegard of Bingen: a Visionary Life* (London, 1989), pp. 175–8; *The Letters of Hildegard of Bingen*, I, trans. Joseph L. Baird and Radd K. Ehrman (New York and Oxford, 1994), nos 50, 50r, 51 (re schisms), 56, 57, 61, 61r, and others.

[94]   See Mayr-Harting, 'The Miracles of St Frideswide', esp. pp. 199–201.

[95]   I cannot now recover the reference to this vivid and obviously impressionistic detail. Contrary to my initial thought, that it was in the Vita prima (which it is not), I now think that I heard it in a paper delivered by the late Conrad Russell to the Merton College 1066 Society, when he was an undergraduate reading the St Bernard Special Subject with R.W. Southern in 1958. For Bob (R.I.) Moore, whom I consulted, tells me that he remembers Conrad citing this very detail in conversation (with irritation!). However, it is given some colour by the observation in the Vita prima that Bernard's growing fame took him ever further afield, and that this brought increasing numbers of recruits to Clairvaux. William of St Thierry says

The story of Christina of Markyate, as depicted in her *Life*, is one of parents who tried to force her into marriage with an eligible citizen of her native Huntingdon, indeed who are described as fearing to lose face if their daughter went ahead with her vocation of celibacy.[96] In their efforts, her mother, Beatrix, was said to have surpassed her father.[97] So Christina found for herself a sympathetic and more tender and loving mother in Mary herself. It should be emphasized that all this should not be taken as necessarily historical fact. If Christina was on such bad terms with her parents, it is hard to understand why they should be named in the obits of the St Albans Psalter, generally associated with her,[98] but it is the kind of storyline that made sense in the mid-twelfth century.

Another difficult child towards his parents, who also became a recluse in the late-twelfth century, was Robert of Knaresborough. His parents were amongst the leading citizens of York; his mother was called Siminima, and is described in uncomplimentary terms obviously emanating from her son (although he subsequently prayed hard for her) as a usurer. What his father did we are not told, but Robert had a brother who became mayor of York.[99] As a youth he was extremely devout – the kind of thing that makes many a parent nervous – and wanted to become a priest. However, he only got as far as to be ordained a subdeacon. When he became a hermit, he left home without a word to his parents (*parentibus inconsultis*). Once settled at Knaresborough, we are not told anything about his adopting Mary as a substitute mother; but he sought out a 'pious matron' not far from his cell, and begged her to help him out, which she did generously.[100] One cannot avoid the impression that in her Robert found his sympathetic mother figure, which he had not found in Siminima.

---

in the Vita prima that he hardly ever returned home empty-handed ('vix aliquando vacuus domum rediret': PL 185: 260C)! So the observation was at least ben trovato as regards St Bernard, and serves also to highlight the family tensions that could arise when a child opted for a religious vocation.

[96]   *Life of Christina*, p. 58.

[97]   Ibid., p. 46.

[98]   However, this association has been questioned by Donald Matthew, 'The Incongruities of the St Albans Psalter', *Journal of Medieval History*, 34 (2008): 396–416. See on the other side, Jane Geddes, 'The St Albans Psalter', in Samuel Fanous and Henrietta Leyser (ed.), *Christina of Markyate. A Twelfth-century Holy Woman* (London, 2005), pp. 197–216; and also Henrietta Leyser in the same volume, p. 8.

[99]   *The Metrical Life of St Robert of Knaresborough*, ed. Joyce Bazire, Early English Text Society 228 (Oxford, 1953). An edition of the Latin prose life is printed here, following P. Grosjean, *Analecta Bollandiana* 57, pp. 364–400, as Appendix A, pp. 113–28. Here, pp. 113, 116, 119.

[100]   *Metrical Life*, pp. 114–15.

Writing this paper has felt a little like painting a diptych, albeit with panels of very uneven sizes. The larger panel has mainly discussed the evidence of widowed mothers and their children in an official survey of 1185. The smaller panel has sketched some of the emotional history of motherhood in the twelfth century. Nothing in the last quarter can be applied directly to shed light on any case in the first three-quarters of the paper. Yet it seems to me that the last part is actually needed to complement the first part.

Chapter 7
Did Mothers Teach
their Children to Read?

Michael Clanchy

This is an important question because medieval learning was primarily associated with an elite class of men, the clergy. If mothers were responsible for initiating reading, then they would have laid the foundations within the home – and not in clerical schools – of an ever-widening literacy inclusive of lay men and women as well as clerics. As Robert Swanson has pointed out, 'such a household context may mean that while the Church had a patriarchal structure, the strongest formative influence on spiritual development would be maternal. Christianity might, then, be considered almost as a matrilineal religion, which makes the available evidence for female literacy and cultural transmission through books and their ownership even more significant'.[1] There is better evidence for mothers teaching in the latter half of the period, notably in the fifteenth century, although it is probable that they had always been involved. In allocating property between men and women, the German lawbook the *Sachsenspiegel* (dating from the early thirteenth century) designates as female gear 'the Psalter and all the books that belong to divine service, which women are accustomed to read' along with domestic animals and furnishings, textiles, shears and cooking utensils.[2] To aid

---

[1]   R.N. Swanson, *Religion and Devotion in Europe, c. 1215–c. 1515* (Cambridge, 1995), p. 71. This subject was first systematically addressed by S.G. Bell, 'Medieval Women Book Owners: Arbiters of Lay Piety and Ambassadors of Culture', *Signs* 7 (1982): 742–68, reprinted in *Women and Power in the Middle Ages*, ed. M. Erler and M. Kowaleski (Athens, GA, 1988), pp. 149–87. I have addressed this question before in 'Learning to Read in the Middle Ages and the Role of Mothers', in G. Brooks and A.K. Pugh (eds), *Studies in the History of Reading* (Reading, 1984), pp. 33–9.

[2]   'Saltere unde alle buke, de to goddes denste horet, de vrowen pleget zu lesene', *Sachsenspiegel, Landrecht*, ed. K.A. Eckhardt (Göttingen, 1955), 1.24.3 cited by D.H. Green, *Women Readers in the Middle Ages* (Cambridge, 2007), pp. 88–9, illustrated by Bell, 'Medieval Women Book Owners', p. 750 (1982), or p. 156 (1988), and by J. Wolf, 'Psalter und Gebetbuch am Hof', in M. Chinca and C. Young (eds), *Orality and Literacy in the Middle Ages: Essays on a Conjunction and its Consequences in Honour of D.H. Green* (Turnhout, 2005), pp. 139–79, at p. 161.

the memory, the manuscripts of the *Sachsenspiegel* contain illustrations of these objects; books are indicated by a drawing of a codex viewed from the side so that its binding and separate pages are visible.

The Psalter, the book of psalms in the Old Testament, was the clergy's principal prayer book because it is the only part of the Bible to be written in the form of a cycle of prayers. Singing and reciting the psalms throughout the canonical hours of the day and night – from Matins before morning through to Compline in the evening – was the principal office of the regular clergy. Lay people's prayer books, therefore, likewise centred on the Psalter and the hours for reciting them. Consequently, lay prayer books were familiarly described as Books of Hours and the commonest liturgy within them was that of the Hours of the Blessed Virgin Mary.[3]

A banal answer to this question – across the thousand years of the Middle Ages in the Latin West from 500 to 1500 and across all social classes (from queens and their courts to the families of day-labourers and serfs) – is that some mothers did teach their children their letters, although many could not because they were too poor or too ignorant. Medieval records are unlikely to give us a rounded picture. If the mother's role in teaching reading was commonplace, it will be taken for granted and only mentioned in exceptional circumstances. Conversely, if it were rare, then mentions of it will likewise be rare. Descriptions of King Alfred and St Louis learning to read at the direction of their mothers are memorable because they are exceptional.

The Case of St Louis

The case of St Louis is more straightforward. A Psalter of English origin, which is still extant, contains a note in French saying: 'This was the Psalter of my lord Saint Louis, who was king of France, from which he learned in childhood'.[4] This

---

[3]   Henrietta Leyser provides an introduction to Books of Hours in *Medieval Women: a Social History of Women in England 450–1500* (London, 1995), pp. 234–6, and see N.J. Morgan, 'Books for the Liturgy and Private Prayer', in N.J. Morgan and R.M. Thomson (eds), *The Cambridge History of the Book in Britain, volume 2, 1100–1400* (Cambridge, 2008), pp. 291–316, and A. Bovey, 'Books of Hours', in M.F. Suarez and H.R. Woudhuysen (eds), *The Oxford Companion to the Book* (Oxford, 2010), 1, pp. 550–52.

[4]   'Cist psaultiers fuit mon seigneur saint looys qui fu roys de france, ou quel il aprist en senfance [sic]', Leiden, Bibliotheek der Rijksuniversiteit, MS Lat. 76A, fol. 30v. N.J. Morgan, *Early Gothic Manuscripts, 1190–1225*, A Survey of Manuscripts Illuminated in the British Isles 3 (Oxford, 1982), 1, no. 14, pp. 60–62. N.J. Morgan, 'Patrons and their Devotions in the Initials of Thirteenth-century English Psalters', in F.O. Büttner (ed.), *The*

was presumably noted after the canonization of Louis IX in 1297. Although prayer books for lay use were associated particularly with women, they might also of course be owned by men. Thus the Psalter from which St Louis had 'learned in childhood' had belonged to his father Louis VIII (1223–1226). As it is of English origin, he may have acquired it in 1216 when he was in England fighting King John. Within the French royal family, particular prayer books and liturgies were associated with the cult of St Louis. Hence there is a Book of Hours associated with Jeanne of Navarre (queen of France 1285–1305) who was active in promoting the cult of St Louis. It contains a rubric stating: 'Here begin the Hours of my lord St Louis king of France'.[5] This statement is accompanied by a miniature of Louis's mother, Blanche of Castile, seated in a professorial chair supervising a male schoolmaster; his function is designated by the birchrods in his right hand and his status by his clerical tonsure. He is instructing the young St Louis at his feet, who uses a pointer to indicate the letters of the book open on his lap (its text is not legible).

This illustrates how reading was initiated by getting the learner to point to each letter or syllable in the Latin text and pronounce it correctly. The text immediately below this miniature is 'Domine, labia mea aperies' ('Lord, open my lips'), the opening words of the Hours of the Virgin Mary. Learning to read in this way did indeed make the student open his lips and annunciate God's praises. Where the method of teaching reading is described in these prayer books, it is done not for its own sake but to demonstrate the child's precocious beginnings in pious worship. Guibert Abbot of Nogent (who was born in the 1060s) recalled how his mother first 'set me to letters; I had grasped their shapes but had scarcely learned to connect their elements' when he was handed over to a cruel male tutor.[6] By contrast (some two centuries earlier), a boy oblate of the abbey of Saint-Germain (in Auxerre) named Esopos 'was delivered by his parents to the holy order when scarcely five years old and, as much as his tender age permitted, he was formed in the first characters of letters more in play than in earnest'.[7] The life of St Bernard of Menton (born in the 920s) describes greater precocity: 'in his second or third year, already thirsting

---

Illuminated Psalter (Turnhout, 1999), pp. 309–22, at p. 318. J. Le Goff, *Saint Louis* (Paris, 1996), p. 582.

5   'Ci commencent les heures monseigneur saint loys roy de france', Paris, BnF, MS n. a. lat. 3145, fol. 85v. M.C. Gaposchkin, *The Making of St Louis* (Ithaca, NY, 2008), pp. 211, 215, Figure 8.

6   'Traditus ergo literis, apices utcunque attigeram, sed vix elementa connectere noram', Guibert of Nogent, *De Vita Sua*, ed. E.R. Labande (Paris, 1981), p. 26.

7   'Qui, cum vix quinque annorum infantiam contigisset, sancto ordini a parentibus mancipatus, prout tenera aetas pati poterat, primis litterarum characteribus ludo quam

to read his mother's prayer book, he combined syllable with syllable connecting element to element'.[8]

The mention of the mother's prayer book is interesting. I concluded in the second edition of *From Memory to Written Record* in 1993 that Books of Hours begin to be made for lay people in the thirteenth century and that:

> the 'domestication' of ecclesiastical books by great ladies, together with the ambitions of mothers of all social classes for their children, were the foundations on which the growth of literacy in fourteenth- and fifteenth-century Europe were constructed. This shift in the focus of literacy from monastic church to noble household was perhaps as significant a cultural change as the shift from memory to written record.[9]

However, I am now aware that aristocratic ladies had possessed personal prayer books long before the development of the regular form of Books of Hours of the Virgin Mary in the thirteenth century. The latter did indeed become 'books for everybody' (as Christopher de Hamel has described them) and they have survived in their hundreds, both as books and as single sheets mainly from the fifteenth and sixteenth centuries.[10] A precious earlier survival is the Psalter made for Clementia von Zähringen in the mid-twelfth century.[11] This is a little book, measuring 11 × 7 cm, designed to be held easily in the user's hands. The life of the Irish hermit Marianus Scotus, who settled at Regensburg in the 1080s, describes how he had written out for poor widows and poor clerics 'many little books and Psalter manuals' ('libellos multaque manualia psalteria').[12] Michelle Brown has marshalled arguments for female ownership of prayer books in Anglo-Saxon

---

serio formabatur', W.S. van Egmond, *Conversing with the Saints: Communication in Pre-Carolingian Hagiography from Auxerre* (Turnhout, 2006), p. 144, n. 21.

[8]   'In biennio aut triennio suo habens facundiam fandi, librum orationum matris iam legere sitibundus, elementum elemento annectens, syllabam syllabae combinabat', P. Riché, 'Recherches sur l'instruction des laics du XIe au XIIe siècle', *Cahiers de Civilisation Médiévale*, 5 (1962): 175–82, at p. 177, n. 18. For syllable formation see n. 73 below.

[9]   M.T. Clanchy, *From Memory to Written Record: England 1066–1307*, 2nd edn (Oxford, 1993), p. 252, and see pp. 13, 245.

[10]   C. de Hamel, *A History of Illuminated Manuscripts*, 2nd edn (London, 1994), title of Chapter 6.

[11]   Baltimore, Walters Art Gallery MS 10. M.T. Clanchy, 'Images of Ladies with Prayer Books: What do they Signify?', in R.N. Swanson (ed.), *The Church and the Book*, Studies in Church History 38 (Woodbridge, 2004), pp. 106–22, at p. 107.

[12]   J.W. Thompson, *The Literacy of the Laity in the Middle Ages* (Berkeley, 1939), pp. 92–3, 110, n. 100.

England.[13] The distinction between nuns and other devout women remained fluid throughout the medieval period.[14]

The role of women in reading is also important because of the significance of the mother tongue. Dante argued in *De Vulgari Eloquentia* that the vernacular is nobler than Latin because it is our first and natural language, whereas Latin is an artifice that has to be learned through grammar from a schoolmaster.[15] Although it is a male master who teaches St Louis in the miniature depicting his beginning reading, it is his mother Blanche of Castile who is shown in the superior position as she supervises both master and pupil. In another manuscript image Blanche is shown enthroned, alongside either her husband (Louis VIII) or her son (St Louis IX), as they direct a monk in the lower half of the picture who is dictating to a scribe-artist.[16] Although he does not articulate this, St Louis would have agreed with Dante that the vernacular was a nobler form of diction. This is the language (Old French) in which he wrote to his children in his own hand in order to emphasize the authenticity and personal nature of his message.[17] (There is a complication here as his mother, Blanche of Castile, presumably had Castilean as her mother tongue, but Castilean would have been close to forms of French in the thirteenth century and Castile also had a stronger tradition than France of writing in the vernacular.[18])

The mother tongue was felt by aristocrats to be superior to Latin because they believed it to be the free and easy language of their noble forbears who had overcome the Roman Empire. In reality the 'barbarian' Franks in France or the Visigoths in Spain had not so much conquered the Romans as infiltrated their culture. This is best demonstrated by their adoption of forms of Roman (that is, 'Romance') speech and their acceptance of Latin as the language in which to record their laws and customs. (Anglo-Saxon literature and lawcodes in Old English are of course exceptions to this rule.) A long and persistent tradition

---

[13]   M.P. Brown, 'Female Book Ownership and Production in Anglo-Saxon England: the Evidence of Ninth-century Prayer Books', in C.J. Kay and L.M. Sylvester (eds), *Lexis and Texts in Early English: Studies Presented to Jane Roberts* (Amsterdam, 2001), pp. 45–67. See also B.J. Muir, 'The Early Insular Prayer Book Tradition and the Development of Books of Hours', in *The Art of the Book: its Place in Medieval Worship* (Exeter, 1998), pp. 9–20.

[14]   J. Jenkins, 'Reading Women Reading: Feminism, Culture, and Memory', in L. D'Arcens and J.F. Ruys (eds), *Maistresse of My Wit: Medieval Women, Modern Scholars* (Turnhout, 2004), pp. 317–34, at pp. 324–5.

[15]   *De Vulgari Eloquentia* 1.1, ed. P.V. Mengaldo (Padua, 1968) pp. 3–4.

[16]   New York, Pierpont Morgan Library MS 240, fol. 8r. Illustrated by C. de Hamel, *The Book: a History of the Bible* (London, 2001), p. 147.

[17]   Thompson, *Literacy of the Laity*, pp. 130–31, 155, n. 70.

[18]   R. Wright, *A Sociophilological Study of Late Latin* (Turnhout, 2002) and R. Wright, *Late Latin and Early Romance in Spain and Carolingian France* (Liverpool, 1982), Chapter 5.

contrasted the literate skills of the clergy with the manliness bred by knighthood. 'Barbarian' warrior mythology still found expression in St Louis's time in the rebellion of the French baronage in 1247, when they declared that 'all of us, the king's chief men, perceive by applying our minds that the kingdom was not won by written law, nor by the arrogance of clerks, but by the sweat of war'.[19] The barons' skill in thinking ('applying our minds', *attento animo* in Latin) is implied to be superior to the literacy of the clergy. More than seven centuries earlier the Ostrogoth Theoderic the Great, the conqueror of Italy (489–493), had been credited with refusing to send his sons to school for fear that they would grow effete.[20] Represented on coins and medals with a moustache and long hair, he and his descendants adopted Roman culture and yet at the same time they were proud to be 'barbarians'.[21]

Centuries later, in the life of Theoderic's namesake, Dietrich Abbot of St Hubert of Liège (who died in 1086), the hagiographer describes a dispute between his mother and father about his upbringing. His father wanted to make Dietrich into what he was himself, that is 'a worldly knight'; so he forcibly had his son 'removed from letters' (meaning that he was brought home from school) and he threatened his wife with dire penalties if she persisted with his clerical education.[22] Needless to say, perhaps, as this is a clerical tale, the mother got her way in the end. In purporting to despise literate culture, the belligerent declaration of the French baronage in 1247 helps explain the much discussed avowal of Wolfram von Eschenbach in *Parzival* (some forty years) earlier that he is distinguished as an author by his lack of book learning: 'I know nothing of letters'.[23] He is not confessing to a deficiency here nor is he expressing humility,

---

[19]   'Nos omnes regni maiores attento animo percipientes, quod regnum non per ius scriptum, nec per clericorum arrogantium, sed per sudores bellicos fuerit adquisitum', Matthew Paris, *Chronica Maiora*, ed. H.R. Luard, Rolls Series (1872–1883), 4, p. 593. Clanchy, *From Memory to Written Record*, p. 37.

[20]   Thompson, *Literacy of the Laity*, pp. 14, 25, n. 109.

[21]   P.E. Dutton, *Charlemagne's Mustache and Other Cultural Clusters of the Dark Age* (New York, 2004), pp. 4–5, 8. B. Ward-Perkins, *The Fall of Rome and the End of Civilization* (Oxford, 2005), pp. 72–4.

[22]   J. Bumke, *Courtly Culture: Literature and Society in the High Middle Ages*, trans. T. Dunlap (Berkeley, CA, 1991), pp. 430–31, 662, nn. 19 and 20. Thompson, *Literacy of the Laity*, pp. 91, 108, n. 86.

[23]   'Ichne kan deheinen buochstap', *Parzival*, 115, 27, cited by A. Wendehorst, 'Wer konnte im Mittelalter lesen und schreiben?', in *Schulen und Studium im sozialen Wandel des hohen und späten Mittelalters* (Sigmaringen, 1986), pp. 9–33, at p. 25, and Wendehorst (translated by A. Davies), 'Who Could Read and Write in the Middle Ages?', in A. Haverkamp and H. Vollrath (eds), *England and Germany in the High Middle Ages: In Honour of Karl J. Leyser* (London, 1996), pp. 55–88, at p. 78.

as is sometimes suggested, but declaring what it means to be a knight who is a poet in his mother tongue. Addressing the women in his audience, he teasingly explains that he would rather be exposed naked in the bath than for anyone to think he had taken anything from a book. In *Willehalm* (which is later than *Parzival*) Wolfram adopts a more solemn tone, as if he were St Augustine or St Bernard, with his opening dedication to God and the Trinity, but he again insists that the skill he has comes from his intelligence and not from what is written in books.[24]

The Case of King Alfred

Like Wolfram's literacy, the enigmatic case of King Alfred (King of Wessex 871–899) has been much discussed. He is a precocious younger son, the sort of aristocratic boy whom a mother in subsequent centuries would have educated as a cleric with the prospect of his becoming a bishop or abbot. According to Asser, his mother showed Alfred and his brothers a book of 'Saxon' or English poetry, which she promised to give to whichever of them could learn it the fastest. This was evidently a small illuminated manuscript, as his mother held it in her hand and Alfred was attracted by the beauty of its initial letter. 'Then he immediately took the book from her hand and went to a master and read. Having read it, he returned to his mother and recited'.[25] The Latin verb for 'read' here is *legere*, which for medieval learners focused usually on correct diction; hence Alfred, after 'reading' with the master, goes to his mother and 'recites' (Latin *recitare*). As reading was often taught directly from Latin (and not from the mother tongue as in Alfred's case), *legere* did not necessarily include understanding the text. 'A boy first learns the alphabet, secondly to form syllables, thirdly to read (*legere*) and fourthly to understand (*intelligere*). At each of these stages he has his own distinct sense of the purpose of that particular step'.[26] Long after Alfred,

---

[24] 'Swaz an den buochen stêt geschriben/des bin ich künstlös beliben/wan hân ich kunst, die gît mir sin', *Willehalm*, 2, 19–20, cited by Green, *Women Readers*, pp. 223–4.

[25] 'Tunc ille statim tollens librum de manu sua, magistrum adiit et legit. Quo lecto, matri retulit et recitavit', Asser, *De Rebus Gestis Aelfridi*, ed. W.H. Stevenson (Oxford, 1904), Chapter 23, p. 20. K.O'B. O'Keeffe, 'Listening to the Scene of Reading: King Alfred's Talking Prefaces', in *Orality and Literacy: Essays in Honour of D.H. Green* (Turnhout, 2005), pp. 17–36, at pp. 20–21, amends the interpretation of this passage in the translation of Asser by S. Keynes and M. Lapidge, *Alfred the Great*, Penguin Classics (London, 1983), pp. 75 and 239, n. 48.

[26] 'Unde sicut puer primo discens alphabetum, secundo sillabicare, tercio legere, et quarto intelligere, habet in quolibet istorum graduum sensum suum distincte intentum circa

John Wyclif in c. 1378 used this evocation of the medieval reader's experience in learning Latin to illustrate the different levels of meaning in Holy Scripture.

Asser's account of King Alfred shows how a mother might introduce a child to reading without understanding Latin. After he had shown her that he could read English, Asser adds that Alfred applied this skill to Latin by learning 'the daily round', that is, 'the services of the Hours and then some psalms and many prayers'. These texts 'were collected together in a single book, which he kept on his person day and night and was never parted from it, as I have seen for myself'.[27] On one occasion Alfred instructed Asser to copy a text into 'the little book which he constantly carried on his person, in which were written out the daily offices and some psalms and certain prayers'.[28] So Alfred possessed his own Book of Hours, which he called his 'handbook'.[29] Perhaps it was of similar dimensions to Clementia von Zähringen's book, as Asser says it 'reached the size of a Psalter' as more texts were added to it.[30] Asser describes the exceptional circumstances in Anglo-Saxon England, where reading might be learned in the vernacular because English had been a written language at least since the time of Augustine's mission from Rome in 597–604. Bede notes how the laws of Aethelbert of Kent, the first king to be converted, were put in writing 'in accordance with the examples of the Romans' and 'in the language of the English'.[31] He makes no comment about the implied contradiction here; if Aethelbert was following 'the examples of the Romans', his laws should have been written down in Latin and not English. The precedents for writing in vernaculars had to come from 'barbarian' models in Germanic/Scandinavian runes and Irish ogams.[32]

---

illud', J. Wyclif, *De Veritate Sacrae Scripturae*, Wyclif Society 29–31 (London, 1905), 1, p. 44, lines 7–11.

[27] 'Post haec cursum diurnum, id est celebrationes horarum, ac deinde psalmos quosdam et orationes multas; quos in uno libro congregatos in sine sua die noctuque , sicut ipsi vidimus, secum separabiliter', Asser, Chapter 24, p. 21.

[28] 'Libellum, quem in sinum suum sedulo portabat, in quo diurnus cursus et psalmi quidam atque orationes quaedam, quas ille in iuventute sua legeret, scripti habebantur, imperavit', Asser, Chapter 88, p. 73.

[29] 'Quem enchiridion suum, id est manualem librum, nominari voluit', Asser, Chapter 89, p. 75.

[30] 'Ad magnitudinem unius psalterii perveniret', Asser, Chapter 89, p. 75. Clementia's Psalter (see n. 11 above), which is incomplete, has 126 folios.

[31] 'Iuxta exempla Romanorum cum consilio sapientium constituit; quae conscripta Anglorum sermone', Bede's *Ecclesiastical History of the English People*, ed. B. Colgrave and R.A.B. Mynors (Oxford, 1969), 2, Chapter 5, pp. 150–51.

[32] S. Kelly, 'Anglo-Saxon Lay Society and the Written Word', in R. McKitterick (ed.), *The Uses of Literacy in Early Medieval Europe* (Cambridge, 1990), pp. 36–62, at pp. 36–8; J. Stevenson, 'Literacy in Ireland', in *The Uses of Literacy*, pp. 33–5.

Alfred confirms that reading was learned directly in English, when he exhorts England's young free men (and women too perhaps) to study his translation of Pope Gregory's *Pastoral Care* until 'they are well able to read English writing'; thereafter (he recommends) a select few should go on to study Latin with a view to being clergy.[33] It was possible to carry over the skill of reading from English to Latin because, as a consequence of Augustine's mission, the written vernacular in England had adopted Latin script together with the addition of a few runes, the letter 'thorn' for example for the phoneme *th*.[34] Nevertheless, it has always been hard to learn to read in English because the Latin alphabet is not suited to it. The young Alfred may have been relieved when he turned from his first book of English poetry to the Latin Psalter in the version by St Jerome, where the pronunciation of the letters was governed by consistent rules which helped even a beginner to sound as if he understood what he was saying. Later on, Asser explains, Alfred became 'literate' (*literatus*), that is, he understood Latin and hence he was able to mastermind the translation of Pope Gregory's *Pastoral Care* and other books that he admired into English.[35]

The book in English from which Alfred first learned to read has not been preserved. This is surprising perhaps, as Asser describes it as a precious manuscript (it had illuminated letters) and its association with Alfred might have led to its being kept, like the book from which St Louis had learned in his childhood.[36] One of the books dating from the sixth century which Augustine of Canterbury brought with his mission from Rome has been preserved, as has the seventh-century Gospel book which was placed in St Cuthbert's coffin.[37] Generally, however, children's reading books are unlikely to be preserved over the centuries, as they got hard usage. Those that have been kept are usually collectors' pieces, like the illuminated Primer of the

---

[33] 'Hie wel cunnen Englisc gewrit araedan', *King Alfred's West Saxon Version of Gregory's Pastoral Care*, ed. H. Sweet, Early English Texts Society 45 (1871), 1, p. 7. Keynes and Lapidge, *Alfred the Great*, p. 126. C. Fell, *Women in Anglo-Saxon England* (London, 1984), p. 100.

[34] N. Orme explains the medieval English alphabet in *Medieval Children* (New Haven and London, 2001), pp. 246–51.

[35] J. Bately, 'Did King Alfred Actually Translate Anything? The Integrity of the Alfredian Canon Revisited', *Medium Aevum*, 78 (2009): pp. 189–215. S. Foot, 'The Making of *Angelcynn*: English Identity before the Norman Conquest', *Transactions of the Royal Historical Society*, 6th series, 6 (1996): 25–49, at p. 37.

[36] See n. 4 above.

[37] *The Making of England: Anglo-Saxon Art and Culture AD 600–900*, ed. L. Webster and J. Backhouse (London, 1991), exhibit no. 1, pp. 17–18, no. 86, p. 121.

Emperor Maximilian (dating from around 1466) or that of Princess Claude of France (dating from around 1506).

A miniature placed beneath the alphabet at the beginning of Maximilian's Primer shows him as a boy beginning instruction with a male tutor in reading the Lord's Prayer ('Pater noster' in Latin), which is written in a bold squared Gothic bookhand.[38] This Primer also contains an alphabet and the texts of the same elementary prayers in German in a more cursive and less weighty script. In the preceding century the Emperor Charles IV (1346–1378) described how at the age of seven he had been sent to the court of King Charles IV of France (1322–1328) to be educated, where it was decided 'that he should be instructed in letters a bit' ('me aliquantulum in litteris erudiret') by his chaplain 'and from this I learned to read the Hours of the Blessed Virgin Mary and, understanding them a bit, I willingly read them daily in the time of my boyhood'.[39] Instruction 'in letters' meant learning Latin. Why was the future Emperor only educated in Latin 'a bit' (the word 'aliquantulum' is repeated in Charles's recollections), considering that a century later the ideal for a prince of the Italian Renaissance was an intensive education in the classics? One answer is that Charles, as Emperor and king of Bohemia, did indeed require some literacy in adulthood, but this was primarily not in Latin but in the fast developing vernacular literatures in French, German, Italian and his mother tongue of Czech. The Emperor Charles IV remembered that King Charles IV of France was 'ignorant of letters'.[40] The French court evidently preserved the traditional warrior ethos of the Franks, where manliness and chivalry were still felt to be at odds with the book learning of the clergy.

---

[38]   Illustrated by B. Wolpe, 'Florilegium Alphabeticum: Alphabets in Calligraphy and Paleography', in A.S. Osley (ed.), *Essays Presented to Alfred Fairbank on his Seventieth Birthday* (London, 1965), pp. 69–74, at plate 20. Comment by Wendehorst, 'Who could read and write?', p. 70.

[39]   'Et ex hoc didici legere horas beatae Mariae Virginis gloriosae et eas aliquantulum intellegens cottidie temporibus meae puericiae libentius legi', *Vita Caroli Quarti: Die Autobiographie Karls IV*, ed. E. Hillenbrand (Stuttgart, 1979), Chapter 3, p. 82, and see the English translation by B. Nagy and F. Schaer, *The Autobiography of the Emperor Charles IV* (London, 2001), p. 24. I owe this reference to Dr Elizabeth Danbury.

[40]   'Rex predictus ignarus esset litterarum', *Vita*, Chapter 3, p. 82.

St Anne Teaching the Virgin Mary

An explicit case of a mother teaching reading occurs in the cult of St Anne as mother of the Virgin Mary that developed in the fourteenth century, particularly in England and thence in France. The Primer of Princess Claude of France (who was born in 1499) is the best example of this. This is a parchment booklet of fourteen pages, measuring 26 × 17.5 cm, and containing an alphabet and the most basic Latin prayers: that is, the Lord's Prayer, the 'Hail Mary' and the Creed followed by a few more prayers and graces at meals. In other words, this is a child's ABC booklet.[41] On its front cover is an accomplished picture in colour showing a kneeling female figure at a prie-dieu, resting her hands on a closed book. On the back cover is another picture of this kneeling figure, who now rests her hands on an open book, while regarding a vision of St Anne teaching the Virgin Mary from another open book.[42] By proceeding from the front cover of this booklet to the back, via the alphabet and the Latin prayers within its pages, the kneeling figure has evidently learned to read – thanks to the example of Anne teaching Mary. This is why both their books are depicted open. The texts of the two books are not made legible by the artist, although they are indicated to be similar to each other in their layout with generous margins and spacing between the lines. The inference is that Princess Claude and the Virgin Mary use comparable prayer books. An inscription across the top of the frame of the back cover reads: 'O mater dei, m[em]ento mei, ave maria gracia plena' ('O mother of God, remember me, hail Mary, full of grace').

---

[41]   I discuss such booklets in 'The ABC Primer: was it in Latin or English?', in E. Salter and H. Wicker (eds), *Vernacularity in England and Wales c1300–1550* (Turnhout, 2011), pp. 15–36, at p. 20, n. 29, for Princess Claude's booklet.

[42]   Cambridge, Fitzwilliam Museum, MS 159, pp. 1 and 14, illustrated in colour and approximately actual size by J. Harthan, *Books of Hours and their Owners* (London, 1977), pp. 134–5, and in black and white but reduced in size by P. Sheingorn, 'The Wise Mother: the Image of St Anne Teaching the Virgin Mary', *Gesta*, 32 (1993): 69–80, at p. 77, Figures 14 and 15, reprinted in M.C. Erler and M. Kowelski (eds), *Gendering the Master Narrative* (Ithaca, NY, 2003), pp. 105–34, at pp. 128–31, Figures 14 and 15. On this image, I have profited from discussions with Professor Pamela Sheingorn and Professor Ayers Bagley.

Figure 7.1 Alphabet and the beginning of the Lord's Prayer in Latin in the Primer of Princess Claude of France

© The Fitzwilliam Museum, Cambridge, MS 159, pp. 2, 1 and 14.

Figure 7.2 Princess Claude, with her book closed, kneels before her patron, Bishop Claude, while St Anne and the Virgin Mary intercede for her

© The Fitzwilliam Museum, Cambridge, MS 159, pp. 2, 1 and 14.

Figure 7.3 Princess Claude, with her book open, kneels before St Anne and the Virgin Mary, while Bishop Claude intercedes for her

© The Fitzwilliam Museum, Cambridge, MS 159, pp. 2, 1 and 14.

The iconography is complicated, as three visionary figures are involved. In addition to Anne and Mary, there is Princess Claude's name-saint, the sixth-century Frankish bishop, Claude of Besançon. He is the dominant figure on the front cover, where he is depicted wearing a golden cope with an image of the Virgin and the Christ Child embroidered on it. Symbolically he represents the male authority of the Church, while conceding by the embroidery on his cope that the Mother of God is to be venerated. He holds aloft his episcopal staff, which is topped by a golden cross instead of a shepherd's crook, to indicate that learning to read is part of learning to pray. In children's ABC booklets the alphabet is invariably preceded by Christ's cross to which the learner commended himself,[43] whereas Princess Claude's booklet contains no such cross because the bishop's staff serves this purpose. On the front cover Princess Claude and Mary are shown 'as equals in age and position'; St Anne 'includes both girls in her maternal protection' in commending them to Bishop Claude and the authority of Christ's cross.[44] On the back cover, by contrast, it is Bishop Claude who now presents his protegé, Princess Claude, to Anne and Mary.

On the front cover the prie-dieu is covered with a cloth powdered with fleur-de-lys symbolizing the kingdom of France and the letter 'A' for Anne, whereas on the back cover the same cloth is powdered with the letter 'C' for Claude. The artist has also made other changes in the details of the front and back covers: the floor carpet has a different colour and pattern; Bishop Claude's cope is different in colour and design; St Anne has a different coloured dress and so likewise does Princess Claude. On the front cover she wears a yellowish dun-coloured dress, whereas on the back she has a dress of black velvet, as if she were in mourning. Possibly the French court was in mourning at the time she learned to read. These differences between the front and back covers of the booklet were perhaps intended by the artist to indicate the passage of time between Claude's starting reading and completing the task.

It has been suggested that the kneeling figure on the front cover is not Princess Claude at all but her mother, Anne of Brittany, and this is why the cloth is powdered with the letter 'A'.[45] On this interpretation, Anne prays for her daughter Claude's success on the front cover, while on the back Claude is

---

[43]   Orme, *Medieval Children*, pp. 248–53.

[44]   P. Sheingorn, 'The Maternal Behaviour of God: Divine Father and Fantasy Husband', in J.C. Parsons and B. Wheeler (eds), *Medieval Mothering* (New York, 1996), pp. 77–99, at p. 90.

[45]   R. Wieck, 'The Primer of Claude de France and the Education of the Renaissance child', in S. Panayotova (ed.), *The Cambridge Illuminations: the Conference Papers* (London, 2007), pp. 267–77, at p. 269.

depicted with her open book (hence the cloth now has the letter 'C' on it). It is true that the kneeling figure on the front cover could depict an adult, rather than a girl of seven or eight, but this is unlikely to be Anne of Brittany, as the left hand of this kneeling figure is made visible to the viewer and it does not bear a wedding ring. In another book, the 'Grandes Heures' made for Anne of Britanny, she is depicted with a ring on the fourth finger of her left hand.[46] The letters 'A' and 'C' on the cloth covering Princess Claude's prie-dieu may refer not to her, but to her saintly patrons: on the front cover St Anne has her hand on Princess Claude's shoulder, while on the back St Claude adopts a similar posture of commendation. The ideal of St Anne teaching the Virgin Mary was not restricted to women. Thus a Book of Hours given by Henry VII of England to his daughter Margaret (who was born in 1489) contains a full-page picture of St Anne teaching Mary with an inscription directing Margaret to remember her father in her prayers.[47]

How the ideal of St Anne teaching the Virgin Mary emerged is not yet fully understood. The canonical scriptures say nothing about Mary's parentage or life before the Annunciation. The apocryphal gospels filled this vacuum by naming her parents as Anne and Joachim and describing how they presented her to the Temple in Jerusalem when she was three years old because Anne had promised to do this.[48] This belief accorded with the practice of giving children to monasteries as oblates at a young age. There was no room in this tradition for Mary being educated at home by her mother. The practice of offering children to monasteries ceased to find favour from the twelfth century onwards and this may be why the story of St Anne and Mary changed. All we know is that the ideal of Anne teaching Mary proliferated in images in the fourteenth and fifteenth centuries in book illuminations, wall paintings, stained glass and sculpture.[49] The latter types of work are significant, as this is public church art, whereas images in books were restricted to their readers or owners. The ideal of Anne as Mary's teacher evidently appealed to patrons and thence to a wider public, although we should not infer that this image emerged spontaneously from mothers in their homes. By and large, art was commissioned by men, even

---

[46]   Paris, BnF, MS lat. 9474. Harthan, *Books of Hours*, pp. 127–8.

[47]   *The Cambridge History of the Book in Britain, Volume 3, 1400–1557*, ed. L. Hellinga and J.B. Trapp (Cambridge, 1999), plate 2.8, and see p. 57, n. 50.

[48]   Sheingorn, 'The Wise Mother', pp. 69–70 (1993), or p. 106 (2003). W. Scase, 'St Anne and the Education of the Virgin', in N. Rogers (ed.), *England in the Fourteenth Century* (London, 1993), pp. 81–96, at pp. 84–6.

[49]   David Park has made a list of English examples in C. Norton, D. Park and P. Binski, *Dominican Painting in East Anglia: the Thornham Parva Retable and the Musée de Cluny Frontal* (Woodbridge, 1987), pp. 51–2.

when – as in the case of Books of Hours made as bridal gifts for example – it was intended for women users.

In the development of the idea of Anne as Mary's teacher, a crucial piece of evidence is a panel painting whose two halves have now been reconstructed.[50] It was probably made for an altar at Thetford priory in Norfolk and dates from after its refoundation as a Dominican house in 1335. The very high standard of this work may be explained by the royal prince, Henry Earl of Lancaster, being the patron of this house. One panel shows the Crucifixion flanked by saints with a Dominican figure at each end, while the second panel shows – among other scenes of Mary's life – St Anne teaching her to read. (This latter panel is quite well known, as it is one of the treasures of the Musée de Cluny or Musée du Moyen Age in Paris.) Mary is shown as a girl, standing at a lectern with an open book on it, while her mother points vigorously at the word 'rex' ('king') in the Latin text. Its large script is made fully legible to the viewer and it reads: 'Audi filia et vide et inclina aurem tuam quia concupuit rex speciem tuam' ('Hearken, daughter, and see and incline thine ear, for the king has desired thy beauty'). The reference here is to the forty-fourth Psalm: 'Hearken, O daughter, and see and incline thine ear, and forget thy people and thy father's house, and the king shall greatly desire thy beauty, for he is the lord thy God'.[51] This text emphasizes the daughter's role as a mediator between her own family and the new one she forms, when she is sent away from her own home as a bride. Because she is betrothed to the king of Heaven, Mary is the mediator for all mankind. Through marriage, medieval women became 'ambassadors of culture' in Susan Bell's words.[52]

In commissioning the Thetford altar panels, the Dominicans were concerned with the theological doctrine that could be extrapolated from the image of Mary being instructed by her mother. They were not aiming to give women a larger role in Christian society, nor were they celebrating mothers and daughters with their books, although they may – if only unconsciously – have been acknowledging the role of their own mothers in pointing them towards literate prayer and a religious vocation when they were boys. In the Thetford image Mary is not being instructed at home, as the elaborate bronze lectern is an ecclesiastical

---

[50]   In addition to Norton, Park, Binski, *Dominican Painting*, David Park has summarized this work in *Age of Chivalry: English Society 1200–1400* (London, 1987), no. 564, pp. 447–9. The Thetford priory panels are also illustrated in colour by N. Coldstream, *The Decorated Style: Architecture and Ornament, 1240–1360* (London, 1994), plates ix and x.

[51]   'Audi, filia, et vide, et inclina aurem tuam; et obliviscere populum tuum et domum patris tui. Et concupiscent rex decorum tuum, quoniam ipse est dominus deus tuus', Psalm 44: 11–12. David Park discusses the theological tradition in Norton, Park and Binski, *Dominican Painting*, p. 50.

[52]   See the title of Bell's article, n. 1 above.

furnishing. St Anne is dressed in black and white, presumably to indicate that she is a widow. Perhaps these colours are also intended to evoke the distinctive black-and-white habits of the Domincan saints, who are depicted at either end of the other Thetford panel. They can be identified as St Dominic himself and St Peter Martyr, an inquisitor who had been assassinated in northern Italy in 1252; he displays the signs of his martyrdom, with blood spurting from an axe through his head and a wound to his heart.

The Ideal of the Virgin Mary as Learner and Teacher

Although the image of Anne teaching Mary was encouraged, and may even have originated, among intellectual male clerics like the Dominicans, it might have also functioned as a model of conduct for women in their homes. Henrietta Leyser has rightly observed:

> As has often been pointed out, these illustrations must be viewed with an open mind. Are they what they seem at first glance? Are these scenes evidence of increasing domestic literacy or should they be seen as new iconographical symbols of the Incarnation? Do we have to choose? The one interpretation should not exclude the other.[53]

In York at the parish church of All Saints, North Street, there is a depiction in stained glass of Anne teaching Mary that may share a patron with a prayer book, the Bolton Hours, likewise containing a full-page picture of Anne teaching. Both the glass and the book can be related to Margaret the wife of Nicholas Blackburn, who was mayor of York in 1412.[54] The glass, which depicts near life-size standing figures, exceptionally shows Anne as a fashionable young woman with a red and white head-dress and a red tunic brocaded with gold; Mary has blonde hair, with a floral or jewelled head-band, and she wears a gold brocaded tunic.[55] She is demonstrably learning to read, in the sense of pronouncing her

---

[53]   Leyser, *Medieval Women*, p. 139.

[54]   P. Cullum and J. Goldberg, 'How Margaret Blackburn Taught her Daughters: Reading Devotional Instruction in a Book of Hours', in J. Wogan-Browne, et al. (eds), *Medieval Women: Texts and Contexts in Late Medieval Britain: Essays for Felicity Riddy* (Turnhout, 2000), pp. 217–36, at pp. 223–33.

[55]   The window is illustrated in colour by A.B. Barton, *A Guide to the Church of All Saints North Street, York* (York, no date), p. 13, and in black and white by E. Duffy, *The Stripping of the Altars: Traditional Religion in England 1400–1580* (New Haven, CT, 1992), plate 82.

Figure 7.4 St Anne teaching the Virgin Mary, stained glass in All Saints Church, North Street, York

© David Titchener.

prayers from a text, as she holds a pointer in her right hand (like the image of St Louis with his mother Blanche of Castile) which rests on the Latin word 'Domine' ('Lord') in the prayer book open in front of her.[56] The large script, with only four lines to the page, reads in English translation: 'Lord, hear my prayer, give ear to my supplication'.[57] This is the beginning of Psalm 142, the last of the Seven Penitential Psalms. Margaret the wife of Nicholas Blackburn is portrayed in another window in the church with her prayer book open at the first of the Penitential Psalms (Psalm 6).[58] An inscription now lost, which was recorded in 1618, referred to Margaret and Nicholas as benefactors of the windows.[59] (Over time the medieval glass has been repaired and removed from one window to another.)

In the stained glass image the large script of Mary's book faces her and it is therefore readable by her, but it is upside-down for the parish congregation viewing the window from below. However, if Margaret Blackburn were the donor, the significance of the text would have been understood by her, as she begins the first Penitential Psalm in one window while Mary pronounces the seventh and final Psalm in the other. Through these images Margaret therefore enters into prayer along with the Virgin Mary, a concept that we have already seen being made visible in the depiction of Princess Claude of France learning to read through the intercession of St Anne and the Virgin.[60] Margaret may also have been the first owner of the prayer book known as the Bolton Hours, which is dated on stylistic grounds to around 1415.[61] Its full-page picture of St Anne is unusual in showing her teaching a group of three girls, who may be identified as the Three Marys, that is, the Virgin Mary and her half-sisters Mary Cleophas and Mary Salome.[62] This trio matches Margaret's own three daughters, Isabel, Alice and Agnes.[63] The text of the Virgin Mary's open book here is 'Domine, labia mea aperies' ('Lord, open my lips'), the opening words of the Hours of the Virgin Mary and an appropriate text for beginning reading. The Bolton Hours also

---

[56]   See n. 5 above.

[57]   'Domine, exaudi orationem meam; auribus percipe obsecrationem [meam]'. This text with its contractions is explicated by E.A. Gee, 'The Painted Glass of All Saints Church, North Street, York', *Archaeologia*, 102 (1969): 151–202, at p. 155.

[58]   Ibid., p. 155.

[59]   Ibid., p. 155.

[60]   See nn. 42–4 above.

[61]   York, Minster Library, MS Additional 2. Cullum and Goldberg, 'How Margaret Blackburn Taught', pp. 218–19.

[62]   Cullum and Goldberg, 'How Margaret Blackburn Taught', p. 230 and illustration 2 at p. 229.

[63]   Ibid., pp. 225, 232.

contain an alphabet and the standard elementary prayers for teaching reading, emphasizing that this is a teacher's book like Princess Claude's booklet.[64]

In Margaret Blackburn we therefore have evidence, although it is circumstantial, of a mother who had a prayer book to teach her daughters and who commissioned (with her husband) stained glass in her parish church showing the exemplary scene of Anne teaching Mary. Margaret would have used the Bolton Hours both at home and in public, when she and her family attended church. There she could contemplate her exemplary window and treasure the knowledge that Mary was depicted in it learning the Penitential Psalms, whose texts were also to be found in her prayer book. Furthermore, the Bolton Hours makes a connection between Anne and the Dominican order, as there is a full-page depiction at folio 185r of St Dominic holding an open book with the single word 'Anna' written on it, while at folio 105r there is a full-page depiction of St Peter Martyr. It looks as if, as at Thetford priory in the preceding century, the Dominicans at York had master-minded the iconography of Anne teaching Mary. Their priory there at Mickelgate was close to the Blackburns' home. It is possible that the scribe of the Bolton Hours, who identifies himself as 'Johannes nomine felix' was a Dominican friar.[65] The Dominicans are known to have produced prayer books for lay use; the scribe's signature in the Bolton Hours may indicate that his name in religion was 'Brother Felix'.

Margaret Blackburn is significant as a pious mother because she does not come from the highest social class, like the mothers of St Louis, King Alfred and Claude of France. In the production of both the prayer book and the stained glass she would have needed the expertise of intellectuals and craftsmen who, given the patriarchal structure of medieval society, were likely to be men. She also of course needed the funding and consent of her husband, whose wishes were paramount in law. Nevertheless, the resultant works of art, in both the Bolton Hours and the window in All Saints church, idealize and celebrate the intellectual and spiritual relationship of a mother with her daughters. This ideal of the mother as teacher took these forms only in the later Middle Ages, when literacy in the homes of the merchant middle class was establishing itself and beginning to measure up to patronage from the aristocracy.

In much the same period in central Europe a parallel image of the Virgin Mary taking the Child Jesus to school served a similar function to the cult in England of Anne teaching Mary. The celebration of the Child Jesus going to school for the first time was not necessarily at odds with the ideal of the mother initiating reading in the home, as it implies that the mother had prepared him

---

[64] Ibid., pp. 231–2. Clanchy, 'The ABC Primer', pp. 22–3. See also nn. 41–2 above.
[65] Cullum and Goldberg, 'How Margaret Blackburn Taught', pp. 219–20.

for school. In the depiction in the parish church at Tuse in Denmark of Jesus going to school, he approaches it with his book already open.[66] (This cycle of fifteenth-century wall paintings had been whitewashed over at the Reformation and was uncovered in 1890.) It is significant that it is Mary, rather than Joseph, who is the prime mover in taking him to school, as this runs counter to the place given to Joseph in St Luke's gospel. In a loose-leaf picture, dating from the fifteenth century and now in Nuremberg, Mary leads the Child Jesus by the hand with Joseph following behind; the Child has 'Ich bin Jesus' on the writing tablet he holds, which might suggest that he had already learned to read and write at home.[67] A woodcut from 1508, which would once have circulated in multiple copies, depicts Mary stepping into a classroom with the Child Jesus, as she declares in the German vernacular: 'I have brought forth my tender and beautiful child and I very much want to let him go to school.'[68] That it was the mother's responsibility to send her boy to school is assumed in a fifteenth-century German poem by Hermann von Sachsenheim.[69]

The ideal of Mary as the teacher of her child developed as a visual motif in a different way in late medieval Italy. The best known example is Boticelli's painting of the 'Madonna with the Book' (dating from around 1480 and now in Milan).[70] While resting the Christ Child on her lap, Mary holds open a prayer book whose Latin text includes the words 'Deo gratias' ('Thanks be to God'). The book rests on a table, as if it were ceremonially open on an altar, and another closed book is visible on a shelf in a corner. On the Child's arm is a golden bracelet in the form of a crown of thorns and he holds up three gold nails to symbolize his crucifixion. He looks up at Mary in acceptance and apprehension, as if he already knows the message of Scripture. The combination here of the book and the Child symbolize the Word made Flesh through the mediation of Mary. This doctrine had been powerfully exemplified at Modena cathedral, where a fresco uncovered in 1967 shows the Child Jesus seated on his mother's lap and holding

---

[66]   M. Clanchy, 'An Icon of Literacy: the Depiction at Tuse of Jesus Going to School', in P. Hermann (ed.), *Literacy in Medieval and Early Modern Scandinavian Culture* (Odense, 2005), pp. 47–73, at pp. 48–9, Figures 1–2.

[67]   Clanchy, 'An icon of literacy', p. 62, Figure 5.

[68]   'Ich han min Kind erzogen zart und schon/Und wolt es gern zu Schul lassen gon', Clanchy, 'An Icon of literacy', pp. 54–6, citing A. Bagley, 'Jesus at School', *Journal of Psychohistory*, 13 (1985): 13–31, at p. 17.

[69]   C. Edwards, 'Mothers' Boys and Mothers' Girls in the Pastourelle', *Forum for Modern Language Studies*, 35 (1999): 70–80, at p. 77.

[70]   Milan, Museo Poldi Pezzoli. R. Lightbown, *Sandro Boticelli: Life and Work* (London, 1989), p. 82 and plate 32 at p. 83. A. Cecchi, *Boticelli* (Milan, 2005), plates 214, 215, and p. 279, n. 68.

open with both hands a small book with quite a number of pages that he appears to be reading (its text is not now legible, although it is writ large).[71] As this life-size image (dating from the latter half of the fourteenth century) is placed immediately above the pulpit used for preaching to the people, its symbolism is evident, since the Child is unrealistically shown completely naked in order to represent the doctrine of the Incarnation where the Word is made Flesh. (The nakedness of Boticelli's Child is modified by a swaddling cloth around him.)

In a parish church near Lucca a fifteenth-century painting shows the Virgin and Child, with the Virgin holding a prayer book open in her left hand that displays her canticle 'Magnificat' ('My soul doth magnify the Lord') from St Luke's Gospel (2: 45–55).[72] The Child Jesus seated on her knee is depicted clothed, unlike Boticelli's Madonna with the Book or the fresco above the pulpit at Modena. He is crowned with a golden crown and wears a dark robe edged with gold brocade from his neck to his ankles. The Child represented here is Christ the King rather than the Word made Flesh. However, the symbolism of his being the Word of God is represented here most exceptionally by his holding a board with the alphabet and two-letter syllables (beginning with 'B' and 'C') displayed on it. (After pronouncing each letter of the alphabet correctly, the new reader proceeded to form syllables from these elements in alphabetical order.[73]) The Child's board, described as a 'tavola' ('table') in Italian or an 'abecedarium' in Latin, would have been a familiar object in any literate home.[74] It served the same function as a slate and enabled children to be initiated into reading without putting their fingers on precious books. The right-hand index finger of the Child in the Lucca painting points to the letter 'g' in the alphabet, which suggests he is depicted thinking about his name in the Tuscan vernacular where it is written 'Gesu' rather than the Latin 'Jesus'.

Would mothers, whether in towns or villages, who saw these public images have come away with the message that they too should be teaching their children to read? Only a minority of families could afford prayer books, although a larger

---

[71]   R. Gibbs, *Tomaso da Modena* (Cambridge, 1989), plates 98–9 and comment at pp. 160–62, 288–9.

[72]   C. Frugoni, 'The Imagined Woman', in C. Klapisch-Zuber (ed.), *A History of Women in the West*, 2, *Silences of the Middle Ages* (Cambridge, MA, 1992), pp. 336–422, at Figure 40 and comment at pp. 397–9. I am grateful to Professor Christine Meek, who obtained a colour transparency of this image for me.

[73]   See nn. 6 and 8 above.

[74]   R. Black, *Humanism and Education in Medieval and Renaissance Italy* (Cambridge, 2001), pp. 35–8. Frugoni, 'The Imagined Woman', p. 398, is mistaken in describing the Child as holding a 'chalk palette'. The object depicted is a framed wooden board with a surface for writing, which has either been painted white or has white paper or parchment fixed to it.

proportion might have possessed prayer rolls or single-sheet woodcuts with short texts like the German vernacular example from 1508.[75] A sixteenth-century broadsheet, headed 'beaulx abc belles heures' ('beautiful ABCs, beautiful Hours'), shows a pedlar hawking dozens of loose unbound booklets which he carries in a tray suspended from his shoulders.[76] These would have been printed items, perhaps including some hand-coloured initials to justify the description 'beautiful [Books of] Hours'. Even before the production of movable metal type (the invention of the mid fifteenth century achieved by Gutenberg), ABC booklets would have become cheaper once they were made of paper rather than parchment.[77] Paper was also a more receptive surface than parchment for the sort of block-printing from woodcuts that preceded Gutenberg's invention.

By 1500 many families in Latin Christendom, ranging from Portugal and Ireland in the west to Poland and Scandinavia in the east, may have possessed ABC booklets containing elementary prayers. This can be no more than a conjecture, but it makes better sense of the scattered and fragmentary evidence than the presumption that most people were entirely illiterate. Nicholas Orme has pointed out that by the thirteenth century, and perhaps much earlier, 'everyone knew someone who could read, and everyone's life depended to some extent on reading and writing'.[78] The Dominicans, who had probably master-minded the pictorial ideal of St Anne teaching the Virgin Mary, may have been reflecting existing social practice rather than introducing something new. Since the Fourth Lateran Council in 1215 bishops and parish clergy had repeatedly enjoined everybody to learn their basic prayers, which now included the 'Hail Mary' as well as the 'Our Father'.[79] Although this legislation did not require the prayers to be in writing, it cannot be a coincidence that ABC booklets contained precisely these texts.[80]

Felicity Riddy has asked: 'Why should we assume that within the household the oversight of reading would have been the responsibility of the male head? Why should we not see reading as a domestic activity that came under the aegis of the wife?'[81] This is what the new images of the Virgin Mary as a learner and

---

[75]   See n. 68 above.

[76]   Paris, Bibliothèque de l'Arsenal, 'Cris de Paris', no. 264, illustrated by M. Mostert, *Oraliteit* (Amsterdam, 1998), p. 85.

[77]   Clanchy, 'An Icon of literacy', p. 64. Clanchy, 'The ABC Primer', p. 21 (printing), p. 30 (multiple copies).

[78]   Orme, *Medieval Children*, p. 240.

[79]   Clanchy, 'The ABC Primer', p. 18.

[80]   Ibid., pp. 24–5.

[81]   F. Riddy, 'Mother Knows Best: Reading Social Change in a Courtesy Text', *Speculum*, 71 (1996): 66–86, at p. 84, n. 65.

teacher suggest. Miri Rubin has placed them in the broad cultural context of the growth of a variety of devotions in the later Middle Ages celebrating 'Mary, local and familiar'.[82] Their inspiration had usually originated from the theological and devotional concerns of reforming male clergy, notably the Dominicans in the fourteenth century and the Cistercians before that. In the twelfth century, for example, St Bernard's sermons on the Song of Songs had found instruction in it for his monks by drawing on ideals of the feminine and the maternal.[83] Caroline Bynum's study of 'Jesus as mother' rightly concludes that this sort of allegorical language does not tell us 'what monks thought of actual women or of their own mothers'.[84] Obviously, however, neither male clergy nor pious ladies could have a monopoly of the feminine and the maternal. Through the dissemination of texts of prayers in people's homes and public images in churches in the fourteenth and fifteenth centuries, clerical learning intersected with the concerns of actual mothers in preparing their children for life in an increasingly literate society.

---

[82]   *Mother of God: a History of the Virgin Mary* (London, 2009), pp. 214, 221.

[83]   *Sancti Bernardi Opera*, ed. J. Leclercq, C.H. Talbot, H. Rochais (8 vols, Rome, 1957–1977), sermon 9 on Canticles, para. 2 and para. 9, 1, pp. 43, 47.

[84]   C.W. Bynum, *Jesus as Mother: Studies in the Spirituality of the High Middle Ages igh M* (Berkeley, CA, 1982), p. 167.

Chapter 8

Who is my Mother?
Honouring Parents in Medieval Exegesis of the Ten Commandments

Lesley Smith

The fourth commandment, 'Honour your father and your mother, that you may be long-lived on the earth the Lord your God shall give you' (Exod. 20: 12), is one of the rare occasions in the Jewish and Christian scriptures when women are referred to as specifically as men.[1] In the words of the first-century Jewish writer, Philo Judaeus, we should honour 'each separately and both in common'.[2] In Scripture as patriarchal as the Hebrew Bible, with its religion of Abraham, Isaac and Jacob, specific (and positive) references to women are worth attention – even when, as here in Exodus, the citation is not to a particular woman, or even to women in general, but to a particular sort of female role. Motherhood is what is being singled out here as worthy of honour.

The Exodus reference is important for its rarity, but also because of where it is to be found – not in just any part of Scripture, but in the Ten Commandments (or Decalogue), one of the fundamental texts of both the Jewish and Christian faiths. The position of the Commandments as part of both religions gives them special importance, serving as a link between the two Covenants. Medieval Christian biblical interpreters were careful to spell out that, contrary to the beliefs of some heretical groups, the Hebrew Bible had not been superseded by the New Testament, but remained part of Christian Scripture. Although, since the coming of Christ, almost all of the 613 *mitzvuot* or laws of the Torah were no longer binding, the Decalogue retained its force: it was just as much a way to God for the Christian as it was for the Jew. This was a Gospel teaching. Jesus is

---

[1] 'Honora patrem tuum et matrem tuam, ut sis longaevus super terram, quam Dominus Deus tuus dabit tibi.' Readers acquainted with some religious traditions may be surprised to see that this is the fourth commandment; a discussion on the history of Decalogue numbering follows later.

[2] Philo Judaeus, *On the Decalogue*, ed. F.H. Colson, The Works of Philo Judaeus, 7 (London, 1937), p. 31.

specific in saying that he comes not to dismantle the Law but to fulfil it, and his immediate reply to the rich young man who asks how he can be perfect is, 'Keep the commandments'.[3]

Here, then, in one of the central ethical texts of both Jews and Christians is a recognition of the role of mothers, and an unequivocal statement that they are to be honoured. Each parent is mentioned independently: a formula such as 'honour your parents' or 'ancestors' is not employed. In a volume devoted to motherhood, then, commentary on this key text is not out of place; and unlike many of the things medieval people wrote about, this precept is one that most, if not all, people in modern society would immediately recognize and subscribe to. Yet this may not mean that medieval concerns were the same as those of today, or that their discussions were framed in similar terms. I shall focus this essay largely on the work of biblical commentators working in Paris and Oxford, from the twelfth to the fourteenth centuries; although they were writing in a scholarly context, most were Franciscan and Dominican friars – members of Orders with a directly pastoral vocation. Their work is interesting in its own right, and also important for its influence on later medieval pastoral traditions.

We must start by situating this commandment vis-à-vis the other nine. The number and ordering of the precepts was an important question for medieval interpreters, both because they considered the details of the biblical text to have meaning, and because they thought that number was an important means of understanding God. Commandments commentators from Augustine onwards were eager to point out the importance of there being *ten* precepts – ten being a perfect number in antiquity and the middle ages with a special affinity to unity and comprehensiveness – and to note connections between this set of ten things and other tens elsewhere in the Bible.[4] The commandments were identified with the Ten Words (*ʿǎśeret haddᵉbārîm*) described in the book of Exodus (Exod. 34: 28; and see Deut. 4: 3, Deut. 10: 4). Augustine of Hippo also coupled them with the ten-stringed instrument of psalm 144: 9, and he made a detailed comparison of the commandments and the Ten Plagues of Egypt, which medieval commentators commonly reprised.[5] For Augustine, the commandments were

---

    [3]   Matt. 5: 17: 'Nolite putare quoniam veni solvere legem, aut prophetas: non veni solvere, sed adimplere'. 'Keep the commandments': Matt. 19: 16–21; Mk 10: 17–21; Lk 18: 18–22.

    [4]   There is not space here to consider the importance of number to medieval commentators, but readers may continue the discussion in, for instance, N. Hiscock, *The Symbol at Your Door: Number and Geometry in Religious Architecture of the Greek and Latin Middle Ages* (Aldershot, 2007), and V.F. Hopper, *Medieval Number Symbolism: its Sources, Meaning, and Influence on Thought and Expression* (Columbia, NY, 1938).

    [5]   Augustine: Sermon 8 on the Ten Plagues of Egypt (*De decem plagis aegyptorum et decem praeceptis legis*); Sermon 9 on the Ten Strings of the Harp (*De decem chordis*), in *Sancti*

individual remedies for each of the plagues. The fourth plague is of dog flies (*cynomyia*). The animals they attack have the general characteristic of all dogs that they do not recognize their parents – by which he means that, when they are old enough to live independently, young dogs do not stay with their parents in a family group, but go off to live alone. Hence it is particularly appropriate that puppies are born blind, to signal that they will not acknowledge their parents.[6] If dogs were to recognize their parents, they would not have to suffer the annoying attacks of the insects; so those children who honour their fathers and mothers will be free from the annoyances of the world. Most of Augustine's couplings of plagues and commandments are less than convincing, but even in this company, the pairing seems far-fetched. Nevertheless, Augustine's exegesis was commonly known to and copied by later commentators such as Rabanus Maurus, Stephen Langton and William of Auxerre.[7]

Exodus tells that the Ten Words were written on two tablets of stone, but Jewish and Christian scholars had different views on how ten should be divided into two, since the Bible does not say how it was done. Whereas Jews thought that there would be five precepts on each tablet, Christians divided them in less straightforward ways, with one tablet containing those commandments pertaining to God and the second those pertaining to one's neighbour.[8] This in itself was open to interpretation, since it had first to be decided how many commandments exactly *did* refer to God, but the commonly accepted arrangement followed Augustine's Trinitarian exposition, with three commandments about God on the first tablet (that is, having no other gods; not taking the Lord's name in vain; keeping the sabbath), and seven about one's

---

Aurelii Augustini. Sermones de vetere testamento, ed. C. Lambot, CCSL, 41 (Turnhout, 1961); English translation in *The Works of St Augustine: a Translation for the 21st Century*, trans. with notes by E. Hill, ed. J.E. Rotelle (Brooklyn, NY, 1990), part 3, sermons: vol. 1, sermons 1–19.

[6]   Augustine, *Sermones*, no. 8, pp. 85–6.

[7]   See for instance, Rabanus Maurus, *Commentarius in Exodum*, lib. 2, c. 13, PL 108: 100–105, and William of Auxerre, *Magistri Guillermus Altissiodorensis. Summa Aurea*, ed. J. Ribaillier, Spicilegium Bonaventurianum, 16–20 (4 vols in 6, Paris and Rome, 1980–1987), here vol. 3(2): lib. 3, tr. 44, c. 5, pp. 844–6. The Langton commentary on Exodus has never been printed; as a base text, I used the version in Oxford, Trinity College, MS 65.

[8]   G.E. Mendenhall, 'Law and Covenant in Israel and the Ancient Near East', *Biblical Archaeologist*, 17 (1954): 26–46 and 49–76, compared the two stone tablets with Hittite tablets of sovereign pacts ('suzerainty treaties'). These took the form of two identical tablets, each of which had the entire text of the pact written on it, one of which was given to each side. Mendenhall suggested that the two tablets of the Decalogue were of this form, with one copy meant for the Israelites, and one for God: see B.S. Childs, *Exodus. A Commentary* (London, 1974), Chapter 17(2A).

neighbour on the second (that is, honouring parents, not killing, not committing adultery, not stealing, not bearing false witness, not coveting one's neighbour's goods, nor his wife). According to this division, the first commandment about God encompasses Exodus 20: 2–6, which includes the acknowledgement of a single God, and the prohibitions of idolatry and graven images. No medieval Christian interpreter could resist the opportunity to involve the Trinity, and the three precepts of the first tablet are an excellent example of how one might do this. Each precept is tied to a single member of the Trinity, with the first commandment specially associated with God the Father, and thus (for instance) with unity and authority, the second with God the Son, and thus with equality, and the third with God the Holy Spirit, and thus with community.[9] It was also routine for medieval commentators to make links across from the precepts of one tablet to those of the other. For example, to be comprehensive, the Law had to cover obligation in thought (or heart), word, and deed, but the balance of these three was reversed on the two tablets. For the first tablet, the best form of obligation was that of the heart, and so the first commandment there is belief in the One God; but for the second tablet, the best form of obligation was obligation by deed, and so the first commandment on this tablet is to honour one's parents.[10] Although honouring might also be taken to be a matter of the heart, here the emphasis is on a more direct provision of charity. Medieval scholars point out the rightness of the first commandment on the first tablet referring to God the Father, and the first commandment on the second tablet to the honouring of one's earthly father. Although it was not unknown for medieval interpeters to conceptualize God (or, at least, Jesus) as mother, no commentator I have come across makes this additional link.

Medieval Christian scholars thought it important that this commandment to honour father and mother should stand in first place on the second stone tablet, as this shows the priority of parents in the scheme of precepts, and thus in God's plan for the world. It is, indeed, notable that this small, domestic commandment about honouring your father and your mother is given first place, before any of the

---

[9]   See, for example, Peter Lombard, *Sententiae in IV libris distinctae*, ed. I.F. Brady (2 vols, Grottaferrata, 1971, 1981), lib. III, d. 37, c. 3. See also Thomas of Chobham, *Thomae de Chobham Summa confessorum*, ed. F. Broomfield, Analecta Mediaevalia Namurcensia, 25 (Louvain, 1968), art. 3, d. 1, q. 8a, p. 27; and William of Auxerre, *Summa aurea*, lib. 3, tr. 44, c. 2, pp. 835–6.

[10]   See, for example, Alexander of Hales, *Glossa in Quatuor Libros Sententiarum*, vol. 3, Bibliotheca Franciscana Scholastica Medii Aevi, 14 (Quaracchi, 1954), lib. 3, d. 37, c. 3. Alexander (d. 1245) was an English master of theology in Paris. He joined the Franciscan Order in 1236, without resigning his chair of theology, which was subsequently filled by Franciscan scholars, giving them an official foothold in the University.

well-known commandments on what might seem to be more important issues, such as killing. Why might this be so? The most obvious point is that (at some time) everyone has a mother and a father. Whereas for many people questions of killing, or even stealing and adultery, might seem distant eventualities, this one is immediate and (for all but the most unfortunate) universally applicable. The singular 'you' of the Latin (rendered 'thou' in older English versions of the text, and an accurate reflection of the singular Hebrew form of the original) is used in order to speak directly to every individual person, and confirm that each commandment is to apply to everyone.

For Jews such as Philo Judaeus, dividing the commandments equally on the two tablets, five and five, this is the fifth commandment, not the fourth, and the last two precepts forbidding covetousness are elided into one. In this ordering, honouring one's father and mother stands as the last precept on the first tablet, forming a bridge between the commandments proper to God and those which concern one's neighbour. This is an apt placement, says Philo, on a border, because parents by nature stand on the borderline between mortal and immortal existence – mortal, because of their own mortality, but immortal because their own act of creation in begetting children assimilates them to God, the generator of all things.[11] In begetting children, Philo adds, parents act as the servants of God, and whoever dishonours the servant – the parent – dishonours the master – God.[12] Thus the precepts of the first tablet, for Philo and the Jews, move from God as spiritual parent to father and mother as temporal parents; and for Philo this movement is something of a litmus test: those who are unable to show reverence to their visible and present parents, 'near at hand and seen by the eye', are most unlikely to be able to show reverence to the invisible God.[13]

For Philo there was another reason for the inclusion of this precept on the first tablet, and that was its positive form: it is the only commandment related to one's neighbour to be cast in positive terms, 'Honour ... ', in the same way that the commandment about the sabbath day begins, 'Remember ... '. Since all the remaining commandments referring to one's neighbour are prohibitions (the famous 'thou shalt not's), Philo thought it more suitable for the positive precepts to stay together on the first tablet.[14] The Franciscan scholar and mystic Bonaventure (d. 1274) gives another reason why honouring parents should come first, which is that kindness should come before blamelessness – these being the

---

[11] Philo, *Decalogue*, p. 61.
[12] Ibid., p. 67.
[13] Ibid., p. 69.
[14] Ibid., p. 33.

two parts of justice, doing good and refraining from evil.[15] The two sides of justice distill to two commandments: do unto others as you would have them do unto you; and do not do unto others anything you would not wish done to you. The more active precept is the better, which is why the positive action of honouring is placed before the negative prohibitions. For other Christian commentators, the uniqueness of this positive form was the reason that the precept should stand at the head of the second tablet, and have priority over the others. The Paris Franciscan master, John of La Rochelle (d. 1245), whose discussion of this commandment is particularly full, states that the positive phrasing is necessary because honour to parents is something that people are likely to omit rather than commit. However, the positive wording also shows the absolute quality of the precept: it is *never* wrong to show honour to parents, although there may be some circumstances in which it may be the lesser of two goods. For instance, if anyone desires to enter a religious Order, they should not put off doing so in order to look after their parents. John resolves this apparent selfishness by noting that no believer should think that they can only aid their parents physically: the prayers of a vowed religious will, in the long run, do parents more good than providing them with food and drink.[16] Simon of Hinton (fl. mid-thirteenth century), from the Dominican house in Oxford, agrees, and adds that this is a positive precept because it seeks to recall humanity's corrupted nature to the natural order of things, by reminding children that their duty is to their parents.[17]

---

[15]   Bonaventure, *Collationes de decem praeceptis*, in *Opera omnia*, 5 (Quaracchi, 1891), Coll. 5, here cc. 3–4, p. 523 ('*et beneficentia melior est quam innocentia*'); English translation, *St. Bonaventure's Collations on the Ten Commandments*, trans. P.J. Spaeth, in *Works of St Bonaventure*, ed. F.E. Coughlin, vol. 6 (St Bonaventure, NY, 1995).

[16]   John's Decalogue commentary is part of a theological treatise known as the *Summa fratris Alexandri*, so-called because of its (and his) association with Alexander of Hales. However, the editors of the Quaracchi edition have shown that John was the most likely author of at least books 1 and 3: *Doctoris Irrefragibilis Alexandri de Hales Summa Theologica seu sic ab origine dicta 'Summa fratris Alexandri'*, ed. V. Doucet, vol. 4 (Quaracchi, 1948), here lib. 3, pt 2, inq. 3, tr. 2, sect. 1, q. 2, tit. 4, cc. 1–4 (a reference which, incidentally, gives a sense of how marvellously John follows the medieval method of dividing a large topic into manageable questions, and approaching, arguing and answering each one, bit by bit).

[17]   The discussion of the Decalogue by Simon of Hinton I have used here is taken from his most popular work (judged by the number of extant manuscripts), the *Summa ad instructionem iuniorum*, which also circulated in an abridged form, the *Exceptiones*. The *Summa* is printed among the works of Jean Gerson, 'Tractatus de decem praeceptis', in *Joannis Gersonii. Opera omnia*, vol. 1, pt. 3 (Antwerp, 1706); the *Exceptiones* are edited from Cambridge, Sidney Sussex College, MS 73 (Δ. 4. 11), in P.A. Walz, 'The "Exceptiones" from the "Summa" of Simon of Hinton', *Angelicum*, 13 (1936): 283–368.

This is the only commandment of either tablet with a promise attached: 'that you may be long-lived on the earth the Lord your God shall give you'. Why is the promise there? Is the commandment so difficult to keep that it needs a bribe or a reward? Is the promise fair? Medieval expositors answer the first question by answering the last: the promise is an especially just one because it is only reasonable that, if you spend time looking after those older than yourself, you should yourself live at least as long as they do. It is because of the justice of the promise that there *is* a promise – it may need no other rationale. Bonaventure, however, regards the promise as part of a much broader landscape. In his opinion, it applies to all the commandments of the second tablet, just as the threat in the first precept ('visiting the iniquity of the fathers upon the children, even to the third and fourth generation of those who hate me', Exod. 20: 5) applies to all those of the first tablet; but it neither is, nor needs to be, repeated after each commandment. The promise is there, he seems to suggest, because the Jews needed an incentive to stop them falling into idolatry and avarice.[18] This was a common accusation against the Jews, and it is one that Bonaventure (not a notably anti-Judaic writer) seems to have taken from the discussion by William of Auxerre, a secular exegete working in Paris, who may have been one of Bonaventure's teachers. As reported by William, 'many people say' rather more unpleasant things, since they add that Jews 'do not wish to provide for the necessities of their parents'.[19] William himself, however, does not think that this is why the precept has the promise ('it is not because of the Jews' avarice'). Rather, he has three more positive proposals: it is there because faith without works is dead; because pro-active works of mercy, such as piety to parents, commend the faithful to God more than a simple omission of an evil act; and because if, out of love for God, someone helps another person to live, then it is a fitting example of divine goodness that they themselves are given life, both now and in the world to come.[20] Thomas of Chobham (d. before 1236), whose written output is concentrated on pastoral works, agrees: with the promise, God invites everyone to undertake the *opera misericordiae*, since it is by these positive works of mercy that God will judge believers at Judgement Day.[21]

However, interpreters are not so blind to reality as not to see that this promise does not always seem to be carried through. Those who show conspicuous *pietas* towards their elders do not always seem to get their reward in this life. The response to this in the standard twelfth-century biblical commentary, the

---

[18] Bonaventure, *Commentaria in quatuor libros Sententiarum*, in *Opera Omnia*, 1–4 (Quaracchi, 1882–1889), here vol. 3, lib. 3, d. 37, dub. 4, p. 833.
[19] William of Auxerre, *Summa aurea*, lib. 3, tr. 44, c. 3, p. 839.
[20] Ibid., pp. 839–40.
[21] Thomas of Chobham, *Summa confessorum*, art. 3, d. 1, q. 8a, p. 29.

Glossa, is that one may live long either in person or in the memory of others: those who come after will remember the good works and the person who did them. Bonaventure has a subtler variation on this theme. For him, quality as well as quantity of life is important. In one of his characteristic threefold expositions of the biblical text, he says that showing honour by reverence leads to a more glorious life; showing honour by obedience leads to a happier life; and showing honour by beneficence or kindness leads to a richer or wealthier life.[22] Hugh of St Cher, an influential Dominican commentator and teacher (d. 1263), on the other hand, thought both rewards could be granted: one will live a longer life in this present world, and obtain future glory in the next. One ought to observe the commandments *intus et foris* – according to their inner (mystical) and outer (literal) meaning; and so it is just to expect both literal and mystical rewards.[23] In the previous century, however, Hugh of St Victor (d. 1142) sounded a warning note to help explain the apparent disjuncture between the promise and its earthly fulfilment: it is not sufficient, he says, to love one's parents on account of their worldly selves, in their humanness alone; you have to love them because of the grace of God shown in them, and for God's sake. Only by loving the spiritual in another person can the faithful person expect a spiritual reward.[24] Nicholas of Lyra, O.F.M. (d. 1349) acknowledges tacitly that justice may not always be seen to be done, but nevertheless, 'it sometimes happens through divine arrangement, secretly, that those honouring their parents do not live long at all, and vice versa; but the whole thing is ordered by God for the better reward of the good and punishment of the evil'.[25] For Nicholas, God's mysterious ways are not always evident to humanity. In Christian doctrine, with its emphasis on the world to come, there is always the possibility of a second chance – an unseen but definite world in which justice reigns, and everyone finally gets their due reward. A question not asked, but an obvious one for a religion with the goal and prize of an eternal spiritual life, is why a Christian with a confident hope of the world to come (in contrast to mainstream Jewish belief, which placed much less emphasis on an afterlife) would want to live long in the land. The joys of this life are not so easily abandoned, it would seem. To get round this, earth could be interpreted as heaven. John Wyclif (d. 1384) follows the line

[22]　Bonaventure, *Collationes de decem praeceptis*, Coll. 5, nos 6–9, pp. 523–4 (Latin); pp. 73–5 (English).

[23]　Hugh of St Cher, *Postilla in totam bibliam* (Paris, 1533), on Exod. 20: 12.

[24]　Hugh of St Victor, *De sacramentis christianae fidei*, ed. and trans. R.J. Deferrari (Cambridge, MA, 1951), I.12.x.

[25]　Nicholas of Lyra, *Postilla litteralis in totam bibliam* (Strassburg, 1492), on Exod. 20: 12.

that 'the earth your Lord God shall give you' is a reference to heaven, which is 'what we most desire'.[26]

The Oxford secular master Robert Grosseteste (d. 1253) adds his own interesting twist to the question of reward. Grosseteste's theological education was not gained by the normal route through the schools, and often his writing does not follow the lines of discussion commonly pursued by the predominantly Paris-trained teaching masters we have heard from so far. His treatise on the Decalogue is very much a case of an author going where his interests take him, rather than where traditional treatments of the material might dictate. He gives the commandment to honour one's parents the longest exposition of any of the Ten, perhaps because, as he notes when condemning superstition, it is in the family that most people's religious education and observance is developed, and where they are most able to practise the Gospel commandment to love.[27] Grosseteste's individuality (copied later by John Wyclif) extends to his adding other rewards for keeping this commandment to the promise of long life.[28] He takes these from examples in the Book of Ecclesiasticus (3: 2–15) which, with the Roman poet Seneca, is his favourite source for his discussion of this commandment, along with a keen eye for the detailed observation of human relations. The extra gifts gained from keeping the commandment are: the joy that one will have in one's own children, who will honour one in return; the blessing of God the Father; the blessing of one's earthly father; the reflected glory that the son receives when it is clear his father is honoured – as opposed to the shame he should bear if his father should be in need; relief from every distress; and relief from the chains of sin.

Grosseteste is unique in talking about parents' treatment of children, and once again his treatment is repeated by Wyclif.[29] Children must be moulded like wax, whilst they are still young enough to take on good habits and learn what

---

[26]   Johannis Wyclif, *Tractatus de Mandatis Divinis*, ed. J. Loserth and F.D. Matthew (London: published for the Wyclif Society by C.K. Paul and Co., 1922), c. 22, pp. 304–305: '*summe appetimus*'. In this area, Wyclif was writing within the tradition of his thirteenth-century models, and the most unusual part of his commentary is that he follows much of the treatise of his Oxford predecessor, Robert Grosseteste.

[27]   *Robert Grosseteste, De decem mandatis*, ed. R.C. Dales and E.B. King, Auctores Britannici medii aevi, 10 (Oxford, 1987), pp. 38–58. Lesley Smith, 'The *De decem mandatis* of Robert Grosseteste', in M. O'Carroll (ed.), *Robert Grosseteste and the Beginnings of a British Theological Tradition* (Rome, 2003), pp. 265–88; J. McEvoy, 'Robert Grosseteste on the Ten Commandments', *Recherches de Théologie Ancienne et Médiévale*, 58 (1991): 167–205.

[28]   Grosseteste, *De decem mandatis*, pp. 40–41; Wyclif, *De mandatis divinis*, c. 22, pp. 306–9.

[29]   Grosseteste, *De decem mandatis*, pp. 48–50; Wyclif, *De mandatis divinis*, c. 23, pp. 328–9.

is right. Sparing the rod definitely spoils the child (Proverbs 13: 24), and it is sinful not to chastise children who sin; for how else will they know the error of their ways? Children treated with laxity, whose moral and religious education is neglected, will not thank you for it when they grow up; on the contrary, they will live to punish the parent who did not teach them to know better. Grosseteste considers both ends of life: children who look on their parents and despise them should think about the future.

> There are those, however, who are either ashamed of, or annoyed and angry with, or even despise the poverty and old age of their parents, and the inconveniences their old age brings, such as failing senses, weakening strength, the ugly shrivelling of wrinkled skin, a curved back, trembling limbs, tottering steps, the stuttering speech of childhood, the praising of the past and disliking of the present, being swift to complain and getting angry over nothing, and many other similar things.[30]

The singularity of Grosseteste's discussion only points up what should now be obvious, that for medieval commentators the children whose mothers and fathers are to be honoured are not children in the sense of minors, but grown-up adults in their own right. In contrast to the Sunday School version of the Decalogue, in which 'Honour your father and your mother' was used as a way of making small children polite and obedient to their elders, medieval commentators always take a different line. We should honour parents at all times, says Nicholas of Lyra, but especially in their old age.[31] In the medieval reading, it is adult children who are to honour their elderly parents, by showing them the reverence that age should be accorded and by providing them with the necessities of life. As Peter Comestor (d. 1178/9) notes, the 'honour' to father and mother must be a double honour, both of showing reverence and ministering to their needs.[32] In a society without social benefits and pensions provided by the State, the protection of the old by the young is considered to be both necessary and reasonable. Moreover, the practicality of providing for their parents' physical needs is always to be coupled with the more affective showing of reverence: the two go hand in hand. In the words of the Gloss, 'A man opens his eyes because of his parents, and begins this

---

[30]   Grosseteste, *De decem mandatis*, p. 47, an exposition of Ecclus 3: 14–15: 'Son, support the old age of your father … And if his understanding fail have patience with him, and despise him not'. The Latin text is in Smith, 'The *De decem mandatis*', p. 276. As I date this work, Grosseteste would have been seventy years old when he wrote this passage.

[31]   Nicholas of Lyra, *Postilla litteralis*, on Ecclesiasticus 3: 2–10: 'Children, hear the judgement of your father'.

[32]   Peter Comestor, *Historia scholastica*, c. 40: *Explicatio decalogi*, PL 198: 1163–1166, here at 1165.

life on account of their love; hence this is the greatest commandment of this tablet ... [and] whoever does not show reverence to parents will not show it to others either.'[33] Philo's interpretation of this point is reminiscent of an older pagan tradition. Children who ignore their parents are worse than beasts, he says, who can often be seen to behave with great piety towards their progenitors. He gives a number of examples from the animal kingdom, including storks, where the old stay in nests whilst their offspring fly off to forage for food for them.[34] 'For children have nothing of their own which does not come from their parents, either bestowed from their own resources or acquired by means which originate from them.'[35]

We can be sure that the commandment refers to adult children when we put it side-by-side with the other Torah *mitzvuot* dealing with relations with one's father and mother. These include Exodus 21: 15, 'He who strikes his father or mother shall be put to death'; Exodus 21: 17, 'He who curses his father or mother shall die the death'; Leviticus 20: 9, 'He who curses his father or his mother, dying let him die'; and Deuteronomy 27: 16, 'Cursed be he who honours not his father and mother'. A feature of these verses is their place amongst the Torah laws which carry the death penalty for those who break them. This most serious of penalties is obviously not directed at small children, but at adults and their relations with their more elderly parents. Such a serious punishment requires that the texts receive careful exegesis. Nicholas of Lyra looks to the Jewish tradition, mediated through the northern French rabbi Solomon ben Isaac, known as Rashi (d. 1105), for advice. Rashi explains that Exodus 21: 15 does not refer to light physical admonition, or any sort of blow struck as a game or in jest, but to serious blows which result in bleeding or bruising.[36] The blows must be struck on purpose and not accidentally. As well as detailing the sort of violence involved, Rashi is equally specific about the type of death penalty they call for: strangulation – although, of course, this would have been the case only in the days of the Temple, when there was a Jewish court that could sentence wrongdoers and carry out punishment. Again quoted by Nicholas, Rashi is specific about the sort of cursing of parents envisaged by Exodus 21: 17 and Leviticus 20: 9. These are not occasional grumbling curses, nor anything said as a joke, but cursing that has become habitual. Strikingly, Rashi adds that the

---

[33]   *Glossa* on Deut. 5: 16: *Biblia latina cum glossa ordinaria* (Strassburg: A. Rusch, [1480/1]).

[34]   Philo, *Decalogue*, p. 65.

[35]   Philo, *Decalogue*, p. 67.

[36]   Nicholas of Lyra, *Postilla litteralis*, on Exod. 21: 15, quoting Rashi, *Pentateuch with Targum Onkelos* ..., tr. M. Rosenbaum and A.M. Silbermann, vol. 2: Exodus (London, 1930), p. 111.

death penalty even applies to those who curse their father and their mother in this most serious manner after their parents' death.[37]

Mention of penalties, however, brings home the point that the Decalogue itself does not carry specific punishments, aside from the general warning that God is a jealous God, who visits iniquity down the generations. Whereas the individual Torah *mitzvuot* have the character of positive injunctions which can be kept or broken, and, if broken, attract penalties, the Decalogue is judged to be of quite another nature. Its laws are descriptive rather than prescriptive: they cannot be broken, in the same way that the law of gravity cannot be broken. The commandments are seen not as matters for individual choice; rather, they lay out the irreducible minimum rules for what it means to be a member of the household of God. Moreover, in spite of the inclusion of the promise of long life, this commandment (and the other nine) should be obeyed out of love, not fear. This question of motive is particularly important for Augustine.[38] On a number of occasions he asks whether it is better to do good and obey God through fear or through love, and his answer is always unequivocal: 'we cling to Christ by love, not fear of punishment ... He who does not sin only through fear of punishment is an enemy to righteousness'. Rashi has an interesting view point on the same question, when he discusses Leviticus 19: 3, 'Let everyone fear his mother and his father'. The Leviticus text, he says, puts mother before father here because it is natural for the child to fear its father more than its mother; and so Scripture puts 'mother' first to show that she, too, should be feared. This is in contrast, he adds, to the commandment, which orders the honouring of the father before the mother, since in this case it is clear that it is much more natural for the child to honour his mother more, since 'she endeavours to win him over by kindly words'.[39]

What exactly does honouring entail? How can a child repay what it owes to its parents? It seems impossible, says Robert Grosseteste, because 'no riches or treasure or secular rank can compare to the gift of life'.[40] Yet honour must be shown. Hugh of St Cher neatly states that honour must encompass the inside and the outside of the person: you must show reverence, and you must

---

[37] Nicholas of Lyra, *Postilla litteralis*, on Exod. 21: 17 and Lev. 20: 9, quoting Rashi, *Pentateuch*, vol. 3: Leviticus (London, 1932), p. 93.

[38] Augustine, Letter 145, in *Epistulae*, pt 3, ed. A. Goldbacher, CSEL, 44 (Vienna and Leipzig, 1904), pp. 266–73, here at pp. 269, 271. See also, for example, Augustine, *Sermones*, 9, nos 8–9, pp. 122–6 or, in general, Augustine, *De spiritu et littera*, PL 44: 199–246. The twin motives of fear and love were commonly discussed by later commentators: see, for example, Bonaventure's second *collatio* on the commandments.

[39] Rashi on Lev. 19: 3: *Pentateuch*, vol. 3, pp. 84–6.

[40] Grosseteste, *De decem mandatis*, p. 42.

provide for the necessities of life.[41] By the time the Observant Augustinian friar Dederich of Münster wrote his hugely popular catechism in the late fifteenth century, more apparently needed to be said. Unlike our earlier writers, working in an academic milieu for a clerical audience, Dederich was writing with a more directly pastoral intent. The difference in detail between his exposition and the earlier scholastics points up what is generally forgotten – that genre is as much an issue in theological writing as it is in literature. Dederich takes us to a vivid and immediate world of painful human relationships. He criticizes those who strike or kick their parents, who desire their death, who hate them, who mock their parents and deride them, who cause them to be poor and miserable, who anger them, who prevent them from making wills or who ignore their wills, who take their inheritance but fail to pay their parents' debts, who do not pray for their parents or have others pray for them, and, finally, who do not help their parents when they fall into poverty.[42]

Dederich seems to be imagining the worst of children, but Bonaventure can see the boot may be on the other foot. It is not necessary, he says, to honour one's parents if they themselves honour bad things and expect you to.[43] Nicholas of Lyra considers the case of another child caught between two stools. Since spiritual help is always better than corporeal help, is it not better for a child to give money to a priest to pray for his parents' souls than to buy them food? No; Nicholas is clear that the precept requires one to make sure one's parents are physically secure before making offerings to God. Indeed, the order of charity ('charity begins at home') means that one may use goods owed to a third party to help one's parents first. However, if those goods have already been vowed to God *before* the parents' difficulty is apparent, then one cannot change the vow and take the goods away. In the same way, a child who has already made vows of religion should not leave his community, against his superior's will, if his parents need him. Yet the precept cannot be dismissed, and it is necessary for a child to fulfill it in some way. Making vows (whether of religion or marriage), is a voluntary act, whereas the commandment is always an obligation. Nicholas resolves this dilemma by agreeing that, although the commandment is always to be obeyed, whatever the circumstances, nevertheless, those circumstances make a difference to how it can be obeyed. Having made a vow of religion, for instance,

---

[41]   Hugh of St Cher, *Postilla*, on Exod. 20: 12.

[42]   Br Dederich von Münster of the Observant Order [Dietrich Kolde], *A Fruitful Mirror or Small Handbook for Christians*, tr. R.B. Dewell, in *Three Reformation Catechisms: Catholic, Anabaptist, Lutheran*, ed. D. Janz (New York, 1982), chapter 11, iv, pp. 55–6.

[43]   Bonaventure, *Collationes de decem praeceptis*, Coll. 5, no. 10, p. 524; p. 75 (English).

means that some ways of helping your parents are no longer open to you, but you should still do your best to help them, as far as you are able.[44]

John of La Rochelle finds a child in an even more difficult position. He asks whether a son should denounce his heretical father.[45] Surprisingly, John distinguishes between a secret heretic, who 'harms only himself' – a most unusual formulation for a Christian theologian who would normally say that the corruption of an individual member damages the whole body of the Church – and the outwardly apostate who corrupts the faith of others. The former should be left in peace, but the latter must be accused: the honour of one's heavenly Father must take precedence over the honour of the father on earth.

Sometimes the whole matter of honouring is conscripted into the service of mendicant concerns. Bonaventure finishes his discussion of the fourth precept with a lengthy narrative example of what it means to honour your mother. It is a story not original to him – indeed, it is sometimes told of master Peter Lombard, bishop of Paris (d. 1160).[46] The story – a perfect Mendicant preaching tool – concerns a famous and beloved master of Paris, whose poor, elderly mother decides to visit him. Arriving in Paris in her usual rough clothes, she is taken up by some kindly ladies, who give her food, dress her in finery, and take her to see her son. However, the master does not recognize her claim to be his mother: 'I do not believe you, because my mother was very poor and unaccustomed to wear anything but a garment of coarse cloth'. The ladies take her away and, retrieving her own clothes and staff, she returns to the master. This time 'in the midst of a great crowd, he recognized his mother, and ... embraced her saying: "Now I know that you are my mother." This story was spread around the city and it was considered that he had done a great good. Afterwards he was made the bishop of Paris.'[47] Clearly, this is a tale meant to appeal to Franciscans, who were especially vowed to poverty. It comes from Bonaventure's set of *Collationes* on the Decalogue, intended primarily for internal circulation among the friars. Nevertheless, it is as interesting for what it does not say as for what it does: the famous master does not alleviate his mother's poverty, for example, or regret that his religious vocation has left him unable to look after her physical needs. He honours her by recognition and reverence, and by acceptance of her

---

[44]   Nicholas of Lyra, *Postilla litteralis*, on Matt. 15: 1.

[45]   John of La Rochelle, *Doctoris Irrefragibilis Alexandri de Hales*, vol. 4, lib. 3, pt 2, inq. 3, tr. 2, sect. 1, q. 2, tit. 4, c. 4, art. 2.

[46]   Peter Lombard, *Sententiae*, vol. 1, pt 1, Prolegomena: *Legenda de adventu matris eius*, pp. 38*–40*.

[47]   Bonaventure, *Collationes de decem praeceptis*, Coll. 5, no. 20, p. 525; pp. 78–9 (English).

poverty, rather than by improving her lot. Beyond the literal world, poverty is our spiritual mother.

This story introduces us to a more than literal reading of the biblical text. This extension of the exegesis into non-literal, 'spiritual' senses of the text is necessary for the patristic and medieval understanding of Scripture. Without it, some parts of Scripture would make no sense at all; but more importantly, for Christian interpreters, it allows them to add a Christological dimension to the Hebrew Bible. So, for instance, they can interpret the Bride and Bridegroom in the Song of Songs as the marriage of the Church and Christ, or as the marriage of the individual soul to Christ. Similarly, although the importance to Christians of the Book of Ruth can be seen in the genealogy at the end of chapter four, which leads from Ruth's son Obed to David, from whose line Christ was born (thus fulfilling the Jewish prophecy about the ancestry of the Messiah), Ruth was also interpreted by Christian exegetes as the Gentile Church, that is, the community of non-Jews who embraced Christianity, just as Ruth embraced Boaz, a 'type' of Christ.

In some cases, the extension of spiritual readings into the biblical text can seem very far-fetched and artificial – as some medieval exegetes themselves acknowledged. Even interpreting David as a type of Christ, for instance, could only be done by ignoring the less noble side of his character, which included ordering an innocent man to be killed. However, in the case of the commandment to honour one's father and mother, at least the first step from a literal to a spiritual interpretation could be more or less automatic, since the formulation of God as father is in itself biblical, and the concept of holy mother Church goes back to the early Church. For John Wyclif, understanding the moral sense of the commandment means that we honour our spiritual parents in the form of all our spiritual superiors, such as priests, and we honour our spiritual mother, 'which is the religion of Christ of Scripture. And ... in the allegorical sense we honour Christ and the Church militant, who are father and mother of all'.[48] Honouring God and the Church as father and mother is very close to being a literal interpretation of the precept. From God as father, it is a short step to priest as father, the earthly representative of God. Who else is my parent? The answer to this is one of many examples among the second tablet precepts of *synechdoche*, as Bonaventure notes, where 'the whole is implied by the part'.[49] 'Parents' applies to all those who have made you what you are: biological parents, of course, but

48   Wyclif, *De mandatis divinis*, c. 22, pp. 294–5.
49   Bonaventure, *Collationes de decem praeceptis*, Coll. 5, no. 4, p. 523; p. 73 (English). Cf. Augustine, *Quaestiones in Exodum* 71.4, in *Quaestiones in Heptateuchum*, CCSL, 33 (Turnhout, 1958), p. 105; Peter Comestor, *Historia scholastica*, c. 40, PL 198: 1165, '*a parte totum intelligitur. Unde et Dominus docens totaliter intelligenda, implevit legem*'.

also godparents, teachers and guides of other sorts – every wise person who has helped you along the way. This broad interpretation of the precept should ensure that everyone in society has someone else who is looking out for them, even if they have no children or living relatives of their own.

In a lengthy exposition, Bonaventure extends the meaning of father and mother up to the point where honour is to be shown to any authority, whether it be monastic, public, ecclesiastical or political; and it should be shown to age, to weakness (even to the extent that those lacking 'sense' should be given 'lessons'), and to friendship.[50] In his hierarchy of honour, likeness to oneself draws the highest obligation. Hence, family comes before anyone else, fellow Christians should be honoured before infidels or non-believers, and members of one's own religious community before outsiders.[51] Since the commandment stands at the head of the precepts pertaining to your neighbour, it might be thought that it should be extended to mean you should honour all your neighbours – in the same way as you should not steal from any of your neighbours. However, this is not the intent. John Wyclif sums up the commentators' view when he says that you should honour only those among your neighbours who deserve it – those who are or who do good.[52]

How far does honour to spiritual parents extend? It must certainly be shown by spiritual obedience to priests, even if they are bad men: if the Church hierarchy tolerates them, then individual believers must show reverence. This is, once more, an anti-heretical position, illustrating that the office of priest was more than its holder, no matter what some heretics might argue. Dederich of Münster once again opens a window onto a contentious world. According to him, the commandment reproves all those who are rebellious against the Church or its prelates, who make light of Church commands, who withold offerings, annoy the clergy, and are a burden to the clergy, who do not heed excommunication orders, who engage in secret marriage ceremonies contrary to Church regulations and at forbidden times, who do not keep fasts or holidays, who do not take part in processions, or who do not show respect for their confessor.[53] This is clearly meant to cover all spiritual eventualities, but as far as material support of clergy goes, things are not so clear. John of La Rochelle states that tithes and other benefits are not necessarily due from needy parishioners, if the local church is

---

[50]   Bonaventure, *Collationes de decem praeceptis*, Coll. 5, nos 11–15, p. 524; p. 76 (English).

[51]   Bonaventure, *Collationes de decem praeceptis*, Coll. 5, nos 16–18, pp. 524–5; p. 78 (English).

[52]   Wyclif, *De mandatis divinis*, c. 22, p. 293.

[53]   Dederich von Münster, *A Fruitful Mirror*, chapter 11, iv, pp. 55–6.

already sufficiently endowed.[54] If the priest of such a church retains anything beyond necessity, rather than giving it away to the poor, he commits sacrilege (a kind of theft, according to John) by holding goods belonging to the Church for improper use.

John is similarly anti-authoritarian as far as fathers from the world of secular power go: kings and princes need only be obeyed in matters concerning the *res publica*.[55] However, for Dederich of Münster this writ might run wide. You are disobeying the precept if you disrespect, never mind attack, the divine right of rulers or of city authorities, fostering dissent, unrest or treason. Even more broadly, you disobey the precept if you deprive someone of an honour or a favour, or keep him from something he is entitled to. This might seem like an extension too far of the commandment, in effect to uphold the status quo, but arguably it is not very wide of the original intention of the precept in a patriarchal society, when family leadership and tribal (or political) leadership were close to the same thing.

Although the Decalogue itself imposes no penalties, Wyclif exposes the dangers of disobedience. There are ten: a shortened life; having no joy in one's children; the loss of one's house through the curses of parents; gaining a bad reputation; being cursed by God; being forgotten; being made a fool of; suffering reproaches; a life which drags on wearily till death; and finally, being stoned.[56] It is lucky that, according to Augustine at least, this commandment is rarely ignored, and children really do usually honour their parents.[57] We may not normally think of Augustine as a man who sees the world through rose-coloured spectacles, but there does seem to be quite a gap between his assurance of familial relations and the harsher light cast by Grosseteste and his observation of those who despise old age, or Dederich of Münster, warning children not to prevent their parents from making a will. Why is there a difference? Augustine's comment is made in a sermon, Grosseteste's treatise on the Decalogue is more pastoral than academic, and Dederich's list is part of a catechism – so the question of genre is less important here. Neither, we might think, is the thousand-year gap between the texts, for it seems unlikely that parent–child relations could really be so different. There is no simple answer, and we should not look for only

---

[54]   John of La Rochelle, *Doctoris Irrefragibilis Alexandri de Hales*, vol. 4, lib. 3, pt 2, inq. 3, tr. 2, sect. 1, q. 2, tit. 4, c. 4, art. 4.

[55]   John of La Rochelle, *Doctoris Irrefragibilis Alexandri de Hales*, vol. 4, lib. 3, pt 2, inq. 3, tr. 2, sect. 1, q. 2, tit. 4, c. 4, art. 3.

[56]   Wyclif, *De mandatis divinis*, c. 22, p. 312.

[57]   Augustine, *Sermones* 9, c. 4, p. 114: '*Multi enim honorant parentes. et raro invenimus parentes conquerentes*'.

one response; it is the very variety of their explanations that makes these writers recognizable as people like ourselves.

In their treatment of the Ten Commandments, we can observe the recurrent paradox of the writings of medieval theologians: one minute, their expectations and concerns, for instance with the importance of number or the spiritual meaning of the text, seem entirely alien, a determinedly contorted interpretative outlook; and the next, their psychological acuity and their concern for the human consequences of the text seem to place them in a world just like our own. Bonaventure's contemporary, the Dominican Simon of Hinton, working in Oxford, asks why the precept does not command parents to honour their children. He knows the answer. It is because parents cannot help themselves from caring for their children: 'succour flows naturally, as from the root to the branch'.[58]

---

[58]   Simon of Hinton, *Exceptiones*, in Walz, 'The "Exceptiones"', p. 310.

Chapter 9
Making Motherhood in Medieval England: The Evidence from Medicine

Monica H. Green

Motherhood. Its very ubiquity has often made it invisible to historians. As the editors of this volume point out, even after forty years of the new women's history of the late twentieth and early twenty-first centuries, motherhood has largely escaped the attention of medieval historians. The subjective experiences of maternity may well remain beyond our grasp for most medieval women not of the elite classes, owing to the lack of private documents such as letters and diaries. Yet other sources yield valuable evidence for ideas about motherhood and may perhaps help us explore the development of behaviours surrounding sexuality and parenting as well.

One source for medieval understandings of motherhood is medical writing, which gives us access to the systems of intellectual discourse and practical interventions developed to understand and intervene in the processes of the female body. Medical writings are, at the moment, still our richest source for lore on how a pregnancy should be best managed, how birth should be assisted, and what procedures need to be followed should any mishap occur. For example, close analysis of the most widely disseminated ensemble of texts on women's medicine, the so-called *Trotula* texts, shows great concern to make the female body reproductively successful. The two texts that focused on gynaecology and obstetrics both shared an assumption – common to the entire Hippocratic-Galenic system of medicine – that regular menstruation was both fundamental to female health and the sign of ability to conceive. If a woman was not menstruating regularly, her uterus was not purging her body of potentially noxious superfluities that were building up. Emmenagogues (substances 'to provoke the menses') make up the largest single category of remedies in medieval gynaecological literature precisely because this function was so central to female health and reproductivity. Texts on women's medicine might also be concerned to 'unmake' or prevent motherhood, either by preventing conception in the first place or expelling a dead foetus that would not emerge spontaneously. Abortion *per se* was almost never mentioned.[1]

From c. 1100 through c. 1300, England was the most richly endowed area in medieval Europe in terms of the number of Latin texts specifically devoted to women's medicine and, in terms of the diversity of texts in circulation, vernacular traditions in England had no rival until German and Dutch traditions began emerging in the later fourteenth century.[2] Ample evidence has been emerging for the past two decades of the circulation of the *Trotula* texts in England: of over ten dozen copies of these twelfth-century southern Italian Latin texts that are extant, at least a quarter were either written in England or migrated there before the end of the Middle Ages. Evidence from inventories and medieval catalogues likewise shows the ready availability of these Salernitan texts in England, and the *Trotula* dominate both the Anglo-Norman and English vernacular traditions.[3] Indeed, I have suggested elsewhere that at least one of the *Trotula* texts, the *De curis mulierum* (*Treatments for Women*, composed around the middle of the twelfth century), may reflect the transcription of Salernitan women's practices by a travelling Englishman who knew he had a ready audience for his work back home.[4]

---

[1]   Of the texts available in post-Conquest England, only one, Theodorus Priscianus's *Gynaecia*, included a chapter on abortifacients. See Monica H. Green, 'Constantinus Africanus and the Conflict Between Religion and Science', in G.R. Dunstan (ed.), *The Human Embryo: Aristotle and the Arabic and European Traditions* (Exeter, 1990), pp. 47–69; and below for further discussion.

[2]   A comprehensive list of all medieval gynaecological texts known as of 1999 (in Latin as well as the various vernaculars), can be found in Monica H. Green, 'Medieval Gynecological Texts: a Handlist', in Green (ed.), *Women's Healthcare in the Medieval West: Texts and Contexts* (Aldershot, 2000), Appendix, pp. 1–36.

[3]   See Monica H. Green, 'A Handlist of the Latin and Vernacular Manuscripts of the So-called *Trotula* Texts. Part I: the Latin Manuscripts', *Scriptorium*, 50 (1996): 137–75 (hereafter, *Trotula* Handlist I); Green, 'A Handlist of the Latin and Vernacular Manuscripts of the So-called *Trotula* Texts. Part II: the Vernacular Texts and Latin Re-writings', *Scriptorium*, 51 (1997): 80–104 (hereafter, *Trotula* Handlist II); Green *Making Women's Medicine Masculine: the Rise of Male Authority in Pre-Modern Gynaecology* (Oxford, 2008), esp. pp. 325–31; and Green, 'Salerno on the Thames: the Genesis of Anglo-Norman Medical Literature', in J. Wogan-Browne, et al. (eds), *Language and Culture in Medieval Britain: the French of England, c. 1100–c. 1500* (York, 2009), pp. 220–31.

[4]   On the transfer of southern Italian medicine to England, see M.H. Green, 'Rethinking the Manuscript Basis of Salvatore De Renzi's *Collectio Salernitana*: the Corpus of Medical Writings in the "Long" Twelfth Century', in Danielle Jacquart and Agostino Paravicini Bagliani (eds), *La 'Collectio Salernitana' di Salvatore De Renzi*, Edizione Nazionale 'La Scuola medica Salernitana', 3 (Florence, 2008), pp. 15–60; and Green, 'Salerno on the Thames'. On the genesis of the *De curis mulierum*, see chapter 1 of Green, *Making Women's Medicine Masculine*.

What is not yet well known is the fact that, for a time, nearly every other specialized Latin text on women's medicine known on the Continent also made its way sooner or later to England.[5] This was in addition to the often quite substantial amount of information on gynaecology and obstetrics that was embedded in general texts on medicine; for example, the text on women's medicine that would prove most popular in Middle English in the fifteenth century was not a translation of the *Trotula* (even though that had been rendered five times into English), but the gynaecological and obstetrical chapters excerpted from the *Compendium medicine* of the mid-thirteenth-century author, Gilbertus Anglicus.[6] Similarly, the most popular Middle English version of the *Trotula* (which still exists in five copies) is not a straightforward translation of the Latin Salernitan text, but a fusion of an Anglo-Norman version of the *Trotula* with two Latin texts of late antique origin that had come to England at least as early as the mid-twelfth century.[7] England's easy engagement with Continental trends in medicine would not be sustained into the fourteenth century, when the new texts coming out of Montpellier and the northern Italian schools usually failed to cross the Channel. One can nevertheless discern ongoing insular traditions of copying and reconfiguring older texts, so it is certainly reasonable to ask whether there was a certain shared character to English views on women's medicine throughout this period.

I offer here a rapid survey of the texts on women's medicine beyond the *Trotula* now known to have been circulating in medieval England from the time of the Conquest up through the later fourteenth century, when Middle English began to assert itself as a force for scientific and medical language. Although a handful of these texts were already known to nineteenth-century editors, most of the identifications are the product of the past three decades, as the

---

[5]   On the important role of surgical texts in the development of obstetrical practices, see Monica H. Green, 'Moving from Philology to Social History: the Circulation and Uses of Albucasis's Latin *Surgery* in the Middle Ages', in Florence Eliza Glaze and Brian Nance (eds), *Between Text and Patient: the Medical Enterprise in Medieval and Early Modern Europe*, Micrologus' Library, 30 (Florence, 2011), pp. 331–72.

[6]   Monica H. Green and Linne R. Mooney, 'The *Sickness of Women*', in M. Teresa Tavormina (ed.), *Sex, Aging, and Death in a Medieval Medical Compendium: Trinity College Cambridge MS R.14.52, its Texts, Language, and Scribe*, Medieval and Renaissance Texts and Studies, 292 (2 vols, Tempe, AZ, 2006), vol. 2, pp. 455–568. For an important reconstruction of Gilbertus's biography, see Michael R. McVaugh, 'Who Was Gilbert the Englishman?', in George Hardin Brown and Linda Ehrsam Voigts (eds), *The Study of Medieval Manuscripts of England: Festschrift in Honor of Richard W. Pfaff* (Tempe, AZ, 2010), pp. 295–324.

[7]   Alexandra Barratt (ed.), *The Knowing of Woman's Kind in Childing: a Middle English Version of Material Derived from the 'Trotula' and Other Sources*, Medieval Women: Texts and Contexts, 4 (Turnhout, 2001).

impact of women's studies has given new importance to the history of women's medicine and as increased studies of Continental medicine have made the trajectories of English medicine more abundantly apparent.[8] I can only hint at the potential of these materials for reconstructing a history of motherhood, but as more work is done to contextualize individual manuscripts and decipher the nuanced recrafting of each text (the subtle additions and deletions, the marginal annotations, the juxtapositions with other texts), we will begin to see more and more of the making of motherhood in high and later medieval England.

To stress the need to understand these discourses on women's medicine as historically contingent phenomena – often operating across several linguistic registers simultaneously – I also examine the genesis of the thirteenth-century Anglo-Norman *Les secrés dé femmes*, which Tony Hunt publishes for the first time elsewhere in this volume. As was already documented in 1997, *Les secrés dé femmes* derives from the sections on making and unmaking motherhood from some version of the earliest form of one of the Latin *Trotula* texts.[9] (I edit the Latin texts in an appendix.) This close analysis makes it abundantly apparent how tightly medicine was connected with the great moral debates of the day, for this text not only exhorts women to learn proper management of their marital relations in order to achieve one of the central Christian goals of marriage, offspring, but it equally exhorts men to turn away from homosexual relations which, by definition, cannot lead to any fertile outcome. The distinctive and obviously deliberate changes that the French/Anglo-Norman translator made give us palpable evidence of the way the new southern Italian medicine was being adopted and adapted in northern Europe as a framework with which to preach to both women and men ideals and expectations of motherhood and fertility.

Latin Texts on Women's Medicine in England, Eleventh to Fourteenth Centuries

The particular character of English medicine, at least in regard to learned writings on women, was established in the late eleventh and twelfth centuries. True, there was some gynaecological material in both Latin and Anglo-Saxon texts known in pre-Conquest England, but it consisted mostly of scattered

---

[8]   A cumulative annotated bibliography of over 375 items of European and North American scholarship published in the past 30 years can be found in Monica H. Green, 'Bibliography on Medieval Women, Gender and Medicine, 1980–2009', posted for free access on *Sciencia.cat*, http://www.sciencia.cat/english/libraryenglish/publicationssc.htm, posted 02 March 2010.

[9]   Green, *Trotula* Handlist II, pp. 89–90.

recipes or charms.[10] No coherent theoretical perspectives on female anatomy or physiology seem to have emerged out of these traditions, leaving England open to the impact of the new traditions on women's medicine entering England from the Continent following the Conquest.

The actual point of arrival of Continental texts is uncertain: we have no catalogue information from this early period or other textual references to confirm the presence of specific texts on women's medicine, and the extant manuscripts I survey below are undated save for modern paleographical estimates. Still, there is no reason to think that the handful of manuscripts that survive represent the only, least of all the earliest copies of the texts that once existed. The data presented in Table 9.1, therefore, can only give us the most minimalist sense of what was once available. Nevertheless, an expanding body of evidence for the rapid transferal of Continental medicine to England in the twelfth century gives us every reason to believe that texts on women's medicine were likewise available to at least certain sectors of literate insular culture within decades or even a few years after they began to circulate on the Continent.[11] I believe, therefore, that it is worthwhile to scrutinize the evidence we do have for women's medicine in England even in this early period, as it probably represents only a fraction of what was once available, and it certainly reflects real interest among specific scribes or commissioners to gather this information together.

One of the earliest texts on women's medicine documented in post-Conquest England is also one of the oldest gynaecological texts in existence. It is found in two manuscripts: the incomplete table of contents is all that remains

---

[10]   On women's medicine in pre-Conquest England, see Marilyn Deegan, 'Pregnancy and Childbirth in the Anglo-Saxon Medical Texts: a Preliminary Survey', in Marilyn Deegan and D.G. Scragg (eds), *Medicine in Early Medieval England* (Manchester, 1989), pp. 17–26; L.M.C. Weston, 'Women's Medicine, Women's Magic: the Old English Metrical Childbirth Charms', *Modern Philology*, 92 (1995): 279–93; László Sándor Chardonnens, 'A New Edition of the Old English *Formation of the Foetus*', *Notes and Queries*, 47 (2000): 10–11; and R.A. Buck, 'Women and Language in the Anglo-Saxon Leechbooks', *Women and Language*, 23 (2000): 41–50. For a comparison of the English tradition of birthing charms with that on the Continent, see William D. Paden and Frances Freeman Paden, 'Swollen Woman, Shifting Canon: a Midwife's Charm and the Birth of Secular Romance Lyric', *PMLA*, 125 (2010): 306–321. Virtually no work has been done on the massive number of recipes dealing with obstetrics and gynaecology from the later medieval period.

[11]   I am currently engaged on a project studying all medical literature in Europe during the 'long twelfth century' (c. 1075 to c. 1225), which includes not only extant manuscripts (currently numbering over 470) but also contemporary catalogues and inventories. Given that we have no catalogue evidence from twelfth-century England save for a handful of male monastic houses, the lack of citations to gynaecological texts in that period hardly constitutes proof that the texts were unknown.

in Harley 4977, written in England early in the twelfth century, but the whole text is found in the second part of what now makes up Sloane 475, written perhaps a couple of decades earlier either in England or in northern France and brought soon thereafter to England.[12] The work is a late-antique Latin version of one of the ancient Greek Hippocratic treatises on women's medicine, called in its twentieth-century edition, *De diversis causis mulierum* (*On the Diverse Conditions of Women*).[13] In its 91 chapters, the text covers an amazing range of gynaecological and obstetrical conditions, from uterine dislocations to fetal death to uterine ulcerations to headache to depression ('Si anima in angustia uel tristitia est'). Besides addressing the pathology and therapy for gynaecological disorders, the text also takes into consideration questions of etiology, diagnosis and prognosis. In the Sloane manuscript, *De diversis causis mulierum* appears as the only text on women in a small, manual-sized (152 x 110 mm) codex that appears to be, given its predominantly diagnostic and prognostic content, a sort of practical vade mecum. The Harley manuscript, in contrast, contains a group of texts, probably recently arrived in England from the Continent, that attempted to re-engage with the theoretical debates among physicians of late Antiquity and bring together a range of materials on therapeutics.[14] Several different texts on women and generation appear here, including treatises on embryology ascribed

---

[12]   London, British Library, MS Sloane 475 is a composite volume made up of two parts of similar age; *De diversis causis mulierum* is found in part 2. The only comprehensive description of the manuscript is Augusto Beccaria, *I Codici di medicina del periodo presalernitano (secoli IX, X e XI)* (Rome, 1956), who identifies Brittany as the locus of origin. An English origin is posited by Richard Gameson, *The Manuscripts of Early Norman England (c. 1066–1130)* (Oxford: University Press, 1999) p. 121 nos 566, 567; see also the description on the British Library Illuminated Manuscripts website, http://www.bl.uk/catalogues/illuminatedmanuscripts/welcome.htm, accessed 5 September 2008, which fails to mention Beccaria's description. Part 2 is mentioned in passing in Debby Banham, 'A Millennium in Medicine? New Medical Texts and Ideas in England in the Eleventh Century', in Simon Keynes, Alfred P. Smyth and C.R. Hart (eds), *Anglo-Saxons: Studies Presented to Cyril Roy Hart* (Dublin, 2006), pp. 230–42, who claims (p. 238) that it is 'paleographically related to Sloane 1621, but the nature of that relationship is not yet clear'.

[13]   This title is actually a misnomer, caused by the corrupt state of the ninth-century manuscript edited in the 1930s. For an edition of St Petersburg, Publicnaja Biblioteka im. M.E. Saltykova-Scedrina, MS lat. F.v.VI.3, s. viii/ix, see Walter Brütsch, 'De diversis causis mulierum, nach einer Petersburger Handschrift aus dem 9. Jahrhundert zum erstenmal gedruckt', unpubl. med. diss. (Freiburg-im-Br., 1922). The fragment of the text in Harley 4977 has readings closer to the St Petersburg copy than the Sloane one.

[14]   See F.E. Glaze, 'Master–Student Medical Dialogues: The Evidence of London, British Library Sloane 2839', in P. Lendinara et al. (eds), *Form and Content of Instruction in Anglo-Saxon England in Light of Contemporary Manuscript Evidence*, Textes et études du moyen âge, 39 (Turnhout, 2007), pp. 467–94.

to the late antique author Vindicianus; a text apparently derived from the ancient Greek author Soranus that addresses the care of the parturient after birth, the choice of the wetnurse, and the care and feeding of the newborn; and then the *Epistola Hippocratis de virginibus* (*The Letter of Hippocrates on Virgins*), which prognosticates the future health of a woman depending on the age she begins to menstruate, and then offers a basic account of gynaecological pathology and a unique conception of female anatomy. The *De diversis causis mulierum* would have made this volume a repository of medical knowledge the likes of which had probably never been seen before in Britain.

However, just at the moment the scribes of Sloane 475 and Harley 4977 were retrieving elements of late antique medicine and looking at it with new eyes, an independent and much stronger spirit of revival and new curiosity in medicine was beginning to impact on medical learning throughout western Europe. Manuscripts Sloane 1621 and Bethesda, NLM, E 8 present another text on women's medicine available in post-Conquest England, important more for the sea change it augured than for its own content. Actually, this can barely be called a 'text' at all as it is just six sentences long. *De urinis mulierum* (*On Women's Urines*) identifies what can be known of a woman on the basis of her urine and gives evidence of the growing importance of uroscopy as an indicator of both character and health. *De urinis mulierum* describes the appearance of urine of, respectively, virgins, non-virgins, menstruating women and women in first, second, third and fourth months of pregnancy.[15] We can divine some sense of how the text might have been used from the general character of the manuscripts where it is found. One is a miscellany of recipes and other medical notes to which nearly two dozen scribes added continually over the course of a half-century. One of those scribes is known to have worked at Bury St Edmunds,[16] which raises the question: what kind of scenario of use can we imagine for these texts in the hands of male clerics? In fact, we need not look far, since already

---

[15]   Here is the entire text collated from London, British Library, MS Sloane 1621, fol. 111r; and Bethesda (MD), National Library of Medicine, MS NLM E 8, fol. 10r: 'Incipiunt urine mulierum puelle virgines faciunt urinam lucidam, idem urinam serenam. Urina mulieris concubite turbida est, et viri semen infundo vasis apparet. Urina mulieris menstruate quasi sanguine est. Urina pregnantis si primum mensem, aut secundum, sive III habuerit, nebulam habet in initiam, et ypostasin albam, et urina nimis clara est. Urina pregnantis que IIII mense iam habuerit, serena est et vini habet colorem et ypostasin albam. Inferius est crassa et lucida'. My thanks to Florence Eliza Glaze for sharing with me her detailed notes on the Bethesda manuscript.

[16]   Rebecca Rushforth, 'The Eleventh- and Early Twelfth-Century Manuscripts of Bury St Edmunds Abbey', unpubl. PhD diss. (Cambridge, 2003), pp. 58–61. My thanks to Dr Rushforth for making a copy of her dissertation available to me, and to Michael Gullick for sharing with me a draft of his own study of this complicated manuscript.

in 1114, we have the story of the physician Faritius, who served as abbot of Abingdon (1100–1117) and is known to have brought *multos libros de physica* into the abbey. King Henry I of England wished to appoint him as archbishop of Canterbury, but the bishops of Salisbury and Lincoln objected that it was unseemly to have as archbishop anyone who inspected women's urine.

It may well be individuals like Faritius – either native Italians or English or Normans who journeyed to the south – who account for another surprising aspect of twelfth-century English medicine: it presents as many witnesses to new texts coming out of southern Italy as can now be found for southern Italy itself. The common Norman domination of both England and southern Italy allowed for the astonishingly rapid transfer of texts, ideas and even medical personnel between the two distant regions. The second manuscript where the text on women's urines appears, National Library of Medicine in the United States, MS NLM E 8, is a massive jumble of notes and recipes, on the one hand, and formal, learned treatises on medicine like a late antique commentary on the Hippocratic *Aphorisms* (with rich layers of notes added by later hands on topics such as the structure of the eyes and the nature of eunuchs, and an extended section *De conceptu* (*On Conception*)), Constantine the African's treatise on surgery, and a recently translated work on pulses by the Greek author Philaretus.[17]

The earliest manuscript to document the presence of the gynaecological texts of the southern Italian corpus is a codex produced in the second quarter or middle of the twelfth century. This manuscript has received attention primarily because of a glossary of 1500 items of *materia medica* with Latin and Anglo-Saxon equivalents, but it also contains Constantinus Africanus' *Viaticum*, *De oblivione* (*On Forgetfulness*) and *De melancholia* (*On Melancholy*) – all of them important works in bringing Arabic medicine into western Europe – and a cluster of texts on women's medicine that were probably redacted in southern Italy just a few decades earlier.[18] First was an abbreviated version of a text seemingly attributed to the Egyptian queen Cleopatra, a work probably pieced together in the late antique period from a variety of previously existing sources, at least some of which were Greek. The abbreviated version omitted three chapters from the

---

[17]   Bethesda (MD), National Library of Medicine, MS E 8, c. 1150. The manuscript is datable because of a list of popes (fol. 148v), which originally ended with death of Pope Lucius II (d. 1145), followed by an entry for Eugenius III (1145–1153) added later.

[18]   On Oxford, Bodleian Library, MS Laud Misc. 567, see N.R. Ker, *A Catalogue of Manuscripts Containing Anglo-Saxon* (Oxford, 1957); M.H. Green, 'The *De genecia* Attributed to Constantine the African', *Speculum*, 62 (1987): 299–323; and Philip G. Rusche, 'The Sources for Plant Names in Anglo-Saxon England and the Laud Herbal Glossary', in P. Dendle and A. Touwaide (eds), *Health and Healing from the Medieval Garden* (Woodbridge, 2008), pp. 128–44.

original, but whittled it down even more decisively by omitting the results or reassurances of the efficacy of many of the medicaments, synonyms and alternative ingredients. A similar process of deletion of terminology and theory deemed no longer relevant characterizes the text *Non omnes quidem,* a work in 78 chapters made up of abbreviated selections from Muscio's *Gynaecia* together with other material. The third text is *De passionibus mulierum,* Version A, an abbreviated version in 39 chapters of a fuller Latin translation of a Greek text ascribed, in its one extant copy, to a female writer, Metrodora. Between them, these three works were probably less important for the reader looking for theories of female physiology or disease than the chapters on women's medicine in Constantine's *Viaticum,* but in their breadth they would have given a sense of confidence that one had assembled a body of material as extensive in its coverage, and as needful of interpretation, as the extensive list of synonyms that closes the volume.

A final manuscript that serves as an important witness to the expanding interest in women's medicine in post-Conquest England is Digby 79, which physically ties southern Italy to England, since parts of it seem to have been made in both places. Of the six texts here on women's medicine (four principally on gynaecology and two more on cosmetics), we find, in the Italian section of the manuscript, the rare work *Inprimis considerandum est utrum culpa uiri uel mulieris.*[19] This is a brief tract on infertility, probably of late twelfth-century Salernitan origin. Like other Salernitan writings on infertility, it identifies the cause in temperamental imbalance. This work is unusual, however, in systematically itemizing the symptoms of each imbalance, including the character of the urine, pulse and hair, and even the quantity and quality of the woman's emitted seed. The woman is tested to determine whether infertility is her 'fault' or that of the man: she is fumigated in her vagina, having been covered up thoroughly to make sure that none of the smoke reaches her nose. If she can still smell it, then that signals that her internal passageways are clear and that the inability to conceive is the fault of the man. Blocked passageways demand further differential diagnosis to determine the cause of the blockage and the derivation of a therapeutic regimen. The manuscript as a whole is a messy but fascinating compilation of Salernitan *praxis,* one that continued to elicit engaged annotations from readers for at least another century.

---

[19]   Oxford, Bodleian Library, MS Digby 79 (SC 1680), s. xiii in. (England and Italy). Besides the text on infertility I describe here, the other gynaecological contents are: the earliest version of Trota's *De curis mulierum*; *De passionibus mulierum B,* cc. 1–9; and pseudo-Theodorus Priscianus, *Ad Octavium filium.* The cosmetics texts are the second version of the Salernitan *De ornatu mulierum* and an otherwise unattested work of probable Salernitan origin I simply call the 'Digby cosmetics'. There is no thorough published description of this manuscript yet; for an interim description, see Green, *Trotula* Handlist I, p. 145.

The English corpus of texts on women's medicine continued to grow in the thirteenth and fourteenth centuries. Again, it is difficult to pinpoint exactly when the texts arrived: some may have been available as early as the others we have surveyed, while others of later composition – like *De naturis mulierum*, an adaptation of mostly obstetrical excerpts from Muscio's *Gynaecia*, apparently redacted in Paris in the late thirteenth or early fourteenth century – were probably brought back to England by returning scholars.[20] However, the bigger question in assessing the historical importance of these texts in defining English views on motherhood is not how many different texts were in circulation, but how they were used. Evidence for ownership of texts on women's medicine by male clerics and scholars becomes ample by the end of the thirteenth century.[21] The task that remains is to find more evidence of how women themselves engaged with these texts and their ideas, whether that be by reading them themselves, commissioning translations or having them interpreted orally for consumption by listening audiences.

Women's Medicine for Women (and their Husbands): *Les secrés dé femmes*

Despite its title, the Anglo-Norman text *Les secrés dé femmes* is not a distillation of women's private lore.[22] Rather, this 165-line tract in octosyllabic and alexandrine verse is a collection of advice on problems of sterility, aids for impregnation, contraceptives, the development of the fetus, regimen for pregnancy, aids for difficult birth (including mechanisms to expel a dead foetus and the afterbirth), and tests to determine the sex of the foetus. Elsewhere in this volume, Tony Hunt presents an edition of the text from Cambridge, Trinity College, MS O.1.20 (1044), a remarkable collection of thirteenth-century French, Anglo-Norman and Latin medical and surgical texts.[23] The *Secrés dé femmes* may well deserve

---

[20]   Green, 'Handlist', p. 22. Although no English copy of the Latin *De naturis mulierum* has been identified, its Middle English translation (which is found uniquely in a late fourteenth-century copy) attests to the text's presence in England.

[21]   Green, *Making Women's Medicine Masculine*, pp. 325–31 and *passim*.

[22]   Indeed, aside from the treatise *De curis mulierum* of the twelfth-century healer, Trota of Salerno, the only medieval gynaecological or obstetrical material that can be said to have come *directly* from female practitioners is a collection of obstetrical remedies transcribed in a Hebrew circumcisor's manual. See Elisheva Baumgarten, '"Thus Sayeth the Wise Midwives": Midwives and Midwifery in Thirteenth-Century Ashkenaz', *Zion*, 65 (2000): 45–74, in Hebrew with English summary.

[23]   See Hunt essay, Chapter 10. Brief excerpts were published in Paul Meyer, 'Les manuscrits français de Cambridge. III. Trinity College O.I.20, Traités de médecine', *Romania*, 32 (1903): 75–101, at pp. 75–77.

the title of the earliest vernacular gynaecological text composed in Europe.[24] Moreover, unique among medieval gynaecological texts, the *Secrés dé femmes* is also an important witness to increasingly vocal and hostile attitudes toward male homosexuality, which is here condemned as a chief contributing factor to infertility, along with squabbling between husbands and wives.

The *Secrés dé femmes* is one of at least seven different medieval French translations of the Latin *Trotula* texts, a group of three texts on women's medicine probably by individuals associated with the southern Italian medical 'school' of Salerno, which was at that time the leading medical centre in western Christian Europe. By the end of the twelfth century, these three texts would be joined into a single compendium and given the title *Trotula*, an epithet that was soon misunderstood as an author's name. The three component texts also continued to circulate independently, and it is one of these, the *Liber de sinthomatibus mulierum* (*Book on the Conditions of Women*, hereafter *LSM*), that served as the basis for the *Secrés dé femmes*.

The Latin *LSM* itself has a rather complicated lineage.[25] It derives in large part from the chapters on women's diseases from the *Viaticum* of Constantinus Africanus (d. *ante* 1098/99), which, in turn, was a translation from the Arabic of a medical encyclopedia by the North African writer Ibn al-Jazzar (d. 979 CE).[26] To the *Viaticum* chapters the *LSM*'s author added small extracts from other Latin medical texts and miscellaneous recipes, some perhaps drawn from

---

[24]   The so-called 'Frauengeheimnisse' ('Women's Secrets', a title not documented in the manuscript itself) is a German-Latin collection of recipes, not a proper text; see L.V. Zingerle, 'Recepte aus dem XII. Jahrhundert', *Germania*, 12 (1867): 463–9. While there is a Hebrew translation of the *Trotula* that seems to predate this Anglo-Norman text by a couple of decades, Hebrew was not the 'vernacular' of French Jews, but rather a learned tongue in the same way Latin was for Christians. The Hebrew *Trotula* is edited from a fragmentary copy in Ron Barkaï, *A History of Jewish Gynaecological Texts in the Middle Ages* (Leiden, 1998), pp. 181–91; and re-edited on the basis of a newly discovered manuscript in Carmen Caballero Navas, 'Algunos 'secretos de mujeres' revelados: El *Šeʾar yašub* y la recepción y transmisión del *Trotula* en hebreo [Some 'secrets of women' revealed. The *Sheʾar yašub* and the reception and transmission of the *Trotula* in Hebrew]', *Miscelánea de Estudios Árabes y Hebraicos, sección Hebreo*, 55 (2006): 381–425.

[25]   For the *LSM*'s history as part of the so-called *Trotula* ensemble, see Monica H. Green, 'The Development of the Trotula', *Revue d'Histoire des Textes*, 26 (1996): 119–203. In all references to the *Trotula* texts here and in the following edition, I identify passages of the Latin texts according to the paragraph divisions employed by Green in 'Development' and used in my edition of the Latin text: *The 'Trotula': a Medieval Compendium of Women's Medicine* (Philadelphia, 2001).

[26]   For an edition and English translation of Book VI of Ibn al-Jazzar's *Zad al-musafir*, see Gerrit Bos, *Ibn al-Jazzar on Sexual Diseases and Their Treatment*, The Sir Henry Wellcome Asian Series (London, 1997).

oral traditions. The *LSM* had an Urtext, an original draft called in one of its two extant manuscripts *Tractatus de egritudinibus mulierum* (hereafter, *TEM*).[27] Not only does the *TEM* lack the prologue of the *LSM*, but it differs textually from it in many respects. Most striking are the differences in vocabulary, which in the *TEM* seem to reflect something closer to contemporary vernacular usages [for example, *flos*, which in the *LSM* is replaced by *menses*; or *natura* (in the sense of 'vagina') which is replaced by *vulva*].[28] The Anglo-Norman translation reflects a text somewhere between the *TEM* and the *LSM* (or perhaps even a conflation of the two), generally giving readings closer to the revised *LSM* but incorporating recipes or, in one case, a reading currently documented only in the *TEM*.[29] The *Secrés* also lacks the prologue that had opened the *LSM* (¶¶1–2, not found in the *TEM*), which recounted in natural philosophical terms the creation of the sexes and the reasons why women, more than men, suffered diseases in their reproductive organs.

The Anglo-Norman *Secrés dé femmes* translates less than a quarter of the contents of the *TEM/LSM*. Skipping over the opening chapters on the causes and cures for menstrual abnormalities, uterine suffocation,[30] other uterine displacements (including prolapse), abnormal heat or cold of the uterus, ulceration of the uterus and itching of the vulva, it goes immediately to the chapters on infertility, opening with the phrase 'Ypocras dit et [nous] enseigne/ Les raisons de femme baraigne' ('Hippocrates says and teaches us/The reasons why women are barren') which translates the Latin ¶74 'Sicut testatur Ypocras, quedam mulieres inutiles sunt ad conceptionem' ('Just as Hippocrates witnesses, certain women are useless for conception'). The next 38 lines of the *Secrés* (ll.

---

[27]　Paris, BnF, MS lat. 7056 (s. xiii med., France or England), fols 97rb–100ra (*olim* 278rb–81ra). A fragmentary copy (¶¶2–33) is found in London, British Library, MS Sloane 783 B (s. xv, England), fols 19r–21r (*olim* 165r–7r). There is also an acephalous Latin-English adaptation of ¶¶6–66 in London, Wellcome Institute for the History of Medicine, Western MS 5650, s. xv (England), fols 62r–7v.

[28]　*Natura* was used twice for 'vagina' in the sole complete copy of the *TEM* (¶¶25 and 36), although *vulva* was the more common term. In the *Secrés dé femmes*, *nature* is used for the vagina of an animal (l. 89) while *naissance* is used for the human vagina (l. 105). In both the Latin and the French texts, *natura/nature* also carries its normal sense of 'nature', 'character', 'Nature' (personified). *Naissance* (and its variants) is used for 'vulva' throughout the other gynaecological text here in Trinity O.1.20, which is drawn ultimately from the Salernitan *LSM*; see Tony Hunt, *Anglo-Norman Medicine* (Cambridge: D.S. Brewer, 1994), 2: 112.

[29]　On the differing readings of the *TEM* and the *LSM*, see pp. 198 (¶¶76a and 78c) and 200–1 (¶97a/101).

[30]　The womb was thought either itself to rise up to the organs of respiration or to give off a noxious fume that caused suffocation. The resulting attack in many respects resembled an epileptic fit and could prove fatal.

3–40) then depart completely from the Latin text, offering instead an account of why some couples are sterile (the first reason being male homosexuality), the sexual debt men and women owe each other, and why men and women should speak well of each other. It then returns to its Latin source and, apart from skipping over a few chapters, it adheres fairly closely to it from here on. The overall fidelity of the translator to his Latin source thus makes the novel additions stand out all the more starkly.

Given the probable composition of this text in the first half of the thirteenth century, the condemnation of male homosexuality is not surprising. The considerable body of work on the history of homosexuality in the last quarter century has produced a consensus on, if nothing else, the fact that the late twelfth and early thirteenth centuries witnessed a pronounced heightening of hostility toward homosexual practices.[31] The prescription that sodomites be burned, for example (line 7), was articulated at an ecclesiastical council in Jerusalem in 1120, and what has been called an 'uncompromising homophobia' seems to have been particularly characteristic of northern France, where there was a spate of synodal legislation against 'sodomy' from 1196 on.[32] What *is* surprising about the *Secrés dé femmes*, however, is to find such an explicit statement in a medical work. Not a single other medieval text on fertility identifies male homosexuality as a cause of infertility.[33] This silence may have been due to an assumption that the diversion of male sexual activity into homosexual couplings was so obvious a cause of non-generation that it need not be mentioned. Perhaps equally influential, however, was the increasing sense, from the mid-thirteenth century on, that 'sodomy' was *nefandum*, a crime so heinous that it ought not even be named.[34] Whatever the reason for the general silence, the unabashed fulminations of this author

---

[31]   Michael Goodich, *The Unmentionable Vice: Homosexuality in the Later Medieval Period* (Santa Barbara, CA, 1979); John Boswell, *Christianity, Social Tolerance, and Homosexuality: Gay People in Western Europe from the Beginning of the Christian Era to the Fourteenth Century* (Chicago, 1980); Mark D. Jordan, *The Invention of Sodomy in Christian Theology* (Chicago, 1997); Allen Frantzen, *Before the Closet: Same-Sex Love from 'Beowulf' to 'Angels in America'* (Chicago, 1998); Helmut Puff, *Sodomy in Reformation Germany and Switzerland, 1400–1600* (Chicago, 2003).

[32]   John W. Baldwin, *The Language of Sex: Five Voices from Northern France around 1200* (Chicago, 1994).

[33]   See Joan Cadden, *Meanings of Sex Difference in the Middle Ages: Medicine, Science and Culture* (Cambridge, 1993), pp. 228–58; and, for a comprehensive list of fertility texts, Green, 'Handlist'.

[34]   Jacques Chiffoleau, 'Dire l'indicible: Remarques sur la catégorie du *nefandum* du XIIe au XVe siècle', *Annales: economies, sociétés, civilisations*, 45 (1990): 289–324; and Puff, *Sodomy*. On the early fourteenth-century efforts of the physician and theologian Pietro d'Abano to open up a space to discuss homosexual activities in a natural philosophical

– who demands not only the burning of 'sodomites' but also the scattering of their ashes to the wind – mark this text as decidedly unusual. In fact, I think it likely, as I will explain in more detail below, that this author (who may not even have been a physician) was not writing for the sake of medical practitioners but was directing his instructions to the general populace. The *Secrés dé femmes* reads more like a *sermon* directed to the laity than a specialized tract on therapy. Indeed, at line 83 he even refers to this treatise as a 'sermon' he is preaching ('*Por sermon dire et proicher*'). Admittedly, not even regular sermons went into this kind of detail about sexual sins; they were, however, characteristically addressed to both men and women, and the need for harmony between husband and wife was a common theme.[35] Thus, while the diatribe against homosexuals makes this tract distinctive, it does seem to fit the genre of marriage sermons better than that of a strictly therapeutic tract. The fact that it came to be included in a compendium of quite specialized works on medicine and surgery may say more about continuing medical concerns over infertility than the text's original purpose or audience.[36]

The didactic character of the *Secrés dé femmes* is further seen in the next lines, which offer a moralizing admonition to husbands and wives. The notion

---

framework, see Joan Cadden, '"Nothing Natural is Shameful": Vestiges of a Debate about Sex and Science in a Group of Late Medieval Manuscripts', *Speculum*, 76 (2001): 66–89.

[35]   David D'Avray, ed., *Medieval Marriage Sermons: Mass Communication in a Culture without Print* (Oxford, 2001), p. 9; and Rudiger Schnell, *Frauendiskurs, Männerdiskurs, Ehediskurs: Textsorten und Geschlechterkonzepte in Mittelalter und Früher Neuzeit* (Frankfurt, 1998), pp. 92–5 and 136–9. Both d'Avray's and Schnell's samples come from the second quarter of the thirteenth century, at the earliest, and so may postdate the text edited here. Marc Boone, 'State Power and Illicit Sexuality: the Persecution of Sodomy in Late Medieval Bruges', *Journal of Medieval History* 22 (1996): 135–53, similarly notes (p. 140) that a study of sermons in the Southern Low Countries showed no mention of sodomy prior to the fourteenth century.

[36]   The corrupt state of the text here in Trinity O.1.20 (see, for example, lines 28–29 and 95) together with indications of Continental origin (see Hunt n. 5), suggest that this copy is some degree removed from the original. The medical material in the *Secrés* is, of course, redundant of the other French version of the *LSM* found on fols 216r–35v, although that fact seems to have been noticed neither by the scribes nor any medieval reader of the manuscript. On the cooptation of gynaecological literature towards the particular goal of rendering women fertile, see Monica H. Green, '"Traittié tout de mençonges": the *Secrés des dames*, "Trotula", and Attitudes Towards Women's Medicine in Fourteenth- and Early Fifteenth-Century France', in Marilynn Desmond (ed.), *Christine de Pizan and the Categories of Difference* (Minneapolis, MN, 1998), pp. 146–78, repr. in Green, *Women's Healthcare*, Essay VI; and Green, 'From "Diseases of Women" to "Secrets of Women": the Transformation of Gynecological Literature in the Later Middle Ages', *Journal of Medieval and Early Modern Studies*, 30 (2000): 5–39.

of the 'conjugal debt' – the obligation of both husband and wife to accede to the sexual demands of their spouse – is of course well known as an element of Christian ideas of marriage as they developed over the course of the Middle Ages.[37] Hildegard of Bingen (1098–1179) is one of the few medical writers to address at length the ways emotional friction between husband and wife can contribute adversely to reproduction.[38] There is no reason to believe our author was influenced by Hildegard's work, of course. Rather, his views simply offer confirmation of how widespread this view of marital sexuality had become.

A further striking feature of this 'sermon' on fertility is that it is clearly addressed as much to women as it is to men. The few medical discussions of sexuality in circulation by the early thirteenth century are addressed (and refer primarily) to men and male sexuality: Constantinus Africanus's *De coitu* (*On Intercourse*), the anonymous late eleventh-century *Liber minor de coitu* (*Lesser Book on Intercourse*), and the pseudo-Galenic *De spermate* (*On the Seed*). Infertility *per se* had not yet become an independent subject of medical interest,[39] and Salernitan writings that mentioned the topic (such as Copho's *Practica*, whose chapters on infertility would later be attached to the *LSM*) acknowledged that both men and women could be the 'cause' of infertility, but tended to focus more attention on the woman.[40] Thus, the *Secrés* is distinctive in recognizing both men and women as equal contributors to the problem of infertility.

Given the likelihood that the author of the *Secrés* is a cleric with quite orthodox religious views, one who was using his Latin source creatively and selectively to fashion a new work to serve his own purposes, it is surprising that he chose to retain the section on contraception (ll. 105–22, ¶¶ 83–7 of the Latin).

---

[37]   Elizabeth M. Makowski, 'The Conjugal Debt and Canon Law', *Journal of Medieval History*, 3 (1977): 99–114. On theological views, see James A. Brundage, *Law, Sex, and Christian Society in Medieval Europe* (Chicago, 1987); and Pierre J. Payer, *The Bridling of Desire: Ideas of Sex in the Later Middle Ages* (Toronto, 1993). On medical and scientific views, see Danielle Jacquart and Claude Thomasset, *Sexualité et savoir médical au moyen âge* (Paris, 1985), English trans. *Sexuality and Medical Knowledge in the Middle Ages* (Oxford, 1988); Mary F. Wack, *Lovesickness in the Middle Ages: the 'Viaticum' and its Commentaries* (Philadelphia, PA, 1990); Cadden, *Meanings*.

[38]   Laurence Moulinier, ed., *Beate Hildegardis Cause et cure*, Rarissima mediaevalia, 1 (Berlin, 2003). Recent research suggests that the *Cause et cure* may not entirely be the authentic work of Hildegard [see Laurence Moulinier, 'Hildegarde ou Pseudo-Hildegarde? Réflexions sur l'authenticité du traité *Cause et cure*', in Rainer Berndt (ed.), *'Im Angesicht Gottes suche der Mensch sich selbst': Hildegard von Bingen (1098–1179)* (Berlin, 2001), pp. 115–46], although this finding in no way diminishes the unusualness of the views in the text.

[39]   Aside from the Salernitan text *Inprimis considerandum est utrum culpa uiri uel mulieris*, all known independent treatises on fertility date from the fourteenth century or later.

[40]   See Green, *The 'Trotula'*, ¶¶129–31.

In justifying the inclusion of contraceptives, the Latin *TEM/LSM* had drawn on a statement in Constantine the African's *Pantegni*, a Latin translation of the *Kamil as-Sina 'a at-Tibbiya* (*Book of the Whole Art of Medicine*) by the tenth-century Persian physician, 'Ali ibn 'Abbas al-Majusi. Constantine, himself a Benedictine monk, said that sexual intercourse should be avoided by women whose uterus was too small to bear children; in such cases, pregnancy might be life-threatening.[41] The author of the Latin *TEM/LSM*, however, went on to note that not all women were able to abstain since (as it was thought) women needed regular sexual activity to maintain health. Thus, contraception is justified on medical grounds and is in no way apologized for. Our French author apparently adhered to this ethic. Lines 105–22, although not a precise translation, in no way mince words: there is no ambiguity about what is being discussed or why.[42] However, neither the Latin nor the French go so far as to advocate abortifacients: all these prescriptions are for preventing *conception* ('sauns conceivre et sauns mort', 'conceivre ne porra', 'de conceivre enfaunt ja mal ne doterez') rather than aborting a conceived foetus. Given the belief that the embryo was not fully human until it was 'ensouled' (fetal ages varied from 30 to 120 days), it seems that this author, like other contemporaries, may have worked within the morally flexible grey zone that any interventions prior to ensoulment were permissible.

Nevertheless, these passages on contraceptives did provoke concerns among both copyists of the Latin *LSM* and other medieval vernacular translators, who displayed various levels of unease with the material. Only one other thirteenth-century French translation of the *LSM* similarly directs contraceptive information to women, and even in this case the section would soon be deleted; the fullest extant copy of this text – which claims to be addressed to a female audience – has suppressed the contraceptive passages in their entirety.[43] Similar

---

[41]   On this passage and the presence of other material in Constantine's works relating to sexuality and contraception, see Green, 'Constantinus Africanus and the Conflict Between Religion and Science'; and Green, *The 'Trotula'*, p. 34. On the *Pantegni* generally, see Charles Burnett and Danielle Jacquart (eds), *Constantine the African and 'Ali ibn al-'Abbas al-Magusi: the 'Pantegni' and Related Texts* (Leiden, 1994).

[42]   Although it has been argued that chemically effective contraceptives seem to have been known in the Middle Ages [see Monica H. Green, 'Gendering the History of Women's Healthcare', *Gender and History*, Twentieth Anniversary Special Issue, 20, no. 3 (November 2008): 487–518], none of these amuletic prescriptions draw on that knowledge. Still, the belief in the power of amulets was real and could even be rationally explained. See Judith Wilcox and John M. Riddle, 'Qust.a- ibn Lūqā's Physical Ligatures and the Recognition of the Placebo Effect: with an Edition and Translation', *Medieval Encounters: Jewish, Christian and Muslim Culture in Confluence and Dialogue*, 1: 1 (1995): 1–50.

[43]   This second French translation of the *Trotula* exists in three different redactions, none of which reflects what must have originally been a complete and quite literal translation

concerns can be found elsewhere. One fourteenth-century copyist of an early version of the Latin *LSM* transposed the passages into cipher.[44] One whole branch of a revised version of the Latin *LSM*, dating from the late twelfth century, deleted the paragraphs in their entirety.[45] Indeed, all late medieval vernacular gynaecological texts addressed to women have suppressed the information on contraceptives lest, as one English translator asserted, 'sume corssed kelots [prostitutes] wold usset'.[46] The Anglo-Norman *Secrés* is thus highly unusual in entrusting contraceptive information directly to women.

Even the title, 'The Secrets of Women', was a novelty. We cannot know, of course, whether the title the work bears in the Trinity manuscript is an addition of the author himself. Be that as it may, whoever did assign the title *Secrés dé femmes* to this text captured the essence of a trend that was to peak in the fourteenth and fifteenth centuries. This was the keen interest among natural philosophers and physicians in both understanding and attempting to control the processes of generation, a topic they labelled 'the secrets of women'. Whereas earlier gynaecological literature (including the full text of the *TEM/ LSM*) was concerned to treat women's diseases broadly defined, there began in the thirteenth century, probably as a result of the new Aristotelian influences in natural philosophical thought, a tendency among both university scholars and physicians to display a narrower, more focused interest in problems of generation alone. This interest manifested itself in several ways, the most important of which (for our purposes) was the habit of excerpting material on generation from pre-existent gynaecological texts.[47] Indeed, the *Secrés* is of particular importance not only because it is so early, but also because it shows this interest so early at a lay level, earlier than among natural philosophers and physicians associated with the universities. Although this *Secrés dé femmes* exhibits far more interest in therapeutic matters than most similarly titled works that would follow in the fourteenth and fifteenth centuries, this redactor's narrowing down of women's

---

of the Latin *LSM*. See Green, 'Handlist II', pp. 90–92. A verse rendition of this prose translation (Fren3 in Green, '*Trotula* Handlist II') pares down the contraceptives to one single recipe, ¶86; see text edited in Hunt, *Anglo-Norman Medicine* 2: 76–107.

[44]   Oxford, Magdalen College, MS 173, fol. 252r.

[45]   On *LSM 3*, see Green, 'Development', pp. 134–5. The contraceptives were, however, reinserted into the proto-ensemble of the *Trotula* compendium and generally remained untouched throughout the later circulation of the Latin texts.

[46]   On this Middle English text, see Monica H. Green, 'Obstetrical and Gynecological Texts in Middle English', *Studies in the Age of Chaucer*, 14 (1992): 53–88, at pp. 65 and 70; and Barratt, *The Knowing of Woman's Kind*. Similarly, there are no contraceptives in a fifteenth-century Dutch translation of the *Trotula* addressed to women that circulated in three different versions; see Green, 'Handlist', pp. 83–4.

[47]   See Green, 'Traittié' and 'From "Diseases of Women"'.

diseases to aspects specifically surrounding fertility would herald a much more widespread phenomenon in the centuries to come.

This little text, then, has much to suggest about attitudes toward sexuality and reproduction in the late twelfth and early thirteenth centuries. The author's Latinity, together with the clear didactic focus of the text and the unusual condemnation of male homosexuality, suggests that he was a priest concerned to provide his flock with clear precepts about sexual behavior. It is clear that he believed that the Latin medical material that came into his hands was a useful source of further information for his parishioners. This brief vernacular text confirms what other contemporary sources have to say about twelfth-century concerns with homosexuality and, at least in this one instance, suggest that the debates among elite Latinate clergy 'trickled down' at certain points to ordinary laity, including women. Whereas the other Anglo-Norman translation of the *Trotula* found in this Trinity manuscript suggests adaptation for medical professionals,[48] the Anglo-Norman *Secrés dé femmes* is indeed 'vernacular' in its objectives as well as its language.

Table 9.1 Latin texts on women's medicine (excluding the *Trotula*) in England, eleventh to fourteenth centuries[a]

Author (if known) and title	Earliest documented presence in England	Earliest English Manuscript(s)
De diversis causis mulierum	Late 11th/ early 12th century	Sloane 475; Harley 4977[b]
Soranus (?), *Ad mulieres postquam peperint*	Early 12th century	Harley 4977
Epistola de virginibus	Early 12th century	Harley 4977
De urinis mulierum	Early 12th century	Sloane 1621; Bethesda, NLM E8; St John's D.4[c]
Gynaecia Cleopatrae (abbreviated version)	Mid 12th century	Laud Misc. 567; St John's D.4; NYAM[d]
Non omnes quidem (an adaptation of Muscio)	Mid 12th century	Laud Misc. 567; St John's D.4; NYAM
De passionibus mulierum A	Mid 12th century	Laud Misc. 567; St John's D.4; NYAM

---

48   Despite its opening address to women ('Bien sachiés, femmes, de ce n'aiés dotaunce, Ci est escrit por voir de lor science'), the text is in fact filled with references to *clercs* and *mires*. See Green, *Making Women's Medicine Masculine*, pp. 170–72; the text is edited in Hunt, *Anglo-Norman Medicine*, 2: 76–107.

De passionibus mulierum B	Early 13th century	Digby 79; St John's D.4
Theodorus Priscianus (pseudo-), *Ad Octavium filium*	Early 13th century	Digby 79; St John's D.4
Inprimis considerandum est utrum culpa uiri uel mulieris	Early 13th century	Digby 79
Cura contra omnes passiones matricis	Late 13th century	Trinity R.14.30
Muscio, fetal images and text	Late 13th century	Ashmole 399
Constantinus Africanus, *De genitalibus membris*	Late 13th century	Ashmole 399; St John's D.4
Theodorus Priscianus, *Gynaecia*	14th century	St John's D.4
Paul of Aegina, *De difficultate parturiendi* (= *De re medica*, Book 3, cap. 251)	14th century	St John's D.4
Caelius Aurelianus, *Gynaecia*	14th century	NYAM
Muscio, *Pessaria*	14th century	NYAM
Gynaecia Cleopatrae (long version)	14th century	Copenhagen 1653[e]
Muscio, *Gynaecia*	14th century	Copenhagen 1653
Johannes de Parma, *Regimen contra sterilitatem*	14th century	Exeter College, MS 35
De naturis mulierum (an adaptation of Muscio)	Late 14th century	[No English MSS, but translated into English by s. xiv ex.]

a: 'Earliest documented presence in England' refers either to the estimated date of the earliest manuscript made in England, or to other documentary witnesses to the text (for example, being listed in a library catalogue). For reasons of space, I have not provided specific citations here. They can be obtained from the author upon request; b: Harley 4977 has been variously localized as either northern France or England. Its provenance prior to the early seventeenth century (when the name 'Elizabeth/Hopton/1610' was inscribed) is uncertain; c: Cambridge, St John's College D.4 [James 79], part 3, dates from the first half of the twelfth century; with 11 different gynecological texts, it stands as the largest collection of its kind since the ninth century. It was written in Italy and may have stayed there through the early thirteenth century, when it was annotated by an Italian hand. By the fourteenth century, however, it had migrated to England; d: New York, New York Academy of Medicine, MS SAFE, s. xiii med. (France). This is probably a manuscript commissioned by the Amiens cleric Richard de Fournival (d. 1260). It had migrated to England by at least the end of the fourteenth century, when it appears in the catalogue to St Augustine's Abbey, Canterbury. See B.C. Barker-Benfield, *St Augustine's Abbey, Canterbury*, Corpus of British Medieval Library Catalogues, 13 (3 vols, London, 2008); e: Copenhagen, Det Kgl. Bibliotek, Gamle Kgl. Samling, MS 1653, s. xi ex, was written in the distinctive southern Italian script called Beneventan at the Benedictine monastery of Monte Cassino. It migrated to England by the fourteenth century. See Francis Newton, *The Scriptorium and Library at Monte Cassino, 1058–1105* (Cambridge, 1999), passim.

Chapter 9

Appendix

What follows are the passages from the Latin *Tractatus de egritudinibus mulierum* (*TEM*) and the *Liber de sinthomatibus mulierum 1* (*LSM 1*) that served as the source(s) for the French translator of *Les secrés dé femmes* (here reprinting the French text as edited later in this volume by Tony Hunt, by kind permission). Comparison of the three texts suggests that the Old French translator was either conflating the two Latin texts or he was using a version intermediate between the two.[1] The *TEM* has been transcribed from Paris, BnF, MS lat. 7056, s. xiii med. (France or England), fols 97rb–100ra (*olim* 278rb–281ra), the only complete copy of the Latin text; and the *LSM 1* from Oxford, Magdalen College, MS 173, s. xiv in. (England), fols 246v–253r (= **O**), with variants noted from Oxford, Bodleian Library, MS Bodley 361, an. 1453–59 (Salisbury), pp. 458–480 (= **Z**).[2] The paragraph numbers refer to the textual divisions of the *TEM/LSM 1* as established by Green in 1996.[3] Punctuation is editorial. Consonantal 'u' and 'i' has been changed to 'v' and 'j', respectively. Square brackets [] indicate text that should be added.

---

[1] A partial Middle English translation of the *TEM* found in London, British Library, MS Additional 34111, fols 72v–73v, presents just such an intermediate form, agreeing with the Paris text of the *TEM* in two passages (¶¶86a and 98), and agreeing with the *LSM 1* in omitting ¶76a and ¶78c but including ¶78. My thanks to Elizabeth L'Estrange for bringing this Middle English MS to my attention and sharing her notes on it.

[2] The full text of **Z** is transcribed in Hunt, *Anglo-Norman Medicine* 2:116–28.

[3] See Green, 'Development'.

Les secrés de femmes	Tractatus de egritudinibus mulierum	Liber de sinthomatibus mulierum
Ypocras dit et [nous] enseigne	[¶74] Quasdam dicit Ypocras non posse concipere	[¶74] Sicut testatur Ypocras, quedam mulieres
Les raisons de femme baraigne;	...	inutiles ad conceptionem ...
Avaunt maudist tot sodomite		
[4] Ke femme laise, a home habite.		
Et ki n'a fait com faire deit		
Et a nature to[l]t sen dreit,		
Il dist que om le devreit arder;		
[8] Por parenté ne por aver		
Justice nel(i) deit respiter,		
Mais au vent la poudre venter,		
Kar il sont taunt de pugnais flair		
[12] Ke a poi ke il n[e] corumpent l'air.		
Ore revendrai a ma ra[i]son,		
Kar del parler n'es[t] or(e) saison.		
Ains voil parler de [la] nature		
[16] Ke om(e) deit a femme par dreiture		
Et femme a home deit son dreit		
Paer; covient que chescun deit		
Aussi cum font les mues bestes		
[20] Ke font en lor saison lor festes		
Et par nature ensemble vivent		
Et fruit font ke le mund mai[n]tenent.		
Home et femme est mult digne chose,		
[24] Trop est fous ke mesdire ose.		
Nous sumus tous de femme trait,		
Ke medit [mult] graunt folie fait.		

Aussi di jo a la parsume:
[28] Fole est femme que mesdit d'ome;
La forme Deu l'image porte
[...]
[...]
[32] Taunt deit plus digne chose estre
Le home ke femme a par dreiture.
Et femme deit metre sa cure
De bien fairë et de bien dire.
[36] Kaunt plus fait mal, de taunt est pire.
Trop ai long[e] demuere faite
Ke aucun[e] raison n'ai estraite
Por quei la femme ne conceit
[40] Kaunt habit d'omë a a dreit.
Il pecche tel orë en l'ome,
Et briefment dirai la some.

Si trop espesse est la semence,
[44] Ne quidez pas ke jo vous mence,
Pas ne poet entrer el marris.
Et si cliers est et trop soutis,
Bien [le] receit et puis le rent,
[48] Si tu [n'] as point d'engendrement.

A chief de fois pesche en la femme;
Si l'uns contre l'autre seme,
Si estreit est le col del marris,
[52] Donc est por nient fait ceste estris,

pre nimia gracilitate vel macie, quasdam uero pre
nimia pinguedine habentes matrices strictas nec
potest semen intrare.

que sunt nimis macre et tenues. Quedam propter
nimiam pinguedinem que circumvoluta ori
matricis¹ non permittit semen intra matricem
recipi quoniam constrictum est orificium.

La semence n'i poet entrer,
Ariere li covient coler.
Et si li marris est trop grasse
[56] De la femme ke bien s'aise
Ke lé conduis scient estopés,
Des [a]chesons i a assés
Ke ne poet entrer la semence
[60] El liu dont femme se deit defence.

Et si li marris n'est vellus,
Kaunt que om mette tot rechiet jus.
Et ce avient en femme de joie
[64] Ke trop est glasaunt cele voie;
La semence poet recoillir,
Mes long tens nel poet retenir,
Ains est come piere glassaunt
[68] Ke gist en ewe que est coraunt.

Home de freide nature
Et si avient par aventure
Kë home est de freide nature
Ki al derain sovre fera,
[72] E la semence s'avauncera.
Kaunt l'un de l'autre s'avaunce,
Lor semence pert l'aliaunce,
Ke il covient que en .i. point soit pris
[76] De lor volenté li delis.

Quedam etiam habent matricem adeo limosam quod non potest semen retinere.

Aliquando contingit ita ex natura hominis habentis semen tenue quod non potest retineri. Quidam adeo frigidi et sicci quod numquam generant.

Quedam habent matrices ita lubricas ut semen infusum non possunt retinere.

Contingit hoc etiam quandoque vicio viri qui habet semen nimis tenue et infusum matrici liquiditate sua elabitur. Quidam autem viri testiculos habent frigide et sicce complexionis, et isti aut numquam aut raro possunt generare, quia semen eorum inutile est generationi.

Kaunt chescun a geté chaaunce,
Adonkes li marris s'avaunce
De cele poison englotir
[80] Dont Deus poet faire son plaisir,
Kar si li plait, mort naistera,
Et si li plait, ce fruit vivera;
A sa volenté tot est fait.
[84] Fors soul pieté cil n'a nul plait
Por sermon dirë et proicher,
Kar tel mei covendra parler.

[French text now skips over Latin chapter with test using urine placed in two jugs to determine whose fault it is that the couple is infertile (¶75)]

Autre

Si femme veut engendrer et conceivre,
[88] Dé coillions de ver face poudre et ens vin le beive.
En la fin de ses flors puis face son voler
A celui ke plus aime, si porra concever.

Autre

Le marris [et] le nature de lievre prendrés,
[92] Vous le seccherés bien et puis poudre ferés
Et le home et la femme en vin le beveront,
Lor volenté ensemble por masle aver front.

[¶75a] Ut femina concipiat faciat pulverem de testiculis porcelli et cum vino bibat in fine menstruorum et cum viro concumbat.

[¶76] Item ut masculum concipiat siccetur matrix et vulva leporis et fiat pulvis et bibat masculus et femina.

[¶75a] Si ergo velit mulier impregnari, desiccet testiculos verris, et inde fiat pulvis et bibat in vino post purgationem menstruorum, et tunc concumbat cum viro et poterit concipere.

[¶76][2] Si velit ut masculum concipiat, accipe matricem et vulvam leporis, et desiccari faciat et bibat vir pulverem distemperatum. Et similiter faciat mulier de testiculo uno leporis in fine menstruorum et iaceat cum viro suo et concipiet masculum.

[deest]

[¶78] Item. Accipiat mulier lanam succidam et intingat cum lacte asine et liget super umbilicum et sit ibi donec vir eius concubuerit cum ea.

[¶78a] Item. Accipe corticem quercus et pulveriza[5] et bibat cum vino et in principio et in fine menstruorum.

[deest]

Autre

Crotes de lievre engloute a la fiez en ses flors,

[¶76a] Item in fine menstruorum transgluciat mulier unum testiculum leporis et coeat cum viro.[3]

[deest][4]

[¶78a] Item fiat pulvis de visco quercus et cum vino bibat in principio florum et in fine.

[¶78c] Item fiat pulvis de lepusculis in noua olla et utatur femina uno crescente luna et altero decrescente et sic istis modis poterit concipere.

---

[96] En lait de anesse laine o tot les somellons,
[...]
Sor vostre nomblil estreit tresbien le liez,
Apré a vostre baron en .i. lit coucherez,
[100] Vous et il ensemble vos volentés facez.

Autre

D[e] busche de chaine .i. sotil poudre ferez,
Au comencement de vos flors o megue le bevez.

[French skips over a recipe employing the liver and testicles of a piglet (¶78b)]

Autre

Vous prendrez del lievre ou .ii. ou .iii. founs
[104] Et en faites poudre en .i. noef pot sor les carbouns.
Ceste poudre userez en decressant et en cressaunt,
Puis faites vos delis, tost concevras enfaunt.

Espermen a femme a petite nassance

Costentin defent femme a petite naissaunce
[108] Que od home ne couche ne receive semence,
Kar por estreit marris mainte femme est morte
Et maint enfaunt peris por trop estreite porte
Por ce que tauntes de tele manere sont
[112] Ke ne poent vivre au secle si aide de home n'ont.
Galiens fait a celes par herbes graunt confort,
Lor volenté front sauns conceivre et sauns mort,
Taunt com sor li avra la femme [afi]
[116] Ne porra conceivre, ce savom nous de fi.

[The French here skips over the instruction to hold a jet stone next to the skin to prevent conception.][7]

El marris de la [chevre] qui n'eut enques foons
Est trové .i. petite piere, de ce tesmoins avoms
Ypocras et Galiens, taunt come le portera
[120] La femme sor sei, conceivre ne porra.

De masle de [mustele] les coillons prendrez
Si ke il voist vive, ne(l) le osciez;
Taunt com en quir de cerf sor vous les porterez
[124] De conceivre enfaunt ja mal ne doterez.

[¶83] Ut femina non concipiat. Constantinus ait in quodam libro[6] quod puelle que strictas habent vulvas et matrices non coeant ne concipiant et moriantur. Sed quia quedam sunt huiusmodi nature quod sine coitu sane non essent, consideraverunt sapientes medici ut coeant et fiat eis medicina ne concipiant.

[¶84] Item in matrice capre que non habet capreolos in ventre aliquando quidam lapis [invenitur]; que hunc super se portauerit non concipiet.[8]

[¶86] Item testiculos mustele vive et dimisse abire ferat ligatos in corio asine, et non concipiet.

[¶83] Constantinus dicit quod virgines que strictas habent matrices et vulvas angustas non debent viris uti propter metum conceptionis, ne moriantur. Sed quia non omnes tales continere possunt, nostro indigent auxilio in hac parte.

[¶84] Mulier si non vult concipere, alliget cum carne sua nuda et ferat secum matricem capre que numquam fetum habuit.

[¶86] Item, accipiatur mustela masculus et auferantur ei testiculi et relinquatur vivus. Hos testiculos ferat mulier in sinu suo ligatos in asinina pellicula,[9] et non concipiet.

French	Latin
[French then omits a recipe for using grains of barley in the afterbirth to prevent subsequent births (¶87); then it skips sections on miscarriage, regimen for pregnancy, swelling of the feet, distention of the belly, aid at birth, narrowness of the birth canal, and unnatural presentation (¶¶88–93)]	
Por mort enfaunt Si l'enfes est mort dedens sa mere Et hom le siet et bien apiere, Pernez moi avrone et muschet [128] Et bibuef[10] autretaunt i met. Triblez lé bien et les batez, Le jus a beivre li donez.	[¶94] Si infans mortuus fuerit in utero, teratur simul et muscus et mater herbarum, et succum bibat. [¶94] Si autem puer mortuus est, accipiatur ruta[11] et arthemesia et terantur simul et bibat succum.[12]
Autre Quisez mai lupins et aloine [132] En ewe, si li donez a beivre.	Vel absinthium et mirta et mater herbarum et piper terantur et cum vino bibat. Bibat aquam ubi lupini sunt decocti vel abscinthium.
Autre Ou [de] bibuef le jus pernez, Od peivre beivre li donez.	[see previous] Piper tritum datum cum vino iuvat.
[French text then skips five very brief recipes for the same (¶¶96–97, 98–99)]	
Autre Pernez mai ruë et bibuef,	[¶97a] Item ruta et mater herbarum et [¶101] Item accipiatur ruta, arthemesia,

absinthium terantur et cum oleo olive coquantur, et parum cere misceatur et super inguina eius mittantur.

opoponacum, abscinthium, terantur cum oleo et modica cera[13] et ponantur super inguina.

[¶100] Quod si adhuc tardet partus vel si puer mortuus est in ea, bibat lac muliebre cum oleo et statim pariet.

[deest]

[136] Aloine et popelia ovec.
Ces .iiii. herbes bien triblerez,
En oile d'olive les quisez.
Virge cirë ovec quisez
[140] Et sor les reines li liez.

Por femme ke targe de enfaunter
Si femme targe d'enfaunter
Por tost mort ou vif fors geter,
Let de femme od oile bevra,
[144] [Et] tost aprés se delivra.

[French text skips the last two recipes of this heading (i.e., expulsion of the dead fetus, ¶¶102–3); then it skips the entire section on retention of the afterbirth and other postpartum conditions (¶¶104–112); it skips the test for determining the sex of fetus (by dropping a drop of woman's blood in water and seeing if it floats or not, ¶113)]

[¶114] Dicit etiam Ypocras quod que masculum portat, colorata est et habet grossiorem mamillam dextram. Que vero feminam, pallida est et synistram mamillam habet grossiorem.

[¶114] Ypocras dicit quod femina que concepit masculum rubicundam habet faciem et dextram mammillam grossiorem. Si uero feminam concepit, pallida est et habet sinistram mamillam grossiorem.

Espeirement de enfaunt
Si vous volez saver en ame
Quaunt porte malle [la] feme,
La face est plus vermaille –
[148] Et si n'est pas de haille –
Si est sa mamele destre
Plus graunt ke la senestre,

Auques vaut viaires
[152] Enplaisaunt ses aferes.

Notes

[1]   ori matricis] ori stomachi **O** orificio matricis **Z**.

[2]   Note that the *LSM* not only combines into one single recipe what both the French and the *TEM* treat as two separate recipes, but it also creates separate instructions for the man and the woman.

[3]   I did not designate a '¶76a' in Green, 'Development', but should have done so, as this is a distinct section of the text of the *TEM* in the Paris MS.

[4]   Although this recipe is not found in the Paris copy of the Latin *TEM*, it does appear in the Middle English translation found in London, BL, Add. 34111. On the difficulties with the French text here, see the notes to Hunt's edition.

[5]   pulveriza] pulverizet **O**.

[6]   *Pantegni, Practica* 1:18, *De mulieribus parvas vulvas habentibus* (ed. in *Opera omnia Ysaac* [Lyons, 1515], pars 2, fol. 62va).

[7]   In the *TEM*, ¶85 reads 'Ut igitur non concipiant habeant secum gagatem ita quod carnem tangat.' In *LSM 1*, it reads 'Invenitur etiam quidam lapis qui gestatus a muliere prohibet conceptionem.'

[8]   Note that the *LSM 1* has substituted the deer's womb itself for the stone found in the womb. It is clear that the translation follows the *TEM* reading.

[9]   asinina] aliqua **O**.

[10]   See Hunt's edition of the OF text for the Continental origins of 'bibuef' (mugwort, *Artemisia vulgaris* L.).

[11]   For the *TEM*'s *muscus*, the *LSM* reads *ruta* here. The substitution is at first glance surprising, since musk (a secretion of the male musk deer) has no relation to rue (*Ruta graveolens* L., or perhaps other species). If, however, the original reading had been *muscata*, which Hunt identifies as sweet woodruff (*Asperula odorata* L.; cf. *Plant Names in Medieval England*, s.v. *muscata* ['anglice wodrove']), this may explain the identification with *ruta* (*Ruta montana* L.), the wild form of which bore the same name in English (see ibid., s.v. *ruta agrestis* ['anglice woderofe']). On the other hand, the error may simply reflect an eye-skip from this recipe to ¶97a/101, which opens similarly. Why the French includes southernwood (*avrone*) when it is not found in either Latin version is unclear.

[12]   The *LSM* adds three more recipes here (none of which appear in the Anglo-Norman *Secrés*): ¶95 (which employs summer savory bound onto the belly), ¶96 (vervain drunk in water or wine), and ¶97 (salt water and ass's milk mixed and drunk).

[13]   The reading in both **O** and **Z** is *zuccara*, but this is clearly an alteration that entered the *LSM* later. Versions 2 and 3 of the *LSM* (whose earliest manuscripts date from the end of the 12th century or beginning of the 13th) still have the original *cera* reading.

Chapter 10
Obstacles to Motherhood

Tony Hunt

The middle ages is dominated by the shining example of motherhood provided by the Virgin Mary, but on a more mundane level we should not ignore the obstacles to motherhood, many of which were dealt with in gynaecological writings that have been carefully studied by Monica Green.[1] Some attention has been paid to issues such as obstetrics,[2] which was mostly represented in the pre-Salernitan period by Muscio's *Gynaecia* (based on Soranus), by Caelius Aurelianus, a number of Hippocratic works, and by a treatise frequently attributed to a woman writer called Cleopatra. Attention was also paid to embryology.[3] In this body of literature we find detailed discussion of alterations of the womb, obstacles to conception, disorders of gestation, causes of miscarriage, difficulties of birth and associated problems. Of the comparatively rare writings in the vernacular, much of interest will be found in a hitherto unedited text, headed *Les Secrés dé femmes*, which was put together from a variety of sources, particularly the *Liber de sinthomatibus mulierum* (hereafter LSM) together, it appears, with an earlier draft, the *Tractatus de egritudinibus mulierum* (TEM), which forms the first component of the complex of texts that came to be known as *Trotula*.[4] The treatise is preserved in Cambridge, Trinity College, MS O.1.20 (1044) fols 21rb–23rb, an Anglo-Norman manuscript written c. 1240, which may be a copy of continental texts, to judge from certain

---

[1] See, for example, M.H. Green, *Women's Healthcare in the Mediaeval West: Texts and Contexts* (Aldershot, 2000), and in this volume. On obstacles to motherhood see C.W. Atkinson, *The Oldest Vocation. Christian Motherhood in the Middle Ages* (Ithaca, NY, 1991).

[2] See the brief remarks of M. Salvat, 'L'Accouchement dans la littérature scientifique médiévale', in *L'Enfant au moyen âge*, Sénéfiance 9 (Paris, 1980), pp. 89–106, and M.H. Green, 'Obstetrical and Gynaecological Texts in Middle English', *Studies in the Age of Chaucer* 14 (1992): 53–88.

[3] Cl. Thomasset, 'Quelques principes de l'embryologie médiévale (de Salerne à la fin du XIIIe siècle)', in *L'Enfant au moyen âge*, pp. 109–21 and P. Pahta, *Medieval Embryology in the Vernacular. The Case of* De spermate, Mémoires de la Société Néophilologique de Helsinki 53 (Helsinki, 1998).

[4] See *The 'Trotula'. A Medieval Compendium of Women's Medicine*, trans. and ed. M.H. Green (Philadelphia, PA, 2001).

lexical items.[5] The *Secrés* follows a collection of versified medical receipts known as the *Physique rimee* (fols 1r–21r), to which it was mistakenly assimilated by Paul Meyer,[6] and is in turn followed (fols 23rb–24va) by miscellaneous prose receipts, also in Anglo-Norman. The text begins with an introduction on aspects of sexual relations between man and wife, including a violent diatribe against homosexuals,[7] which is not in the LSM, and then proceeds to extol the natural relationship of man and woman and to examine a variety of topics, often with therapeutic prescriptions. Infertility of the male may be caused by the thickness of his seed, which prevents its entry into the womb, or else by its thinness, which causes it to slip out, or by infertility. Other topics include contraception,[8] aids for expelling the dead foetus, and methods of determining the sex of the foetus. In other words, *Les Secrés dé femmes* deals with obstacles (*impedimenta*) to birth and motherhood in a comparable manner to LSM c. 11 *Contra sterilitatem mulierum*,[9] and it does so in a mixture of octosyllabic (ll.1–86, 125–152) and do-decasyllabic verse (ll.87–124).

[fol. 21rb],

       Ypocras dit et [nous] enseigne[10, a]
       Les raisons de femme baraigne;
       Avaunt maudist tot sodomite
4   Ke femme laise, a home habite.[b]
       Et ki n'a fait com faire deit

---

[5]   The plant name *bibuef* (*Artemisia vulgaris*), which belongs to the language of northeast France is found in the text we print below at lines 128, 133 and 135. For further details see T. Hunt, *Anglo-Norman Medicine* 2 (Cambridge, 1997), pp. 12–13.

[6]   P. Meyer, 'Les manuscrits français de Cambridge. III. Trinity College O.I.20, Traités de médecine', *Romania*, 32 (1903): pp. 75–101, at 77.

[7]   See J.T. Noonan, *Contraception. A History of its Treatment by the Catholic Theologians and Canonists* (Cambridge MA, 1966), pp. 226–7 and J. Boswell, *Christianity, Social Tolerance, and Homosexuality. Gay People in Western Europe from the Beginning of the Christian Era to the Fourteenth Century* (Chicago, IL, 1980) and M. Kuefler, *The Boswell Thesis* (Chicago, IL, 2006), esp. pp. 179–212 (M. Kuefler, 'Male Friendship and the Suspicion of Sodomy in Twelfth-Century France'). See also M.D. Jordan, *The Invention of Sodomy in Christian Theology* (Chicago, IL, 1997).

[8]   See Noonan, *Contraception* for a discussion of contraceptive methods, especially those in Avicenna's *Canon of Medicine* and in Albert the Great, on pp. 200–230. See also M.A. Hewson, *Giles of Rome and the Medieval Theory of Conception* (London, 1975).

[9]   The Anglo-Norman translation of the LSM [hereafter LSM(AN)] is found in the Trinity manuscript on fols 216r–235v and is printed by Hunt, *Anglo-Norman Medicine*, pp. 76–107. See the section headed *Del marris* ('On the womb'). It declares concerning women 'De lor *secrés* tot i est devisé' (prologue, l.5).

[10]   LSM(AN) 717 'Ce nus dit Ypocras, que tot le bien enseigne'.

    Et a nature to[l]t sen dreit,   [fol. 21va]
    Il dist que om le devreit arder;
8   Por parenté ne por aver
    Justice nel(i) deit respiter,ᶜ
    Mais au vent la poudre venter,
    Kar il sont taunt de pugnais flair
12 Ke a poi ke il n[e] corumpent l'air.
    Ore revendrai a ma ra[i]son,
    Kar del parler n'es[t] or(e) saison.
    Ains voil parler de [la] nature
16 Ke om(e) deit a femme par dreiture
    Et femme a home deit son dreit
    Paer; covient que chescun deit
    Aussi cum font les mues bestes
20 Ke font en lor saison lor festes
    Et par nature ensemble vivent
    Et fruit font ke le mund mai[n]tenent. [sic]
    Home et femme est mult digne chose,
24 Trop est fous ke mesdire ose.
    Nous sumus tous de femme trait,
    Ke medit [mult] graunt folie fait.
    Aussi di jo a la parsume:
28 Fole est femme que mesdit d'ome;
    La forme Deu l'image porte   [fol. 21vb]
    [...]
    [...]
32 Taunt deit plus digne chose estre
    Le home ke femme a par dreiture.
    Et femme deit metre sa cure
    De bien fairë et de bien dire.
36 Kaunt plus fait mal, de taunt est pire.
    Trop ai¹¹ long[e] demuere faite
    Ke aucun[e] raison n'ai estraite
    Por quei la femme ne conceit
40 Kaunt habit d'omë a a dreit.
    Il pecche tel orë en l'ome,
    Et briefment dirai la some.
    Si trop espesse est la semence,

---

¹¹ MS *i a.*

44 Ne quidez pas ke jo vous mence,
    Pas ne poet entrer el marris.
    Et si cliers est et trop soutis,
    Bien [le] receit et puis le rent,
48 Si tu [n'] as point d'engendrement.[12]
    A chief de fois pesche en la femme;[13, d]
    Si l'uns contre l'autre seme,
    Si estreit est le col del marris,
52 Donc est por nient fait ceste estris.[14]
    La semence n'i poet entrer,
    Ariere li covient coler.   [fol. 22ra]
    Et si li marris est trop grasse
56 De la femme ke bien s'aise[15]
    Ke lé conduis seient estopés,
    Des [a]chesons i a assés
    Ke ne poet entrer la semence[e]
60 El liu dont femme se deit defence.[16]
    Et si li marris n'est vellus,[17]
    Kaunt que om mette tot rechiet jus.
    Et ce avient en femme de joie[18]
64 Ke trop est glasaunt cele voie;
    La semence poet recoillir,
    Mes long tens nel poet retenir,
    Ains est come piere glassaunt
68 Ke gist en ewe que est coraunt.

    Home de freide nature[19]
    Et si avient par aventure
    Kë home est de freide nature

---

[12] Cf. LSM [74] 'quod contingit quandoque vicio viri qui habet semen nimis tenue et infusum matrice liquiditate sua foras labitur'.
[13] See LSM [74] and LSM(AN) 722–725.
[14] 'effort, struggle'.
[15] 'lives well, indulges herself'.
[16] MS *se deit sence.*
[17] 'rough'.
[18] 'good-time girl', one of the earliest attestations.
[19] Rubric written at the end of ll.68–9. Cf. LSM [74] 'Quidam vero testiculos habent frigidos valde et siccos. Illi raro aut numquam generant quia semen eorum inutile est generatione'.

Ki al derain sovre fera,
72 E la semence s'avauncera.
Kaunt l'un de l'autre s'avaunce,
Lor semence pert l'aliaunce,
Ke il covient que en .i. point soit pris
76 De lor volenté li delis.
Kaunt chescun a geté chaaunce, [fol. 22rb]
Adonkes li marris s'avaunce
De cele poison englotir
80 Dont Deus poet faire son plaisir,
Kar si li plait, mort naistera,
Et si li plait, ce fruit vivera;
A sa volenté tot est fait.
84 Fors soul pieté cil n'a nul plait
Por sermon dirë et proicher,
Kar tel mei covendra parler.

Autre
Si femme veut engendrer et conceivre,[20]
88 Dé coillions de ver face poudre et ens vin le beive.
En la fin de ses flors puis face son voler
A celui ke plus aime, si porra concever.

Autre
Le marris [et] le nature de lievre prendrés,[21]
92 Vous le seccherés bien et puis poudre ferés
Et le home et la femme en vin le beveront,
Lor volenté ensemble por masle aver front.

Autre
Crotes de lievre engloute a la fiez en ses flors,[22] [fol. 22va]
96 En lait de anesse laine o tot les somellons,[23]

---

[20] See LSM [82]; LSM(AN) ll.741–4.
[21] See LSM [76]; LSM(AN) ll.745–8. The word 'nature' (vulva) is rendered in LSM(AN) l.745 by 'nassance'.
[22] See LSM [78]
[23] The evidence of TEM here ('Item in fine menstruorum transgluciat mulier unum testiculum leporis et coeat cum viro') suggests emendation to *Coillion de lievre engloute en la fin de ses flors* (cf. 99) and the omission of a line (to include 'intingat' from LSM 'Accipiat mulier lanam succidam et intingat cum lacte asine'). The latter seems to rule out

[...]

Sor vostre nomblil estreit tresbien le liez,

Apré a vostre baron en .i. lit coucherez,

100   Vous et il ensemble vos volentés facez.

Autre

D[e] busche de chaine .i. sotil poudre ferez,[24]

Au comencement de vos flors o megue le bevez.

Autre

Vous prendrez del lievre ou .ii. ou .iii. founs

104   Et en faites poudre en .i. noef pot sor les carbouns.

Ceste poudre userez en decressant et en cressaunt,

Puis faites vos delis, tost concevras enfaunt.

Espermen a femme a petite nassance

Costentin defent femme a petite naissaunce[25]

108   Que od home ne couche ne receive [fol. 22vb] semence,

Kar por estreit marris mainte femmë est morte

Et maint enfaunt peris por trop estreite porte

Por ce que tauntes de tele manere sont

112   Ke ne poent vivre au secle si aide de home n'ont.

Galiens fait a celes par herbes graunt confort,[26]

Lor volenté front sauns conceivre et sauns mort,

Taunt com sor li avra la femme [afi]

116   Ne porra conceivre, ce savom nous de fi.

El marris de la [chevre] qui n'eut enques foons[27]

Est trové .i. petite piere, de ce tesmoins avoms

Ypocras et Galiens, taunt come le portera

---

the interpretation (*AND²*, vol. A–C, p. 83) *l'aine* 'turnip, coleseed', of which there is no reference in the source. This leaves us with the problem (for both rhyme, form and sense) of *somellons*, which is not otherwise recorded save in the form *sommeron*(e). Is it intended to be a rendering of 'lana *succida*' ('unwashed wool, still greasy with the sweat, suint, of the sheep), that is, 'suors'?

24   See LSM(AN) ll.755.

25   See LSM [83] and p.235 n.43. See LSM(AN) ll.763–6.

26   Galen replaces the Constantine of the earlier Latin LSM.

27   See LSM [84] In Oxford, Magdalen College, MS lat.173 part of this section is written in cipher.

120 La femme sor sei, conceivre ne porra.[28]

De masle de [mustele] les coillons prendrez[29]

Si ke il voist vive, ne(l) le osciez;

Taunt com en quir de cerf sor vous les porterez

124 De conceivre enfaunt ja mal ne doterez.   [fol. 23ra]

Por mort enfaunt

Si l'enfes est mort dedens sa mere[30]

Et hom le siet et bien apiere,

Pernez moi avrone[31] et muschet

128 Et bibuef autretaunt i met.

Triblez lé bien et les batez,

Le jus a beivre li donez.

Autre

Quisez mai lupins et aloine[32]

132 En ewe, si li donez a beivre.

Autre

Ou [de] bibuef le jus pernez,

Od peivre beivre li donez.[33]

Autre

Pernez mai ruë et bibuef,

136 Aloine et popelia ovec.

Ces .iiii. herbes bien triblerez,

En oile d'olive les quisez.

Virge cirë ovec quisez

140 Et sor les reines li liez.

Por femme ke targe de enfaunter

Si femme targe d'enfaunter

---

[28] This combines LSM [84] 'Mulier si non vult concipere, carne sua nuda ferat secum matricem capre que numquam fetum habuit' and [85] 'Invenitur autem quidam lapis gagates qui gestates a muliere prohibet conceptionem vel etiam gustatus'.

[29] See LSM [86] and LSM(AN) ll.771–74.

[30] See LSM [94].

[31] MS *ravone*.

[32] See LSM [94].

[33] See above ll. 12ff.

Por tost mort ou vif fors geter,
Let de femme od oile bevra,
144 [Et] tost aprés se delivra.   [fol. 23rb]

Espeirement de enfaunt
Si vous volez saver en ame[34]
Quaunt porte malle [la] feme,
La face est plus vermaille –
148 Et si n'est pas de haille –
Si est sa mamele destre
Plus graunt ke la senestre,
Auques vaut viaires
152 Enplaisaunt ses aferes.

Notes

[a] A similar introductory line is found in LSM(AN) 717.

[b] *Abiter a*, 'to copulate with'.

[c] MS *ne li. Respiter* 'to spare, show leniency to'.

[d] The text is closer to that in Oxford, Bodleian Library, MS Bodl. 361 'Sicut testatur Ypocras, quedam mulieres inutiles sunt ad conceptum qui nimis sunt macre et tenues. Quedam propter nimiam pinguedinem que circumvoluta orificio matricis non permittit semen intra matricem recipi, quoniam constrictum est orificium. Quedam habent matrices ita lubricas ut semen infusum non possint retinere. Contingit etiam quandoque viri istud qui habet semen nimis tenue et infusum matrici liquiditate sua elabitur' (Hunt, *Anglo-Norman Medicine*, p. 125). Compare LSM [74] 'Quedam mulieres sunt inutiles ad concipiendum ... quia sunt nimis pingues et caro circumvoluta orificio matricis constringit eam, nec permitit semen viri in eam intrare. Quedam habent matricem ita lenem et lubricam quod semen receptum non potest interius retineri, quod contingit quandoque vicio viri qui habet semen nimis tenue et infusum matrice liquiditate sua foras labitur' (*The Trotula*, ed. Green, p. 94).

[e] See LSM(AN) 725ff 'A la fiez [li] rest la marris ensi grans/Que ne poet la semence [si] retenir dedens./Ne la poet retenir marris par la sentence./Et mult homes refunt qu'espandent la semence'.

---

[34]   See LSM [114] and LSM(AN) ll.845–52. The first rhyme word *ame* (*asme*) suggests the reordering of l.144 where the MS has *Quaunt feme porte malle*.

Chapter 11

A Mother's Past and her Children's Futures: Female Inheritance, Family and Dynastic Hospitals in the Thirteenth Century

Sethina Watson

As my doctoral supervisor, Henrietta Leyser impressed upon me how the high middle ages, widely recognized for its emerging institutions, was also very much a *peopled* age and a society being actively, often consciously, forged by its people.[1] Its structures did not simply emerge; they were created, as much by the beliefs or ambition of the creators as by a more pragmatic concern to 'sort things out'. She met my interest in the constitutional forms of religious houses with her own sense of the distinctiveness of any circumstance and, especially, of the people in the midst of change who were confronted with competing challenges and often answerable to strong convictions. Their labour to find workable solutions shaped and even accidently built the structures that survived them. This awareness has been my key to the early histories of several hospitals whose development in the decades between c. 1220 and c. 1240 has been particularly opaque. The hospitals at North Creake, Lechlade, Brackley and Kersey have two long-recognized features in common: on the one hand, they were foundations by laity that developed an unusually strong liturgical element, in some cases transforming into Augustinian priories; on the other, their twisting constitutional development in these years has been seen as migratory, even rudderless. Yet both these features were due to a third, unrecognized factor:

---

[1]   I grateful to the British Academy for funding the archival work upon which this study is based and, for consultation of their archives, to the Master, Fellows and Scholars of Christ's College, Cambridge; the President and Fellows of Magdalen College, Oxford; the Provost and Fellows of King's College, Cambridge; and the Warden and Fellows of New College, Oxford. My thanks also to Jocelyn Wogan-Browne, Tim Ayers and Emma Cavell for advice on earlier drafts of this essay.

they were founded or reconstituted in these decades by heiresses in the lower aristocracy or barony.

Since the early work of these women was conducted during their marriages, it is obscured by charters in their husbands' names and only revealed in their widowhood. It is a pattern familiar to scholars who have stressed the discrete identities of aristocratic women as they proceed to the status of wife then widow.[2] This course is recognized as the female lifecycle, a term which rightly aims to capture the legal and social stages of a woman's life, as well as appreciating its biological phases.[3] Lifecycle has proven particularly effective in the recent study of aristocratic women of the twelfth and thirteenth centuries, prompting fresh routes into difficult material and illuminating the lives of even lesser-known women, including those of the gentry.[4] Yet its very success has fostered an awareness of, and indeed emphasis on, the identities of the single woman, wife and widow at the expense of other, perhaps more enduring identities within family and society.[5] It may also lend an episodic quality to aristocratic women's lives in contrast to the sustained or strategic endeavours that are so readily appreciated

---

[2]   For important discussions of the ways in which marriage and widowhood could construct female identity, and the theatres of activity for aristocratic women, see Louise J. Wilkinson, *Women in Thirteenth-Century Lincolnshire* (London, 2007), pp. 1–2, 7–9, 13–91; Susan M. Johns, *Noblewomen, Aristocracy and Power in the Twelfth Century Anglo-Norman Realm* (Manchester, 2003), pp. 53–80; Emma Cavell, 'Aristocratic Widows and the Medieval Welsh Frontier: the Shropshire Evidence', *Transactions of the Royal Historical Society*, 6th series, 17 (2007): 57–82. For the legal and political status of aristocratic widows: Linda E. Mitchell, *Portraits of Medieval Women: Family, Marriage, and Politics in England 1255–1350* (Basingstoke, 2003), esp. pp. 43–55.

[3]   The defining studies are P.J.P. Goldberg, *Women, Work and Life Cycle in a Medieval Economy: Women in York and Yorkshire, c. 1300–1520* (Oxford, 1992); Pauline Stafford, 'Women and the Norman Conquest', *Transactions of the Royal Historical Society*, 6th series, 4 (1994): 221–49, at pp. 239–40. Both consider lifecycle within sophisticated contexts: Goldberg examines marriage as an aspect of women's lives, negotiated within a shifting economic milieu; Stafford stresses the relevance of stage of life to inheritance as part of wider issues of status and position in family.

[4]   Notably, the work of Wilkinson and Johns, above. For unmarried status more broadly, Cordelia Beattie, *Medieval Single Women: the Politics of Social Classification in Late Medieval England* (Oxford, 2007).

[5]   The restricted rights of married women in law also fostered depictions of motherhood in legal discussions and romance as a similarly episodic bond. Both play on social fears of the compromised loyalties of widowed mothers who have remarried and borne children with their new husband, Noël James Menuge, 'A Few Home Truths: the Medieval Mother as Guardian in Romance and Law', in Noël James Menuge (ed.), *Medieval Women and the Law* (Woodbridge, 2000), pp. 77–103. For an example of an ongoing bond of sisterhood, see Mitchell, *Portraits of Medieval Women*, pp. 11–28.

in their male counterparts.[6] Establishing the complex early histories of these hospitals allows us to discover the women behind their unusual constitutional development, and in so doing restore to these houses their constitutional rudder. To do so, we must discover both the aristocratic heiresses, whose formative role has been obscured by the forms of legal record, and the family context in which and for which they worked. For behind their actions was a personal and social role that transcended lifecycle, enduring through the more transient identities of wife and widow: motherhood.

The North Creake hospital provides an unusually rich case study (and subsequent model) for interpreting similar houses. Each was created or reconstituted by an heiress and mother, its form revised in response to her children's fortunes. The women's actions reveal that their identity as mothers was not dictated, as was their legal identity, by marital status; instead, motherhood was a station often assumed early in life and held continuously until, and even after, death. In contrast to their episodic legal identities, as mothers these women show a continuity of purpose, acting as conscious links between past and future by refashioning their inheritance for their children's futures. Leyser's work has demonstrated how aristocratic mothers tended their young children;[7] a study of dynastic hospitals extends this picture of active motherhood beyond their children's youth. It suggests that aristocratic women could take a distinctive role in formulating the future of their family, tending their children financially, politically and spiritually into adulthood and even after death. The North Creake case study is also remarkable because it illuminates a minor family of the lowest aristocracy in the early thirteenth century, a time when the families of even great magnates can be shrouded in mystery. The actions of Alice de Nerford, the woman at its centre, suggest that

---

[6]   For studies of women's strategic pursuits, see Helen J. Nicholson, 'Margaret de Lacy and the Hospital of Saint John at Aconbury, Herefordshire', *Journal of Ecclesiastical History*, 50 (1999): 629–50; Mitchell, *Portraits of Medieval Women*, esp. pp. 43–55. The literature on lordship is considerable, recent studies across this period include, David Crouch, *The Beaumont Twins: the Roots and Branches of Power in the Twelfth Century* (Cambridge, 1986); Daniel Power, *The Norman Frontier in the Twelfth and Early Thirteenth Centuries* (Cambridge, 2004); Marc Morris, *The Bigod Earls of Norfolk in the Thirteenth Century* (Woodbridge, 2005); R.R. Davies, *Lords and Lordship in the British Isles in the Late Middle Ages*, ed. Brendon Smith (Oxford, 2009); Brock Holden, *Lords of the Central Marches: English Aristocracy and Frontier Society, 1087–1265* (Oxford, 2008); Max Lieberman, *The Medieval March of Wales: the Creation and Perception of a Frontier, 1066–1283* (Cambridge, 2010).

[7]   Henrietta Leyser, *Medieval Women: a Social History of Women in England 450–1500* (London, 1995), pp. 122–41.

even the smallest inherited income could be a creative tool for refashioning the children's future, with mother as creative agent.

Because Alice's creative agency is missing from the histories of her foundation, the North Creake house remains a constitutional conundrum with a series of conflicting histories. The standard history remains that of the *Victoria County History* in 1906, which relies on G.A. Carthew's 1864 account of the house's creation, itself simply quoting the 1821 *Index Monasticus*.[8] All relate how Robert de Nerford and his wife Alice built a hospital in the reign of Henry II at North Creake, where they later established a church in 1206. Here, briefly, the *VCH* parts company with its sources, attributing the church's foundation to a widowed Alice in contrast to the earlier histories, which credit Robert.[9] All agree that this was transformed into an Augustinian priory by its first master, with Alice's consent, and in 1231 elevated to an abbey under Henry III, to whom Alice had granted patronage. When he published a translation of its cartulary, A.L. Bedingfeld proposed a revised history, suggesting that the house began as a private chapel, established by the couple in c.1206 on land brought to the marriage by Alice.[10] The hospital was added shortly after 1217 by Alice. This in turn was transformed into a priory when the master and brethren adopted the Augustinian Rule in 1227, with Alice's consent. The house came into its own only after Alice granted its patronage to the king, who raised it to an abbey and generously added estates in Rothersthorp (Northamptonshire), Ilston and Thurnby (Leicestershire), as well as other incomes and bequests. Neither of these contradictory modern histories could settle the course of the house's unusual constitutional migration, nor the reasons behind it. Only Bedingfeld attempted the latter, suggesting that a rapidly increasing endowment, fuelled by local benefaction, drove the series of elevations in status. This proposal is undermined, however, by the cartulary's

---

[8]   *VCH Norfolk*, ii, pp. 370–72; G.A. Carthew, 'A Cellarer's Account Roll of Creak Abbey', in *Norfolk Archaeology*, 6 (1864): 314–59, at pp. 314–15; Richard C. Taylor, *Index Monasticus: or the Abbeys and Other Monasteries, Alien Priories, Friaries, etc.* (London, 1821), p. 22.

[9]   Other early sources also present Robert as the church's founder, e.g. Samuel Lewis, *A Topographical Dictionary of England*, 7th edn (4 vols, London, 1848), i, p. 720; Francis Blomefield, *An Essay towards a Topographical History of the County of Norfolk* (11 vols, London, 1807), vii, p. 75.

[10]   *A Cartulary of Creake Abbey*, trans. A.L. Bedingfeld, Norfolk Record Society, 35 (Norwich, 1966) [herein *Cart. Creake*], pp. xiii–xvii. Despite Bedingfeld's more critical investigation of the sources for foundation, scholarship continues to rely on the *VCH* account, notably David Knowles and R. Neville Hadcock, *Medieval Religious Houses: England and Wales* (London, 1971), pp. 142, 168, 328, 381; Miri Rubin, *Charity and Community in Medieval Cambridge* (Cambridge, 1987), p. 138. Also, J.C. Dickinson, *The Origins of the Austin Canons and their Introduction into England* (London, 1950), p. 293.

own evidence that the house attracted few notable grants beyond its founders' endowments and by successive episcopal interventions, from its earliest days as an abbey, for the peculiarly impoverished house.[11] Although Bedingfeld elevated Alice's role, the few histories that use his work continue to credit Robert with the hospital's foundation, noting, of course, his wife's consent.[12]

Included among the house's rich archives is a brief medieval history, which aims to relate how the Augustinian abbey came into being.[13] It survives on the first folios of the abbey's cartulary, in the same hand as the original cartulary, and so was either written or copied in the first decade of the fourteenth century.[14] Bedingfeld complained that it was 'obscure and chronologically faulty',[15] but its detail is tantalizingly specific and often, as we shall see, verifiable. It serves as the

---

[11]   *Cart. Creake*, pp. xvi–xvii. For its poverty just five years after becoming an abbey, Cambridge: Christ's College Muniments [herein CCCM], Creake Abbey, At/35a; and twenty-five years later, *English Episcopal Acta* (London, 1980–) [herein *EEA*] 32, no. 144. By c. 1240 its poverty was such that 'it is known to go begging, to the public ignominy of its order' ('cogerentur in sui ordinis ignominia puplice mendicare'), *EEA* 21, no. 130.

[12]   A.J. Musson, 'Nerford , Robert (d. 1225)', *Oxford Dictionary of National Biography*, Oxford University Press, 2004 [http://www.oxforddnb.com/view/article/19781, accessed 27 November 2009].

[13]   The abbey's archive is preserved among the muniments of Christ's College, Cambridge, to whom the estates of the defunct abbey were given by Margaret Beaufort in 1507 after they reverted to the Crown in 1506. There is also a cartulary of the house: London, British Library [hereafter BL], Add. MS 61900. Bedingfeld publishes a faithful translation of the cartulary, but because its original compiler omitted witness lists and dates, and Bedingfeld did not consult the originals in the archive, his dating throughout is unreliable and sometimes wildly inaccurate. All deeds naming Abbot John, for example, refer to le Chevre (1281–1303) not Harpley (1334–1352). This essay uses the manuscript text and my own dating – with references following the earlier, continuous foliation – and indicates the deed numbers in Bedingfeld's translation. The cartulary was compiled in the early fourteenth century, and probably 1303–1307 since the original compilation is almost entirely thirteenth-century material with only six deeds mentioning Abbot Thomas of South Creake (1303–1334) (*Cart. Creake*, nos 41, 45–6, 119, 209–210). Other deeds were inserted later, including one of 1307 on fol. 34v (no. 105) by the original scribe, but seemingly after the cartulary had been compiled. Additions were also made mid-fourteenth century (after 1357) on fols 48r–53r (nos 149–167); later fourteenth century (after 1379) on fols 55v, 76v (nos 168, 242); c. 1400 of a 1304 deed on fol. 42v (no. 131); and after 1477 on fol. 53r–v (no. 168). For the abbey's dissolution, *Cart. Creake*, pp. xxii–xxiii.

[14]   BL, Add. MS 61900, fols 1r–2r, printed with many minor errors in William Dugdale, *Monasticon Anglicanum* (6 vols in 8, London, 1817–1830) [hereafter *MA*], vi, pp. 487–8 (i). The precis here relies on the manuscript text. The medieval account provides those dates not in brackets; I have supplied dates for the events it gives in brackets.

[15]   *Cart. Creake*, p. xiii.

basis for the modern histories whose attempts to navigate the confusion of dates have led to such diverse accounts of the abbey's creation.[16] It describes how a little church (*ecclesiola*) was founded in 1206 on forty acres of uncultivated land, called Lingerescroft, once held by William Pouchard from Castle Acre Priory. Its dedication to the Virgin Mary was chosen by Lord Robert de Nerford, a noble man married to the noble lady Alice. Here mass was first celebrated by Master Adam of Walsingham, dean of Burnham, in the first year (1216–17) of the reign of King Henry son of John, when Pandulf was made Bishop of Norwich (in 1222).[17] Robert had been made principal warden of Dover Castle (in 1220) by the Justiciar, Hubert de Burgh, and later, flush with victory in the naval battle of Saint Bartholomew's day (1217), he established at the urging of his wife a chapel with a hospital for a master, four chaplains and thirteen paupers. When Robert died shortly thereafter, patronage fell to Alice, daughter of John Pouchard, by right of inheritance. Sometime later, the master, William de Geyste, received the canonical habit from Thomas de Blundeville, Bishop of Norwich (1226–1236), and became prior of the brethren, now canons, to whom he also gave the habit. Its chapel and land were dedicated in 1221 by Geoffrey, Bishop of Ely (1225–1228), the nephew of Alice and brother of Hubert de Burgh. In 1231, on the advice of a council of great and wise men, Alice handed patronage to the king because she feared that her own heirs, being less well provided for, might despoil her house. The illustrious king received the patronage, and so it was through his confirmations and grants of liberties and protection, supported by papal privileges, that the almshouse came to be called abbey.[18]

Alice is a constant presence in this medieval account, either granting her consent to, or fearing, male action. Indeed, her position seems peculiarly precarious since the heirs who threatened her house were, we know from the cartulary deeds that follow, her own sons. Even though the account is fortified by the actions or advice of great men, there remains little sense of any directing vision for the house and certainly not from Alice, who seems to lack the support

---

[16] Taylor and Blomefield also construct their histories on this medieval account. Their dating to the reign of Henry II of the hospital's foundation (by Taylor) and the chapel's (by Blomefield) finds no support in the medieval account, which dates the first to *t.* Henry III and the second to *t.* John. Taylor, *Index Monasticus*, p. 22; Blomefield, *History of Norfolk*, vii, p. 75.

[17] Pandulph was elected in 1215 but not consecrated until 1222, *EEA* 21, p. xxi.

[18] 'Et sic eadem domus elemosinarium cum situ xl acrorum cum circumadiacentibus cum pertinentiis ex dono predicte fundatricis et per confirmacionem et libertatum concessionem et proteccionem venerabilium Regis Henrici tercii et aliorem per litteras et privilegia concessa stabilita et confirmata in habitatoribus eiusdem loci a Domino papa Gregorio Nono nominatur Abbatia.' BL, Add. MS 61900, fol. 2r.

of her own family. However, this impression is wrong. Rendered amenable to the will of others, Alice is placed at the edge rather than the centre of her family. Her substantial networks, which fostered her family's rise, have been hidden; so, too, has her creative determination in the face of challenges to her family's future and so to the role of her religious institution.

The early history of the house is in fact intertwined with the heady, then dashed, ambition of a Norfolk family, whose fortunes (through Alice) were tied to Hubert de Burgh, one of the major figures of his age. Hubert was from a Norfolk family of humble origins whose minor estates were in Norfolk and Suffolk and included a half knight's fee that Hubert inherited in Creake.[19] Hubert had risen swiftly through service first in John's household and then to the Crown when John became king, eventually rising to the highest of national offices when, in 1216, he was appointed Justiciar of England.[20] In May 1219, he also became regent of England for the young king and, effectively, the most powerful man in the kingdom. Hubert was a man to hitch one's fortunes to; he was also a man keen to elevate his family. Alice was closely related to Hubert, although precisely how remains unclear since Hubert's own parentage remains mysterious. The cartulary history calls him her *nepos*, and for this reason scholars have conjectured that Hubert's mother was Alice's sister.[21] Unsurprisingly, Alice herself has attracted less attention, although more can be identified of her family. A 1212 suit records that Alice, wife of Robert de Nerford, and her sister Matilda, wife of Richard de Bellehus, were daughters and co-heiresses of John Pouchard, son of William Pouchard, and his widow Ita.[22] Since Hubert's

---

[19]   S.H.F. Johnston, 'The Lands of Hubert de Burgh', *English Historical Review*, 50 (1935): 418–32, at pp. 418–21; *Rot. Chart.*, pp. 158b–9. Hubert inherited the Creake estate from Emma de Bella Fago, whose family had been granted it by Henry I, TNA C53/19, m.8; *Calendar of the Charter Rolls* (London, 1904–) [herein *CChR*], i, p. 49; *Liber Feodorum: the Book of Fees, Commonly called Testa de Nevill*, ed. H.C. Maxwell Lyte (London, 1920) i, p. 129.

[20]   For Hubert's career at this time, see Clarence Ellis, *Hubert de Burgh: a Study in Constancy* (London, 1952), pp. 12–53; D.A. Carpenter, *The Minority of Henry III* (London, 1990), esp. pp. 135–45. For its wider context see ibid. and Nicholas Vincent, *Peter des Roches, an Alien in English Politics* (Cambridge, 1996), pp. 114–41.

[21]   Mussen, 'Nerford', *DNB*. This has been convincingly refuted by S.H.F. Johnston, whose alternative suggestion that Alice de Nerford was a widow of Hubert's paternal uncle is unconvincing given the consistently close ties between Alice and the de Burghs. See Johnston, 'Lands of Hubert de Burgh', p. 421; Ellis, *Hubert de Burgh*, p. 191.

[22]   *Curia Regis Rolls of the Reigns of Richard I, John and Henry III* (London, 1922–) [herein *CRR*] vi, pp. 199–200. William Pulchehardus held one knight's fee in Norfolk from William de Wormegai in 1166, *Red Book of the Exchequer*, ed. Hubert Hall (3 vols, London, 1965), I, p. 399.

mother was also named Alice and was not a party in the division of this estate, she appears to have been neither a full nor a half-sister of Alice de Nerford,[23] but it seems that the close connection between the de Burghs and the de Nerfords probably came through Hubert's mother, Alice, rather than his unknown father. Through Hubert's own grant, we know that his mother was buried at Walsingham, a priory just four miles from North Creake.[24] Hubert and his brothers were of a similar generation to Alice de Nerford,[25] suggesting that his mother may have been sister to Ita or John and so aunt to Matilda and Alice de Nerford. Indeed, Alice may have been named after Hubert's mother; certainly, she named her own youngest son Hubert. Hubert, his family and *familia*, as we shall see, were constantly behind the promotion of Alice's own family and her North Creake foundation.

Alice had married Robert de Nerford, a minor member of another Norfolk family, a cadet branch of the family who held the Narford fee, near Castle Acre.[26] If not for Alice, his life may have passed unrecorded. He first appeared as a defendant in law suits over her inherited land in North Creake and her sister's estates in the Tresgoz fee, the latter noting that he was in royal service in 1212.[27] In 1220 he acted as warden for the heir of William de Tresgoz, the tenant in chief from whom the inherited lands were held.[28] We see his own career from late 1215 when, quite suddenly, he was active in Kent, receiving seisin of land there from Hubert de Burgh and acting as a royal official under the sheriff, with particular responsibility for royal ships and galleys.[29] This location and date is

---

[23]   For the division of women's inheritance between daughters at this time, see S.F.C. Milsom, 'Inheritance by Women in the Twelfth and Early Thirteenth Centuries', in M.S. Arnold, et al. (eds), *On the Laws and Customs of England: Essays in Honor of Samuel E. Thorne* (Chapel Hill, NC, 1981), pp. 60–89; Scott L. Waugh, 'Women's Inheritance and the Growth of Bureaucratic Monarchy in Twelfth- and Thirteenth-Century England', *Nottingham Medieval Studies*, 34 (1990): 71–92.

[24]   *Pro anima Aleysie matris nostre*, BL, MS Cotton Nero E.vii, fol. 91r (86r); Johnston, 'Lands of Hubert de Burgh', p. 419. Lacking a witness-list, the charter can be dated 1227–32 by Hubert's titles.

[25]   Both branches reached adulthood c. 1190. Hubert was active in John's service by 1198 and his elder brother, William (d. 1205), by 1185. The careers of Alice's sons suggest that the eldest were born c. 1190–1200. For the de Burghs, Johnston, 'Lands of Hubert de Burgh', pp. 418n, 421; for the de Nerford sons, n. 58, below.

[26]   Joldewin then his son, William, held the fee, *CRR* xi, nos 1799, 2493; xii, no. 1499.

[27]   *CRR* vi, pp. 2, 155, 295–6.

[28]   *CRR* vi, pp. 199–200; ix, pp. 144, 381.

[29]   *Rotuli Litterarum Clausarum*, ed. T.D. Hardy (2 vols, London, 1833–1834) [herein *RLC*] i, pp. 230, 259, 265b; *Rotuli Litterarum Patentium*, ed. T.D. Hardy (London, 1835) [herein *RLP*], pp. 170b, 177, 178.

important, since in June of that year Hubert had been made sheriff of Kent and, once again, castellan of Dover. Throughout his career, Hubert held a succession of offices and many castles, but Dover Castle remained his most constant prize.[30] He gained its custody in 1200, shortly after John became king and two years later was warden of the Cinque Ports and guardian of the seas. Although he lost these offices several years later, he was to regain Dover, along with Canterbury castle and the offices of sheriff of Kent and Surrey, on the same day he became justiciar in 1215.[31] Dover was the scene of his greatest feats of heroism, when he valiantly held the castle against sieges by Louis's invading French forces through the summer of 1216 and again in 1217.[32] It was from here, too, that '*Hubertus victor miraculosus*' set out on 24 August (St Bartholomew's day), 1217, and steered the English navy to victory against the French at the Battle of Sandwich, securely ending Louis's designs upon the English Crown.[33] By the end of 1217 the Justiciar was again in Dover, overseeing the extensive rebuilding programme that would continue through the 1220s and create one of the mightiest castles in England; indeed, by 1221 £4865 had passed through Hubert's hands for this purpose.[34] In following years the castle remained in Hubert's custody, but the building works were overseen by the constables and keepers of the works, notably Robert and Richard de Nerford and Jocelyn de Oye.[35] It was in Dover, too, that Hubert maintained his own hospital, the *Maison Dieu*, and when he was finally made an earl in 1227, it was as 'Earl of Kent'.[36] A new man, without an ancient baronial seat, Hubert may have chosen Dover, 'the key to England', as the place worthy of this honour.[37] Certainly, it was a place of the highest personal importance to Hubert throughout his years on the national stage: as royal official (custodian of the castle), justiciar (hero of its siege), regent (the great rebuilder) and then as Earl of Kent. Dover Castle was the site and symbol of his national

---

[30]   His biographer has accused Hubert of having 'an insatiable appetite for castles', Ellis, *Hubert de Burgh*, p. 12. Of them all, Dover was foremost.

[31]   Ibid., pp. 12, 14, 26.

[32]   Matthew Paris's dramatic recreations of the sieges and battle were probably drawn from conversations with Hubert. Paris, *Chronica Majora* (7 vols, London, 1872–1883), iii, pp. 3–5, 26–9; Carpenter, *Minority of Henry III*, p. 138.

[33]   Paris, *Chronica Majora*, iii, p. 29; Henry Lewin Cannon, 'The Battle of Sandwich and Eustace the Monk', *English Historical Review*, 27 (1912): 649–70, at pp. 660–67.

[34]   R.A. Brown and H.M. Colvin 'The Royal Castles 1066–1485' in H.M. Colvin (ed.), *The History of the King's Works* (2 vols, London, 1963), ii, pp. 533–894 (633–5).

[35]   *RLC* i, p. 654; ii, p. 33b. For Richard and Jocelyn, *History of the King's Works*, ii, p. 635. For Robert, see below.

[36]   *CChR* i, pp. 81–3.

[37]   *clavis enim Angliae est*. The phrase is reputedly Hubert's, Paris, *Chronica Majora*, iii, p. 28.

status; that he entrusted it to Robert suggests his personal connection to and confidence in Alice's husband.

Robert's professional life was tied to both Hubert and Dover Castle. It is likely that he was, as the abbey's medieval history states, among the victors of the St Bartholomew's day naval battle. Circumstantially, it would have been odd that he was absent from both Hubert and Dover only at this most crucial moment; more directly, Robert had by March 1216 been given responsibility for the royal ships and galleys at Dover that formed the core of the navy that day.[38] For these reasons, he was probably also present at the sieges of the castle in the summers of 1216 and 1217.[39] By December 1220, Robert was constable of Dover Castle and directing royal operations at its port, all still under Hubert. In 1221 he was personally receiving £12 p.a. from the farm of royal mills in Kent via the sheriff (Hubert), and by 1222 was taking 20 marks p.a. from the royal exchequer 'for his maintenance in our service'. He was also receiving £100 each term for the castle building works, money that previously had been paid directly to Hubert.[40] From 1223 he is named frequently in royal dispatches, receiving regular payments for the running of the castle, accounting for the building works there, overseeing and despatching the royal ships, and acting on the king's behalf to conduct inquests, seize goods, secure the safe passage of foreign embassies and commission a trebuchet.[41] In December 1223, he was still Hubert's constable when the Justiciar had to surrender his royal castles, including Dover, when the king obtained his majority. Robert's ongoing custody after this moment has been seen as one indicator of Hubert's continued, and even increasing, local power at this time.[42] Robert also occurs as a witness in a charter confirming a land purchase by Hubert de Burgh.[43] In 1224, while still constable, Robert was also sent overseas as a royal ambassador.[44] It was lucrative work and during these heady years Robert gained substantial royal gifts, consolidating

---

[38] *RLP* p. 177; Carpenter, *Minority of Henry III*, p. 21.

[39] The Crown pledged rebels' estates in Kent to those who stayed with Hubert through the second siege, Ellis, *Hubert de Burgh*, p. 39. Unfortunately, it is not clear whether Robert received any.

[40] 'ad se sustentandum in servicio nostro', *RLC* i, pp. 458, 508, 514, 546, 596b; ii, p. 3b; *Building Accounts of King Henry III*, ed. H. M. Colvin (Oxford, 1971), pp. 20–25.

[41] *RLC* i, pp. 532, 562a/b, 570, 577 a/b, 582b, 584, 596b, 599b, 600, 609b, 622, 630, 634, 636b, 637b, 647; ii, p. 7; *Bldg. Accts. Hen. III*, pp. 22–6; *CRR* xi, no. 890. For an early occurrence, *Patent Rolls of the Reign of Henry* III, 6 vols (London, 1901–1913) [herein *PR*] 1216–25, pp. 305–306.

[42] Carpenter, *Minority of Henry III*, pp. 327–8.

[43] *PR* 1225–32, p. 164. The charter can be dated between Jan. 1215 and March 1225, by the consecration of Benedict, Bishop of Rochester, a witness, and Robert's death.

[44] *RLC* i, pp. 582, 589.

incomes in Kent and Leicester.[45] This, too, was fostered under his patron and relative, the Justiciar, to whom Robert's own rise was so intimately tied, and his years of swiftest ascendency mirror those of Hubert. Then, quite suddenly in October 1224, Robert's name disappeared from the flow of royal directives regarding the castle.

It was during his time as constable, at the height of his success, that Robert and Alice began their hospital at North Creake. Its core endowment was Alice's inherited estates. The forty acre Lingerescroft site, which her father and grandfather had held from Castle Acre Priory, was supplemented by her other possessions in the nearby vills of North Creake and Burnhamthorpe, and by Alice's portion of the parish church of All Saints, Wreningham.[46] The existence of an earlier *ecclesiola* on the site is unlikely and appears to be a fabrication by the abbey's historian. His account is at pains to argue that the abbey was free from tithes and all exactions on grounds that its site was dedicated to a church before the Lateran Council of 1215.[47] There is no reference among the abbey's many early evidences either to an earlier chapel or to the date of 1206;[48] indeed the surviving body of material contradicts both. For his account of the *ecclesiola*, the author relies on an agreement witnessed by Adam de Walsingham, dean of

---

[45]   *RLC* i, p. 588b; ii, pp. 4, 40; *CRR* xi, no. 106; *Calendar of the Fine Rolls of the Reign of Henry III* (Woodbridge, 2007–) [herein *CFR*] 1223–34, no. 39; *CChR* i, p. 238.

[46]   BL, Add. MS 61900, fols 3v, 4r–5v, 6v–8r; *Cart. Creake*, nos 4, 6–11, 15–6.

[47]   The account opens with the assertion that the *ecclesiola* was established there, on land given by Philip de Candous to Castle Acre Priory 'longe tempore ante concilium Lateranensem' and had no secular or ecclesiastical service, 'because whatsoever was granted to religious men or to any church before that time was free of rent and tithe for ever' ('et quicquid ante illud tempus conferebatur religiosis, sive alicui ecclesie, sive de terris, redditibus, decimis, ratum, et firmum haberetur imposterum'). To support this, the abbey historian claims that the priory imposed the 10s rent when it enfeoffed William Pulchard. In fact, the rent was a charge incumbent on the holding and payable to Philip and his heirs; and William already held the property when Philip gave it to the priory, BL, MS Harl. 2110, fol. 44r; BL, Add. MS 61900, fols 1r, 6v–7r; *Cart. Creake*, nos 1, 15. The *ecclesiola* seems to be a tool to back-date the Creake house as a church and to a date safely before Lateran IV and the general interdict.

[48]   One of the earliest deeds, a c. 1224 grant to Robert de Nerford, mentions land at Shammer beside 'the land of St Mary de Crek', which was later confirmed by his son as being beside 'terram ecclesie sancte marie de Crek' (BL, Add. MS 61900, fols 9v–10r; *Cart. Creake*, nos 23, 25). The priory then abbey of North Creake were always referred to as 'the church of St Mary *in the meadows* of Creake' in order to distinguish it from the church of St Mary, North Creake, which was the parish church. Shammer is an area just to the east of North Creake, distant from the Lingerescroft site, but behind the parish church. The reference seems to be to land belonging to the parish church. There are no deeds that suggest that the North Creake priory held other strips of land in Shammer.

Burnham, whom he claims conducted the first mass. The agreement survives in its original, but does not mention a pre-existing church; instead it gives Alice the new right to found a hospital and, with it, to erect a chapel so that divine services might be conducted there.[49] Its date of April 1225, written prominently across its base, was ignored by the abbey's historian, who worked instead to manufacture an alternative chronology. The year-dates he supplies all relate to the early chapel, but because they are threaded throughout his account they lend the narrative its air of nonsensicality. With the elements of this argument for pre-Lateran IV religious status removed, the account is remarkably accurate, and largely verifiable.

In fact, work began on the house quite suddenly between 1223 and 1225. During this time, Robert purchased an additional forty acres of land from an indebted Roger de Geddings and secured four further acres in the town of Creake; the former he confirmed to the hospital, together with the endowment from Alice's inheritance, a windmill and patronage of the parish church of St Margaret, Hapton.[50] His confirmations 'to my hospital on Lingerescroft, and to the brothers who serve and shall serve God there' can be dated c.1224, after Robert secured Hapton church from the heirs of William Puleys in the king's court at the end of 1223.[51] Building was clearly underway, since the chapel, which was added to the hospital, was completed by April 1225.[52] The chapel's dedication to SS Bartholomew and Nicholas had been planned from at least 1223 when, on 12 May, Robert secured two yearly fairs at Burnhamthorpe on the

---

[49]   CCCM, Creake Abbey, At/26. Significantly, the author did not go on to copy the agreement into the cartulary.

[50]   BL, Add. MS 61900, fols 4r–v, 6r, 9v (*Cart. Creake*, nos 6, 7, 13, 23, 24). The four acres were Alice's dowry, defended in the king's court in 1219 and 1220, *CRR*, viii, pp. 164–5, 190. Janet Senderowitz Loengard, '"Of the Gift of her Husband": English Dower and its Consequences in the Year 1200', in Julius Kirshner and Suzanne F. Wemple (eds), *Women of the Medieval World: Essays in Honour of John H. Mundy* (Oxford, 1985), pp. 215–55.

[51]   'hospitalis meo in Lingyerescrofte et fratribus ibidem deo servientibus et servituris', BL, Add. MS 61900, fol. 4r–v (*Cart. Creake*, nos 6–7); *CRR* xi, nos 382, 1220. In 1221 Robert secured twenty-four acres in Hapton and Fundenhall (both near Wreningham) through a claim secured in a charter witnessed by Thomas de Burgh and Thomas Blundeville, Hubert's brother and nephew, *CRR* x, pp. 56–7. I cannot find mention of these among the abbey's archives, but it is possible they related to claims regarding Hapton and Wreningham churches.

[52]   CCCM, Creake Abbey, At/26. For the date see below. A charter of William son of John de Burnhamthorpe grants 1½ roods of land 'capelle sancti Bartholomei et sancti Nicholai quas Dominus Robertus de Nerford construxit in terram qui vocatur Lyngerescroft'. The deed, confirmed by his son, would appear to date to the later 1220s. BL, Add. MS 61900, fol. 70r–v (*Cart. Creake*, nos 216–7). In a c. 1300 note, the hospital of St Bartholomew was said to be outside the abbey's east gate, CCCM, Creake Abbey, roll, 7(dorse).

vigils and feasts of these saints, together with a weekly market on Wednesdays.[53] Robert's charters can all be dated between late 1223 and early 1225, although it is possible that his purchase of Hapton, by 1221, may have been an early act to gather an endowment. The timing is important because the hospital for the poor in Dover, which Hubert seems to have founded, was begun in, or slightly before, 1221 and may have served as the de Nerfords' inspiration.[54]

Alice's absence from the written record does not mean that her actual role was marginal. The hospital's histories were drawn from its early charters in Robert's name, but legal documents do not seek to reflect the complex, lived relationships behind the actions they record.[55] Indeed, they aimed to codify sometimes messy, particular circumstances in a clear statement of legal action that was thus in a recognizable, and so standardized, form. This creates problems in understanding the machinations behind any act of legal constitution, but the difficulty is heightened for a married woman, who did not grant property under her own name in common law.[56] Deeds were contracted in her husband's name, with her legal consent noted. In equating this legal formula of consent with simple agreement, as the various histories of the North Creake house have done, the picture becomes one of male actors (both constructive and potentially destructive) and of female compliance. The above account might suggest, similarly, that Alice was an observer in her family's rise under the careers of Hubert and Robert. If the constitutional creation of an institution was as much the consequence of social deliberation and politicking as legal record, the rise of a family was even more so. Because the form of record creates a legal smokescreen, reconstruction of Alice's role in the creation of her family's fortune and hospital during her married years must rely largely on circumstantial, but cumulative evidence.

In these years Alice was at the centre of her family and may even have seen herself as mother to a new dynasty. Robert's career was in his own name, and his success contingent in no small part upon his own talents, but it was Alice's

---

53   *RLC* i, p. 545b; *CFR* 1222–23, no. 169.

54   A royal charter of protection, issued December 1221, is the earliest reference to the Dover hospital. It was issued at the same time as a royal grant in favour of Hubert de Burgh, *PR* 1216–25, pp. 322–3. For Hubert's 1227–8 foundation deed, *MA* vi, p. 657 (vii).

55   For a parallel circumstance in the creation of hermitages, see Henrietta Leyser, *Hermits and the New Monasticism: a Study of Religious Communities in Western Europe* (London, 1984), p. 38.

56   Paul Brand, 'Family and Inheritance, Women and Children', in Chris Given-Wilson (ed.), *An Illustrated History of Late Medieval England* (Manchester, 1996), pp. 58–81, at pp. 63–5; Robert C. Palmer, 'Contexts of Marriage in Medieval England: Evidence from the King's Court circa 1300', *Speculum*, 59 (1984): 42–67, at pp. 50–51; Wilkinson, *Women in Thirteenth-Century Lincolnshire*, pp. 6, 17–18.

family tie that propelled and sustained this minor local figure in his royal career. The hospital was built on Alice's inherited estates and in the heart of her Norfolk home, indeed on a site near Hubert's own inheritance. This was effected with Robert's active support, but it is notable that many of the deeds in his name relate to Alice's inherited possessions and that his acquisitions were attested by the de Burghs, her family. While Robert's charters record the hospital's legal foundation, the memory of the social (and pious) act of foundation is preserved by the canon's account of c.1300, which relates that Robert established the hospital and chapel 'through the desire and common determination of that devout woman, Lady Alice, his wife'.[57]

Alice's family circumstances are therefore fundamental to understanding the creation of the North Creake house. She was a local heiress whose family ties had transformed the career of her husband and so, too, the fortunes of her family. For Alice was mother to a large family: her sons with Robert included Nicholas, John, Richard, Hubert and possibly William. With the exception of Hubert, probably the youngest, all are recorded in royal service, and in substantial posts, in the years between 1225 and 1227.[58] Hitched as they were to Hubert de Burgh, the family's fortunes must have seemed, at this moment in 1223 and 1224, to be limitless. In imitating Hubert's hospital foundation in Dover, they may have seen their own creation as a gesture of baronial pretension. Its twin dedication to SS Bartholomew and Nicholas had unusual significance to the family. Both first appear in the 1223 grant for fairs on their vigils and feast days, and were confirmed in 1227.[59] The first dedication clearly celebrated St Bartholomew's day (24 August) and Robert's heroic victory in the naval battle of that day.[60] It was also, helpfully, an excellent date for a fair. The same could not be said for St Nicholas's day (6 December), in the heart of winter, whose inconvenience prompted the removal of the fair in 1285–86 to

---

[57]   'per voluntatem et consensum devote mulieris Domine Alicie predicte uxoris sue', BL, Add. MS 61900, fol. 1v. In my translation I have chosen to stress the sense of 'shared will' that is in line with how *consensum* was used when an abbot or abbess acted legally on behalf of their monastic body.

[58]   For Nicholas (by 1224), Richard (by 1225), John and William (by 1227), see *RLC* ii, pp. 4, 11, 40, 55, 65, 94b, 108b, 115, 126b, 140b, 167b, 181b, 189b; *CFR* 1226–7, no. 326; *Bldg. Accts. Hen. III*, pp. 68, 82, 84. Hubert is first mentioned in 1236 with his brother, Richard, in a suit at Dover, *Close Rolls of the Reign of Henry III* (London, 1902–1975) [herein *CR*] 1234–7, p. 335.

[59]   *RLC* i, p. 545b; ii, pp. 100b, 116.

[60]   It was not the only hospital built to celebrate the victory: the grateful citizens of Sandwich constructed a hospital and chantry to St Bartholomew in thanksgiving, Cannon, 'Battle of Sandwich', pp. 668–9.

St Michael's Day (29 September).⁶¹ It was thus not selected for its economic benefit but, rather, because the saint's feast itself had significance. This suggests that its identification with the name of Alice and Robert's eldest son and heir was not mere coincidence, but perhaps aimed to align the hospital's identity with their son's, or to recognize a family saint after whom Nicholas was named. Either way, the dedication was intertwined with this Robert and his heir, and the charitable foundation a status symbol for the rapidly rising family, in the heart of their homeland. As such, it may have been part of a new mythology creating roots for a family destined, it must have seemed, for a future on the national stage.

For many women, such a circumstantial picture is as much as can be drawn, since their actions remain hidden behind deeds in their husband's name. This is not the case for Alice, because widowhood suddenly withdraws the legal screen. The charters of the following years reveal her determined vision for family and hospital, and the wider familial and local networks integral to its pursuit. They illuminate how Alice, in using her inherited estates as her hospital's endowment, reinvented her local, gentry past in service of her family's aristocratic future. Indeed, they show how Alice was herself that link between past and future, in her person as daughter and mother, and in her status as heiress and as relative of the de Burghs.

We are able to see Alice's actions because all went suddenly, badly wrong for the de Nerford family. Before the hospital's chapel was dedicated, Robert died. Administrative records support the abbey historian's claim that he died peacefully.⁶² He was apparently ailing by October 1224, when his name abruptly disappears from royal dispatches to Dover Castle.⁶³ His last recorded act, in early November, was to petition to transfer his tenure of land in Wytherdale (?Leicestershire), held for his maintenance in royal service, to his son and heir Nicholas in order that he be likewise maintained; this was granted at Westminster in the presence of the Justiciar, Hubert de Burgh.⁶⁴ By 10 April 1225, Robert was dead. At this date, Alice, in her widowhood, put her seal to the first of several unusual deeds for her hospital: an agreement in her name, with the archdeacon of Chester, who as the local parish rector, in which she provided two pieces of land 'de hereditate sua' to secure the rights to chaplains

---

⁶¹   *Cart. Creake*, p. xvi.

⁶²   BL, Add. MS 61900, fol. 1v.

⁶³   He was last named as constable in September and received 10 marks pay (half his annual salary) at the end of October and repayments for expenses in early November. Hubert remained custodian of the castle, receiving £1000 annually. *RLC* i, pp. 647, 650b, 652b, 654; ii, pp. 3b, 6b, 7, 8, 20b, 33b; *Bldg. Accts. Hen. III*, pp. 24–6.

⁶⁴   *RLC* ii, pp. 7 and 11.

in the hospital chapel and burial in its cemetery.[65] The agreement states that Alice was the founder, who built and sought permission for her hospital and its chapel, and whose desire it was to establish chaplains there. Alice and the rector both swore oaths to observe the agreement and set their seals at the centre of its base, between those of Adam de Walsingham, dean of Burnham; William, prior of Coxford; Robert de Creake, the parish patron; and the archdeacons of Sudbury, Shropshire and Coventry. This was done, it states, in her new chapel in the presence of many local knights and clerics. It must have been an important local occasion, with Alice and her wishes firmly at its centre.

The ecclesiastical politics behind Alice's charter are unusual. To secure spiritual services within a hospital, a founder required consent from the parish rector and an agreement that protected parochial rights; unless the parish was in a peculiar jurisdiction, the right to effect such agreements fell to the diocesan or, through him, the archdeacon. Alice's agreement was obtained under Alan de Beccles, archdeacon of Sudbury and official for an absent Bishop Pandulf.[66] With no bishop present, however, the chapel could not be consecrated at this time, rendering the agreement an unfinished act that secured rights to celebrate divine service but not an altar for their performance. Exceptionally, too, the deed is not in the name of any ecclesiastical official, and even lacks an address.[67] Despite the array of archdeacons, there is none here *as* archdeacon, for the local archdeacon is absent. This is all the more remarkable because the archdeacon of Norfolk at this time was Geoffrey de Burgh, Alice's *nepos*. Together, these oddities suggest

---

[65]   CCCM, Creake Abbey, At/26. 'Noverint universi ad quos presens scriptum pervenerit quod cum nobilis mulier Alicia quondam uxor Roberti de Nerford pro salute fidelium fundare proposuerit hospitale ad sustentacionem pauperum in pratis de Lingerescroft, volens capellanos constituere (corrected from instituere) qui perpetuo ibidem divina celebrant. Ex adverso oponente se eidem magistro Roberto archidiacono Coventrensi ... et quod locus ille situs esset ut dicebat in parochia de Norcrek et ex eidem loci et hospitalis et capelle construccione sue posset ecclesie primodicunt gravari eandem amicabiliter compositione hoc fine et sub hanc subiecta forma utriusque partis contencio et contradiccio conquievit. Videlicet quod dicta Alicia tempore viduitatis sue pro conservitanda idempnitate ecclesie de Crek spontanea et libera voluntate sua dedit ecclesie de Norcrek dicas pecias terre in campis de Crek apud Watermeres de hereditate sua ... Prenominatus vero archidiaconus rector dicte ecclesie de Crek attendens prepositum boni operis et salubre concessit dicte Alicie quod libere et absolute et sine omni contradiccione possit ibidem hospitale construere ad sustentacionem pauperum et capellam erigere, cimiterium habere et capellanos ibidem (iñ)constituere'.

[66]   Pandulph was in Rome from February 1225 until his death in Septeptember 1226, *EEA* 21, p. xxii. For Alan's career, ibid., pp. xliv–v.

[67]   It is not under any name but, lacking title, address and greeting, begins with the *notificatio*.

that the timing of Alice's agreement was dictated by local exigency, in defiance of ecclesiastical protocol. Might that urgency have been Robert's death, and a desire to bury him in their hospital? If so, it underscores Alice's regional influence, in marshalling available ecclesiastical officials, and her local persuasiveness, in wresting such a swift and accommodating agreement from the parish.[68] This explanation would also make sense of the puzzling statement in the medieval account that Geoffrey de Burgh, Bishop of Ely, consecrated the chapel and surrounding site. Geoffrey became Bishop of Ely just a few months later, in June 1225, and could have acted for the absent diocesan at any time before the next bishop's appointment in October 1226.[69] That bishop turned out to be Thomas de Blundeville, nephew to Hubert de Burgh. Along with the de Burghs and their *familia*, Thomas was to stand beside Alice as tragedy continued to strike and the widowed mother responded by reinventing her foundation.

Robert had hoped for a smooth transition to his heir when he secured his royal estates to Nicholas, but in May, only a month after Alice's burial agreement, controversy arose within the family, when Nicholas was challenged by his brothers for the inheritance of Robert's movable goods in Kent.[70] The instigator was probably Richard, the third son, who had assumed his father's place at Dover Castle, overseeing the building works from February 1225. Nicholas, meanwhile, made a career outside Kent, receiving rewards in Suffolk (January 1226), Leicester (January 1227) and Yorkshire (April 1227) for his royal service.[71] Then, quite suddenly, between April and early June 1227, Nicholas died. His heir was his brother John, and just as Robert's royal holdings and service were transferred to Nicholas, so John received his brother's lands in Leicester, to be held similarly from the king for royal service.[72] This was supplemented in 1229

---

[68]   On the same occasion Robert de Creake, patron of the church, ratified the 'constitucionem et ordinacionem domine Alicie quondam uxor Roberti de Nerford super libertatibus hospitalis fundati in pratis de Lingerescroft', BL, Add. MS 61900, fol. 6v (*Cart. Creake*, no.14). As with the parish agreement, its first witness is Ralph de Maidstone, Archdeacon of Chester.

[69]   In a similar circumstance in July 1225, Alan de Beccles induced the Bishop of Llandaff to consecrate an altar at Stoke by Clare priory, *EEA* 21, p. xlv; *Stoke by Clare Cartulary*, ed. Christopher Harper-Bill and Richard Mortimer, Suffolk Records Society: Suffolk Charters 4–6 (3 vols, Woodbridge, 1982–1984) i, no. 103.

[70]   *RLC* ii, p. 40.

[71]   *Bldg. Accts. Hen. III*, pp. 26, 64, 82; *RLC* ii, pp. 55, 65, 94b, 108b, 115, 126b, 140b, 167b, 181b.

[72]   *RLC* ii, p. 189b; *CFR* 1226–7, no. 326. John's earlier career is unknown. A John de Nerford, cleric, was presented to Shalford church in Surrey in 1224 and 1226, a church in the king's gift. Both presentations were made under the Justiciar, Hubert de Burgh. *PR* 1216–25, p. 497; 1225–32, p. 28.

with £10 annual salary from the royal farm of a tenement in Bedfordshire.[73] In the years before Nicholas's death, Alice had acted in small ways to secure her hospital, establishing a third fair for the hospital 'at Lingerescroft' in February 1226 on the vigil and annunciation of the Virgin, which she changed three months later to the vigil and day of the translation of Thomas the Martyr.[74] With the exception of her parish agreement, Alice's actions as a hospital founder were conventional, even conservative, and limited largely to securing minor incomes. The death of her eldest son, however, inaugurated a period of frantic activity and singular creativity.[75]

Between 1227 and 1228 Alice reformed her hospital, issuing ordinances that defined the number, duties and government of the hospital brethren.[76] Their earliest date can be fixed by the titles of its first witness: Hubert de Burgh, Earl of Kent (from 1227) and Justiciar of England. In her charter Alice de Nerford, daughter of John Pouchard, states that she has established a hospital, to be named St Mary of the Meadows, with thirteen beds to receive paupers. Through the communication and counsel of men of religion who fear God she has also established five priests, one to be master, who must celebrate divine services and minister to the poor. Lay brothers should conduct the business of the house and tend the poor. There are provisions for oaths on admission, common living, wearing habits, supplying food and clothing to the brethren and food to the poor, receiving brethren, and electing and removing the master through the counsel of

---

[73]   *CR* 1227–31, p. 188.

[74]   *RLC* ii, pp. 100b, 116. The feast of the Annunciation, 25 March, may have commemorated Robert's death or simply been an expression of local devotion to the Virgin, who had a shrine at nearby Walsingham. The second change may be an early sign of the influence of Thomas Blundeville, who had a particular devotion to St Thomas. Overseeing the fortification of the Cinque ports, Thomas was working with Robert at Dover Castle from July 1224 until at least October, when Robert was ailing. Curiously, Thomas established a weekly fair on the episcopal manor of Homerfield on St Nicholas's day in September 1227, just months after Nicholas's death, *EEA* 21, pp. xxv–vii, no. 12; *RLC* i, pp. 614, 638b, 639, 650b.

[75]   The final confirmation was issued on 29 May 1227, probably shortly after Nicholas's death; its four annual fairs were on the feasts and vigils of St Bartholomew, St Nicholas, the translation of St Thomas, and the Annunciation of the Virgin. Hubert de Burgh had presided over the sealing of letters close at Westminster on the previous day, *RLC*, ii, p. 187a–b. The original grant was made in March, *CChR* i, p.26.

[76]   Three originals survive, with minor variations, CCCM, Creake Abbey, At/1, 1b and 1c. Two retain fragments of Alice's seal, which has an image of a standing lady and the probable inscription [*Sigillum Alicie d*]*e Ne*[*rford*]. At/1b was copied, without its witness list, into the cartulary, from which it was edited by Dugdale, BL, Add. MS 61900, fols 2r–3r; *Cart. Creake*, no. 2; *MA* vi, p. 488. It was at this time that Alice apparently confirmed her grant of a portion of the church of All Saints, Wreningham, *Cart. Creake*, no. 4.

the bishop. Although she reserved to her heirs the right to consent to the choice of master, she explicitly prevents them acting in the affairs of the house against the will of the brothers, by seizing or altering the use of its goods or by intruding any steward to oversee the house. Any future increase in income was to be applied to an increase in the number of beds, brethren or priests, as the brothers should judge fit.[77] This is the only known set of detailed ordinances issued to an English hospital in the name of a private lay person before the fourteenth century. Similar ordinances can be found in contemporary hospitals from the second quarter of the thirteenth century, but they were issued for lay founders by the diocesan.[78] Since Alice's ordinances allocated certain jurisdictions to the bishop, they must have been carried out in concert with the local diocesan, Thomas Blundeville. Indeed this kinsman was almost certainly one of the men of religion whose communication and counsel underpinned her arrangements for the priests.[79] Alice's sons were not mentioned. No charter for the hospital survives in Nicholas's name, but his heir and brother, John, confirmed at this time his father's final purchase for the hospital, of four acres in the town of Creake.[80]

These ordinances signal a shift in the hospital's constitution. Their purpose was to establish and regulate a body of priestly brethren, whose spiritual service would be supported by lay brothers who would manage the house's income and charity. In so doing, Alice was creating a new liturgical body in her hospital, and it was for this reason that she required the advice of men of religion. There are two likely, and not mutually exclusive, reasons behind her actions. Just as the hasty parish agreement followed her husband's death, so these liturgical reforms follow closely upon her son's death. The burial sites of Robert and Nicholas are unknown, but Alice's two unusual deeds suggest that they may have been buried here. Rarely were aristocratic founders or their families buried in hospitals at this early date, but the other rare instances, as we shall see, occurred in houses that had, or acquired, a strongly liturgical character. If this is the case, it raises

---

[77]   The cartulary text adds 'et heredum meorum', missing from the three original charters.

[78]   From the late-thirteenth century, regulations were also issued by the Crown. For the rules of lay founders, Sethina C. Watson, '*Fundatio, Ordinatio* and *Statuta*: the Statutes and Constitutional Documents of English Hospitals to 1300', unpubl. D.Phil. thesis, University of Oxford, 2004, pp. 282–6.

[79]   I have not been able to discover a letter or charter in Blundeville's name, but it is likely that some correspondence formed the basis for much of the detail in her ordinances. The text is neither naïve nor quirky, and fits comfortably beside contemporary regulations issued by bishops to other lay foundations.

[80]   This he gave 'ad sustentacionem iij pauperum in predicto hospitale', probably to complete a full cohort of thirteen paupers. BL, Add. MS 61900, fols 9v–10r; *Cart. Creake*, nos 23, 25. John also witnessed several grants to the house, notably Ralph of Gatley's gift of lands that his father had given his anchorite sisters, CCCM, Creake Abbey, At/6 and 10.

the poignant possibility that Alice, in the wake of her son's death, was now converting her hospital into a family mausoleum.

This new liturgical body may also have been the first step in a process to transform the house into a priory. The prior and canons first occur in a 1228 agreement providing rents to Castle Acre Priory in exchange for free tenure of the Lingerescroft site.[81] The deed was sealed with the seals of the two houses and of Lady Alice 'patrone et fundatricis sepedicte domus sancte marie de pratis'; its first witness was Bishop Thomas Blundeville and one of its last was Reyner de Burgh. Bishop Thomas had just assisted the now-widowed Nesta de Cockfield and her husband, Thomas de Burgh (Hubert's brother), in re-establishing the hospital of Kersey (Suffolk) as a priory. Shortly before his death, Thomas de Burgh had entrusted custody of Kersey to the bishop, his nephew.[82] As early as 1225 Nesta and Thomas had intended a house of canons, dedicated to SS Mary and Anthony. The house is only fleetingly termed a 'hospital' thereafter, in Blundeville's confirmation of May 1228.[83] Kersey was henceforth known as a 'church of canons' and it is here that Nesta instructed that she be buried.[84] Similarly, the canon who wrote the medieval history of North Creake Abbey states that the North Creake brethren received their canonical habit from Thomas de Blundeville. The bishop's presence at the 1228 agreement to free

---

[81]   CCCM, Creake Abbey, At/3; BL, Add. MS 61900, fols 7r–8r; *Cart. Creake*, no. 16; and a copy in the Castle Acre priory cartulary, BL, MS Harl. 2110, fols 44v–45r. The chirograph was effected during the judicial eyre of Norfolk in May–August of 1228, since Martin de Pattishall, Hugh Abbot of St Edmunds, Thomas Heyden and William de Insula, justices, were witnesses. For Martin's eyre, which exhausted his fellow justices, see *Royal and Other Historical Letters Illustrative of the Reign of Henry III*, ed. Walter Waddington Shirley (2 vols, London, 1862–1866), i, no. 281; David Crook, *Records of the General Eyre* (London, 1982), pp. 82–3. The house was still termed 'hospital' in royal and archiepiscopal deeds until January 1228, but not thereafter: *MA* vi, p. 488 (iii); TNA C/53/18, m.14 (*CChR* i, p. 26); *The Register, or Rolls, of Walter Gray, Lord Archbishop of York*, ed. James Raine, Surtees Society 56 (Durham, 1872), p. 16. The 1225 parish agreement had explicitly stated that the chaplains were not to be classed as monks or regular canons, CCCM, Creake Abbey, At/26.

[82]   *EEA* 21, no. 71. Blundeville's original letter is Cambridge, King's College muniments, KER/621.

[83]   Two charters in Thomas de Burgh's name were witnessed by his brother, Geoffrey, before becoming Bishop of Ely in 1225, and Thomas's own grant is 'Deo et ecclesiae beatae Mariae et sancti Antonii'. These deeds, now missing, are *MA* vi, p. 593 (v–vi; see also i–iv). Others survive to the chapel or church of SS Mary and Anthony, witnessed by Thomas: Cambridge, Kings College muniments, KER/20–23, 25–32. Blundeville's 1228 confirmation to the 'hospital' of Nesta's earlier grants, along with her grant of the parish church 'for the support of the canons serving God and the sick and poor resorting there' may repeat phrases from his predecessor's confirmation *EEA* 21, no. 72 and App II, no.11.

[84]   *MA* vi, p. 592 (iv).

their site suggests therefore that this was in fact a necessary preliminary for the transformation into a priory.[85] At about this time, in a charter witnessed by John de Burgh (Hubert's son) and Raymond de Burgh, Alice confirmed her grants to 'the house of Blessed Mary of the Meadows near Creake and the canons there serving God and to serve God in perpetuity, which house I, Alice, have founded'.[86] Thereafter the house was known as a priory of canons.[87] An otherwise confusing variation among the three original deeds of Alice's 1227x28 ordinances supports the idea that the priory was planned, or hoped for, when her ordinances were drafted. The three copies are identical with the exception that one omits all references to the thirteen beds for the poor and charges the lay brethren to serve the priests instead of the poor.[88]

The claim that Alice was acting to transform her hospital into a family mausoleum is reinforced by a third tragedy. By July 1231, her next son, John, had died and was certainly buried at the priory. A royal charter of this date granted to the priory, where John's body now rested, the lands in Leicester that Nicholas de Nerford and then John, his brother, had held for their royal service.[89] A fuller grant issued by the king at Castle Matilda in Elveyn in August identified these as estates at Ilston and Thurnby and added £10 of rents in Rothersthorp, also previously held by Nicholas.[90] Its first witness was Hubert de Burgh. These incomes constitute the full package of lands that historians of the house have attributed to the king's own generosity as patron. They should instead be understood as products of the efforts of Hubert. Their form also had another,

---

[85]   If so, this suggests a more specific date of 1228–29 for its transformation than the 1226–31 offered in *EEA* 21, App II no. 21.

[86]   'domui beate Mariae de Prato iuxta Crek' et canonicis ibidem Deo servientibus et imperpetuum servituris quam, videlicet, domum ego Alicia in honorem beatae Virginis Mariae fundavi', BL, Add. MS, 61900 fol. 3r–v; *Cart. Creake*, no. 3; *MA* vi, p. 488 (iii). The lands were confirmed to the canons of the church of St Mary *de Pratis* by the king on May 8, 1229, *CChR* i, p. 95.

[87]   With one exception: in April 1230, the king granted Alice twenty oaks 'ad hospitale suum de Creic in Norf' hospitandum', *CR* 1227–31, p. 314; but see, *prioratui* and 'canons of the church', *CChR* i, p. 95; *CR* 1227–31, p. 490.

[88]   CCCM, Creake Abbey, At/1. Endorsed 'prima fundacionis' and with a medieval note this was the foundation deed exhibited the during the 1429 episcopal visitation of the abbey.

[89]   'quam rex postea commiserat Johanni de Nereford', fratri suo, qui nuper obiit, commisit priori et canonicis juxta Crek', ubi corpus ipsius Johannis requiescit', *CR* 1227–31, pp. 537–8.

[90]   CCCM, Creake Abbey, At/27 and 28r, and Additional (b)1, fol. 5r–v. A charter issued three days later at Elveyn confirms that the income from Rothersthorp had also been held first by Nicholas and then by his brother John, CCCM, Creake Abbey, At(28)v. For confirmations, *CChR* i, p. 139; *CR* 1227–31, pp. 550, 570; *CCR* 1231–34, pp. 96–7.

more poignant meaning. These lands and incomes that had once supported first Nicholas then John in their royal careers now sustained prayers at the site of at least one, but probably both, of their burials. Their transition from the profits of the worldly ambition of Alice's sons to incomes for their commemoration reflects the transformation of the North Creake house more generally, from charitable status symbol into liturgical site of remembrance and spiritual observance. It also suggests how, for Alice as mother of the family, unguarded optimism had been replaced by loss and mourning.

Another, more famous, fall was scuppering the fortunes of her younger sons. From 1229, the influence of Hubert de Burgh had been waning, culminating in his sensational ejection as Justiciar in July 1232. His situation had become particularly unsure after his rival, Peter des Roches, returned to England in August 1231.[91] Family members may have felt the winds change as early as 1228, when Bishop Blundeville's relations with the king had soured.[92] Alice's sons were out of favour by 1229. Richard, who had continued to oversee the building works of Dover Castle, abruptly disappears from the accounts in early 1229; John, too, was last given payment for his service to the king in 1229.[93] Thereafter Alice's sons appear rarely in royal records, and then only in local controversies.[94] In these years, too, there was a push to secure the site and revenues of the North Creake house.[95] By October 1231, several months after John's death, the family's decline must have seemed irreversible. It was then that Alice, as the abbey's history narrates, 'foreseeing that her heirs would be less provided for and fearing that they might thus inflict great harm and dilapidation on the house, and wishing to guard against this despoiling in the future, consulted a council of great and wise men who advised her to surrender the right of her and her heirs in the advowson and lordship of the church, and the patronage of the house, to the lord king and his heirs and successor kings; and this was done'.[96] These words, which initially seemed to suggest that Alice was alienated from her family, now

---

[91]   David Carpenter, 'The Fall of Hubert de Burgh', *Journal of British Studies*, 19 (1980): 1–17; Ellis, *Hubert de Burgh*, p. 128.

[92]   *EEA* 21, p. xxvi.

[93]   *Bldg. Accts. Hen. III*, p. 84; *CR* 1227–31, p. 188.

[94]   *CRR* xvi, no. 1053; xvii, no. 1857; *CR* 1227–31, p. 171; *CPR* 1234–7, p. 335; *CChR* i, p. 238.

[95]   *CChR* i, p. 95; *CR* 1227–31, pp. 173, 314, 490, the latter concerning the additional forty acres secured for the site from Roger de Geddings, BL, Add. MS 61900, fol. 4r–v, *Cart. Creake*, nos 6–7.

[96]   BL, Add. MS 61900, fols 1v–2r, ed. *MA* vi, p. 487 (i). 'Videns predicta Domina Alicia quod heredes sui minus essent providi et timens ne forte gravamina aut dilapidacionem domui predicte inferrent et huius dispendium precavere volens in futurum, consilio vocato tunc magnatis et sapientibus ab eis consulebatur quod ipsa redderit ius suum advocacionis

suggest she was acting on behalf of her deceased children, and possibly with the support of her living children. As the family had fallen, so had Alice's hopes for their future and for her house. The royal incomes that had once sustained her sons' careers now supported prayers at their graves. She had lost two heirs in quick succession and, if either or both had married, significant portions of the family estate would be tied up with their widows, as dower.[97] The uncertain futures of her younger sons, denuded now of Hubert's patronage, placed in jeopardy the family incomes that were now in the hands of the priory, and so the spiritual care of her family. In fact, her family worked to support her house. Her next son, Richard, and his son, Robert, both confirmed Alice's benefactions.[98] The 'great and wise men' who advised her clearly included her *nepos*, Hubert. The foundation charter of Henry III, which established his patronage of the abbey, was issued on 26 October 1231. On that same day, it was enrolled in the charter roll between two deeds: a royal grant to Hubert's hospital in Dover and a royal confirmation, also issued that day, of Hubert's own gifts to his hospital.[99] The transfer of patronage was, in fact, copying Hubert's own grant of patronage of his Dover hospital to the king in 1229.[100]

Henry III took little interest in his new house, and even its transformation into an abbey must be credited to Alice. William was first termed 'abbot' in a deed witnessed by John de Nerford, and so before July 1231, and early grants were secured to the abbot and canons 'at the prompting (*instantiam*) of the noble matron Alice de Nerford'.[101] Henry did not further endow the house, and subsequent confirmations were secured from popes and bishops.[102] The de Burgh *familia* continued to promote the hospital. John de Burgh, Hubert's son, gave 20s annual rent for the souls of his father and mother, and Ralph de Blundeville, archdeacon of Norwich, 'moved by pity over the deficiencies of the poor little

---

et dominii Domino Regi H. prenominato et heredibus et successoribus suis regibus de se et heredibus suis inperpetuum ecclesie et patronatum prefate domus; quod et factum est.'

[97]   Senderowitz Loengard observes that 'The death of two married brothers in rapid succession could cripple a family for more than a generation, perhaps permanently', in her 'Of the Gift of her Husband', p. 240.

[98]   BL, Add. MS 61900, fol. 5r–v; *Cart. Creake*, nos 9–11.

[99]   TNA C53/25, m. 2–3; *CChR* i, p. 141. For his charter of protection in February, 1232, *PR* 1225–32, p. 463.

[100] *MA* vi, 657 (v), where it is misdated to 1239. For its 1229 enrolment, *CChR* i, p. 101.

[101] CCCM, Creake Abbey, At/5 and 6. And see *CR* 1227–31, p. 490.

[102] A 1231–41 papal confirmation that the monastery observe the Augustinian rule also confirmed the incomes from Rothersthorp and Ilston, and the grant of a messuage in London from Richard of St John. This is the first deed on a roll of thirteenth century papal and episcopal charters, many mentioning the poverty of the house, CCCM, Creake Abbey, roll, 7. The first membrane is calendared in Carthew, 'North Creake Abbey', pp. 155–6.

house of canons' confirmed another portion of the church of Wreningham into their hands in 1237.[103] One final record of royal benefaction survives: in 1232 the king commissioned a choir cope and vestments for the abbey which, once completed, were to be handed to Richard of St John to present to the abbey.[104] Richard was a benefactor of the abbey, and he was also Hubert's personal chaplain, especially active in his service in the years around 1230.[105] Despite their efforts, by the late 1230s the house was falling into poverty. It had, however, settled into its final form.

Its period of formation and reinvention from c. 1224 to 1231 had, like the fortunes of the de Nerford family, been brief and twisting. Indeed, its constitutional form was inexorably linked through Alice to the family's fortunes, and the house itself was an expression of her sense of her family's status and needs. Its transformations from charitable hospital to liturgical community, to priory and, finally, to an abbey surrendered to the king were the responses of a family whose swift ascendency was undone by death and political exclusion. In their own way, they reveal how the national fortunes of a great man might ricochet in the localities through the minor figures tied to his fortunes. The house served Alice's family, first as an expression of dynastic ambition but later, as tragedy struck, as mausoleum and site of remembrance and spiritual service. Behind the difficult work was Alice, tending the needs of her family, her actions informed by her own motherhood. Unlike the legal and social statuses of wife and widow, this was not a transient identity. Her role as mother did not shift with her marital status, even if the legal forms of its expression altered. Indeed, as performed by Alice, her motherhood was fundamentally about continuity. In transmitting her inherited estates to her new house, she acted as a link between generations and provided a visible tie between local past and national future. In securing these estates to a house of charitable then spiritual service, her actions first anchored her family as they scattered geographically and later tended their souls in perpetuity as, one by one, they died.

Alice's dynastic hospital was short-lived and unusual, but it was not without parallel. Two other hospitals were developed by women heiresses, then reinvented to serve as family burial sites. The hospital of St John the Baptist, Lechlade, was established by Isabella de Mortimer and her second husband Peter fitzHerbert in c. 1228, and is said to have been developed into an Augustinian priory by

---

[103]   BL, Add. MS 61900, fols 72r, 73v; *Cart. Creake*, nos 226, 234; CCCM, Creake Abbey, Add. (b)1 fols 4v–5r, and At/35a. Ralph uses the first person plural in his deed.

[104]   *CCR 1231–4*, p. 25.

[105]   Ellis, *Hubert de Burgh*, pp. 86, 116–17.

Richard Earl of Cornwall, her successor as lord of her manor.[106] By contrast, the hospital of St John the Baptist, Brackley, was already in existence when Margaret de Quincy inherited it with her portion of the earldom of Leicester and, unrecognized in the histories of the house,[107] transformed it into a site of liturgical service. As with the North Creake house, reinstating these heiresses at the centre of their houses' development returns a constitutional *animus* to their apparent migrations in form. As with Alice, Isabella's and Margaret's actions were prompted by the fortunes of their families, adapting the use of inherited estates to respond to their children's needs.

The role of Lechlade hospital was intertwined with the fortunes of the Mortimer children and with the utility of the manor itself. Lechlade (Gloucestershire), with Longborough, was the lesser of the two estates that had constituted the English barony of Isabella's father, Walkelin de Ferrers. The second estate, at Oakham (Rutland), gave the barony its name and had been the focus of Walkelin's attention. It was here that he built his fortified hall, completed shortly before his death in 1201 and still surviving.[108] He entrusted Lechlade to his younger son, Hugh (d. 1204).[109] The estates escheated to the Crown as a Norman estate when Isabella's eldest brother chose to remain in the lost duchy, but Isabella intervened to purchase the manors at considerable cost from King John.[110] In contrast to her father, Isabella gave priority to Lechlade over Oakham, clearly preferring the former's proximity to the lands of her husband, Roger de Mortimer, Baron of Wigmore, a marcher lord whose main estates and royal offices were held in Herefordshire and Shropshire.[111] By the time of her death almost fifty years later, Oakham was worth nearly £11 p.a., but Lechlade drew almost £50 annually, £20 in rents and tolls and £30 from a demesne estate that included two mills, a fishery, a dovecot and a herbage.[112] Isabella's adult life coincided with the span of years that saw the barons of Wigmore, once marginal

---

[106]   *VCH Glouc.* ii, p. 125; D.A. Carpenter, 'A Noble in Politics: Roger Mortimer in the Period of Baronial Reform and Rebellion, 1258–1265', in Anne J. Duggan (ed.), *Nobles and Nobility in Medieval Europe* (Woodbridge, 2000), pp. 183–203, at pp. 186, 188, 203.

[107]   *VCH Nhants*, ii, p. 151; John Clarke, *The Book of Brackley: the First Thousand Years* (Buckingham, 1987), pp. 40–43.

[108]   *VCH Rutland*, ii, pp. 8, 10–11.

[109]   Carpenter, 'A Noble in Politics', p. 192; Holden, *Lords of the Central Marches*, p. 149.

[110]   She secured Lechlade (with Longbridge) in 1205 and Oakham in 1207, each for 300 marks, *RLC* i, pp. 30b, 97.

[111]   For the barons of Wigmore, J.J. Crump, 'The Mortimer Family and the Making of the March' in Michael Prestwich, R.H. Britnell and Robin Frame (eds), *Thirteenth Century England* VI (Woodbridge, 1997), pp. 117–26, esp. pp. 117–22.

[112]   The demesne included 202 acres of land, 648 acres of meadow, and pasture for twenty-four oxen, thirty-two cows and 200 sheep. Additional incomes came from freeholders,

marcher lords, emerge as some of the most powerful barons in England.[113] On the Gloucestershire border with Oxfordshire, Lechlade was securely within England and on the great road from London to Wales. It thus offered a geographical presence that mirrored the Mortimers' political expansion in these years, beyond the march and into the heart of national politics. Roger was the first to take his place as one of the leading barons under John, but little was done with the manor during his lifetime. The only certain initiative was taken in 1210, when the couple obtained an annual three-day fair at Lechlade on the feast day of St Lawrence, the patron saint of the parish church.[114]

It is only after Roger's death in 1214 that activity began at Lechlade.[115] The barony fell to their son, Hugh, but Isabella retained Oakham and Lechlade, although her tenure was interrupted briefly when the Crown seized both estates in 1219 for default of payment.[116] Married now to Peter fitzHerbert, Isabella used Lechlade to provide for her younger sons, as her father had done before.[117] Initially, her son Roger had held lands in Longborough, part of her Lechlade estate. By 1224 they were in the hands of another son Ralph, who was sued by Hugh for its custody in the king's court. Ralph rebuffed the suit, referring his brother to the rightful defendants in whose name he held the lands: Peter fitzHerbert and Isabella, their mother.[118] Rather than pursue his case against Isabella, Hugh appears to have abandoned his suit. The bridge at Lechlade, now the highest on the Thames, was probably built during these years, and certainly by 1228, when Isabella's use of Lechlade changed abruptly. At this date the manor was held directly by Isabella and Peter and work was suddenly underway, in Peter's name, on a hospital. It is first mentioned in September 1228, when Peter obtained a royal licence to build a gate over the causeway of Lechlade Bridge, in front of the hospital he had built.[119] In 1231 Peter and

---

burgesses, market tolls, villeins, cottars and rustics. *Calendar of Inquisitions Miscellaneous*, i, no. 457; *CChR* i, p. 392.

[113]   Crump, 'Mortimer Family', esp. p. 126.

[114]   *VCH Glouc.* vii, p. 117; *CPR 1396–9*, pp. 384–5.

[115]   For Roger's death, *Pipe Roll 16 John*, ns 35 (London, 1962), p. 120; *RLC* i, pp. 170, 208.

[116]   *RLC* i, pp. 343b, 371, 382b, 390; *CPR 1216–25*, p. 29; CFR 1217–18, no. 180; 1218–19, nos 97, 154–5.

[117]   Hugh de Ferrers had been Walkelin's second son, Carpenter, 'A Noble in Politics', p. 192. Isabella's children were all Mortimers. She and Peter fitzHerbert were childless, although Peter had an heir by an earlier wife; G.E. Cokayne, *Complete Peerage*, ed. Vicary Gibbs and H.A. Doubleday (London, 1926), V, p. 465n.

[118]   *CRR* xi, pp. 298, 403.

[119]   'quod permittat Petrum filium Hereberti levare quondam portam super calcetum pontis Lechelad' coram hospitali quod ibidem construxit', *CR 1227–31*, p. 82.

Isabella secured an archiepiscopal indulgence for the hospital, by 1233 grants of papal protection, liberties and immunities from the bishop, and by 1234 the right for the hospital to hold a five-day fair in the meadow below the bridge.[120] Isabella's work continued apace after Peter's death in 1235, the charters now in her own name.[121] In that year five royal oaks were secured for building at the hospital.[122] She developed the borough, too, establishing a market at Lechlade and securing from the abbot of Cirencester, who held the hundred, jurisdiction over the market in her court there, which included the right to use a pillory and ducking stool.[123] During Peter's lifetime, the couple also claimed judicial privileges, erecting a gallows in Lechlade from which thieves were hung.[124]

Isabella's efforts were shaped by events in her children's lives. She and Roger had had at least five children who survived into adulthood: a daughter, Joan, and sons Hugh,[125] Roger, Ralph and Philip.[126] In the decade before 1224, all

[120]   The episcopal grants are mentioned in the papal protection, Oxford, New College Archives, charter no. 14063, cal. *Original Papal Documents in England and Wales from the Accession of Pope Innocent III to the Death of Pope Benedict XI (1198–1304)*, ed. Jane E. Sayers (Oxford, 1999), no. 182; *Reg. Walter Gray*, p. 44; *CR 1231–4*, p. 398.

[121]   For the delivery of Lechlade into the hands of Isabella, newly widowed, *CCR 1234–7*, p. 102.

[122]   *CR 1234–7*, p. 145.

[123]   *The Cartulary of Cirencester Abbey, Gloucester*, ed. C.D. Ross (3 vols, London, 1964–1977), i, no. 231/369, and for legal custom, and the burgesses of Lechlade, see ibid., ii, p. 623.

[124]   Ibid., iii, no. 378; ii, no. 650.

[125]   It is possible, although unlikely, that Hugh was Isabella's stepson. The second section of Wigmore Abbey's *Fundationis et Fundatorum Historia*, written 1399–1401, states that Hugh was the son of a first wife, Milicent de Ferrers, daughter of the earl of Derby. R.W. Eyton's belief that this was a confusion with Milicent, wife of Ralph I, and mother of Hugh I (d. 1149) is reinforced by a 1225 charter of Hugh *junioris*, in which he conceded four virgates of land to Reading Abbey 'pro salute anime mee et pro animabus Rogeri patris mei et Isabelle matris mee et omnium antecessorum et successorum meorum', BL, MS Harl. 1708, fol. 56v; Cotton Vespasian Exxv, fol. 241r–v; cal. *Reading Abbey Cartularies: British Library Manuscripts Egerton 3031, Harley 1708 and Cotton Vespasian E xxv*, ed. B.R. Kemp, 2 vols, Camden 4th series, 31 (London, 1986–1987), no. 1071. R.W. Eyton, *Antiquities of Shropshire*, 12 vols (London, 1854–60), iv, p. 207. For the *Historia, MA* vi, pp. 348–55 (350); and its dates, Chris Given-Wilson, 'Chronicles of the Mortimer Family, c. 1250–1450', in Richard Eales and Shaun Tyas (eds.), *Family and Dynasty in Late Medieval England*, Harlaxton Medieval Studies, 9 (Donington, 2003), pp. 67–86, at pp. 71–2.

[126]   The same 1399–1401 passage in the *Historia* states that Isabella had sons Ralph, Philip and Robert. I can find no evidence of an adult child, Robert. The *Historia* might be referring to her deceased infant son, but it is more likely a confusion of her son Roger with Robert de Mortimer, son of a Robert who was perhaps brother to Hugh II (d. 1181). Robert junior married Margaret de Say, widow of Isabella's brother Hugh de Ferrers (d. 1204), in

were taking their place in the world. In 1212 Joan married the Beauchamp heir, Walter, whose wardship her parents had purchased in 1211, and soon had two sons, William and James.[127] Hugh became baron of Wigmore in 1214 and was married to Annora, daughter of William de Broase, while Philip seems to have been a companion of Hugh, witnessing his 1226–27 grant of land to Reading Abbey, together with his heart and entrails for burial.[128] In 1225, however, Joan died.[129] The previous year, Roger's death prompted Longborough's transfer to Ralph.[130] After 1226–27, Philip also disappears from the record.[131] But it was the childless Hugh's sudden death, 'shattered and struck' in a tournament in November 1227 that inaugurated Isabella's activity.[132] Ralph now succeeded to the Wigmore barony and with her family's future now vested in her last remaining son, Isabella began to develop Lechlade as a new centre for the barony. The new bridge made Lechlade a reliable route from London to the west and Wales, and the gate built across its causeway in 1228, in front of the hospital, proclaimed a traveller's arrival in the Marcher barony. The town was soon reinforced by market privileges and public gallows, its political status developed by a hall, or possibly even the hospital itself, where the royal court first stayed in July 1229 dispatching a series of royal business.[133] At a distance from the settlement, but integral to bridge and gate, and with its fair in the nearby meadow, the hospital might have been conceived as part of Lechlade's political infrastructure. Yet it soon developed a more spiritual function for the family. The building programme of 1235 was probably to create a chapel, whose chaplain was established in a charter of 1237–46 by which the hospital brothers acknowledged Isabella's endowment

---

1210 and died in 1219. *MA* vi, p. 350; *CPR 1216–25*, p. 223; *Book of Fees*, p. 140; *CFR 1218–19*, no. 321; *CFR 1219–20*, no. 19; 1229–30, no. 364; *Annales Monastici*, ed. H.R. Luard (5 vols, London, 1864–1869), p. 411.

[127]   *The Beauchamp Cartulary Charters 1100–1268*, ed. Emma Mason, Pipe Roll Society, n.s. 43 (London, 1280), p. xxiii.

[128]   Probably made at Hugh's deathbed. BL, MS Harl. 1708, fols 56v–57r; *Reading Abbey Cartularies*, no. 1072.

[129]   *Annales Monastici*, iv, p. 418; Beauchamp Cartulary, p. xxiii.

[130]   *CRR* xi, pp. 298, 403.

[131]   There was another Hugh de Mortimer who had married Alice, daughter of Henry de Thobun. Alice later claimed her dower from Isabella's lands in 1244, including lands in Lechlade, *CRR* xviii, no. 1246. I cannot identify this Hugh, although it is possible that he was a son of Philip or Roger.

[132]   *MA* vi, p. 350; *CFR 1227–8*, nos 31–2, 66; 1228–9, no. 255; *PR 1225–32*, pp. 169 and 171; Crump, 'Mortimer Family', pp. 123–4. For Annora's dowry, *PR 1225–32*, p. 501; 1232–47, p. 80.

[133]   *CR 1227–31*, p. 189; *CFR 1228–9*, nos 248–51.

to provide a chaplain and a lamp before the altar of the Virgin Mary.[134] The deed was witnessed by Bishop Walter de Cantilupe, who would enforce Isabella's conditions, and by local lords who included William de Beauchamp, Isabella's grandson. The chaplain was to celebrate in perpetuity for her soul and that of lord Hugh de Mortimer, junior, her son. Like his father, Hugh had been buried at the Mortimer abbey at Wigmore,[135] but Isabella was creating her own site of commemoration for herself and her deceased child.

There is another date of great importance to the hospital, for in 1247 the brothers assumed the Augustinian rule.[136] Richard Earl of Cornwall acquired the manor after Isabella's death and has been credited with establishing the Augustinian canons,[137] but they were in fact introduced under Isabella and at a moment of great insecurity for her family. In August 1246, her son Ralph had died leaving his son, Roger, by his wife Gwladys, the daughter of Llywelyn Prince of Gwynedd, who entered into his father's estates in February 1247.[138] Roger would become the first Baron Mortimer and a powerful man in his own right, but on Ralph's death he was just fourteen years old. Within months he was married to Maud de Braose, whose sister Eva had married Bishop Cantilupe's nephew, William.[139] The security of the hospital, and the future tenure of Lechlade itself, was under threat at this time. In 1244 the king had made it plain that the aging Isabella's estates would, upon her death, escheat to the Crown, apparently as *terra Normanorum*.[140] With a young grandson in wardship, and without Mortimer uncles to protect Isabella's estate, her arrangements would be in jeopardy after her death. Isabella worked hard, and with the support of Bishop Cantilupe, to secure the services in her hospital and the manor to the Mortimer heir. Two days before Ralph died, she gained royal confirmation, enrolled in the charter rolls, of the hospital's endowment, notably her own gifts of its site,

---

[134]   In the Mortimer cartulary, BL, MS Harl. 1240, fol. 48v (44v). Date limits are supplied by the consecration of Bishop Cantilupe and the death of Abbot Hugh of Cirencester in 1250, witnesses, but can probably be refined by the confirmation of Isabella's grant of the mill, its core endowment, and the chapelry in 1246, *CChR*, i, p. 296.

[135]   The barons of Wigmore were buried at the abbey from its foundation in 1179 by Hugh II through the fourteenth century, Davies, *Lords and Lordship*, p. 34; for Isabella's husband and sons, *MA* vi, p. 350.

[136]   Oxford, New College archives, charter no. 14,065; *Orig. Papal Docs.*, no. 330.

[137]   Lewis, *Topographical Dictionary*, iii, p. 46; Carpenter, 'A Noble in Politics', p. 203.

[138]   Carpenter, 'A Noble in Politics', pp. 184–5. For their marriage in 1230, *Annales Monastici*, iv, p. 421.

[139]   *CR* 1242–7, p. 484; *CPR* 1247–58, p. 156; *Calendarium Genealogicum Henry III and Edward I*, ed. Charles Roberts (2 vols, London, 1865), i, p. 46; Holden, *Lords of the Central Marches*, pp. 207 and 225.

[140]   *CRR* xviii, no. 1246.

the bridge, the chapelry and its mill.[141] The following year they obtained papal charters of protection, confirming her gift of the site, and undertaking not to compel the house to receive papal appointments to its benefice.[142] It was the latter that first mentioned their status as Augustinians, and its timing suggests a wary savvy in planning for the house and the probable guidance of Bishop Cantilupe. The bishop continued to work with Isabella, confirming the arrangements between parish and hospital and supplying a rule to accommodate the diverse community.[143] An Augustinian community would provide the house, and with it her family's tenure of Lechlade, with greater security.[144]

Isabella also acted to secure Lechlade for the Mortimer line, handing her manor to Roger shortly before she died and issuing a letter instructing her tenants to obey him.[145] Her fears were justified for, together with Oakham, the manor was seized as an escheat by the king on her death in April 1252. Roger fought hard yet unsuccessfully to regain Lechlade, by 'force of arms' and labyrinthine legal suits whose pursuit, David Carpenter has argued, dictated his changing political stance during the baronial rebellion.[146] Like his father and brother before him, Ralph had been buried at the Mortimer Abbey of Wigmore, but Isabella had chosen to be buried in the chapel within the hospital's enclosure.[147] The hospital brethren issued a charter acknowledging 60 marks from William

---

[141]   TNA C 53/38, m. 6; *CChR*, i, p. 296. The deed is witnessed by, among others, the Bishop of London, Ralph fitzNicholas and John Maunsel, the chancellor of St Paul's.

[142]   Oxford, New College archives, charter nos 14,064–5, 13907; *Orig. Papal Docs*, nos 329, 329A, 330.

[143]   The Latin text of the rule is missing, but a translation, omitting names, is available in Adin Williams, *Lechlade: Being a History of the Town, Manor and Estates, the Priory and the Church* (Cirencester, 1888), pp. 65–6. Its probable date is 1247–52, but certainly before 1259, when Bishop Walter imported the Lechlade customs into the newly Augustinian hospital of St Mark's, Bristol, *EEA* 13, no. 48.

[144]   Other religious houses, such as Biddlesden Abbey, had been established in an attempt to secure a controversial claim to an estate, Richard Dace, 'Lesser Barons and Greater Knights: the Middling Group within the English Nobility c. 1086–c. 1265', *Haskins Society Journal*, 10 (2001): 57–77, at p. 73.

[145]   The letter no longer survives, but there is a brief medieval description in the Mortimer cartulary: 'La lettre Is' de Mortemer per quele ele ad mandez a ses tenants de Lecchelade destre entendantez a Roger de Mortemer'. It was preceded in the cartulary by the charter of Walkelin de Ferrers granting his son Hugh, Isabella's brother, the manors of Lechlade with Longbridge, a deed which Isabella must have retained and passed onto Roger, probably at this moment. BL, MS Harley 1240, fol. 28r. For later testimony of this event, Carpenter, 'A Noble in Politics', p. 188.

[146]   *CR* 1251–3, p. 220; Carpenter, 'A Noble in Politics', pp. 190–201, esp. pp. 188–9. Roger did not attempt to recover her other manor, Oakham.

[147]   *Beauchamp Cartulary*, no. 79; *MA* vi, pp. 350–52.

de Beauchamp (her grandson) and her other executors to support a chaplain there to celebrate for her soul. The chaplain would be presented to William and the Beauchamp heirs, and the Bishop of Worcester would, again, ensure that the brethren obeyed the charter's terms. It was witnessed by two more of her grandchildren: Roger de Mortimer and James, William's brother. Isabella worked hard for the Mortimer dynasty, but harder still for her children. Her identity as a mother may be signalled through her name, for this heiress of the de Ferrers estates, carrying out her work when married to and widowed by Peter fitzHerbert, remained in her deeds 'Isabella de Mortimer'. More assuredly, it is signalled through her use of the inherited estates, and especially the manor that lay closest to the geographical interests of her children. Initially used to support her younger sons, Lechlade was reinvented as a political seat when the Mortimer inheritance fell to her only remaining son, then further secured for his young heir, her grandson. Her hospital was a means by which this could be accomplished as baronial status symbol, commemorative site for her own and her son Hugh's souls, hoped-for tenurial anchor, and finally, as she was buried surrounded by the sons (and perhaps daughters) of her own daughter and youngest son, her own mausoleum. Throughout, Lechlade was a creative tool by which Isabella responded to and shaped the fortunes of her children. In choosing a site so different from their ancient seat of Wigmore, more prominent in England and on the road to London, Isabella was complementing patrimony with her own inheritance, once stamped with her own personality and, in burial, ongoing presence.

The hospital of St John the Baptist, Brackley (Northamptonshire), was not established by an heiress but under Robert II, Earl of Leicester, in c. 1150.[148] When the earldom was divided in 1204 upon the death of his grandson, Robert IV, the patronage of Brackley came into the hands of his sister Margaret de Beaumont, wife of Saher de Quincy, who would be Earl of Winchester in 1207.[149] The couple initially did nothing with the new house, but began work quite suddenly in c. 1218. At some point after 1217, but before his death on Crusade in 1219, Saher gave Littlehay Wood to the house and confirmed both the endowment of the Earls of Leicester and a grant of Andrew fitzWilliam, each 'at the petition and with the agreement of my wife Margaret and my son and heir, Roger'; he also added his own gift of the church of Gask in Perthshire.[150] These

---

[148]   *MA* vi, p. 751 (iv).

[149]   *RLC* i, pp. 24b–25; Sidney Painter, 'The House of Quency, 1136–1264', *Medievalia et Humanistica*, 11 (1957): 3–9.

[150]   Oxford, Magdalen College Archives [hereafter MCA], Brackley charters A11, D116, D219, B179; MS 273, fols 27r, 29v–30r; *The Collection of Brackley Deeds at Magdalen College*, W.D. Macray (Buckingham, 1910), p. 58.

efforts were not simply to support the existing house. The expanded dedication to SS John and James first appears in these deeds, and a contentious suit with the parish rector over rights to burial and spiritual services in the hospital, settled in 1219, suggests an expansion of its spiritual provision.[151] By the early 1220s, under the widowed countess and her son, the hospital was being rebuilt.[152] From the beginning, mother and son had worked together on the hospital and during the course of their lives Margaret (d. 1235) and her son Roger (d. 1264) transformed the house, granting substantial properties that eventually helped support a body of 11 priests.[153]

As with Isabella's hospital at Lechlade, work was prompted by the sudden death of Margaret and Saher's firstborn son, Robert, in 1217.[154] In contrast to the lost Lechlade archive, Brackley's has been preserved at Magdalen College, Oxford. Its trail of deeds reveals how Margaret sought to commemorate many of her children, not only the dynastic heir, as Isabella may have done. From 1217, when her son Robert's heart was interred near the hospital's high altar, Margaret used the hospital as a site to enact maternal care through spiritual ministration. Saher's own grant of Gask Church was for the soul of Robert, but the grants urged by Margaret and Roger were for the souls of Robert and another deceased son, John.[155] To their memory was soon added that of a third son, Saher, the three being commemorated, with Saher the elder, by Margaret's alms.[156] Before her own death, Margaret was also to commemorate her widowed daughter Loretta in a bequest of the mill at Halse, her nearby manorial seat.[157] Margaret

---

[151]   MCA, Brackley charters 187; MS 273, fol. 6r–v.

[152]   *RLC* i, pp. 461b, 552b; ii, pp. 9b, 11, 166.

[153]   MCA, MS 273, fols 9v–12r, 13v–18r, 19r, 27r–28v.

[154]   Wilkinson, *Women in Thirteenth-Century Lincolnshire*, p. 31n. Robert's marriage to Hawise, sister of the Earl of Chester, had produced a young daughter, Margaret, who was disinherited in favour of her uncle, Roger, ibid., pp. 30–35.

[155]   'pro anima Roberti de Quincy Primogeniti mei et pro anima Johannis de Quincy filii mei peticione et assensu predicte Margarite uxoris mei et predicti Rogeri de Quincy filii mei', MCA, Brackley charters, A11, D219; MS 273, fols 5v, 29v–30r.

[156]   'pro anima domini mei Seheri Comitis Winton' et pro animabus filiorum meorum Roberti Roberti [sic] et Seheri et Johannis', MCA, MS 273, fol. 30r. There is another grant by Roger de St. Andrew, Margaret's nephew, 'pro anima Seheri Comitis Winton' avunculi mei et pro animabus Roberti de Quinci et fratrum suorum'. It is witnessed by Margaret, Countess of Winchester, *domina mea*, and Roger de Quincy. MCA, Brackley charters, D103, C87.

[157]   'pro salute anime Lorette filie mee', MCA, Brackley charter, B180; MS 375, fol. 10r–v. For Saher's provision for his widowed daughter, see MCA, Brackley charter, 12. Another daughter, Orabel (Arabella), wife of Richard de Harcourt settled a suit against the hospital regarding her marriage portion in 1236, MCA, MS 273, fols 19r–20r.

never remarried, and when she died in 1235 her heart was buried before the high altar, beside her son Robert's.[158]

Roger continued this devotion to family and hospital, providing richly and almost continuously for the hospital until his death in 1264.[159] In the years after his mother's death, he worked to endow three chaplains in the hospital, and a light to burn before the altar of the Blessed Virgin Mary.[160] The two wives who pre-deceased him were buried and commemorated there.[161] A series of grants by Roger, his second wife Matilda and her father, Humphrey de Bohun, Earl of Hereford, made provision for Matilda's burial at the hospital and for chaplains to celebrate there for her soul in perpetuity.[162] In 1256 Roger endowed two more chaplains to celebrate for the soul of his first wife, Helen, the mother of his children, and for the soul of his brother, a second Robert, who died in 1257.[163] In one affecting grant, about five years after his mother had died, Roger bequeathed his own body to the house and income to provide a 3lb candle. This, he directed, should burn before the great altar during all masses and the canonical hours, suspended above the raised tombs where the hearts of his mother and brother lay.[164] Of the eleven chaplains established by 1279, three were to celebrate for Roger's soul, one for his brother Robert, two for his sister

---

[158] MCA, Brackley charters, B229.

[159] *Brackley Deeds*, pp. 14–41.

[160] Concluded by 1241, MCA, Brackley charters, B117, C114, C125, D124.

[161] Roger had three wives, the last of whom outlived him, Matthew Paris, *Chron. Maj.*, v, p. 341.

[162] MCA, Brackley charters, 183, B106, B108, C109. He also enacted a final bequest by Joan de Eu, lady of Criol, purchasing income to support a chaplain and providing a golden girdle and comb to buy a chalice ('cum quadam zona et quodam pectine aureis ad quemdam calicem emendum'), MCA, Brackley charters, C108; MS 273, fol. 11v. I have been unable to identify this Joan, whom the charter also calls 'Comitisse Britannie'. She would appear to be related to Matilda, whose mother Maud was the daughter of the Count of Eu. A Joan who was the daughter of Roger's younger brother, Robert, married Humphrey de Bohun, son of Earl Humphrey and Maud d'Eu, but she outlived Roger by many years, *CPR* 1258–66, p. 504; 1266–72, p. 472.

[163] MCA, Brackley charters, A4; Matthew Paris, *Chron. Maj.*, v, p. 99. For Robert's daughters, Joan and Hawise, aged nineteen and fourteen at Roger's death, *Calendar of Inquisitions Post Mortem*, I, no. 587; *Calendarium Genealogicum*, *Henry III* and *Edward I*, ed. Charles Roberts, i, pp. 111–12.

[164] 'debet pendere super tumulos cordium Margarete bone memorie Comitisse Winton' matris nostre et domini Roberti de Quency fratris nostri que ante magnum altare in predictorum apostolorum ecclesia tumulantur et super corpus nostrum quod ego delego concedo et confirmo', MCA, Brackley charters, B229; MS 273, fol. 12r. Its witness list suggests a date similar to charter B183.

Loretta, two for his wife Matilda and one for his wife Helen.[165] Roger's daughter and heir, Helen, also established a chaplain at the hospital, but somewhat grudgingly since she had wanted the chaplain to celebrate in her nearby chapel at Halse.[166] Her husband, Alan de la Zouche, was buried at the hospital, which then obtained a series of episcopal indulgences in 1318 for those who visited the hospital to pray for the faithful departed.[167]

With the support of her son, Margaret came the closest of the three women to establishing a dynastic hospital on her inherited estates. The Brackley house did serve as a family mausoleum and a site of commemoration for Margaret, her children and the wives of her heir, but the de Quincy name died with Roger, and the familial ties to the house dissipated in the following decades. The ambitions of Alice de Nerford and Isabella Mortimer did not even survive their deaths. Alice's dynastic dreams had died while she had lived, as her family failed and its fortunes crashed; and despite her best efforts, Isabella's Lechlade manor and hospital were seized by the Crown and so lost to her family. In all three cases, however, the reshaping of each hospital must be understood in relation to the estates of each heiress and her creative use of her inheritance to tend the political and spiritual needs of her children.

For the social historian motherhood presents an unusual challenge. As the metaphors of mother church, mother Mary and Jesus as mother reveal, this was one of the most fundamental, and powerful, of human relationships.[168] Yet it is one that is largely absent from documents. The problem is illustrated in the diplomatic of the very charters that are our chief sources for the high middle ages, whose gifts are given 'pro anima patris et matris et omnium antecessorum et successorum'. This standard phrase reflects the omnipresence of motherhood, biologically and even emotionally, together with the sense of obligation visited upon children; but it also obscures the distinctiveness of the relationships themselves. For the role of mother must have been constructed as much by time, circumstance, class and context as by the varieties of individual personality and forms of expression. As many studies have shown, simply finding women behind the legal sources can be a challenge; placing them within their family in order to explore this often less-public, largely unrecorded relationship can only be done haphazardly.

The hospitals of North Creake, Lechlade and Brackley permit insight into a social, even dynastic aspect of motherhood. They suggest how a distinction

---

[165]   MCA, Brackley charters, *Brackley Deeds*, p. 65.
[166]   Ibid.
[167]   MCA, Brackley charters, D250/4, 5, 9, and 10.
[168]   See, esp. Caroline Walker Bynum, *Jesus as Mother: Studies in the Spirituality of the High Middle Ages* (London, 1982), pp. 110–69.

might exist between the father's inheritance – the patrimony – and the mother's, which unfortunately we cannot call 'matrimony'. The former was the lineage estate, passed by this time from father to son, with its established *caput* and family abbey; the latter, by contrast, did not have an established meaning within the family's past but therefore offered a creative tool to reinvent its future. In all three examples, the women supplied that creative *animus*, using their inherited estates to define new political and spiritual centres for their family, their hospitals offering a means to inscribe these new meanings on the maternal estate. Alice used her estates to imagine a new dynastic anchor for a family scattered in royal service; Isabella first to provide materially for her younger sons then, with their deaths, to form a political presence, en route to London, for the Wigmore heir; Margaret, in her hospital, to develop a familial site of remembrance and spiritual care. All three were creatively *responsive* to changes in the family, and particularly to the circumstances of their adult children. They might have tended the dynastic heir, but they seem unexpectedly responsive to their children rather than to the dynasty. The loss of his heir provided the impetus for work on each hospital, yet the work was not simply in service of the dynasty. Each heir died before fulfilling his dynastic role and so proved a barren branch, cut off in its prime, as also were other adult brothers, often the next heir: Nicholas and John de Nerford, Hugh and Roger de Mortimer, and Robert and John de Quincy. Of these, only Robert had a child, a daughter Margaret, who was disinherited in favour of her uncle.[169] The women's labours thus created legacies for sons who had died before creating their own, and remembered children who might otherwise be forgotten. It suggests an identity in motherhood that is at odds with the more transient statuses bequeathed in law, of single, married or widowed woman; and at odds, too, with the stages of lifecycle, with a temporal role provided at birth and relinquished upon death. Motherhood could begin in a woman's teens, its responsibilities and attachments survive into her widowhood and even after the death of her children, and her vision of the children's future could extend beyond her own death. Aristocratic mothers were thus a generative link between past and future, not only biologically but consciously and creatively, intervening to fashion different futures for her children from her own past and, in the site and endowment of a hospital, to tie their fortunes to a place of maternal origin.

The emotional ties of motherhood, so effectively articulated in Leyser's own work, are more difficult to access, yet something more than constitutional pragmatism seems to lie, unwritten, behind the actions of these women.[170] The

[169] Wilkinson, *Women in Thirteenth-Century Lincolnshire*, pp. 31–4.
[170] Leyser, *Medieval Women*, p. 132.

particularly liturgical, even Augustinian, character of each hospital, long noted by scholars, developed in each case after multiple bereavements in a brief period. It is hard not to see escalating desperation behind Alice's responses to the deaths of her sons, and grief in Margaret's commemoration of first two, then three and four of her children. The burial of Margaret's own heart twenty years later beside her eldest son's testifies to an emotional attachment that endured beyond his death and that she wished to be expressed after her own.[171] The limited glimpses of Isabella's actions reveal that she endowed a chaplain for her eldest son and that her daughter's children remained close to her, even acting as executors after her death. As the latter suggests, daughters may not have been as absent as their invisibility in the record might indicate. Margaret's daughter Loretta was commemorated by two chaplains by her mother and brother; and the husband of another daughter, Arabella, makes occasional appearances among the Brackley deeds. Significantly, it was the childless children who were tended by commemorations at the hospitals, notably those who reached adulthood but not old age. The escalation of spiritual provision that followed these deaths suggests a depth of grief for the children and a sense of hope lost for their, and perhaps the family's, future.

These ties are reinforced by two further glimpses of these women as mothers. Wigmore Abbey's *Historia* preserves a tale of a young, pregnant Isabella, travelling with her husband through the village of Snitton when she fell ill. Her illness induced labour and she delivered a boy who was baptized but quickly died. The grieving Isabella then implored her husband to return the village to the canons, convinced that its unlawful seizure by him had induced this misfortune and so transformed the hope she had had in great comfort from her son's life into great sadness at his death.[172] In early 1240, a few years after his mother's death, Roger de Quincy made an unusual grant to Brackley hospital. This charter directed that an open sarcophagus be placed in the hospital, to the right of his mother's heart. This was to be filled with winnowed wheat from Margaret's – now his – grange in nearby Halse, 'one sarcophagus' of wheat on each of three annual festivals

---

[171]   For the suggestion that heart burial could 'emphasis[e] the emotional and religious aspects of interment', and especially attachment to family, see Danielle Westerhof, 'Celebrating Fragmentation: the Presence of Aristocratic Body Parts in Monastic Houses in Twelfth- and Thirteenth-Century England', *Cîteaux: Commentarii Cistercienses*, 56 (2005): 27–45, at p. 31; Elizabeth A.R. Brown, 'Death and the Human Body in the Later Middle Ages: the Legislation of Boniface VIII on the Division of the Corpse', *Viator*, 12 (1981): 221–70, at pp. 227–9.

[172]   'pria a sun seigneur humblement et devotement en lermant ... et dist, qe per encheson de ceo, si aveit grant torment en enfantant, et aveit esperance de aver en grant solaz de la vye de sun fiz, si aveit ele graunt tristure de sa mort', *MA* vi, p. 348.

including Easter until Roger's death, and four festivals annually thereafter.[173] I can find no parallels among English aristocratic or monastic tombs for such a striking gesture. It perhaps owes its form to Robert Grosseteste, the diocesan, who had intervened at the hospital the previous year on Roger's behalf;[174] the maternal devotion that it captures, however, was Roger's. Since Margaret's heart burial was before the high altar, this empty sarcophagus lay open, permanently, in front of the congregation in the hospital, a constant expression of Margaret's absent presence. Its filling with winnowed wheat on certain feast days draws daringly upon thirteenth-century imagery of the Eucharist as bread, and Christ himself as wheat.[175] Margaret's heart and her own absent body were thus a source of nourishment, in perpetuity, to the sick poor of the hospital as it had been, it implies, to her children. It is an image from her son that answers the maternal identity suggested by the women's own labours. As mothers, each of these women made from her care and her own family's past a place that tended her children's needs both in this world and the next. Through their bodies and, creatively, through their own inheritance they helped fashion the futures of their children even, and perhaps especially, when those futures failed dynastically.

---

[173] 'unum sarcofagum qui iacebit ad dexteram cordis domine Margarete de Quency matris nostre, ter plenum frumenti vannati singulis annis inperpetuum ad tres terminos anni: videlicet unum sarcofagum plenum ad festum sancti Thome apostoli et unum alium ad pascha et tertium ad festum sancti petri ad vincula, recipienda de grangia nostra de halsou', MCA, Brackley charters, B183; MS 273, fol. 27r–v.

[174] He had invalidated an election to substitute a candidate more acceptable to Roger, *Rotuli Roberti Grosseteste, Episcopi Quondam Lincolniensis Epistolae*, ed. H.R. Luard (London, 1861), pp. 179–80.

[175] Roger's deed pre-dates the first celebration of Corpus Christi, whose feast did not arrive in England until 1318. From the fourteenth century, the Eucharist was more often portrayed as flesh than wheat. Miri Rubin, *Corpus Christi: the Eucharist in Late Medieval Culture* (Cambridge, 1991), pp. 37–9, 199–200; Caroline Walker Bynum, *Holy Feast, Holy Fast: the Religious Significance of Food to Medieval Women* (Berkeley, CA, 1982), pp. 47–69.

Chapter 12

Becoming the Theotokos: Birgitta of Sweden and Fulfilment of Salvation History

Samuel Fanous

The degree of spiritual authority acquired by Birgitta of Sweden (1303–1370) during the turbulent decades of the Avignon Papacy is remarkable.[1] Born in a noble family, her mother, Ingeborg Bengtsdotter, was a daughter of the Folkunga clan, the reigning Swedish dynasty that had occupied the Swedish throne since 1250.[2] A mother of eight children (all of whom lived), she devoted herself to a

---

[1]   I am grateful to Vincent Gillespie, Roger Ellis, Tore Nyberg and Ann Hutchinson, who read and commented on earlier versions of this paper. Any errors or infelicities are of course my own.

On Birgitta (or Bridget) generally, see Eric Colledge, '*Epistola solitarii ad reges*: Alphonse of Pecha as Organizer of Brigittine and Urbanist Propaganda', *Mediaeval Studies*, 18 (1956): 19–49; Roger Ellis, '"Flores ad fabricandam ... coronam": an Investigation into the Uses and Abuses of the Revelations of St Birgitta of Sweden in 15th Century England', *Medium Ævum*, 51 (1982): 163–86; J.H. Hallendorff and A. Schück, *History of Sweden*, trans. L. Yapp (Stockholm, 1929); Ingvar Andersson, *A History of Sweden* (London, 1955); Johannes Jørgensen, *Saint Bridget of Sweden*, trans. I. Lund (2 vols, London, 1954), a flowery but useful account of Birgitta's life, whose sources should be verified; H.T. Gilkær, *The Political Ideas of St. Birgitta and her Spanish Confessor, Alfonso Pecha*: Liber Celestis Imperatoris ad Reges: a Mirror of Princes, trans. M. Cain, Odense University Studies in History and Social Sciences, 163 (Odense, 1993), pp. 216–18; *Birgitta, hendes værk og hendes klostre i Norden*, ed. Tore Nyberg (Odense, 1991) and Nyberg, *Birgittinsk festgåva. Studier on heliga Birgitta och Birgittinorden* (Uppsala, 1991); Birger Bergh (ed.), *Heliga Birgitta. Åttabarnsmor och profet* (Stockholm, 2002); Birgit Klockars, *Birgitta och böckerna. En undersökning av den heliga Birgittas källor* (Stockholm, 1966); Bridget Morris, *St Birgitta of Sweden* (Woodbridge, 1999); Claire Sahlin, *Birgitta of Sweden and the Voice of Prophecy* (Woodbridge, 2001); and Karin Schuback (ed.), *Birgitta – feminist, politiker och helgon. En antologi från Birgittajubileumsåret 2003 vid Linköpings universitet* (Linköping, 2005).

[2]   Strictly speaking, Birgitta was not of the line of Magnus Ericsson (the reigning king) but was his third cousin. Her father, Birger Petersson, served as the *lagman* ('lawman', judge) of the province of Uppland from 1290 until his death (except in 1316–1318), and sat on

vocation of visionary prophecy comparatively late in life, moving to Rome at the age of 47. Unstinting in her criticism of the moral degeneracy and apostasy in contemporary society, her oracles acquired a unique prophetic status. Having correctly prophesied the death of pope Urban V if he should return to Avignon, she succeeded in gaining from his successor permission to found her Order of Birgittine nuns.[3] The totality of her vision, encompassing a universal mission for the re-establishment of piety and morality in Christendom – through the spread of her Order – is astounding in its scope and extent. Moreover, this ideal was conceived not by ignoring or mitigating her status as mother, but by incorporating it fully into her vision. While Birgitta's revelations have been widely discussed, her sources, motivation and direct models have not been fully appreciated. Looking first briefly at Birgitta's biblical identity created both by her amanuenses and by the saint, this essay will examine Birgitta's perception of her own biblical prophetic identity, her assimilation of contemporary events to the history of the Egyptian and Babylonian captivity, her perception of her new Order as the fulfilment of Ezekiel's vision of the Temple, her use of the ceremonies of Moses' Temple, and her synthesis of these into highly matriarchal, Marian-centred vision for her Order, based on the model of the first-century apostolic community.

---

the Rigsråd (Privy Council) which elected the new monarch, usually the king's offspring. Birgitta's brother, Israel, inherited Birger's title as the Uppland's *lagman*, becoming, like his father, the *de facto* first peer of the realm. Six years after she married Ulf Gudmarsson, the son of a *lagman* (of Västergötland) in 1316, he became a *lagman* (of Närke) and by the early 1330s, a member of the Rigsråd (Privy Council). Eventually, Birgitta's son, Birger, also sat on this assembly. Birgitta was tutor to the queen, Blanca of Namur, and became the godmother of King Magnus and Queen Blanca's first child, Eric. Ulf died in 1344, after which Birgitta moved to Rome, where she sought papal permission for her Order and Rule.

   [3]   In the aftermath of legislation promulgated at the Council of Lyons (1274), new religious Orders, like the Birgittines, had to subordinate their own Rule to one of the four existing monastic *regulae* – the Birgittines chose the Rule of St Augustine – according their own Rule the lesser status of 'Constitutions'. The Birgittine Rule had been received in the 1340s as a direct revelation from God by the Saint and was first approved by the Roman Curia in 1370, but in a form that undermined its more radical innovations. It was not until the outbreak of the Papal Schism in 1378, in response to the enthusiastic support of his papacy by followers of what would become the Birgittine Order, that Urban VI approved the Rule substantially in the form of its first reception. Additions to the Rule to adapt it to local situations were permitted: Syon Abbey had Additions in English for the nuns and the lay brothers, and in Latin for the monks. I am indebted to Roger Ellis for this point.

Clerical Alignment

One of the problems in attributing sources and motives in the writings of saints, especially women saints, is the recovery of the voice and person of the saint, which sometimes lies submerged beneath a sea of clerical artifice, predictable by its nature and recognizable by its very ubiquity.[4] Moreover, when putative saints turned to pen their own spiritual memoirs, they did not adopt an entirely new style but borrowed the hagiographer's manner of discourse. Conversely, while the roles of saint and hagiographer were in theory clearly defined, considerable overlap in the editorial process from the twelfth century onwards meant that, in practice, saints increasingly played a more active part in the creation of their own *vitae*. Thus, an autobiographic element crept into saints' lives and a degree of hagiographic presentation characterized writings by the saints. Not only did this foster a closer generic relation, but it also created a literary environment where the putative saint could practise the hagiographer's techniques without prejudice to inherent contradictions arising from this crossover of roles. The enormous popularity of saints' lives in the middle ages and the wide association of hagiography with biographical *imitatio* – describing an individual in terms designed to recall a predecessor – in the collective consciousness ensured that the saintly author's use of the mimetic topos would be consumed and digested in a hagiographic context. Thus, the hagiographer's regard for his subject's literary appearance and the saint's authorial concern with self-representation could

---

[4] Birgitta's *vita* was written by her two Swedish confessors, Peter Olavsson (d. 1390), the Prior of the Cistercian Monastery in Alvastra, and Master Peter Olavsson of Skänninge (d. 1378), a theologian and secular priest who was to become the first Confessor General of Vadstena, the mother house of the Birgittine Order. The shorter *vita*, now Uppsala, University Library, MS C 15, formed the basis for what became the standard life, the *Processus Vita*, prepared by the Spaniard, Alphonse of Pecha, former Bishop of Jaén, who resigned his office for that of a hermit and became Birgitta's principal confessor towards the end of her life and the chief editor of the *Revelations*. Their *attestationes* are edited in I. Collijn (ed.), *Acta et processus canonizacionis beate Birgitte* (hereafter *A&P*), Samlingar utgivna av Svenska Fornskriftsäilskapet (hereafter SSFS), 2, 1 (Uppsala, 1924–1931): Prior Peter (named as Birgitta's *secundus confessor*, p. 268): pp. 472–562; Master Peter: pp. 255–92; and Alphonse: pp. 363–414. On Master Matthias's role as Birgitta's first confessor see *A&P*, pp. 267, 324, 486, and more generally, Anders Piltz, 'Magister Mathias of Sweden in his Theological Context: a Preliminary Survey', in Monika Asztalos (ed.), *The Editing of Theological and Philosophical Texts from the Middle Ages*, Acta Universitatis Stockholmiensis, Studia Latina Stockholmiensia, 30 (Stockholm, 1986), pp. 137–60; and 'Introduction', Carl–Gustaf Undhagen (ed.), *Sancta Birgitta: Revelaciones, Lib. I cvm Prologo Magistri Mathie*, Kungl. Vitterhets Historie och Antikvitets Handlingar (hereafter KVHAA) (Uppsala, 1977), pp. 9–10, 38–50.

acquire an identical appearance through their mutual application of *imitatio*. Mediated and heavily redacted by her amanuenses–confessors, Birgitta's vast collection of visions received over a lifetime, filling nine books (containing extensive repetition), bears the heavy stamp of clerical authority.[5] Yet occasionally, Birgitta's voice rings through her visions. The use of highly personal motifs, such as images and phrases from Swedish law (inherited through both sides of the family and sustained in marriage), the language and imagery of mothering and biblical antecedents applied almost as cultural metaphors to describe everyday events, points to the author as the source.

The complex enterprise of establishing Birgitta's sanctity began while she was still alive through her promotion by biblical types. While Birgitta maintained a highly developed sense of biblical self-identity (as we shall see), her confessors were engaged in a parallel enterprise of developing biblical resonances to her persona so as to counter the problematic nature of Birgitta's ministry, which sharply challenged received conventions regarding the public role of women – especially mothers – and their engagement in preaching and ecclesiastical reform. Counterpointing her *vita* with sustained references to prophetic biblical models, they sought to approbate her preaching and defend her from the obvious charge of exercising clerical prerogative. Their account of Birgitta's calling provides a compact example of this technique. As Ezekiel fell with fear before the theophany in the shining cloud (Ez., 1: 26–2: 1), Birgitta was thrice called in her prayers by a voice from a shining cloud. Twice she fled in terror, but on the third occasion, the thundering voice called her to become

---

5   In addition to Book I (see previous note) Birgitta's revelations are edited in the following critical editions: Carl-Gustaf Undhagen and Birger Bergh (eds), *Birgitta: Revelaciones, Lib. II*, SSFS 2, 7.2 (Uppsala, 2001); Ann-Mari Jönsson (ed.), *Sancta Birgitta: Revelaciones, Lib. III*, SSFS 2, 7.3 (Stockholm, 1998); Hans Aili (ed.), *Sancta Birgitta: Revelaciones. Lib. IV*, SSFS, 2, 7: 4, KVHAA (Uppsala, 1992); Birger Bergh (ed.), *Sancta Birgitta: Revelaciones, Lib. V: Liber Questionum*, SSFS 2, 7: 5, KVHAA (Uppsala, 1971); Birger Bergh (ed.), *Sancta Birgitta: Revelaciones Lib. VI*, SSFS, 2, 7: 6, KVHAA (Uppsala, 1991); Birger Bergh (ed.), *Sancta Birgitta: Revelaciones, Lib. VII*, SSFS 2, 7: 7, KVHAA (Uppsala, 1967); Hans Aili (ed.), *Sancta Birgitta: Revelaciones, Book VIII* SFSS 2, 7.8 (Stockholm, 2002); Lennart Hollman (ed.), *Den heliga Birgittas Reuelaciones Extrauagantes*, SFSS, 2, 5 (Uppsala, 1965); Sten Eklund (ed.), *Opera Minora I, Regula Salvatoris*, SSFS, 2, 8: 1 (Uppsala, 1975); Sten Eklund (ed.), *Opera Minora II: Sermo Angelicvs*, KVHAA, SSFS, 2, 8: 2 (Uppsala, 1972). References are cited by book and chapter in the text. See also the critical edition of the Middle English *Revelations* printed in Roger Ellis (ed.), *Liber Celestis of Bridget of Sweden*, EETS OS, 291 (Oxford, 1987). For modern translations, see: Marguerite Tjader Harris (ed.), *Birgitta of Sweden, Life and Selected Revelations*, trans. Albert Ryle Kezel, Classics of Western Spirituality (New York, 1990); *The Revelations of St. Birgitta of Sweden*, trans. Denis Searby and Bridget Morris, vols 1 & 2 (New York, 2006, 2008).

the spouse of Christ, to adopt a life of prophecy and missionary activity, and directed her to test this vision through her confessor, Master Matthias, an expert in the discernment of spirits.[6] Master Matthias's Prologue to Book I written before 1349 (when she left for Rome) gives a glimpse of some of the problems encountered by the phenomenon of a laywoman in receipt of divine oracles: God could not be expected to speak to a secular woman; her visions proceeded from a false spirit; and her true intentions were vainglorious. He accounts for the incredulity Birgitta's visions aroused among her compatriots, particularly the nobles, by comparing her with Christ, who was not accepted by his own people (I. Prol.). He credits her with postponing God's judgement on Sweden and its people, aligning her to the figure of an Old Testament prophet whose quasi-thaumaturgic presence defers the wrath of God against a sinful people.

The task of approbating Birgitta fell chiefly to Alphonse, the divinely appointed editor of the *Revelations* who compiled the individual revelations (*Extrav.*, 49).[7] His greatest contribution to Birgitta's *approbatio* was the creation of a set of criteria for discernment of spirits ('discretio spiritum'), culled from the Scriptures and patristic sources and applied to Birgitta and her visions, in his masterful *Epistola solitarii ad reges* as Preface to the *Liber Celestis Imperatoris ad Reges*, Book VIII.[8] These criteria would acquire and maintain high influence in the contentious matter of the discernment of spirits over the course of

---

[6] *A&P*, pp. 73–101 (pp. 80–81 for the call narrative). Note here the conflation of two stories, viz. the calling of Samuel (I Sam. 3) through the three-fold call and the verification by superiors, so characteristic of hagiography. For the use of this technique in the *vitae* of Ursulina of Parma and Catherine of Siena, see: Simon Zanachi, *Vita Vrsulinae Virgine, Acta Sanctorum*, vol. 7, 1 April, 725–39 (728); and Catherine of Siena, *Vita Catherinae*, 876, both cited in M.S. Costello, 'Women's Mysticism and Reform: the Adaptation of Biblical Prophetic Conventions in Fourteenth–Century Hagiographic and Visionary Literature', unpubl. PhD diss. (Northwestern University, 1989), pp. 147ff., 174ff.

[7] Alphonse's position as editor-in-chief of the *Revelations* is repeated on Birgitta's deathbed (*A&P*, p. 98). He prepared the first edition (*Liber Alfonsi*) in 1377 for examination by the canonization commission appointed by Gregory XI. On the contents of this edition, Alphonse's role in shaping the text into books and chapters and supplying rubrics, and the critical discussion regarding the textual history of the *Revelations*, see 'Introduction', *Lib. I*, pp. 14ff, and Rosalynn Voaden, *God's Words, Women's Voices: the Discernment of Spirits in the Writings of Late-Medieval Women Visionaries* (York, 1999). Cf. Arne Jönsson, *Alfonso of Jaén: His Life and Works with Critical Editions of the* Epistola Solitarii, *the* Informaciones *and* Epistola Serui Christi, Studia Graeca et Latina Lundensia, 1 (Lund, 1989); and Bergh, 'On the History of the Text', *Lib. V*, pp. 13ff.

[8] *Epistola solitarii*, I.1, in Jönsson, *Alfonso of Jaén*. Jönsson draws attention to Alphonse's title of his book, the *Epistola solitarii* not the *Epistola eposcopi*, taking advantage of the status of hermits, who deemed to be expert in the discernment of spirits.

successive centuries.⁹ Yet Alphonse did not accomplish the monumental task of approbating Birgitta's visions by *discretio* alone. In the *Epistola* and in his related works, he creates a biblical identity for Birgitta largely through the use of biblical metaphors, a technique employed by all three of Birgitta's confessor-amanuenses. Avignon becomes Egypt, a potent symbol of captivity; the Pope is the hard-hearted Pharaoh refusing God's Word from the mouth of his messenger, stubbornly clinging to signs; and the pleasures which attract the *carnalis cardinales* become the fleshpots of Egypt (*Infomaciones*, 45, 55). Alphonse warns the kingly readership of the *Liber celestis* against Pharaoh's incredulity and hard-heartedness (*Epistola*, 1, I.29). In describing spiritual visions, he uses the example of Pharaoh's dream of the ears of corn and the burning bush to validate Birgitta's revelations (V.7). He compares the composition of the *Revelations* to the work of the Evangelists and asks the reader to believe that they were written by the very finger of God in Birgitta's heart, as was the law on stone tablets (A&P, p. 86; *Epistola*, 1). Alphonse's language is intentional, influencing his own apprehension of these events and seeking to shape the reader's perception of Birgitta's mission through select rhetorical strategies that vivify her biblical persona and give powerful scriptural dimension to her prophecies. It lends subtle approbation by lifting her message from the intractability of papal politics to the biblical plane of Moses and the Exodus, buttressing the method of *discretio*.¹⁰ The cumulative effect of these biblical references is to map out a

---

⁹ The work was re-arranged by Jean Gerson in his tract *De probatione spirituum* composed, ironically, to attack St Birgitta at the Council of Constance (1414–1418) (Colledge, '*Epistola solitarii*', pp. 44–6). See Paschal Boland, *The Concept of Discretio Spirituum in John Gerson's 'De Probatione Spirituum' and 'De Distinctione Verarum Visionum A Falsis'*, The Catholic University of America Studies in Sacred Theology, 2nd series, 112 (Washington, DC, 1959).

¹⁰ A similar technique is deployed by Adam of Easton, whose magnificent *defensorium* in support of Birgitta against the now lost Perugian *Libellus* carefully aligns Birgitta and her text with biblical characters and the Scriptures. He compares her receipt of the *Regula* with St Paul's divine receipt of the Epistles and declares the parallel processes *similis sive minus*. Birgitta's dictated the *Sermo Angelicus* 'sicud fecit Moyses per angelum plebi sue'. Similarly, he states: 'Notandum quod ista devota domina Brigitta in suis dictis habet modum loquendi scripture sacre, unde est signum manifestatum quod a Spiritu Sancto fuerat inspirata' ('It is noted that this devout lady Bridget in her sayings possesses the way of speaking of Holy Scripture, which is a manifest sign that she was inspired by the Holy Spirit') [edited in J.A. Schmidtke, 'Adam Easton's Defence of St Brigitta from Bodleian MS Hamilton 7 Oxford University', unpubl. PhD diss. (Duke University, 1971), pp. 173–4, 199, 288]. See further W.A. Pantin, 'The Defensorium of Adam of Easton', *English Historical Review*, 51 (1936): 675–80; and James Hogg, 'Cardinal Easton's Letter to the Abbess and Community of Vadstena', in Hogg (ed.), *Studies in St. Birgitta and the Brigittine Order* (2 vols, Salzburg, 1993), 2.20–26.

terrain of sanctity in the *Revelations* in which Birgitta recedes into the figure of the saint, making it more difficult for criticism to gain a foothold in the edifice of her hagiographic identity.[11]

Birgitta's Biblical Identity

Birgitta had access to a Bible, probably a free Swedish translation of the Pentateuch made in the early fourteenth century by Master Matthias, perhaps at her request (*A&P*, p. 78).[12] The influence of his strong biblically centred theological approach on Birgitta is evident throughout her *Revelations*,[13] which contain more than 200 direct biblical quotations and even more unattributed references and allusions. Moses and the Old Testament prophets figure largely, and in addition to the Ezekiel reference in her calling, Isaiah is frequently cited, particularly his prophecies regarding the Virgin and the Messiah (I.17, 37, IV.126, VI.56, VII.25). Even where there is no single direct source, the style and tone of many of Birgitta's revelations echo biblical dialectic. For example, she borrows the rhetorical style of the Old Testament prophets to add authority to her visions, particularly her oracles to Clement VI (IV.63, VI.63). God frequently defines himself by his deeds in her revelations, a pattern fundamental to God's oracles to Israel's prophets.[14] It is no coincidence that Birgitta's very first revelation begins in this style: 'I am the creator of heaven and earth, one in Godhead with the Father and the Holy Spirit. I am he who spoke with the prophets and patriarchs and whom they expected' (I.1).[15] The history of God's

---

[11]   Roger Ellis, 'A Note on the Spirituality of St Bridget of Sweden', in James Hogg (ed.), *Spiritualität heute und gestern, Analecta Cartusiana*, 35: 1 (1982): 157–66 (p. 160): 'even as we read, we feel the person disappearing into the Saint'.

[12]   Klockars, *Birgitta och böckerna*, p. 59.

[13]   Master Matthias was one of the foremost theologians in Sweden, a gifted biblical scholar, and a D.D. of the University of Paris. See Piltz, 'Master Matthias', who discusses his strong biblical orientation and his concern for a theologically-based approach to biblical exegesis.

[14]   A.C. Charity, *Events and their Afterlife: the Dialectics of Christian Typology in the Bible and Dante* (Cambridge, 1966), pp. 22–3.

[15]   'Ego sum creator celi et terre, unus in deitate cum Patre et Spiritu sancto, ego, qui prophetis et patriarchis loquebar et quem ipsi expectabant. Ob quorum desiderium ei ixusta promissionem meam assumpsi carnem.' Adam of Easton says Birgitta's visions must be true since, 'per hoc quod ipsa modo prophetarum utitur in loquendo: "Hec dicit Dominus" et post subiungens totum quod fuerat revelatum' ('Bridget uses the method of the prophets in speaking: "Thus sayeth the Lord", and afterwards took down all that was revealed', Schmidtke, 'Defence of St Brigitta', p. 177).

dealings with Israel, so succinctly summarized in this locution, is perhaps the most influential biblical phenomenon in Birgitta's thought. Her early revelations contain numerous references to the life of Moses. Books I (received entirely in Swedish) and II contain more than 20 references to the Exodus.[16]

Birgitta also employs biblical images to interpret contemporary circumstances typologically. In their love for the world and neglect of their spiritual children, corrupt priests (worse than Judases [IV.132]) are like the Israelites worshipping the golden calf while Moses was atop the mountain with God. They regard Christ as the Israelites did Moses: he had been absent for a long time and no one knew when he would return (IV.132). Birgitta allegorizes every part of the calf: its feet represent sloth, impatience, foolish merriment and covetousness; its neck and throat, the priests' greed and insatiable desires; and the whole calf symbolizes perfect love of the world (I.48). The seven plagues that visited the Egyptians will descend upon priests (VI.132). They are accursed with the curse of David (I.47).[17] Her contemporaries' reception of Christ and his message is likened to the Israelites' reception of Moses' message (I.60, VIII.49) and their praying to the golden calf (I.48, 53). Sweden has been badly led astray by King Magnus, who has not been to it as Moses was to Israel (VIII.49). Queen Blanca, in her malignant beauty, is a Jezebel (VIII.12, 10, 14). Birgitta applies typology reflexively, placing herself within the interpretative framework. God's anger towards the immorality of Cyprus was so great that it became a Gomorrah *ardens igne luxurie* that God would punish and which she ardently wished, like Abraham, to save from destruction (VII.16). The wayward son of the noble Orsinis who wrongly seized his neighbour's vineyard becomes a King Ahab who wrongly took Naboth's vineyard (III Kgs, 21: 17–19); Birgitta becomes Elijah, warning him of imminent judgement (IV. 46). She prays for the salvation of the world as if she were an Old Testament prophet ('Descendere ad liberandum populum suum Israel', III.5; cf. Jer., 31: 7). Called to the bed of a sick child, she spread out her mantle over the infant who immediately recovered and arose (I Kgs, 18: 17–24; *A&P*, pp. 359–60, 387).[18] Christ compares Birgitta and her predicament directly to the prophets and their circumstances, with Jeremiah, for

---

[16]   For example, the receipt of the Ten Commandments is referred to in five revelations (I.10, 26, 45, 47, 48), as is the Crossing of the Red Sea (I.15, 45, 48, 53, 60). I have made extensive use of Klockars's highly useful indexes to Birgitta's revelations.

[17]   'Non ex ira, vel voluntate mala sed ex iustitia.' ('Not from wrath or ill will but from justice.') Note, once again, Birgitta's strong sense of divine justice.

[18]   The parallel with Elijah's healing of the widow's child (I Kgs, 18: 17–24) is conflated with Jesus' healing of Jairus' daughter as she adds, 'Non moritur puer, sed dormit' (cf. Lk, 9: 52). In a real sense, all experience could be interpreted by reference to the past, for history was primarily the record of God's intervention in the course of human affairs, working out

example, while the stubborn pope influenced by the corrupt cardinals is Israel's king who listened to evil counsellors opposed to Jeremiah (IV.141). In the manner that Israel's prophets and patriarchs symbolized their people, Birgitta represents to Christ the faithful:

> Truly my daughter, although I speak to you I understand by you all who follow the holy faith by works of charity. For as in one man Israel is represented, so also by you are all true believers understood. (IV.18)[19]

The universalism of Birgitta's visions reflects her deep concern for the state of Christendom. Her pre-occupation with Moses, Israel, the prophets and salvation history stemmed from her profound awareness of the parallels between Moses, the prophets and their times, and between herself and her times. Called in the manner of Ezekiel's calling (by design or fact), she perceived her world, like the prophet's, in terms of crisis and judgement, comprising God's friends and enemies. Ezekiel had lived through the greatest crisis in Israel's history, witnessing the desolation of Judah and Jerusalem, the loss of the promised land to a foreign power, the destruction of the Temple (IV Kgs, 25: 8–17; Jer., 39, 52; II Chr., 36: 15–21), and the exile of its people and leaders (IV Kgs, 24: 10–20). The sons of Israel had brought about its destruction by defiling the sanctuary (Ez., 5: 11), following after other gods (8: 7–9), worshipping idols (14: 3–5), defiling themselves by adultery and fornication (23: 37–38), and making themselves unclean (20: 30–31; 22: 26; 36: 18). They had violated divine justice and behaved wickedly (7: 10, 23; 18: 7–9; 22: 11–12). Israel's sins are reversed in Ezekiel's vision of the Temple. Righteousness is restored and the divine presence returns to dwell among the Israelites. Ezekiel thus attempts a complete programme of reform to re-establish the covenant in its proper setting. God would again rule the land not from Mt Sinai but from a new mountain some distance away on which the Temple seen by Ezekiel in spirit would be built.

Birgitta, too, felt that she was living through the Christendom's darkest days. Even before she left Sweden, she was appalled by the nobility's overweening pride and obsession with every form of physical gratification (I.1), exemplified

---

the divine purpose of salvation. Moreover, the Bible did not contain two distinct histories of Israel and the early Church but a single universal history. See below, p. 276.

[19] 'Verumptamen, filia, quamuis tibi loquor, per te tamen omnes intelligo, qui fidem sanctam sequuntur operibus caritatis. Sicut enim in uno homine Israel omnes Israhelite intelligebantur, sic per te omnes veri fideles intelliguntur.'

to her by King Magnus's homosexuality (VI.80). She railed against the moral laxity of Magnus's councillors, who bitterly resented her strong influence over him, and prophesied against the people of Sweden (for example, I.27, *Extrav.*, 73), earning the opprobrium of leading figures in the Swedish court (*A&P*, pp. 19, 492–94, 583). Things were no better in Naples and Cyprus (VII.11, 19, 27, 28). Rome's decadence, at the heart of Christendom, was especially shocking and grievous: monks and nuns openly disregarded religious observances, living in fornication and luxury (IV.33, *Extrav.*, 8). Priests neglected their office, caring primarily for their own temporal affairs and teaching only love of the world (I.59; IV.43, 132–133). The Pope and the Curia had exiled themselves to Avignon, indulging in immorality (I.23, 41). In Birgitta's revelations, Christ wept over Rome as a prophet over Jerusalem, lamenting the loss of her justice, the transformation of her princes into murderers, the destruction of her gates, the tearing down of her walls, the desolation of her watchtowers, the selling of her sacraments, the profane use of her sacred vessels, and the ruin of her altars at the hands of loveless ministers (III.27, IV.10, VI.26). Everywhere, sin, vice and wickedness were rampant. God had become old in men's hearts and was ignored (VI.88). His wrath had never been greater in a thousand years, as the Plague amply testified (IV.134; *Extrav.*, 74). The final age (the first two being from Adam to Christ and from Christ to Birgitta's day), the Age of Apostasy, had arrived and would last until the End Times and the Judgement (VI.67). Things could hardly be worse.

Birgitta had done everything in her power to return the popes to Rome and to reverse the prevailing moral decline through her prophetic preaching. Alphonse was to deliver in person Birgitta's most scathing revelation about Gregory XI (IV.142) but, convinced that the Pope's relatives and the French cardinals (or as he called them, the *carnalis cardinales*), preferring the high life in Avignon to the comparative austerities of Rome, would have plotted his death had they known of his mission, he travelled from Rome to Avignon secretly.[20] Cardinal Beaufort (who became Gregory XI on Urban V's death) refused to deliver to Urban V Birgitta's earlier revelation of imminent punishment (IV.138), perhaps from fear of reprisal.[21]

As Israel's crisis culminated in and was reversed by Ezekiel's vision of the Temple (Ez., 40–48), Birgitta received divine instructions for founding Vadstena, which she imaged as the mother house of a reforming Order throughout

---

[20]   *Informaciones*, 37, in Jönsson, *Alfonso of Jaén*, p. 189, 43–6.

[21]   On Birgitta's view of the godlessness of era, see Ingvar Fogelqvist, *Apostacy and Reform in the Revelations of St Birgitta*, Bibliotheca Theologiae Practicae, 51 (Stockholm, 1993).

Christendom.[22] The plans are 'received' and described visually, as Birgitta sees in spirit the new monastery section by section, just as Ezekiel had seen the Temple (*Extrav.*, 29).[23] In unparalleled detail, Birgitta specified Vadstena's orientation, construction materials, the dimensions of its constituent components, and the number and size of its altars, railings, quires, porches, naves and arches (*Extrav.*, 28, 31). No other founder of a religious Order left such detailed instructions to their followers. On the contrary, such guidelines are generally characterized by their generality and brevity. Why she should have devoted so much attention to the architectural minutia of her convent and its rites at the expense of more basic issues has never been suitably explained.[24]

The Old Covenant Re-established

The first peculiarity is the rubric stipulating that the Birgittine monastery church must face west. Vadstena, the royal castle donated in 1346 by King Magnus and Queen Blanca to Birgitta for her envisioned Order, could not be entered from the west because that side abutted water. Its altars therefore had to face west, so this stipulation may simply reflect practicality. However, in discussing church orientation, Durandus, while acknowledging Roman exceptions and thus implicitly recalling the very important church of St John Lateran, stressed the

---

[22]   The *Regula Salvatoris* was probably received in 1346 by the shores Lake Vättern (while Birgitta travelled to Stockholm). She was divinely instructed to found a monastery on the site of its reception (*Regula*, Prol., 30). For the date of this revelation, see Eklund's introduction.

[23]   The style, 'Vidi a magna domo ... diendi a muro isto vidi ... post hec vidi' (*Extrav.*, 29), is highly evocative of Ezekiel.

[24]   Bertil Berthelson's exhaustive analysis of Brigittine architecture hardly addresses symbolism, concentrating instead on the parallels between the daughter houses and Vadstena [*Studier i Birgittinerordens byggnadsskick: Anläggningsplanen och dess tillämpning* 1, KVHAA 63 (Lund, 1947)]. More recent studies look further at aspects of Birgitta's instructions in relation to the architecture: Stephan Borgehammer, 'St. Birgitta, An Architect of Spiritual Reform', *Birgittiana*, 5 (1988): 23–47 (p. 35). Mereth Lindgren cites Ezekiel as a possible prototype: 'Altars and Apostles: St Brigitta's Provisions of the Altars in the Abbey Church at Vadstena and their Reflection of Birgittine Spirituality', in Alf Härdelin (ed.), *In Quest of the Kingdom, Ten Papers on Medieval Monastic Spirituality*, Bibliotheca Theologiae Practicae, 48 (Stockholm, 1991), pp. 245–82. See also Gunnel Wentzel, 'Birgittiner', *Reallexikon zur deutschen Kunstgeschichte*, Bd 2 (1984), cols 750–67; R.W. Dunning, 'The Building of Syon Abbey', *Transactions of the Ancient Monuments Society*, ns. 25 (1981): 16–26; and Per Sloth Carlsen, 'Lægteranordningerne I den birgittinske klosterkirke – et udviklingsforløb, in Nyberg, *Birgitta, hendes værk*, pp 146–65.

necessity of eastward orientation and cited as biblical precedent the eastward facing entrances of Solomon's Temple and Moses' Tabernacle.[25] In allegorizing the various names given to a church, he included *templum* and *tabernaculum*, although, unlike the other precedents, he regarded the Temple and Tabernacle as particularly appropriate on account of the divine instruction given to Moses and the work of Solomon as precedents.[26] Like its predecessors (the Tabernacle and Solomon's Temple), Ezekiel's Temple also faced west. While it has always been assumed that the *Regula Salvatoris* stipulated westward orientation to reflect practicality, it is entirely possible that Birgitta may have had the biblical models in mind when choosing Vadstena.

Second, a watery location for the monastic church seems an essential component of the Birgittine vision. Again, this may be no more than virtue born of geographical necessity, as Vadstena was bounded by a lake. However, water is a very important aspect of Ezekiel's Temple that distinguishes it from its predecessors, spreading from beneath its altars to the east (Ez., 47: 1–12). The Church interpreted this allegorically as the water that flowed from Christ's side and incorporated these verses into the Paschaltide liturgy in the antiphon *Vidi aquam* sung during the Asperges.[27] In Ezekiel, the river is interpreted allegorically as a fertile, life-giving source, feeding many fish and bearing fruit by the river bank, becoming a source of physical and spiritual blessing for the whole world. The *Revelations* associate the re-Christianization of Christendom with the spread of the Order.[28] Thus Vadstena's restorative spirituality is envisioned as spreading universally, like a river, through the generation of daughter houses, reconciling Christendom with God.

Third, the architecture itself is evocative of the Temple. The latter's three main entrances, each with symbolic resonance (Ez., 46: 9), were located on the eastern, northern and southern sides and were segregated, with the east gate open only for the prince on the sabbath (Ez., 46: 9). Vadstena was to have three main entrances: in the eastern, western and northern sides (between the church and monastery). Moreover, each door is segregated: the eastern door, the Door

---

[25]   V. d'Avino (ed.), Durandus of Mende, *Rationale Divinorvm Officiorvm*, 5.1.57 (2 vols in 1, Naples, 1859), p. 340: 'Templum quoque Salomonis, et tabernaculum Moysi, leguntur ab oriente ostia habuisse' ('Also we read that the Temple of Solomon and the Tabernacle of Moses had their doors on the east'), and therefore faced west. But see Borgehammer, 'St. Birgitta', p. 35; and Tore Nyberg, 'Byggandsföreskrifter för birgittineklostern', *Fornvännen*, 87 (1992): 255–59.

[26]   *Rationale*, 1.1.4–5, pp. 12–14.

[27]   F.H. Dickinson (ed.), *Missale ad Usum Insignis et Praeclare Ecclesia Sarum* (Burntisland, 1861–1883), p. 357.

[28]   Ellis, 'A Note', pp. 166–7.

of Remission for the laity; the western door, the Door of Reconciliation and Propitiation for the brethren; and the northern door, the Door of Grace and Glory for the nuns alone (*Extrav.*, 31).

Fourth, steps, expressing transition from secularity to sanctity, are integral to the Temple design, with seven steps leading to the outer courtyard and eight to the inner court and the Temple proper. Birgitta's rubrics specify stairs with six steps of precise width leading to the dais. Of course, the architecture of many churches incorporated altar steps, so this may be nothing more than ordinary convention. On the other hand, the Birgittine steps do not merely serve a practical function but are one of the high points of Birgittine symbolism, as we shall presently see.

Fifth, the Temple was constructed around three basic chambers: the outer and inner courts, and the Temple proper for the priests alone (Ez., 40: 45–6). Birgitta's description of Vadstena emphasizes its three-fold design and segregation with a space for the laity, brethren and nuns. Moreover, the strictly segregated priestly area in the northernmost part of the Temple is exactly where the brethren's quire is placed, behind the altar.

Sixth, Ezekiel's Temple is built around a series of linear and concentric square measurements, which create a square whole. The three alcoves on the northern and southern side of the porch are all identically sized squares (Ez., 40: 7). The outer court is 100 cubits square (Ez., 40: 19), as is the inner court (40: 47), and the Temple area itself (41: 13–14). The outer court contains 30 rooms, all square (40: 17). One of the striking aspects of Birgitta's architectural rubrics is the number of square measurements it contains. For example, the nave was to be triple-vaulted with five cross-vaults, producing 15 perfect squares, each 20 by 20 ells. The brothers' quire, like the inner Temple itself, was also square (*Extrav.*, 28).

Practical considerations produced manifold architectural variation in monastic houses.[29] Rievaulx, for example, had to be sited north–south because of the narrow river valley hemming it in and similar exceptions to eastward orientation were generally a matter of necessity, not design. Form, however, did follow liturgical function, in some cases producing complex designs, such as at Deerhurst, where the extensive chambers, galleries and annexes were probably used for liturgical chant, drama and the display of relics. Doorways, west end porches and processional arches were born of an emphasis on processions in some Orders. Sectarian priorities also affected design, the rounded churches favoured by the Knights Templar in imitation of the Holy Sepulchre in Jerusalem being a prime example. The Mendicant emphasis on preaching tended to eliminate

---

[29]   For an overview of monastic architecture, see G.H. Cook, *English Monasteries in the Middle Ages* (London, 1961).

interior divisions and created more open spaces.[30] The austerity of the Cistercian spirit, exemplified in St Bernard's rejection of Cluniac ornamentation,[31] was reflected in a marked early rejection of architectural superfluity, such as towers, stained glass, and even transepts and apsidal east ends.[32] Thus, inasmuch as Birgitta's frame of mind was characterized by a strong biblical identity and deep identification with Moses and the prophets, her application of elements from these sources to her architectural designs is not unprecedented, although the source seems unique.[33]

Ezekiel's Temple was not uniquely different from the Tabernacle, Solomon's Temple or its successors (Zerubabel's and Herod's Temples), but was a continuation of Israel's Temple tradition. Just as the architecture of Vadstena mirrors the Temple proportions, its ceremonies re-enact the Temple rites. The order of consecration of nuns prescribed in the *Regula Salvatoris* contains numerous idiosyncrasies and elements that have never been adequately explained, and which find echoes in the ceremony of the consecration of Israel's priests. The Birgittine liturgy began not with the usual procession into the nave (as in other consecration rites) but, uniquely, at the church door itself, where the candidate was met by the bishop, who solemnly examined her before the congregation.[34] The Old Testament rite for priestly consecration began not in the Tabernacle, but at the Tabernacle gate, where Aaron was met by Moses, who ceremonially cleansed him at the opening of the consecration rite in the presence of the entire congregation (Ex., 29: 4; Lev., 8: 4–6). Before she entered the church, the nun was therefore ceremonially prepared, like Aaron at the monastery gate, for her sacred ministry.

The *Regula* gives very precise instructions regarding the nun's vesting. On removing her secular clothes, she was vested with shoes, a tunic, cowl, mantle,

---

[30]   J. Burton, *Monastic and Religious Orders in Britain 1000–1300* (Cambridge, 1994), pp. 136–40.

[31]   'Apologia', in *Opera*, 2.61–108 (pp. 104–107) and for the context, 3.63–79, and C.H. Talbot, 'The Cistercian Attitude Towards Art: the Literary Evidence', in C. Norton and D. Park (eds), *Cistercian Art and Architecture in the British Isles* (Cambridge, 1986), pp. 56–64.

[32]   C. Holdsworth, 'The Chronology and Character of Early Cistercian Legislation on Art and Architecture', in *Cistercian Art and Architecture*, pp. 40–56, and for a very useful checklist, C. Norton, 'Table of Cistercian Legislation on Art and Architecture', in *Cistercian Art and Architecture*, pp. 315–93. For the developments in the later Middle Ages, N. Coldstream, 'Cistercian Architecture from Beaulieu to the Dissolution', in *Cistercian Art and Architecture*, pp. 139–59.

[33]   Ingvar Fogelqvist, 'The New Vineyard: St. Birgitta of Sweden's *Regula Salvatoris* and the Monastic Tradition', in Härdelin (ed.), *In Quest of the Kingdom*, pp. 203–44.

[34]   The rite of profession is described in *Regula*, 10–11.

mantle clasp, wimple, veil and the *corona*, a distinctive garment signed with five round red dots extending over the forehead (*Regula*, 4, 11). The overall appearance created by the unique head garment, which bore no relation to the other monastic headdress, was one of significant distinction. The occasional suggestion that Birgitta's eccentricity lies behind these peculiarities can be discounted immediately not only on account of the general significance of symbolism to Birgitta and her scrupulous attention to detail in the *Regula*, but also because the greatest symbolism was attached to every liturgical vestment in the middle ages. Durandus devoted nearly an entire book of his lengthy *Rationale* to commentary on the symbolism of vestments, from the humble amice to the princely mitre.[35] Several perfectly reasonable influences have been suggested for these vestments, including Birgitta's own daily habit in Rome[36] and iconographic precedent.[37] All monastic dress derived ultimately from St Benedict's *Rule*, the tunic, scapular and hood evolving into the vestments of the new Orders of the eleventh and twelfth centuries.[38] The Cistercians (Birgitta had resided at the monastery in Alvastra) were particularly close to the Benedictines in dress except for colour (white). While liturgical vestments underwent considerable evolution in the middle ages and the monk's habit differed markedly from Order to Order, the nun's habit tended to alter less. Most wore a variation of the Benedictine garb consisting of the tunic, gown, wimple and veil. Differences between the Benedictine, Cluniac and Cistercian nun's habits were marked more by colour than style.[39] Not only is Birgitta's specificity unusual among monastic *regulae*,

---

[35]   *Rationale*, 3, pp. 177–238.

[36]   R. Ellis, *Viderunt Eam Filie Syon: the Spirituality of The English House of a Medieval Contemplative Order from Its Beginnings to the Present Day*, Analecta Cartusiana, 68 (Salzburg, 1984), pp. 14–16.

[37]   Sister M. Patricia [Torstensson] O.Ss.S. Vadstena ['The Foundation of the Abbey in Vadstena', in Hogg, *Studies in St. Birgitta*, pp. 5–19 (pp. 8–9)] says Birgitta may have seen a similar habit in the Gisela manuscript at the Cistercian nunnery in Rulle (near Osnabrück). Less obviously, M.B. Tait ('The Brigittine Monastery of Syon [Middlesex] with Special Reference to Its Monastic Usages', unpubl. DPhil. thesis (University of Oxford, 1975), pp. 215–16) suggests Crusader heraldry as a possible source and observes that the Trinitarians, a branch of the Augustinian Order, had a blue and red cross on their scapular and cap.

[38]   Benedict, *The Rule of St Benedict*, 55, ed. and trans. J. McCann (London, 1952), pp. 124–6. The *Rule of St Augustine* (5) does not even specify items of clothing but concentrates on their appropriate use [L. Verheijn (ed.), *La Règle de Saint Augustin*, Études Augustiniennes (2 vols, Paris, 1967)], 1.418–19.

[39]   Janet Mayo, *A History of Ecclesiastical Dress* (London, 1984), pp. 32–8. For a useful checklist of variations in monastic Orders, see R.A.S. MacAlister, *Ecclesiastical Vestments: their Development and History*, The Camden Library (London, 1896), pp. 234–53.

but its incorporation into the consecration rite is unique (*Regula*, 10–11).[40] All nuns in every Order were vested during the profession ceremony, although typically with the habit, ring, and above all, the veil. The action associated with the blessing and imposition of the veil was the high point of the ceremony and regarded as quasi-sacramental in the standard rites. In the Birgittine rite, the veil was not distinguished as the pre-eminent vestment, but is one of six garments imposed by the bishop of equal significance. Only the corona was singled out for special treatment, being imposed apart from the other garments. The heart and climax of the traditional ceremony of profession, the solemn prayer of consecration, is entirely absent in the Birgittine rite.[41]

The idea of incorporating the entire monastic habit, including shoes (the candidate approached the bishop barefoot), into the vesting at the consecration seems peculiar to Birgitta.[42] Moreover, the absence of prayers of consecration throws greater emphasis upon the vesting ceremony in its totality. Moses had received precise instructions regarding the vesting of Aaron with the tunic, robe, ephod, girdle, breastplate, mitre and the distinctive golden plate to be worn upon his forehead, inscribed with the seal 'Sanctum Domino' (Ex., 28). Moreover, after Aaron was ceremonially cleansed at the Temple gate, his vesting with all the holy garments took place within the divine rite of priestly consecration (Ex., 29: 1–9; Lev., 8: 1–13). The dangers of making associations with Levitical priestly dress were realized by nineteenth-century liturgical historians who, in their zealous search for a jettisoned Catholicism created by the Tractarian movement, uncritically observed intuitive parallels between medieval liturgical vestments and Mosaic ones and assumed as corollary what appeared to them self-evident.[43] This suggestion cannot therefore be proven, as the origins of the Birgittine nuns' habits are likely to be enmeshed in a complex web of visual and verbal stimuli.[44] However, in this context, the growing pre-occupation with the Old Testament and the increased tendency from the twelfth century onwards to

---

[40]   Tait ('Brigittine Monastery', pp. 198–208) has discussed the peculiarities associated with the Birgittine rite of consecration.

[41]   Tait, 'Brigittine Monastery', p. 207; cf. the Additions to the Rule of St Saviour, prepared at Syon Abbey, from London, British Library, MS Arundel 146, in G.J. Aungier, *The History and Antiquities of Syon Monastery* (London, 1840), Appendix, p. 316.

[42]   The Syon Additions allowed the Abbess *in tyme of grete colde* to permit the candidate to arrive at the church door in shoes (Aungier, *History and Antiquities*, p. 303).

[43]   MacAlister, *Ecclesiastical Vestments*, pp. 1–19; cf. Mayo, *Ecclesiastical Dress*, pp. 11–22; J.G. Davis (ed.), *A Dictionary of Liturgy & Worship* (London, 1972), pp. 365–83 (p. 366).

[44]   Tait's suggestion regarding the nuptial elements of the Rite, including the parallel between the examination by the Church door and the first part of the marriage ceremony (*Regula*, 11), are interesting ('Brigittine Monastery', pp. 208–10).

search for biblical origins cannot be ignored. The long tradition of commentary in support of Levitical precedents for the liturgy, beginning in the fifth century with Rabanus Maurus, culminated in the work of Ivo of Chartres and its appropriation by Hugh of St Victor.[45] Commentators found precedents in the minutiae of Hebrew ritual not only for Christian ceremonies and observances but also for liturgical vestments. This trend Judaized the liturgy by introducing various Old Testament rites, particularly from the sacerdotal code, through which altars and churches were dedicated with formulas and gestures heavily reminiscent of the Levitical Law. The entry of the celebrant and officiants into the church echoed the return of the king to Jerusalem.[46] The Mass was compared in detail with the sacrifices of the Old Testament.[47] No lesser authority than Durandus advocated Aaronic dress as direct precedent for clerical and episcopal dress and illustrated his exposition of contemporary clerical dress by copious reference to Aaron, Moses and Levite priestly dress.[48] Moreover, he included an entire chapter on the exposition of the Levitical priestly dress.[49] In light of Birgitta's strong Moses-identity and the other Temple parallels with Vadstena, it seems probable that Aaronic precedents at least indirectly inspired the Birgittine habit. In particular, the corona and Aaron's mitre, both bearing a sacred inscription and worn upon the forehead, seem to warrant relation. If so, the inspiration of Levitical dress for monastic vestments is unprecedented, for liturgical vestments evolved from the civilian dress of the late Roman empire, and were not derivative from the Jewish priesthood.

Once professed, the new nun faced another peculiarity unique to the Birgittine: she was excluded from all offices and activities for seven days but resided within the monastery (*Regula*, 11).[50] Various attempts have been made to explain this puzzling rubric, including an appeal to Birgitta's maternal instincts, which would not have overlooked the need for a gentle transition from the world to the cloister. It is, however, the Exodus context which provides a satisfactory

---

[45]   Rabanus Maurus, *De Clericorum Institutione*, 1.14–16, PL 108: 297–420 (306). Ivo of Chartres, *De significationibus indumentorum sacerdotalium*, PL 172: 519–224; Hugh of St Victor, *De sacramantis Christianae fidei*, 2.4, PL 176: 434–8 (M.D. Chenu, *Nature, Man and Society in the Twelfth Century*, trans. J. Taylor and L.K. Little (Chicago, IL, 1968), pp. 150–54).

[46]   Honorius of Autun, *Gemma animae, sive de divinis officiis et antiquo ritu missarum*, 1.72–73, PL 172: 566–7. Cf. Amalarius of Metz, *De ecclesiasticis officiis*, 3.5, PL 101: 1107–13.

[47]   Innocent III, *De sacro altaris mysterio*, PL 217: 773–916.

[48]   *Rationale*, 3.1.2; cf. 3.1.9, 3.1.13, 3.7.4, 3.8.2, 3.8.10, 3.13.2, 3.13.8, 3.15.2, pp. 178, 181, 182–3, 196, 197, 201, 209, 211–212, 215.

[49]   *Rationale*, 3.19, pp. 230–39.

[50]   At Syon, the nun was immediately lead to the chapter and thereupon stood at the bottom of the choir (Aungier, *History and Antiquities*, p. 316).

solution. Once the ceremonies of consecration were complete, Aaron and his priestly sons remained sequestered within the Tabernacle confines for seven days while their consecration continued to be effected (Ex., 29: 35; Lev., 8: 33; Ez., 44: 26). The day of profession was one of the most important in the life of any nun or monk and the impression made upon the novice and community was lasting, contributing to the identity of the Order. The impact, therefore, of the Mosaic and Levitical parallels within the Birgittine consecration rite was likely to have confirmed and contributed to the Order's Exodus identity.

As well as Vadstena's architecture and rites, its spirituality is also based on the Temple vision. Of the virtues of the Temple cult, allegorized through its life-giving river, holiness to God and purity of its priesthood, whose earlier corruption had caused the Temple's destruction, are emphasized by Ezekiel above all others (Ez., 44: 21–28). The moral perfection associated with Yahweh was reflected in the express and strict prohibition in Ezekiel's vision of the Levitical priesthood from maintaining any private possessions. This emphasis is precisely mirrored in Birgitta's revelations dealing with the Order and the *Regula*, where, as the antithesis of widespread contemporary clerical corruption, purity of heart and mind is an undercurrent, exemplified in the strict prohibition of private possessions (*Regula*, 18).[51] Of course, the idea of personal property is antithetical to the essence of communal life and is enshrined in monastic *regulae*,[52] but abuses were notorious and it was generally the stricter Orders that enforced this rule with success.[53] Even so, the unusually harsh Birgittine punishment differs considerably from the others with satisfaction consisting of penance and dire public humiliation. Even death could not mitigate the seriousness of the crime or its denunciation; on the contrary, it escalated it (*Regula*, 18). Thus, in its severity the Birgittine prohibition against private possessions is unique, drawing attention to itself and the biblical precedent.

In the Old Testament, God's presence among his people centred on the Temple. Divinity and humanity converged in the 'tent of meeting' where the

---

[51] The Syon Additions detail disciplines for *lyght defawtes, greuous defautes, more greuous defautes*, and *most greuous defautes* (Aungier, *History and Antiquities*, pp. 252–63). Private possessions are treated in the last.

[52] *Rule of St Benedict*, 55, pp. 124–6; *Règle de Saint Augustin*, 1.3–5, pp. 417–19. While a Carthusian monk had many possessions in his cell, this was necessarily for the maintenance of solitude; proprietorship was forbidden [A Carthusian Monk (ed.), Guido I, *Consuetudines Cartusiae*, 28, 57, SC, 313 (Paris, 1984), pp. 222–4].

[53] M.D. Knowles, *The Religious Orders in England* (3 vols, Cambridge, 1948–1959), 2.90–114, 167–74, 240–47; Eileen Power, *Medieval English Nunneries c. 1275–1535*, Cambridge Studies in Medieval Life and Thought (Cambridge, 1922), pp. 211–12, 303–309, 315–40.

shekina glory rested on the Temple Mount and God tented among his people. Ezekiel had seen the terrible sight of the departure of the glory of the Lord prior to the destruction of the Temple (Ez., 10: 18). In the Temple vision, the glory of the Lord, like the roar of rushing waters, re-entered it and filled the land with its radiance (Ez., 43: 3–5; 44: 4). The Temple once again became God's footstool (43: 7). Birgitta had seen what seemed to her the departure of godliness and religious fervour from Sweden, Naples and Cyprus, and above all, Rome. By abandoning divine service for the pleasures of the flesh, God's people had effectively exiled his presence from them (VI.88). Her response to the burden of widespread godlessness, spiritual torpor and papal exile was to found an Order that would reverse these developments. The nuns were to lead the people of God out of their bondage like Miriam, leading the children of Israel thorough the Red Sea, singing to the glory of God (*Extrav.*, 4). The Virgin informed Birgitta that the Temple in Jerusalem would never be rebuilt. Instead, the fulfilment of the Temple seen in the spirit by Ezekiel would be Vadstena (*Extrav.*, 39). In the same revelation, the Order is described as a fire raging through the house. Surely, this fire is the glory of the Lord, returning once again to Ezekiel's Temple, to be built not in Jerusalem but in the unlikely setting of the Kingdom of Sweden, and radiating from thence throughout the world (*Regula*, 26). Not only is Vadstena declared to be Ezekiel's Temple, but is directly compared with the Tabernacle (*Extrav.*, 18). The parallel is made even clearer in a revelation to Birgitta, stating that King Magnus was not worthy to build the monastery at Vadstena because of his sins: 'He shall not build a house unto me like Solomon' (*Extrav.*, 27).[54] It is therefore most interesting that a letter signed by the abbess, confessor general, *ac vterque conuentus monasterij Watzstenensis*, to Henry V in 1415 continues this theme, entreating the King to construct the then future Syon as Solomon consumated the Temple.[55] Likewise, the divine comparison of the nuns to

---

[54]   'non edificabit michi domum vt Salomon'.

[55]   C. Silfverstolpe (ed.), *Svenskt Diplomatarium från och med år 1401* (3 vols, Stockholm, 1875–1902), 2082 (3.389). The Tabernacle and the Temple had attracted interpretative commentary from apostolic times. Bede allegorized the Tabernacle and the Temple, respectively, as the Church militant and Church triumphant [D. Hurst (ed.), *De Templo* and *De Tabernaculo*, Opera, CCSL, 119A (Turnhout, 1969)]. Much of Bede's commentary on the Tabernacle was incorporated into the *Glossa Ordinaria* and was therefore adopted by later writers [*Glossa Ordinaria*, especially on Ex., 24: 12–30: 21 (PL 113: 265–84)]. The commentaries on the Tabernacle by Peter of Poitiers and Peter of Celle were largely dependant on Bede and also interpreted the Tabernacle as a sign of Christ and the Church [Peter of Celle, *De tabernaculo I* and *De tabernaculo II*, ed, G. de Martel, CCCM 54 (Turnhout, 1983), pp. 171–219, 220–43]. P.S. Moore and J.A. Corbett (eds), Peter of Poitiers, *Allegoriae super tabernaculum Moysi*, Publications in Mediaeval Studies, 3 (Notre Dame. IN, 1938). Richard of St Victor used the Ark to illustrate his six stages of

Miriam leading the children of Israel through the Red Sea, singing to the glory of God (*Extrav.*, 4) finds an echo in the *Myroure of our Ladye*, where the nuns' singing of the offices is likened to the song of Miriam, and the priests' singing to the song of Moses.[56]

The New Apostolic Community

Leading Christendom out of exile from sin into the promise land of reform, Birgitta modelled her Order closely on the apostolic community of the first century, limiting its number to seventy-two in direct imitation:

> There shall be sixty sisters and not more. They shall have priests who shall say Mass daily ... These priests shall be thirteen in number after the thirteen apostles, of which the thirteenth, Saint Paul, did not work least. Then there shall be four deacons, who may be priests if they so desire. They shall signify the four great doctors of the Church: Ambrose, Augustine, Gregory, and Jerome. Next there shall be eight laymen who shall serve the priests. This makes sixty sisters, thirteen priests, four deacons and eight servants, which is the same number as the thirteen apostles and seventy-two disciples. (*Regula*, 12.)[57]

---

contemplation and the Tabernacle and its components to clarify and expand these ideas (Richard of St Victor, *Benjamin Major*, PL 196: 63–192; *Nonnullae Allegoriae Tabernaculi Foederis*, PL 196: 191–202). For Gregory, the obscurity of the literal text of Ezekiel's Temple invited allegorization, primarily on the active and contemplative life [Gregory, *Homiliae in Ezechielem Prophetam*, ed. and trans. C. Morel, SC 327, 360 (Paris, 1986, 1990); ed. and trans. M. Borret, SC 352 (Paris, 1990)]. Jerome concentrated on the literal sense of the text drawing out its theological implications. Andrew of St Victor, also following the literal sense, focused his *expositio* on the language of the text and its visual imagery [F. Glorie (ed.), Jerome, *In Ezechielem*, CCSL 75 (Turnhout, 1964); M.A. Signer (ed.), Andrew of St Victor, *In Ezechielem*, CCCM 6 (Turnhout, 1991)]. For a summary, see A.G. Holder, 'The Mosaic Tabernacle in Early Christian Exegesis', *Studia Patristica*, 25 (1993): 101–106.

[56]   J.H. Blunt (ed.), *The Myroure of our Ladye*, EETS ES, 19 (1873), pp. 35–6. The relatively large number of references to Moses and the Exodus by way of reference or explication of liturgical observance suggests that the compiler of the Syon Breviary was aware of the significance of the parallel not only in the Birgittine canon but in Birgitta's perception of the Order (pp. 53, 88, 89, 111, 112, 153, 204–5, 206–7, 211, 250, 296). See Ann M. Hutchinson, '*The Myroure or our Ladye*: a Medieval Guide for Contemplatives', in Hogg, *Studies in St. Birgitta*, 2.215–27.

[57]   'Sorores erunt sexaginta et non plures. Que clericos habebunt, qui cottidie de tempore missam et officium ... Ipsi quidem sacerdotes debent esse tredecim iuxta numerum tredecim apostolorum, quorum Paulus, tercius decimus, non minimum laborem sustinuit; deinde quatuor dyaconi, qui eciam sacerdotes possunt esse, si volunt, et ipsi figuram habent

Just as by tradition the Virgin Mary was given the place of honour in the apostolic community, the abbess was placed at the head of the Birgittine community (*Regula*, 1).[58] Everything about the community is representative of the apostolic community (Lk, 10: 1), including the priests' and the deacons' vestments, which, in an echo of the nuns' vestments, represent the New Covenant through abstract symbols of the Passion, the Eucharist, the Church Fathers and Pentecost (*Regula*, 12, 13). Birgitta dramatically extended the literalism of her symbolic structures by ordaining for thirteen altars in representation of the twelve apostles and St Paul, two on each of the six steps of the high altar dais, the thirteenth being the high altar itself (*Extrav.*, 28, 34). Each altar was dedicated to a disciple and inscribed with a brief summary of the disciple's qualities.[59] The provision for multiple altars in a monastic church for the priest-monks to say masses is common enough in Cistercian, Benedictine and Cluniac houses. It is also true that Carthusian charterhouses restricted their numbers to thirteen or fourteen monks, although this does not seem expressly symbolic.[60] However, the Birgittine correlation between brethren and altars seems altogether alien to the Carthusians. The closest example is the Chapel of the Nine Altars at Fountains Abbey, emulated at the Cathedral Priory in Durham, although again this was lacking in apostolic symbolism and was hence distant from the Birgittine example.[61] One would very much like to know how the thirteen altars were used. For example, on the feast day of an apostle, was the Mass offered on the altar of its dedication with special ceremony? Were all thirteen ever used simultaneously, perhaps on solemnities? Did, as seems likely, the correspondence between the thirteen priests and altars reinforce the apostolic symbolism inherent in the community's number and contribute to its apostolic climate? This becomes even more the case if, as seems not unlikely, each priest had his own altar at which he habitually served in the same way as he had his own cell. Were this so, the

---

quatuor precipuorum doctorum, Ambrosii, Augustini, Gregorii et Ieronimi; deinde octo laici, qui laboriubus suis clericis necessaria ministrabunt. Computatis igitur sexaginta sororibus, tredecim sacerdotibus, quatuor dyaconis et octo eorum seruitoribus tantus omnium personarum erit numerus, quantus erat tredecim apostolorum et septuaginta duorum discipulorum.'

[58]   A entire chapter of the *Sermo Angelicus* (19) is devoted to Mary's ministry to the local community after the Ascension.

[59]   For the significance of position of each apostle's altar relative to the thirteen, see T.S. Nyberg, 'The Thirteen Apostles in the Spiritual World of St. Birgitta', in Hogg, *Studies in St. Birgitta*, 1.192–208; and Lindgren, 'Altars and Apostles'.

[60]   *Consuetudines Cartusiae*, 78.1, SC 313, p. 284.

[61]   R. Gilyard–Beer and G. Coppack, 'Excavations at Fountains Abbey, North Yorkshire, 1979–80: the Early Development of the Monastery', *Archaeologia*, 108 (1986): 147–88 (p. 151).

identity of the priest might naturally have been subsumed to some measure into the identity of the relevant disciple, whose virtues were inscribed on his altar of dedication, with each priest, perhaps, cultivating the qualities of his altar's patron disciple and reflecting these to the community. Or was use of the altars governed by a rota, so that each priest might serve on all the altars over a period? Whatever the details, the correlation between the thirteen priests and altars undoubtedly added to the community's literal apostolic identity and reinforced the general imitative climate at Vadstena.

The Virgin Mary, the apogee of the community's structure, is represented by the abbess, who in contrast to the customary choice of a widow and in remarkably concrete imitation, was by preference to be a virgin (*Extrav.*, 21).[62] Her humility and simplicity literally influence the building, whose roof was to be of moderate height so that nothing there appeared 'nisi quod humilitatem redoleat' (*Extrav.*, 30), and the preaching heard within, which was to be characterized by simplicity and effectiveness (*Extrav.*, 23). As she divided her earthly time into three parts, the nuns were to alternate periods of prayer and manual labour with recitation (*Extrav.*, 30). The entire community, even the confessor general, was subordinate to the abbess in every way, by their number and place in the choir below the women (*Regula*, 14). Reciprocally, her pre-eminence was to be expressed primarily through her humility (*Extrav.*, 21). She not only represented the Virgin Mary, but was also the head of a community that Birgitta envisioned as a literal reconstitution of the apostolic, post-Ascension community, where the Virgin Mary was pre-eminent: 'Of reverence for the most blessed Virgin, my mother, to whom this Order is dedicated, she is to be head and ruler, for the Holy Virgin, whom she represents here on earth, was after my ascension head and queen of my apostles and disciples' (*Regula*, 14; cf. *SA* 19).[63] In this astonishingly literal manner, the abbess, the nuns, the priests and the deacons were *specula* of the divine *imago*, reflecting to one another the same ideal of Mosaic and apostolic perfection.[64] Like the first apostolic community, Vadstena's mission was primarily to be a witness among the community. This was achieved first and foremost through the prayers of the nuns. It was also achieved

---

[62]   The apostolic profile of the community is discussed in Ellis, *Viderunt Eam Filie Syon*, pp. 26ff.

[63]   'Que ob reuerenciam beatissime Virginis, Matris mee, cui hic ordo dedicatus est, caput esse debet, quia ipsa Virgo, cuius abbatissa gerit vicem in terris, acendente me in celos caput et regina extitit apostolorum et discipulorum meorum.'

[64]   The idea is not entirely unique to St Birgitta, though it is nowhere expressed so forcefully or literally. See T.J. van Bavel, 'The Evangelical Inspiration of the RSA', *Downside Review*, 93 (1975): pp. 83–99: 'The ideal that the monk Augustine has here before his eyes is the first Christian community of Jerusalem' (p. 87).

through preaching – *continuacio verba dei*. Priests were to expound the Gospel in the vernacular before all the nuns every Sunday at Mass and before the laity on all feast days in straightforward biblical sermons in the vernacular (*Regula*, 15; cf. *Extrav.*, 10, 19, 23).

Birgitta's highly self-conscious placement of the Order within the framework of the Old and New Testament communities is well evinced in her decision regarding the use of an organ at Vadstena.

> The children of Israel ... had many things with which they were stirred to devotion. They had trumpets, harps, and other stringed instruments with which they were incited to the praise of God ... Therefore now that the Truth, prefigured in types, has come ... it is fitting I should be served in truth and with the whole heart. (*Extrav.*, 10; cf. *Extrav.*, 4)[65]

We can almost see her decision-making process. She considers the probity of the organ against the two influential touchstones for Vadstena, the Israelite community and the New Covenant. Where no synthesis is possible, it is the more relevant model of the apostolic community, so strikingly represented by the Order's structure, that guides her choice. This combination of literal embodiments of the Old and New Testament communities seems unique, although the fusion of the two ideals, of course, is not. Bede interprets the twelve names born on Aaron's shoulders as representing the twelve apostles and the seventy bells around the hem of his robe as pre-figuring the number of the disciples.[66] Thus, as the apostolic community of Luke 10: 1 was pre-figured in Aaron's dress, the Old Covenant and the Law, which Christ came not to abolish but to fulfil (Matt., 5: 17), are represented and restored in Vadstena. Of course, it is unnecessary to suggest Bede as a direct precedent, since the Old Testament was continually quarried by biblical commentators for parallels with the New Testament, although the incorporation of this exegesis into the *Glossa Ordinaria* would have given it the widest dissemination possible.[67]

---

[65] 'Filii Israhel ... multa habebant, quibus ad deuocionem excitabantur. Habebant quippe tubas, organa et citharas, quibus accendebantur ad laudem Dei ... Ideo quia nunc venit veritas ipsa, presignata in figuris ... dignum est, vt in veritate et toto corde michi seruiatur.'

[66] *De Tabernaculo*, 3.6, CCSL, 119A, pp. 111–12.

[67] *Glossa Ordinaria*, PL 113: 281.

Birgitta's Marian Self-identity

Birgitta's and Vadstena's self-identities were shaped by the perceived correlations with the prophets and the Virgin Mary. It is difficult to underestimate Birgitta's devotion to the Virgin Mary and her role in Birgitta's piety. Birgitta had read of the details of her life in the *Legendariet* and these now worked their way into the *Revelations*. She speaks in over 150 revelations and the scenes of her life are revisited in detail in Birgitta's revelations.[68] Each shared in the other's experience of childbirth. The Virgin appeared to Birgitta when she was in peril during childbirth, entered her and eased her delivery. Birgitta's children were therefore to be the Virgin's (*A&P*, p. 79). In Jerusalem, Birgitta had been granted a vision of the Nativity, the details of which were to have a profound influence on its contemporary iconographic representation (VII.21–23).[69] Mary, Joachim's daughter, had promised to act as mother to the children of Birgitta, Birger's daughter, when she found it difficult to tear herself from them and obey the command to go on pilgrimage to Rome (*Extrav.*, 63). Each also shared in the other's experience of their sons' death. Birgitta had been granted an intimate vision of the Crucifixion in Jerusalem (VII.15). The Virgin had acted as a metaphorical midwife, delivering Birgitta's son, Charles, in his passage *in illo arto spacio* from life to death, protecting him from demons (VII.13). Moreover, Birgitta had been called to be a spouse of Christ (*A&P*, pp. 80–81).[70]

The image of birthing is central to Birgitta's Marian identity, encapsulated and dramatized in Birgitta's experience one Christmas Eve when she resided at the Cistercian Monastery in Alvastra. Her heart leapt for joy 'ac si infans ibi jaceret voluens et reuoluens se'. Prior Peter and Master Peter witnessed the

---

[68] Klockars, *Birgitta och böckerna*, p. 170, who notes strong similarities between Birgitta's version of Marian events and those in the *Fornsvenska legendariet*, an old Swedish legendary, compiled by a Dominican who was largely influenced by the *Legenda Aurea*, and dating from the mid–fourteenth century with earlier parts. As Kristina Bosdotter testified, Birgitta retired after breakfast to the servants' hall to read from 'librum in lingua materna conscriptum de vita sanctorum et eorum passionibus' (*A&P*, p. 66): ('a book written in [her] mother tongue of the lives and passions of the saints'). See further Kari Elisabeth Børresen, 'Religious Feminism in the Middle Ages: Birgitta of Sweden', in Louise D'Arcens and Juanita Feros Ruys (eds), *Maistresse of my Wit: Medieval Women, Modern Scholars* (Turnhout, 2004), pp. 295–312.

[69] Henrik Cornell, *The Iconography of the Nativity of Christ*, Uppsala Universitets Årsskrift 1.3 (Uppsala, 1924), esp. pp. 1–45.

[70] On the congruence between Mary and Birgitta as teachers, see Katherine Zieman, 'Voices in Dialogue: Reading Women in the Middle Ages', in Linda Olson and Kathryn Kerby-Fulton (eds), *Voices in Dialogue: Reading Women in the Middle Ages* (Notre Dame, IN, 2005), esp. pp. 319–27.

phenomenon and felt this movement 'super vestes ipsus domine Brigide, quas habebat supra cor' (*A&P*, p. 500). The Virgin explained this motion:

> Daughter ... just as you do not know how the exultation and movement of your heart came to you so suddenly, so the coming of my son into me was wondrous and swift. For when I consented to the angel announcing to me the conception of the Son of God, at once I sensed in me something marvellous and vigorous ... Therefore, daughter, do not fear this illusion, but rejoice because this movement which you feel is a sign of the coming of my son into your heart. Assuredly, this movement of your heart will remain with you and will grow according to the capacity of your heart. (VI.88)[71]

The comparison between Birgitta's heartfelt joy and the Virgin's sensation of joy in her womb on consenting to Gabriel's message, together with the assurance that Birgitta's *mirabilis motu* will grow, clearly suggests that Birgitta will give birth – but to what? Birthing imagery is not alien to the *Revelations*. To a mother of eight, its metaphorical propriety is self-evident. The Virgin Mary employs it to describe her care of Charles, Birgitta's son, in the hour of his death and Christ compares his redemptive work to the physical act of giving birth (VI.19). The symbolic potency and universalism of the image of birthing Christ in the soul is evident in Christian spirituality from Origen to Bonaventure.[72] The *Speculum Virginum*, from which Prior Peter read to Birgitta in a vernacular translation, encouraged the nun Theodora to give birth to Christ spiritually in imitation of Mary.[73] This form of imitation and mental role-playing, with its intense focus on the meditation of the humanity of Christ, was fundamental to the Bernardine–Franciscan tradition of devotional piety. Contemplation was intended to

---

[71] 'Filia ... Nam sicut tu ignoras, quomodo tam subito tibi cordis exultacio et motus aduenit, sic aduentus filii mei in me mirabilis fuit et festinus. Nam quando ego consensi angelo nuncianti michi concepcionem filii Dei, statim sensi in me mirabile quoddam et viuidum ... Ideo, filia, non timeas illusionem sed gratulare, quia motus iste, quem tu sentis, signum aduentus filii mei est in cor tuum ... Motus vero iste cordis tui perseuerabit tecum et augebitur iuxta capacitatem cordis tui.'

[72] See Claire Sahlin, '"A Marvellous and Great Exultation of the Heart": Mystical Pregnancy and Marian Devotion in Birgitta of Sweden's *Revelations*', in Hogg, *Studies in St. Birgitta*, 1.108–28 (p. 110). See also chapter 3 in Sahlin's *Birgitta of Sweden*, pp. 78–108. St Francis had used the metaphor to describe the exemplary life: 'Matres, quando portamus eum in corde et corpore nostro per amorem, et sinceram conscientiam, et partur imus eum per sanctam operationem', *Epistola ad Fideles II*, in *Bibliotheca Patristica Medii Ævi* 4.1 (Paris, 1880), pp. 216–23 (p. 221). ('We are mothers to him when we bear him in our hearts and souls by love with a pure and sincere conscience, and give birth to him by doing holy works.')

[73] Sahlin, 'Mystical Pregnancy', p. 113.

stimulate the affections, leading to identification with the paradigm, which in turn generated imitation of virtues.[74] The widespread urge in the late middle ages to participate imaginatively with the Gospel events went a step further, leading in some cases to a blurring of the distinction between identification and literal forms of imitation. From here, it was but a small step from the deeply internalized role-playing of devout contemplation to the conscious self-representation in the form of the contemplated paradigm.

This mimetic way of seeing beyond the signifiers into the world of signification itself has its parallel in the figural view of history. For Birgitta, as for her contemporaries, the Bible did not contain two distinct histories of Israel and the early Church but a single universal history. The present and even the future were but different stages of the story of salvation, which began at Creation and would end in Judgement. In this radically linear course of universal governance, history repeated itself, imposing ancient precedents on the present. Events did stand alone on their historical completeness, but were best understood in relation to the divine purpose in which circumstances, while retaining their historical integrity, figurally re-enacted archetypes. These historical recurrences were regarded as incarnations of divine meaning revealed by God's providence and gesturing beyond themselves, in one direction towards the archetype and the historical fulfilment, in the other towards their ultimate apocalyptic consummation. In a sense, an event became more 'real' by incorporation into a corresponding archetype of salvation history, where it acquired transcendent universal significance.[75] While Birgitta's spiritual pregnancy appears to be a sign of contemplative union, a formula reiterated by Christ (II.18), it is limiting to confine her mystical pregnancy to the level of signification. For *imitatio* is not merely a matter of exciting the affections through signification, but of union with the sign through prolonged contemplation, of becoming. Birgitta therefore

---

[74]   See Ewart Cousins, 'Francis of Assisi and Christian Mysticism', in S.T. Katz (ed.), *Mysticism and Religious Traditions* (Oxford, 1983), pp. 163–90; Cousins, 'The Humanity and the Passion of Christ', in J. Raitt (ed.), *Christian Spirituality 2: High Middle Ages and the Middle Ages* (New York, 1987), pp. 375–91.

[75]   On the figural view of history, see Erich Auerbach, *Mimesis: the Representation of Reality in Western Literature*, trans. W.R. Trask (Princeton, NJ, 1953), esp. 70–76, pp. 151–8; Beryl Smalley, *Historians in the Middle Ages* (London, 1974); Thomas J. Heffernan, *Sacred Biography: Saints and Their Biographers in the Middle Ages* (Oxford, 1988), pp. 72–99; and C.W. Jones, *Saints' Lives and Chronicles in Early England* (Ithaca, NY, 1947), pp. 51–67. On the development of typology, see Jean Daniélou, *From Shadows to Reality: Studies in the Biblical Typology of the Fathers*, trans. W. Hibberd (London, 1960); Chenu, *Nature, Man and Society*; W.H. Lampe and K.J. Woollcombe, *Essays on Typology*, Studies in Biblical Theology, 22 (London, 1957); Erich Auerbach, 'Figura', in *Scenes from the Drama of European Literature*, trans. Ralph Manheim, Theory and History in Literature, 9 (New York, 1959), pp. 11–76.

does not merely *identify* with Mary, in a real sense she *becomes* the God Bearer. It is the Spirit that enters her and produces this palpable feeling.

As Mary gave birth to Word, Birgitta becomes the Theotokos, re-birthing the Logos through her revelations, begetting spiritual children through her personal witness, and bringing forth Vadstena and the Order (VI.88). Spiritual generation is summarized in Birgitta's calling *propter salutem aliorum* (*A&P*, p. 81). Just as the Virgin Mary was an active participant in the work of salvation, Birgitta's ministry will re-introduce Christianity to the world. Her revelations, declared to be inspired by the Holy Spirit, are several times compared with the Scriptures and are thus a continuation of the divine revelation of the Word (*Extrav.*, 49; *A&P*, p. 86).[76] The revelations are given for the purpose of begetting spiritual children (I.52) and Birgitta is specifically instructed in this task.[77] The Virgin comments directly on the health of Birgitta's spiritual children through extended use of the birthing image.[78] She applies the birthing metaphor in this passage to encompass the birth of the Order by comparing Birgitta to St Francis, who, although he had been ill for a time, recovered, bore fruit and became a great intercessor.[79] She reminds Birgitta of her earlier promise that, should she perish before all her prophecies were fulfilled, the Order would nevertheless come into existence and that she would even be regarded as a nun at Vadstena and partake of all that God promised her. Vadstena's abbess *in perpetua* was its earthly mother, Birgitta, as its heavenly mother was the Virgin Mary.

Birgitta's Marian self-perception is reflected in the Order's strong Marian identity. The interplay between Moses, the prophets and the Virgin Mary is explored in the *Sermo Angelicus*, the Birgittine office for matins in honour of the Virgin dictated to Birgitta by an angel. The Virgin becomes the prism

---

[76] This passage from the *Extravagantes* compares Birgitta and Alphonse to the evangelists, and the task of editing the *Revelations* and the guidance of the Spirit in this operation to the work of the evangelists. It is thus not entirely surprising that the Lübeck Brigittines ranked the *Revelations* with the Gospels, apparently a somewhat widespread claim repeated in Tortsch's *Onus Mundi*, a contemporary apocalyptic work in the Joachimite tradition (F.R. Johnston, 'English Defenders of St. Bridget', in Hogg, *Studies in St Birgitta*, 1.263–75, p. 270; Ellis, 'Flores ad Fabricandam', pp. 169ff.).

[77] 'Ego per te volo generare michi multos filios, non carnales sed spiritualis' (I.20). ('I desire through you to beget many children, not physically but spiritually.')

[78] 'Si femina, quando est infirma, parit, omnes filii eius, quos parit, infirmantur. Sed tu paries filios fortes et sanos et Deo deuotos' (*Extrav.*, 67). ('If a woman gives birth while she is ill, all the children she bears will be ill. But the children you bear are strong, healthy and devoted to God.')

[79] Birgitta is compared directly with the founders of major religious Orders, St Anthony (II.7), St Benedict (III.21), St Dominic (III.17) and once again St Francis (VII.20) (Ellis, 'A Note', p. 166).

through which the various strands of salvation history fuse, from the Creation, Exodus, prophets, Incarnation, Crucifixion, Assumption, to the unfinished work of redemption, the Order's solemn task. Repeatedly, the prophets' sorrow at Israel's rejection of God and the Law is contrasted with their joy in the foreknowledge of Mary's role as the Godbearer. Their witness to the invocation of God's wrath through Israel's sin is contrasted with their foreknowledge of Israel's reconciliation through Mary (*SA* 9). Their sorrow at the destruction of Jerusalem's Temple, wall, and gates by God's enemies, and Satan's spiritual destruction of Jerusalem, is contrasted with their joy in foreseeing the formation of the new *templum Dei*, Mary's body, the most glorious gate through which Christ as a valiant giant would be armed to champion his people and overcome his enemies and the devil (*SA* 9):

> The prophets likewise sorrowed because the Temple was laid waste wherein sacrifices ought to be offered to God; but they rejoiced in foreseeing that the temple of thy body would be formed which was to receive God himself with all joy. They sorrowed by reason that the walls and gates of Jerusalem, having been destroyed, the enemies of God had entered the city, destroying it materially while Satan did so spiritually; but they rejoiced in thee, O Mary, most glorious Gate, for they knew beforehand that God himself, as a most valiant giant, would be armed in thee, by which he would overcome the devil and all other enemies. Thus were the prophets and the patriarchs most comforted in thee, most glorious Mother.[80]

Birgitta, as we have seen, was the prophet who lamented Christendom's demise and saw God's approaching wrath. She had witnessed the destruction of Rome's gates, walls and altars, and the desecration of its sacred vessels through clerical, episcopal and papal neglect and decadence (III.27):

> And now I must speak to Rome like the prophets to Jerusalem. Formerly, justice dwelt in the city, her chiefs were princes of peace, but now they have become slayers of men. Oh Rome, if thou had known this day, thou would weep and not rejoice ... Now her gates are destroyed ... Her walls are torn down and without

---

[80]   'Dolebant insuper prophete, quia templum, in quo oblaciones Dei offerri debebant, erat desolatum; exultabant vero preuidentes, quod templum tui benedicti corporis creari debebat, quod ipsum Deum cum omni consolacione in se suscepturum erat. Dolebant eciam, quia destructis muris et portis Iherusalem inimici Dei fuerant ingressi expugnantes eam corporaliter, Sathanas autem spiritualiter; sed exultabant de te, o Maria, porta dignissima, prescientes in te ipsum Deum, fortissimum gigantem, assumpturum arma, quibus Dyabolum et omnes inimicos deuincere debebat. Et sic vere prophete sicut et patriarche de te, o dignissima mater, permaxime consolati fuerunt.'

watchmen ... The sacred vessels are sold, God's sacraments are served out and exchanged for money and the favour of men. The altars are laid waste, for he who handles the sacred vessels does it with loveless hands. (See also IV.10, 33; cf. VI.26)[81]

The close parallels between the two passages and the strikingly similar imagery are clear. They suggest that they were both written at a time when Birgitta (in the second passage) reacted strongly against the excesses she witnessed and resolved (in the first) to amend, through the spread of the Order, the ruin of the capital of Christendom and by extension, its cities and towns. Viewed in this light, Birgitta is the prophet who grieves over the destruction of Rome as the prophets lamented the destruction of the Temple. She witnesses the metaphorical destruction of Rome's altars as the prophets had beheld the physical devastation of the Temple altars. The sacred vessels in Rome had been removed for personal use just as the Temple vessels had been stolen by Nebuchadnezzar for his pleasure. Birgitta is also a very literal type of the Virgin whose agency brings forth a champion to fight against the devil, the apostolic zeal and piety to be re-fostered within Vadstena, which would re-convert Christendom. In giving birth to this Order, she is thus a universal mother figure and a type of the Virgin. Moreover, as the fulfilment of Ezekiel's Temple, Vadstena itself becomes a new maternal temple, metaphorically ringed by the *porta dignissima*, the Virgin Mary, giving birth to and cultivating an apostolic zeal and evangelical fervour to vanquish the world, the devil and the *inimici Dei* who had destroyed Rome, its gates, walls and altars. For as Ezekiel had attempted a complete programme of reform that would re-establish the covenant in its proper setting, Birgitta's *Revelations* set out a sweeping agenda of evangelical reform for universal re-conversion.

Thus, as the nuns read daily of salvation history in the *Sermo Angelicus* and the Virgin's role in it, they regarded a *speculum* of their own mission and the role they had been ordained to fulfil. The story of God's dealings with Israel told through the prophets and the Virgin Mary was being retold in the history of Christendom through the Birgittines. Built after the very model of God's meeting place in the Old Testament and professing its nuns in a liturgy suffused with elements from the Aaronic rite of priestly consecration, their Order was to

---

[81]   'Nunc autem ego possum loqui de roma sicut propheta loquebatur de iherusalem. Olim inquiens habitauit in ea iusticia et principes eius principes pacis. Nunc autem versa est in scoriam et principes eius homicide. O si cognosceres dies tuos, o roma, fleres vtique et non gauderes ... Nunc autem porte eius desolate sunt ... Muri eius depressi sunt et sine custodia ... Vasa diuina venduntur contemptibiliter quia sacramenta dei propter pecuniam & fauorem mundanum dispensantur. Altaria vero desolata sunt quia qui celebrant cum valis manus habent a caritate dei vacus.'

serve as the *locus* of God's presence within his community. In its commitment to prayer it was to continue the work of Moses and the prophets, re-establishing an observance of the Law, invoking divine mercy for the entire state of Christendom, and calling God's people to repentance through preaching. Mirroring literally through its numbers, vocations and virginal, matriarchal head the apostolic community, it was to obey Christ's command to his disciples to go into all the world, disseminating the Gospel through its own self-propagation in many lands.

Chapter 13

Mothers and Orphans in Fourteenth-century London

Caroline M. Barron and Claire A. Martin

The administrative records of the City of London might not seem a likely source of rich material to illuminate the attitudes to mothers and mothering prevalent in medieval London, but in one respect they throw unexpected light on children and their parents.[1] By the early fourteenth century it had been established as civic custom that, on the death of a freeman (or citizen) of London, his underage children (boys were usually considered to come of age when they were twenty-one, and girls when they married) became the responsibility of the mayor and aldermen. There were two parts to this responsibility: the practical concern for the well-being of the fatherless child and the need to ensure that any inheritance due to the child was safeguarded until the child came of age.

As a result of the development of this civic custom, the records of the city, and in particular the City's Letter Books which survive from 1272, record, amongst all the other civic business, decisions taken by the court relating to individual orphans (sometimes including their ages), their parents and step-parents, their appointed guardians and their coming of age, when they came to court to receive their inheritances and the mayor and aldermen relinquished their responsibilities. Not all stages of this process, or all details, have survived for every orphan. It is clear that there were orphan children of London citizens who never came to the attention of the court and there were orphans for whom guardians were appointed but there is no further evidence about their fate. The ways in which this 'wardship' of the fatherless children of London citizens worked out in practice has been the subject of several studies.[2] This information can be

---

[1] We are grateful to Professor Martha Carlin for reading an earlier draft of this paper and providing much useful advice.

[2] See: Elaine Clarke, 'City Orphans and Custody Laws in Medieval England', *The American Journal of Legal History*, 34 (1990): pp. 168–87; Barbara Hanawalt, *Growing Up in Medieval London: the Experience of Childhood in History* (New York , 1993), chapter 6; Caroline M. Barron, *London in the Later Middle Ages: Government and People 1200–1500* (Oxford, 2004), pp. 268–73.

used by historians in a number of ways, for example to assess life expectancy and survival rates among the urban population over a two-hundred-year period.[3] We have used in our sample the City's Letter Books G and H, which cover the years 1352–1398, when it is known that there was a high mortality rate and so there were particularly large numbers of orphans claiming the attention of the court.[4] The fluctuation in the number of orphan cases is shown in Figure 13.1.

It would seem that the number of orphaned families who came under the jurisdiction of the mayor and aldermen increased slightly between the 1350s and the 1370s, but was declining again by the end of the century. This probably reflects mid-century outbreaks of the plague. If this study were extended retrospectively into the 1340s, it might reveal that the level of orphan business in the 1350s was itself an increase on the number of orphans who came to the notice of the court in the earlier part of the century.

The aim of this study has been to use this material to assess the attitude of the court (as expressed in the entries to be found in the City's Letter Books) to the surviving mothers of the children, and to supplement the material to be found in the Letter Books we searched for surviving wills of the citizen fathers to see what instructions they may have given for the care of their children. However, the evidence provided by the wills is important in another way because we know (in most cases) when the father drew up his will and when it was proved (that is, he was dead by that date), and so this information can be used, in conjunction with the records in the Letter Books, to find out the length of time between the death of a father and the intervention by the court in appointing guardians for his children. It is possible carry out this analysis because the wills of London citizens were enrolled in the city's court of Husting from the middle of the thirteenth century, although by no means all wills were enrolled.[5] From the last quarter of the fourteenth century there survive, in addition, wills enrolled in the two ecclesiastical courts of the London Commissary and Archdeaconry.[6] Even so, it has only been possible to find about one-third of the wills of the

[3]   Barbara Megson, 'Life Expectations of the Widows and Orphans of Freemen in London 1375–1399', *Local Population Studies*, 57 (1996), pp. 18–29.

[4]   *Calendar of the Letter Books of the City of London A–L*, ed. R.R. Sharpe (11 vols, London, 1899–1912); hereafter *LB*, followed by the relevant letter, for example, *LBA*, *LBF*, and so on.

[5]   *Calendar of Wills proved and Enrolled in the Court of Husting, London 1258–1688*, ed. R.R. Sharpe (2 vols, London, 1889–1890); hereafter *HW*. We have used Sharpe's calendar, which is very accurate, and he always includes in his synopses information about the wives and children of the testator. He does not, however, include the names of the executors. It is probable that it was the executors who, apart from the mother, were often appointed as guardians of orphan children.

[6]   *Index to Testamentary Records in the Commissary Court of London 1374–1488*, ed.

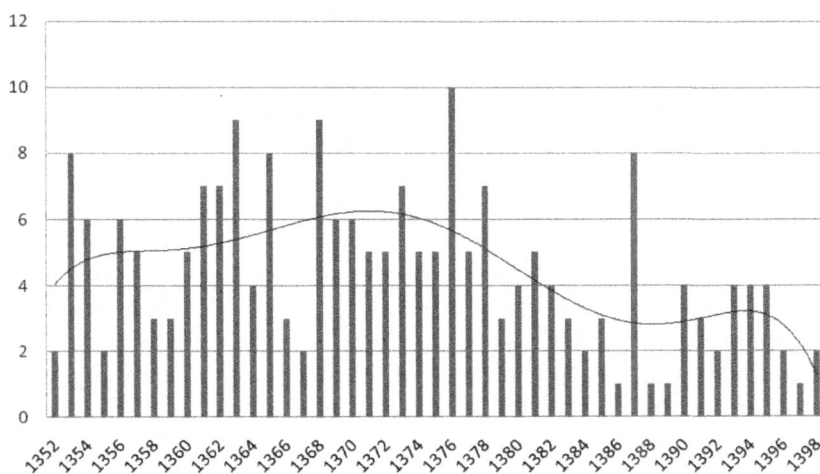

Figure 13.1 Number of orphaned families allocated a guardian per year
Source: Letter Books G and H.

fathers whose children came before the mayor and aldermen as orphans. Study of the references to orphans found in the City's Letter Books in the years 1352–1400 produced the names of 186 deceased fathers, but only sixty-seven had left surviving wills, although we know that a further twenty-three fathers certainly left a will but no copy of it has survived.[7] This means that, although ninety (48 percent) of the deceased fathers are known to have made wills, only 36 percent of these wills were available for use in this study.[8]

Who were chosen by the court of aldermen to act as guardians of civic orphans? The legal process and definition of orphanage, which meant that a female parent was, in law, the same as no parent at all, would appear on the surface to place very little value on the role and significance of mothers. Statistical analysis of the appointment of guardians initially suggests support

---

M. Fitch (London, 1969); *Testamentary Records in the Archdeaconry Court of London 1363–1649*, ed. M. Fitch (London, 1979)

[7] These twenty-three wills are known to have existed either because the existence of a will is referred to in the Letter Books, or because the name of the testator is included in the list of contents of the register of the Archdeaconry Court, but the early folios have not survived, see Fitch, *Archdeaconry*, pp. xi–xii.

[8] Claire Martin prepared the spreadsheet on which the details of the 186 orphan cases were recorded, together with information gleaned from the father's will where this was available. Most of the conclusions in this essay derive from information in this spreadsheet.

for this assessment. In total, over this period, 316 orphans [173 (55 percent) male and 143 (45 percent) female] were dealt with by the court.[9] For these orphans, 216 guardians were assigned, of whom 165 were male, twenty-one were female, and in thirty cases a man and woman were appointed together as joint guardians. It might be expected that male guardians would be favoured, given that guardianship usually included not only the care of a child but also financial responsibility for protecting the orphan's inheritance and employing it in such a way as to produce an acceptable return.

Let us first consider the twenty-one cases in this sample in which a woman was appointed by the court to act as the sole guardian. In two cases it was a female relative who was appointed: in 1352 Alice de Grantham was given the custody of her sister Isabella, and in 1377 the court agreed, after a legal dispute, that John Padyngton should be in the custody of his grandmother (his mother's mother), rather than in the custody of his mother, Juliana, and her new husband, as his father had specified in his will.[10] In four cases a woman was chosen to act as a guardian, but her relationship to the orphan is not known. In March 1354, John Fabe, who was twelve, was committed by the court to the guardianship of a widow, Avice atte Brome, but by November of that year she had remarried and together with her new husband came to court to be relieved of the guardianship, since neither she nor her husband exercised a trade or craft which they could teach to young John, so his guardianship was transferred to a pewterer.[11] Six-year-old Cecilia de Basyngstoke was committed to the guardianship of Johanna le Blake, the recent widow of a vintner, who may have wished for a young companion.[12] In two cases it appears that women may have taken over orphans as apprentices: John Tamworth was fourteen when he was committed to the

---

[9]   Megson found a similar proportion of male to female orphans, 53 percent male and 47 percent female, see 'Life Expectations', p. 25; and cf. Table 2 in Hanawalt, *Growing Up*, p. 223.

[10]   *LBG*, p. 2; the case of young John Padyngton was complicated by the fact that, when his father Henry died in August 1375, he had also left a daughter Katherine, born to his late servant Johanna atte Pitte. His estate was to be divided into three parts: for Juliana, John and Katherine. Henry appointed his wife Juliana as the guardian of his son during his minority. By the autumn of 1377, Juliana was remarried to a man named Robert Louth and the guardianship of John was disputed between William Whetley, a cordwainer, one of the executors of Padyngton's will, and Johanna Mitford, his grandmother. She won. London Metropolitan Archives, Husting Roll 103/217; *HW*, ii, pp. 181–2; *LBH*, pp. 82–3.

[11]   *LBG*, pp. 19, 32. William Fabe's will does not survive. Avice seems to have been anxious to divest herself of her responsibilities, because two weeks after arranging the apprenticeship of John Fabe, the guardianship of Katherine, the seven-year-old daughter of her late husband John atte Brome, was allocated by the court to Thomas atte Hale. It seems likely that Katherine was the stepdaughter of Avice, *HW*, i, p. 682; *LBG*, p. 32.

[12]   *LBG*, p. 36; *HW*, i, p. 684.

guardianship of Goda Bysouth, and William Pountfreit was also fourteen when the court appointed Margery, the wife of the mercer and alderman Richard Nottingham, as his guardian. Nine years later William came to court and acknowledged satisfaction for his inheritance.[13]

Of particular interest to us here are the fifteen cases where a mother was appointed as the sole guardian of her children. In five of these cases we have a record of the appointment of the guardians and also a copy of the father's will. In all these five cases the mother was appointed by the court as a guardian very soon after the death of her husband. In three cases, the husband in drawing up his will had left instructions about the guardianship of his children and committed them to his wife. Thomas Hore, a fishmonger, drew up his will on 5 June 1370, leaving the custody of his three sons and their estate to his wife Agnes. His will was proved in October 1372, and in November of that year the court appointed Agnes as the guardian of her sons.[14] However, the instructions in wills could be complex. When Eustace de Glaston drew up his will in April 1374 he left two daughters, Alice and Mathilda, and two sons, James and John. It would seem that Alice and John may have been the children of his first wife, Margery, because only James and Mathilda were allocated to the guardianship of Eustace's wife Margaret. Alice was to be handed to the custody of Katherine and Richard Norton, and John to the custody of John de Glaston, his uncle. The guardianship of the two children who were handed into the custody of their mother seems never to have come before the court, but in August 1377 the guardianship of both Alice and her brother John was committed to the custody of Katherine Norton.[15] However, by this time Katherine was herself a widow and so in the following month she came to court to be appointed as the guardian of her own children, John and Johanna Norton.[16] Three years later Katherine came again before the court and asked to be discharged from the guardianship of John de Glaston because the money which she received for his maintenance was insufficient. Clearly Johanna had been in charge of the inheritance as well as the person of young John, and she brought nearly £65 owing to him into court

---

[13] *LBH*, p. 52; *LBG*, p. 136. Richard Nottingham appears to have died c. 1363, soon after his wife took on the guardianship of William, which suggests that she may have taken him on to secure the future of her husband's business. No will survives for Nottingham, A.B. Beaven, *The Aldermen of the City of London* (2 vols, London, 1908–1913), i, p. 387.

[14] *HW*, ii, 151; *LBG*, p. 301.

[15] *LBH*, p. 71; perhaps Richard her husband had died in the intervening three years.

[16] 12 September 1377. In his will (not surviving) Richard de Norton asked John Welde (possibly a baker, see *LBG*, p. 130) to join Katherine in the guardianship of their children but Welde declined to act and so Katherine took on the responsibility on her own, *LBH*, p. 75.

and was discharged.[17] It would seem that she retained the guardianship of Alice de Glaston, who later married and claimed her inheritance in 1388, by which time Katherine Norton was dead.[18] In this case we can see a London woman who was considered to be responsible not only for her own children but also for the children of another Londoner whose relationship to her is not clear; Richard de Glaston may have been a neighbour or a fellow craftsman, but the absence of surviving wills for either Katherine or her husband makes it difficult to determine the nature of the relationship.

In another complex case John Gille, a draper, in January 1380 drew up a long and detailed will in which he specified that his wife Johanna was to be the guardian of his daughter Margaret (aged five) and to give security at the Guildhall for her custody and her legacy. In the following month Johanna came to court and took on the guardianship not only of her daughter but also Richard, son of William Robynet, who was eighteen.[19] It seems likely that John Gille, her husband, had taken on the guardianship of Richard, the son of a fellow draper, perhaps to act as his apprentice since he left a bequest to him in his will. Johanna may have wished to retain Richard to help to run the business after her husband's death. The family seems to have done well; Richard Robynet took over his patrimony in February 1383, by which time Johanna Gille had married Nicholas Extone, who had just been elected an alderman and was to be mayor of London in 1386–1388.[20] Young Margaret, by June 1387, had married John Sibille, a common councilman for Bishopsgate ward, and her property was handed over to her husband.[21] Johanna herself was appointed one of Exton's executors when he drew up his will in 1393 and appears to have outlived her husband.

In the remaining ten instances where a mother was appointed by the court as the sole guardian of her children, we have no surviving copy of the husband's will, so we cannot know what his instructions might have been, nor the length of the gap between the father's death and the mother's appearance in court to claim the custody of her children.[22] In an unusual further case, the court appointed

---

[17]   *LBH*, p. 72. It is not clear what happened to John de Glaston at this point, but two years later he came to court and asked that the money owing to him might be delivered to John de Glaston, his uncle, who had probably taken on his guardianship, and this was done, Ibid., pp. 72, 75–6.

[18]   Alice married John Carton or Gartone, *LBH*, p. 72.

[19]   *HW*, ii, pp. 218–9; *LBH*, pp. 160–61.

[20]   Beaven, *Aldermen*, i, p. 397.

[21]   *LBH*, pp. 161, 333. Margaret seems to have been no more than twelve when she was married to Sibille.

[22]   John Goldesburgh was committed to his mother, Juliana, January 1367, *LBG*, p. 214; Richard and Alice atte Hale were committed to their mother, Agnes, November 1368,

Johanna Staunford as the guardian of her eight-year-old son John, 'his father having been absent abroad a long season'. She had to be his *de iure* guardian in order to receive the bequest of 40s left to her son by John Cornwaille, who had recently died.[23]

What is clear from this juxtaposition of the wills of dead fathers and the appointment by the court of aldermen of their widows to act as guardians of the young children is that, in four out of the five cases where we have both the will and the date of appointment, this took place within a month of the father's will being proved.[24] In three cases the father had specified that the mother was to act as the guardian, and in the other cases the court took that decision.

However, if we turn to consider the cases where the guardians who were appointed were the mother with her new husband, or the new husband on his own, the picture is very different. There are forty-one cases in this sample where it is clear that the mother has remarried and that is the reason for her appearance (or that of her new husband) in court. In the earlier part of this period it was usual for the mother to come into court with her new husband and they would together be appointed as joint guardians, but what appears to become more common over the fifty years (this may simply reflect a change of recording procedure) is that, when the widow remarried, it was the new husband on his own who provided the sureties rather than the married couple together, although the fact that he had married the orphan's mother is recorded. The first recorded such case of the stepfather coming to court is that of the six-year-old son of Adam de Glendone, who was committed in February 1372 by the mayor and aldermen to John Blakeneye, a mercer who had 'married the orphan's mother'.[25]

LBG, p. 234; John, Richard and Alice Askote were committed to their mother Lucy, July 1375, *LBH*, p. 8; William Goldyngham, aged seventeen, and his brother Thomas, aged thirteen, were committed to their mother, Isabella, September 1376, *LBH*, p. 45; Thomas Dannger, aged fourteen, and his brother Richard, aged five, together with their property and that of their sister Emma were committed to their mother Juliana in May 1378; a month later the guardianship of Emma was committed to Edmund Haryngeye, *LBH*, pp. 91–2; Simon, John and Robert Harpesfeld were committed to their mother Johanna in August 1378, *LBH*, p. 96; Idonea Camber was committed to the widow of her father (possibly therefore a stepmother rather than mother) in February 1383, *LBH*, p. 210; Thomas Codham was committed to his mother Alice in January 1387, *LBH*, p. 295; Agnes Wallere was committed to her mother Mathilda in January 1394, *LBH*, p. 405.

[23] 13 December 1379, *LBH*, pp. 138–9; John Cornwaille is probably the currier who died in 1379, see Fitch, *Archdeaconry Wills*, p. 93.

[24] The exception is that of the guardianship of John Bradley, whose father's will was proved in April 1371 and his mother was not appointed as his guardian until August of that year, *HW*, ii, p. 140; *LBG*, p. 286.

[25] *LBG*, p. 292.

There are thirteen (out of forty-one) of these cases where the mother has remarried where we have a copy of the father's will and can know something of his wishes for his children and also the date of his death. We also know the date on which his widow and her new husband (or the husband alone) came into court to take over the guardianship, and the average length between these two events is eighteen months. These remarriages range from the precipitate single month that it took for Johanna, the widow of John Redeford, a glover, to take her four sons together with her into a new marriage and guardianship with another glover, John de Cornewaille, to the more decorous four years that Isabella Stodeye took to marry Philip Derneford.[26] When Adam Stodeye had drawn up his will in 1375, his wife was pregnant with their daughter Agnes; by the time she was five, and her mother had remarried, Agnes was committed to the guardianship of her new stepfather.[27] It seems clear that in all these cases where a mother and her new husband entered into formal guardianship, often many months after the death of the father, the mother has in fact been acting as the guardian of her children and it is only her remarriage that has made it necessary for her new husband, or both together, to come to court and be formally appointed as guardians. In all these thirteen cases the children had a surviving mother (or possibly in some cases a surviving stepmother) and she was accepted as the appropriate guardian for her children and their property. These children were not left untended when their fathers died: they were left in the care of their mothers.

Then there is a further group of guardians appointed by the court who were not the mothers nor the mother's new husband, but on the face of it complete strangers. In some cases they were relatives, or the executor of the father, or someone who had been named as a guardian in the father's will. Yet in the majority of cases we do not know what the link was between the orphan and the new guardian and, doubtless, there must have been cases when they were comparative strangers to each other. In this group there are forty cases where it is, however, possible to know the date when the father's will was proved and the date when these new 'stranger' guardians were appointed for his children. These range from the one month it took for the court to appoint a guardian for seven-year-old Juliana atte Brome[28] to the gap of over eleven years between the drawing up of the will of Edmund de Hemenhale at the height of the plague in June 1349 and the appointment of Thomas Cheyner, another mercer, to act as the guardian

---

[26]   *HW*, ii, pp. 145–6; *LBG*, p. 296. The court may have had some reservations about the speed of this remarriage since the children and their properties were only committed to John de Cornwaille for three years.

[27]   *HW*, ii, p. 185; *LBH*, p. 141.

[28]   *HW*, i, p. 682; *LBG*, p. 32.

of his two children in December 1360, by which time Thomas was aged sixteen and Margaret twelve.[29] The *average* length of time between proving the will and appointing a 'stranger' guardian was, however, thirty-four months. Here again it seems clear that the mother must have been taking care of her children so that the appointment of guardians was not necessary. This might become necessary if she died, or if the children needed to be apprenticed or required, in some way, the extra protection of the court to ensure their well-being.

So this apparent preference for male guardians that appears in the orphan records in the City's Letter Books is misleading. It is necessary to read the silences and to compare the dates when the guardians were appointed with the date of the will of the orphan's father. The default guardianship enjoyed by the mother often went unrecorded, but it can be inferred from the gap that commonly occurred between the father's death and assignment of guardians.

The wills have proved useful in this study because they have enabled us to demonstrate that the London mother was the default guardian of her underage children. Her guardianship was assumed by the court and she rarely came into court to take up her guardianship formally unless she remarried, usually several months after the death of the orphan's father. The appointment of 'stranger' guardians (usually male, although couples were sometimes appointed) by the court of aldermen seems to have taken place only if there was no surviving mother (or stepmother) or she had died, or there was some other reason that made the appointment of strangers necessary. Such a case occurred during the plague outbreak of 1361. In May of that year, Robert de Guldeford, a draper, drew up his will and appointed his wife Johanna as the guardian of their son, Henry, and three daughters, Roesia, Mathilda and Margery. Robert died within two weeks and his widow then drew up her will and appointed guardians for two of her children, perhaps because the other two had already died. Johanna chose for the guardian of her son Henry the rector of her parish church of St Augustine at Paul's Gate, Thomas de Kendale. Her daughter Roesia was to remain in the custody of John de Utlicote and these two men were also appointed as her executors. However, Johanna also was dead by December of that year, presumably again of plague. The court then, within a month, appointed the two guardians she had named to look after Henry who was nine, and Roesia who was eleven.[30]

In the years between 1352 and 1398 there are sixty-seven wills surviving of fathers who left underage children who later came to the attention of the court. In at least nine of those wills there is no mention of a surviving wife; in at least twenty other cases the husband specified that he wished his wife to act as the

29 *HW*, i, p. 608; *LBG*, p. 125.
30 LMA, Husting Roll 89/264; *HW*, ii, pp. 60–61; *LBG*, pp. 134–5.

guardian of their children, sometimes requiring her to offer security at Guildhall and sometimes saying that there was no need for her to do this.[31] William Potenham, for example, specified that his wife was to be the guardian of his children and of their property up to the age of sixteen years 'without rendering any account for the same'.[32] When John Stable, a mercer, died in 1360 he left three young children and his wife Johanna was pregnant. He left property to his wife and their children and a sum of money to his two apprentices, who were to trade with it and from the profits they were to give half to his wife 'for the maintenance of their children' and the other half they were to keep for their trouble. It would seem that Johanna did not survive because in October 1363 two of the children, Thomas and Isabella, who were four and three, were handed over to the guardianship of another mercer, although it is clear that her husband had intended that she should continue to run their household and care for their children.[33] Sometimes the father specified that the mother should act as sole guardian only until she remarried. In 1360, for example, John Derham left custody of his children to his wife Cecilia but, if she remarried, she and her new husband were to give surety at the Guildhall for the return to the children of their property when they came of age.[34] Henry Padyngtone demonstrated considerable faith in his wife Juliana. His will of 1375 left her custody of their son John and specified that she need not give security at the Guildhall.[35] This case only came into court two years later because Juliana had married Robert Louthe and so was required by the court to provide sureties. At this time William Whetley, cordwainer, one of Padyngtone's executors, claimed the guardianship of John from Juliana and her new husband on the grounds that this was in accordance with the terms of Henry Padyngtone's will. Whetley's motivation, however, may have been principally financial because the boy's maternal grandmother, Johanna Mitford,

---

[31]   Wills of John de Mymmes, Richard de Wycombe, Robert Guldeford, Osbert Wynter, Richard Bacoun, William atte Hale, Thomas Hore, Eustace de Glastone, Henry Padyngtone, John Gille, Robert Cok, John Clenhond, William Potenham and Geoffrey Patrik, *HW*, i, p. 558; *HW*, ii, pp. 19–20; 60–61; 48; 79–80; 118–19; 151; 165; 181–2; 218–19; 268; 300; 308; 147–8; John Hothom, *LBH*, p.177.

[32]   *HW*, ii, p. 308.

[33]   *HW*, ii, p. 63; *LBG*, p. 156.

[34]   *HW*, ii, pp. 12–13. This demonstrates the standard process although, in this case, other unknown events meant it was not followed. Within two months of their father's will being proved, the guardianship of Derham's four children was assigned to three separate guardians. Only one of his daughters was returned to Cecilia's guardianship, two years later. Why the instructions of this will were not carried out is unclear, *LBG*, pp. 120, 157. In 1352 John Merwe also specified that his wife was to have custody as long as she remained 'a chaste and honest widow', *HW*, i, pp. 659–60.

[35]   *HW*, ii, pp. 181–2.

widow of John Mitford, draper, successfully claimed the guardianship as John's next of kin on the grounds that she had nothing to gain from his death.[36] There are no details in Paddyngtone's will, however, that shed any light on exactly what that financial motivation may have been.

In our sample of sixty-seven wills there are eight cases where a father named a guardian other than his widow in his will. In three cases it would appear that there was no surviving widow, so this is understandable, but in five of these eight cases, it is known that the father actually had a surviving widow who could have acted as guardian but the husband seems to have excluded her from the custody of the children.[37] When John Mount, a glasier, drew up his will in October 1376, he specified that the custody of his daughter Alice should go to Henry Abbot, a goldsmith, and his wife Alice, who was Alice's godmother. Alice's mother Johanna had died, and although Mount left a widow, Katherine, he clearly thought that his daughter would be better off with the Abbots, to whom he entrusted various goods for Alice and 40s. to keep her for a year after his death with the nuns at Stratford so that she might be taught there.[38] In a similar case the father appointed two different men as masters or guardians for his two sons who were probably the children of his first wife Alice, rather than his widow Lucy. Even so, it was more than three years before the court appointed the two men as guardians, which suggests that they may have remained with their stepmother for a time. One of the boys was only eight when his father died.[39]

In the remaining three cases it would appear, however, that the father specifically excluded the biological mother from the guardianship of her children. However, here, as elsewhere, it seems probable that the mayor and aldermen exercised some discretion in carrying out the wishes of a deceased father. This is clear in two of these three cases. Although the court appointed Peter Sterre as the guardian of Sarah Martyn, as her father wished, this did not in fact happen until four years after her father's will had been proved. Martyn had left a widow, Margery, who was probably Sarah's mother, and it seems that

---

[36]   *LBH*, p. 82.

[37]   In three of these cases it seems apparent that the widow so denied custody of her children was indeed their biological mother as there is no reference in the will to the father having a deceased first wife.

[38]   Mount's will is copied into London Metropolitan Archives, Archdeaconry Register, MS 9171/1 fol. 41r; 19 November 1376, Henry Abbot is given the guardianship of Alice by the court. Six years later Alice had died, unmarried, and Abbot handed her inheritance back to the court, who allocated it to Katherine, the widow of John Mount; she was inaccurately described as 'mother of the orphan', although it is quite clear from Mount's will that she was not Alice's mother, *LBH*, p. 49.

[39]   *HW*, ii, p. 133; *LBG*, pp. 307–8, 320–21.

she was allowed to retain custody of her daughter for three or four years because of her daughter's age. Sarah was five when her guardianship was assigned to Sterre so she was only about a year old when her father died.[40] Something similar probably occurred in the case of William Knyghtcote, as his wishes also seem to have been superseded, at least for a time, by the rights of his widow, the mother of his children. In 1383, Knyghtcote left custody of his children to John Otteley, a mercer, but it was not until four years later that Otteley was formally given the guardianship of Margaret and Margery. Their sister Idonia, meanwhile, remained in the custody of their mother Johanna, who had probably been caring for all her daughters during the intervening time.[41] In this case the ages of the girls are not stated but it is probable that Idonia was the youngest as she was the last to marry and claim her inheritance. Margaret and Margery were probably assigned to the guardianship of Otteley when they were deemed old enough to leave their mother, and would have been joined later by their younger sister. Otteley was given custody of Idonia's portion at the same time that he took over the guardianship of her sisters, but there is no record of his formal appointment later as her guardian.[42] In the third case, the court may have followed the wishes of the testator. William Tonge, in 1390, left four children and a widow, Avice, who was also his executrix. His will makes no mention of a previous wife but demands that his children's inheritance be kept at the Guildhall until 'good men be found ready to bring up his said children'. Despite apparently being their mother, and competent enough to be chosen by her husband to act as his executrix, Avice was not permitted to be guardian of his children and she was also required to remain unmarried in order to continue to enjoy her dower.[43] Tonge seems to have been quite a bossy man since his daughters' inheritances were to be reduced if they married without discretion or lived immodestly, and his sons could not enjoy their inheritances before they were twenty-five. It appears, however, that Avice played an active role as the executrix of her husband.

The evidence collected for this study suggests that the wishes of testators with regard to the custody of their children seem generally to have been respected. In only two cases is it clear that the chosen guardian refused the appointment. Richard de Nortone, who died in about 1377, wanted the guardianship of his children to be held jointly by his wife Katherine and John Welde, but Welde refused and Katherine held the guardianship alone; since she was the mother of

---

[40]   *LBG*, p. 147. *HW*, ii, p. 9.

[41]   *LBH*, p. 316. *HW*, ii, p. 237.

[42]   *HW*, ii, pp. 278–9.

[43]   *HW*, ii, 278–9; *LBH*, pp. 357–8. There is no record of the appointment of guardians by the court but only of Avice's activities as the executor of her husband's estate on behalf of the children, *LBH*, pp. 357–8.

the children, this would not a have been a dramatic departure from the normal procedure.[44] Richard Russell died in May 1374 and in the same month his executors were summoned to the mayor and aldermen to give surety for their guardianship of Richard and Lucy, his orphan children. Richard appears not to have a left a widow, which may explain why it was noted that, while waiting for the appearance of the executors, the children 'were to remain in the charge of Adam de Bury, the mayor'. It is interesting to speculate what Mrs Bury may have thought of this arrangement. When the executors appeared they refused the guardianship of the children and returned their inheritances. By August of that year a guardian was found for Richard, but it is not clear what happened to his sister Lucy.[45] On only one occasion would it appear that a mother gave up the guardianship of her children; Cassandra Scut, in July 1377 on her remarriage, surrendered the guardianship of Thomas and Johanna to John Walcote, but as she is described simply as 'the widow of Richard Scut', rather than as the mother of the two children, she may have been their stepmother.[46] We have also seen how Juliana Padyngtone lost custody of her son to her mother, following a dispute and her remarriage.[47] So mothers (or stepmothers) did not always choose to assert their rights, or may have been unable to do so, or their new husbands may have been unwilling to take on the extra responsibilities.

The illegitimate children of London citizens also show up in this survey and, although the children appear to have had the same rights and protection as legitimate orphans, it is not quite so clear that the primary role of the mother of illegitimate children was so respected. When Roger Longe died in 1375 he left two legitimate sons and a bastard son who was probably the child of Maud Beccote, to whom he left generous bequests in his will 'for her marriage' and further money should she prove to be *enceinte*. Longe's wife Lucy was dead and so the court assigned the three boys within months to three separate guardians. Whether Maud Beccote wished to act as a guardian is not clear, but neither the boys' father, nor the court, chose to appoint her.[48] On the other hand when Thomas Wirlyngworth died in 1365, he left substantial bequests to Cristina, the daughter of John Ippegrave, together with the guardianship of her three sons, who were probably also his sons. Five years later, one of the sons had died, and Cristina and her husband came to court and were appointed as the guardians of the two remaining boys.[49] However, the case of Alice Reyner indicates the

---

[44]   *LBH*, p. 75.

[45]   *HW*, ii, p. 160; *LBG*, p. 326.

[46]   *LBH*, pp. 70–71. There is no surviving will for Richard Scut.

[47]   See above, footnote 36.

[48]   *HW*, ii, pp. 185–6; *LBH*, pp. 31–2.

[49]   *HW*, ii, pp. 87–8; *LBG*, pp. 261–2.

limitations to the rights of the mothers of illegitimate children. Alice was the daughter of John Reyner and his servant Margaret. By his will of 1375, Reyner had left money to Alice (for her marriage or apprenticeship) and bequests to her mother. He also left bequests to the children of John Bryan, a fishmonger, one of whom was his godson. Shortly after Reyner's death, John Bryan accepted responsibility for the bequest on behalf of his own children and at the same time, took over the guardianship of Reyner's illegitimate daughter Alice.[50] Margaret later petitioned the mayor, claiming that Bryan planned to marry her daughter Alice (for a sum) to his apprentice, Richard Fraunceys, without the permission of the court.[51] Clearly she would not have complained to the mayor if she had been happy about this marriage. If she had been accepted as Alice's guardian she would have been able to prevent the marriage. As it was, Bryan took the precaution of obtaining the formal consent of the mayor and aldermen to the marriage of wealthy young Alice to Fraunceys, and the financial arrangements between him and Richard Fraunceys were settled to their satisfaction.[52] We do not know what happened to Margaret, but her inability to control her daughter's marriage is a good indication of the restricted rights of the mothers of illegitimate children who, however, appear to have suffered no disadvantages through their illegitimate birth.

It would appear from the cases that we have studied in this fifty-year sample that the mayor and aldermen left the widows of London citizens to get on with the task of bringing up their underage children and also, very often, left them to manage the inheritance that their fathers had left to maintain and educate or train their children. It is worth remembering in this context that London custom was particularly generous to widows, who were entitled to a dower consisting of the house in which she and her husband were living at the time of his death, and this she could occupy until she remarried. She was also entitled to a third (or a half if there were no children) of the lands and tenements that had belonged to her husband at the time of their marriage. This she could enjoy for her life, whether she remarried or not. Over and above her claim upon her husband's landed estate, the London widow was entitled by the custom of *legitim* to a share of her husband's movable goods, again a half or a third, depending upon whether there were children or not. Of course, though, if the children were underage, the widow often also took responsibility for

---

[50]   Reyner's will does not survive, but details are found in *LBH*, p. 3; see also *LBH*, pp. 10–11, 28. The case of Alice Reyner is discussed by Hanawalt, *Growing up*, pp. 97–100 and 245–6.

[51]   LMA, Mayor's Court File CLA/024/02/001/63. The bill is not dated.

[52]   *LBH*, 11, 28 and H. T. Riley, ed., *Memorials of London and London Life* (London, 1868), pp. 446–7.

their portions of their father's estate. In addition to these generous provisions, the widow of a London citizen was entitled to claim the status of citizen or freewoman for herself, and so could do business in her own right and secure for her goods the privileged status enjoyed by London merchants and craftsmen in other English markets. She was also not only allowed, but expected, to continue the training of her husband's apprentices (and her own also if she had them) and in many wills London merchants and craftsmen left legacies to their apprentices with instructions that they were to remain with their widows and complete their terms.[53] John de Bonyndon, an apothecary who died in 1361, instructed his three apprentices to continue to serve his wife, who was to maintain their household and care for their three children.[54] So city custom made it possible for widows to be economically self-sufficient, and to maintain a home that they could run for themselves and their children.

In the period on which this study has focused, the years 1352–1398, the orphaned children of 186 citizen fathers occupied the attention of the court and were recorded in the City's Letter Books. In the case of sixty-seven of the these families, it has been possible to locate the wills of the father who had died. A comparison between the date when the father died and the appearance of his widow and/or children in court has shown that there was a considerable gap between the death of the father and the appointment of guardians for his children, and it has been suggested here that the reason for this was that, in practice, the mother was a prime carer for her children and guardians had to be appointed in court only when the mother remarried (to protect the children from a marauding stepfather) or when, later, they had to be apprenticed, or married, or their mother had died and it was necessary to find a 'stranger' to take over the care of the children.

However, there is another piece of 'silent' evidence which needs to be considered. If we look not at the records of the court of aldermen but rather at all the wills enrolled in the court of Husting, we are presented with a surprising statistic. In a sample decade, 1358–1368, a period of high mortality because of the second outbreak of plague in 1361–1366, there are 118 enrolled wills in which the testator left underage children. Of these 118 orphan cases, only eighteen, or 15 percent, ever attracted the attention of the court of aldermen. This means that, in 85 percent of the cases when citizens died leaving their children as orphans, it was their widows who were left to care for them, maintain their inheritance and see them married and trained. It is abundantly clear that,

---

[53] See Caroline M. Barron, 'Introduction: the Widow's World in later Medieval London', in Caroline M. Barron and Anne F. Sutton (ed.), *Medieval London Widows 1300–1500* (London, 1994), pp. xiii–xxxiv, esp. pp. xvii–xxi; xxvii–xxviii.

[54] *HW*, ii, p. 40.

although there would appear to be a large number of orphan cases coming before the court, the intervention by the mayor and aldermen in the fate of city orphans, was, in fact, the exception rather than the rule. The mothers were left to get on with the job because, then as now, they were recognized as the people who, in almost every case, were likely to provide the best care for their children.

Chapter 14

Mother or Stepmother to History?
Joan de Mohun and her Chronicle

Jocelyn Wogan-Browne

The fact that the texts of a family may be part of its agency and in particular of the political imagination of its women is increasingly recognized by scholars of medieval history and literature. A mid fourteenth-century chronicle made at the abbey of Wigmore for its lay patrons, the Mortimers, acknowledges female roles in the memory and history of a family through its account of what a bad 'mother to history' would do. Not to attend to lineage and memorialization, says *Wigmore*, is to become a stepmother, rather than a mother, to culture:

> Negligence de escoter et en memoire retenier les eovres notables et profitables de antiquité est *marastre dé virtues et destrueresse*, et la prise de euz en memoire planté del sage ovesqe la siwte de lor ensample est *mere et norice de bons mœurs.* [Italics mine][1]

> [Failure to listen and to commit to memory the noteworthy and beneficial deeds of antiquity is *the stepmother and destroyer of virtues* and the understanding of them rooted in memory by the wise together with the following of their example is *the mother and nurturer of good customs.*]

---

[1]   This essay is dedicated with great respect and affection to Henrietta Leyser, begetter of much fine historiography of medieval women and men; of good scholars within her family and her teaching; and of generously undertaken scholarly enterprises for the common good. I thank Sethina Watson, Christopher Baswell, John Spence and Robert W. Hanning and his Columbia Medievalists' discussion group for much valuable help. For the Wigmore Chronicle see J.C. Dickinson and P.T. Ricketts (ed. and trans.), 'The Anglo-Norman Chronicle of Wigmore Abbey', *Transactions of the Woolhope Naturalists Field Club*, 39 (1969): 413–45 (the editors omit the *marrastre* metaphor from their translation, so the full effect of *Wigmore's* statement has been somewhat muffled); C. Given-Wilson, 'Chronicles of the Mortimer Family c. 1250–1450', in Richard Eales and Shaun Tyas (eds), *Family and Dynasty in Late Medieval England: Proceedings of the 1997 Harlaxton Symposium* (Donington, 2003), pp. 67–86.

Women's roles in the construction and keeping of memory have been given increased study in recent years, and metaphors of women as mothers, good or bad, to history, need not be seen as only figurative. The Latin commissions by royal women of earlier insular culture – Edith and her life of her husband Edward the Confessor, Edith-Matilda, queen of Henry I, to William of Malmesbury, Adeliza of Louvain's lost biography of Henry I, for example – have some descendants across the Conquest at noble and gentry level:[2] the first vernacular post-Conquest historiography, Gaimar's *Estoire des Engleis*, was composed for Lady Constance Fitzgilbert in Lincolnshire, and literary and other forms of cultural patronage remained a recognized role for women in both secular and religious lives.[3] The question of what happens when we read such histories from the perspectives of their mothers (or stepmothers) is worth pursuing in many dimensions, although my example here will be single and in some ways small-scale. It nevertheless casts light on some particularly crucial themes of dynastic creation and maintenance.

Little known till now, but shortly to become available thanks to the scholarship of Dr John Spence, is the fourteenth-century chronicle composed in French and associated with Lady Joan de Mohun (d. 1404), wife of John de Mohun, lord of Dunster Castle, Somerset, (d. 1375).[4] The chronicle was probably

---

[2]   Elizabeth Tyler, *Crossing Conquests: Royal Women and the Politics of Fiction in Eleventh-Century England* (Toronto, in press); William of Malmesbury, *Gesta regum Anglorum*, trans. and ed. R.A.B. Mynors, R.M. Thomson and M. Winterbottom (2 vols, Oxford, 1998–1999), I, pp. 6–9; *Estoire des Engleis /History of the English by Geffrai Gaimar*, trans. and ed. Ian Short (Oxford, 2009).

[3]   Henrietta Leyser, *Medieval Women: a Social History of Women in England 450–1500* (London, 1995 and repr.), pp. 240–56; Ian Short, 'Patrons and Polyglots: French Literature in Twelfth-Century England', *ANS*, 14 (1991): 229–49; Loveday Gee, *Women, Art and Patronage from Henry III to Edward III, 1216–1377* (Woodbridge, 2002); J. Wogan-Browne, 'Cest livre liseez ... chescun jour': Women and Reading *c*.1230–*c*.1430', in Wogan-Browne (ed.), *Language and Culture in Medieval Britain: the French of England c. 1100–c. 1500* (York, 2009), pp. 239–53.

[4]   See John Spence, 'The *Mohun Chronicle*: an Introduction, Edition and Translation', *Nottingham Medieval Studies* 55(2011): 153–219, for a pre-publication sight of which I am grateful to the author. See also his invaluable broader account of Anglo-Norman prose history writing: J.W. Spence, 'Anglo-Norman Prose Chronicles and Their Audiences', in *English Manuscript Studies, 1100–1700: XIV, Regional Manuscripts*, ed. A.S.G. Edwards (London, 2008), pp. 27–59, and on the genealogical aspects of *Mohun* and other chronicles, John Spence, 'Genealogies of Noble Families in Anglo-Norman', in Raluca L. Radulescu and Edward D. Kennedy (eds), *Broken Lines: Genealogical Literature in Medieval Britain and France* (Turnhout, 2008), pp. 63–77. Dr Spence has also contributed an edition of the *Mohun Chronicle* Prologue to J. Wogan-Browne, Thelma Fenster and Delbert Russell (eds), *Vernacular Literary Theory and Practices 1100–1500: the French of England* (forthcoming).

composed by Abbot Walter de la Hove of Newenham, a Cistercian foundation of the Mohuns.[5] According to John Osborne, clerk of Joan de Mohun, Constable of Dunster Castle, and author in 1350–1351 of a Mohun register, the abbot of Newenham had given an account of Mohun events and possessions in his Red Book 'for the utility and profit of the lords of Dunster and most of all to the praise and glory of his most noble lady, Lady Joan de Mohun' and this book is most probably to be identified with the *Mohun Chronicle*.[6]

The *Mohun Chronicle* is not mentioned in Antonia Gransden's survey of history writing in medieval Britain, understandably so: only the first quire of the chronicle is extant and that in a single fragmentary mid fourteenth-century manuscript, British Library Additional MS 62929, decorated formally but modestly with flourished and coloured capitals, and containing only the opening

---

[5]   On Walter de Hove see James Davidson, *The History of Newenham in the County of Devon* (London, 1843), pp. 75–87; *The Heads of Religious Houses in England and Wales II 1216–1377*, ed. David M. Smith and Vera C.M. London (Cambridge, 2001), pp. 297–8. De Hove's abbacy began in 1338 and his successor was installed by 1361, but it is not known if de Hove's abbacy continued after 1348. *Mohun* must be before 1350–51 but may be earlier.

[6]   'ad utilitatem et proficuum dominorum de dunstor et maxime ad laudem et magnificentiam nobilissime domine sue domina Johanna de mohune': Osborne's statement is extant in the early seventeenth-century transcription of Richard St George, Norrey King at Arms, in London, British Library, Add. MS 47176, fol. 24v, and was identified by Sir Herbert Maxwell-Lyte as taken from now lost folios from the Mohun Register extant in BL, MS Egerton 3724: H.C. Maxwell-Lyte, *A History of Dunster* (2 vols, London, 1909), I, pp. vii–viii, 49. In an indenture of 1349 Osborne styles himself 'general attourne Monsur Johan de Mohun' [*Documents and Extracts Illustrating the History of Dunster*, ed. H.C. Maxwell-Lyte, Somerset Record Society 33 (London, 1917–1918), pp. 83–4], but he will also have dealt extensively with Joan as the Mohun possessions were made over to her (see n. 46 below). The application of Osborne's remark to the chronicle cannot be completely unambiguous [it is for instance possible that, although the extant Newenham Cartulary and the Newenham Register (Oxford, Bodleian Library, MS Top. Devon d. 5 and BL, MS Arundel 17 respectively) do not show signs of having had red covers, either of them, rather than the chronicle itself, may have been the book in question, since events and possessions might well be noted in any of these genres of text]. John Osborne, the 'clerk and servant' of Lady Joan, would also be a possible candidate for the chronicle authorship, but *Mohun*'s emphasis on the value of the histories written by 'gent de religion' favours monastic authorship. The presence in Bodleian Library, MS Top. Devon d. 5 of Anglo-Norman passages on the kings of France 'apres la destruccion de troie' from Pharamon to Louis VIII (fols 88v–89r) and one on the kings of England from the Anglo-Saxon heptarchy to Edward III (fols 104v–110r) suggests preparation at Newenham towards the information offered in *Mohun*: and the style and hands of the cartulary and the chronicle are very similar. For a full account and a careful scrutiny of Maxwell-Lyte's arguments see now Spence, 'The *Mohun Chronicle*', pp. 169–72.

quire of *Mohun*.[7] A few further passages survive in extracts made by sixteenth-and seventeenth-century antiquaries.[8] Moreover, the text's opening as we have it is largely concerned with semi-legendary origin stories of the kind often considered to have little to contribute to history conceived as the record of events.

Yet, however modest the extant survival, the intentions of the *Mohun Chronicle* were grand, and they have much to reveal of the seigneurial mentalities and lineage concerns in which women were often cultural as well as biological players. The prologue promises a history moving from Adam to the Incarnation, the settlement of England, the history of the popes, the archbishops of Canterbury and the kings of France and England, and finally to the story of

> coment la noble lignage des Mohuns vint odve William, conquerour d'Engleterre,
> et combien des grandz seignurs William de Moion le Veil aveit a sa retenance
> adonqes; et puis del decent des Mohuns jusqes a cesti jour. (Fol. 1r, 38–40)

> [how the noble lineage of the Mohuns came with William, Conqueror of England,
> and how many great lords William de Moion the Older had in his retinue at that
> time, and then about the descent of the Mohuns up to the current day.]

Universal history is thus pressed into service to place the Mohun lineage in relation to the Roman, Christian and Anglo-French successions in world affairs.

We can observe here a doubling and updating of diasporas by which links to Normandy and the Conqueror make Normandy 'the Troy of the English nobility'.[9] William de Mohun, as it happens, did actually come from Normandy, from Moyon, near St Lo – and he is in Domesday Book as having been rewarded by the Conqueror with English lands[10] – but the grand retinue assigned to him by

---

[7]   Antonia Gransden, *Historical Writing in England, c. 1307 to the Early Sixteenth Century*, vol. 2 (London, 1996, repr.; 1974, 1982). *Mohun* was partially edited by Ethel Lega-Weekes, 'The Mohun Chronicle at Haccombe', *Devon Notes and Queries*, 4 (1906–1907): 17–22: see also H.C. Maxwell-Lyte, 'The Mohun Chronicle at Haccombe', *Devon Notes and Queries*, 4 (1906–1907): 249–52 (p. 251 on the chronicle as the Red Book of Newenham).

[8]   Spence (ed.), 'The *Mohun Chronicle*' provides editions and translations of the extant early modern transcriptions from *Mohun*.

[9]   See Elisabeth van Houts, 'The Ship List of William the Conqueror', *Anglo-Norman Studies*, 10 (1987): 159–83; Gudrun Tscherpel , 'The Political Function of History: the Past and Future of Noble Families', in Eales and Tyas (eds), *Family and Dynasty*, pp. 87–104, at p. 91.

[10]   K.S.B. Keats-Rohan, *Domesday People: a Prosopography of Persons Occurring in English Documents, 1066–1166. I. Domesday Book* (Woodbridge, 1999), p. 476, H.C. Maxwell-Lyte, *Dunster and its Lords 1066–1881* (printed in Exeter for private circulation, 1882), p. 1.

the *Mohun Chronicle* comes courtesy of a misreading of a list of the Conqueror's companions in a twelfth-century history of the Normans, the *Roman de Rou*, by the Jersiaise poet Wace. (In Wace's verse history, William de Mohun is *one* of, not *the lord* of, the fifty-seven names among which he figures.)[11] The historical 'error' here in *Mohun* – making William de Mohun the overlord of so many *grandz seignurs* among the Conqueror's companions – is an opportune one that trumps the more usual claim simply to have participated in the Conquest.

As John Spence has shown, many sources have been drawn on in the *Mohun* prologue: in addition to the *Roman de Rou*, a version of Josephus for an opening image of Adam inscribing two pillars with all human knowledge so it may survive fire and flood, Martinus Polonus's *Chronicle of Popes and Emperors*, perhaps Higden's *Polychronicon*, the continental *Pseudo-Turpin Chronicle*.[12] However, most important, and echoing through the prologue, are the perspectives of the *Brut*, the portmanteau medieval name for the vast array of French, Middle English and Latin re-workings that followed Geoffrey of Monmouth's account of the originary Trojan diaspora and the foundation of Britain, his *History of the Kings of Britain*. The impact of this work on both clerical and lay audiences as a supplement and challenge to Bedan history, as a reinvention and extension of Virgilian Roman history and ultimately as the stimulus for a more secular non-Augustinian historiography is well established.[13] However, the *Brut* that was most influential throughout the fourteenth and fifteenth centuries, the prose *Brut* composed in the French of England at the beginning of the fourteenth century (with subsequent reworkings in Middle English and Latin), has only recently had its first modern edition.[14] It is this *Brut* and its variants that formed the basis of most people's 'vision of history'. The name *Brut* invokes, even more than that of

---

[11] *Roman de Rou*, ed. A.J. Holden, SATF (3 vols, Paris, 1970–1973), 2, vv. 8487–8544: only vv. 8487–8 concern William de Moion: they state that he came over with some companions, but the following fifty-six lines constitute a separate listing of other knights.

[12] Spence (ed.), 'The Mohun Chronicle', pp. 161–7.

[13] See Francis Ingledew, 'The Book of Troy and the Genealogical Construction of History: the Case of Geoffrey of Monmouth's *Historia regum Britanniae*', *Speculum*, 69 (1994): 665–704; Richard Waswo, 'Our Ancestors, the Trojans: Inventing Cultural Identity in the Middle Ages', *Exemplaria*, 7 (1995): 269–90; Alan Shephard and Stephen D. Powell (eds), *Fantasies of Troy: Classical Tales and the Social Imaginary in Medieval and Early Modern Europe* (Toronto, 2003).

[14] *The Oldest Anglo-Norman Prose* Brut *Chronicle*, trans. and ed. Julia Marvin (Woodbridge, 2006). For the manuscripts of the Anglo-Norman prose *Brut*, see Ruth J. Dean with Maureen B.M. Boulton, *Anglo-Norman Literature: a Guide to Texts and Manuscripts*, ANTS OPS, 3 (London, 1999), nos 36, 42–49. For a general catalogue of *Brut* manuscripts in insular languages see Lister M. Matheson, *The Prose Brut: the Development of a Middle English Chronicle* (Tempe, AZ, 1988).

Arthur, the whole identity and history of Britain and the changing successions of peoples and lineages in it.[15]

Brut themes and perspectives are pervasive in seigneurial historiography, as they are in romance and other literature, and will have been known to nobles, gentry and the administrative and professional groups associated with them among whom such histories were produced.[16] Sir Thomas Gray's own Anglo-Norman *Scalacronica* (begun 1355–1356), Trevet's *Chroniques* for Princess Mary, granddaughter of Eleanor of Provence (1330s?), the 'ancestral romance' of *Fouke Fitz Waryn* (in an early fourteenth-century prose *remaniement* of a late thirteenth-century poem) and the *Wigmore Chronicle* earlier cited deploy *Brut* material, for instance, although seldom quite with *Mohun*'s particular plangency.[17] *Mohun* itself explicitly links the necessity of lineage commemoration and the transience noted by the *Brut*: we must, we ought to, it claims,

> put into writing the doings, sayings, names, lines of succession and good customs of our kin, and particularly of our founding ancestors, because it is thanks to their good deeds that we live and rejoice on earth and they live and rejoice in heaven; and because many things are forgotten with the passage of time, old age, various wars, and sudden changes of lineage [*par cours de longtenps, par grande age, par diverses gueres, et par sodeine mutacions des lignages*], unless they are recorded in a book by men of religion ... And because of such changes no living people has a greater need to learn the history of the world and of the holy church than the great lords of England, for many reasons, and particularly because England has often been troubled by war since the time of Brutus, and still it is not stable, nor

---

[15]   As Ingledew points out, the *Brut* was assimilated to universal and biblical history: the dual use of *Brut* and Bible is characteristic of historiography as practised and consumed by both the lay and religious alike: 'Book of Troy', pp. 665–6.

[16]   On the audiences of prose historiography see Spence, 'Anglo-Norman Prose Chronicles'; *Oldest Prose* Brut, ed. Marvin; and Julia Marvin, 'The Vitality of Anglo-Norman in Late Medieval England: the Case of the Prose *Brut* Chronicle', in Wogan-Browne (ed.), *Language and Culture*, pp. 303–19. Joan de Mohun's brother, Bartholomew Burghersh the younger, is recorded by Froissart as quoting a prophecy from the *Brut* [Anthony Verduyn, *Oxford Dictionary of National Biography* (*ODNB*) *s.v.* Burghersh, Bartholomew, the younger].

[17]   For information on these texts see Dean and Boulton, *Anglo-Norman*, nos 74, 70, 156, 64. The Wigmore Chronicle manuscript includes a genealogy of the Mortimers' descent from Brutus: see Given-Wilson, 'Chronicles of the Mortimer Family', p. 70; images reprod. in Mary E. Giffin, 'A Wigmore Manuscript at the University of Chicago', *National Library of Wales Journal*, 7 (1951–1952): 316–25, plate VI (University of Chicago Library, MS 224, fols 51v–52r). For Trevet, a convenient full edition is Nicolas Trevet, *Les Cronicles*, ed. Alexander Rutherford, unpubl. PhD Diss., University of London, 1932. *Fouke Fitz Waryn* is translated by G.S. Burgess in *Two Medieval Outlaws* (Woodbridge, repr. 2007).

will it ever be [*nomeement pur ceo qe Engleterre ad esté puis le tenps Brutus par guerre troblé sovent, et enqore n'est ele pas bien estable, ne james serra*]. (Fol. 1r, 19–29; fol. 1v, 10–15)

Here indeed is a sense of how the grand themes of the *Brut* shape and express mentalities. The very notion of lineage as it developed from the twelfth century is hypostasized on stasis and immobility, on inalienable territory and continuous name, and yet the *Brut* template for lay historiography is inevitably founded on transience, on the changes that drive the historical perception of succession. Change –*mutacion* – is at once the terror of lineage and the precondition of its continuity. The *Brut* derives much of its power from this tension between the ever renewed desire for duration and the mutabilities of Britain's persistent multi-ethnicity and its *sodeine mutacions des lignages* – the changes of time, old age, sudden death, wars and the resulting changes in lordships, territories and names that are so vividly present in the lives of elite families.[18] Joan and John de Mohun must have known the longing for continuity: they had no sons and there were no Mohuns after their day living in the *caput* of the Mohun honour at Dunster Castle.[19]

In this context, *Mohun* gives the *Brut's* central convention of mutable toponymy striking treatment:

Further, one finds that several regions, towns, and surnames of great lords have changed: for example, England, which in earlier times was called Albion, then Great Britain; ... and London first had the name New Troy, afterwards Trinovant; York had the name Eborak, afterwards Kaer Ebrak.[20] And so, just as the names of regions and of great towns have changed with the passage of time, in the same way the surnames of the conquerors have changed, and in particular the name of the noble lineage of the Mohuns has changed, for the reasons given above. For

---

[18]   By the late thirteenth century Anglo-Norman *mutacion* and *transmutacion* had an additional, legal sense of 'transfer of an estate or of possesssion', see AND s.v. *transmutacion* and *Earliest English Law Reports*, ed. Paul Brand, 4 vols, Selden Society 111–12, 122–3 (London: 1996–2007), vol. 3, pp. 237, 296; vol. 4, p. 547.

[19]   Dunster Castle passed to the Luttrells, see p. 312 below: the barony devolved to the Lestranges: see n. 39 below.

[20]   Name-change, closely associated as it is with *translatio studii et imperii*, is a pervasive topos of *Brut* literature: see Gioia Paradisi, '"Par muement de langages". Il tempo, la memoria e il volgare in Wace', *Francofonia*, 45 (2003): 27–45 and Laurence Mathey-Maille, 'L'Etymologie dans le *Roman de Rou* de Wace', in Keith Busby, Bernard Guidot and Logan E. Whalen (eds), *De sens rassis. Essays in Honor of Rupert T. Pickens* (Amsterdam, 2005), pp. 404–14; Laurence Mathey-Maille, *Écritures du passé. Histoires des ducs de Normandie* (Paris, 2007), esp. pp. 214–17.

the first of them who ever came to this land were accustomed to be called by the surname "Moion", as it is written in the book of the conquerors and as it is found in ancient charters which the family has had made to the benefit of various abbeys and priories, until the time of the first John de Mohun, who removed a syllable of the surname "Moion" and had himself called "Mohun". [*'le quil dil sournon "Moion" osta un silable et fist apeler "Mohun".*] (Fol. 1r, 26–1v, 1–10).

There may have been pragmatic reasons for care about the Mohun surname – there was also a Mohaut of Hawarden in Flintshire,[21] to be distinguished from the Moions and their pre-Conquest origins in Moyon near St Lo in Normandy. However, the chronicle's intense focus on the *mutacion* of a syllable within the framework of the history of the world does more than this: it meets the anxieties attending *sodeine mutacions des lignages* with continuity in the lineal dignity of the Mohuns, the 'ancient charters which the family has had made to the benefit of abbeys and priories' (fol. 1v, 8–9 above) witnessing to the early surname. Against implacable transience, the chronicle presents a prehistory for the Mohun name in which linguistic change is a continuing form of Mohun agency: that syllable has not been effaced by time, but has been removed (*osta*) by the first John de Moion and the name *made* to become ('*fist* apeler') 'Mohun'.

The themes of the *Mohun* prologue suggest that its composer enters into the seigneurial anxieties of the Mohuns (if he was the abbot of Newenham, the fate of his abbey's founding family was not of course irrelevant to the abbey's own prospects, nor presumably was his own skill at brokering transience in representing their history) and that he shares their ethos. The prologue's sentiments, he asserts,

> must be cherished and heard gladly by all high-ranking men. For the good qualities of the world have diminished and the hearts of lords grown less resolute, so that a man never remembers as willingly as he once did the works of the ancients or the stories in which the great deeds are to be found that teach how one should have faith in God and live honorably in the world. (Fol. 2r, 1–8)

At the end of this passage, in the prologue's resonant concluding motto, the *Mohun Chronicle* offers, in the face of the change and transience it records, the fragile carapace of the chivalric memory of honour: 'car, *vivere sanz honur est morir*': 'to live without honour is to die' (fol. 2r, 9).[22]

---

[21]   The Mohaut barony died out in 1329 [*The Complete Peerage of England, Scotland Ireland, Great Britain and the United Kingdom* (henceforth CP), ed. G.E.C. Cockayne, vol. IX (1936), (repr. as a Microprint Edition, Stroud, 1982), vol.4, pp. 16–17].

[22]   The ending of the *Mohun* Prologue, including this phrase, is from an early-thirteenth-century version of the *Pseudo-Turpin Chronicle*, which circulated in England alongside the

Especially given the chivalric inflections of the *Brut* in *Mohun*, a quick reading might see the chronicle as inscribing an alliance between clerical and military men occlusive of women. However, apart from the respect paid by her clerk, John Osborne, to Joan de Mohun in the matter of Mohun records and the well established pattern of noblewomen's textual patronage in collaboration with their clerics and religious, *Mohun's* concern with a lineage of fighting and founding males is not at all incompatible with female involvement. As Elisabeth van Houts and others have shown, women have cultural duties in relation to memory as well as to begetting and may identify their interests for these purposes with their matrimonial lineage.[23] Joan is perfectly likely to have carried out the female roles of guardian of memory and lineage and family publicist. Espousing the dynastic hopes and sense of genealogical perspective so strongly represented by the *Brut* was scarcely something to be refused by elite women.[24]

And yet, male foundations may not constitute the only model of pertinence for women in *Brut* historiography. Prior to Brutus's foundation, *Mohun* presents an alternative and slightly scandalous stepmother for British history. After its formal prologue, *Mohun* moves briefly through a five ages universal chronicle scheme directly to the story of Albina (fol. 2r/22–2v/33). This at last increasingly well-known story is the prequel to British history: the narrative of an alternative female foundation in Albion. Its earliest known versions are Anglo-Norman verse and prose of, probably, the mid to late thirteenth centuries (subsequently translated into Latin and English), and it is a frequent, though not automatic, inclusion in many of the multitudinous manuscript versions of the prose *Brut*, right through to the second half of the fifteenth century.[25] The most common forms of the story

---

Anglo-Norman *Pseudo-Turpin: the Old French Pseudo-Johannes Version of the Pseudo-Turpin: a Critical Edition*, ed. R.N. Walpole (Berkeley, CA, 1976), I, p. 130, 'Prologue' ll. 15–20.

[23]   Elisabeth van Houts, *Memory and Gender in Medieval Europe 900–1200* (Basingstoke, 1999).

[24]   If *Mohun* was in some way an initiative of Abbot Walter's for the benefit of his house (as Phillip Morgan has kindly suggested to me), it would still be significant that Joan's clerk presents her as the de Mohun figure for whom documents and accounts are to be made (n. 6 above).

[25]   For the early verse version *Des Grantz Geanz*, see Dean and Boulton, *Anglo-Norman*, no. 36 and for the other Anglo-Norman versions of the Albina story, Dean and Boulton, *Anglo-Norman*, nos 37–41. For a foundational study based on the verse version but of general significance, see Lesley Johnson, 'Return to Albion', *Arthurian Literature*, 13 (1994): 19–40; for a prose version (Dean and Boulton, *Anglo-Norman*, no. 41) see Julia Marvin, 'Albine and Isabelle: Regicidal Queens and the Historical Imagination of the Anglo-Norman Prose *Brut* Chronicles', *Arthurian Literature*, 18 (2001): 143–91; for a translation into Latin see Julia Crick and James Carley, '*De Origine gigantum*: an annotated edition', ibid., 41–114. An important paper by Julia Crick, 'Albion before Albina' (given at Medieval Academy,

narrate the exiling of the daughters of the King variously of Greece or Syria for plotting to kill, or in some versions actually killing, their husbands on their wedding night. The women feel that their husbands, sub-kings to their father, are of lower rank than themselves, and resent what they perceive as disparagement (a perspective for which *Magna Carta* offers some support).[26] When the sisters' plot is variously either achieved or disclosed, they are set adrift in punishment, and their rudderless boat arrives at an island in the North Sea. The eldest sister, Albina, takes seisin of the land, which she names after herself as Albion. Lacking males, the women mate with incubi, and produce giants. Their descendant giants are eventually conquered and killed off when Brutus arrives, and thus more officially founds – through war and ethnic cleansing – a postcolonial society that is now going to be called Britain, and become not Albina but *Brut* territory and story.

As Christopher Baswell has written, 'if empire typically maps itself across a feminized geography, then that territorial body, or its receptive and marriageable heiress, has to arrive first'.[27] Yet although the Albina story occurs at the beginning of the *Brut* in sixteen out of twenty-six manuscripts of the Short Version and in many other *Brut* versions and manuscripts, it hardly ever becomes part of 'history', but remains always a prologue to it.[28] As Baswell argues, the paradoxes of Albina's position – 'a founder erased, a position both original and marginal, beginner of an alternate and unnerving lineage' – are replicated codicologically in the *Brut*: Albina is excluded from the carefully numbered sequence of chapters that begin with the arrival of Brutus, and almost none of 'the hundreds of copyists of the Anglo-Norman or Middle English redactions … ever chose to revise the *Brut*'s chapter numbers'.[29]

Vancouver, April 2008), illuminates the earlier history of the Albina story: see now also her 'Edgar, Albion and Insular Dominion', in Donald Scragg (ed.), *Edgar, King of the English 959–975* (Woodbridge, 2008), pp. 158–70.

[26]   Provision against unsuitable marriages enforced by the king on their daughters and widows had been one of the barons' concerns in *Magna Carta*: the Anglo-Norman term is current in the revisions of *Magna Carta* and in the law books, *t.* Edward II (see AND s.v. *desparagement*).

[27]   Christopher Baswell, 'Albyne Sails for Albion: Gender, Motion and Foundation in the English Imperial Imagination', in Peregrine Horden (ed.), *Freedom of Movement in the Middle Ages: Proceedings of the 2003 Harlaxton Symposium* (Donington, 2007), pp. 157–68, at p. 162.

[28]   Even the version closest to being an independent poem introduces itself as the origin story 'of the great giants' ('*des grantz geanz*') who first held Britain, incestuous, cannibal and associated with primordial chaos as these are, rather than as the story of Albina and the sisters from whom the giants were bred: see *Des Grantz Geanz*, ed. Georgine E. Brereton (Oxford, 1937), p. 2, vv. 1–4.

[29]   Baswell, 'Albyne Sails for Albion', ibid., p.165 and n. 22.

The *Mohun Chronicle*'s version of the Albina story, however, integrates it into the Brutus era:

> Brutus came first to this land twelve hundred years before the birth of our lord Jesus Christ. And this was in the third age between Abraham and David. The histories by Gildas say that this was at the time that Eli was judge among the sons of Israel. This land was named Britain the Great after Brutus's name. But before the coming of Brutus, this kingdom was called Albion after a woman who was the first creature of human lineage who ever came to this land. She was called Albina, and she was daughter to a king of Greece who had thirty daughters and no sons. (Fol. 2r, 23–33)[30]

Mohun also, uniquely among all the many Albina variants as far as I know, focuses on Albina *and on one other sister*. Among the thirty daughters of the sonless king of (in this version) Greece, these two alone plot poisoning rather than throat-cutting and not of their husbands, but of 'all their *sisters* and their father, so as to have the whole realm of Greece to themselves' (*totes lour seors et lour pere, d'avoir a elles meismes tot le roialme de Grece entier*, fol. 2v, 2–3). Their plot fails and the two sisters are set adrift in a rudderless boat, but once arrived at the nameless land in the North Sea, in again, an unparalleled motif, the younger sister disputes Albina's seisin of the land, thus provoking a double landing:

> A wind sprang up and drove them to Dartmouth beyond the shores of Greece (*a Dertemuth hors de Grece*). And the ship came in to the land. Then the elder sister, Albina, jumped out of the ship and said, 'This land is mine, and I alone will hold it'. The other replied that she would have half of it. Then a great struggle sprang up between them, with the result that the younger sister was not allowed to get out of the ship. But a wind came and drove her to Southampton and she took land there. Thus she was there, and the other sister at Dartmouth. (Fol. 2v, 7–14)[31]

---

[30] 'Avant la nativité nostre seignur ihu crist mil cc ans vint Brutus primes en ceste terre. Ceo fust en la tierce age parentre Abrahim et Dauid. Les estories de Gildas dient qe ceo fust en le tenps qe Ely fust juge des filz Israël. Apres le non de Brutus fust ceste tere nomee Britaigne la grande, mais avant la venue Brutus fust cesti roialme apelé Albion après une feme qe fust la primere creature de humeine lignage qe en nul tenps vint en ceste tere. La quele fust apelé Albine, et ele fust fille au un Roi de Grece, le quil Roi avoit XXX filles et nul fils' (fol. 2r, 23–33).

[31] 'Sourvint un vent et les chacia a Dertemuth hors de Grece. Et vint la neoft a la terre. Donques la eisné seor Albine sailli hors del neoft et dist, "Ceste terre est a moi. Et ieo l'avra soulle". L'autre respondi q'elle avreit la moitié. Puis grand contak sourdi entre elles, issint qe la poisné seor ne fust pas seofferte issir hors del neoft. Mais un vent vint et la chacia a Hamptone et la prist ele terre. Donques elle fust la et l'autre a Dertemuth' (fol. 2v, 7–14).

Mohun is also the only Albina version to specify the site of the sisters' landfall apart from the version in Sir Thomas Gray's *Scalacronica*.[32] In *Mohun*, although the landfall is not, as one might perhaps expect, at Dunster, but divided between Dartmouth and Southampton, the sisters' destinations show a well-informed grasp of regional priorities. Dunster Haven, though it was a medieval port for Gascon wine and also for a largely insular wool and clothmaking trade, was gradually silting up: moreover, being on the north side of the Devon peninsula, Dunster is in any case not where one would first land 'hors de Grece'. Rather, with their Dartmouth and Southampton landings, the sisters focus each half of the country on one of the two major medieval ports of the south west coast. Dartmouth, the home base of Edward III's navy, was of high strategic and defence value and Southampton was the major early port between Winchester and Normandy and, from the thirteenth century onwards, a vital port for the continental wool trade. Up river from Dartmouth is Totnes, site of Brutus's landfall in Britain. Dunster is about equidistant from both these south coast ports. The Mohun *Chronicle* is *au courant* in its updating of Brutus' Totnes to Albina's Dartmouth: Totnes had had jurisdiction over the settlement at the mouth of the Dart, but only up to the early fourteenth century when Dartmouth was taken over by the crown.[33] A historiographic template for the entire country's

[32]   Gray has thirty-three sisters plotting to kill their husbands and their boat lands them all in Galloway on the south west coast of Scotland (Cambridge, Corpus Christi College, MS 133, fol. 29v). The sisters land at the Rhins peninsula ('rennes de Galewey', fol. 29v, col. b), which stretches from Stranraer in the north to the Mull of Galloway in the South. The specific force of Gray's Galloway allusion is not clear to me, other than that, having begun *Scalacronica* in 1355–56 as a prisoner of the Scottish Wars in Edinburgh Castle, and being himself from a northern family, he would have been aware of northern and Scottish topographies. However, his very different handling of Albina exemplifies adaptation for particular regional and lineage perspectives, just as the *Mohun* version's view-point is south western.

[33]   Maryanne Kowaleski, 'Shipping and the Carrying Trade in Medieval Dartmouth', in Marie-Luise Heckmann and Jens Röhrkasten (eds), *Von Nowgorod bis London. Studien zu Handel, Wirtschaft und Gesellschaft im mittelalterlichen Europa. Festschrift für Stuart Jenks zum 60. Geburtstag*, Nova Mediaevalia. Quellen und Studien zum europäischen Mittelalter, 4 (Göttingen, 2008), pp. 465–87, at pp. 465–70, whom I thank for this reference and much helpful information on ports. For Totnes records see Hugh R. Watkin, *The History of Totnes Priory and Medieval Town* (Torquay: published by the author, 1914): for a burgage in Dartmouth in which the Mohuns had a share from 1272 to 1307 see also Watkin, *Dartmouth, vol 1, Pre-Reformation*, Parochial Histories of Devonshire, 5 (Torquay, 1935), p. 10. Like Totnes, Southampton's name was resonant through its inclusion in legendary histories: in Geoffrey of Monmouth, Southampton is a destination for one of the major roads of Britain ('usque ad Portum Hamensis extensa', see Michael D. Reeve (ed.) and Neil Wright (trans.), *The History of the Kings of Britain: an Edition and Translation* of De gestis Britonum (Historia regum Britanniae) (Woodbridge, 2008), III, 39, p. 53.

foundation seems here to have been applied with specific customization to the *Mohun* perspective on Britain as the two sisters' contest makes the south west coast the gateway to Albion.

Such competition with Albina is unknown except in *Mohun*, but competition between inheritors was certainly possible in a system that allowed parcenary inheritance among daughters to take precedence over more distant male heirs. John Hudson notes that, from the late twelfth century, direct female heirs were preferred to collateral male heirs: 'a daughter is to be preferred to a nephew in inheritance from the father'.[34] According to the law-code *Britton*, where a tenancy in chief from the king, 'descends to several daughters or their issue, as one heir, the eldest shall do homage to us for all her parceners, and the others shall do homage to the eldest'.[35] However, Bracton cites 'another way and another form where several parceners, co-heirs having one right, claim by the assise, as several women of whom some are married and some not'.[36] Further divisions of property could thus be made among younger female siblings (especially if unmarried and therefore unable to transmit property to their husbands), so that a younger sister could indeed claim land.[37]

The treatment of Albina and her sister in *Mohun* is of special interest in a family that produced only daughters. Very good marriages were made for them all, but as they were daughters, this could not sustain the Mohun name, however helpful to the family in its position and connections.

Elizabeth de Mohun was married at the age of six to William Montague, Earl of Salisbury, in 1349, immediately after the annulment of his marriage with Joan of Kent, and eventually had one son, who was accidentally killed by his own father in a tournament in 1382;[38] Maud or Matilda de Mohun died in 1397, having married Sir John le Strange of Knockin, and having had one son, Richard, through whom the de Mohun barony ultimately went to the Stranges and the

---

[34]   John Hudson, 'Court Cases and Legal Arguments in England, c.1066–1166', *Transactions of the Royal Historical Society*, 6th series, 10 (2000): pp. 91–115, at p. 111.

[35]   'De Mariage', in F.M. Nichols, ed., *Britton* (2 vols, Oxford, 1865), Book III, chapter 3; online at www.anglo-norman.net/texts/.

[36]   Bracton, *De Legibus Et Consuetudinibus Angliæ*, vol. III, p. 250, online at http://hlsl5.law.harvard.edu/bracton/.

[37]   For the background see S.F.C. Milsom, 'Inheritance by Women in the Twelfth and Early Thirteenth Centuries', in M.S. Arnold, T.A. Green, S.A. Scully and S.D. White (eds), *On the Laws and Customs of England: Essays in Honor of Samuel E. Thorne* (Chapel Hill, NC, 1981), pp. 60–89, at pp. 69–71. See further work on Albina and legal discourse forthcoming by my former graduate student Laura J. Shafer.

[38]   John L. Leland in *Oxford Dictionary of National Biography on-line*, s.v. William Montague, second earl of Salisbury, 1328–1397.

Table 14.1 The Mohun daughters and their marriages

Joan de Burghersh (d. 1404)	*m.*	**(shortly before 1341) John de Mohun V, Lord of Dunster (d. 1375)**
(i) Elizabeth (1343–1415)	*m.*	William Earl of Salisbury (1328–1397)
	one son, d. 1382.	
(ii) Maud/Matilda (d. 1397)	*m.*	Sir John le Strange of Knockin
	one child, Richard	
(iii) Philippa (d. 1431)	*m.*	(i) Walter Lord Fitzwalter (d. 1386) (ii) Sir John Golafre (d. 1396) (iii) (by 1398) Edward, Duke of York (d. 1415)

Stanleys.[39] The third daughter, Philippa, married (i) William, Lord Fitzwalter, (ii) Sir John Golafre, a chamber knight of Richard II and (iii) Edward, Duke of York, and she had no children by any of her marriages.[40] In their life-time, Joan and John de Mohun's sonlessness was compounded by the increasingly shaky hold the Mohuns had on their property, which was repeatedly mortgaged by this financially declining family.[41]

Joan herself was the daughter of Bartholomew Burghersh the elder (d. 1355), soldier and diplomatic envoy, and chamberlain to Edward III.[42] Her uncle, Henry Burghersh, Bishop of Lincoln (d. 1340) obtained the marriage of

---

[39]   At the death of this child's last surviving aunt, Philippa, in 1431, the barony was taken out of abeyance and devolved, through him and his mother Maud, coheir of John de Mohun, to the Stranges and the Stanleys (CP IX, p. 25).

[40]   The *Westminster Chronicle* notes the marriage of Sir John Golafre to 'filiam domini de Mohoun, que quondam fuit copulata domino filio Walteri': *The Westminster Chronicle 1381–1394*, ed. L.C. Hector and Barbara F. Harvey (Oxford, 1982), pp. 406–407 and n. 4. Philippa's last and most illustrious husband, whom she married in 1398, died at Agincourt in 1415 and Philippa herself died in 1431, see Rosemary Horrox, *ODNB, s.v.* Edward duke of York *c.* 1373–1415, under Family Life.

[41]   See further n. 46 below.

[42]   Anthony Verduyn, *ODNB, s.v.* Bartholomew Burghersh the elder (d. 1355).

the fifth John de Mohun (c. 1320–1375) and custody of his lands on the death of John's grandfather in 1330, and John was married to Joan de Burghersh in or before 1341.[43] In this year John de Mohun was given livery of his inheritance, the lordship of Dunster Castle. John de Mohun did well as a military man, fighting against the Scots and the French (1346–1347). He was a member of the Black Prince's household (of which his father-in-law was master) and part of the close-knit group of earls, barons and knights who fought at Crécy and who were the original members of the order of the Garter when the first liveries were given in 1348.[44] This group included his wife's brother, Bartholomew Burghersh the younger and, after 1349, his daughter's husband, William Montague. However, his military world was failing by this time: there would be no further major military successes between the Black Prince and Henry V, and John de Mohun, although regularly summoned to Parliament and once (in 1342) to a council, held only commissions in his own Somerset region and no civilian office at court: he does not seem to have been as successful in peacetime as in war. As a baron he failed his family in custodianship and succession – he began spending his inheritance as soon as he got it, died with debts outstanding and produced no sons.[45]

The *Mohun Chronicle* might well be seen in the context of very real threats of transience both felt and resisted by the Mohuns, dependent as they were on traditional landholding, but not apparently producing enough income to carry on much longer. At the period of *Mohun*'s composition, most probably shortly before the mid-century, the Mohuns were manoeuvring to hold onto Sir John's inheritance, largely by transferring it temporarily to his wife. From 1346 to 1350 they conveyed, reconveyed and mortgaged Dunster Castle, and the Mohun lands fell largely into Joan de Mohun's hands: in 1355 Sir John made over to his wife forty-three title deeds relating to their Dunster manors and

---

[43]   CP IX, pp. 23–4; Nicholas Bennett, *ODNB, s.v.* Henry Burghersh (c. 1290–1340). John's marriage and lands were subsequently transferred to the Bishop of Norwich and in 1334 his marriage was in the custody of Bartholomew Burghersh the elder, Joan's father (Maxwell-Lyte, *History of Dunster*, I, pp. 43–4; Robert W. Dunning, *ODNB, s.v.* John Mohun, 1320?–1375).

[44]   *ODNB, s.v.* John Mohun (1320?–1375) and under Founding Knights of the Order of the Garter.

[45]   His will of 1342 already mentions creditors (Mawell-Lyte, *History of Dunster*, I, p. 46). In the *Mohun Register* (London, BL, MS Egerton 3724, Davis no. 1285), there is an advice poem drawing on estate management manuals and conduct books and probably designed for John de Mohun ['En sa veillesce siet le prodhom', ed. Ruth J. Harvey, *Anglo-Norman Anniversary Essays*, ed. Ian Short, ANTS OPS, 2 (London, 1993), pp. 159–78, at p. 161; Dean and Boulton, *Anglo-Norman*, no. 396, also 395].

other holdings.[46] However, although Dunster Castle had been mortgaged, the brilliant marriage between the six-year-old Elizabeth de Mohun and the Earl of Salisbury had been made (in 1349), and John de Mohun's successful relations with his fellow soldiers and relatives in the royal circle were being consolidated both by this marriage and his inclusion in the founding members of the Order of the Garter (1348–1349). Joan de Mohun's vision for her chronicle may have involved affirming, through the representation of their place and topography in the great founding history of the *Brut*, that the Mohuns belonged by ancient right at the heart of the elite. More specifically, in the inclusion of the by no means obligatory Albina story, her version of the *Brut* narrative organizes a properly ancient past of female foundresses for a family where daughters were the future. It provides a political tool for her daughters, especially as an assertion of Mohun prestige that might bolster Elizabeth de Mohun's status as she entered the family of the Earls of Salisbury.[47] There were reasons both positive and negative for turning to the past to affirm present prestige and to try to build a future.

There may be further ways in which we can use Joan's chronicle to think about her own career. John de Mohun died in 1375, and a year later, Joan completed the sale of her own life-interest in Dunster to Elizabeth Luttrell for a large sum, and shut up the castle of Dunster on its Somerset Tor.[48] She went off to spend what turned out to be a widowhood of some thirty years at court and also in Canterbury. Joan outlived Elizabeth Luttrell, who never had her side of the bargain in person, although the Luttrells did get Dunster Castle in the end. A friend of, or at the least in high favour with, Richard II and Queen Anne, Joan

---

[46]   For details, see Maxwell-Lyte, *History of Dunster*, I, pp. 46–50. The Mohuns recovered the castle in 1355, at which point the forty-three manors were handed over. Maxwell-Lyte calculates that by 1348 Joan had a life interest in almost all the manors belonging to her husband in England (p. 48).

[47]   There may have been only two daughters at mid-century: if the third daughter, Philippa, was born in 1345 directly after the others, she would have been about eighty-six at her death in 1431 and fifty-three when she married the twenty-five-year-old Duke of York. This is not absolutely impossible, but Philippa may have been born significantly later than her sisters, and if this was after the chronicle was completed, it bears on the unusual choice of two sisters in its Albina narrative. I am grateful to Sethina Watson for valuable discussion and encouragement to think further about *Mohun*'s occasion and purposes.

[48]   The text of the agreement (in French) is quoted from Dunster Castle Muniments I, 32, by Maxwell-Lyte, *History of Dunster*, I, p. 53. A deposit of 200 *livres* was part of the agreement in case it was not carried through owing to objection from the de Mohun daughters. They had been co-heirs until Joan sold the reversion to Elizabeth Luttrell, and Elizabeth and Philippa de Mohun and their husbands as well as Maud/Matilda's son, Richard Lord Strange of Knockin, challenged the agreement after Joan's death (ibid., pp. 83–6).

also continued skilfully dealing in land and money with them both, exchanging an annuity by which her service was rewarded for the manor of Macclesfield and later acquiring the lease of Leeds Castle in Kent.[49] Like some other widows and daughters of the founding Knights of the Garter, Joan and her daughter, the Countess of Salisbury, were given livery of the Order of the Garter in 1384.[50] Joan was among the three ladies of court *'specialiter'* compelled to abjure the court by the Appellants in their purge of Richard II's counsellors in 1387–1388.[51] It is true that these women were merely banished, not, like Richard's favourite counsellors, executed, but that initial banishment by the Appellants and the fact that Joan was back in court by the 1390s[52] suggests that she was both privately and publicly acknowledged as someone valued by the king. Joan died in 1404 and was not buried beside her husband: she commissioned her own stone monument in the Black Prince's Chapel of Our Lady in the crypt of Canterbury cathedral.[53] This she had inscribed with both her maiden and her married name: 'Johane de Borwasche ke feut dame de Mohun'.[54] The monument shows her not in widow's weeds but in fashionable low-cut clothing with jewelled buttons,[55] a woman who had prospered by movement, by financial acuity, by trading in, not

---

[49]   Maxwell-Lyte, *Dunster and its Lords*, p. 21. Nigel Saul notes that Joan was Richard II's friend: *Richard II King of England 1367–1400* (New Haven, CT, 1997), p. 318 n. 110: she was sometimes referred to as the king's 'cosyn'.

[50]   These were awarded in that year to the widows and daughters of original Knights of the Garter, founded in 1348: these included John de Mohun (KG 1348), Bartholomew Burghersh the younger (KG 1348) and both Elizabeth de Mohun's husbands: see Hugh E.L. Collins, *The Order of the Garter 1348–1461: Chivalry and Politics in Late Medieval England* (Oxford, 2000), pp. 302, 289. Collins comments on the political signals sent by distributing livery to kinswomen (pp. 80–81).

[51]   The *Westminster Chronicle* notes that, following the arrests and the forced abjurations of the court on 1 January 1388, there were also three ladies who abjured the court, 'scilicet domina de Ponyngg, domina de Mohon, et domina de Molyns' (that is, Blanche, Lady Poynyngs, widow of Sir John Worth, a steward of Joan of Kent and executor of her will; Joan de Mohun; Margery, widow of Sir William de Moleyns, d. 1381), see *The Westminster Chronicle 1381–1394*, ed. Hector and Harvey, pp. 230 and 231 and nn. 15–17. The women are also noted in *The St Albans Chronicle: The Chronica maiora of Thomas Walsingham*, ed. John Taylor, Wendy Childs and Leslie Watkiss (Oxford, 2003), p. 848.

[52]   Nigel Saul notes that Joan was back in favour in the 1390s (*Richard II*, p. 370).

[53]   Joan de Mohun founded a chantry in the crypt in 1396, but masses were said for her in the cathedral in the 1370s, and in early 1371–1372, some three years before John de Mohun's death, 'Lady de Maun' is recorded as donating £66 13s 4d and an iron grille at the west end (paid for in 1378–1380): Nicholas Pevsner and Priscilla Metcalf, *The Cathedrals of England: the South-East* (London, 2005), pp. 16–17.

[54]   Maxwell-Lyte, *History of Dunster*, 1, p. 55.

[55]   Reproduced as an engraving based on the etching in Stothard's 'Monumental

by holding onto land, and by using the skills of a courtier in her successful service as a lady in waiting – a woman, that is, who had organized a different future for herself once John de Mohun and, with him, her lineage responsibilities, had gone to the grave. For John de Mohun, soldier and baron in a changing world, that grave was a tomb in the family Augustinian foundation of Bruton in Somerset, not a monument in the Black Prince's chapel in Canterbury.[56]

In her will of October 1404, Joan de Mohun gives a psalter bound in white to Archbishop Arundel (fol. 218v, l. 5), one of her executors; and another 'beautiful' *Legenda sanctorum* and a 'book with painted pictures' ('unum librum pictum', fol. 218v, l. 6) to her son-in-law, the Duke of York. The duke's wife, Joan's daughter Philippa, gets the maternal blessing and some of Joan's best red wine ('unum rubrum meliorum quem habeo', ibid., l. 7) and is not mentioned among those living people for whom masses are to be said. Something of Joan's personality may be evidenced in the way in which, having thus dismissed Philippa, she gives 'to the countess of Salisbury my daughter', a cross which 'I used to say I will leave to the one I love best' together with a legendary.[57] Joan's youngest daughter Maud/Matilda had died in 1397: neither she nor her son, Joan's only living grandchild, are mentioned in the will.

Might not Joan's widowhood be viewed as the celebration of a different model of family, predicated not on male but female heirs, and on the inevitable but planned *mutacions des lignages* experienced by women in their mobility and disposal through marriage? In this model, not all wealth is gained through hanging on to land (such as the large and forbidding Dunster Castle, perhaps, after the Black Death, encumbered with labour problems), but through the mobile and dispersable system of court service and the trading of its rewards for annuities and shorter land tenures. Careers of Joan's kind are often seen in

---

Effigies' in Maxwell-Lyte, *Dunster and its Lords*, opposite p. 23 and in Maxwell-Lyte, *History of Dunster* I, as a photograph opposite p. 54.

[56]   *ODNB, s.v.* John de Mohun: Bruton was specified in John de Mohun's extant will, made in 1342 (Maxwell-Lyte, *History of Dunster*, I, pp. 46, 51).

[57]   'Item: lego comitisse de Salesburiensis filie mee unam crucem quam solebam dicere quem magis dilexero. illi legabo hunc crucem et eidem filiee mee lego unam legendum sanctorum', Lambeth Palace Library, Archbishop Arundel's register, vol. 1, fol. 218v, 7–8. The rest of the will (fols 218v–219r) involves Joan's household of servants, Canterbury churchmen and her then clerk, Philip Caxton (I thank Lambeth Palace Library for access to Arundel's Register). One *mutacion* Joan would not permit: in the initial agreement between her and Christ Church Priory in a deed of 1395, she stipulates that, in exchange for 350 marks sterling and gifts to the priory, her monument in the undercroft at Canterbury is to be permanently hers, not to have its name changed, and to be properly maintained: 'nec nomen illius tumbe mutabitur. sed honorifice custodietur' [*Inventories of Christ Church Canterbury*, ed. J. Wickham Legg and W.H. St John Hope (Westminster, 1902), pp. 99–100].

modern historiography as a form of 'bastard feudalism', dependent on affinity and its more temporary rewards, not on fixed ancestral land tenure,[58] and can usefully be thought about specifically in regard to women.

Joan's aims seem to have had less to do with stasis in land and lineage and more to do with financial security and domestic comfort (she got a dispensation of her rent for Leeds castle from Richard II when Queen Anne's death left Joan to pay for roof repairs), with display (Joan and her daughter Elizabeth in those garter robes) and so, perhaps, with pleasure and sociability.[59] Richard II's court was early noted by Gervase Matthew as importantly inclusive of women, and Joan de Mohun suggests some of the ways in which women could deploy the more mobile forms of power and reward.[60] Philippa, the daughter to whom Joan does her bare duty in her will, seems to have learned from this model and to have reproduced it on her own account. Having had not only no male heirs, but no children at all by her first two husbands, her third marriage, made by a woman not outstandingly rich, much older than the Duke of York, and with no history of heir production, seems extraordinarily like the marriage of a fascinating woman free to go after what she wanted. Certainly, in his will, Edward of York speaks of her as 'ma tresamee compaigne Phelippe', and leaves her 'mon lit de plumes et leopars' as well as lesser beds and other favoured objects.[61]

Joan and her daughters all turned out to have exceptionally long careers to organize and ones open to *mutacions* planned and unplanned, both as wives and widows. Even the shorter-lived second daughter, Maud/Matilda, must have been at least in her fifties when she died, and Joan and Philippa, like Elizabeth de Mohun (with her own tragic experience of sonlessness) lived at least into their seventies. The successes of Joan and Philippa, in particular, must have been partly a matter of skill as well as of luck. From their viewpoints, the instabilities of this world may have come to seem less tyrannical and more opportune than allowed for in the representation of such matters in historiographical orthodoxy. The figures of these women remind us that women are not only images *for* historiography, but themselves have histories with outcomes. As with the story of Albina and her sisters, what seems lack or loss may also become adventure,

58   Michael Hicks, *Bastard Feudalism* (London, 1995).
59   Maxwell-Lyte, *History of Dunster*, I, p. 54 [online at The National Archives, Ancient Petitions SC/8/221/11003 (1399)].
60   Gervase Mathew, *The Court of Richard II* (London, 1968), p. 28.
61   *Chichele's Register*, ed. E.F. Jacob (4 vols, Oxford, 1938–1947), II, p. 64. Edward's will was proved in November 1415. The will of Philippa's sister Elizabeth, Countess of Salisbury, proved January 1415, leaves 'a madame de York ma soire une anel dore ove une grand diamond' ('to Madame de York, my sister, a gold ring with a large diamond'), several other gold rings, and a gilded hanap and ewer, ibid., p. 16.

opportunity and the foundation of a different life. The Albina narrative that re-surfaces at the beginning of variant *Bruts* as the inauguration of history, memory, territory is often returned to the margins, but may nonetheless inspire alternative resolutions of the tension between stasis and change epitomized in the *Brut*.

Joan's own career seems an oscillation between centres and margins: from birth close to Edward III's household to the provinces and back to London and Canterbury, from a failing barony to an intimate position of favour at court where, although in one way at the margins of the political centre, she is also, as her Garter robes, expulsion, and return suggest, a figure of emblematic importance and resonance. For that matter, Camden reports that Joan de Mohun was supposed to have secured from her husband for a Common for their tenants as much land as she could walk round barefoot in a day.[62] This of course is the updating of a historiographical template familiar from many stories of female foundation – Dido and the bull-hide at Carthage, Domneva's white hind on the Isle of Wight – and many others, in which territory is carved out of the patrimony by female vision and ingenuity. That this template should be attached to Joan suggests that she too was perceived as a defender and definer of territory with the capacity to make history, indeed, that, like Albina, she moves flexibly amidst legend and historiography. She may have been a stepmother in some models of history – as for the great historian of the Mohuns, Sir Herbert Maxwell-Lyte, who reproaches her with ascendancy over her husband and unduly speedy action after his death, and who is unpleasantly struck by the fact that 'on the only occasion since the Norman Conquest on which Dunster Castle has passed by sale, it was sold by one woman and bought by another'.[63] Yet, like Albina herself, Joan de Mohun seems to have mothered a version of history in which women's agency plays a part.

[62] Maxwell-Lyte, *Dunster and its Lords*, p. 19: William Camden, *Brittania*, trans. Philemon Holland and rev. Edmund Gibbon, 3rd edn, vol 1 (London, 1753), col. 68.

[63] Maxwell-Lyte, *History of Dunster*, I, p.49; *Dunster and its Lords*, p. 20. For some of the constraints on widows' dowers via actions of waste and other legal instruments, see further Paul Brand, '*In perpetuum*; the Rhetoric and Reality of Attempts to Control the Future in the English Medieval Common Law', in J.A. Burrow and Ian Wei (eds), *Medieval Futures: Attitudes to the Future in the Middle Ages* (Woodbridge, 2000), pp. 101–13, at pp. 109–11; Leyser, *Medieval Women*, pp. 168–75.

Bibliography

A. Manuscripts

Baltimore

Walters Art Gallery, 10

Bethesda (MD)

NLM, E 8

Budapest

Széchényi Bibl. nat., clma 316

Cambridge

Christ's College Muniments, Creake Abbey, At/35a
Corpus Christi College, 133
Fitzwilliam Museum, 159
St John's College, D.4
Trinity College
    O.1.20
    R.14.30

Chicago

University of Chicago Library, 224

Copenhagen

Det Kgl. Bibliotek, Gamle Kgl. Samling, 1653

Leiden

Bibliotheek der Rijksuniversiteit, MS Lat. 76A

London

British Library
    Add. MS 11880
    Add. MS 47176
    Add. MS 61900
    Add. MS 62929
    Arundel 17
    Arundel 146
    Cotton Nero E.vii
    Cotton Vespasian E.xxv
    Egerton 3724
    Harl. 1240
    Harl. 1708
    Harl. 2110
    Harl. 4977
    Sloane 475
    Sloane 783 B
    Sloane 1621
Wellcome Institute for the History of Medicine
    Western MS 5650

Montpellier

Bibliothèque de la Faculté de médecine, 55

New York

New York Academy of Medicine, MS SAFE
Pierpont Morgan Library, 240

Oxford

Bodleian Library
    Ashmole 399
    Bodl. 361

Digby 79
Laud Misc. 567
Top. Devon d. 5

Exeter College, 35
Magdalen College Archives
    Brackley charters, 12
    Brackley charters, A4
    Brackley charters, A11
    Brackley charters, B117
    Brackley charters, B179
    Brackley charters, B229
    Brackley charters, C87
    Brackley charters, C108
    Brackley charters, C114
    Brackley charters, C125
    Brackley charters, D103
    Brackley charters, D116
    Brackley charters, D124
    Brackley charters, D219
    Brackley deeds, D136
Magdalen College Library
    273
    lat.173
New College archives
    charter no. 14063
    charter no. 14064
    charter no. 14065
Trinity College
    65

Paris

BnF
    Arsenal, 'Cris de Paris', no. 264
    lat. 7056
    lat. 9474
    nouv. acq. lat. 3145

Rheims

Bibliothèque municipale, 1395

St Petersburg

Publicnaja Biblioteka im. M.E. Saltykova-Scedrina, MS lat. F.v.VI.3

Stuttgart

Württembergerische Landesbibliothek, Cod. Bibl. 2° 23

Uppsala

University Library, C 15

Utrecht

Bibliotheek der Rijksuniversiteit, Utrecht, cod. 32

York

Minster Library, Additional 2

B. Primary Printed Sources

Aelredi Rievallensis Opera Omnia, I, ed. A. Hoste and C.H. Talbot, CCCM 1 (Turnhout: Brepols, 1971).

The Life of Ailred of Rievaulx by Walter Daniels, ed. F.M. Powicke (London: Nelson, 1950).

Alcuin, *De virtutibus et vitiis*, PL 101: 613–39.

Alexander of Hales, *Doctoris Irrefragibilis Alexandri de Hales Summa Theologica seu sic ab origine dicta 'Summa fratris Alexandri'*, ed. V. Doucet (Quaracchi: Coll. S. Bonaventura, 1924–1948).

Alexander of Hales, *Magistri Alexandri de Hales Glossa in Quatuor Libros Sententiarum*, vol. 3, Bibliotheca Franciscana Scholastica Medii Aevi, 14 (Quaracchi: Coll. S. Bonaventura, 1954).

Alfred, *King Alfred's West Saxon Version of Gregory's Pastoral Care*, ed. H. Sweet, EETS, 45, 50 (2 vols, London: published for Early English Text Society by N. Trübner & Co, 1871–1872).

Amalarius of Metz, *De ecclesiasticis officiis*, 3.5, PL 1011: 107–13.

Andrew of St Victor, *In Ezechielem*, ed. M.A. Signer, CCCM 6 (Turnhout: Brepols, 1991).

Annales Bertiniani, ed. F. Grat, J. Vielliard and S. Clémencet (Paris, 1964), trans. J.L. Nelson (Manchester: University of Manchester Press, 1991).

Annales Mettenses Priores, ed. B. von Simson, MGH SS rerum Germanicarum in usum scholarum [10] (Hannover, 1905); trans. P. Fouracre and R.A. Gerberding, *Late Merovingian France: History and Hagiography 640–720* (Manchester: University of Manchester Press, 1996).

Annales Monastici, ed. H.R. Luard (5 vols, London: Longman et al., 1864–1869).

Anselmi Opera Omnia, ed. F.S. Schmitt (2 vols, Stuttgart–Bad–Cannstatt: F. Frommann, 1968–1984).

Antiquities of Shropshire, ed. R.W. Eyton (2 vols, London: J.R. Smith, 1854–1860).

Asser, *De Rebus Gestis Aelfridi*, ed. W.H. Stevenson (Oxford: Clarendon Press, 1904).

Augustine, *Confessiones*, trans. R.S. Pine-Coffin (Harmondsworth: Penguin Classics, 1961).

Augustine, *Confessions*, trans. with intro. and notes Henry Chadwick (Oxford: Oxford University Press, 1991).

Augustine, *Confessions*, ed. J.J. O'Donnell (Oxford: Oxford University Press, 1992).

Augustine, *Enarrationes in Psalmos*, ed. E. Dekkers and I. Fraipont, CCSL, 38, Pss. I–L (Turnholt: Brepols, 1956).

Augustine, *Epistulae*, pt 3, ed. A. Goldbacher, CSEL, 44 (Vienna & Leipzig: F. Tempsky, 1904).

Augustine, *Quaestiones in Exodum* in *Quaestiones in Heptateuchum*, CCSL, 33 (Turnhout: Brepols, 1958).

Augustine, *Sermones de vetere testamento*, ed. C. Lambot, CCSL, 41 (Turnhout: Brepols, 1961).

Augustine, *De spiritu et littera*, PL 44: 199–246.

Augustine, *The Works of St Augustine: A Translation for the 21st Century*, trans. with notes E. Hill, ed. J.E. Rotelle (Brooklyn, NY: New City Press, 1990).

The Beauchamp Cartulary Charters 1100–1268, ed. E. Mason, Pipe Roll Society, n.s. 43 (London: J.W. Ruddock for the Pipe Roll Society, 1980).

Bede, *Ecclesiastical History of the English People*, ed. B. Colgrave and R.A.B. Mynors (Oxford: Clarendon Press, 1969).

Bede, *De Templo* and *De Tabernaculo*, ed. D. Hurst, Opera, CCSL, 119A (Turnhout: Brepols, 1969).

Benedict, *The Rule of St Benedict*, ed. and trans. J. McCann (London: Burns and Oates, 1952).

Bernard of Clairvaux, *Sancti Bernardi Opera*, ed. J. Leclercq, C.H. Talbot, H. Rochais (8 vols, Rome, 1957–1977).

Bernard of Clairvaux, *Sancti Bernardi Vita Prima*, in PL 185: 225–416; trans. Martinus Cawley, *Bernard of Clairvaux. Early Biographies* (Lafayette, OR, Guadalupe, 2000).

Bernard of Clairvaux, *Sermones in laudibus Virginis Matris*, in *Opera Bernardi*, ed. J. Leclercq and H. Rochais, vol. 4, trans. Marie-Bernard Saïd, *Homilies in Praise of the Blessed Virgin Mary* (Kalamazoo, MI: Cistercian Publications, 1993).

Birgitta, *Acta et processus canonizacionis beate Birgitte*, ed. I. Collijn, Samlingar utgivna av Svenska Fornskriftsäilskapet, 2, 1 (Uppsala: Almqvist & Wiksells, 1924–1931).

Birgitta, *Den heliga Birgittas Reuelaciones Extrauagantes*, ed. L. Hollmann, SFSS, 2, 5 (Uppsala: A & W, 1965).

Birgitta, *Heliga Birgitta. Åttabarnsmor och profet*, ed. B. Bergh (Stockholm: Historiska Media, 2002).

Birgitta, *Liber Celestis of Bridget of Sweden*, ed. R. Ellis, EETS OS 291 (Oxford: Oxford University Press, 1987).

Birgitta, *Opera Minora I: Regula Salvatoris*, ed. S. Eklund, SSFS, 2, 8:1 (Uppsala: Svenska fornskriftsällskapet, 1975).

Birgitta, *Opera Minora II: Sermo Angelicvs*, ed. S. Eklund, KVHAA, SSFS, 2, 8:2 (Uppsala: Svenska fornskriftsällskapet,1972).

Birgitta, *The Revelations of St. Birgitta of Sweden*, trans. D. Searby and B. Morris, vols 1 and 2 (New York: Oxford University Press, 2006, 2008).

Birgitta, *Sancta Birgitta: Revelaciones, Lib. I cvm Prologo Magistri Mathie*, ed. C.-G. Undhagen, Kungl. Vitterhets Historie och Antikvitets Handlingar (Uppsala: Svenska fornskriftsällskapet, 1977).

Birgitta, *Sancta Birgitta: Revelaciones, Lib. II*, ed. C.-G. Undhagen and B. Bergh, SSFS 2, 7:2 (Uppsala: Svenska fornskriftsällskapet, 2001).

Birgitta, *Sancta Birgitta: Revelaciones, Lib. III*, ed. A.-M. Jönsson, SSFS 2, 7:3 (Stockholm: Almqvist and Wiksell, 1998).

Birgitta, *Sancta Birgitta: Revelaciones. Lib. IV*, ed. H. Aili, SSFS, 2, 7:4, KVHAA (Uppsala: Svenska fornskriftsällskapet, 1992).

Birgitta, *Sancta Birgitta: Revelaciones, Lib. V: Liber Questionum*, ed. B. Bergh, SSFS 2, 7:5, KVHAA (Uppsala: Svenska fornskriftsällskapet, 1971).

Birgitta, *Sancta Birgitta: Revelaciones Lib. VI*, ed. B. Bergh, SSFS, 2, 7:6, KVHAA (Uppsala: Svenska fornskriftsällskapet, 1991).

Birgitta, *Sancta Birgitta: Revelaciones, Lib. VII*, ed. B. Bergh, SSFS 2, 7:7, KVHAA (Uppsala: Almqvist & Wiksell, 1967).

Birgitta, *Sancta Birgitta: Revelaciones, Book VIII*, ed. H. Aili, SFSS 2, 7:8 (Stockholm: Almqvist & Wiksell International, 2002).

Bonaventure, *Collationes de decem praeceptis*, in *Opera omnia*, 5 (Quaracchi: Coll. S. Bonaventura, 1891).

St Bonaventure's Collations on the Ten Commandments, trans. P.J. Spaeth, in *Works of St Bonaventure*, vol. 6, ed. F.E. Coughlin (St Bonaventure, NY: Franciscan Institute, 1995).

Bracton, H., *De Legibus et Consuetudinibus Angliæ*, vol. 3, online at http://hlsl5.law.harvard.edu/bracton/.

Building Accounts of King Henry III, ed. H.M. Colvin (Oxford: Clarendon Press, 1971).

Caesarius of Heisterbach, *Dialogus miraculorum*, ed. J. Strange (Cologne: J.M. Heberle, 1851; reprinted Ridgewood, NJ: Gregg Press, 1966).

Calendar of the Charter Rolls (London: PRO, 1904–).

Calendar of the Fine Rolls of the Reign of Henry III (Woodbridge: Boydell, 2007–).

Calendar of Wills Proved and Enrolled in the Court of Husting, London 1258–1688, ed. R.R. Sharpe (2 vols, London: J.C. Francis, 1889–1890).

Calendarium Genealogicum Henry III and Edward I, ed. C. Roberts (2 vols, London: Longmans, Green, 1865).

Charles IV, *Vita Caroli Quarti Die Autobiographie Karls IV*, ed. E. Hillenbrand (Stuttgart: Fleischhauer und Spohn, 1979); and English translation by B. Nagy and F. Schaer, *The Autobiography of the Emperor Charles IV* (Budapest: Central European University Press, 2001).

Chichele's Register, ed., E.F. Jacob (4 vols, Oxford: Clarendon Press, 1938–1947).

Christina of Markyate, *The Life of Christina of Markyate, a Twelfth-Century Recluse*, ed. C.H. Talbot (Oxford: Clarendon Press, 1959); revised with an Introduction and Notes, S. Fanous and H. Leyser (Oxford: Oxford University Press, 2008).

Chronicon Roskildense in *Scriptores Rerum Danicarum* 2, ed. M.Cl. Gertz (Copenhagen: Penguin, 1970).

The Cartulary of Cirencester Abbey, Gloucester, ed. C.D. Ross (3 vols, London: Oxford University Press, 1964–1977).

Close Rolls of the Reign of Henry III (London: HMSO, 1902–1975).

Conciliorum Oecumenicorum Decreta, ed. Joseph Alberigo (Basel: Herder, 1962).

Conciliorum Oecumenicorum, series ii, vol. 3.1 (Berlin: Walter de Gruyter, 2008).

Concilium Universale Nicaenum Secundum. Concilii Actiones I–III, ed. E. Lamberz, Acta Council of Meaux–Paris (845), ed. A. Boretius, MGH *Capitularia regum Francorum* (Hannover: Hahn, 1893).

A Cartulary of Creake Abbey, trans. A.L. Bedingfeld, Norfolk Record Society, 35 (Norwich: Norfolk Record Society, 1966).

Crook, D., *Records of the General Eyre* (London: HMSO, 1982).

Curia Regis Rolls of the Reigns of Richard I, John and Henry III (London: HMSO, 1922).

Dante, *De Vulgari Eloquentia*, ed. P.V. Mengaldo (Padua: Antenore, 1968).

De ordine palatii, ed. T. Gross and R. Schieffer, MGH Fontes iuris germanici antique (Hannover: Hahn, 1980).

Decretum Gelasianum de libris recipiendis et non recipiendis, ed. E. von Dobschütz Texte und Untersuchungen, 38.4 (Leipzig: Hinrichs, 1912).

Br. Dederich von Münster of the Observant Order [Dietrich Kolde], *A Fruitful Mirror or Small Handbook for Christians*, trans. R.B. Dewell, in *Three Reformation Cathecisms: Catholic, Anabaptist, Lutheran*, ed. D. Janz (New York: E. Mellen, 1982).

Dhuoda, *Handbook for her Warrior Son: Liber Manualis* (Cambridge: Cambridge University Press, 1998); Latin text with English trans. M. Thiébaux, *Dhuoda. Manuel pour mon fils*, ed. P. Riché, ed. with trans. B. de Vregille and C. Montdésert, SC, 225 (Paris: Cerf, 1975).

Documents and Extracts Illustrating the History of Dunster, ed. H.C. Maxwell-Lyte, Somerset Record Society, 33 (London: Harrison and Sons, 1917–1918).

Durandus of Mende, *Rationale Divinorvm Officiorvm*, ed. V. d'Avino (2 vols in 1, Naples: J. Dura, 1859).

Eadmer of Canterbury, *Tractatus de conceptione sanctae Mariae*, ed. H. Thurston and P.T. Slater (Breisgau: Herder, 1904).

Earldom of Gloucester Charters, ed. R.B. Patterson (Oxford: Clarendon Press, 1973).

Einhard, *Vita Karoli*, c. 7, ed. L. Halphen, *Vie de Charlemagne* (Paris: Les Belles Lettres, 1938).

Estoire des Engleis/History of the English by Geffrai Gaimar, ed. and trans. I. Short (Oxford: Oxford University Press, 2009).

Facsimiles of Early Charters from Northamptonshire Collections, ed. F.M. Stenton, Northants Record Society, 4 (Lincoln: J.W. Ruddock and Sons, 1930).

Flodoard, *Historia Remensis Ecclesiae*, ed. M. Hartmann, MGH SS, 36 (Hannover: Hahn, 1998).

Fouke Fitzwaryn, trans. G.S. Burgess in *Two Medieval Outlaws* (Woodbridge: Boydell and Brewer, reprinted 2007).

Francis of Assisi, *Epistola ad Fideles II*, in *Bibliotheca Patristica Medii Ævi*, 4.1 (Paris: Imprimerie de la Bibliothèque ecclésiastique, 1880), pp. 216–23.

Fredegar, *The Fourth Book of the Chronicle of Fredegar*, ed. J.M. Wallace-Hadrill (London: Nelson, 1960).

Genealogiae Karolorum, ed. G. Waitz, MGH SS, 13 (Hannover: Hahn, 1881), pp. 242–8.

Gerson, J., 'Tractatus de decem praeceptis', in *Joannis Gersonii. Opera omnia*, vol. 1, pt 3 (Antwerp, 1706).

Glanvill, *De Legibus et Consuetudinibus Anglie = The Treatise on the Laws and Customs of the Realm of England, Commonly Called Glanvill*, ed. G.D.G. Hall (London: Nelson, 1965).

[Godric of Finchale], *De Vita et miraculis S. Godrici*, ed. J. Stevenson, Surtees Society, 20 (London: J.B. Nichols and Son. 1847).

Gregory, *Homiliae in Ezechielem Prophetam*, SC 327, ed. and trans. C. Morel; SC 352, ed. and trans. M. Borret; SC 360, ed. and trans. C. Morel (Paris: Editions du Cerf, 1986, 1989, 1990).

Gregory of Tours, *Decem Libri Historiarum*, V.49, ed. B. Krusch and W. Levison, MGH SS Rerum Merovingicarum, I.1 (Hannover: Hahn, 1951).

Grosseteste, R. *Robert Grosseteste, De decem mandatis*, ed. R.C. Dales and E.B. King, Auctores Britannici medii aevi, 10 (Oxford: Oxford University Press for the British Academy, 1987).

Guibert de Nogent, Autobiographie, ed. E.-R. Labande (Paris: Belles Lettres, 1981), trans. P.J. Archambault, *A Monk's Confession. The Memoirs of Guibert of Nogent* (University Park, PA: Pennsylvania State University Press, 1995).

Guibert of Nogent, *De Vita Sua*, ed. E.R. Labande (Paris: Belles Lettres, 1981).

Guido I, *Consuetudines Cartusiae*, ed. A Carthusian Monk, SC, 313 (Paris: Editions du Cerf, 1984).

Henry of Huntingdon, *Historia Anglorum*, ed. Diana Greenway (Oxford: Clarendon Press, 1996).

The Letters of Hildegard of Bingen, I, trans. J.L. Baird and R.K. Ehrman (New York and Oxford: Oxford University Press, 1994).

Hincmar of Rheims, *Carmina*, ed. L. Traube, MGH Poetae III (Berlin: Weidmannschen, 1891), pp. 410–12.

Hincmar of Rheims, *De divortio Lotharii regis et Theutbergae reginae*, ed. L. Böhringer, MGH, Concilia IV.I (Hannover: Hahn, 1992).

Honorius of Autun, *Gemma animae, sive de divinis officiis et antiquo ritu missarum*, 1.72–73, PL 172: 566–7.

[Hugh of Lincoln], *Magna Vita S. Hugonis*, I, ed. D. Douie and H. Farmer (London: Nelson, 1961).

Hugh of St Cher, *Postilla in totam bibliam* (Paris, 1533).

Hugh of St Victor, *Hugh of St Victor on the Sacraments of the Christian Faith* (De sacramentis), ed. and trans. R.J. Deferrari (Cambridge, MA: Medieval Academy of America, 1951).

Hugh of St Victor, *De sacramentis Christianae fidei*, PL 176: 173–618.

Index to Testamentary Records in the Commissary Court of London 1374–1488, ed. M. Fitch (London: HMSO 1969).

Innocent III, *De sacro altaris mysterio*, PL 217: 773–916.

Inventories of Christ Church Canterbury, ed. J. Wickham Legg and W.H. St. John Hope (Westminster: Constable, 1902).

Ivo of Chartres, *De significationibus indumentorum sacerdotalium*, PL 172: 519–224.

Jerome, *In Ezechielem*, ed. F. Glorie, CCSL 75 (Turnhout: Brepols, 1964).

Le Roman de Rou de Wace, ed. A.J. Holden, Société des anciens textes français (3 vols, Paris: A. & J. Picard, 1970–1973).

Liber Feodorum: the Book of Fees, Commonly called Testa de Nevill, ed. H.C. Maxwell Lyte (London: HMSO, 1920).

Malachi, *Vita. Malachiae*, p. 310, trans. R.T. Meyer, *The Life and Death of Saint Malachy the Irishman* (Kalamazoo, MI: Cistercian Publications, 1978).

Menologium Graecorum Basilii Porphyrogeniti imperatoris jussu editum, PG 117: 19–614.

New Testament Apocrypha, ed. E. Hennecke and W. Schneemelcher, trans. R.McL. Wilson (2 vols, Philadelphia, PA: Westminster Press, 1963).

Nicholas of Lyra, *Postilla litteralis in totam bibliam* (Strassburg, 1492).

Nicolas Trevet, *Les Cronicles*, ed. A. Rutherford, unpublished PhD dissertation, University of London, 1932.

Niketas, *Life of St Philaretos the Merciful Written by His Grandson Niketas: A Critical Edition*, ed. L. Rydén, Studia Byzantina Upsaliensia, 8 (Uppsala: Almqvist & Wiksell International: 2002).

Ordericus Vitalis, *The Ecclesiastical History of Orderic Vitalis*, ed. M. Chibnall (6 vols, Oxford: Clarendon Press, 1969–1980).

Original Papal Documents in England and Wales from the Accession of Pope Innocent III to the Death of Pope Benedict XI (1198–1304), ed. J.E. Sayers (Oxford: Oxford University Press, 1999).

[Ormulum], *The Ormulum, with the Notes and Glossary of Dr R.M. White*, ed. R. Holt (Oxford: Clarendon Press, 1878).

Oxford Dictionary of National Biography, ed. L.N. Goldman (Oxford: Oxford University Press, 2004).

Paris, M., *Matthaei Parisiensis ... Chronica Maiora*, ed. H.R. Luard, Rolls Series (7 vols, London: Longman, 1872–1883).

Paschasius Radbertus, *Cogitis me/Epistula beati Hieronymi ad Paulum et Eustochium de assumptione sanctae Mariae virginis*, ed A. Ripberger (Freiburg: University of Freiburg, 1962), text reprinted CCCM, 56C (Turnhout: Brepols, 1985).

Paschasius Radbertus, *Expositio in Matthaeum Libri XII* I. 16, ed. Beda Paulus, CCSL, 56, 56A, 56B (3 vols, Turnhout: Brepols, 1984).

Paschasius Radbertus, *De partu virginis*, ed. E.A. Matter, CCCM, 56C (Turnhout: Brepols, 1985).

Paschasius Radbertus, *Vita Adalardi*, PL 120: 1507–56.

Patent Rolls of the Reign of Henry III (6 vols, London: HMSO, 1901–1913).

Peter of Celle, *De tabernaculo I, II*, ed. G. de Martel, CCCM, 54 (Turnhout: Brepols, 1983).

Peter Comestor, *Historia scholastica*, PL 198: 1053–1721.

Peter Lombard, *Magistri Petri Lombardi Sententiae in IV libris distinctae*, ed. I.F. Brady (2 vols, Grottaferrata: Coll. S. Bonaventura, 1971, 1981).

Philo Judaeus, *On the Decalogue*, ed. F.H. Colson, Works of Philo Judaeus, 7 (London and Cambridge, MA: Harvard University Press, 1937).

Pseudo-Matthaei Evangelium, ed. J. Gijsel, CCSA, 9 (Turnhout: Brepols, 1997).

Rabanus Maurus, *De Clericorum Institutione*, 1.14–16, PL 108: 297–420.

Rabanus Maurus, *Commentarius in Exodum*, PL 108: 100–10.

Rashi, *Pentateuch with Targum Onkelos ...*, trans. M. Rosenbaum and A.M. Silbermann, vol. 2: Exodus (London: Shapiro, Valentine and Co., 1930); vol. 3: Leviticus (London: Shapiro, Valentine and Co., 1932).

Ratramnus of Corbie, *De partu sanctae Mariae*, ed. J.M. Canal, *Marianum*, 30 (1968): 53–160.

Reading Abbey Cartularies: British Library Manuscripts Egerton 3031, Harley 1708 and Cotton Vespasian E xxv, ed. B.R. Kemp, Camden, 4th series, 31 (2 vols, London: Royal Historical Society, 1986–1987).

Records of the Templars in England in the Twelfth Century: the Inquest of 1185, ed. B.A. Lees (London: Humphrey Milford, Oxford University Press, for the British Academy, 1935).

Red Book of the Exchequer, ed. H. Hall (3 vols, London, 1965).

Richard of St Victor, *Benjamin Major*, PL 196.63-192.

Richard of St Victor, *Nonnullae Allegoriae Tabernaculi Foederis*, PL 196. 191–202.

[Robert of Bethune], *The Life of Robert of Bethune by William of Wycombe*, trans. with intro. and notes B.J. Parkinson, unpublished B.Litt. thesis, Oxford University, 1952.

[Robert of Knaresborough], *The Metrical Life of St Robert of Knaresborough*, ed. Joyce Bazire, Early English Text Society, 228 (Oxford: Oxford University Press, 1953).

[Robert of Knaresborough], 'Vita S. Roberti Knaresburgensis', ed. P. Grosjean, *Analecta Bollandiana*, 57 (1939): 364–400.

Rotuli de Dominabus et Pueris et Puellis de XII Comitatibus (1185), ed. J.H. Round, Pipe Roll Society, 35 (London: Pipe Roll Society, 1913).

Rotuli Litterarum Clausarum, ed. T.D. Hardy (2 vols, London: private publication, 1833–1834).

Rotuli Litterarum Patentium, ed. T.D. Hardy (London: Eyre and Spottiswoode, 1835).

Rotuli Roberti Grosseteste, Episcopi Quondam Lincolniensis Epistolae, ed. H.R. Luard (London: Longman et al., 1861).

Royal and Other Historical Letters Illustrative of the Reign of Henry III, ed. W.W. Shirley (2 vols, London: Longman et al., 1862–1866).

Ruyijun zhuan, ed. and trans. C.R. Stone, *The Fountainhead of Chinese Erotica: the Lord of Perfect Satisfaction (Ruyijun zhuan)* (Honolulu, HI: University of Hawai'i Press, 2003).

Sacrorum conciliorum nova et amplissima collectio, ed. G.D. Mansi (31 vols, Florence: Antonius Zatta, 1758–1798).

Stoke by Clare Cartulary, ed. C. Harper-Bill and R. Mortimer, Suffolk Records Society: Suffolk Charters 4–6 (3 vols, Woodbridge: Boydell and Brewer for the Suffolk Records Society, 1982–1984).

Stuttgart Psalter, facsimile: the *Stuttgart Psalter*, ed. E. DeWald (Princeton, NJ: Department of Art and Archaeology, Princeton University, 1930).

Symeon, M., *Annales*, ed. I. Bekker, Corpus scriptorum historiae Byzantinae, 33 (Bonn: Eduard Weber, 1838), pp. 603–760.

Synaxarium Ecclesiae Constantinopolitanae: Propylaeum ad Acta Sanctorum Novembris, ed. Hippolyte Delehaye (Brussels: Apud Socios Bollandianos, 1902).

Testamentary Records in the Archdeaconry Court of London 1363–1649, ed. M. Fitch (London: British Record Society, 1979).

The Complete Peerage of England, Scotland Ireland, Great Britain and the United Kingdom, ed. G.E.C. Cockayne (London: St Catherine's Press, 1936); reprinted as a Microprint Edition, Stroud: Sutton, 1982).

The Heads of Religious Houses in England and Wales II 1216–1377, ed. D.M. Smith and Vera C.M. London (Cambridge: Cambridge University Press, 2001).

The History of the Kings of Britain: An Edition and Translation of De gestis Britonum (Historia regum Britanniae), ed. M.D. Reeve and trans. N. Wright (Woodbridge: Boydell Press, 2008).

The Myroure of our Ladye, ed. J.H. Blunt, EETS ES 19 (London: N. Trübner, 1873).

The Register, or Rolls, of Walter Gray, Lord Archbishop of York, ed. J. Raine, Surtees Society, 56 (Durham: Andrews and Co. for Surtees Society, 1872).

Thegan, *Vita Hludowici imperatoris* 2, ed. E. Tremp, MGH Scriptores rerum Germanicarum in usum scholarum, 64 (Hannover: Hahn 1995), trans. P. Dutton, *Carolingian Civilization: A Reader* (New York: Broadview Press, 1996).

Theophanes, *Chronographia*, ed. Karl de Boor (2 vols, Leipzig: Teubner, 1883–1885).

Thomas of Chobham, *Thomae de Chobham Summa confessorum*, ed. F. Broomfield, Analecta Mediaevalia Namurcensia, 25 (Louvain: Nauwelaerts, 1968).

Thomas of Walsingham, *Chronica Majora*, ed. J. Taylor, W. Childs and L. Watkiss (Oxford: Clarendon Press, 2003).

Transcripts of Charters Relating to Gilbertine Houses, ed. F.M. Stenton, Lincoln Record Society, 18 (Horncastle: W.K. Morton and Sons, 1922).

Utrecht Psalter, facsimile: *Utrecht Psalter. Vollständige Faksimile-Ausgabe*, ed. K. van der Horst and J.H.A. Engelbregt (2 vols, Graz: Akademische Druck- und Verlagsanstalt, 1984).

Vita Herluini, in A.S. Abulafia and G.R. Evans (eds), *The Works of Gilbert Crispin*, Auctores Britannici Medii Aevi, 8 (London: Oxford University Press for the British Academy, 1986).

Walter Daniels, *The Life of Ailred of Rievaulx*, ed. and trans. F.M. Powicke (Oxford: Clarendon Press, 1978).

Wharton, H., *Anglia Sacra ii* (London: Richard Chiswell, 1691).

William of Auxerre, *Magistri Guillermus Altissiodorensis. Summa Aurea*, ed. J. Ribaillier, Spicilegium Bonaventurianum, 16–20 (4 vols in 6, Paris: CNRS, 1980–1987).

William Camden, *Brittania*, trans. P. Holland, rev. E. Gibbon, 3rd edn (London: R. Ware, J.P. Kingston, T. Longman et al., 1753).

William of Malmesbury, *Gesta regum Anglorum*, ed. and trans. R.A.B. Mynors, R.M. Thomson and M. Winterbottom (2 vols, Oxford: Clarendon Press, 1998–1999).

Wyclif, J., *Tractatus de Mandatis Divinis*, ed. J. Loserth and F.D. Matthew (London: published for the Wyclif Society by C.K. Paul and Co., 1922).

Wyclif, J., *De Veritate Sacrae Scripturae*, Wyclif Society, 29–31 (London: Wyclif Society, 1905).

C. Secondary Sources

Age of Chivalry: English Society 1200–1400 (London: Kingfisher and Royal Academy of Arts, 1987).

Airlie, S., 'The Nearly Men: Boso of Vienne and Arnulf of Bavaria', in A.J. Duggan (ed.), *Nobles and Nobility in Medieval Europe: Concepts, Origins, Transformations* (Woodbridge: Boydell, 2000), pp. 25–41.

Airlie, S. 'Private Bodies and the Body Politic in the Divorce Case of Lothar II', *Past and Present*, 161 (1998): 3–38.

Airlie, S., '*Semper fideles*? Loyauté envers les Carolingiens comme constituant de l'identité aristocratique', in R. Le Jan (ed.), *La royauté et les élites dans l'Europe carolingienne* (Lille: Université Charles-de-Gaulle, 1998), pp. 129–43.

Andersson, I., *A History of Sweden* (London: Weidenfeld and Nicholson, 1955).

Andrewes, L., *A Pattern of Catechistical Doctrine and Other Minor Works*, Minor Works of Bishop Andrewes (Oxford: John Henry Parker, 1846).

Armstrong, R.J., J.A. Wayne Hellmann and W.J. Short (eds), *The Life of Saint Francis by Thomas of Celano* in *Francis of Assisi. The Saint. Early Documents* (Hyde Park, NY: New City Press, 1999).

Aston, M., *England's Iconoclasts*, I – (Oxford: Oxford University Press, 1988–).

Atkinson, C.W., *The Oldest Vocation. Christian Motherhood in the Middle Ages* (Ithaca, NY: Cornell University Press, 1991).

Atkinson, C.W., '"Your Servant, My Mother": the Figure of Saint Monica in the Ideology of Christian Motherhood', in C.W. Atkinson, C.H. Buchanan and M.R. Miles (eds), *Immaculate and Powerful: the Female in Sacred Image and Social Reality* (Boston, MA: Beacon Press, 1985), pp. 139–72.

Auerbach, E., 'Figura', in *Scenes from the Drama of European Literature*, trans. R. Manheim, Theory and History in Literature, 9 (New York: Meridian, 1959), pp. 11–76.

Auerbach, E., *Mimesis: the Representation of Reality in Western Literature*, trans. W.R. Trask (Princeton, NJ: Princeton University Press, 1953).

Aungier, G.J., *The History and Antiquities of Syon Monastery* (London: J.B. Nichols, 1840).

Bagley, A., 'Jesus at School', *Journal of Psychohistory*, 13 (1985): 13–31.

Baldwin, J.W., *The Language of Sex: Five Voices from Northern France around 1200* (Chicago, IL: University of Chicago Press, 1994).

Balmelle, C., *Les demeures aristocratiques d'Aquitaine: Société et culture de l'Antiquité tardive dans le Sud-Oeust de la Gaule*, Aquitainia Supplément, 10 (Bordeaux: de Boccard, 2001).

Banham, D., 'A Millennium in Medicine? New Medical Texts and Ideas in England in the Eleventh Century', in S. Keynes, A.P. Smyth and C.R. Hart (eds), *Anglo-Saxons: Studies Presented to Cyril Roy Hart* (Dublin: Four Courts Press, 2006), pp. 230–42.

Barkaï, R., *A History of Jewish Gynaecological Texts in the Middle Ages* (Leiden: Brill, 1998).

Barker-Benfield, B.C., *St Augustine's Abbey, Canterbury*, Corpus of British Medieval Library Catalogues, 13 (3 vols, London: British Library in association with the British Academy, 2008).

Barratt, A. (ed.), *The Knowing of Woman's Kind in Childing: A Middle English Version of Material Derived from the 'Trotula' and Other Sources*, Medieval Women: Texts and Contexts, 4 (Turnhout: Brepols, 2001).

Barron, C.M., 'Introduction: the Widow's World in Later Medieval London', in C.M. Barron and A.F. Sutton (eds), *Medieval London Widows 1300–1500* (London: Hambledon, 1994).

Barron, C.M., *London in the Later Middle Ages: Government and People 1200–1500* (Oxford: Oxford University Press, 2004).

Bartlett, R., *England under the Norman and Angevin Kings, 1075–1225* (Oxford: Clarendon Press, 2000).

Barton, A.B., *A Guide to the Church of All Saints North Street, York* (York: no date).

Baswell, C., 'Albyne Sails for Albion: Gender, Motion and Foundation in the English Imperial Imagination', in P. Horden (ed.), *Freedom of Movement in the Middle Ages: Proceedings of the 2003 Harlaxton Symposium* (Donington: Shaun Tyas, 2007), pp. 157–68.

Bately, J., 'Did King Alfred Actually Translate Anything? The Integrity of the Alfredian Canon Revisited', *Medium Aevum*, 78 (2009): pp. 189–215.

Baumgarten, E., '"Thus Sayeth the Wise Midwives": Midwives and Midwifery in Thirteenth-Century Ashkenaz', *Zion*, 65 (2000): 45–74.

Beattie, C., *Medieval Single Women: the Politics of Social Classification in Late Medieval England* (Oxford: Oxford University Press, 2007).

Beattie, J., *Other Cultures: Aims, Methods and Achievements in Social Anthropology* (London: Cohen and West, 1964).

Beaven, A.B., *The Aldermen of the City of London* (2 vols, London: Eden Fisher & Co., 1908–1913).

Beccaria, A., *I Codici di medicina del periodo presalernitano (secoli IX, X e XI)* (Rome: Edizioni di Storia e Letteratura, 1956).

Becker, P.-A., 'Dhuodas Handbuch', *Zeitschrift für romanische Philologie*, 21 (1897): 73–101.

Belfour, A.O. (ed.), *Twelfth-Century Homilies in Ms. Bodley 343*, Early English Text Society, 137 (London: Oxford University Press, 1909; reprinted 1962).

Bell, M., *Wulfric of Haselbury, by John, Abbott of Ford*, Somerset Record Society, 47 (London: Somerset Record Society, 1933).

Bell, S.G., 'Medieval Women Book Owners: Arbiters of Lay Piety and Ambassadors of Culture', *Signs*, 7 (1982): pp. 742–68; reprinted in M. Erler and M. Kowaleski (eds), *Women and Power in the Middle Ages* (Athens, GA: University of Georgia Press, 1988), pp. 149–87.

Bennett, C., 'The Conversion of Vergil: the *Aeneid* in Augustine's *Confessions*', *Revue des Études Augustiniennes*, 34 (1988): 47–69.

Benton, J.F., *Culture, Power and Personality in Medieval France*, ed. T.N. Bisson (London: Hambledon, 1991).

Benton, J.F., *Self and Society in Medieval France* (New York: Harper & Row, 1970).

Berthelson, B., *Studier i Birgittinerordens byggnadsskick: Anläggningsplanen och dess tillämpning* 1, KVHAA, 63 (Lund: H. Ohlssons, 1947).

Beyers, R., '*De nativitate Mariae*: problèmes d'origine', *Revue de théologie et de philosophie*, 122 (1990): 171–88.

Black, R., *Humanism and Education in Medieval and Renaissance Italy* (Cambridge: Cambridge University Press, 2001).

Blomefield, F., *An Essay Towards a Topographical History of the County of Norfolk* (11 vols, London, 1805–1910).

Boland, P., *The Concept of Discretio Spirituum in John Gerson's 'De Probatione Spirituum' and 'De Distinctione Verarum Visionum A Falsis'*, The Catholic University of America Studies in Sacred Theology, 2nd series, 112 (Washington, DC: Catholic University Press, 1959).

Bondurand, E., *L'éducation carolingienne, Le Manuel de Dhuoda (843)* (Paris: Picard, 1887).

Bonney, R., 'The Rise of the Fiscal State in Europe, c. 1200–1815', in R. Bonney (ed.), *The Rise of the Fiscal State in Europe, c. 1200–1815* (Oxford: Oxford University Press, 1999), pp. 1–14.

Boone, M., 'State Power and Illicit Sexuality: the Persecution of Sodomy in Late Medieval Bruges', *Journal of Medieval History*, 22 (1996): 135–53.

Borgehammer, S., 'St. Birgitta, An Architect of Spiritual Reform', *Birgittiana*, 5 (1988): 23–47.

Børresen, K.E., 'Religious Feminism in the Middle Ages: Birgitta of Sweden', in L. D'Arcens and J. Feros Ruys (eds), *Maistresse of My Wit: Medieval Women, Modern Scholars* (Turnhout: Brepols, 2004), pp. 295–312.

Bos, G., *Ibn al-Jazzar on Sexual Diseases and Their Treatment*, The Sir Henry Wellcome Asian Series (London: Kegan Paul, 1997).

Boswell, J., *Christianity, Social Tolerance, and Homosexuality: Gay People in Western Europe from the Beginning of the Christian Era to the Fourteenth Century* (Chicago, IL: University of Chicago Press, 1980).

Bovey, A., 'Book of Hours', in M.F. Suarez and H.R. Woudhuysen (eds), *The Oxford Companion to the Book* (2 vols, Oxford: Oxford University Press, 2010), vol. 1, pp. 550–52.

Brand, P. (ed.), *Earliest English Law Reports*, Selden Society 111–12, 122–3 (4 vols, London: Seldon Society, 1996–2007).

Brand, P., 'Family and Inheritance, Women and Children', in C. Given-Wilson (ed.), *An Illustrated History of Late Medieval England* (Manchester: Manchester University Press, 1996), pp. 58–81.

Brand, P., '*In perpetuum*; The Rhetoric and Reality of Attempts to Control the Future in the English Medieval Common Law', in J.A. Burrow and I. Wei (eds), *Medieval Futures: Attitudes to the Future in the Middle Ages* (Woodbridge: Boydell, 2000), pp. 101–13.

Brandes, W., *Finanzverwaltung in Krisenzeiten: Untersuchungen zur byzantinischen Administration im 6.–9. Jahrhundert*, Forschungen zur byzantinischen Rechtsgeschichte, 25 (Frankfurt am Main: Löwenklau Gesellschaft, 2002).

Brereton, G.E. (ed.), *Des Grantz Geanz* (Oxford: Blackwell, 1937).

Brooks, E.W., 'On the Date of the Death of Constantine the Son of Irene', *Byzantinische Zeitschift*, 9 (1900): 654–7.

Brown, E.A.R., 'Death and the Human Body in the Later Middle Ages: the Legislation of Boniface VIII on the Division of the Corpse', *Viator*, 12 (1981): 221–70.

Brown, M.P., 'Female Book Ownership and Production in Anglo-Saxon England: the Evidence of Ninth-century Prayer Books', in C.J. Kay and L.M. Sylvester (eds), *Lexis and Texts in Early English: Studies Presented to Jane Roberts* (Amsterdam: Rodopi, 2001), pp. 45–67.

Brown, P., *Augustine of Hippo. A Biography* (Berkeley, CA: University of California Press, 2000).

Brown, P., *The Body and Society: Men, Women and Sexual Renunciation in Early Christianity* (New York: Columbia University Press, 1988).

Brown, P., *The Cult of the Saints: Its Rise and Function in Latin Christianity* (Chicago, IL: University of Chicago Press, 1981).

Brown, P., *A Life of Learning*, Charles Homer Haskins Lecture for 2003, American Council of Learned Societies Occasional Paper, 55 (2003).

Brown, P., 'The Rise and Function of the Holyman in Late Antiquity', *Journal of Roman Studies*, 61 (1971): 80–101.

Brown, R.A. and H.M. Colvin 'The Royal Castles 1066–1485', in H.M. Colvin (ed.), *The History of the King's Works* (2 vols, London: HMSO, 1963), vol. 2, pp. 533–894.

Brubaker, L., 'Sex, Lies and Textuality: the *Secret History* of Prokopios and the Rhetoric of Gender in Sixth-Century Byzantium', in L. Brubaker and J.M.H. Smith (eds), *Gender in the Early Medieval World: East and West, 300–900* (Cambridge: Cambridge University Press, 2004).

Brubaker, L. and J. Haldon, *Byzantium in the Iconoclast Era, c. 680–850* (Cambridge: Cambridge University Press, 2011).

Brundage, J.A., *Law, Sex, and Christian Society in Medieval Europe* (Chicago, IL: University of Chicago Press, 1987).

Brütsch, W., 'De diversis causis mulierum, nach einer Petersburger Handschrift aus dem 9. Jahrhundert zum erstenmal gedruckt', unpublished medical dissertation (Freiburg-im-Br., 1922).

Buck, R.A., 'Women and Language in the Anglo-Saxon Leechbooks', *Women and Language*, 23 (2000): 41–50.

Bullough, D., 'Early Medieval Social Groupings: the Terminology of Kinship', *Past and Present*, 45 (1969): 3–18.

Bumke, J., *Courtly Culture: Literature and Society in the High Middle Ages*, trans. T. Dunlap (Berkeley, CA: University of California Press, 1991).

Burgmann, L., 'Die Novellen der Kaiserin Eirene', *Fontes Minores*, 4 (1981): 1–36.

Burnett, C. and D. Jacquart (eds), *Constantine the African and 'Ali ibn al-'Abbas al-Magusi: the 'Pantegni' and Related Texts* (Leiden: E.J. Brill, 1994).

Burton, J., *Monastic and Religious Orders in Britain 1000–1300* (Cambridge: Cambridge University Press, 1994).

Bynum, C.W., *Holy Feast, Holy Fast: the Religious Significance of Food to Medieval Women* (Berkeley, CA: University of California Press, 1987).

Bynum, C.W., *Jesus as Mother: Studies in the Spirituality of the High Middle Ages* (Berkeley, CA: University of California Press, 1982).

Caballero Navas, C., 'Algunos "secretos de mujeres" revelados: El *Šeʾar yašub* y la recepción y transmisión del *Trotula* en hebreo' ['Some "Secrets of Women" Revealed. The *Sheʾar yašub* and the Reception and Transmission of the *Trotula* in Hebrew'], *Miscelánea de Estudios Árabes y Hebraicos, sección Hebreo*, 55 (2006): 381–425.

Cabaniss, A. (trans.), *Charlemagne's Cousins: Contemporary Lives of Adalard and Wala* (Syracuse, NY: Syracuse University Press, 1967).

Cadden, J., *Meanings of Sex Difference in the Middle Ages: Medicine, Science and Culture* (Cambridge: Cambridge University Press, 1993).

Cadden, J., '"Nothing Natural is Shameful": Vestiges of a Debate about Sex and Science in a Group of Late Medieval Manuscripts', *Speculum*, 76 (2001): 66–89.

Cameron, A., 'The Theotokos in Sixth-Century Constantinople: A City finds its Symbol', *Journal of Theological Studies*, 29 (1978): 79–108.

Cannon, H.L., 'The Battle of Sandwich and Eustace the Monk', *English Historical Review*, 27 (1912): 649–70.

Carlsen, P.S., 'Lægteranordningerne I den birgittinske klosterkirke – et udviklingsforløb', in T. Nyberg (ed.), *Birgitta, hendes værk og hendes klostre i Norden* (Odense: Odense universitetsforlag, 1991), pp 146–65.

Carpenter, D.A., 'The Fall of Hubert de Burgh', *Journal of British Studies*, 19 (1980): 1–17.

Carpenter, D.A., *The Minority of Henry III* (London: Methuen, 1990).

Carpenter, D.A., 'A Noble in Politics: Roger Mortimer in the Period of Baronial Reform and Rebellion, 1258–1265', in A.J. Duggan (ed.), *Nobles and Nobility in Medieval Europe* (Woodbridge: Boydell, 2000), pp. 183–203.

Carthew, G.A., 'A Cellarer's Account Roll of Creak Abbey', *Norfolk Archaeology*, 6 (1864): 314–59.

Cavadini, J., *The Last Christology of the West: Adoptionism in Spain and Gaul, 785–820* (Philadelphia, PA: University of Pennsylvania Press, 1993).

Cavell, E., 'Aristocratic Widows and the Medieval Welsh Frontier: the Shropshire Evidence', *Transactions of the Royal Historical Society*, 6th series, 17 (2007): 57–82.

Cecchi, A., *Botticelli* (Milan: Motta, 2005).

Chandler, C.J., 'Barcelona BC 569 and a Carolingian Programme on the Virtues', *Early Medieval Europe*, 18 (2010): 265–91.

Chardonnens, L.S., 'A New Edition of the Old English *Formation of the Foetus*', *Notes and Queries*, 47 (2000): 10–11.

Charity, A.C., *Events and their Afterlife: the Dialectics of Christian Typology in the Bible and Dante* (Cambridge: Cambridge University Press, 1966).

Chazelle, C., *The Crucified God in the Carolingian Era: Theology and the Art of Christ's Passion* (Cambridge: Cambridge University Press, 2001).

Chenu, M.-D., *Nature, Man and Society in the Twelfth Century*, trans. J. Taylor and L.K. Little (Chicago, IL: University of Chicago Press, 1968).

Chibnall, M., *The Empress Matilda: Queen Consort, Queen Mother and Lady of the English* (Oxford: Blackwell, 1991).

Chiffoleau, J., 'Dire l'indicible: Remarques sur la catégorie du *nefandum* du XIIe au XVe siècle', *Annales: economies, sociétés, civilisations*, 45 (1990): 289–324.

Childs, B.S., *Exodus. A Commentary* (London: SCM, 1974).

Christophilopoulou, A., 'He antibasileia eis ton Byzantion', *Symmeikta*, 2 (1970): 1–144.

Clanchy, M.T., 'The ABC Primer: Was it in Latin or English?', in E. Salter and H. Wicker (eds), *Vernacularity in England and Wales c1300–1550* (Turnhout: Brepols, 2010), pp. 15–36.

Clanchy, M.T., 'An Icon of Literacy: The Depiction at Tuse of Jesus going to School', in P. Hermann (ed.), *Literacy in Medieval and Early Modern Scandinavian Culture* (Odense: University Press of Southern Denmark, 2005), pp. 47–73.

Clanchy, M.T, *From Memory to Written Record* (London: Edward Arnold, 1979); 2nd edn (Oxford: Blackwell, 1993).

Clanchy, M.T., 'Images of Ladies with Prayer Books: What Do They Signify?', in R.N. Swanson (ed.), *The Church and the Book*, Studies in Church History, 38 (Woodbridge: Boydell and Brewer, 2004), pp. 106–22.

Clanchy, M.T., 'Learning to Read in the Middle Ages and the Role of Mothers', in G. Brooks and A.K. Pugh (eds), *Studies in the History of Reading* (Reading: Centre for the Teaching of Reading, 1984), pp. 33–9.

Clarke, E., 'City Orphans and Custody Laws in Medieval England', in *The American Journal of Legal History*, 34 (1990): 168–87.

Clarke, J., *The Book of Brackley: The First Thousand Years* (Buckingham: Barracuda, 1987).

Claussen, M., 'Fathers of Power and Women of Authority: Dhuoda and the *Liber Manualis*', *French Historical Studies*, 19 (1996): 785–809.

Clayton, M., *The Apocryphal Gospels of Mary in Anglo-Saxon England* (Cambridge: Cambridge University Press, 1998).

Cokayne, G.E., *Complete Perrage*, ed. V. Gibbs and H.A. Doubleday (London: St Catherine's Press, 1926).

Coldstream, N., 'Cistercian Architecture from Beaulieu to the Dissolution', in C. Norton and D. Park (eds), *Cistercian Art and Architecture* (Cambridge: Cambridge University Press, 1986), pp. 139–59.

Coldstream, N., *The Decorated Style: Architecture and Ornament, 1240–1360* (London: British Museum Press, 1994).

Colledge, E., '*Epistola solitarii ad reges*: Alphonse of Pecha as Organizer of Brigittine and Urbanist Propaganda', *Mediaeval Studies*, 18 (1956): 19–49.

Collins, H.E.L., *The Order of the Garter 1348–1461: Chivalry and Politics in Late Medieval England* (Oxford: Clarendon Press, 2000).

Conybeare, C., *The Irrational Augustine* (Oxford: Oxford University Press, 2006).

Cook, G.H., *English Monasteries in the Middle Ages* (London: Phoenix House, 1961).

Cooper, K., 'Contesting the Nativity: Wives, Virgins, and Pulcheria's Imitatio Mariae', *Scottish Journal of Religious Studies*, 19 (1998): 31–43.

Cooper, K., 'Empress and *Theotokos*: Gender and Patronage in the Christological Controversy', in R.N. Swanson (ed.), *The Church and Mary*, Studies in Church History, 39 (Woodbridge: Boydell, 2004), pp. 39–51.

Cooper, K., *The Fall of the Roman Household* (Cambridge: Cambridge University Press, 2007).

Cornell, H., *The Iconography of the Nativity of Christ*, Uppsala Universitets Årsskrift 1.3 (Uppsala: A.-b. Lundequistska bokhandeln, 1924).

Costello, M.S., 'Women's Mysticism and Reform: The Adaptation of Biblical Prophetic Conventions in Fourteenth-Century Hagiographic and Visionary Literature', unpublished PhD dissertation (Northwestern University, 1989).

Cousins, E., 'Francis of Assisi and Christian Mysticism', in S.T. Katz (ed.), *Mysticism and Religious Traditions* (Oxford: Oxford University Press, 1983), pp. 163–90.

Cousins, E., 'The Humanity and the Passion of Christ', in J. Raitt (ed.), *Christian Spirituality 2: High Middle Ages and the Middle Ages* (New York: Crossroad, 1987), pp. 375–91.

Crick, J., 'Edgar, Albion and Insular Dominion', in D. Scragg (ed.), *Edgar, King of the English 959–975* (Woodbridge: Boydell, 2008), pp. 158–70.

Crick, J. and J. Carley, '*De Origine gigantum*: An Annotated Edition', *Arthurian Literature*, 18 (2001): 41–114.

Crouch, D., *The Beaumont Twins: The Roots and Branches of Power in the Twelfth Century* (Cambridge: Cambridge University Press, 1986).

Crump, J.J., 'The Mortimer Family and the Making of the March', in M. Prestwich, R.H. Britnell and R. Frame (eds), *Thirteenth Century England*, VI (Woodbridge: Boydell, 1997), pp. 117–26.

Cullum, P. and P.J.P., Goldberg, 'How Margaret Blackburn Taught her Daughters: Reading Devotional Instruction in a Book of Hours', in J. Wogan-Browne et al. (eds), *Medieval Women: Texts and Contexts in Late Medieval Britain: Essays for Felicity Riddy* (Turnhout: Brepols, 2000), pp. 223–33.

Dace, R., 'Lesser Barons and Greater Knights: The Middling Group within the English Nobility c. 1086–c. 1265', *Haskins Society Journal*, 10 (2001): 57–77.

Daniélou, J., *From Shadows to Reality: Studies in the Biblical Typology of the Fathers*, trans. W. Hibberd (London: Burns & Oates, 1960).

Davidson, J., *The History of Newenham in the County of Devon* (London: Longman, 1843).

Davies, R.R., *Lords and Lordship in the British Isles in the Late Middle Ages*, ed. B. Smith (Oxford: Oxford University Press, 2009).

Davis, J.G. (ed.), *A Dictionary of Liturgy and Worship* (London: SCM, 1972).

Davis, R.H.C., 'An Oxford Charter of 1191', in his *From Alfred the Great to Stephen* (London: Hambledon, 1991).

D'Avray, D.L. (ed.), *Medieval Marriage Sermons: Mass Communication in a Culture without Print* (Oxford: Oxford University Press, 2001).

De Hamel, C.F.R., *The Book: A History of the Bible* (London: Phaidon, 2001).

De Hamel, C.F.R., *A History of Illuminated Manuscripts*, 2nd edn (London: Phaidon, 1994).

De Jong, M., 'Becoming Jeremiah: Paschasius Radbertus on Wala, Himself, and Others', in R. Corradini et al. (eds), *Ego-Trouble: Authors and Their Identities in the Early Middle Ages* (Vienna: Akademie der Wissenschaften, 2010), pp. 185–96.

Dean, R.J., with M.B.M. Boulton, *Anglo-Norman Literature: A Guide to Texts and Manuscripts*, ANTS OPS 3 (London: ANTS, 1999).

Deegan, M., 'Pregnancy and Childbirth in the Anglo-Saxon Medical Texts: A Preliminary Survey', in M. Deegan and D.G. Scragg (eds), *Medicine in Early Medieval England* (Manchester: Centre for Anglo-Saxon Studies, University of Manchester, 1989), pp. 17–26.

Demus, O., *Romanesque Mural Painting*, trans. M. Whittal (London: Thames & Hudson, 1970).

Dickinson, F.H. (ed.), *Missale ad Usum Insignis et Praeclare Ecclesia Sarum* (Burntisland, 1861–1883).

Dickinson, J.C., *The Origins of the Austin Canons and their Introduction into England* (London: SPCK, 1950).

Dickinson, J.C. and P.T. Ricketts, ed. and trans., 'The Anglo-Norman Chronicle of Wigmore Abbey', *Transactions of the Woolhope Naturalists Field Club*, 39 (1969): 413–45.

Dobson, R.B. and S. Donaghey, *The History of Clementhorpe Nunnery* (London: published for the York Archaeological Trust by the Council for British Archaeology, 1984).

Doran, S., *Monarchy and Matrimony: The Courtships of Elizabeth I* (London: Routledge, 1996).

Douglas, D.C. and G.W. Greenaway (eds), *English Historical Documents 1042–1189* (London: Eyre and Spottiswoode, 1953).

Dronke, P., *Women Writers of the Middle Ages* (Cambridge: Cambridge University Press, 1984).

Duby, G., *The Chivalrous Society*, trans. Cynthia Postan (London: Edward Arnold, 1977).

Duffy, E., *The Stripping of the Altars: Traditional Religion in England 1400–1580* (New Haven, CT: Yale University Press, 1992).

Dugdale, W., *Monasticon Anglicanum*, new edn (6 vols in 8, London: Longman, etc., 1817–1830).

Dumville, D., 'Kingship, Genealogies, and Regnal Lists', in P. Sawyer and I. Wood (eds), *Early Medieval Kingship* (Leeds: University of Leeds, 1977), pp. 72–104.

Dunn, G., 'The Ancestry of Jesus According to Tertullian: *ex David per Mariam*', *Studia Patristica*, 36 (2001): 349–55.

Dunning, R.W., 'The Building of Syon Abbey', *Transactions of the Ancient Monuments Society*, ns. 25 (1981): 16–26.

Dutton, P.E., *Charlemagne's Mustache and Other Cultural Clusters of the Dark Age* (New York: Palgrave Macmillan, 2004).

Dutton, P.E., *The Politics of Dreaming in the Carolingian Empire* (Lincoln, NE: University of Nebraska Press, 1994).

Eckhardt, K.A. (ed.), *Sachsenspiegel, Landrecht* (Göttingen: Musterschmidt, 1955).

Edwards, C., 'Mothers' Boys and Mothers' Girls in the Pastourelle', *Forum for Modern Language Studies*, 35 (1999): 70–80.

Ehrlich, T.L., *Landscape and Identity in Early Modern Rome: Villa Culture at Frascati in the Borghese Era* (Cambridge: Cambridge University Press, 2002).

Elkins, S., *Holy Women of Twelfth-Century England* (Chapel Hill, NC: University of North Carolina Press, 1988).

Ellis, C., *Hubert de Burgh: A Study in Constancy* (London: Phoenix House, 1952).

Ellis, R., '"Flores ad fabricandam ... coronam": an Investigation into the Uses and Abuses of the Revelations of St Birgitta of Sweden in 15th Century England', *Medium Ævum*, 51 (1982): 163–86.

Ellis, R., 'A Note on the Spirituality of St Bridget of Sweden', in J. Hogg (ed.), *Spiritualität heute und gestern, Analecta Cartusiana*, 35 (1982): 157–66.

Ellis, R., *Viderunt Eam Filie Syon: The Spirituality of The English House of a Medieval Contemplative Order from Its Beginnings to the Present Day*, Analecta Cartusiana, 68 (Salzburg: Institut für anglistik und amerikanistik, 1984).

Fanous, S. and H. Leyser (eds), *Christina of Markyate: A Twelfth-Century Holy Woman* (London: Routledge, 2005).

Fell, C., *Women in Anglo-Saxon England* (London: British Museum, 1984).

Ferber, J., 'Theophanes' Account of the Reign of Heraclius', in E. Jeffreys, M. Jeffreys and A. Moffat (eds), *Byzantine Papers: Proceedings of the First Australian Byzantine Studies Conference, Canberra, 17–19 May 1978*

(Canberra: Humanities Research Centre, Australian National University, 1981), pp. 32–42.

Flanagan, S., *Hildegard of Bingen: A Visionary Life* (London: Routledge, 1989).

Fogelqvist, I., *Apostacy and Reform in the Revelations of St Birgitta*, Bibliotheca Theologiae Practicae, 51 (Stockholm: Almqvist and Wiksell, 1993).

Fogelqvist, I., 'The New Vineyard: St. Birgitta of Sweden's *Regula Salvatoris* and the Monastic Tradition', in A. Härdelin (ed.), *In Quest of the Kingdom* (Stockholm: Almqvist & Wiksell, 1991), pp. 203–44.

Foot, S., 'The Making of *Angelcynn*: English Identity before the Norman Conquest', *Transactions of the Royal Historical Society*, 6th series, 6 (1996): 25–49.

Foss, C., 'Theodora and Evita: Two Women in Power', in C. Sode and S. Takács (eds), *Novum Millennium: Studies in Byzantine History and Culture, Presented to Paul Speck* (Aldershot: Ashgate, 2001), pp. 113–22.

Fouracre, P., *The Age of Charles Martel* (Harlow: Longman, 2000).

Fouracre, P., 'The Origins of the Carolingian Attempts to Regulate the Cult of Saints', in J. Howard-Johnston and P.A. Hayward (eds), *The Cult of Saints in late Antiquity and the Early Middle Ages: Essays on the Contribution of Peter Brown* (Oxford: Oxford University Press (1999), pp. 143–65.

Frantzen, A., *Before the Closet: Same-Sex Love from 'Beowulf' to 'Angels in America'* (Chicago, IL: University of Chicago Press, 1998).

Frugoni, C., 'The Imagined Woman', in C. Klapisch-Zuber (ed.), *A History of Women in the West*, 2, *Silences of the Middle Ages* (Cambridge, MA: Belknap Press of Harvard University Press, 1992), pp. 336–422.

Fulton, R., *From Judgement to Passion: Devotion to Christ and the Virgin Mary, 800–1200* (New York: Columbia University Press, 2002).

Fulton, R., '"Quae est ista quae ascendit sicut aurora consurgens?": the Song of Songs as the Historia for the Office of the Assumption', *Mediaeval Studies*, 60 (1998): 55–122.

Gailor, T.F., *Some Memories* (Kingsport, TN: Southern Publishers, 1937).

Gameson, R., *The Manuscripts of Early Norman England (c. 1066–1130)* (Oxford: Oxford University Press, 1999).

Ganshof, F.L., *Frankish Institutions under Charlemagne*, trans. B. Lyon and M. Lyon (New York: Norton, 1970).

Gaposchkin, M.C., *The Making of St Louis* (Ithaca, NY: Cornell University Press, 2008).

Garver, V.J, 'The Influence of Monastic Ideals upon Carolingian Conceptions of Childhood', in A. Classen (ed.), *Childhood in the Middle Ages and Renaissance* (Berlin: Walter de Gruyter, 2005), pp. 67–85.

Geary, P.J., *Aristocracy in Provence: The Rhône Basin at the Dawn of the Carolingian Age*, Monographien zur Geschichte des Mittelalters, 31 (Stuttgart: Anton Hiersemann, 1985).

Gee, E.A., 'The Painted Glass of All Saints Church, North Street, York', *Archaeologia*, 102 (1969): 151–202.

Gee, L., *Women, Art and Patronage from Henry III to Edward III, 1216–1377* (Woodbridge: Boydell and Brewer, 2002).

Genicot, L., *Les Généalogies*, Typologie des sources du moyen âge occidental, Fasc. 15 (Turnhout: Brepols, 1998).

Gibbs, R., *Tomaso da Modena* (Cambridge: Cambridge University Press, 1989).

Giffin, M.E., 'A Wigmore Manuscript at the University of Chicago', *National Library of Wales Journal*, 7 (1951–1952): 316–25.

Gijsel, J., *Die unmittelbare Textüberlieferung des sog. Pseudo-Matthäus* (Brussels: Koninklijke Academie voor wetenschappen, 1981).

Gilchrist, R., *Gender and Material Culture: The Archaeology of Religious Women* (London: Routledge, 1994).

Gilkær, H.T., *The Political Ideas of St. Birgitta and her Spanish Confessor, Alfonso Pecha:* Liber Celestis Imperatoris ad Reges: A Mirror of Princes, trans. M. Cain, Odense University Studies in History and Social Sciences, 163 (Odense: Odense University Press, 1993), pp. 216–18.

Gilsdorf, S., *Queenship and Sanctity: The* Lives *of Mathilda and the* Epitaph *of Adelheid* (Washington, DC: Catholic University of America Press, 2004).

Gilyard-Beer, R. and G. Coppack, 'Excavations at Fountains Abbey, North Yorkshire, 1979–80: The Early Development of the Monastery', *Archaeologia*, 108 (1986): 147–88.

Given-Wilson, C., 'Chronicles of the Mortimer Family c. 1250–1450', in R. Eales and S. Tyas (eds), *Family and Dynasty in Late Medieval England: Proceedings of the 1997 Harlaxton Symposium* (Donington: Shaun Tyas, 2003), pp. 67–86.

Glaze, F.E., 'Master–Student Medical Dialogues: The Evidence of London, British Library Sloane 2839', in P. Lendinara et al. (eds), *Form and Content of Instruction in Anglo-Saxon England in Light of Contemporary Manuscript Evidence*, Textes et études du moyen âge, 39 (Turnhout: Brepols, 2007), pp. 467–94.

Goldberg, P.J.P., *Women, Work and Life Cycle in a Medieval Economy: Women in York and Yorkshire, c.1300–1520* (Oxford: Clarendon Press, 1992).

Goodich, M., *The Unmentionable Vice: Homosexuality in the Later Medieval Period* (Santa Barbara, CA: ABC–Clio, 1979).

Goody, J., *The Development of the Family and Marriage in Europe* (Cambridge: Cambridge University Press, 1983).

Gransden, A., *Historical Writing in England, c. 1307 to the Early Sixteenth Century* (2 vols, London: Routledge, 1996, reprinted; originally published by Routledge and Kegan Paul, 1974, 1982).

Graus, F., *Volk, Herrscher und Heiliger im Reich der Merowinger: Studien zur Hagiographie der Merowingerzeit* (Prague: Nakladatelství Ceskoslovenské Akademie Věd, 1965).

Green, D.H., *Women Readers in the Middle Ages* (Cambridge: Cambridge University Press, 2007).

Green, M.H., 'Bibliography on Medieval Women, Gender and Medicine, 1980–2009', posted for free access on *Sciencia.cat*, http://www.sciencia.cat/english/libraryenglish/publicationssc.htm.

Green, M.H., 'Constantinus Africanus and the Conflict between Religion and Science', in G.R. Dunstan (ed.), *The Human Embryo: Aristotle and the Arabic and European Traditions* (Exeter: Exeter University Press, 1990), pp. 47–69.

Green, M.H., 'The De genecia Attributed to Constantine the African', *Speculum*, 62 (1987): 299–323.

Green, M.H., 'The Development of the Trotula', *Revue d'Histoire des Textes*, 26 (1996): 119–203.

Green, M.H., 'From "Diseases of Women" to "Secrets of Women": the Transformation of Gynecological Literature in the Later Middle Ages', *Journal of Medieval and Early Modern Studies*, 30 (2000): 5–39.

Green, M.H., 'Gendering the History of Women's Healthcare', *Gender and History*, Twentieth Anniversary Special Issue, 20, no. 3 (November 2008): 487–518.

Green, M.H., 'A Handlist of the Latin and Vernacular Manuscripts of the So-Called Trotula Texts. Part I: The Latin Manuscripts', *Scriptorium*, 50 (1996): 137–75.

Green, M.H., 'A Handlist of the Latin and Vernacular Manuscripts of the So-Called Trotula Texts. Part II: The Vernacular Texts and Latin Re-Writings', *Scriptorium*, 51 (1997): 80–104.

Green, M.H., *Making Women's Medicine Masculine: The Rise of Male Authority in Pre-Modern Gynaecology* (Oxford: Oxford University Press, 2008).

Green, M.H., 'Medieval Gynecological Texts: A Handlist', in M.H. Green (ed.), *Women's Healthcare in the Medieval West: Texts and Contexts* (Aldershot: Ashgate, 2000), Appendix, pp. 1–36.

Green, M.H., 'Moving from Philology to Social History: The Circulation and Uses of Albucasis's Latin *Surgery* in the Middle Ages', in F.E. Glaze and B. Nance (eds), *Between Text and Patient: The Medical Enterprise in Medieval and Early Modern Europe*, Micrologus' Library, 30 (Florence: SISMEL/Edizioni del Galluzzo, 2010), pp. 331–72.

Green, M.H., 'Obstetrical and Gynecological Texts in Middle English', *Studies in the Age of Chaucer*, 14 (1992): 53–88.

Green, M.H., 'Rethinking the Manuscript Basis of Salvatore De Renzi's *Collectio Salernitana*: The Corpus of Medical Writings in the "Long" Twelfth Century', in D. Jacquart and A. Paravicini Bagliani, *La 'Collectio Salernitana' di Salvatore De Renzi*, Edizione Nazionale 'La Scuola medica Salernitana', 3 (Florence: SISMEL/Edizioni del Galuzzo, 2008), pp. 15–60.

Green, M.H., 'Salerno on the Thames: The Genesis of Anglo-Norman Medical Literature', in J. Wogan-Browne et al. (eds), *Language and Culture in Medieval Britain: The French of England, c. 1100–c. 1500* (York: York Medieval Press, 2009), pp. 220–31.

Green, M.H., '"Traittié tout de mençonges": the *Secrés des dames*, "Trotula", and Attitudes Towards Women's Medicine in Fourteenth- and Early Fifteenth Century France', in M. Desmond (ed.), *Christine de Pizan and the Categories of Difference* (Minneapolis, MN: University of Minnesota Press, 1998), pp. 146–78; reprinted in Green, Women's Healthcare, essay VI.

Green, M.H., *The 'Trotula': a Medieval Compendium of Women's Medicine* (Philadelphia, PA: University of Pennsylvania Press, 2001).

Green, M.H. and L.R. Mooney, 'The Sickness of Women', in M.T. Tavormina (ed.), *Sex, Aging, and Death in a Medieval Medical Compendium: Trinity College Cambridge MS R.14.52, Its Texts, Language, and Scribe*, Medieval and Renaissance Texts and Studies, 292 (2 vols, Tempe, AZ: Arizona Center for Medieval and Renaissance Studies, 2006), vol. 2, pp. 455–568.

Grierson, P., *Catalogue of the Byzantine Coins in the Dumbarton Oaks Collection and the Whittemore Collection, III: Leo III to Nikephoros III 717–1081. Part 1: Leo III to Michael III (717–867)* (Washington, DC: Dumbarton Oaks, 1973).

Guerreau-Jalabert, A., 'L'Arbre de Jessé et l'ordre chrétien de la parenté', in I. Prat (ed.), *Marie: Le culte de la vierge dans la société médiévale* (Paris: Beauchesne, 1996), pp. 137–70.

Guerreau-Jalabert, A., 'La désignation des relations et des groupes de parenté en latin mediéval', *Archivium latinitatis medii aevi (Bulletin du Cange)*, 46–47 (1988): 65–108.

Guerreau-Jalabert, A., 'Sur les structures de parenté dans l'Europe mediévale', *Annales: économies, sociétés, civilizations*, 36 (1981): 1028–49.

Guisso, R.W.L., 'The reigns of the empress Wu, Chung-tsung and Jui-tsung (684–712)', in D. Twitchett (ed.), *Cambridge History of China*, iii: *Sui and T'ang China, 589–906*, part 1 (Cambridge: Cambridge University Press, 1979), pp. 290–332.

Guisso, R.W.L., *Wu Tse-T'ien and the Politics of Legitimisation in T'ang China* (Bellingham, WA: Western Washington, 1978).

Hallendorff, J.H. and A. Schück, *History of Sweden*, trans. L. Yapp (Stockholm: C.E. Fritze, 1929).

Halsall, G., *Settlement and Social Organization: The Merovingian Region of Metz* (Cambridge: Cambridge University Press, 1995).

Hanawalt, B., *Growing Up in Medieval London: The Experience of Childhood in History* (New York: Oxford University Press, 1993).

Harris, M.T. (ed.), *Birgitta of Sweden, Life and Selected Revelations*, trans. Kezel, Albert Ryle, Classics of Western Spirituality (New York: Mahwah, 1990).

Harthan, J., *Books of Hours and their Owners* (London: Thames & Hudson, 1977).

Harvey, R.J. (ed.), 'En sa veillesse siet le prodhom', in I. Short (ed.), *Anglo-Norman Anniversary Essays*, ANTS OPS 2 (London: ANTS, 1993), pp. 159–78.

Hector, L.C. and B.F. Harvey (eds), *The Westminster Chronicle 1381–1394* (Oxford: Clarendon Press, 1982).

Heene, K., *The Legacy of Paradise: Marriage, Motherhood and Woman in Carolingian Edifying Literature* (Frankfurt: Peter Lang, 1997).

Heffernan, T., *Sacred Biography: Saints and Their Biographers in the Middle Ages* (Oxford: Oxford University Press, 1988).

Heidecker, K., *The Divorce of Lothar II: Christian Marriage and Political Power in the Carolingian World*, trans. Tanis Guest (Ithaca, NY: Cornell University Press, 2010).

Hellinga, L. and J.B. Trapp (eds), *The Cambridge History of the Book in Britain, 3, 1400–1557* (Cambridge: Cambridge University Press, 1999).

Herrin, J., *Women in Purple: Rulers of Medieval Byzantium* (London: Weidenfeld and Nicolson, 2001).

Heslop, T.A., 'The Virgin Mary's Regalia and Twelfth-century English Seals', in A. Borg and A. Martindale (eds), *The Vanishing Past: Studies Presented to Christopher Hohler* (Oxford: BAR, 1981), pp. 53–62.

Hewson, M.A., *Giles of Rome and the Medieval Theory of Conception* (London: Athlone Press, 1975).

Hicks, M., *Bastard Feudalism* (London: Longman, 1995).

Hiscock, N., *The Symbol at Your Door: Number and Geometry in Religious Architecture of the Greek and Latin Middle Ages* (Aldershot: Ashgate, 2007).

Hogg, J., 'Cardinal Easton's Letter to the Abbess and Community of Vadstena', in J. Hogg, *Studies in St. Birgitta and the Brigittine Order, Spiritualität heute und gestern, Analecta Cartusiana*, 35:19 (Salzburg: Institut für Anglistik und Amerikanistik, Universität Salzburg, 1993), vol. 2, pp. 20–26.

Hogg, J. (ed.), *Spiritualität heute und gestern, Analecta Cartusiana*, 35:1 (Salzburg: Institut für Anglistik und Amerikanistik, Universität Salzburg, 1982).

Hogg, J. (ed.), *Studies in St. Birgitta and the Brigittine Order, Spiritualität heute und gestern, Analecta Cartusiana*, 35:19 (2 vols, Salzburg: Institut für Anglistik und Amerikanistik, Universität Salzburg, 1993).

Holden, B., *Lords of the Central Marches: English Aristocracy and Frontier Society, 1087–1265* (Oxford: Oxford University Press, 2008).

Holder, A.G., 'The Mosaic Tabernacle in Early Christian Exegesis', *Studia Patristica*, 25 (1993): 101–106; vol. 1 (Stockholm, 1875–1884); vol. 2 (Stockholm, 1879–1887); vol. 3 (Stockholm, 1885–1902).

Holdsworth, C., 'The Chronology and Character of Early Cistercian Legislation on Art and Architecture', in C. Norton and D. Park (eds), *Cistercian Art and Architecture* (Cambridge: Cambridge University Press, 1986), pp. 40–56.

Holum, K., *Theodosian Empresses: Women and Imperial Dominion in Late Antiquity* (Berkeley, CA: University of California Press, 1982).

Hopper, V.F., *Medieval Number Symbolism: Its Sources, Meaning, and Influence on Thought and Expression* (New York: Columbia University Press, 1938).

Hudson, J., 'Court Cases and Legal Arguments in England, c. 1066–1166', *Transactions of the Royal Historical Society*, 6th series, 10 (2000): 91–115.

Hudson, J. (ed.), *History of the Church of Abingdon* (Oxford: Clarendon Press, 2002).

Hunt, A., *Anglo-Norman Medicine*, vol. 2 (Cambridge: Cambridge University Press, 1997).

Hunt, A., *Plant Names of Medieval England* (Cambridge: D.S. Brewer, 1989).

Hunter, D., *Marriage, Celibacy, and Heresy in Ancient Christianity: The Jovinianist Controversy* (Oxford: Oxford University Press, 2007).

Hutchinson, A.M., '*The Myroure or our Ladye*: A Medieval Guide for Contemplatives', in J. Hogg, *Studies in St. Birgitta and the Brigittine Order, Spiritualität heute und gestern, Analecta Cartusiana*, 35:19 (Salzburg: Institut für Anglistik und Amerikanistik, Universität Salzburg, 1993), vol. 2, pp. 215–27.

Hutton, G. and E. Smith, *English Parish Churches* (London: Thames & Hudson, 1952, rev. 1957).

Hyams, P.R., *Rancor and Reconciliation in Medieval England* (Ithaca, NY: Cornell University Press, 2003).

Hyams, P.R., 'Warranty and Good Lordship in Twelfth-century England', *Law and History Review*, 5 (1987): 437–503.

Ingledew, F., 'The Book of Troy and the Genealogical Construction of History: The Case of Geoffrey of Monmouth's *Historia regum Britanniae*', *Speculum*, 69 (1994): 665–704.

Innes, M., 'A Place of Discipline: Carolingian Court and Aristocratic Youth', in C. Cubitt (ed.), *Court Culture in the Early Middle Ages* (Turnhout: Brepols, 2003), pp. 59–76.

Innes, M., *State and Society in the Early Middle Ages: The Middle Rhine Valley, 400–1000* (Cambridge: Cambridge University Press, 2000).

Iogna-Prat, D., 'Le culte de la Vierge sous le règne de Charles le Chauve', *Les Cahiers de Saint-Michel de Cuxa*, 22 (1992): 97–116.

Iogna-Prat, D. (ed.), *Marie: Le culte de la vierge dans la société médiévale* (Paris: Beauchesne, 1996), pp. 65–98.

Jacquart, D. and C. Thomasset, *Sexualité et savoir médical au moyen âge* (Paris, 1985), English trans. *Sexuality and Medical Knowledge in the Middle Ages* (Oxford: Polity Press/Princeton, NJ: Princeton University Press, 1988).

Jaeger, C.S., 'The Loves of Christina of Markyate', in S. Fanous and H. Leyser (eds), *Christina of Markyate. A Twelfth-Century Holy Woman* (London: Routledge, 2005), pp. 99–115.

James, E., *Empresses and Power in Early Byzantium* (Leicester: Leicester University Press, 2001).

Jenkins, J., 'Reading Women Reading: Feminism, Culture, and Memory', in L. D'Arcens and J.F. Ruys (eds), *Maistresse of My Wit: Medieval Women, Modern Scholars* (Turnhout: Brepols, 2004).

Johns, S.M., *Noblewomen, Aristocracy and Power in the Twelfth Century Anglo-Norman Realm* (Manchester: Manchester University Press, 2003).

Johnson, L., 'Return to Albion', *Arthurian Literature*, 13 (1994): 19–40.

Johnston, F.R., 'English Defenders of St. Bridget', in J. Hogg, *Studies in St Birgitta and the Brigittine Order*, Spiritualität heute und gestern, Analecta Cartusiana, 35:19 (Salzburg: Institut für Anglistik und Amerikanistik, Universität Salzburg, 1993), 1.263–75.

Johnston, S.H.F., 'The Lands of Hubert de Burgh', *English Historical Review*, 50 (1935): 418–32.

Jones, A.H.M., *The Later Roman Empire 284–602* (2 vols, Oxford: Basil Blackwell, 1964).

Jones, C.W., *Saints' Lives and Chronicles in Early England* (Ithaca, NY: Cornell University Press, 1947).

Jönsson, A., *Alfonso of Jaén: His Life and Works with Critical Editions of the Epistola Solitarii, the Informaciones and Epistola Serui Christi*, Studia Graeca et Latina Lundensia, 1 (Lund: Lund University Press, 1989).

Jordan, M.D., *The Invention of Sodomy in Christian Theology* (Chicago, IL: University of Chicago Press, 1997).

Jørgensen, J., *Saint Bridget of Sweden*, trans. I. Lund (2 vols, London: Longmans, Green, 1954).

Junod, E. and J.-D. Kaestli, *L'histoire des Actes Apocryphes des Apôtres du III au IX siècle. Le cas des Actes de Jean* (Geneva: La Concorde, 1982).

Keats-Rohan, K.S.B., *Domesday People: A Prosopography of Persons Occurring in English Documents, 1066–1166 I Domesday Book* (Woodbridge and Rochester: Boydell, 1999).

Kelly, S., 'Anglo-Saxon Lay Society and the Written Word', in R. McKitterick (ed.), *The Uses of Literacy in Early Medieval Europe* (Cambridge: Cambridge University Press, 1990), pp. 36–62.

Ker, N.R., *A Catalogue of Manuscripts Containing Anglo-Saxon* (Oxford: Clarendon, 1957).

Keynes, S., and M. Lapidge, *Alfred the Great* (London: Penguin, 1983).

Klockars, B., *Birgitta och böckerna. En undersökning av den heliga Birgittas källor* (Stockholm: Almqvist & Wiksell, 1966).

Knowles, M.D., *The Religious Orders in England* (3 vols, Cambridge: Cambridge University Press, 1948–1959).

Knowles, M.D. and R.N. Hadcock, *Medieval Religious Houses: England and Wales* (London: Longman, 1971).

Kowaleski, M., 'Shipping and the Carrying Trade in Medieval Dartmouth', in M.-L. Heckmann and J. Röhrkasten (eds), *Von Nowgorod bis London. Studien zu Handel, Wirtschaft und Gesellschaft im mittelalterlichen Europa. Festschrift für Stuart Jenks zum 60. Geburtstag*, Nova Mediaevalia. Quellen und Studien zum europäischen Mittelalter, 4 (Göttingen: V&R unipress, 2008), pp. 465–87.

Kuefler, M., *The Boswell Thesis* (Chicago, IL: University of Chicago Press, 2006).

Lambot, C., 'L'Homélie du Pseudo-Jérôme sur l'Assomption et l'Évangile de la Nativité de Marie d'après une lettre inédit d'Hincmar', *Revue Bénédictine*, 46 (1934): 265–82.

Lampe, W.H. and K.J. Woollcombe, *Essays on Typology*, Studies in Biblical Theology, 22 (London, 1957).

Lawrence, C.H., *The Life of St Edmund of Abingdon by Matthew Paris* (Oxford: Alan Sutton, 1996).

Lea, H.C., *History of Sacerdotal Celibacy in the Christian Church*, 4th edn (London: Watts & Co., 1932).

Leclercq, H., 'L'épiscopat de saint Bertrand', in F. Cabrol and H. Leclercq (eds), *Dictionaire d'Archéologie Chrétienne et de Liturgie* (15 vols, Paris: Letouzey et Ané, 1924–1953), x, cols 1490–522.

Lega-Weekes, E., 'The Mohun Chronicle at Haccombe', *Devon Notes and Queries*, 4 (1906–1907): 17–22.

Le Goff, J., *Saint Louis* (Paris: Gallimard, 1996).

Le Jan, R., *Famille et pouvoir dans le monde franc (viie–xe siècle). Essai d'anthropologie sociale* (Paris: La Sorbonne, 2003).

Le Jan, R., *La société du haut Moyen Âge, vi^e–ixe siècle* (Paris: Armand Colin, 2003).

Leongard, J.S., 'Rationabilis dos', in S.S. Walker (ed.), *Wife and Widow in Medieval England* (Ann Arbor, MI: University of Michigan Press, 1993).

Lewis, S., *A Topographical Dictionary of England*, 7th edn (4 vols, London: S. Lewis & Co., 1848).

Leyser, H., 'Clerical Purity and the Re-ordered World', in M. Rubin and W. Simons (eds), *Christianity in Western Europe, c. 1100–c. 1500* (Cambridge: Cambridge University Press, 2009), pp. 11–21.

Leyser, H., *Hermits and the New Monasticism: A Study of Religious Communities in Western Europe 1000–1150* (London: Macmillan, 1984).

Leyser, H., *Medieval Women: A Social History of Women in England, 450–1500* (London: Weidenfeld and Nicolson, 1995).

Leyser, K., 'The German Aristocracy from the Ninth to the Twelfth Centuries. A Historical and Cultural Sketch', *Past and Present*, 41 (1968): 25–53.

Leyser, K., 'Maternal Kin in Early Medieval Germany: A Reply', *Past and Present*, 49 (1970): 126–34.

Leyser, K., *Rule and Conflict in an Early Medieval Society: Ottonian Saxony* (London: Edward Arnold, 1979).

Lieberman, M., *The Medieval March of Wales: The Creation and Perception of a Frontier, 1066–1283* (Cambridge: Cambridge University Press, 2010).

Lightbown, R., *Sandro Botticelli: Life and Work* (London: Thames & Hudson, 1989).

Lilie, R.-J. with I. Roschow, *Byzanz unter Eirene und Konstantin VI. (780–802)* (Frankfurt-am-Main: Peter Lang, 1996).

Limberis, V., *Divine Heiress: The Virgin Mary and the Creation of Christian Constantinople* (London: Routledge, 1994).

Lindgren, M., 'Altars and Apostles: St Brigitta's Provisions of the Altars in the Abbey Church at Vadstena and their Reflection of Birgittine Spirituality', in A. Härdelin (ed.), *In Quest of the Kingdom, Ten Papers on Medieval Monastic Spirituality*, Bibliotheca Theologiae Practicae, 48 (Stockholm: Almqvist & Wiksell, 1991), pp. 245–82.

Little, L.K. and B.H. Rosenwein, *Debating the Middle Ages: Issues and Readings* (Oxford: Blackwell, 1998).

Loengard, J.S., "'Of the Gift of her Husband': English Dower and its Consequences in the Year 1200", in J. Kirshner and S.F. Wemple (eds), *Women of the Medieval World: Essays in Honour of John H. Mundy* (Oxford: Blackwell, 1985), pp. 215–55.

MacAlister, R.A.S., *Ecclesiastical Vestments: Their Development and History*, The Camden Library (London, 1896).

MacLean, S., *Kingship and Politics in the Late Ninth Century: Charles the Fat and the End of the Carolingian Empire* (Cambridge: Cambridge University Press, 2003).

MacLean, S., 'Queenship, Nunneries and Royal Widowhood in Carolingian Europe', *Past and Present*, 178 (2003): 3–38.

Macray, W.D., *The Collection of Brackley Deeds at Magdalen College* (Buckingham, 1910).

Magdalino, P., 'Paphlagonians in Byzantine High Society', in S. Lampakis (ed.), *Byzantine Asia Minor (6th–12th c.)*, Institute for Byzantine Research, International Symposium, 6 (Athens, 1998), pp. 141–50.

Magnou-Nortier, E., ' La chute de Rome a-t-elle eu lieu?', *Bibliothèque de l'Ecole de Chartes*, 152 (1994): 521–41.

Maitland, F.W. et al., *Essays on the Teaching of History* (Cambridge: Cambridge University Press, 1901).

Makowski, E.M., 'The Conjugal Debt and Canon Law', *Journal of Medieval History*, 3 (1977): 99–114.

Mango, C. and R. Scott (ed. and trans.), *The Chronicle of Theophanes Confessor: Byzantine and Near Eastern History, AD 284–813* (Oxford: Oxford University Press, 1997).

Marvin, J., 'Albine and Isabelle: Regicidal Queens and the Historical Imagination of the Anglo-Norman Prose *Brut* Chronicles', *Arthurian Literature*, 18 (2001): 143–91.

Marvin, J., ed. and trans., *The Oldest Anglo-Norman Prose* Brut *Chronicle* (Woodbridge: Boydell Press, 2006).

Marvin, J., 'The Vitality of Anglo-Norman in Late Medieval England: The Case of the Prose *Brut* Chronicle', in J. Wogan-Browne (ed.), *Language and Culture in Medieval Britain: The French of England c. 1100–c. 1500* (Woodbridge: York Medieval Press with Boydell, 2009), pp. 303–19.

Matarasso, P., *The Cistercian World. Monastic Writings of the Twelfth Century* (London: Penguin, 1993).

Matheson, L.M., *The Prose Brut: The Development of a Middle English Chronicle* (Tempe, AZ: CMERS, 1988).

Mathew, G., *The Court of Richard II* (London: John Murray, 1968).

Mathey-Maille, L., *Écritures du passé. Histoires des ducs de Normandie* (Paris: Champion, 2007).

Mathey-Maille, L., 'L'Etymologie dans le *Roman de Rou* de Wace', in K. Busby, B. Guidot and L.E. Whalen (eds), *De sens rassis. Essays in Honor of Rupert T. Pickens* (Amsterdam: Rodopi, 2005), pp. 404–14.

Matthew, D., 'The Incongruities of the St Albans Psalter', *Journal of Medieval History*, 34 (2008): 396–416.

Maxwell-Lyte, H.C., *A History of Dunster*, 2 vols (London: St Catherine Press, 1909).

Maxwell-Lyte, H.C., *Dunster and its Lords 1066–1881* (printed in Exeter for private circulation, 1882).

Maxwell-Lyte, H.C., 'The Mohun Chronicle at Haccombe', *Devon Notes and Queries*, 4 (1906–1907): 249–52.

Mayo, J., *A History of Ecclesiastical Dress* (London: B.T. Batsford, 1984).

Mayr-Harting, H., 'The Idea of the Assumption of Mary in the West, 800–1200', in R.N. Swanson (ed.), *The Church and Mary*, Studies in Church History, 39 (Woodbridge: Boydell, 2004), pp. 86–111.

Mayr-Harting, H., 'The Miracles of St Frideswide', in H. Mayr-Harting and R.I. Moore (eds), *Studies in Medieval History, Presented to R.H.C. Davis* (London: Hambledon, 1985), pp. 193–206.

Mayr-Harting, H., *Religion, Politics and Society in Britain, 1066–1272* (Harlow: Pearson, 2011).

McEvoy, J., 'Robert Grosseteste on the Ten Commandments', *Recherches de Théologie Ancienne et Médiévale*, 58 (1991): 167–205.

McGuire, B.P., 'Bernard and Mary's Milk: A Northern Contribution', in B.P. McGuire, *The Difficult Saint. Bernard of Clairvaux and his Tradition* (Kalamazoo, MI: Cistercian Institute Publications, 1991), pp. 189–225.

McGuire, B.P., *Brother and Lover: Aelred of Rievaulx* (New York: Crossroad, 1994).

McGuire, B.P., *Friendship and Community: The Monastic Experience 350–1250* (Kalamazoo, MI: Cisterican Institute Publications, 1988).

McKitterick, R., *The Carolingians and the Written Word* (Cambridge: Cambridge University Press, 1989).

McNamara, J., 'The *Herrenfrage*: The Restructuring of the Gender System, 1050–1150', in C.A. Lees (ed.), *Medieval Masculinities. Regarding Men in the Middle Ages* (Minneapolis, MN: University of Minnesota Press, 1994), pp. 3–29.

McVaugh, M.R., 'Who Was Gilbert the Englishman?', in G.H. Brown and L. Ehrsam Voigts (eds), *The Study of Medieval Manuscripts of England:*

Festschrift in Honor of Richard W. Pfaff (Tempe, AZ: Arizona Center for Medieval and Renaissance Studies; and Turnhout: Brepols, 2010), pp. 295–324.

Megson, B., 'Life Expectations of the Widows and Orphans of Freemen in London 1375–1399', *Local Population Studies*, 57 (1996): 18–29.

Mendenhall, G.E., 'Law and Covenant in Israel and the Ancient Near East', *Biblical Archaeologist*, 17 (1954): 26–46 and 49–76.

Menuge, N.J., 'A Few Home Truths: The Medieval Mother as Guardian in Romance and Law', in N.J. Menuge (ed.), *Medieval Women and the Law* (Woodbridge: Boydell, 2000), pp. 77–103.

Meyer, P., 'Les manuscrits français de Cambridge. III. Trinity College O.I.20, Traités de médecine', *Romania*, 32 (1903): 75–101.

Milsom, S.F.C., 'Inheritance by Women in the Twelfth and Early Thirteenth Centuries', in M.S. Arnold, T.A. Green, S.A. Scully and S.D. White (eds), *On the Laws and Customs of England: Essays in Honor of Samuel E. Thorne* (Chapel Hill, NC: University of North Carolina Press, 1981), pp. 60–89.

Mitchell, L.E., *Portraits of Medieval Women: Family, Marriage, and Politics in England 1255–1350* (New York: Palgrave/Macmillan, 2003).

Moore, P.S. and J.A. Corbett (eds), Peter of Poitiers, *Allegoriae super tabernaculum Moysi*, Publications in Mediaeval Studies, 3 (Notre Dame, IN: Notre Dame University Press, 1938).

Moore, R.I., *The Discovery of the Individual 1050–1200* (Toronto: University of Toronto Press, 1987).

Moore, R.I., 'Duby's Eleventh Century', *History*, 69 (1984): 36–54.

Moore, R.I., 'Family, Community, and Cult on the Eve of the Gregorian Reform', *Transactions of the Royal Historical Society*, 30 (1980): 49–69.

Moore, R.I., *The First European Revolution, c. 970–1215* (Oxford: Blackwells, 2000).

Morgan, N.J., 'Books for the liturgy and private prayer', in N.J. Morgan and R.M. Thomson (eds), *The Cambridge History of the Book in Britain, volume 2, 1100–1400* (Cambridge: Cambridge University Press, 2008), pp. 291–316.

Morgan, N.J., *Early Gothic Manuscripts, 1190–1225*, A Survey of Manuscripts Illuminated in the British Isles, 3 (Oxford: Harvey Miller, 1982).

Morgan, N.J., 'Patrons and their Devotions in the Initials of Thirteenth-Century English Psalters', in F.O. Büttner (ed.), *The Illuminated Psalter* (Turnhout: Brepols, 1999), p. 318.

Morris, B., *St Birgitta of Sweden* (Woodbridge: Boydell, 1999).

Morris, M., *The Bigod Earls of Norfolk in the Thirteenth Century* (Woodbridge: Boydell, 2005).

Mostert, M., *Oraliteit* (Amsterdam: Amsterdam University Press, 1998).

Moulinier, L. (ed.), *Beate Hildegardis Cause et cure*, Rarissima mediaevalia, 1 (Berlin: Akademie Verlag, 2003).

Moulinier, L., 'Hildegarde ou Pseudo-Hildegarde? Réflexions sur l'authenticité du traité *Cause et cure*', in R. Berndt (ed.), *'Im Angesicht Gottes suche der Mensch sich selbst': Hildegard von Bingen (1098–1179)* (Berlin: Akademie Verlag, 2001).

Muir, B.J., 'The Early Insular Prayer Book Tradition and the Development of Books of Hours', in M.M. Manion and B.J. Muir (eds), *The Art of the Book: its Place in Medieval Worship* (Exeter: University of Exeter Press, 1998), pp. 9–20.

Mulder-Bakker, A.B., 'Introduction', in A.B. Mulder-Bakker (ed.), *Sanctity and Motherhood: Essays on Holy Mothers in the Middle Ages* (New York: Garland, 1995), pp. 16–23.

Neel, C., trans. with intro., *Handbook for William: A Carolingian Woman's Counsel for her Son* (Lincoln, NE: University of Nebraska Press, 1991; reprinted with Addendum on historiography, Washington, DC: Catholic University of America Press, 1999).

Nelson, J.L., *Charles the Bald* (London: Longman, 1992).

Nelson, J.L., 'Dhuoda', in P. Wormald and J.L. Nelson (eds), *Lay Intellectuals in the Carolingian World* (Cambridge: Cambridge University Press, 2007), pp. 106–20.

Nelson, J.L., 'Queens as Jezebels: The Careers of Brunhild and Balthild in Merovingian History', in D. Baker (ed.), *Medieval Women: Dedicated and Presented to Professor Rosalind M.T. Hill on the Occasion of her Seventieth Birthday*, Studies in Church History, Subsidia, 1 (Oxford: Basil Blackwell, 1978), pp. 31–77.

Nelson, J.L., *The Frankish World, 750–900* (London: Hambledon, 1996).

Nelson, J.L., 'Was Charlemagne's Court a Courtly Society?', in C. Cubitt (ed.), *Court Culture in the Early Middle Ages* (Turnhout: Brepols, 2003), pp. 39–57.

Nelson, J.L., 'Women at the Court of Charlemagne: A Case of Monstrous Regiment?', in Nelson, *The Frankish World, 750–900* (London: Hambledon Press, 1996), pp. 223–42.

Newton, F., *The Scriptorium and Library at Monte Cassino, 1058–1105* (Cambridge: Cambridge University Press, 1999).

Nichols, F.M., ed., *Britton* (2 vols, Oxford: Clarendon Press, 1865), online at www.anglo-norman.net/texts/.

Nicholson, H.J., 'Margaret de Lacy and the Hospital of Saint John at Aconbury, Herefordshire', *Journal of Ecclesiastical History*, 50 (1999): 629–50.

Noonan, J.T., *Contraception. A History of its Treatment by the Catholic Theologians and Canonists* (Cambridge, MA: Belknap Press of Harvard University Press, 1966).

Norton, C., 'Table of Cistercian Legislation on Art and Architecture', in C. Norton and D. Park (eds), *Cistercian Art and Architecture* (Cambridge: Cambridge University Press, 1986), pp. 315–93.

Norton, C., D. Park and P. Binski, *Dominican Painting in East Anglia: The Thornham Parva Retable and the Musée de Cluny Frontal* (Woodbridge: Boydell, 1987).

Nyberg, T. (ed.), *Birgitta, hendes værk og hendes klostre i Norden* (Odense: Odense University Press, 1991).

Nyberg, T., *Birgittinsk festgåva. Studier on heliga Birgitta och Birgittinorden* (Uppsala: Teologiska institutionen vid Uppsala universitet, 1991).

Nyberg, T., 'Byggandsföreskrifter för birgittineklostern', *Fornvännen*, 87 (1992): 255–59.

Nyberg, T., 'The Thirteen Apostles in the Spiritual World of St. Birgitta', in J. Hogg, *Studies in St. Birgitta and the Brigittine Order, Spiritualität heute und gestern, Analecta Cartusiana*, 35:19 (Salzburg: Institut für Anglistik und Amerikanistik, Universität Salzburg, 1993), vol. 1, pp. 192–208.

O'Donnell, J.J., *Augustine: A New Biography* (New York: Harper Perennial, 2005).

Oexle, G., 'Die Karolinger und die Stadt des heiligen Arnulf', *Frühmittelalterliche Studien*, 1 (1967): 250–364.

O'Keeffe, K.O.'B., 'Listening to the Scene of Reading: King Alfred's Talking Prefaces', in M. Chinca and C. Young (eds), *Orality and Literacy: Essays on a Conjunction and its Consequences in Honour of D.H. Green* (Turnhout: Brepols, 2005), pp. 17–36.

Orme, N., *Medieval Children* (New Haven, CT: Yale University Press, 2001).

Ozment, S., *When Fathers Ruled. Family Life in Reformation Europe* (Cambridge, MA: Harvard University Press, 1983).

Pächt, O. et al. (eds), *The St Albans Psalter* (London: Warburg Institute, 1960).

Paden, W.D. and F.F. Paden, 'Swollen Woman, Shifting Canon: A Midwife's Charm and the Birth of Secular Romance Lyric', *PMLA*, 125 (2010): 306–21.

Pahta, P., *Medieval Embryology in the Vernacular. The Case of* De spermate, Mémoires de la Société Néophilologique de Helsinki, 53 (Helsinki: Société Néophilologique, 1998).

Painter, S., 'The House of Quency, 1136–1264', *Medievalia et Humanistica*, 11 (1957): 3–9.

Palmer, R.C., 'Contexts of Marriage in Medieval England: Evidence from the King's Court circa 1300', *Speculum*, 59 (1984): 42–67.

Pantin, W.A., 'The Defensorium of Adam of Easton', *English Historical Review*, 51 (1936): 675–80.

Paradisi, G., '"Par muement de langages". Il tempo, la memoria e il volgare in Wace', *Francofonia*, 45 (2003): 27–45.

Patzold, S., *Episcopus. Wissen über Bischöfe im Frankenreich des späten 8. bis frühen 10. Jahrhunderts* (Ostfildern: Thorbecke, 2008).

Payan, P., *Joseph. Une image de la paternité dans l'Occident médiévale* (Paris: Aubier, 2006).

Payer, P.J., *The Bridling of Desire: Ideas of Sex in the Later Middle Ages* (Toronto: University of Toronto Press, 1993).

Pevsner, N. and P. Metcalf, *The Cathedrals of England: The South-East* (London: Folio Society, 2005).

Piltz, A., 'Magister Mathias of Sweden in his Theological Context: A Preliminary Survey', in M. Asztalos (ed.), *The Editing of Theological and Philosophical Texts from the Middle Ages*, Acta Universitatis Stockholmiensis, Studia Latina Stockholmiensia, 30 (Stockholm: Almqvist & Wiksell, 1986), pp. 137–60.

Poole, A.L., *Obligations of Society in the XII and XIII Centuries* (Oxford: Clarendon Press, 1946).

Power, D., *The Norman Frontier in the Twelfth and Early Thirteenth Centuries* (Cambridge: Cambridge University Press, 2004).

Power, E., *Medieval English Nunneries c. 1275–1535*, Cambridge Studies in Medieval Life and Thought (Cambridge: Cambridge University Press, 1922).

Power, K., *Veiled Desire: Augustine's Writing on Women* (London: Darton, Longman and Todd, 1995).

Prinz, F., *Frühes Mönchtum im Frankenreich: Kultur und Gesellschaft in Gallien, den Rheinlanden und Bayern am Beispiel der monastischen Entwicklung* (4. bis 8. Jahrhundert), 2nd edn (Munich: R. Oldenbourg, 1988).

Prosopographie der mittelbyzantinischen Zeit, ed. R.-J. Lilie et al. (6 vols, Berlin: De Gruyter, 1998–2002).

Prosopography of the Byzantine Empire, I, 641–867, CD ROM, ed. J.R. Martindale (Aldershot: Ashgate, 2001).

Puff, H., *Sodomy in Reformation Germany and Switzerland, 1400–1600* (Chicago, IL: University of Chicago Press, 2003).

Reimitz, H., 'Anleitung zur Interpretation. Schrift und Genealogie in der Karolingerzeit', in W. Pohl and P. Herold (eds), *Vom Nutzen des Schreibens. Soziales Gedächtnis, Herrschaft und Besitz im Mittelalter* (Vienna: Akademie der Wissenschaften, 2002), pp. 167–81.

Reimitz, H., 'Ein karolingisches Geschichtsbuch aus Saint-Amand. Der Cvp 473', in C. Egger and H. Weigl (eds), *Text – Schrift – Codex. Quellenkundliche*

Arbeiten aus dem Institut für Österreichische Geschichtsforschung, Mitteilungen des Instituts für Österreichische Geschichtsforschung, Erg. bd. 35 (Vienna: Oldenbourg, 2000), pp. 34–90.

Reimitz, H., 'Geschlechterrollen und Genealogie in der fränkischen Historiographie', in C. Ulf and R. Rollinger (eds), *Frauenbild und Geschlechterrollen bei antiken Autoren an der Wende von der Spätantike zum Mittelalter* (Cologne: Böhlau, 2007), pp. 335–54.

Reuter, T., 'The End of Carolingian Military Expansion', in P. Godman and R. Collins (eds), *Charlemagne's Heir* (Oxford: Clarendon Press, 1990), pp. 391–405.

Reuter, T., 'Plunder and Tribute in the Carolingian Empire', *Transactions of the Royal Historical Society*, 35 (1985): 75–94.

Reynolds, S., *Fiefs and Vassals* (Oxford: Oxford University Press, 1994).

Riché, P., 'Les bibliothèques de trois aristocrates laïcs carolingiens', *Le Moyen Âge*, 69 (1963): 87–104; reprinted in P. Riché, *Instruction et vie religieuse dans le Haut Moyen Âge* (London: Variorum, 1981).

Riché, P., 'Recherches sur l'instruction des laics du XIe au XIIe siècle', *Cahiers de Civilisation Médiévale*, 5 (1962): 175–82.

Riddy, F., 'Mother Knows Best: Reading Social Change in a Courtesy Text', *Speculum*, 71 (1996): 66–86.

Riley, H.T., ed., *Memorials of London and London Life* (London: Longmans, Green & Co., 1868).

Ringrose, K.M., *The Perfect Servant: Eunuchs and the Social Construction of Gender in Byzantium* (Chicago, IL: University of Chicago Press, 2003).

Rosenwein, B., *Anger's Past* (Ithaca, NY: Cornell University Press, 1998).

Rosenwein, B., *Emotional Communities in the Early Middle Ages* (Ithaca, NY: Cornell University Press, 2006).

Rothschild, N. Harry, *Wu Zhao: China's Only Woman Emperor* (New York: Pearson, 2008).

Rubin, M., *Charity and Community in Medieval Cambridge* (Cambridge: Cambridge University Press, 1987).

Rubin, M., *Corpus Christi: The Eucharist in Late Medieval Culture* (Cambridge: Cambridge University Press, 1991).

Rubin, M., *Mother of God: A History of the Virgin Mary* (London: Allen Lane, 2009).

Rusche, P.G., 'The Sources for Plant Names in Anglo-Saxon England and the Laud Herbal Glossary', in P. Dendle and A. Touwaide (eds), *Health and Healing from the Medieval Garden* (Woodbridge: Boydell, 2008), pp. 128–44.

Rushforth, R., 'The Eleventh- and Early Twelfth-Century Manuscripts of Bury St Edmunds Abbey', unpublished PhD dissertation (Cambridge, 2003).

Sahlin, C., *Birgitta of Sweden and the Voice of Prophecy* (Woodbridge: Boydell, 2001).

Sahlin, C., "'A Marvellous and Great Exultation of the Heart": Mystical Pregnancy and Marian Devotion in Birgitta of Sweden's *Revelations*', in J. Hogg, *Studies in St. Birgitta and the Brigittine Order, Spiritualität heute und gestern, Analecta Cartusiana*, 35:19 (Salzburg: Institut für Anglistik und Amerikanistik, Universität Salzburg, 1993), vol. 1, pp. 108–28.

Salvat, M., 'L'Accouchement dans la littérature scientifique médiévale', in *L'Enfant au moyen âge*, Sénéfiance, 9 (Paris: CUERMA, 1980), pp. 89–106.

Sanders, I.J., *English Baronies* (Oxford: Clarendon, 1960), p. 74.

Saul, N., *Richard II King of England 1367–1400* (New Haven, CT: Yale University Press, 1997).

Scaravelli, I., 'Per una mariologia carolingia: Autori, opere e linee di ricerca', in C. Piastra (ed.), *Gli studi de mariologia medievale: Bilancio storiografico* (Florence: Edizione del Galluzzo, 2001), pp. 65–85.

Scase, W., 'St Anne and the Education of the Virgin', in N. Rogers (ed.), *England in the Fourteenth Century* (Stamford, CA: Paul Watkins, 1993), pp. 81–96.

Scheffzyck, L., *Das Mariengeheimnis in Frömmigkeit und Lehre der Karolingerzeit* (Leipzig: St Benno Verlag, 1959).

Schmid, K., 'The Structure of the Nobility in the Earlier Middle Ages', in T. Reuter (ed. and trans.), *The Medieval Nobility* (Amsterdam: North Holland, 1979), pp. 37–59.

Schmidtke, J.A., 'Adam Easton's Defence of St Brigitta from Bodleian MS Hamilton 7 Oxford University', unpublished PhD dissertation (Duke University, 1971).

Schnell, R., *Frauendiskurs, Männerdiskurs, Ehediskurs: Textsorten und Geschlechterkonzepte in Mittelalter und Früher Neuzeit* (Frankfurt, 1998), pp. 92–5 and 136–9.

Schönbach, A.E., 'Über Evangelionkommentare des Mittelalters', *Sitzsungeberichte Wien*, 146 (1903): 1–176.

Schuback, K. (ed.), *Birgitta – feminist, politiker och helgon. En antologi från Birgittajubileumsåret 2003 vid Linköpings universitet* (Linköping: Filosofiska fakulteten, Linköpings universitet, 2005).

Schulenburg, J.T., *Forgetful of Their Sex: Female Sanctity and Society, ca. 500–1100* (Chicago, IL: University of Chicago Press, 1998).

Select Charters and Other Illustrations of English Constitutional History from the Earliest Times to the Reign of Edward the First, arranged and edited by William Stubbs, 9th edn, ed. H.W.C. Davis (Oxford: Clarendon Press, 1921).

Sharpe, K., *Selling the Tudor Monarchy: Authority and Image in Sixteenth-Century England* (New Haven, CT: Yale University Press, 2009).

Sharpe, R.R., *Calendar of the Letter Books of the City of London A–L*, ed. R.R. Sharpe (11 vols, London: Guildhall, 1899–1912).

Shaw, B.D., 'The Family in Late Antiquity: The Experience of Augustine', *Past and Present*, 115 (1987): 3–51.

Sheingorn, P., 'The Maternal Behaviour of God: Divine Father and Fantasy Husband', in J.C. Parsons and B. Wheeler (eds), *Medieval Mothering* (New York: Yale University Press, 1996), pp. 77–99.

Sheingorn, P., 'The Wise Mother: The Image of St Anne Teaching the Virgin Mary', *Gesta*, 32 (1993): 69–80; reprinted in M.C. Erler and M. Kowelski (eds), *Gendering the Master Narrative* (Ithaca, NY: Cornell University Press, 2003), pp. 128–31.

Shephard, A. and S.D. Powell (eds), *Fantasies of Troy: Classical Tales and the Social Imaginary in Medieval and Early Modern Europe* (Toronto: Centre for Reformation and Renaissance Studies, 2003).

Short, I., 'Patrons and Polyglots: French Literature in Twelfth-Century England', *ANS* 14 (1991): 229–49.

Silfverstolpe, C. (ed.), *Svenskt Diplomatarium från och med år 1401* (3 vols, Stockholm, 1875–1902).

Smalley, B. *Historians in the Middle Ages* (London: Thames & Hudson, 1974).

Smith, J.M.H., 'Did Women have a Transformation of the Roman World?', *Gender and History*, 12 (2000): 552–71.

Smith, L., 'The *De decem mandatis* of Robert Grosseteste', in M. O'Carroll (ed.), *Robert Grosseteste and the Beginnings of a British Theological Tradition* (Rome: Istituto storico dei Cappuccini, 2003), pp. 265–88.

Southern, R.W. (ed.), *The Life of St. Anselm* (Oxford: Clarendon Press, 1972).

Southern, R.W., *The Making of the Middle Ages* (London: Hutchinson's Universal Library, 1953).

Southern, R.W., 'The Place of England in the Twelfth-Century Renaissance', in *Medieval Humanism and Other Studies* (Oxford: Basil Blackwell, 1970).

Southern, R.W., *Saint Anselm. A Portrait in a Landscape* (Cambridge: Cambridge University Press, 1990).

Southern, R.W., *Saint Anselm and his Biographer. A Study of Monastic Life and Thought 1059–c. 1130* (Cambridge: Cambridge University Press, 1966).

Speck, P., *Kaiser Konstantin VI: Die Legitimation einer fremden und der Versuch einer eigenen Herrschaft: Quellenkritzsche Darstellung von 25 Jahren byzantinischer Geschichte nach dem ersten Ikonoklasmus* (2 vols, Munich: Wilhelm Fink Verlag, 1978).

Spence, J., 'The Mohun Chronicle: An Introduction, Edition and Translation', Nottingham Medieval Studies (forthcoming).

Spence, J.W., 'Anglo-Norman Prose Chronicles and Their Audiences', in A.S.G. Edwards (ed.), *English Manuscript Studies, 1100–1700: XIV, Regional Manuscripts* (London: British Library, 2008), pp. 27–59.

Spence, J.W., 'Genealogies of Noble Families in Anglo-Norman', in R.L. Radulescu and E.D. Kennedy (eds), *Broken Lines: Genealogical Literature in Medieval Britain and France* (Turnhout: Brepols, 2008), pp. 63–77.

Spiegel, G.M., 'Genealogy. Form and Function in Medieval Historiography', in G.M. Spiegel, *The Past as Text. The Theory and Practice of Medieval Historiography* (Baltimore, MD: Johns Hopkins University Press, 1997).

Stafford, P., 'La Mutation Familiale: A Suitable Case for Caution', in J. Hill and M. Swan (eds), *The Community, the Family and the Saint: Patterns of Power in Early Medieval Europe* (Turnhout: Brepols, 1998), pp. 103–25.

Stafford, P., *Queens, Concubines, and Dowagers: The King's Wife in the Early Middle Ages* (London: Leicester University Press, 1983).

Stafford, P., 'Sons and Mothers: Family Politics in the Early Middle Ages', in D. Baker (ed.), *Medieval Women: Dedicated and Presented to Professor Rosalind M.T. Hill on the Occasion of her Seventieth Birthday*, Studies in Church History, Subsidia, 1 (Oxford: Basil Blackwell, 1978), pp. 79–100.

Stafford, P., 'Women and the Norman Conquest', *Transactions of the Royal Historical Society*, 6th series, 4 (1994): 221–49.

Stark, J.C. (ed.), *Feminist Interpretations of Augustine* (State College, PA: Penn State Press, 2007).

Stenton, D.M., *The English Woman in History* (London: George Allen and Unwin, 1957).

Stevenson, J., 'Literacy in Ireland', in R. McKitterick (ed.), *The Uses of Literacy in Early Medieval Europe* (Cambridge: Cambridge University Press, 1990), pp. 11–35.

Stofferahn, S., 'The Many Faces in Dhuoda's Mirror: The *Liber Manualis* and a Century of Scholarship', *Magistra: A Journal of Women's Spirituality in History*, 4 (1998): 89–134.

Stoll, B., 'Drei karolingische Matthäus-Kommentare (Claudius von Turin, Hrabanus Maurus, Ps. Beda) und ihre Quellen zur Bergpredgt', *Mittellateinisches Jahrbuch*, 26 (1991): 36–55.

Stone, C.R., *The Fountainhead of Chinese Erotica: The Lord of Perfect Satisfaction* (Ruyijun zhuan) (Honolulu, HI: University of Hawai'i Press, 2003).

Swanson, R.N., *Religion and Devotion in Europe, c. 1215–c. 1515* (Cambridge: Cambridge University Press, 1995).

Swanson, R.N., *The Twelfth-Century Renaissance* (Manchester: Manchester University Press, 1999)

Tait, M.B., 'The Brigittine Monastery of Syon [Middlesex] with Special Reference to Its Monastic Usages', unpublished DPhil thesis (University of Oxford, 1975).

Talbot, C.H., 'The Cistercian Attitude Towards Art: The Literary Evidence', in C. Norton and D. Park (eds), *Cistercian Art and Architecture in the British Isles* (Cambridge: Cambridge University Press, 1986), pp. 56–64.

Taylor, R.C., *Index Monasticus: Or the Abbeys and Other Monasteries, Alien Priories, Friaries, etc.* (London, 1821).

Thomasset, C., 'Quelques principes de l'embryologie médiévale (de Salerne à la fin du XIIIe siècle)', in *L'Enfant au moyen âge*, Sénéfiance, 9 (Paris: CUERMA, 1980), pp. 109–21.

Thompson, J.W., *The Literacy of the Laity in the Middle Ages* (Berkeley, CA: University of California Press, 1939).

Thompson, S., *Women Religious: The Founding of English Nunneries after the Norman Conquest* (Oxford: Clarendon Press, 1991).

Tilly, C., *Coercion, Capital and European States, AD 990–1990* (Oxford: Basil Blackwell, 1990).

Torstensson, Sister M.P., O.Ss.S. Vadstena, 'The foundation of the abbey in Vadstena', in J. Hogg, *Studies in St. Birgitta and the Brigittine Order, Spiritualität heute und gestern, Analecta Cartusiana*, 35:19 (Salzburg: Institut für Anglistik und Amerikanistik, Universität Salzburg, 1993), vol. 1, pp. 5–19.

Tremp, E., *Studien zu den Gesta Hludowici imperatoris des Trierer Chorbischofs Thegan* (Hannover: Hahn, 1988).

Trollope, A., *The Warden* (London: Longman, Brown, Green and Longmans, 1855).

Tscherpel, G., 'The Political Function of History: The Past and Future of Noble Families', in R. Eales and S. Tyas (eds), *Family and Dynasty in Late-Medieval England*, Harlaxton Medieval Studies, 9 (Donington: Shaun Tyas, 2003), pp. 87–104.

Twelfth-Century Paintings at Hardham and Clayton, introductory essay by C. Bell (Lewes: Miller's Press, 1947).

Twitchett, D. and H.J. Wechsler, 'Kao-tsung (reign 649–83) and the Empress Wu: The Inheritor and the Usurper', in *Cambridge History of China*, iii: *Sui and T'ang China, 589–906*, part 1, ed. D. Twitchett (Cambridge: Cambridge University Press, 1979), pp. 242–89.

Tyler, E., *Crossing Conquests: Royal Women and the Politics of Fiction in Eleventh-Century England* (Toronto: University of Toronto Press, forthcoming).

Ullmann, W., *A Short History of the Papacy* (London: Routledge, 1972).

Van Bavel, T.J., 'The Evangelical Inspiration of the RSA', *Downside Review*, 93 (1975): 83–99.

Van Caenegem, R.C. (ed.), *Royal Writs in England from the Conquest to Glavill*, Selden Society 77 (London: B. Quaritch, 1959).

Van der Horst, K., 'The Utrecht Psalter: Picturing the Psalms of David', in Van der Horst et al. (eds), *The Utrecht Psalter in Medieval Art* (Utrecht: HES, 1996), pp. 23–84.

Van Egmond, W.S., *Conversing with the Saints: Communication in Pre-Carolingian Hagiography from Auxerre* (Turnhout: Brepols, 2006).

Van Houts, E., *Memory and Gender in Medieval Europe 900–1200* (Basingstoke: Macmillan 1999).

Van Houts, E., 'The Ship List of William the Conqueror', *Anglo-Norman Studies*, 10 (1987): 159–83.

Van Houts, E., 'Women and the Writing of History in the Early Middle Ages: The Case of Abbess Matilda of Essen and Aethelweard', *Early Medieval History*, 1 (1992): 53–68.

van't Spijker, I., 'Family Ties: Mothers and Virgins in the Ninth Century', in A.B. Mulder-Bakker (ed.), *Sanctity and Motherhood: Essays on Holy Mothers in the Middle Ages* (New York: Garland, 1995), pp. 165–90.

Verheijen, L. (ed.), *La Règle de Saint Augustin*, Études Augustiniennes (2 vols, Paris: Études Augustiniennes, 1967).

Vincent, N., *Peter des Roches, an Alien in English Politics* (Cambridge, 1996).

Voaden, R., *God's Words, Women's Voices: The Discernment of Spirits in the Writings of Late-Medieval Women Visionaries* (York: York Medieval Press, 1999).

Wack, M.F., *Lovesickness in the Middle Ages: The 'Viaticum' and its Commentaries* (Philadelphia, PA: University of Pennsylvania Press, 1990).

Walpole, R.N. (ed.), *The Old French Pseudo-Johannes Version of the Pseudo-Turpin: A Critical Edition* (Berkeley, CA: University of California Press, 1976).

Walz, P.A., 'The "Exceptiones" from the "Summa" of Simon of Hinton', *Angelicum*, 13 (1936): 283–368.

Ward, E., 'Caesar's Wife: The Career of the Empress Judith/Elizabeth Ward', in P. Godman (ed.), *Charlemagne's Heir: New Perspectives on the Reign of Louis the Pious* (Oxford: Oxford University Press, 1990), pp. 205–27.

Ward-Perkins, B., *The Fall of Rome and the End of Civilization* (Oxford: Oxford University Press, 2005).

Waswo, R., 'Our Ancestors, the Trojans: Inventing Cultural Identity in the Middle Ages', *Exemplaria*, 7 (1995): 269–90.

Watkin, H.R., *Dartmouth, Vol 1, Pre-Reformation*, Parochial Histories of Devonshire, 5 (Torquay: The Devonshire Association for the Advancement of Science, Literature, and Art, Parochial History Section, 1935).

Watkin, HR., *The History of Totnes Priory and Medieval Town* (Torquay: published by the author, 1914).

Watson, S.C., '*Fundatio, Ordinatio* and *Statuta*: The Statutes and Constitutional Documents of English Hospitals to 1300', unpublished DPhil thesis, University of Oxford, 2004.

Waugh, S.L., 'Women's Inheritance and the Growth of Bureaucratic Monarchy in Twelfth- and Thirteenth-Century England', *Nottingham Medieval Studies*, 34 (1990): 71–92.

Webster, L. and J. Backhouse, *The Making of England: Anglo-Saxon Art and Culture AD 600–900* (London: British Museum, 1991).

Weidemann, M., *Das Testament des Bischofs Berthramn von Le Mans vom 27. März 616*, Römisch-Germanisches Zentralmuseum Monographien, 9 (Mainz: Dr Rudolf Habelt, 1986).

Wendehorst, A., 'Wer konnte im Mittelalter lesen und schreiben?', in J. Fried (ed.), *Schulen und Studium im sozialen Wandel des hohen und späten Mittelalters* (Sigmaringen: J. Thorbecke, 1986), pp. 9–33.

Wendehorst, A. (trans. A. Davies), 'Who Could Read and Write in the Middle Ages?', in A. Haverkamp and H. Vollrath (eds), *England and Germany in the High Middle Ages: In Honour of Karl J. Leyser* (London: German Historical Institute and Oxford: Oxford University Press, 1996), pp. 55–88.

Wentzel, G., 'Birgittiner', *Reallexikon zur deutschen Kunstgeschichte*, Bd 2 (1984), cols 750–67.

Werner, K.F., 'Untersuchungen zur Frühzeit des Französischen Fürstentums (9–10 Jahrhundert)', *Die Welt als Geschichte*, 20 (1960): 87–119.

Werpehowski, W., 'Weeping at the Death of Dido: Sorrow, Virtue, and Augustine's Confessions', *The Journal of Religious Ethics*, 19 (1991): 175–91.

Westerhof, D., 'Celebrating Fragmentation: The Presence of Aristocratic Body Parts in Monastic Houses in Twelfth- and Thirteenth-Century England', *Cîteaux: Commentarii Cistercienses*, 56 (2005): 27–45.

Weston, L.M.C., 'Women's Medicine, Women's Magic: The Old English Metrical Childbirth Charms', *Modern Philology*, 92 (1995): 279–93.

Whittow, M., 'Early Medieval Byzantium and the End of the Ancient World', *Journal of Agrarian Change*, 9 (2009): 134–53.

Whittow, M., *The Making of Orthodox Byzantium, 600–1025* (Basingstoke: Macmillan Press, 1996).

Wickham, C., *Framing the Early Middle Ages* (Oxford: Oxford University Press, 2005).

Wickham, C., 'La chute de Rome n'aura pas lieu', *Le moyen âge*, 99 (1993): 107–26.

Wieck, R., 'The Primer of Claude de France and the education of the Renaissance child', in S. Panayotova (ed.), *The Cambridge Illuminations: The Conference Papers* (London: Harvey Miller, 2007).

Wilcox, J. and J.M. Riddle, 'Qustā ibn Lūqā's Physical Ligatures and the Recognition of the Placebo Effect: With an Edition and Translation', *Medieval Encounters: Jewish, Christian and Muslim Culture in Confluence and Dialogue*, 1:1 (1995): 1–50.

Wilkinson, L.J., *Women in Thirteenth-Century Lincolnshire* (London: Royal Historical Society, 2007).

Williams, A., *Lechlade: Being a History of the Town, Manor and Estates, the Priory and the Church* (Cirencester, 1888).

Wills, G., *Saint Augustine* (London: Phoenix, 2000).

Wilmart, A., *Auteurs Spirituels* (Paris: Bloud and Gay, 1932, 1971).

Wogan-Browne, J., ''Cest livre liseez ... chescun jour': Women and Reading c.1230–c.1430', in J. Wogan-Browne et al. (eds), *Language and Culture in Medieval Britain: The French of England c. 1100–c. 1500* (York: York Medieval Press, 2009), pp. 239–53.

Wolf, J., 'Psalter und Gebetbuch am Hof', in M. Chinca and C. Young (eds), *Orality and Literacy in the Middle Ages: Essays on a Conjunction and its Consequences in Honour of D.H. Green* (Turnhout: Brepols, 2005), pp. 139–79.

Wollasch, J., 'Eine adlige Familie des frühen Mittelalters. Ihr Selbstverständnis und ihre Wirklichkeit', *Archiv für Kulturgeschichte*, 39 (1957): 150–88.

Wolpe, B., 'Florilegium Alphabeticum: Alphabets in calligraphy and paleography', in A.S. Osley (ed.), *Essays Presented to Alfred Fairbank on his Seventieth Birthday* (London: Faber & Faber, 1965), pp. 69–74.

Wood, I., 'Genealogy Defined by Women: The Case of the Pippinids', in L. Brubaker and J.M.H. Smith (eds), *Gender in the Early Medieval World: East and West, 300–900* (Cambridge: Cambridge University Press, 2004), pp. 234–56.

Wood, I., *The Merovingian Kingdoms, 450–751* (London: Longmans,1994).

Wood, I., 'Review of P. Geary, *Aristocracy in Provence*', in *French History*, 1 (1987): 118–19.

Wood, I., 'The Secret Histories of Gregory of Tours', *Revue belge de philologie et d'histoire*, 71 (1993): 253–270.

Wright, D.F., 'From "God-Bearer" to "Mother of God" in the Later Fathers', in R.N. Swanson (ed.), *Church and Mary*, Studies in Church History, 39 (Woodbridge: Boydell, 2004), pp. 22–30.

Wright, R., *Late Latin and Early Romance in Spain and Carolingian France* (Liverpool: F, Cairns, 1982).

Wright, R., *A Sociophilological Study of Late Latin* (Turnhout: Brepols, 2002).

Zieman, K., 'Voices in Dialogue: Reading Women in the Middle Ages', in L. Olson and K. Kerby-Fulton (eds), *Voices in Dialogue: Reading Women in the Middle Ages* (Notre Dame, IN: Notre Dame University Press, 2005), pp. 307–34.

Zingerle, L.V., 'Recepte aus dem XII. Jahrhundert', *Germania*, 12 (1867): 463–9.

Henrietta Leyser: Principal Publications

Belief and Culture in the Middle Ages: Studies Presented to Henry Mayr-Harting, ed. with R. Gameson (Oxford: Oxford University Press, 2001), including her essay 'Two Concepts of Temptation', pp. 318–26.

'Beryl Smalley (1905–1984)', in H. Damico and J.B. Zavadil (eds), *Medieval Scholarship: Biographical Studies on the Formation of a Discipline, 1: History* (New York: Garland, 1995), pp. 313–24.

'*Cher Alme': Texts of Anglo-Norman Piety*, ed. A. Hunt, trans. J. Bliss, with an Introduction by HL (Tempe, AZ: Arizona Center for Medieval and Renaissance Studies, 2010).

'Clerical Purity and the Re-ordered World', in M. Rubin and W. Simon (eds), *Christianity in Western Europe, c. 1100–c. 1500* (Cambridge: Cambridge University Press, 2009), pp. 11–21.

'Cultural Affinities', in B. Harvey (ed.), *The Twelfth and Thirteenth Centuries, 1066–c. 1280* (Oxford: Oxford University Press, 2001), pp. 167–200, 269–70.

Hermits and the New Monasticism: A Study of Religious Communities in Western Europe 1000–1150 (London: Macmillan, 1984).

'Hugh the Carthusian', in H. Mayr-Harting (ed.), *St Hugh of Lincoln. Lectures Delivered at Oxford and Lincoln to Celebrate the Eighth Centenary of St Hugh's Consecration as Bishop of Lincoln* (Oxford: Clarendon Press, 1987), pp. 1–18.

The Life of Christina of Markyate, ed. with S. Fanous, trans. C.H. Talbot (Oxford: Oxford University Press, 2008).

Medieval Women: A Social History of Women in England, 450–1500 (London: Weidenfeld and Nicholson, 1995; reprinted Phoenix, 1996 and 2005).

'Medieval Women and the Women Medievalists', *Journal of British Studies*, 37 (1998): 441–6.

'Peter Damian, *The Life of St. Romuald of Ravenna*', trans. in T. Head (ed.), *Medieval Hagiography: An Anthology* (New York: Garland, 2000), pp. 295–315.

'Piety, Religion, and the Church', in N. Saul (ed.), *The Oxford Illustrated History of Medieval England* (Oxford: Oxford University Press, 1997), pp. 174–206.

Presenting the Past. Book 1, Invasion and Integration, with H. Middleton (Oxford: Oxford University Press, 1986).

'Women and the Word of God', in D. Wood (ed.), *Women and Religion in Medieval England* (Oxford: Oxbow Books, 2003), pp. 32–45.

Index

CPSIA information can be obtained at www.ICGtesting.com
Printed in the USA
BVOW06*2005010616

449699BV00009B/37/P

9 781409 431459